I CONFESS

I CONFESS

THE TRUTH ABOUT AMERICAN COMMUNISM

BY

BENJAMIN GITLOW

Communist candidate for Vice-President of the United States in 1924 and 1928; formerly member of the ruling Political Committee of the American Communist Party and of the Executive Committee and Praesidium of the Communist International.

WITH AN INTRODUCTION BY

MAX EASTMAN

NEW YORK

E. P. DUTTON & CO., INC.

PUBLISHERS

PRINTED IN THE U. S. A.

FIRST EDITION

INTRODUCTION

THIS book is a faithful and resolutely candid account from the inside—and what is more important, from the top—of a vital phase of recent American history. The history is secret, and might well have remained so but for the extraordinary poise and courage of this man, Ben Gitlow, and his ultimate recovery of clear vision and unmixed devotion to his ideals. A thousand congressional investigations could not expose the facts exposed in this book. A thousand research experts, convinced of them, could not make them convincing. The work of the Communist Party in the United States has involved a series of fanatical crimes, not only against American law or American "ism," but against the party's own principles and ideals—against the working class. Nothing less than a confession by one of those guilty of leadership in these crimes of insane zealotry could adequately reveal them.

In every case where the author describes an event or situation with which I had personal contact—and that means a good many both here and in Moscow—his statement of the facts, in so far as that can be separated from political or personal feelings toward them, is unassailable. In a number of cases he lays bare the essentials more objectively than I could. His book is true history. Every judicious person from the inside to the remote fringes of the Communist movement, whether he says so or not, will know that it is. Personally I failed to detect on any vital issue the dominance of any motive other than that of unmitigated truth-telling.

Of course Ben Gitlow's judgments of men and their motives are his own, and they must be. Human motives are rarely single, and I am not sure the author has always borne in mind that his opponents, like him, were moved in their factional maneuvers, and their dirty trickery in general, by super-zealotry as well as by the mere thirst of power. To this I must add, however, that his depiction of persons in the movement who happen to have been more or less intimately known to me, is often startlingly perspicacious. I could endorse a surprisingly large number of his characterizations. They will be read by thoughtful people in touch with the movement, even when not with endorsement, nevertheless with a sharp sense of their honesty and acuteness.

Thanks to his native gift, and guiding principle, of truthfulness, Gitlow has written an historical and political work of vital importance, and one which will probably never be replaced. No one studying American reflections of the Russian revolution—as such reflections of the French revolution are still elaborately studied—will ever be able to ignore this book.

MAX EASTMAN.

August 8, 1939

ERRATA

Page 181, line 16, omit the word "unborn"
Page 260, line 3, read "Flicken" for "Ficken"
Page 361, line 7 and line 3 from bottom, name is "Borucho-vitch" and not "Burochovitch"
Page 372, line 6 from bottom, read "I.W.A." and not "I.W.W."
Page 470, lines 20 and 21, read "sixteen thousand" instead of "sixteen million"
Page 487, line 21, read "Trotsky" and not "Trosky"

CONTENTS

PART III: FROM LEADER TO OUTCAST

PRELUDE

PRELUDE

A REBEL IS BORN

In the spring of 1891 two young Russian Jewish men rented for ten dollars a month the ground floor and basement of a two-story frame dwelling in Elizabethport, New Jersey, a village near the southern shores of Newark Bay and on the eastern outskirts of Elizabeth. The thin fellow with the shocks of wavy black hair was my father; the other, short, stocky and blond, my father's boyhood friend, Morris Rippenbein. Several days later (I was told it was a Saturday morning) a strange group of foreigners was the object of curiosity to the Americanized Scotch, Irish, English and German settlers as it came to occupy the premises. Rippenbein and his young wife, who had recently arrived from Russia, together with my father, mother and older brother, Sam, two years old, made up the tired hungry group. A can of salmon was the only meal that day for the grown-ups. Sam was given a roll and butter which my mother had brought with her from New York. The rent and the rooms were divided equally between the two families. My parents occupied the one large room on the ground floor, Rippenbein and his wife the two smaller rooms. The two basement rooms were shared together, although not in the fall and winter, when they were too damp and cold to be occupied. The place was infested with rats and had no improvements. There was an outhouse in the yard, water was drawn from a well, kerosene lamps furnished the light. My mother liked the place because it was in the country. The air was exhilarating, the bright rays of the sun danced through the windows, and two tall trees majestically stood guard in the front yard. Compared to the dirty tenements of Hester Street with their dark rooms and the noise, crowds, dirt and foul odors of the East Side, the Elizabethport place was paradise indeed.

But times were bad and work scarce. My parents found it difficult to pay their five dollars rent each month. My father worked only part time. The family income had to be replenished by my mother working at home. The shirt factory from which she obtained her work was far away. To reach the place my mother had to take a street car and then walk an interminably long road with a large clumsy heavy bundle of shirts. One miserable fall day dark with rain my mother lost her way. Besides the bundle of shirts, she was heavy with child. She arrived at the factory when it was dusk, drenched to the skin. The forelady saw her condition; when paying her off, she refused to give her any more work until "the thing was over." My mother begged for the work, said she needed it badly, explained that her condition did not interfere with her doing it. But her pleading was of no avail. Mother returned home tired, despondent and despairing of the future. To make matters worse, the Rippenbeins moved away, leaving my destitute parents with the full burden of the rent. Worrying, her mind constantly on the new life that was about to be born, mother helped my father to find tenants for the rooms left vacant by the Rippenbeins: these went to an elderly woman and her daughter. Into this world of tyrannical petty worries I was born about an hour after noon of Tuesday, December twenty-second, 1891.

No physician officiated at my delivery. I was pulled into the one-room world of my family by a German midwife in her middle forties, who received six dollars in cash of the recently-collected sublet money for her services. My father came home from the factory at two o'clock in the afternoon. He did the shopping and house work until late in the evening. When he went to bed he soon fell fast asleep, exhausted from the day's work and the excitement of the event. My mother fell asleep later. About midnight I awoke and kept crying incessantly. Weak as she was, scarcely twelve hours after delivery, instead of awakening my tired father, mother got up to look at me herself. My face was covered with soot. The kerosene lamp was ablaze. A terrible tragedy was impending. But my mother did not become panicky. She picked me up in her arms and awakened the elderly lady who shared the rooms with us. The latter awakened my father, then carried Sam, who had slept soundly through it all, out of the house. After my father had put the fire out and tidied up the room, my mother returned. Physically strong and firm in character, mother sent my father right back to bed, because he had to be up early in the morning to go to work, herself emptied the ashes from the cold stove, made a new fire, put a large kettle of water on, bathed my brother and me and put us to bed, washed all the linen accumulated as a result of the confinement, hung the clothes up to dry, and only then retired for the night. The very next day, the day after the confinement, my mother was out of bed, attending to her domestic duties as if nothing had happened. In the one large room that was our home nothing remained to remind one that a day before a baby was born.

Five weeks later, during a big snowstorm, the family moved back to New York, for my father, although not directly involved in a fight between some workers and the boss of the factory in which he was employed, as a class-conscious worker, sided with his fellow employees and lost his job. At five weeks I was the son of a despairing unemployed tramping the sidewalks of New York in quest of work.

As I look back in retrospect upon my boyhood days I find that lasting impressions have been made upon me by the social life in my parents' home, the constant coming and going of friends, the Socialist activities that emanated from our house, the discussions and the stories that the immigrants told about their personal and political experiences in Tsarist Russia. Growing up largely in the Socialist movement, stories about underground Russia fascinated me. I would listen intently to the adventures of the Russian revolutionary leaders, of their experiences with the police, the days and years spent in prisons and their exile to the wastes of Siberia. I would grow indignant hearing how the Tsar mistreated the people. I thrilled at the stories of the underground movement, of the conspiring activities, how deeds of violence against the Tsarist oppressors were planned. I marvelled when they explained how they transmitted messages in code by a system of telegraphic knocks upon the wall. I learned also how they crudely wrote out by hand the pamphlets and proclamations that were then distributed secretly by passing them in an endless chain from one person to another. The stories of personal experiences when raids were made by the secret police upon revolutionists' homes held me spellbound. I anticipated every incident that would be related. I also listened to discussions, very idealistic in their essence, in which the participants showed how Socialism would transform the world, and to arguments over methods of how Socialism was to be achieved. But don't for one moment imagine that my parents and their circle of radical immigrants lived with their past in Russia and the other countries from which they came. Far from it. They were eagerly interested in the world in which they lived. I was only a little tot when I heard the stories about the Molly Maguires, the Homestead Steel Workers Strike, the heroism of the Anarchist martyrs. They took a keen interest in the economic development of the United States, discussing organization of the trusts and their significance from all angles, as well as eagerly following the political issues before the country.

I was about four years old when the family moved to Cherry Street near the East River. On the north side of the street lived the Jewish immigrant families; on the south side, the Irish. A block below the tenement in which we lived were warehouses, factories and a large livery stable. The river was close by. The busy docks, the barges lying lazily tied up to the wharves, the puffing toilers of the river—the tugs, the ferries and other river craft of all description—the many children, the excitement, the noise and the congestion of the East Side stirred my youthful imagination and left a lasting impression upon me. During the Spanish-American war we lived in Brooklyn. I was then about six, an ardent American patriot who hated the Spaniards for their mistreatment of Cuba. The radical circle that came to our house was interested and excited over the war with Spain. They were unanimous in their support of the United States. The Hearst papers, which they read and believed, influenced them tremendously.

In New York City I learned more about the Socialist movement. I attended mass meetings, listened to street corner orators, read Socialist newspapers and argued Socialism with the boys at school. The most impressive meeting I attended during that period was the one at which I first heard Mother Jones, the intrepid leader of the miners, and Ben Hanford, the Socialist agitator. It took place in Bohemian Hall on Seventy-Sixth Street. I sat in the balcony. A noisy, enthusiastic crowd of men and women was present. A small band played the "Marseillaise," the cornet shrieking defiance (it seemed to me) of the whole capitalist world. I was all eyes and ears, determined to see and hear everything. Until then Mother Jones had been a mythical figure to me. I had heard many stories about her heroism and devotion to the miners' cause. Now I was to see her in person. When the chairman introduced her I was nervous with anticipation. A tall, strong-featured elderly woman took the platform amid the outburst of applause, her voice was clear, powerful. It rang out in condemnation of the injustice meted out to the miners. When she finished, the band played, and the very ceiling seemed to vibrate as the crowd rose to its feet and cheered. Ben Hanford followed her. He was tall, good-looking and impressed me very much. His voice, deep, gently resonant, was most appealing, as in simple language he delivered the Socialist message. I was sure that his promise of a better world under Socialism would come true. I left the meeting, convinced that in the end Socialism would be victorious.

My daily life really began after working hours. The most important single factor was Frederick C. Howe's forum at Cooper Union, which in those days exerted considerable influence upon the lives of the thinking youth of the city, especially those politically and socially minded. A motley crowd came to listen and learn. Many came to ask questions by which to justify their political philosophy. The Socialists were most active in this respect. I attended these lectures often. I listened. I studied the crowds there. Attending the Cooper Union forum was like attending a living university. It was vibrant with the life of the times. Nor did my evening end with the closing of the hall, for crowds gathered outside it, and groups of intensely serious people discussed Philosophy, Religion, Politics, Socialism, Anarchism, Astronomy, Economics—there was no limit to the range of inquiry. The Socialists, who were very numerous then, would cleverly turn every topic under discussion into one on Socialism. At times a group would gather around some itinerant worker who would tell about the wonders of other parts of the country and of the world.

There, exchanging experiences and views, were tramps, hoboes, cranks, workers, students and professional people, all representing numerous nationalities. There I would be found, a tall lad for my age, listening and absorbing what was being said. I went from group to group. I found that men in rags could be profoundly philosophic and far from ignorant. I learned from the lips of men themselves how they lived, how they felt about life. When I reached home and went to bed, I would turn over in my mind the things that left an impression upon me. I would try to fathom the problems confronting mankind. In my mind would be the faces of those whom I had seen and heard, men unnamed, of unrecorded fame, who had kindled in me a spark of affection and admiration for them, men who had given me a feeling for the world as it was and as it might be. It was at that time, in 1909, that I joined the Socialist Party and became active in the radical labor movement.

PART I

FROM REVOLUTIONARY IDEALISM TO POWER POLITICS

CHAPTER I

FROM SOCIALISM TO COMMUNISM

In March, 1917, when it seemed as if the German Kaiser and his allies were winning the war in Europe and America seemed secure in its peace after re-electing the President who had kept it out of war, Nicholas II, Emperor of All the Russias, abdicated the throne on which the Romanov dynasty had sat for over three centuries. This news struck the world like a thunderbolt. But it was a welcome surprise. It augured the clearing of the war-clouded sky. It betokened glad tidings to Socialists throughout the world, who gathered all over the face of the earth to discuss the implications of this historic event to the sacred cause of Socialism—the liberation of the working class.

The small club rooms of the Socialist Branch in New York to which I belonged were crowded with happy men and women, whose smiling faces and expressions of ecstasy showed with what intense emotion they welcomed the news. To those among them who had played their parts in the 1905 Revolution and, after its defeat, stumbled through the dark days of reaction that followed, it was an occasion of great rejoicing, for at last they were celebrating the defeat of the autocracy and the victory of the Russian people over the Tsar. One such old comrade turned to me and said, "At last it has happened! The mighty Tsar is no more! Who could have foretold in 1905, when the Tsar seemed almighty and invincible, that he would be overthrown in so short a time! The great Russian people have proven that they are mightier than any despot. My people are free! It is hard to believe."

To many of us the Russian Revolution was that break in the war for which we had been hoping and waiting. We saw in it the beginning of a world-wide revolutionary wave of resentment against the sordid capitalistic orgy of carnage—popular resentment that would end the war by driving from power those who were responsible for it. Eventually the world would rise out of its shambles like the fabled phenix, resplendent in the beauty and youthful vigor of Socialism. Surely, no one could now regard that hope as utopian. Yesterday it seemed as if civilization was to be doomed to the boom of cannon and eternal destruction. Now the most backward people on earth were beginning to assert themselves. Russia showed the way. Others would follow. Peace and a new freedom seemed on the very threshold of this war-ridden world.

The Russian Revolution revived our faith in Socialism and in the ultimate success of our movement. That was why Socialists everywhere followed its development with intense interest. When the Bolshevik uprising took place in November we in New York were perplexed, because we had never heard about Bolshevism before. But the Bolsheviks' denunciation of the war, their demand for peace, and uncompromising declarations in favor of Socialism struck in us a responsive chord. Then we understood: the bolsheviks were the *revolutionary* Socialists, the true votaries of orthodox Marxism. The Bolshevik Revolution, many of us felt, was the Socialist phase of the epoch-making events which the Russian masses were enacting. We were now witnessing in Russia a social upheaval of world-wide magnitude in which the overthrow of the Tsar's government was only an incident.

The ending of the World War in 1918, followed by the revolutionary developments in Europe, seemed to indicate that the end of capitalism was at hand, as the red banners were being unfurled in one country after another. It was a sign that the Russian Revolution was spreading. Socialism was becoming a fighting revolutionary force. We accepted the Bolshevik Revolution as our revolution, the Bolshevik leaders as our leaders. We worshiped Lenin and Trotsky as the heroes of the Revolution. Their influence upon us was tremendous.

We did not stop to weigh and examine the program and philosophy of Bolshevism. Why should we? Bolshevism had shattered capitalism in Russia and was calling upon the revolutionary Socialists to overthrow it in their own countries. Theirs was the militant call to action for which we had been waiting. The Revolution was on the march. We could not lose time. We had to march with it.

The Socialist movement of the United States was caught in this whirlwind of revolutionary enthusiasm. The Socialist Party was at its mercy like a tiny boat caught in a storm at sea, for the party which had hailed the Bolshevik Revolution was in turn subjected to Bolshevik attacks, was given blow after blow from which it never recovered. The Bolsheviks split it. They called upon those of us who heeded their call to sever our ties with the "opportunists" and "social patriots" who stood pat in the way of the Revolution. The Socialist Party, which I joined in 1909, when I was eighteen years old, became by 1919 the battleground of an internecine war between its Right and Left Wings. Erstwhile comrades turned into ruthless enemies. The party whose guiding principle was democracy fell a prey to Lenin's philosophy, based upon the repudiation of democracy, and the Socialist movement was split with ease. Inspired by Bolshevism, the Left Wing did not hesitate to use all means, fair or foul, to wreck the Socialist Party. When Lenin called for the extermination of the "yellow" Socialists, we understood that the first prerequisite for the building of the Communist Party was that its foundation should rest upon the wreckage of the Socialist Party.

In 1919, when I helped to wreck the Socialist Party, I had in back of me ten active years of devoted service to the movement. Joining the Socialist Party had seemed to me the proper and necessary thing to do. My father and mother were Socialists. Our home in the lower East Side of New York City was a gathering place for radical Russian immigrants. As a boy I was thrilled by their stories of adventure in the fight against Tsarism and fascinated by their descriptions of the utopian paradise Socialism would establish. I believed that Socialism would create a new society, free from exploitation, a republic of liberty and justice for all.

The Harlem Branch which I joined had its headquarters in a stuffy basement at 104th Street and Lexington Avenue. The Branch had about sixty members, all foreign born. They looked at me with amazement when they heard that I was born in the United States, because I was the first American-born member to join their branch. The Socialist Party at the time was a large and growing organization. Its fifty thousand members were scattered all over the country. In the last presidential elections it had polled over eight hundred thousand votes. Most of its members were foreign-born and belonged to the foreign-language federations. The native American elements were just beginning to join in larger numbers than heretofore. The organization was very democratic. Every action, every decision of the party was thoroughly discussed by the mass of its members. Suppression of opinion was unknown. Though the professionals and intellectuals exerted great influence over the party, its membership was nevertheless distinctly working-class in composition.

A few months later, as it was natural for a Socialist to do, I joined the union of my trade, the Retail Clerks Union of New York, which was attempting to organize the department store workers. I soon became a member of its executive board, and at the first general election was elected its president. The union employed one paid organizer, all the elected officials serving without pay. The union was helped by a group of women who were active in the woman's suffrage movement and in the Women's Trade Union League. Among them was the liberal Elizabeth Dutcher, who threw her whole soul into the work; Mrs. James P. Warbasse; Mrs. O. H. P. Belmont, who gave us the use of the suffrage headquarters she maintained on 41st Street; Mrs. J. Sargent Cram; and the vivacious Inez Millholland, who was very popular with the girl members of our union.

My first fight in the Socialist Party was over the Negro question. One of the Negro members of the Party, a cigar maker, had refused to go out on strike when his shop was called out by the Cigar Makers International Union. The Socialist Party of Local New York condemned him for his action and suspended him from the party. He defended himself on the ground that the union discriminated against Negroes by refusing to accept them into the union. I fought against his suspension on the grounds that the action of the union in discriminating against Negroes was deserving of severe censure and that the Negro worker had registered such censure in the way he believed would be most effective. Some of the old party members attacked my viewpoint and threatened to expel me from the party for defending scabbing. I fought them tooth and nail and upbraided them for their failure to fight against all forms of race discrimination.

The Socialist Party was never a party of one mind, never "monolithic," as the Bolsheviks would want their party to be. It was rather the battleground for sharp differences of opinion, for contending viewpoints. The most important clashes were over the question of industrial unionism and the advocacy of violence. With the rise of the I. W. W. this controversy divided the party into virtually two warring camps. Hillquit represented one camp, Haywood, the other. Haywood favored industrial unionism, reinforced by the tactics of sabotage and violence, which Hillquit opposed. Haywood wanted to split and smash the American Federation of Labor, in order to build the I. W. W. as the one big union, which Hillquit opposed. At the 1912 convention Hillquit put through an amendment to the constitution calling for the expulsion of all those members of the party who advocated crime, sabotage and violence as means of working class action. The matter went to a referendum of the party membership.

At first I favored Haywood's position, but as the discussion proceeded I broke with Haywood, because I opposed his contempt for political action and did not favor his proposal for smashing the American Federation of Labor. I voted in favor of Hillquit's amendment, even though I did not believe in his blanket condemnation of violence. I believed that there were occasions during trade union and political struggles when the use of violence was necessary. However, I was of the opinion that the public advocacy of violence as proposed by Haywood could only end in making the trade unions and the Socialist party a prey to *agents provocateurs* and persecution by the government. Hillquit's amendment, known as Article 2, Section 6, won. Its victory inflicted deep wounds on the Party. Many thousands of the young and most brilliant members of the party voluntarily left its ranks. Many of Haywood's supporters accepted the defeat and remained in the Party. These later formed the Left

Wing opposition, out of which the Communist Party was subsequently organized.

The following year an economic crisis hit the country. It was a year of breadlines, unemployment and discontent. Hungry workers paraded the streets demanding food. The jobless invaded the churches for lodgings. Demands were made upon the government that something be done to relieve the plight of the unemployed. An unemployed movement sprang up, the spearhead of which were the members of the I. W. W. and the Anarchists, with the Socialist Party playing a minor and very unimportant rôle. Yet I was drawn into it. My first meeting with the leaders of the movement took place at the home of Joseph O'Brien in Greenwich Village, New York City's Bohemia. O'Brien and his wife, Mary Heaton Vorse, were ardent supporters of the I. W. W. Most of us squatted on the floor during the deliberations. Here I met Elizabeth Gurley Flynn, the fiery-tongued orator and organizer of the I. W. W. She sharply criticized the Anarchists, and particularly Emma Goldman, for disregarding I. W. W. decisions and for pursuing an independent policy. Later Big Bill Haywood dropped in. He gave a glowing account of the heroic struggles of the I. W. W. and heartened his listeners by promising that, as soon as the unemployed movement in New York developed, an order would be issued for the foot-loose I. W. W. members to converge on New York, to help in the fight of the jobless. In the dim light of the room, his massive hulk, his voice ringing with emotion and tenderness, and his one eye, from which flashed in turn both hate and love, Haywood appeared as a powerful dreamer of intrepid spirit who was ready to risk all in the attainment of his goal.

After Haywood had concluded, we decided to hold a meeting on Rutgers Square in defiance of police orders. I was to be the first speaker, because I was not a member of the I. W. W., was a native of New York and was president of a trade union. Before departing for Rutgers Square we were informed that Lincoln Steffens, heading a group of prominent liberals, would be present to back up our right to speak, and when we arrived there Lincoln Steffens and his group were already on hand. As the chairman was about to introduce me, the I. W. W. unemployed leader leaped upon the platform and proceeded to speak, disregarding the decision that had been made that I was to be the first speaker. He was the most surprised man in the world when the police did not interfere, spoiling his attempt to become a martyr. Later, when the unemployed movement became the target of bitter opposition, I saw him battered by policemen's clubs, during an unemployed demonstration on Union Square, until he fell unconscious in a pool of his own blood.

The months preceding the World War were full of adventure for radicals. The strikes in Rockefeller's mines in Colorado aroused us to a pitch of feverish excitement. In protest against the burning of the miners' tent colony at Ludlow resulting in the death of men, women and children, we paraded together with Upton Sinclair, displaying mourning bands on our sleeves, in front of the Rockefeller offices at 26 Broadway. The Socialists, Anarchists, Liberals and members of the I. W. W. jointly participated in a mighty protest movement against the outrage. Then followed the hearings in New York of the United States Committee on Industrial Relations, packed to the doors with radicals, who came to hear their own people testify and to enjoy the gruelling cross-examination to which the capitalists were subjected by Frank P. Walsh, the committee's chairman, and by the labor members on the committee.

Then came the second half of 1914. The outbreak of the World War shook the American Socialist Party to its very foundations. We all believed that our brother parties in Europe would prevent the war. We were heartsick when we learned that the Socialist parties of the warring countries flagrantly violated their pledges that workers would never shoot each other. Instead they were actually supporting the capitalist governments of their respective countries at war. The Socialist Party of the United States, however, maintained throughout an attitude opposed to the war, although many of its members took sides, some supporting the Allies, others the Entente. I was steadfast in my opposition to the war as a capitalist shambles for imperialist profits. In this I was not unlike the majority of my party, whose prestige was enhanced during the war years, notwithstanding fluctuations in membership from 118,000 in

1912 to 93,500 in 1914, down to 79,000 in 1915 and up to 83,000 in 1916, when in the presidential elections of that year on an anti-war and peace platform, the Party, for the first time without Debs as its candidate and fighting against Woodrow Wilson's popularity as the man who had kept the country out of war, polled over half a million votes. The war situation was the acid test of our Socialism. The American Socialist Party passed through that test far more creditably than its fraternal parties in the major countries of Europe.

When the United States Government declared war in April, 1917, five months after Wilson had pledged the country to peace, the American people were profoundly shocked. The Socialist Party, in convention assembled, answered the declaration of war with its famous St. Louis Resolution in opposition to the war. We thus demonstrated the utter unreliability of liberal-democratic pacifism. We denounced those Socialists who came out in support of the war as traitors to the Party and to the proletariat. Socialist Party members everywhere plunged into the anti-war campaign, notwithstanding that the Party as such did not lead and direct it. Although we recruited comparatively few members, the periphery of our sympathizers extended considerably, for we became the anti-war party that had remained true to its pledge. Our influence was best expressed through numerous peace organizations which immediately grew to large proportions. The peace movement was spontaneous, clearly indicating that the people of the United States were opposed to American participation in the war and were determined to preserve democracy at home during its duration.

I plunged into the anti-war campaign. I joined the People's Council, a peace movement which attracted radicals and liberals of every shade of opinion. Almost every night I spoke against the war before tremendous crowds. It seemed that people everywhere were seeking the answer to the one question: "What can be done to prevent the country's actual participation in the war?" The anti-war groups were totally unprepared for the situation and could give no satisfactory answer. The government, on the other hand, pursued a very cautious policy. The peace groups were allowed to blow off steam with little interference. Government pressure was applied slowly. I believe, from my experience in the anti-war campaign, that decisive in the situation was the outstanding fact that the people, though anxious for peace, were not ready for any violent or revolutionary changes to attain it. The leaders of the anti-war movement, though they all loudly shouted against the war, were not ready to back up their defiance with action.

One meeting in particular bears out this point. The government had decided upon conscription. The next day was registration day. The Anarchists called a meeting in Hunt's Point Palace in the Bronx. The hall was packed to the doors. The stairs leading to the hall were lined with government agents and police. The square outside was a mass of seething humanity upon which the police played powerful searchlights. Tense excitement prevailed. The noise from the crowd outside reached those lucky enough to get in. Alexander Berkman and Emma Goldman were the principal speakers. But neither speaker was able to arouse the crowd, which listened intently to every word they uttered, to the necessary pitch of enthusiasm. The crowd was distinctly disappointed. Why the disappointment? Because both Emma Goldman and Alexander Berkman had failed to give the audience an answer to the question which was uppermost in its mind. The people wanted to know what they were to do tomorrow, the day of registration for conscription. The speakers proposed no concrete action. They merely told their listeners to follow their own conscience.

The war had become a grim reality. The Socialist Party entered the political campaign of 1917, expecting to capitalize heavily on the country's anti-war sentiment. I was nominated for the Assembly in the Third Assembly District of the Bronx. My campaign was directed chiefly against the war. I was threatened with arrest many times. The campaign was successful. I was elected to the Assembly by a good majority. For the first and only time in its career the Socialist Party elected ten Assemblymen and five members of the Board of Aldermen, polling a record vote in New York City. We ten Socialist Assemblymen took our office very seriously. We were no mere politicians; we were crusaders—and the Assembly was a bigger and better rostrum. We attended all the sessions, even when most of the other members were absent. For example, my Democratic neighbor must have been sworn in when I was, on the first day, but I never saw him until two or three days before the closing of the term.

Our caucus leader was Abraham Shiplacoff. We always met in the modest apartment house, where we established our headquarters and in which several of our colleagues lived. We worked out a legislative program of reforms, drew up the bills accordingly and introduced them for passage. But the work of the Socialist delegation was of a negative character, its bills completely ignored. Our work was therefore mainly confined to voting against obnoxious bills and criticizing them. We were tolerated but not liked. Our way of thinking, our attitude on public matters, our ideas of what the concern of the government should be were out of harmony with the ideas and attitudes of the Republican and Democratic legislators, from whom it was most difficult to get any attention on matters of interest to the workers and the poor city dwellers generally. The greatest weakness of our legislative activity consisted in the fact that we sought to enact into law our whole Socialist platform of reforms, instead of concentrating on one or two important political measures. Our second weakness consisted in the fact that we were completely ignorant of the needs of the rural population and were practically unconcerned with its lot, and at that time the farmers of New York State, through their various organizations, exerted considerable influence upon the legislature.

When the legislature adjourned I began to take stock of the Socialist movement, for the war shook to the very foundations my faith in the movement. I had become firmly convinced that the socialist parties of the warring countries were betraying the interests of the working class, in supporting the war. The Bolshevik Revolution further convinced me that the prevailing position of modern Socialism—that Socialism could be attained peacefully and through a gradual accumulation of reforms—was wrong. I looked upon the reformist Socialists with contempt. I deduced from the war that brutal force and violence were the final arbitrators, and concluded that Socialism would come as the result of revolution in which the masses would use force and violence in overthrowing their oppressors. My break with pre-war Socialism followed. I became a *revolutionary* Socialist and forthwith joined the ranks of the Left Wing. I pledged myself to work for the transformation of the Socialist Party into a revolutionary Socialist organization. This was in the Spring of 1918. A year later I was expelled from the party. After my expulsion, I was drafted by the Left Wing to carry on the work of its organization.

The Bolshevik Revolution gave the Left Wing Socialists the program they were looking for. The wrecking of the Socialist Party became its first step in winning the Socialists for a program of revolution. The splitting of the Socialist movement followed quickly. It was much easier to destroy than to build. I engaged in the crime of wrecking the Socialist movement. My actions were motivated by the highest ideals and by the belief that I was thereby hastening the victory of Socialism. It was not difficult to wreck the American Socialist Party, because its composition was mostly non-American, and the Bolshevik Revolution exerted a profound influence upon its foreign-born membership. In 1918, prior to the split, the American Socialist Party had over 70,000 members in its foreign-language-speaking federations. These federations dominated, because not only did they control the bulk of the party membership, but also because they had large cultural, economic and financial resources. But the foreign-born members were not all confined to the foreign language federations. Approximately half of the membership of the so-called "American" or English-speaking branches were likewise foreign-born. It is not an exaggeration to state that in 1918 the bulk of the membership of the American Socialist Party was made up of the foreign-born. About the year 1912, it was evident that the Socialist Party was beginning to take root in the United States. Had this process not been curtailed by the outbreak of the World War and especially by the split up after the Bolshevik Revolution, there is no doubt in my mind that the American Socialist Party would have become an important political party, its activities greatly influencing American life. The party certainly withstood the blows of the war quite well. Unfortunately, it could not help succumbing to the general demoralizing influences and reactionary trends set loose by the war; with its overwhelming foreign-born membership, it could not withstand the impact of the Bolshevik Revolution, for the triumph of Bolshevism electrified the foreign-born, and through them the Dybbuk of Bolshevism took hold of the party. Romantics among the native-born succumbed to it along with the comrades whose roots were abroad. For the overwhelming majority of the party—the romantic native-born as well as the others—Bolshevism meant the people's protest against the war and victory for revolutionary Socialism. The party, without at once realizing it, was celebrating not only a decisive turning point in international Socialism but in American Socialism as well.

The first news of the Tsar's overthrow was received with great rejoicing. It stimulated above all those elements in the party that comprised the Slavic and Jewish federations, because most of their members hailed from Tsarist Russia. These federations were: The Russian Federation, the Jewish Federation, the Ukrainian Federation, the Lithuanian Federation, the Esthonian Federation, the Polish Federation, the Lettish Federation and such allied Slavic federations as the Bulgarian and, the Yugo-Slav. The Slavic language federations began to grow very rapidly. Those who had immigrated from Tsarist Russia began to look forward to the time when they would return to their native land, and as many as could left for Russia immediately. Among the latter were several staff members of the *Novy Mir,* Russian Socialist paper published in New York, such as, Leon Trotsky, Nicholas Bukharin, Volodarsky, who played stellar roles in the Bolshevik Revolution, and lesser luminaries, like Boris Reinstein, for many years active in the Socialist Labor Party, and Bill Shatoff of the I. W. W., as well as scores of other assorted radicals.

Notwithstanding the presence of Russian Bolsheviks on our shores, the Socialist Party membership knew very little about Bolshevism prior to 1917, many of us hearing about it that year for the first time. For example, the Socialist Propaganda League, which later became extremely pro-Bolshevik, ignored Lenin when he wrote them in 1915, and apparently threw his letter into the waste basket. Only after Lenin's death, when a thorough search was made of Lenin's personal papers, was a draft of the first part of the letter found. After the downfall of the moderate Socialist Kerensky, a large section of the party became definitely pro-Bolshevik, all of us of that persuasion believing that Bolshevism was synonymous with the principles of revolutionary socialism and orthodox Marxism. A new defiant spirit arose which drew its inspiration directly from Bolshevik Russia. This new spirit clashed with the spirit that dominated the Socialist movement before the war. It needed only a signal from Bolshevik Russia to arouse those imbued with the new spirit to war upon the old. The Russian Bolsheviks wasted no time in giving us the signal. They gave the order that the Socialist "traitors" must be destroyed. We set up the hue and cry against all Socialists who refused to accept Bolshevism, and the civil war in the American Socialist Party was on in earnest.

Of all those who returned from Russia in the early days of the Bolshevik Revolution, John Reed made the greatest impression. Wherever he spoke he was greeted by wildly enthusiastic audiences. I was determined that the people of the Bronx should hear from John Reed the truth about Russia. The old time Socialists of the Bronx organization opposed my proposal for a John Reed meeting. They were afraid that the authorities might break up the meeting and arrest the speakers. But I succeeded in overcoming their opposition, and the meeting was decided upon. In agreeing to speak, John Reed wrote me as follows:

> I shall be glad to accept. I hope that it *will* be a grand demonstration, and that you do not spoil the opportunity by introducing on the platform men who are likely to moderate their protest, or attempt to apologize for the *government of the United States in its intervention in Russia.*

The meeting took place in Hunt's Point Palace on September 13, 1918. The place was packed to the doors. Thousands were turned away. That was the largest demonstration for Bolshevik Russia so far held in the United States.

I spoke at that meeting before Reed. When I finished, he shook my hand and said he was very glad to make my acquaintance, because for the first time since he had returned to the United States had he heard a truly proletarian speech. That was how we met. I saw that he was nervous, very pleased with the large turn out and bubbling over with enthusiasm. I liked him at once because he was so typically American in his reckless abandon. Besides, his smile was captivating. When he arose to speak, the crowd greeted him wildly, standing, waving red bunting, applauding, cheering to the echo. Reed did not know what to do. He pleaded with them to stop, but they cheered more loudly and demonstratively than before. He turned to us on the platform for advice. But we could not help him. When he finally did get to speak, he spoke simply, with conviction and emotion. Although he was no orator, his earnestness and his fighting mood were truly impressive. At times he fairly leaped off the platform as he spoke. Now and again he dropped a few Russian words, which unfailingly drew loud applause and vociferous cheers from the crowd. His words seemed to carry a genuine message from the land of revolution and a challenge to the whole capitalist world. His descriptions of Red Russia and its people were vivid and indicated that the Russian people in their fight for freedom and a new world had made a deep impression upon him. What was most striking to me was the great impatience that was apparent in his talk. He spoke rapidly, as if in a very great hurry. It seemed that John Reed felt that the revolution was near in America and time must not be lost in preparing for it. John Reed's whole demeanor showed that he was certain of it and was eager to play his part in the momentous events that were to take place.

After this meeting John Reed was arrested and later indicted by the federal authorities. But Reed was not the only pilgrim who had seen the red star over the new Bethlehem. Many others followed, returning from the wondrous land of Bolshevism with words that set us all aflame. Bolshevism began to sweep the membership of the Socialist Party like a prairie fire. The sober leaders of the Socialist Party, grouped around Morris Hillquit, became very apprehensive of the new current, but they did not dare openly to obstruct its course. They sensed in it the flood that would engulf them. At the beginning they refrained from attacking Bolshevism, and the press which they controlled carried glowing accounts of events in Red Russia. But this calm before the storm did not last very long. The Bolshevik revolution had given the Left Wing what it had lacked—a program around which to organize. The Left Wing was quick to take advantage of this, by claiming for itself the Bolshevik leadership of America. Its organization grew rapidly. New York City became the hotbed of American Bolshevism. The New York Left Wingers propagandized the country. The fight between the Lefts and the Rights in the Socialist Party soon took on national proportions. The Socialist Party was divided into warring camps. The Lefts looked upon the Rights as Mensheviks and counter-revolutionists. Peace between the two factions was out of the question.

The Russian Federation of the Socialist Party became the idol of the Left Wing. We looked upon its membership as the true Bolshevik kernel in the party, little realizing that the Russian Federation members who allocated to themselves the glory of the Bolshevik Revolution had little or nothing to do with it. Many Socialists believed that only the Russians understood Bolshevism and were fitted to speak on its behalf. Had they investigated the Russian Federation, they would have discovered that the majority of its large membership had joined after the success of the Bolshevik Revolution, that most of them were actually ignorant of what Socialism or Bolshevism really stood for. The leaders of the Russian Federation did nothing to dispel these misconceptions. They wallowed in the esteem accorded them. Not only did they let the American Socialists know that when it came to Bolshevism they knew all about it, but they went further and insisted that they alone should be recognized as the leaders of the Left Wing.

The first important step taken in consolidating our organization in the Socialist Party was taken at the Convention of the Left Wing Section of the Socialist Party, Local Greater New York, held February 16, 1919 in Odd Fellows Hall on St. Mark's Place. The small hall was filled to capacity. Great enthusiasm reigned. All the outstanding figures of the Left Wing were present, including Rose Pastor Stokes, John Reed, Jim Larkin, as well as the leaders of the Russian, Lettish, Lithuanian and other Slavic Federations. Louis C. Fraina, an expert in copying the ideas of the Bolshevik leaders and attaching his name to them, prepared the program for the convention under the title, *Manifesto and Program of the Left Wing Section of the Socialist Party of Local Greater New York.* It had nothing to do with American conditions. It might just as well have been written by the Man in the Moon. It urged upon the American people "the organization of Workmen's Councils, as the instruments for the seizure of power and the basis for the proletarian dictatorship, which is to replace the overthrown government; workmen's control of industry, to be exercised by industrial unions or soviets; repudiation of all national debts, with provisions to safeguard small investors; expropriation of the banks; expropriation of the railways and the large (trust) organizations of capital; the socialization of foreign trade." What we proposed that the American people should do in 1918 was precisely what the Bolsheviks did after they seized power in Russia. The program was drawn up as if a revolution was around the corner in the United States and would be similar in all its aspects to the revolution in Russia. This *Manifesto and Program* proved that we had lost all sense of reality and that we either ignored American conditions as unimportant or were totally ignorant of them. To transform the Socialist Party into a Bolshevik party, we proposed the elimination of the reform planks in its platform, the building of revolutionary industrial unions, the repudiation of the Second (The Socialist) International and the election of delegates to an International Conference to be held in Moscow, called by the Communist Party of Russia. Only lunatics or hopeless romantics could even consider such a program. We, however, discussed it in all seriousness. We argued with passion over every clause, for we sincerely believed we were preparing a guide for the coming revolution in the United States.

Very much seen and heard at the convention was Nicholas Hourwich, son of Professor Isaac Hourwich, famous economist and authority on immigration. He was the theoretical and ideological leader of the Russian Federation. Probably because his father had been friendly with Lenin in his youth, he actually believed that he was the outstanding exponent of Bolshevism in America. His egotism knew no bounds. When he spoke, his small reddish beard bristled with excitement and he was oblivious of everything else around him. He spoke with great speed, his words jumbled in an incoherent cataract. Behind his thick lenses his eyes flared with nervous tension. Short of stature and impressed with his own importance, he was a ludicrous-looking individual dressed in black, pockets crammed full of papers and documents, a bundle of newspapers and magazines always under his arm. When, finally, we bundled him off to Russia, to escape arrest, shipping him off as a coal stoker on a vessel Russia bound, he looked upon his departure from the United States as a temporary interlude. But the Communist International willed otherwise. He never returned.

At the first Left Wing convention there was plenty of talk. Everybody talked. If talk could make revolution, the Left Wing would have won in the United States. Yet despite all the debates and wranglings, an organization was actually established and a city committee of fifteen elected to carry on its work. This committee consisted of the following: Nicholas I. Hourwich, Fanny Horowitz, Jay Lovestone, James Larkin, Harry Hilzik, Edward I. Lindgren, Milton Goodman, John Reed, Joseph Brodsky, Dr. Julius Hammer, Jeanette D. Pearl, Carl Brodsky, Mrs. L. Ravitch, Bertram D. Wolfe and myself. An executive committee was also elected to carry out the daily activities of the organization, composed of the following: Nicholas I. Hourwich, George Lehman, James Larkin, L. Himmelfarb, George C. Vaughn, Benjamin Corsor, Edward I. Lindgren, Maximilian Cohen and me. With the exception of Larkin, Lindgren, and myself, the rest of the members of the executive committee were entirely unknown in the Socialist Party and had never before acted in a leading capacity in the movement. The West Side Branch of the Socialist Party, known as the Irish Branch, situated at 43 West 29th Street, became our headquarters. A small room there was turned over to the Left Wing. Here we established also the business and editorial offices of our official paper, *The New York Communist,* publication of which was started in April, 1919. John Reed was its editor. These headquarters became the center of feverish Left Wing activity.

Soon after the Left Wing organization was established, Ludwig C. A. K. Martens, who was appointed the official representative of the Soviet Government in January, 1919, announced the opening of his bureau at 110 West 40th Street. Martens was a quiet, mild-tempered man. He did not look like a Russian. Fair of complexion, with blond hair and mustache, he looked more like a middle class German business man than what went for the accepted description of a Bolshevik. He was indeed of German descent and an engineer by profession. He was a member of the Russian Federation and belonged to the faction that did not like Hourwich. He was at a loss as to how to conduct the affairs of his bureau and ended by following two distinct courses. One course sought to placate American business men by attempting to convince them that it would be profitable for them to do business with Russia. The other course was to cooperate very closely with the Left Wing in carrying on Soviet Government Communist propaganda. I conferred with him often on Left Wing matters and received from him from time to time financial help for our organization and its press. Martens was not a strong man. He leaned very heavily on his advisors—namely, Santeri Nuorteva, a Finnish Communist, his secretary; Dr. Hammer, whose generous financial assistance made the establishment of the "Embassy" possible; and Gregory Weinstein, one of the editors of *Novy Mir.* Weinstein was an able writer, well versed in the movement, a good lecturer and speaker and in addition a fairly capable politician.

The appointment of Martens and the opening of his "Embassy" led to one of the sharpest controversies in the Left Wing. The leaders of the Russian Federation, who were very jealous of Martens' appointment—which was especially true of Hourwich, who had personally written to Lenin asking for the appointment—tried to gain control of Martens' "Embassy." They demanded that Martens and his "Embassy" submit to the supervision and control of a committee set up for that purpose by the Russian Federation. When Martens refused, they sought to get the Left Wing officially to endorse their proposal. Nicholas Hourwich became the leader of the fight against Martens. Martens' official supporters in the Left Wing were Dr. Hammer and Gregory Weinstein. The American elements in the Left Wing did not support Hourwich. The one notable exception was Louis C. Fraina, who catered to the leaders of the Russian Federation. He wanted powerful support behind him in the Left Wing whenever it was necessary. Larkin, Reed and I fought the Russian Federation's attempt to boss Martens. However, there was more to the fight than just that. It was the first sign that some of the American elements in the Left Wing resented the domination of the Russian Federation leaders.

The meetings on the Martens controversy were decidedly violent in character. Nick Hourwich, spectacles perched on his thin pointed nose, red with rage, his eyes flashing scorn, spoke heatedly in his thick Russian accent. "You are Mensheviks, Socialist traitors and counter-revolutionists," he shouted at all who dared to oppose him. His followers listened to him as if he were a demi-god. They sat taut in their seats, eyeing their opponents with piercing glances of hate. In fighting Hourwich, arguments were useless. Yet I argued for hours. John Reed did likewise, till he almost collapsed from exhaustion and exasperation. The meetings never ended before three or four in the morning. When a vote went against the Russian Federation, Hourwich would stand up, fuming with anger, call us counter-revolutionary bastards, after which he would proceed to walk out of the meeting in protest followed by all his supporters, who snarled and cursed at us. But when he discovered that his bolting did not have any effect, he would return at the head of his cohorts, declaring that he returned to do his Bolshevik duty by watching the proceedings in order to prevent us from committing more treachery against the movement. The declaration made, the Martens fight would start all over again. During one of these hectic nights I remember Nick Hourwich's consternation when Harry Winitsky interrupted him and called him an American cadet. Hourwich knew that in Russia the Cadets represented a political party made up of the bourgeoisie, the party of Constitutional Democrats, outlawed by the Bolsheviks as White Guards and counter-revolutionists. He fairly screamed: "How dare you call me a Cadet? Don't you know that a Cadet is a counter-revolutionist? I am a Bolshevik, not a Cadet."

"But, Comrade Hourwich," interjected Winitsky with sweet reasonableness, "I said you were an *American* cadet, not a Russian one."

Hourwich was flabbergasted. "What is it you call an American cadet?" he demanded.

"Oh," replied Winitsky, "Don't you know? Why, an American cadet is a pimp."

In spite of all the dissensions within the Left Wing, the organization grew to such an extent that the Right Wing leaders of the Socialist Party became alarmed. They soon realized that if they did not take drastic steps at once, the Left Wing would take over the party. Hillquit gave the signal for action against the Left Wing in his famous declaration of "Clear the Decks" published in the New York *Call* on May 21, 1919, on the eve of the meeting of the New York State Executive Committee of the Socialist Party. The meeting took place in Albany. I was present as a member of the State Committee from the Bronx organization. The block of Left Wing State Committee men, all of whom had been elected to the Committee before the Left Wing organization was formed, was on hand. A bitter fight took place over Hillquit's proposals for the reorganization of the party and the expulsion of the Left Wingers. Hillquit, who had control of the State committee, forced his proposals through, though he did not have the support of the majority of the party membership. One of the Left Wing Bloc, Harry Waton, rose and, pointing his finger at Hillquit, shouted: "You are Right Wing enemies of the revolution! Go ahead with your dirty work! Expel us from the party! We will soon meet you in bloody battles on the barricades!"

Following that meeting, all members of the Left Wing were expelled from the Socialist Party and summarily removed from all leading positions and committees. The fight between the Lefts and the Rights by this time had spread to the entire country. A referendum of the Socialist Party membership had just been completed on the election of a new National Executive Committee and a delegate to the International Socialist Congress. When the results were announced they showed that the Left Wing slate had swept the elections and that Hillquit for the first time was beaten as a delegate to the international congress by Kate Richards O'Hare, who had been endorsed by the Left Wing. The Left Wing endorsed her because she had been convicted and sent to prison for opposition to the war. She was, however, not a supporter of the Left Wing. The old National Executive Committee took the unprecedented action of voiding the elections. They went even further. They suspended all the federations which supported the Left Wing and expelled the whole Michigan State organization. By this time the split in the Socialist Party was an accomplished fact and the breach between the two factions could no longer be bridged. The Left Wing immediately took steps to consolidate its forces on a national scale by calling a National Conference to be held in New York City on June 21, 1919.

But before the conference took place other troubles were to beset the Left Wing and the radical labor movement. A reaction against all Reds set in. Returned soldiers were organized into groups whose function it was to attack radical headquarters and newspapers. The Socialist *Call* was viciously attacked by such a group. When a report reached the Left Wing headquarters that a similar group was coming to attack it, preparations were immediately made to meet the attack. Comrades were hastily gathered together and armed with long iron pipes. Buckets of hot boiling water were kept in readiness. The stairway leading to the first floor was lined with armed men ready to fight to the last man for our headquarters. James Larkin was in charge of the defense forces. I eagerly awaited the attack, as did all those inside. But it never came. At the same time the Lusk Committee, appointed by the New York State Legislature to investigate seditious activities, became active in breaking into Socialist and Left Wing headquarters, destroying property and stealing cash and records. The Left Wing definitely had its hands full. Some supporters were frightened away from the organization by the terror and persecution of those days, but their numbers were few. We managed to keep our forces intact. Our spirit was far from broken by these early attacks. In fact, it was spurred on to greater enthusiasm and sacrifice.

The Left Wing Conference was held the very day the Lusk Committee broke into our headquarters on West Twenty-ninth Street between Broadway and Sixth Avenue in New York. This forced the conference into semi-secrecy and made it necessary to move from one hall to another during the sessions, in order to avoid detection. About a hundred delegates were present, representing every important Socialist center in the country. Among them was Charles E. Ruthenberg, secretary of the Cleveland local of the Socialist Party. It was the first time we in New York had seen him. His fame as a Left Wing leader had reached us long before he did. From Ohio also came Alfred Wagenknecht, State Secretary of the Socialist Party there, who later was to become the financial wizard in raising funds for Communist purposes. From Kansas came Louis E. Katterfeld, a Kansas farmer, prominent in Socialist Party national office affairs, who later became the leader of the underground Communist Party. William Bross Lloyd, Chicago Socialist millionaire, was present, as was his private secretary, Isaac E. Ferguson, who became the first secretary of the National Left Wing organization at the close of the conference. Also, James P. Cannon, a member of the I. W. W. and editor of a Socialist paper in Kansas City, Missouri. New York sent a large delegation, which included Jim Larkin, John Reed, Rose Pastor Stokes, Jay Lovestone, myself and many others. The Russian Federation and the group of Slavic language federations were all represented by delegates, among whom Nick Hourwich and Alexander I. Stoklitzky were the most vociferous. Present also was a delegation headed by Dennis E. Batt, representing the Michigan State Socialist Party, which had just been expelled from the National party.

That the ultimate aim of the Left Wing in the Socialist Party was to capture the Socialist Party and change it into a Communist Party cannot be denied. The Left Wing Conference was called in order to organize the Left Wing forces on a national scale in preparation for the national convention of the Socialist

Party. But there were many in the Left Wing who, for one reason or another, were impatient and wanted to have the Communist Party organized forthwith. The question of the immediate formation of the Communist Party became the most hotly debated question before the Left Wing National Conference rather than the question of what steps to take to organize the forces within the Socialist Party, for which the conference had been called.

How did this come about? In New York one of the prominent leaders of the New York Left Wing was Harry Waton, who conducted a Marxian study group. His chief lieutenant was Morris Zucker. At the City Convention of the New York Left Wing on the eve of the opening of the National Conference, Harry Waton and Morris Zucker argued for the passage of a motion calling upon the National Left Wing Conference to organize immediately the Communist Party of the United States. He argued that the Socialist Party could not be reformed or captured by the Left Wing, that to work in that direction was a waste of time, the historical moment demanding the immediate formation of a Communist Party. He carried the City Convention by storm. "Why wait?" the membership cried. "Let us have the real thing, the Communist Party, right away." The question therefore could not be kept out of the National Left Wing Conference. Not only was Harry Waton present as a delegate supported by a delegation from the City Convention, but, what was even more important, the Russian Federation and the group of Slavic Federations also favored this step.

Opposed to the immediate organization of the Communist Party was the overwhelming majority of the Americans of the Left Wing, though a few of the American leaders were beginning to compromise on the question because they wished to gain the support of the Russian and Slavic Federations. Outstanding in this respect was Louis C. Fraina, whose whole demeanor gave to many the impression that he considered himself the Lenin of America. The others were Jay Lovestone, Bertram D. Wolfe, Charles E. Ruthenberg and Isaac E. Ferguson. Had the Federation leaders not been afraid of a break at the conference on this question, they would have forced the proposition through. John Reed, Jim Larkin, L. E. Katterfeld, Wagenknecht, myself and a large enough number of out-of-town delegates fought against the proposal and insisted that only after the National Convention of the Socialist Party had refused to recognize the will of the majority of its members in favor of the Left Wing should the Left Wing split the Socialist Party and organize a Communist party. The National Left Wing Conference did not dare, in the face of the stubborn opposition that developed, to vote in favor of the immediate formation of a Communist Party. When the proposition was defeated, Harry Waton called the delegates "betrayers" and bolted the conference. Then we passed a resolution calling for the mobilization of the membership to capture the Socialist Party Convention for the Left Wing. The leaders of the Russian Federation, their supporters in the Left Wing and the Michigan Delegation had no intention of carrying out this resolution, and after the Conference adjourned they at once began to organize the split in the Socialist Party by calling for the immediate organization of a Communist Party.

The following nine were elected to the National Council: Louis C. Fraina, Boston; Charles E. Ruthenberg, Cleveland; Isaac E. Ferguson, Chicago; John J. Ballam, Boston; James Larkin, New York; Eadmonn MacAlpine, New York; Benjamin Gitlow, New York; Maximilian Cohen, New York, and Bertram D. Wolfe, New York. It should be noted that not a single leader of the language federations was included among those elected to the National Council. The federation delegates were in a majority and could easily have dominated the committee. Their omission was not accidental. Nor was it due to the fact that the Russian Federation leaders and the leaders of the other language federations had come to the conclusion that the native elements must take over the leadership of the movement. There was no danger of any such altruism or adherence to principle on their part. It should also be noted that in spite of the fact that the Michigan delegation was a large one and represented one of the largest state organizations, not a single representative from Michigan was included in the National Council. The explanation is that the Russian Federation and the group of

Slavic Federations around it made a deal with the Michigan delegation to go ahead immediately with the organization of a Communist Party. Though they voted for the decisions of the National Conference to carry on a fight in the Socialist Party, they had a tacit understanding among themselves to sabotage the National Council and the decisions of the conference. That was why they had declined to accept membership on the National Left Wing Council.

Immediately after the conference, the National Council of the Left Wing established offices in the same building that housed the headquarters of the New York Left Wing. Isaac E. Ferguson became the secretary. *The Revolutionary Age*, published in Boston by the Lettish club, was turned over to the National Council of the Left Wing. I was appointed business manager of the paper. The first issue published by the National Council in New York appeared on July 5, 1919.

Then began the era of double dealing, lying, disregard of decisions, breaking of promises, and horsetrading for personal gain and position, which has characterized the internal politics of the Communist movement to the present day. It seemed as if the newly-born Bolshevik leaders in the United States had very little to learn from the ward heelers of Tammany Hall. That was the only American thing about them. No sooner was the conference over than evidence began piling up about the duplicity of the Language Federation leaders. They refused to support the National Council. They openly carried on a vicious campaign against it. They withdrew all financial support and withheld the membership dues to which the Council was entitled. The Russian Federation went further. They ordered large bundles of *The Revolutionary Age*, which they destroyed and then refused to pay for. When the Council issued a call for funds it was sabotaged. The leaders of the Language Federations backed up this campaign against the Council by making deals with individual leaders of the National Council as to their future positions and jobs in the Communist Party that they were going ahead to organize.

In the early part of July, the Russian and Slavic Federation leaders issued a call, together with the expelled Michigan State

Socialist Party, for a convention to be held in Chicago on September 1, 1919, for the purpose of organizing the Communist Party. This call was signed by four members of the Michigan organization and S. Kopnagel of the Lettish Federation, I. Stilson of the Lithuanian Federation and Alexander Stoklitzky, National Secretary of the Russian Federation. The Federation leaders who signed the call looked upon the Michigan organization as a non-Communist group, because they laid too much stress on educational activities and attached little importance to the trade unions. Besides, there were too many native Americans in the Michigan organization. They made the deal with them, however, in order to force certain Left Wing leaders into line. When the deal with these Left Wing leaders was finally consummated, it was with the understanding that the Michigan crowd was to be eliminated.

The split of the Socialist Party was carried through by the Russian Federation with great rapidity. There was a reason for their haste. They hoped to organize a Communist party in the United States which they would control and by that fact to become the directors of Soviet policy in the United States and, what is more important, secure control of Soviet appointments for themselves as representatives for the various Soviet agencies to be established in the United States. They actually believed that the Soviet Government would appoint only those people who would be recommended by the Communist Party once it was organized and recognized by the Soviet Government.

On July 27, three weeks after the first issue of *The Revolutionary Age* appeared in New York, the Russian Federation leaders called a conference in New York, composed of representatives of the National Council and the Central Executive Committee of the Lettish, Lithuanian, Esthonian, Ukrainian, Polish and Russian Federations. The representatives of the National Left Wing Council were Ferguson and myself. It is necessary to keep in mind that the central committees of the above-mentioned federations formed a so-called revolutionary council which was dominated by the leaders of the Russian Federation. This council considered itself the only genuine Bolshevik and trustworthy revolutionary body in the United

States. Needless to say, this council had met in caucus before Ferguson and I arrived. It had made all the decisions in advance and from these they had decided to yield not one iota. At that time the Russian leaders claimed that a good Bolshevik was one who would not compromise on the smallest point and would fight for that point to the bitter end.

These federations represented over ninety percent of the Left Wing of the Socialist Party. And they were growing daily because the foreign-born workers were joining them in droves. For example, it was a common practice for Alexander Stoklitzky, the National Secretary of the Russian Federation, when addressing meetings of Russian workers, to hold up a membership card in the Russian Federation and declare that the card was the equivalent of a passport to Russia; that if any worker wanted to go back to his native country he could only do so by joining the Russian Federation and getting a membership card, the only passport Bolshevik Russia would honor. The members of the Russian Federation, who were anxious to go back to Russia, backed up their leaders, because they did not want to jeopardize their chances and incur the disfavor of their leaders who acted as if they were representative of the new Russian government.

This Council not only dominated the Left Wing, it dictated its policies, and sought to exercise complete control over its leaders. It steadfastly maintained that the American comrades could not be trusted because they did not understand Russian Bolshevism. Their reasoning was based on the premise that only those who were born in the territory that formerly comprised the Russian Empire had the attributes that went to make Bolsheviks. When Ferguson and I entered the room we found the other Council members already seated solemnly around a long oblong table. Their demeanor was stern and serious. They were the revolutionary council and were acting their part. I tried to convince them that the only position to follow was the one adopted by the National Conference. I argued in vain. They sat glued to their seats, waiting with obvious boredom for me to finish. To them it seemed the height of impudence for a mere ignorant American to appeal to *them* against their dogmatic self-assured wisdom. When I finished speaking, they began to converse among themselves in Russian, not even bothering to give us a translation. Everyone who spoke knew English and could speak it and on previous occasions they had done so. But now it was different. After they finished their Russian conversation, they informed us that they rejected the proposals of the National Council. They insisted that the National Council endorse their proposals for organizing a Communist Party right away. They demanded that we should not participate in the Emergency Convention called by the Socialist Party. We were then forthwith dismissed from the meeting like two schoolboys who had just received a spanking. Isaac Ferguson was very much distressed. He felt that the National Council should capitulate to the Russian Federation. I pleaded with him to the contrary. His reply to me was, "After all, comrade, whenever it comes to a question of revolutionary tactics, I feel inclined to follow the Russian comrades. Have they not lived and been brought up in a country where the revolution has been successful?" Today the same intellectual cowardice and lack of independence finds its counterpart in the subservience of present-day Communist leaders to Stalin.

John Reed was in Chicago at the time, attending the sessions of the newly-elected National Executive Committee of the Socialist Party, which the Right Wing of the Socialist Party refused to recognize. When Reed returned I held a conference with him and Jim Larkin, at which we decided to fight tooth and nail against the Russian Federation and for the decisions of the National Left Wing Conference. On that very day the National Council decided to capitulate to the Russian Federation, Larkin and I being the only members to vote against capitulation. Reed publicly supported our position, though he was not a member of the National Council. Those who capitulated were Fraina, Ruthenberg, Ferguson, Ballam, Dr. Cohen and Wolfe.

We immediately took the fight to the New York membership. The Kings County Socialist Party, the largest single section in the New York Left Wing, decided to participate in the Socialist Party Convention; so did Local Queens. We were outvoted by the Manhattan membership, though we carried a number of the branches. In The Bronx we lost the decision by one vote, due to the tactics of Jay Lovestone, who kept disturbing the meeting and interfering with the vote to such an extent that a number of members left the hall in disgust. John Reed, MacAlpine and I resigned from the staff of *The Revolutionary Age,* because of our opposition to the policy of the National Left Wing Council. On August 15 we launched a paper called *The Voice of Labor.* John Reed was the editor and I the business manager. This paper made phenomenal headway. In a very short time it attracted a paid circulation of over 25,000 copies.

About three days before the memorable September 1, 1919, Jim Larkin, John Reed and I discussed the question of going to the Socialist Party convention to represent the New York Left Wing. Money was needed. Among the three of us we had fifty cents. How to get more? We decided to call a meeting of our supporters immediately, hold elections for delegates to the convention and then and there try to raise the necessary funds. The next day the meeting was held. The three of us were elected delegates and the money was raised to send us to Chicago. I left with Reed for Chicago immediately. John Reed was as jubilant as a college boy going to a football game. It was my first trip to Chicago. I was to see a stretch of the country I had not yet seen. John Reed and I little guessed what the immediate future would hold in store for us. We discussed plans of what we would do. We did not expect to capture the Socialist Party. The split in our own ranks made that impossible. But we were agreed that as a result of our participating at the Socialist Party convention we would get the support of the radical element in the Socialist Party to build a genuine American Communist Party, for which we believed there was a great need. Both Reed and I in our discussions on the train had come to the conclusion that with the Russian Federation and the other Language Federations dominating the movement, no movement that was worthwhile could be founded. The American Communist Party, we decided, had to be an American party led by Americans, in the same way that the Bolshevik Party was a Russian party led by Russians.

A little over a month before, the Left Wing had formulated

a program at its National Conference. All the Left Wing leaders who were soon to launch the Communist movement were present and helped to formulate it. This program, as we have seen, gives an insight into the minds of the Communists in 1919, and what they stood for. The National Left Wing program was an elaboration of the program of the New York Left Wing. It was, however, more specific on three important points: first, in its definite break with the official Socialist movement and non-Communist working-class political organizations, as for example a Labor Party; second, in definitely opposing the American Federation of Labor and calling for the splitting of that organization; third, by its disavowal of democracy. The program, in its entirety, was nothing more or less than a declaration of war against democratic government, the Socialist Party and the trade union movement. On the Labor Party and the Socialist Party it stated:

> A Labor Party is not the instrument for the emancipation of the working class; its policy would in general be what is now the official policy of the Socialist Party—reforming capitalism on the basis of the bourgeois parliamentary stage . . . *There can be no compromise either with Laborism or the dominant moderate socialism.*

From this language it is clear that the Left Wing was preparing for a war to the bitter end against all non-Communist working-class political organizations. On the American Federation of Labor the program went on to say:

> Our task is to encourage the militant mass movements in the A. F. of L. *to split the old unions,* to break the power of unions which are corrupted by imperialism and betray the militant proletariat.

The existing trade unions were considered instruments of American imperialism which must be split and destroyed. On democracy the program clearly declared:

> In form a democracy, the bourgeois parliamentary state is in fact an autocracy, the dictatorship of capital over the proletariat. . . . The proletarian revolution disrupts bourgeois democracy . . . which must be destroyed.

On my way to Chicago I certainly could not foresee that Bolshevism, seeking a monopoly of the labor movement by the destruction and annihilation of all non-Communist working-class organizations and advocacy of proletarian dictatorship, by the destruction of existing progressive forces of civilization and its opposition to democratic principles, was preparing the way for reaction in the form of Fascism. I was convinced that Bolshevism was a system of revolutionary theory and practice which would enable the working class to overthrow Capitalism and institute Socialism. I was going to Chicago to build a Bolshevik party for the United States. I foresaw that many difficulties would have to be overcome, but entertained no doubts as to the ultimate success of the cause to which I had devoted my life. John Reed, I am sure, entertained very optimistic views as to the future success of the Communist venture in the United States. I listened to him talk about his plans for the future, of his trip to Russia after the Chicago conventions. He sensed then that Moscow was destined to play a very important part in the development of the Communist movement. That Moscow would set itself up as the undisputed boss of the movement he did not and could not at that time foresee. We arrived in Chicago in the morning and rented a room at the Atlantic Hotel. Here we stayed until the convention was over.

Chicago was the journey's end for the Left Wing of the Socialist Party. It also marked the end of the period which owed its inspiration to the war and to the early phases of the Bolshevik Revolution. The movement attracted many of the best and most militant elements of the Socialist Party. These, however, were not attracted by a consideration of the needs of the country and of the American working class. Because of the apparent success of the Bolshevik revolution, its championship of Socialism, and its open declarations against war, they accepted its principles even though in so doing they abandoned positions they had steadfastly maintained as to the democratic foundations upon which Socialism must rest. Attracted also were many youthful elements who became inspired with the romance of the Russian revolution, but who had little or no idea of what Socialism or Bolshevism really was. The base of the movement was provided by the membership of the Russian Federation and the other Slavic federations, the majority of whom were motivated by nationalist emotion rather than Socialist conviction. To these must be added a considerable group of adventurist, unprincipled job-seeking individuals, mostly confined to the leadership, who expected the revolution to spread rapidly throughout the world and hoped thereby to bask in its glory. Besides, many of them realized that there were many advantages to be gained by breaking with the Socialist movement and tying up with a new movement that would be connected with the ruling class of such a mighty country as Soviet Russia.

Among all those I met at the time in the Left Wing movement I cherish most my association with John Reed and Jim Larkin. With John Reed I worked closely on *The Revolutionary Age, The Voice of Labor* and *The New York Communist*. We were independent rebellious spirits at that time. The Communist International and the Moscow leaders had not yet put us into party strait-jackets. We mixed the seriousness of our work with adventure and play. An idea struck us to publish a fake *Socialist*. It was done. An exact replica of the *Socialist* was printed. The articles were written by John Reed and Eadmonn MacAlpine. The bundle was deposited at the Rand School Book Store. When the Right Wing Socialists bought it and began to read the contents, they fumed and protested at their own editorial board, only to discover the hoax later by recognizing a slight difference in the type used. For that exploit we were charged with forgery by the Right Wing. We, however, enjoyed a good laugh at the seriousness with which they took the incident. Then there was the attempt to liberate Eugene V. Debs from Moundsville prison by force. Jim Larkin organized all the preliminaries. In on the scheme were Jim Larkin, members of the Irish Republican forces, who were to carry out the plan, John Reed, Louis C. Fraina and I. On the day the plan for Debs' liberation was to be carried out, and without Debs' knowledge, the authorities transferred him from Moundsville, West Virginia, prison to Atlanta, Georgia.

John Reed and I also worked on a bold but fantastic plan to break the blockade of Soviet Russia with an American merchant ship loaded with food. John had succeeded in interesting a captain who was ready to run his ship, flying the American flag, through the blockade established by the British and French naval authorities. The United States had not joined the blockade. Martens agreed to defray the expenses of equipping the ship with a cargo of foodstuffs. He was afraid to take the responsibility of hiring the captain and the ship specifically for that purpose. We therefore tried to raise the money through private sources. We did not succeed, because those with money who professed to be friends of Soviet Russia either refused or were afraid to underwrite the expedition. Because of the nature of the proposed exploit the funds could not be raised publicly.

The cause then was uppermost in our minds. Other things mattered not. John Reed often wandered about penniless. I received just enough money for the barest necessities. Regular wages were out of the question. But we worked all hours of the day and night. No time was taken off for careful planning; indeed, there was no time for serious thinking, let alone constructive planning. We were in a fight right now against the Socialist Party which was a preliminary to the revolutionary struggles which were to follow. We failed to give serious attention to the fact that on the eve of the Chicago conventions the country was going through a hysterical Red scare. The Attorney General's office under the supervision of A. Mitchell Palmer was exploiting the Red scare for all it was worth. The Seattle General Strike and the Winnipeg General Strike and the many "outlaw" strikes that broke out in defiance of government edicts and the express orders of the labor leaders increased the hysteria against the Reds. Attacks upon our meetings and headquarters by men dressed in the uniforms of the returned soldiers, aided by government agents and police, were common occurrences. Every device for stirring up anti-Red sentiment was employed. Plots were unearthed, bombs discovered, and some even exploded. The anti-Red hysteria was fanned into a high pitch of frenzy by reactionary politicians who hoped thereby to gain political advancement, by all the open shop and anti-labor interests of the country, by a large section of the press and by labor spy agencies, who now saw a splendid chance to sell their stock-in-trade to the industrial interests. Certain wealthy individuals were also persuaded by these spy agencies that their persons and possessions were in immediate danger of a Bolshevik revolution.

Lumped together as Reds were all factions of the Socialist Party, the I. W. W., the Anarchists, liberals and trade unionists. This atmosphere permeated the city of Chicago on the eve of the three conventions which marked the split of the Socialist Party and the organization of the Communist movement. If we who had participated at the three conventions had been awake to the situation confronting the labor movement, we would have come to Chicago with only one purpose in mind—to unite our forces in order that we might more effectively fight the wave of reaction which was sweeping the country. But there was not one among us who gave the question of unity a thought. We drifted with the prevailing tide. To us the internal war in the Socialist Party was of the utmost importance. It alone mattered, for we believed that its outcome would to a very large extent determine the course of the social revolution in the United States.

The Socialist Party convention took place at Machinists Hall, 113 South Ashland Boulevard, on the second floor of the main auditorium. The Left Wing Convention, which culminated in the organization of the Communist Labor Party, took place on the first floor of the same building, in the room which the Left Wing delegates had hired for caucus purposes. The Russian Federation's Communist Party convention was held at "Smolny," named after the headquarters of the Bolshevik Government in Petrograd, the Chicago Smolny being the headquarters of the Russian Federation. Max Eastman characterized this convention as the Slavic-American Communist Convention.

As soon as our bags were deposited, Reed and I went to Machinists Hall, to meet the other Left Wing delegates, and to organize our forces for the Socialist Party Convention. We arrived at the hall bright and early. Comrades Katterfeld and Wagenknecht had made all arrangements for registering the Left Wing delegates and for holding caucus meetings. The Socialist Party convention was to open that morning. The arrangements committee was meeting during the morning at the National Headquarters of the Socialist Party. We had dispatched a number of comrades there to find out what were the plans of the Right Wing Old Guard for the convention. We soon found out that delegates had to register at the National Headquarters, where only those who were not contested would be allowed to sit in the convention as accredited delegates. Each delegate who was approved by the arrangements committee received a white card of admission. As soon as we found this out, we called together a hurried caucus of our delegates. Only a few were present. It was clear to us that by this arrangement the Old Guard was determined to exclude a sufficient number of our delegates to maintain a majority for itself. The "Democratic Socialists," as they liked to call themselves, in an emergency which threatened their control of the Party, quickly found ways to overthrow democratic procedure. We decided that they should not succeed in excluding the Left Wing delegates. The strategy we worked out was that as many Left Wing delegates as it was possible to summon together should immediately enter the convention hall and take their seats. These delegates were to be prepared, when the convention was called to order, to participate in all the preliminaries of organizing the convention—namely, in the election of a temporary chairman and the election of a credentials committee to determine who were the delegates entitled to vote.

But the Old Guard had much more convention experience than we had. Their convention forces were manipulated by Julius Gerber, the secretary of the New York County organization of the Socialist Party. A man with years of experience in party organization and conventions, Gerber was alive to all moves and left nothing to chance. No sooner had we entered the hall than Gerber came rushing in, ordering all to leave. I was in the rear of the hall when John Reed and Gerber engaged in a tussle. It did not last long. The arrangements committee had seen to it that police were on hand, and with their aid all of us were cleared out of the hall and the doors locked. Reed immediately drew up a protest regarding the use of the police, which the executive board of the Die and Tool Makers Lodge No. 113

signed and presented the next day to the Socialist Party Convention. This protest stated in part:

> We call upon you to take steps to remove the police or make such arrangements as will satisfy us that you are not responsible for the presence of the police. . . . We are not asking this to put hardships on you, but for the best interests of the Socialist Party and the labor movement in general.

The Socialist movement as well as the trade union movement looked upon the police with disfavor, for it was an unwritten law to exclude police from the internal affairs of the Socialist Party and the trade unions also. In resorting to the police, the Old Guard showed how desperate was its position. Without police assistance they would have had to submit to the organization of the convention by the Left Wing, which would have been in a majority, or else bolt their own convention. How strong the Left Wing delegation was, is indicated by the vote for chairman of the convention. Seymour Stedman, a lawyer from Chicago, received 88 votes, and Joseph Coldwell of Rhode Island, a Left Wing delegate, received 37 votes, these representing the number of Left Wing delegates who had received white cards and were allowed to take their seats. At the Left Wing caucuses there were present about 100 delegates from 23 states, most of them representing English-speaking sections of the Socialist Party and a good cross section of the country. When the Socialist Party Convention voted down a motion of its Left Wing delegates that action on the contested delegates be taken up as the first order of business, the Left Wing delegates bolted the Convention. Though the Emergency Convention of the Socialist Party opened on Saturday morning, August 30th, the Convention of the excluded Left Wing delegates which founded the Communist Labor Party did not officially open until September 1st, after the excluded California Delegation had submitted a statement to the Socialist Convention which we drew up, and which ended as follows:

> That unless the convention takes the above action [action on contested delegates] before transacting other business, the delegates from California, representing the overwhelming sentiment

of their constituents, do join with the delegates refused seats and the comrades of the expelled and suspended federations and states, in the immediate formation of a real revolutionary Socialist Party in the United States,—the Communist Party of America; and we urge all comrades having the good of the working class of the United States and the world at heart to at once leave this reactionary convention and repair to the floor below to help us organize the proletariat of America for the final victory over capitalism.

The few remaining Left Wing delegates at the Socialist Party Convention bolted after the reading of this alternate statement. Downstairs they were met by a cheering, excited crowd of the Left Wing Section of the Socialist Party. The convention was called to order. Delegates and visitors rose spontaneously. Our singing of the International fairly shook the building and ended with thunderous applause for Revolutionary Socialism and Communism.

John Reed and I made up a steering committee of two during our stay in Chicago. We worked out every detail of strategy together. In our tactics we consulted during the lunch periods with Max Eastman, who was reporting the conventions for the *Liberator*. At these meal time conferences there was often present, besides Eastman, Henry M. Tichenor, who owned and edited a Socialist paper called *The Melting Pot*. We dined together at a Chinese restaurant on West Madison Street. Eastman usually gave us good advice, some of which we accepted. He was not so sure that the course we had mapped out would suit America. In the main he was in sympathy with what we were doing, but critical. Reed was all enthusiasm. He seemed to be driven by an impatience and a desire for action rather than calm deliberation. But he knew his shortcomings, the fact that he was new in the political movement, and he readily sought advice and accepted it.

Our meetings at the Chinese restaurant were not confined to the politics of the convention. Reed liked to reminisce about his rich experiences and adventures. He never tired of telling about his experiences as a war correspondent in Germany and how he used to embarrass the representatives of the general staff and the foreign office. However, when Reed spoke about the I. W. W. his eyes would sparkle with delight, his words expressing a deep sympathy and love for the organization. The I. W. W. was part of the fiber that made up John Reed. He knew it and had been in it in its days of fighting activity and romance. The I. W. W. strikes thrilled him. The free speech fights, and the heroic struggles of the Wobblies in the bull pens, were reminiscent of the bold, pioneer spirit of the West, and John Reed was of the West. This movement of roving workers, traveling up and down the country in carefree abandon, militant and anarchistic in their defiance of authority and exploitation, struck a responsive chord in John Reed. Besides the I. W. W. was a movement of action and song, the songs that always stirred within his poetic breast. Max Eastman on these occasions was usually restrained, his humor subdued and philosophical. Tichenor, when he was present, was the life of the party. Reed used to lean over the table, the better to hear this man of the Middle West, in appearance like Clarence Darrow, tell his ribald stories. He used to roar with glee at their simple, sturdy humor.

The convention of the Russian Federation Communists opened up at the "Smolny" on September 1. No sooner was Fraina elected chairman of the convention than the factional struggle broke loose. There were three factions represented: The Russian Federation, which, together with the other Slavic federations, controlled the largest bloc of votes; the Michigan delegation, which disagreed with the Russian Federation on what a Communist Party should be, but united with it in splitting away from the Socialist Party; and the English-speaking delegation, which had violated the decisions of the National Left Wing Conference in order to go along with the Russian Federation in organizing the Communist Party. The convention was therefore conducted on the basis of negotiations among the caucuses representing these factions. The delegates tried to create the impression that they alone represented the true and genuine Communist forces of the country. They soon denounced the other conventions in Chicago in typical Communist style, classifying the Emergency Convention of the

Socialist Party as Right Wing, the Communist Labor Party Convention as the expression of American Centrism, and their own as the real Left, the true Bolshevik convention. In the unity negotiations with the Communist Labor Party, they gave ample expression of their self-glorification as the saints of Communism. They claimed that they represented the only *conscious* Communist elements. The proposal of the Communist Labor Party to unite the two conventions in order that only one Communist party should emerge from Chicago they rejected by a vote of 75 to 31.

The Ruthenberg minority, by splitting the National Left Wing under pressure from the Russian Federation, was largely responsible for the chaos which prevailed in Chicago. The Russian Federation would never have issued the call for the organization of a Communist Party in defiance of the English-speaking membership, if the Ruthenberg group had not gone along. For all their disdain for the Americans, they realized that without an English-speaking wing they could not organize a Communist party in the United States. True, they united with the Michigan delegation to force a split in the Left Wing. But they neither trusted the Michigan comrades nor considered them Communists. At the Chicago Convention the Russian Federation began to tighten its hold on the Ruthenberg faction. Against the obstinate wall of Russian Federation delegates, little could be done. Ruthenberg therefore sought the admission of the Communist Labor Party Convention delegates on the basis of equality. With them added, a better showing could be made against the Russian Federation majority. However, the question of unity was not looked upon as a question of principle but as a political question involving merely the jockeying for power at the convention.

When defeated upon this question, the Ruthenberg faction staged a sit down strike. All its members who held convention positions and membership on committees resigned. Ferguson, reporting the convention in the *Communist*, the official organ of the Communist Party, of September 27 characterized the act as follows: "The minority 'strike on the job' had its quick effect." But this "effect" did not bring about the unity of the

Communist forces. It had the effect of forcing the Russian Federation to come to an understanding with the Ruthenberg faction. And in the deal that was made, unity with the Communist Labor Party was forgotten.

That the Ruthenberg faction never took unity of the Communist forces seriously is further brought out in the first number of the official organ of the Communist Party, edited by Fraina and Ferguson, both members of this faction at the convention, which declared editorially:

> That there are communist elements in the Communist Labor Party is a fact, and particularly the comrades of the Pacific Coast. But it is equally a fact that these comrades have the opportunity of affiliating with the Communist Party. They are now being misled by the Lore-Katterfeld-Wagenknecht Centrists and by the Reed-Carney emotionalists.

What was not reported, however, was the fact that the Russian Federation was prepared to admit John Reed the "emotionalist" to their convention, but under no circumstances was I to be admitted. I was to be driven completely out of the movement, because of my opposition to Russian domination. This final proposal was submitted to Reed personally by Ruthenberg. He had hoped by informing Reed of this fact to cause a break between us and bring about the downfall of the Communist Labor Party Convention. Reed immediately took up the matter with me, never for one moment leaving any doubt that he scorned the offer and detested its motives. I think that Ferguson, officially reporting the Convention for the Party in its official press, characterized it more properly than he intended, in saying:

> For one thing the fact that the Federation delegates were largely Slavic emphasized the close union between the organization of the Communist Party here and the parent organization which came into being at Moscow in March of this year—the Communist International. It was the Russian expression of Marxism which predominated this convention, the Marxism of Lenin, and the party traditions of the Bolsheviki.

The Communist Party organized in "Smolny Institute," Chicago, was dominated by foreign-born workers and owed its organization entirely to Russian Bolshevik inspiration. The Communist Party I helped to organize at the same time, though its delegates represented the American elements in the Left Wing of the Socialist Party, also owed its organization to the same inspiration. The difference between the Communist Party and the Communist Labor Party was evident in the desire of the Communist Labor Party to apply what it believed to be Bolshevism to American conditions. The Communist Party, on the other hand, was oblivious of America. Its heart was in Russia and its head full of Bolshevik abstractions.

The closing days of the Communist Labor Party Convention took place at one of the I. W. W. headquarters on Throop Street. Before every session Reed and I discussed questions of policy. Reed, more than I, understood that we would face a fight in Moscow on the question of recognition by the Communist International. He realized that he would have to gain recognition of the Communist Labor Party by overcoming the opposition of the Communist Party. Because of the fight for recognition that would have to be fought out in Moscow, we were very careful to hew close to what we believed to be Bolshevism. This brought about a clash between us and the American delegates from the Middle West and other states, who although opposing the policies of the Right Wing of the Socialist Party, were not yet fully prepared to accept what we presented to them as Revolutionary Socialism and Bolshevism. At the same time, we had to counteract the charge that we were a centrist organization. This brought us into conflict with a small group of Eastern delegates, who refused to accept the theories of Bolshevism in their entirety, like Louis B. Boudin and Ludwig Lore, who had maintained an independent position in the Left Wing controversy. These elements were branded as centrists, because they preferred to take a position to the left of Social-Democracy, yet hesitated in accepting the extreme positions of Bolshevism. The Russian Bolsheviks directed their fire at this time against the centrists, insisting that their influence had to be destroyed first, if the world revolution was to be successful. To be called a centrist was the most damning charge that could be hurled against a Communist.

Our task was therefore twofold: We had to induce the convention to adopt our Bolshevik program and in addition defeat the so-called centrists, notably Lore and Boudin. We succeeded by the sheer weight of argument and oratory in overcoming the opposition of the Western delegates to the program. But Boudin was obstinate. He had the reputation of being one of the foremost Marxian scholars in the Socialist movement. He argued that the program was un-Marxian, that it was in total disagreement with the Communist Manifesto of Marx and Engels. He had delivered a terrific attack just before adjournment for lunch. John Reed was very much worried. As we went to the Chinese restaurant to eat, he turned to me and said: "Ben, we must do something to kill the effect of Boudin's speech. He made a deep impression. I don't know what to say in answer to him."

"Don't worry," I said, "I have the Communist Manifesto with me, and I have just the quotation you need to show up Boudin." We sat down at the table and I showed him the quotation. His eyes sparkled with glee. He could not wait for the time when he was going to spring his surprise. As soon as the convention reopened John Reed asked for the floor. He launched a sharp attack upon Boudin, and ended by flashing his copy of the Communist Manifesto and read from it to prove that Boudin did not know what he was talking about. Boudin shouted back, all excited, "Let me see that copy." Reed handed it to him. He read it, hesitated, and then exclaimed that it was a poor and false translation from the original German.* I followed up the attack. In reporting the incident, Max Eastman stated:

> Therefore, it was a practical, as well as theoretical, triumph for the majority when Ben Gitlow, walking up to the front of the hall like a great sombre mountain unloosed the crackling thunder of his eloquence to the effect that Boudin had deliberately employed his knowledge of Marx to destroy and dilute the scientific

* The English translation of the Communist Manifesto had been approved by Engels.

integrity of this platform, and Boudin, crying "It's a damn lie," got up and fled like a leaf out of the storm.

When Boudin grabbed his portfolio under his arm, took up his cane and fled from the hall I was relieved and John Reed chuckled with glee. We had demonstrated how to deal effectively with centrists. But our troubles were not yet over. Ludwig Lore was elected to the National Executive Committee. This came as a distinct surprise. John Reed became panicky. I also realized the gravity of our situation. The Slavic federations' Communist Party would seize upon the election of Lore as convincing proof that the Communist Labor Party was a party of Centrism. Something had to be done. I was a good parliamentarian. Comrade Wagenknecht was chairman of the session. When he announced the complete results of the balloting, he asked if there were any objections or reasons why the vote should not stand. I directed Reed to object and state his reasons. Meanwhile, I rushed to the back of the platform, got hold of Wagenknecht and Katterfeld, and explained to them why the election of Lore would be bad for us. A motion to reconsider the elections was carried. I spoke on the kind of an executive we needed and explained why Lore should not be elected. On the second balloting Lore was defeated and our Bolshevik skirts were clean. I did not run for the executive and neither did Reed. I knew that if I had accepted, the Communist Party would have charged that I split the Communist forces because I wanted to be elected to the National Executive Committee. I preferred not to give them that opportunity. Instead, I ran for the Labor Committee and received the highest vote. John Reed, as had been planned, ran for International delegate and was elected.

When Reed and I came to Chicago together, we were determined not to capitulate to the Russian Federation. We were out to build an American Communist Party, a party that would make the Revolution in the United States as the Bolsheviks had made it in Russia. I had put my whole being into the work of organizing such a party. Throughout the convention I labored with that one object in mind. I was very serious in my purpose and fostered no personal ambitions. The leadership which came to me I accepted, fully conscious of its responsibilities. I was twenty-six years old at the time. What spurred me on were not the cold abstractions of theories, nor political ambitions. Injustice, human suffering, the callous exploitation of workers, the brutality of our system and the useless extermination of human life were the basic motivating causes of my rupture with capitalism. I treasured human values above all other considerations. It was for safeguarding these human values that I had become first a Socialist, then a Communist.

Reporting the Chicago conventions, Max Eastman wrote in part: "The most powerful figure in the militant group—and the best speaker, I should say, in all three conventions—was Ben Gitlow." But Max Eastman evidently had not seen in Chicago a stranger who left a lasting impression on me, a certain minister, his garb old and threadbare, who came to one of our caucus meetings and whose name I never learned. He was very much disturbed over what was going on. He accosted me—why, I don't know—and in all seriousness said, "What is taking place here will not end well for the labor movement. It means strife, internal conflict, frightful suffering; eventually, war and devastation." The manner in which he said it struck home. Here was a Socialist who was wrought up over what was happening to the Socialist movement. He spoke in a low voice, with no venom. There was a note of sadness in his tone, as if some great personal tragedy was in store for him. Through all these years I have not forgotten his words. The sincerity with which he said them impressed me. The marks of poverty were clearly expressed on his haggard face. He looked at me and at all the world with a calm, saddened stare. Perhaps I thought for a moment that he might be right. A comrade passed by and jeeringly asked me what the "skypilot" had to say. I just shrugged my shoulders. Yet in more than one way, his words have come true.

Before the Russian Revolution the Left Wing of the Socialist Party was pro-I. W. W. in its sentiment. The Left Wing felt that the I. W. W. put into practice the tactics of revolutionary Socialism. It was therefore no wonder that the Chicago conventions were greatly influenced by the I. W. W. At the same time what was going on in Chicago also had an effect upon the I. W. W. When the Communist Labor Party Convention was transferred to the I. W. W. hall, the Wobblies gathered at the rear of the hall and closely followed what went on. Many of them realized the new movement was going to play an important part in the growth of the I. W. W. A number of the I. W. W. members said that the Communist movement was dynamite for the I. W. W., that it would end in wrecking their movement. A number of them were obviously impressed and took the position that the Communist movement was adding that understanding of government and politics that was lacking in the I. W. W.

John Reed and I took the first opportunity we had, during a lull in the convention, to visit William D. Haywood at the general headquarters of the I. W. W. on West Madison Street. Haywood, in his shirt sleeves, was seated at his desk. He was very glad to see us. Reed he knew well, but he met me for the first time. He was now an old man in appearance, and when he looked with his one eye through his spectacles it was difficult to realize that here was a man whose whole life from boyhood on was a struggle against adversity on behalf of Labor. He spoke in a low musical voice. The conventions that went on in Chicago interested him very little. The I. W. W. was uppermost in his mind, and most important was the job of organizing a defense for the I. W. W. boys in prison. Haywood had just been released from jail on bail pending an appeal on his case. He had been convicted in August, 1918, together with 99 other members of the I. W. W., charged with interfering with the progress of the war. The war was over now, but the conviction still stood. He went into detail, telling what he was doing to organize the defense forces and raise the necessary funds for legal and other purposes. I could see from the way he spoke that he was deeply affected by the fate of his fellow-workers. Haywood impressed me very much by the simplicity of his character. His sensitive feelings revealed a big man with a big heart. There was, however, a little note of pessimism in his voice. He was somewhat discouraged at the losses the I. W. W. had sustained. He was a little troubled about his future, intimating that if he returned to prison he would end his days there. He asked us to help in the defense of the I. W. W. prisoners, because only through a display of working-class solidarity could their release be obtained.

When asked about his opinion of the Russian Revolution, he replied, "Yes, it seems they have done a good job in Russia." We asked him to acquaint himself with what was going on in Chicago and with the Communist movement. He said he had been busy working on the defense, but certainly would look into the matter at the first opportunity. I saw him again one evening at the I. W. W. headquarters in front of Jackson Park. Here a large frame house with a veranda had been converted into an I. W. W. hall. The place was full of Wobblies, many of whom were dressed in overalls. They gathered in groups on the porch, arguing among themselves. In one corner Haywood was reclining on a rocker. Grouped around him were a score of Wobblies. He did not look at all like the robust fighting miner that he was when I first saw him in New York. With his spectacles and the bald spot bordered by fringes of light blond hair here and there turning gray, he looked more like a genial retired locomotive engineer from the Middle West. The Wobblies looked up to him like a father. In fact, his demeanor towards them was like that of a grandfather to his loving grandchildren. I greeted him. It was the last time I greeted him in America. When next I saw him he was an exile in Moscow.

The conventions finished, the following remained the result of their deliberations: the Socialist Party, which it had taken many years to build, was decimated, while the Communist movement was started with three splits at its birth—namely, the Communist Party, dominated by the Russian Federation; the Communist Labor Party, consisting of the English-speaking representatives of the Left Wing of the Socialist Party; and the Michigan State Socialist Party, which soon became the Proletarian Party of America. Our Communist message fell upon deaf ears, as far as the American people were concerned. But our failure to impress the American people did not prevent our penetration of the labor movement. The Chicago experience did not only represent a split in the Socialist Party, it represented much more than that: it registered the official date when we started the civil war in the labor movement. This war has become more general with the growth of the Communist movement, wider and more violent in its scope. It has divided the working class, raised havoc among the liberals and sown dissension in all ranks.

Before the Chicago Conventions the Left Wing had approximately sixty thousand members. Most of them were foreign-born, belonging to the foreign-language-speaking federations of the Socialist Party. About a tenth—roughly, six thousand members—were either American-born or belonged to the English-speaking branches. Of these, many were psychologically unfit for a revolutionary movement that sought to constitute itself the government of the United States. After the Chicago Conventions both Communist parties were even more foreign-born in their complexion than the Left Wing had been. The splits in Chicago scattered the sixty thousand Left Wingers. Only a fraction of this number joined the new Communist parties. The return home from Chicago was that of armies with few laurels to show, tired and exhausted, straggling from the field of combat, their ranks greatly decimated. The Socialist Party, which boasted over a hundred thousand members before the split, was left with somewhat over twenty-five thousand. The Communist Labor Party and the Communist Party together had slightly less than that.

But what stands out as a result of the Chicago experience is the Russian character of the movement. The determination of the Russian Federation to control the movement out of Russian nationalist considerations certainly characterized its early phases. When better contact was established with Soviet Russia and the Communist International, the Russian heritage was not cast off, the Party did not become more American, but instead more Russian. The Russians still rule, although the dominance of the Russian Federation has been done away with and their leaders have been replaced by American leaders. For the Russians now rule from Moscow. Their decisions and orders must be obeyed. The American Communist Party is only a tool in their hands, its leaders their puppets, who must dance to every tune they play. John Reed and I had fought against the domination of the Russian Federation, little realizing that what we were fighting against was only a danger signal of what was yet in store for us.

On our way back to New York I took the opportunity of the long train ride to relax from the strain and excitement of the Chicago days. I had some forebodings of the future. I told John Reed that we were not going to have an easy time of it, that the rank and file would not be pleased by the turn of events in Chicago. Many of them in Chicago had expressed themselves to me. They were dissatisfied. They blamed the personal ambitions of the leaders for the split in the movement. But Reed was not troubled by what I had to say. I ended by saying, "The die has been cast. We will have to fight the thing through." Reed, however, was jubilant. He often remarked, "Ben, we have a Communist Party and I think a good Bolshevik program for America. Moscow will have to sit up and take notice of us." He now spoke as the International Delegate of the Communist Labor Party of the United States. He repeatedly kept harping on the fact that he must go to Moscow without delay to present the Party's credentials to the Bolsheviks and to affiliate it with the Communist International. My mind was on what we must do to build the party in the United States, John Reed's on how to get recognition for it from Moscow.

CHAPTER II

THE RED RAIDS OF 1919

THE Communist Labor Party first established its national headquarters in Cleveland, but soon afterwards moved to New York, where its headquarters were established at 108 East 12th Street, in a house rented for us by Dr. Julius Hammer, who not only paid the rent but later bought the house and turned it over to our party. Here we also established the headquarters of the Labor Committee, which I headed; the business and editorial offices of *The Voice of Labor,* which was the organ of the Labor Committee, edited by John Reed and managed by myself; and the New York City headquarters of the party. Before the office was actually established, John Reed, as had been decided, left for Moscow. The necessary money was raised by Max Eastman, the necessary sailor's papers secured through the efforts of Jim Larkin, for Reed was leaving for Europe as a stoker. One night, dressed in his work clothes, Reed hurriedly came in and said good-bye. It was his last farewell, for I was never to see him again.

The Communist Labor Party had its hands full in getting started. All kinds of difficulties were in the way. The factional fight with the Communist Party not only took up a great deal of time but also drove many members away from us. The reaction in the country was becoming more pronounced. On October 16th, the secretary, organizers and editors were arrested and charged with violating the anti-syndicalist laws. This happened at an organization meeting in Cleveland. From all over the country we received reports of the hostility of the federal and local authorities. The press kept up an incessant barrage against us. Many of our meetings were either broken up or prohibited. Our activities, and especially the activities of our rival, the Communist Party, helped to add oil to the flames and gave the reaction every reason to proceed against us. We openly called for the violent overthrow of the United States Government. We isolated ourselves by attacking the A. F. of L. as an agent of the capitalist government and calling upon the workers to build new unions that would not be afraid to use their economic power for revolutionary purposes. When strikes took place we called upon the workers to turn them into revolutionary channels, the Communist Party actually calling upon them, as it did in the strike of the Brooklyn street car men, to overthrow the government and establish soviets. We existed in a state of semi-legality, always expecting to be attacked and arrested.

On November 7th most of the meetings we organized for the celebration of the anniversary of the Bolshevik Revolution were prohibited by the police, who saw to it that the halls we had hired remained darkened and closed. Most of us however did not realize how far both the local and national government was prepared to go. We knew that the Lusk Committee was busy investigating us, but we did not expect that the investigations would soon lead to arrests and indictments. We were therefore caught by surprise when the famous Lusk Committee raids came. On the night of November 8th, I was addressing a meeting of the Lettish Club in upper Manhattan in celebration of the Russian Revolution. In the middle of my speech about fifty police, detectives and operatives swooped down upon us in the name of the Lusk Committee. All the men present were lined up against the wall and searched for membership cards. I had some confidential papers in my possession which involved Ludwig Martens, the official Soviet representative to the United States. I slipped them out of my pocket and dropped them behind the radiator in front of which I was standing. When the examination was over about twenty-five of us were huddled into a patrol wagon and taken to police headquarters. But we were not a dejected crowd. We were in the best of spirits. We were, after all, revolutionists, ready to sacrifice all for the revolution, so that a mere arrest and a ride in a patrol wagon was a trifling incident.

The police headquarters was alive with excitement. Policemen and detectives were running to and fro. We were taken to a large room, which to me looked like an auditorium capable of seating a thousand persons. Many comrades from all parts of the city were already there. Nobody knew what it was all about. New batches of comrades were being brought in continually. Soon after I arrived Jim Larkin was brought in. He was given a seat next to me. On the platform in front of the room was seated Archibald Stevenson, the counsel for the Lusk Committee and actually its head, and a number of men and women who acted as interrogators and interpreters. Most of those examined were released. When I appeared before them I had only time to tell them my name. I was immediately placed in the custody of two detectives who proceeded to take me to the rear of the hall. My insistence on knowing why I was being detained was left unanswered. The same thing happened to Jim Larkin. I knew that I was being held for something serious—how serious, I did not know. Out of the thousands brought to police headquarters, the Lusk Committee detained about thirty persons. About three o'clock Sunday morning we were locked up in the cells in the basement. I was tired and hungry. So were all of us. But that did not dampen our spirits. Jim Larkin and I were put in one cell, a narrow contraption of steel and cement about four feet wide and seven feet long. A cot made of latticed iron strips was suspended with iron chains from the wall. The cot was very narrow. No mattress, sheets, blankets, pillows or bedding of any kind were supplied. At the head of the cot facing the cell door was a porcelain toilet bowl. Jim Larkin and I were to spend all of Sunday and a part of Monday together in that cell. We had large overcoats which we used for bedding. But when we lay down the thick iron lattice work penetrated through, making it impossible to sleep. Every bone in our bodies ached. Jim Larkin tried it, I tried it, time and time again. It was no use. Once when I got off the cot I laughed for all I was worth, for there was big Jim Larkin, of Dublin, Ireland, over six feet tall, seated on the toilet bowl, fast asleep. But we Reds were not a sad lot. We yelled through the bars to one another, called the authorities and our keepers all kinds of names and sang revolutionary songs all through the night.

There was method in the treatment we received. We were arrested on Saturday night, so that no legal steps could be taken before Monday for our release. In the meantime Stevenson could create sentiment against us through the reports he gave the press of his citywide raids upon the Reds. Through these raids he sought so to dramatize the situation that public opinion would be against us and the judges before whom we would be arraigned should be properly impressed. In addition, spending as we did almost two days cooped up in a little cell, unable to wash, shave or even comb our hair, did not improve our appearance when we were brought into court. We emerged with dirty shirts, our clothes creased and disheveled, looking like desperate criminals who could be guilty of any crime. Before arraignment and in violation of the law, we were fingerprinted and "mugged," and those horrific photographs were later published in the official report of the Lusk Committee. After we had been kept waiting an eternity in the court room of Chief Magistrate McAdoo, our attorney, Walter Nelles, informed us that the reason for the delay was Archibald Stevenson's inability to make up his mind as to the crime with which to charge Larkin and me. He finally decided to make it criminal anarchy, under the statute that was passed by the New York Legislature against the Anarchists during the hysteria following the assassination of President McKinley.

When arraigned before the judge on this charge, we pleaded not guilty. Bail was immediately set at $25,000.00 each. A friend of mine, a Socialist in the real estate business, offered free and clear real estate for much more than double the amount set, to secure the bail. A hurried consultation took place between the prosecuting attorney and the magistrate's court, Archibald Stevenson and Judge McAdoo, and a ruling was handed down that the bail must be in cash or Liberty Bonds. The moment bail was set at the exorbitant figure of $25,000.00 I knew that I faced a serious charge. I looked upon the case as a challenge to the newly organized Communist Labor Party. As much as I desired freedom and as little as I enjoyed the prospect of many years in prison, I nevertheless realized that, from the Party standpoint, the greatest publicity possible must be made out of the case, my own liberty and personal comfort being secondary. Cash bail not being on hand, Jim Larkin and I were handcuffed together. I bade farewell to my friends and parents, who were in the court room. Larkin and I laughed at Archibald Stevenson, who expected us to collapse when the bail was refused. Put in the custody of a couple of detectives of Geegan's Bomb Squad, we were escorted to the Tombs. Larkin and I were lodged in one cell on the main floor.

"Well, Jim," I said, "How do you like our new hotel?"

"It has all the improvements. If the service is all right, I suppose it will be satisfactory," he replied in his haughty Irish manner.

The cell was fairly large. An upper and a lower cot extended from the wall. Each of us was provided with a thin mattress, two cheap shoddy blankets and a pillow. A porcelain toilet bowl with no separate seat and a small wash basin with running water completed the equipment. The smell of disinfectant and bed bug exterminator pervaded the whole place. Above us stretched four tiers of cells. In all, it was a dirty, foul-smelling place infested with vermin and bedbugs. Prisoners came and went, some out on bail, others to face trial, and some to Sing Sing; the vermin and the bedbugs stayed on, and with them the sickening aura of their alleged exterminators, which by no means enhanced the palatability of the utterly abominable food. The mush and the hash were awful to look at, let alone eat. I never saw a prisoner touch the stuff. Many threw it down on the floor in demonstrative disgust. Most of the prisoners bought their own food from the commissary, a privately run concession which did a thriving business. The prices were controlled and therefore reasonable, though the food was not of the best quality. I must add that, on the whole, I found the keepers considerate. But during the few days Larkin and I stayed in the Tombs our attorneys succeeded in having our bail reduced to ten thousand dollars each, in either cash or Liberty Bonds. Dr. Julius Hammer supplied the Liberty Bonds, and one fine morning we breathed free air again.

The period I was out on bail awaiting trial was marked by continual blows against the Communist movement. The attacks of the United States Attorney General's office and the deportation activities of the United States Labor Department took on the character of a nation-wide crusade against the Reds. Besides, all the leaders of the Communist Party and of the Communist Labor Party had been indicted on state charges either in New York, Ohio or Illinois. Most of them had been apprehended and were out on bail awaiting trial. To hold meetings of the executive committee, we had to move from place to place to cover up our trail, in order to avoid being raided. I remember particularly one meeting of the executive of the Communist Labor Party, held in the offices of the *New Yorker Volkszeitung,* the oldest German Socialist Paper in the United States, at 15 Spruce Street. Ludwig Lore was the editor of the paper and present at the meeting. A worker on the staff rushed in with a long tape from the news ticker, shouting excitedly at Ludwig Lore, "Comrade Lore, it's very important news. We must not miss it. We must feature it." He started reading from the ticker, "Nationwide raids started this evening by Attorney General Palmer against the Communists throughout the country. . . ." As he read, citing one city after another—Patterson, New York, Pittsburgh, Chicago, Boston—the National Headquarters of the Communist Labor Party in New York, various city headquarters, clubs, newspapers, and the like, we realized for the first time the nationwide scope and thoroughness of the raids. It was uncanny to think that only a few minutes before I had left our national headquarters on Twelfth Street and that now it was already in the hands of federal authorities with all our records gone.

We immediately decided to postpone the meeting of the executive committee, to take place later at an attorney's home in Brooklyn. Each one present was assigned to go out on a tour of inspection, to see what had taken place and to gather all available information. I went to the National Headquarters on Twelfth Street. A large van stood in front of the place. Into it federal agents were loading papers, records, files, books and literature taken from our headquarters. Then I went from one place to another. All our local headquarters showed the physical effects of the raids. Besides, all were still under strict guard by federal agents. These raids, followed by deportation proceedings, were evidently conducted by the federal government for that express purpose, because all caught in a place who could not prove citizenship were turned over to the immigration authorities. Ellis Island in New York was jammed with thousands of our foreign-born members. Defense machinery had to be hurriedly set up, to handle the task of locating those arrested, securing a hearing for them and procuring their release on bail.

Attorneys Charles Recht, Isaac Shorr and Walter Nelles immediately came to our assistance in handling the legal matters involved. Money to pay for defense had to be raised, bail secured, public opinion aroused against the deportation activities and order created in the organization out of the chaos resulting from the raids. Money came pouring into the defense channels immediately, bail to a very large extent was raised by the frantic relatives of those being held. However, no sooner did we overcome the effects of one raid than another one started with equally devastating effects.

These raids were very costly to the movement. They struck at its very heart and terrorized its foreign-born membership. Thousands of members dropped out. The organization was very badly crippled. A simple necessity as vital to any organization as conducting correspondence with its members and local subdivisions became impossible for the time being. Organizers had to be sent out to reestablish contacts, and when they returned the reports were very disheartening, because most of the former contacts had been lost completely and the new ones established to replace them were only a fraction of the old. For all practical purposes the movement in the smaller towns and cities was almost completely wiped out. The Communist Labor Party and the Communist Party suffered alike in this respect. A few months after the Chicago conventions both parties together had only from eight to ten thousand members. In fact, so badly was the movement disorganized that it was impossible to check up on its membership in order to determine its actual number.

The movement went into a state of semi-illegality. The underground character of the movement consisted at the time in holding all meetings strictly secret and in breaking up our large branches into small units of from ten to fifteen members. When the movement shortly afterwards went completely underground, the units consisted of a maximum membership of ten. Meetings took place in private homes and were carefully guarded. All the members and officials of the party assumed fictitious names. We believed that in going underground we were giving evidence of the revolutionary character of our movement, for we reasoned that before the Russian Revolution the Bolshevik Party too was an underground party. We ascribed the attacks of the government to the capitalist fear of the revolution we Communists would soon lead—a revolution, which like the Russian Revolution, would dislodge the present government and put the Communists into power. Many with whom I spoke said in effect, "It is now possible to know which Communists can be depended upon when the revolution comes, because all the cowards have now left the party." They were sure that in the underground party we would learn, as the Bolsheviks did, how to engage in conspiratorial and revolutionary activities.

The few members we retained welcomed the change into an illegal party. The conspiratorial atmosphere surrounding the underground movement was so romantic as to be enticing. One joined a small group, the leader of which was appointed, not elected. Meetings were held in different places under a veil of secrecy, with always the possibility of a sudden raid. One lost his real name and adopted a party name. Sometimes we adopted more than one name. For example, I went under two names, Tom Paine and John Pierce. Many times the legal and the illegal, as we called the underground names, became confused. At an underground meeting we sometimes called a comrade by his right name; whereupon, he would protest most violently. Very often at public meetings, where the real name should have been used, the illegal one was used instead, much to the chagrin of those who knew the person under his real name. Needless to say, the members of the foreign-language federations got a real thrill out of underground party life, as they hid in their secret meeting places and romanced about their fantastic plans. Divorced from the politics of the country, having little or nothing to do with the problems of the workers, they could plot and counter-plot, in comparative safety. Through their benevolent and cultural organization they were able to reestablish a good part of their membership in the underground, so that while the English-speaking membership was greatly reduced, the numerical superiority of the foreign-speaking membership was very much higher than before. The result was that the underground Communist movement was less American and more than ever dependent for its finances on the foreign-language federations. Shortly, however, the influx of money from the Communist International of Moscow lessened this financial dependency.

From the day I was released on bail to the time I was indicted by the Grand Jury there was always excitement and trouble. The Lusk Committee and the federal government never ceased their attacks. Martens was hailed before the Lusk Committee and subjected to a gruelling examination as to his credentials and finances. The Lusk Committee followed up the raids in New York City by raids in cities upstate. The indictment was handed down in November, 1919. I was again brought into court, pleaded not guilty and continued on bail until my trial took place in the Extraordinary Criminal Trial Term of the Supreme Court presided over by Justice Bartow S. Weeks. The District Attorney decided that my case should come up first. Others indicted on the same charge were James Larkin, Charles E. Ruthenberg, Isaac E. Ferguson and Harry Winitzky, secretary of the New York Local of the Communist Party. We were indicted, except Winitzky, for publishing the left-wing Manifesto in the July 5, 1919 issue of *The Revolutionary Age*. We had neglected to build up a defense movement around the cases and now it became necessary to proceed with all haste. The securing of a good trial lawyer who knew how to defend the labor viewpoint became imperative. Our executive committee decided to secure the services of Clarence Darrow, the famous Chicago lawyer who in 1907 had ably defended William D. Haywood and many other labor cases. Comrade Daniel

Curley was immediately dispatched to Chicago to induce Darrow to take charge of the case. Curley succeeded in this mission, a retainer was telegraphed to Chicago and Darrow became my attorney.

Curley was one of my closest companions in the movement. I first made his acquaintance at the Left Wing headquarters on 29th Street. He took care of the headquarters and did odd jobs. When I had charge of *The Revolutionary Age,* Curley helped to mail the paper. He had a ready wit and could tell stories rich in humor and imagination. He was of Irish Canadian stock, having been born in Canada at a trading post of the Hudson Bay Company of which his father was in charge. He was a mixture of Irish stubbornness and frontier individualism. Rebellious in spirit, he was subservient to no one and was usually at odds with everyone except me. If I wanted any thing done I had just to ask him and it was forthwith attended to. He enjoyed arguments, was well informed and a good talker, and in a dispute his tongue was sharp, his sarcasm cut to the bone. Once he debated Larkin on the question of trade unionism. Larkin, who towered over him in stature, spoke in a loud voice and was no respector of personalities. It seemed as if Larkin would just crush him with his size, domineering manner and loud voice. But Curley just smiled. A devilish glint lit up his eyes as he took the platform. Curley began to unravel a story, full of superlative descriptions of how Jim Larkin, the Irish labor leader, sipped tea on an English lawn with an English Countess:

> "And shall I put one or two lumps of sugar in your tea, Mr. Larkin?" asked the Countess. And what do you think this Irish labor leader just off the docks of Dublin replied? "Two, if it please, your ladyship."

He went through all the mannerisms. The audience roared with laughter. Jim Larkin listened in amazement, then lost his temper. He challenged Curley to a fight and called him all kinds of ugly names. Larkin completely forgot about the debate. Curley, however, did not. When the debate was over, I asked

Curley, "How about that story—was it true, what you said about the Countess and Jim?"

"Oh, that, why, it never took place! I just made it up to get Jim Larkin's goat."

In the days of the Left Wing a spirit of comradeship prevailed which one cannot find in the radical movement today. Our Left Wing headquarters were always open. All felt themselves on an equal plane. The most modest rank and file comrade did not hesitate to discuss questions with the leaders or to join with them in fun and jokes. One of Reed's pastimes on 29th Street was to call a certain comrade over for the purpose of discussing a question of Marxism with him, just because he liked to watch the solemn expression on his face when he discussed Marx. On these occasions Reed would purposely take the most ridiculous position on Marx, in order to arouse the ire of the comrade over his ignorance. A crowd would soon gather and the argument, once started, would wax furious for hours. Every now and then Reed, with a very serious mien, would interrupt, "But, comrade, Karl Marx never said that. Did you not read in volume three on page 600 that Marx said the direct opposite?" "That is impossible," the exasperated comrade would protest excitedly, "I'll bring volume three with me next time to prove you are wrong and don't remember what you read."

I was too busy to worry about my case. I did not see Darrow until the eve of the trial. He was not enthusiastic about the case. "Oh, I know you are innocent, but they have the country steamed up. Everybody is against the Reds." He seemed not a little frightened when I told him I intended to stand by every Communist principle and to defend my position regardless of the consequences. I was indicted on two counts for publishing in *The Revolutionary Age* and the Left Wing Manifesto and Program, and for printing in the same paper an article by Nikolai Bukharin entitled, "The Communist Program." These, the indictment charged, advocated the overthrow of the United States government by force, violence and illegal means. When Darrow realized that I was determined to defend the views of both the Manifesto and the Bukharin article he insisted that there was no use in my taking the stand. I agreed to his proposal, provided that he would allow me to address the jury on my own behalf in my own way. He agreed, saying, "Well, I suppose a revolutionist must have his say in court even if it kills him."

The trial opened in an atmosphere of hysteria. The court room was filled with detectives. Everyone who came to witness the proceedings was carefully scrutinized. From the very start Judge Weeks showed his prejudice. The prosecutor, Assistant District Attorney Rorke, took advantage of every opportunity to create a hostile attitude. The selection of the jury was a long and tedious affair in which the judge bent over backwards to please the prosecution and was obdurate as far as the defense was concerned. We had very little to pick from, because the special jury panel selected from what was known as the "silk stocking district," was made up of individuals, who, being ultra conservative, obviously could be depended upon to bring in the verdict against the Reds, as desired by the prosecutor.

During the trial, the prosecutor tried to bring in all kinds of extraneous matters for the purpose of blackening my character. But these attempts were so crude that even Judge Weeks could not allow them, and upheld Darrow's objections. One, for instance, was to try to introduce checks and money orders received by me as manager of *The Revolutionary Age,* in an effort to prove that I was pocketing the money and making plenty out of the revolutionary business. He knew very well that *The Revolutionary Age* had no bank account and that it was heavily in debt. Furthermore, he also knew that its editors and I as its manager seldom got paid and that, when we did, it was a mere pittance, usually about ten dollars every other week.

I followed the trial closely. From the very start I was of the opinion that the verdict would be against me. However, I could not help but be angry at the Judge. Weeks appeared to me everything but impartial. His interpretation of the law, his narrow definitions of what constituted legal means in effecting a change of government, left the jury no other recourse but to convict. Time and time again he stressed the fact that the only legal way of bringing about a change is through the ballot box and that all other methods were illegal. To demonstrate on behalf of political objectives through mass demonstrations or by means of the strike in his opinion constituted a criminal act.

In summing up the case, the prosecutor made an appeal to the prejudices of the jury, to their hundred percent Americanism and coupled it with a personal attack upon me which pictured me as the worst blackguard in America. I did not mind his speech, because I expected it and realized that he did not believe the half of it. I knew that he expected to make political capital for himself out of the case and through it perhaps elevate himself to the office of District Attorney of New York.

The speech of Darrow I discussed with him before he delivered it. I knew it was to be one of his flowery appeals to the jury, seeking, through arousing their sympathy and feelings for righteousness, to get them into a mood favorable for an acquittal. Upon my insistence his speech also included a defense of the right of revolution and an attack upon the hysteria which was sweeping the country. On the question of revolution he said:

> For a man to be afraid of revolution in America, would be to be ashamed of his own mother. Nothing else. Revolution? There is not a drop of honest blood in a single man that does not look back to some revolution for which he would thank his God that those who revolted won.

Later on he said—and emphatically, too—

> It is utterly idle to talk about the abolition of a government by voters. It cannot be done.

In attacking the red hysteria, he said,

> If Lincoln would have been here today, Mr. Palmer, the Attorney-General of the United States, would send his night riders to invade his office and the privacy of his home and send him to jail.

It was clear that evasion was not the tactic which I adopted. I was determined to fight out the issue squarely, insisting upon my right to advocate the communist program for revolution in the United States.

When I rose to address the jury, I was nervous. It was a new experience. I had addressed hundreds of meetings of all kinds. An audience never frightened me. But here in court it was different. I could feel that the room was surcharged with hostility. I felt that the jury would somehow be impatient and would not quite understand what I would say to them. I had not written my speech, but I had it well mapped out in my mind. I did not expect what followed. From my knowledge of other labor cases it had never happened before. The Judge continuously interrupted me and objected to what I had to say. Whenever my attorney rose to my defense he overruled him. It was obvious that the judge wanted to break up my talk, disconnect my thoughts and finally spoil whatever effect a continuous well-thought-out speech would have upon the jury. I criticized capitalism, attacked the war, defended the Russian revolution and what I believed to be its system of democracy in industry. I ended my speech with this defiant note:

> Well, gentlemen of the jury, I think that when you read the manifesto of the Left Wing Section of the Socialist Party, you will understand what the fundamental principles involved in the manifesto are. I want you to realize that I believe in those principles, that I will support them and that I am not going to evade the issue. My whole life has been dedicated to the movement of which I am a member. No jails will change my opinion in this respect. I ask no clemency. I realize that as an individual I have a perfect right to my opinions, that I would be false to myself if I tried to evade that which I supported. Regardless of what your verdict may be, I maintain that the principles of the Left Wing Manifesto and Program on the whole are correct, that capitalism is in a state of collapse, that capitalism has brought untold misery and hardships to the working man, that thousands of men in this democratic republic are in jails today on account of their views, suffering tortures and abuse, and nothing . . .

Here the judge again interrupted, stating

> Again the defendant must cease from making statements. There is no evidence before the court that anyone is in jail or suffering tortures and abuse. Proceed.

I concluded:

> All I ask of you gentlemen of the jury is to consider the language of the manifesto, to realize that the manifesto stands for a new order in society, a new form of government, that the Communists believe in a new form of society and necessarily in a new form of government and will bend all their efforts in that direction.

When the Judge closed the case by giving his instructions to the jury it was with great effort that I could control myself. As he spoke I felt that I was like a fly caught in a spider's web. Every word was calculated to impress the jury adversely. When he finished I turned to Charles Recht, who was assisting Darrow, and said, "It is all over now. The jury can do nothing else than bring in a verdict of guilty." The jury filed out. I felt relieved that the trial was over. The nervous strain of that day in court made my temples throb. I knew that in a very short time the course of my life would change. Darrow did not even wait to hear the verdict. He knew what to expect. The jury deliberated about three quarters of an hour and returned with the expected verdict of guilty.

Weeks sentenced me to the maximum—five to ten years in Sing Sing at hard labor. When my attorney sought clemency, the judge interrupted Recht and said, "I am sure that what you are saying does not meet with the approval of your client and that if he were asked he would make no such plea for clemency." He was right, for I directed Recht not to proceed further. Then the judge thanked the jury in a speech in which he took notice of the fact that I had not accumulated private property by saying,

> A young man, twenty-eight years of age, of intelligence, a striking example of the educational system of this country, able-bodied, of full intellect, confesses he owns no property. Employed at forty-one dollars a week the last time he was employed and never accumulated any property!

Evidently Judge Weeks judged a man's worth only by the property he accumulated and held in scorn those who were propertyless.

The sentence given, I was seized by two officers, taken immediately to the Tombs and lodged in a cell on the main tier. The realization that I was no longer a free man struck home. Recent events went through my head in a kaleidoscopic whirl. I took very little notice of the many doors that were opened and shut behind me, the steps up and down, the short walk across the Bridge of Sighs from the criminal court building to the Tombs. When I was locked up in my cell I was in a daze. I sat down on the cot. I was certain I would spend the entire ten years in prison, for I knew that the hysteria against the Reds was in full force and I did not expect it to abate very soon. I kept thinking to myself: ten years in prison will be a long time—I am twenty-eight years old; when I come out, I shall be thirty-eight. Who knows what will happen during that period?

I rose and paced up and down like a wild beast in a cage. The walls of my cell seemed to move about me in confusing circles. The strain of the day was taxing my mental and nervous system to its capacity. Again I heard the district attorney shout his abuse, again I heard the Judge's harsh interruptions. Before me I saw his undersized figure, his prominent hooked nose; he looked like a vulture ready to pounce upon me and destroy me. What a little fellow he was—and how great his hate of me! My temples throbbed fitfully. This will never do, I said to myself. I am not the only one who has ever gone to prison. Many have gone, some for a very much longer time and some never to see the outside again. If they were able to do so, why can't I? I have made my fight. What is there to be ashamed of? Nothing! Then came a period of calm.

Although I felt keenly the separation from my many friends and the family I loved, I began to feel at home in my surroundings. The din of the Tombs seemed somehow familiar. Let the future bring what it would, I was determined to face it. I breathed a sigh of relief, threw myself on the cot and soon was fast asleep. Undisturbed sleep is man's greatest boon and perhaps the only time when he is really at peace with himself. When I awoke next morning the past was history. My new life as a prisoner began.

CHAPTER III

AMERICA'S FIRST COMMUNIST PRISONER IN SING SING

The Tombs became my home, its prisoners my companions. Those who have never been imprisoned cannot realize how closely prison draws together individuals from different walks of life, of different views, of entirely divergent psychological make-ups. The least common denominator of all the members of a prison community, the one factor that draws them together, is, of course, their imprisonment: all are captives, all enemies of the law. I was surprised how many of the prisoners were glad to make my acquaintance. They expressed indignation over my verdict. What in the hell was the country coming to when men such as I were being sent to prison! The respect with which they treated me pleased me because of its genuineness. In their many and varied ways they all sensed that I was in prison because I was fighting injustice. As one short fellow who came to my cell put it, "Pal, I'm glad to make your acquaintance. It's pretty rotten with the law when they begin to put a fellow like you in the pen. But I am with you. I am against the law, too."

During my stay in the Tombs I met all kinds of men: pickpockets, murderers, robbers, burglars, forgers, bigamists. All kinds of criminals entered and left the Tombs. Some were old; others, mere boys. Some, shrewd, mentally alert; others, undeveloped and below normal. One nervous fellow, a forger, was a cocaine addict. When he did not have the drug he was miserable. His despondency ended the moment he received his packet. Regardless of the strict rules against the use of drugs and their smuggling into the Tombs, the drug addicts succeeded in obtaining their supply regularly. I was never able to find out how they obtained it.

For exercise we were permitted to walk around the cell block an hour at a time, three times a day. We kept up a dizzy pace, getting nowhere, like squirrels turning the wheels of their cages. Only once were we let out in the yard. How exhilarating was the air! The blue sky overhead had never before looked so strange and so beautiful! But the yard was so small! It was surrounded by buildings on three sides, and on the fourth by a high stone wall. I soon got tired of the dizzy pace in the endless circle. All I could see was the gray wall and the red brick of the buildings.

Prison accustoms its inmates to limited spaces. If any ordinary person were told to walk up and down in a four by seven foot room for an hour or two at a time, he would soon rebel; and, if forced to do so, might even go crazy. Yet prisoners pace for hours up and down their narrow cells for relaxation. How do they do it? Go to the zoo and watch the animals in their cages. You'll get the idea.

A monstrosity in the Tombs was the visiting room, where relatives and friends were permitted to talk to the prisoners for fifteen minutes. It was long and narrow, with two parallel rows of wire cages made of a thick, close iron mesh. Each cage was as wide as a narrow telephone booth. In one row of cages the prisoners sat; in the opposite row, about two feet apart, sat the visitors,—all yelling and screaming at the top of their voices to their own dear ones, because in no other way was it possible to carry on a conversation.

The most horrible sight I ever witnessed in all my prison experiences was that of a young boy going stark mad. He was involved in some shooting affray. Picture to yourself a boy of about eighteen, shrieking in a high-pitched voice hysterical with terror, "Take him away! Don't shoot! Don't shoot!" His lean frame stretches upwards, so that he appears much taller than he actually is. Every muscle of his body twitches in convulsive fear. His eyes, glassy and large, bulge out of his head as they stare in sheer fright. Froth comes from his mouth. His boyish face, getting redder and redder, is contorted in agony and fear, his head moving from side to side in jerky spasms, as if to throw off an attack. His screams, ebbing into moans, are frightful to hear. When he is taken from his cell, two keepers must hold him with all their strength. He keeps wriggling in their grasp, frothing at the mouth, and his eyes stare, horror-stricken. With much effort the keepers force him down into a chair. He stretches himself upward, lets out an inhuman yell and shrieks, "Oh, the pistol! Take it away! Don't shoot me! Don't shoot me!" A sedative is administered, the shrieking and yelling dies down, the awful moaning continues. The ambulance from Bellevue comes. He is taken away.

I stayed in the Tombs longer than I was supposed to, because Sing Sing was quarantined, due to an influenza epidemic among its prisoners. The day I was informed that I would be transferred to "the Big House up the river," as Sing Sing was called, one of the prisoners came to my cell and said, "Well, pal, I am glad to see you leave this dump. Sing Sing is a fine place, a country home on the Hudson. You'll get lots of fresh air, good food, a nice clean cell, every one with running hot and cold water, a hospital bed to sleep on with a fine mattress, white sheets, pillow cases and warm blankets." I didn't expect all that, but I was sure that it would be a great relief to get away from the foul air and dirty surroundings of the Tombs. I did not know, but somehow felt that conditions in Sing Sing would be better. I had my sentence of five to ten years to do and I felt that the sooner I began doing it the better.

The next morning a number of prisoners were herded together by the keepers, handcuffed in pairs and marched to the prison yard. There we were placed in the custody of two deputy sheriffs, who put us into the sheriff's wagon which was already waiting for us. It was exceedingly cold that morning. New York was having a very severe winter. But I welcomed the cold air. I felt as if I had been liberated. The sky overhead was free, majestic, limitless. The prison gate opened for the sheriff's wagon with its human cargo. I enjoyed the ride. The city now looked strange to me, as though I had been away from it for many years. I was fascinated by all I saw. My fellow-prisoners enjoyed themselves by cursing every policeman we passed on our way. The deputy sheriffs were very considerate with me.

The stout fellow excused himself for putting "the cuffs" on me, as he called the handcuffs. "We had to do it," he said. "We were given the strictest orders to that effect." I did not mind.

During the ride my fellow-prisoners asked :"Say, Bud, how much time you got?"

"Five to ten," I answered, laughing.

"Oh, that's sleeping time. You can do that sleeping on one side."

When I found out what long stretches they were being sent up for, the shortest being ten years, I began to appreciate their humor. Many of them had sentences of life imprisonment. The only first-timer besides myself was a young Irish-American lad of about eighteen, who had received ten to twenty years for robbery. The others had been to prison before.

Our destination was Grand Central Station, where we were to board a train for Ossining. At the station the crowds gaped at us, as if we were dangerous beasts. One mother pulled her child close to her and clasped it tightly in her arms for protection. I was amused at the way people looked at us. Once on the train, the deputy sheriffs held a secret conversation, then unlocked my handcuffs and let me sit as if I were a free man.

On the way they spoke to me freely. They could not understand why I should be going to prison. They frankly declared that my case was a flagrant miscarriage of justice. I discussed local politics with them, mostly about Tammany Hall and the city administration. The stout deputy complained about the new Tammany Hall. "Before," he said, "everybody had a chance to get a job if he was regular. Now only the Catholic Micks are getting the jobs." The deputy sheriffs treated the prisoners like human beings, giving us cigars and cigarettes and on the train providing us with coffee and sandwiches. They spoke to us in a friendly manner, as if we were all old friends. We looked like a sociable crowd enjoying a pleasure trip.

The train ride was soon over. From Ossining we walked slowly up the long hill to Sing Sing Prison. From the distance I saw the gray oblong structure that was to be my home. Every moment of that walk on that cold winter's day was precious. A beautiful scene unfolded. The bleak prison on top of the hill.

The Hudson River, frozen from shore to shore, a silver ribbon, glistening under the melancholy colors of the departing sun. In the distance rose the Palisades, like the massive walls of an ancient feudal castle. Beyond the prison, hills, with ghostlike trees, their bare branches like outstretched arms tapered by fingers thinned to the bone. Everywhere snow covered the ground. I felt no fear in approaching the place. I confess, it appealed to me. I began to wonder what was in store for me. Perfectly calm, I took a fatalistic attitude and was prepared for anything that was to follow.

We entered the warden's office—a quiet, warm, business-like office. We were registered. The convict clerks, as they put down our history, eyed us shrewdly and intimated that things would not be so bad, after all. Registration over, each one was given a card. We were taken to the big gate at the southwest corner of the prison adjacent to the old death house. The keeper in charge of us shouted to the guard on the wall who controlled the gate, "Eight on the count." The two deputy sheriffs were on hand to see that we were safely delivered. The massive door swung open. We passed through, eight state prisoners, eight felons. The door closed behind us.

Many may wonder what are the feelings one experiences the first time he enters prison. I can only speak for myself. I felt as if I had just finished a period of my life, one that was already buried in the past. I regretted having lost my liberty, but I was not sad or dejected. I felt a little uncertain of the future and a little nervous, not because I was in prison, but because I did not know what were to be my immediate new experiences and how I would adjust myself to them. The old-timers seemed happy enough. They had been here before. They brought packages with them, knowing what a man needed here and what was allowed.

The keeper mustered us up in a double line. "Forward march," he shouted. He marched us up to the state shop. Here we were again registered in an office at the head of the stairs. We were told to undress completely. Each one was then given a coarse towel and a small chunk of brown soap. We were then ordered to go under the shower four at a time to take a bath. The four of us washed as best we could under the one shower, but before we were half finished we were ordered out. Another batch of four went under the shower.

All our clothes were taken away. New underwear was thrown at us—with our prison numbers stamped on them. Each one was given a shirt, socks, a pair of heavy crude shoes, a gray pair of pants and a gray jacket with metal buttons. All the clothing supplied to us was prison made, ill-fitting, of rough cheap material. It is said that clothes make the man. Truer still is the fact that prison garb makes the prisoner. I was amazed at the transformation. My fellow convicts no longer looked the same. They turned to me and said, "Your own mother wouldn't know you now." The convicts working in the state shop knew of me as soon as I came in. They gave me a warm welcome. I remember one of them turning to another and saying in Yiddish, *"Nu zeh vos zai hoben gemacht von a Mensch."* ("Now see what they have made from a man.") They told me not to worry, that things would be all right. I remember the sympathetic expressions on their faces—I have met it time and time again—a feeling on their part that my crime consisted simply of trying to make the world better and that a grave injustice had been done by sending me to prison. When I look back upon my prison life, it was this feeling on the part of my fellow-prisoners, the genuine concern over my welfare, their expressions of gratitude and sympathy, that I cherish above everything else.

From the state shop we were marched into the mess hall. The inmates eyed the newcomers. Many a hello and broad smile greeted the old-timers in the line who had been there before. But I was the center of attraction. I was pointed out continuously. We were seated at a table. All we got for supper was white prison bread, a cup of bitter black coffee without sugar, and a couple of spoonfuls of corn starch jelly on a plate. Nothing to grow fat on and not very satisfying. Then we were marched out of the mess-hall down through the yard to the bucket rack, which was situated in the rear of the yard facing the Hudson River. The cast iron buckets with their lids off—ugly, dirty, foul-smelling contraptions—stood in rows. We were each directed to take one off the rack. We took up our buckets and were marched back to the cell block.

I was locked in a cell on the ground floor. It was in a prison building about a hundred years old, built of massive blocks of limestone and iron bars, painted a dismal gray. The cell block, oblong in shape, towered in the center of the building five tiers high. Through the narrow windows of the prison building the light fell in parallel shafts. We were placed in cells situated in the so-called "receiving flats"—a section of the ground floor tier facing the darkest section of the prison—set aside for newcomers. Each of us was locked alone in a dark and dismal cell no more than seven feet long and about three feet wide. An iron cot, on which was thrown a thin mattress and a shoddy blanket, protruded from the wall. The floor of the cell was of stone. Rough limestone boulders with their jagged surfaces made up the walls. The ceiling was no more than seven feet from the floor. A small electric bulb supplied scanty light. A tin cup attached to the door of each cell was filled with water. The bucket, which I placed underneath my cot, was my lavatory for the night. Such bad living quarters I had not expected. It was my first unpleasant impression—and it came as a shock. Yet I did laugh when I recalled that in the Tombs I had been told to expect a room with hot and cold running water and all the comforts of a hospital bed. The prospect of living several years in a place like this was not a pleasant one.

My experience in prison, however, has been that always in one's darkest moments a ray of light just squeezes itself in. As soon as the keeper was gone the prisoner charged with looking after the receiving flats stopped in front of my door and said "You're Gitlow aren't you?" I replied, "Yes." He said, "It's a damn shame you're here, but it's not as bad as it looks. These are only the receiving flats. Tomorrow morning you will get your regular cell. It won't be so bad. You can fix it up and make it comfortable. Besides, you won't spend much of your time in the cell anyway. And the five to ten years—you will do that in three to nine years. That's a small bit; it will be over before you roll on your other side. If you want any smokes or other things, just let me know." Gratefully, I thanked him. Later I heard the noise of marching men, the clatter of feet walking upstairs, the slamming of doors and boisterous voices. Then a bell rang out loudly, followed by the shouts on all tiers, "Close all doors!" The keepers started to lock the cells. The count began. A few minutes later, the count completed, a bell rang, cell doors opened, and I heard the sound of hurrying feet. The cell block filled with voices and noise. Someone stopped in front of my door.

I looked at the man, a prisoner whom outside I would have taken for a prosperous business or professional man. He introduced himself as Doctor ——— "I am very glad to make your acquaintance," he told me. "I have read all about you in the papers. I want to help you and be of service to you. You will find that if you know how to conduct yourself, your stay here will be relatively comfortable and you will not get into trouble. Tomorrow you will be assigned to a cell. I have taken care that you get a cell on a tier that is kept clean by a Negro friend of mine, Jim. He will provide your cell with a good mattress, blankets and things you need. Later you will know what to get from home to supplement what they give you here. You will be assigned to Yard Two for work. In Yard Two ask for Jimmie Hughes. I have arranged with him to take care of you." Cheered, I thanked him, too. I was not alone. Men I never knew or met always came forward to help me at a time I needed help. Later in Auburn Prison and in Dannemora State Prison it was the same.

The cell was very cold. The limestone cells in Sing Sing are always damp and in the winter very cold. In the summer they are hot and the stones become so wet that the moisture drips from the walls. I was very tired. The first day had been a long one, full of excitement and mental agitation. I undressed and in my prison underwear stretched myself out on the cot, pulled the blanket over me and passed the night in blessed sound sleep. I awoke to the clatter of banging on my door. I got up and discovered it was morning.

We were lined up, each one with a bucket in his hand, and marched to the bucket rack. We emptied our buckets. Unlike the regular prisoners, who left them in the racks, we took them back with us to our cells. When the whistle blew we were marched into the mess-hall, where corned beef hash, consisting of mashed potatoes and shredded corned beef, was served with coffee and bread. After that we were taken to Yard Two and registered. Then came trips to the doctor for a superficial examination; to the school, to determine our mental development; to the principal keeper's office, where we were given to understand that we were prisoners, that we had to obey the rules, that we had no rights and that whatever considerations we did receive were precious privileges.

We were led to the Bertillon office, which had a small building of its own situated in the yard and separated from the administration building. Here we were photographed, front, left and right view. We were fingerprinted, each finger of each hand separately, then both hands, including the palms in full. Our footprints were also taken. We had to undress, and were examined all over for identification marks; all marks noted were registered on the card. A description followed—color and texture of hair, color of eyes, shape of ears, general description. Then the measurements began. The head was measured in width and length, the length of nose, arms, hands, legs, and feet. I was completely catalogued, deprived of the slightest possibility to elude identification.

The visit to the chaplain's office, for every new prisoner goes through the chaplain's hands, was both interesting and instructive. Before I went there I was warned to be on my guard, for the chaplain was very shrewd; in his polished and suave manner he might lead me into saying something that I would later regret. But I was rather intrigued by the idea of talking with him. The chaplain was Father Cashin, a Catholic. When I entered his office he asked me courteously to sit down. His face lit up in an inviting pleasant smile. He was well-built, a light-complexioned man with the straight chiseled features of the Irish. He looked at my card, studied it a while and then said, "I see that you are Jewish." "Yes," I answered, "I am Jewish. But not from a religious standpoint. As you undoubtedly know, I am an atheist." He smiled and continued, "I see that you are different from the other men who come here. You probably have good reasons for believing as you do. But now you are in prison and subject to the rules of the prison. My advice to you is to stay out of trouble while here. Being an intelligent man, you, I am sure, will obey the rules and follow the advice I am about to give you. There are all kinds of men here, some good and some bad beyond redemption. Most of them are ignorant, mentally undeveloped, but some are intelligent and, in spite of their being here, not bad. However, remember you are in a prison. And the best rule to follow in a prison is to be yourself, use your own judgment, confide nothing to your fellow-prisoners. Don't trust the best of them. You have heard the remark that walls have ears. They have ears in Sing Sing. You may pass a remark and you will never know how it got about."

I thanked him for his advice and told him that I came to prison to serve my sentence, that I had no intention of making trouble, that I intended to live up to the rules. He continued, telling me that he had charge of the library, that the library in Sing Sing was one of the best prison libraries in the country, that it contained a fine collection of books. He supposed that I would be interested in books and assured me that in the prison library I could find almost all the reading matter I would want. Then with a twinkle in his eyes he went on: "But I suspect that you will like to receive certain books that we do not have in our library and that you will like to get papers as well. I want to inform you now that I have the authority over all printed matter that comes into the prison. I alone can decide what books and papers are to be allowed in and what not. But I will not judge you by the ordinary standards. I will allow you to get the books and papers you desire, provided you will promise now that you will read them yourself and will not pass them around to the other inmates in the prison." I gave him that promise. Did I keep it? Of course not! I am sure he never expected me to, but just put it that way in order to protect himself if anything happened. He inquired about the law under which I was sentenced. It was new to him. I explained. He smiled good-naturedly, was very glad to make my acquaintance and hoped we would be friends.

After we were completely examined and documented, we

were enrolled in the Mutual Welfare League, the prisoners' self government organization in Sing Sing. Before the Mutual Welfare League was instituted by Warden Thomas Mott Osborne, an advocate of prison reform, the prison system, known as the old system, was based on harsh discipline. The régime which instituted the reforms, known as the new system, consisted of a less rigid and less brutal discipline, more freedom within the confines of the prison for the inmates, and the opportunity accorded them to supplement the discpline of the prison authorities with regulation of the men's conduct through their own organization, democratically chosen and administered. The office of the Sergeant of the Mutual Welfare League was situated next to the P. K.'s (Principal Keeper's) office. Lined up in the Sergeant's Office, we stood quietly at attention, while the Sergeant enrolled us in the League, gave each one a button, informed us of the rules of the prison, explained how important it was for us not to jeopardize the many privileges we now enjoyed in consequence of the League. The speech finished, we were marched back to Yard Two, full-fledged prisoners of one of the most famous prisons in the world.

Yard Two was an old one-story red brick structure that had been salvaged from a prison fire. Surrounding it were heaps of bricks. All the new prisoners were assigned to Yard Two before they were assigned to their regular jobs or transferred to other prisons. Prisoners who had broken rules and were punished were also assigned to Yard Two, as were the sick and the infirm and the gangs who worked outside the prison walls. Yard Two was the most colorful and interesting place in the whole prison. It took on the appearance of a pioneer camp on some Western frontier. I shall always remember one of its keepers, an Irishman, six-feet-six, well-built, in his early fifties, extremely gruff in manner. He always shouted out his orders in a voice charged with his dire retribution for disobedience, yet, notwithstanding the menace of his manner and his towering height, he was really a very gentle and kindly soul. He liked his charges and his charges liked him. The angrier he got, the more they kidded him. He towered above the whole motley lot of us and epitomized Yard Two.

The yard was divided into corners, coops and sections, each the claim of a particular group of prisoners. All around the walls were lockers of different sizes and shapes, made of old boxes and boards. Clothes lines were stretched across the yard on which the prisoners had hung their wash to dry—socks, underwear, shirts. Before the center of the rear wall was a large blow furnace, the remains of the blacksmith shop that had been Yard Two before the fire. This furnace was a very interesting and important institution. It was the communal cooking range. Around this range fifteen or twenty prisoners at a time would gather to cook their meals. Soup, macaroni, chops, hash, bacon and eggs, flapjacks, a dozen pots of coffee, all would be cooking at the same time. And the cooks were all experts. They would toss their flapjacks high in the air to turn them over and catch them just right on the pan. Around this community stove the busy cooks of all shapes and sizes argued, yelled, played pranks and had one hell of a broiling time. Yard Two was always full of men. Everywhere the groups could be seen arguing or washing or otherwise occupied. Jimmie Hughes had the largest place in Yard Two. I threw in my lot with Jimmie Hughes. He was a jovial Negro of excellent features who was greatly respected by the prisoners and the attendants as the leader of the Negro group, which, as I soon learned, he most certainly was.

In Sing Sing, if you had the wherewithal and the proper connections, there was no need to eat in the mess hall, where, except on special holidays, the food was far from good. Only a few dozen prisoners took their breakfast there, about fifty percent their noon-day meal and a mere handful gathered in the mess hall for the supper the state served them in the evening. Jimmie Hughes was one of those who never ate in the mess hall. An excellent cook, he was famous for his pies. He would come into the mess hall to collect a bucketful of the prunes served for supper that the men would not touch, and cook them into prune pies. These he disposed of at a quarter each, selling as many as he baked. I took my meals with Jimmie. His assistant was a short jet black Negro, an expert at gambling in all its forms. As a youngster he had been picked up by a gambling man in the South. They went the rounds of gambling houses, race tracks, resorts, saloons and cafes. He would laugh, telling me how they would rope in the suckers and how crooked every gambling game was. He was a quiet, unassuming little fellow who would chuckle to himself every once in a while. Besides helping Hughes at whatever Hughes put him to do, he would wash the dishes and clean up the corner—the Hughes domain—three times a day.

Through Hughes I made very important contacts. I soon discovered that the most reliable underground chain in Sing Sing was the one operated by the Negroes, consisting of Negro convicts working at strategic places, including the warden's office. Through this channel I could secure desired messages or articles from the outside or send communications to the Communist organizations which the censor would not otherwise permit or which I did not want the censor to see. It was done quickly, confidentially and faultlessly. Every time I used the services of the chain I paid a quarter. It was well worth it. Through my contact with this chain I knew what was going on in the prison, learned about orders received by the warden affecting the prison as soon as they were received. When drafts of Sing Sing prisoners to other prisons were contemplated, I learned in advance the names of those on the draft. I want to pay tribute to this Negro chain. It could be trusted implicitly. A job turned over to it was never discovered. Letters given to the chain to mail never reached the hands of the authorities. It maintained the highest moral code in this respect. I used the chain frequently. I never once had occasion to doubt in the slightest degree that my trust in them would be violated. Jimmie Hughes was also a help to me in many other ways. We were on terms of warmest friendship. This helped me materially with the whole Negro population of Sing Sing. As long as I was Jimmie Hughes' friend I was O. K. I could be trusted, and what was worth still more, they respected me.

I was warned by the prison authorities that a strict rule in prison was the one against having money in one's possession, infraction of this rule being severely punished because one had no need for cash in prison. Money could be deposited to my account. With it I could buy almost any necessity either at the store of the Mutual Welfare League or from the stores in Ossining. The rules provided that one could spend no more than $6.00 a week at the League store. But this rule was never followed. One could spend as much as desired.

I soon discovered that cash in one's pocket was a very valuable asset. I obtained my first cash by buying a carton of cigarettes at the League store on money deposited to my account with the prison authorities and selling it for cash. Rules or no rules, I soon found out how to get money into the prison. I smuggled it in myself through the visiting room. I had it sent in through the Negro chain by having a letter mailed to me with money. I soon discovered that obeying all the rules got you nowhere. All rules were generally being broken. Indeed, very often those who most strictly adhered to all the rules found themselves in trouble. In all my prison experiences I always did the things I thought it was possible for me to get away with, whether it meant breaking the rules or not. I was never brought up before the prison authorities for infraction of the rules. As far as they were concerned, my conduct was unimpeachable.

I found the inmates courteous, friendly, and helpful. The keepers were not intimate with me, but in the main treated me humanely and courteously. Had I been a bank robber, or labor union racketeer, I would have been given many privileges and favors. But I was a new type of prisoner. Though classified as an ordinary felon, they knew that I was not the type of criminal they were accustomed to take care of. They knew that I was sentenced for my political views. They expected me to be honest and incorruptible—and therefore kept their distance. But I very quickly adjusted myself to prison life. In the prison shop I made contact with tailors, who, for a small consideration in cash, made me a pair of prison trousers and a prison jacket to measure. We were allowed to wear gray shirts which we could buy at the store or have sent in from outside. Sweaters could be worn in place of the prison jacket, provided they were in gray. The only garment that marked one off as an inmate was the gray trousers. These trousers, tailored, well-pressed, clean, made one look far from the prison picture of a convict dressed in stripes. (My prison number in Sing Sing was 70900; my cell, 243.)

I came to Sing Sing after Major Lawes had been appointed Warden. Many of the prisoners were afraid that under Lawes the reforms that had been instituted by Wardens Brophy, Osborne and Kirchwey would be abrogated and the hated old system installed once more. But they were mistaken in their fears. The régime at Sing Sing was a very liberal one. It had its shortcomings, there were of course abuses but, in the main, it was very considerate of the welfare and comfort of the men. What were its main faults? The food was very poor and inadequate. It is true that most men could supplement their prison fare by getting food at the store or by having food sent to them by their relatives and friends. If they could procure food, they were permitted to do their own cooking. With cash, food staples could be bought from the prisoners who worked in the storehouse. Food supplies which the store-house received for the inmates were peddled by the prisoners working there and, I suspect, with the knowledge and collusion of the keeper in charge. Sugar, milk, fine cuts of meat, canned stuffs, found their way under coats and sold for a quarter or fifty cents or more, depending upon what one wanted. The finest cakes and the warden's delicious bread was sold by the inmates who worked in the bake-shop. The Negro cook who took care of the keepers' meals, and prepared the meals for the death-house, would deliver, for a cash consideration or its equivalent, a cooked meal from soup to dessert. The prison laundry washed prison underwear for one free each week. But if special service was wanted, it was possible to obtain it from the convicts who worked in the wash-house. The laundry came back washed spotlessly, everything pressed as neatly as by the finest laundries outside.

The prison regulations provided that you get a shave twice a week at the prison barber shop. The inmates were then not allowed to have razors of any kind in their possession. A haircut was given once a month. Without any difficulty one could, for a stipulated amount, arrange with a barber for haircuts and shaves as often as wanted. We could select a good barber and get as good service as we could get outside, if not better. One barber shop, run strictly as a private enterprise by a convict, was patronized by both prisoners and keepers. So crowded was this shop that customers always had to wait in line for their turn. One's cell could be kept spotlessly clean by paying the prisoner in charge of one's tier a stipulated amount every month for keeping it so. Even the bucket was cleaned and taken care of for one by the convict in charge of the bucket rack, if paid for. The bucket would even be taken from the cell and put back for the night. Of course the prisoners who had no money, or could not devise some way of making money, were badly off, and greatly envied their more fortunate associates.

The prisoners in Sing Sing were always afraid of being drafted to other prisons. Drafts took place every few months, sometimes, if secrecy was desired, at midnight or two in the morning. The reason for the drafts is obvious. The overwhelming majority of men sent to Sing Sing from New York State come from the City of New York. New York is the world's greatest breeding spot for criminals. The world's richest city is the world's most criminal numerically. Sing Sing, being the nearest state prison to New York City, necessarily becomes the receiving station for the metropolis' army of criminals. Sing Sing is not large enough to accommodate all of them. It, therefore, becomes necessary from time to time to send batches of them to the other prisons, notably, Clinton Prison at Dannemora in the Adirondack Mountains, to Auburn, the oldest prison in New York state, and to Comstock. But the prisoners resent being transferred, for Sing Sing is the most liberal prison in the state, and, being near to New York City, is more accessible to relatives and friends. Sing Sing, because it is a famous institution and is visited by thousands of sightseers, is very careful of its reputation. This results in a cautious application of the meting out of punishment for infraction of rules. In Sing Sing a convict has more free time, more fresh air, more diversions and entertainments to help him spend his time than in other prisons in the state. The régime is humane, and the contact with the outside world fairly well maintained; both from the prisoner's standpoint are very important and desirable. Hence the drafting of prisoners is responsible for many abuses. Those who have political connections and those who have money can find ways and means of either staying at Sing Sing or being transferred back to Sing Sing in a few months' time.

Abuses were also rife in the assignment of prisoners to the different jobs in the prison industries, maintenance, or administration. Jobs varied in quality from good to definitely bad, yet often the value of a job depended on how hard it was for an inmate to get it. The men were not always assigned to jobs on the basis of their fitness for the work. It was common gossip among prisoners that political pull and paying the price demanded for the job had a lot to do with one's assignment to a desirable post. From my observations the conclusions of the prisoners appeared to be correct, because rich men and those with political pull always did get the good jobs, the poor and those without pull getting the jobs that were undesirable.

I was kept in Yard Two for a long time, working about an hour or two a day at the odd jobs to which I was assigned; such as, washing windows and "manicuring" bricks. The metropolitan press carried a story that I was assigned to heavy work on a frozen coal and rock pile. But there was no rock pile in Sing Sing. "Manicuring" bricks consisted in picking out a few bricks from the mass of bricks left by the ruins of the fire, putting them into a wheelbarrow, and carting them to another part of the yard, where they were piled up. When the newspapers reported I was sweating on the rock pile, I was either visiting the various prison departments for registration and examination or else was sitting around in Yard Two listening to the stories or woes of my fellow convicts.

After sitting around in Yard Two for many months, I was finally given a job in the knitting shop. The inmates considered this shop the worst one to work in. The shop was run by Kennedy, a disciplinarian of the old system. The men feared and hated him. He was always finding fault with some one. One of the keepers in charge of the men in this shop was unfit to guard dogs, let alone men. He looked more criminal than the men he was in charge of, and there were some really ugly fellows among the hundred men there. My first job was assisting the packer. When the cutter, who supplied the work to the operators on the machine, finished his term and was released from prison I got his job. From then on my troubles began. At first Kennedy wanted to be satisfied that I knew my work, which he soon found out I could do very well. But when he saw me standing around doing nothing, because whatever had to be done was finished quickly, he started complaining that I was not doing enough work.

I decided to teach Mr. Kennedy a lesson. I gave him a "lay-down," as the clothing workers would call it. Whenever he passed through the shop I was busy working. He did not know I was working in my own way, turning out as far as I was able a perfect job, the kind of a job that necessarily took a great deal of time. I took my time placing the patterns on the lay, and figured and refigured in order to save materials. I succeeded in shortening the lays two to three yards from the lengths specified by Mr. Kennedy. He came to investigate and found everything in order. He was satisfied. In working with the electric cutting machine, I cut as if I were cutting men's suits made out of the most expensive woolen worsteds. It was very tiring to take my time cutting cheap flannel nightgowns for inmates of state insane asylums, pajamas, aprons, house dresses, etc., for the various state institutions. I hewed close to the line, made all curves perfect, and above all, deliberately took my time about it. Work of such quality was never before turned out in Sing Sing. But I gained my point. The work was not coming out fast enough for the operators on the machines, who had to sew the cut parts up into the various garments. Mr. Kennedy fumed. But he could not complain that I was not working, because whenever he looked toward the cutting table he found me busy at work. Finally, he asked me what was the matter. I told him there was nothing wrong; that I was working as well as I knew how, that I could not work otherwise. If he did not like the way I worked, he could put me at other work or make a change, since he had the power to do what he desired. He fumed and blustered and sent me out of the office.

As the cutter of the knit shop I also took care of the stock room, which was stacked with all kinds of piece goods. The cutter before me used to dispose of a few yards of piece goods from time to time in return for pocket money, cigarettes and favors. The inmates bought the materials to sew up into sheets and pillow cases, well-fitting underwear, handkerchiefs, and the like, which they used themselves, sold, or exchanged for other articles. When I was placed in charge of the cutting table my fellow prisoners came around, leaned over the table, looked knowingly and confidentially into my eyes, passed a few hints about the stock room and waited to see if I would bite. I knew very well what they wanted. I laughed and said: "See here, I am not selling anything. There is no use your trying to induce me to. I am no screw either. I am not here to watch over you or any of the prison property. Keep this in mind as far as I am concerned. I see nothing and hear nothing. Whenever you see the stock room door open, remember that. The rest is up to you, you can do as you please." Like old hands at a familiar game they understood me well. Whenever the stock room door was left open, they found the opportune time to sneak around my back, enter the stock room and make away with a bolt or two of goods. The market for sheets and pillow cases in particular became well supplied, and all demands on the part of prisoners for the same was immediately met, for a consideration of course.

In the Spring Jim Larkin arrived, and later on Harry Winitsky.

When Harry Winitsky arrived in Sing Sing he immediately became the talk of the prison. You must know Harry Winitsky to appreciate the humor of it all. On his arrival in Sing Sing, Harry weighed exactly three hundred and twenty-five pounds. There were no prison clothes on hand to fit him. But they had to give him gray pants. So the story went round that three men in the state shop who were assigned to make the pants in a hurry did not know whether they were making a pair of pants or a tent. Some said they actually got lost in the cloth and were missing on the count. Winitsky got his pants, but he did not get a belt with them. When he emerged in the yard he carried a bundle in one arm and held his pants up with the other. Every once in a while he let go, and down slid his pants.

"Some baby elephant," the prisoners said to me. "They'll have to blast the cell block to get him in."

One day Jim Larkin came to me for advice on how to mail a letter out without having it censored by the prison authorities. I informed him about the Negro chain. But when I asked him for the letter, he refused to give it to me. Evidently he was suspicious; either he did not trust me or the chain. Later when he informed me what he had done I became furious. As much as I argued with him that he had made a mistake, he refused to admit it, his Irish obstinacy showing up to perfection. Larkin had been foolish enough to turn over his "kite," as such letters are called, to the one keeper in the knit shop who was most despised and least trusted by the prisoners. A few days later the keeper informed him upon returning the letter that he had opened it, read it and that its contents were of such a nature that he was afraid to mail it.

We found out later that the letter was not opened by the keeper to whom it was entrusted, but by the proper prison authorities. Returning the letter to Jim was a bit of strategy: the authorities wanted to find it on his person. Soon thereafter Jim was called out to the visiting room to meet some one who came to see him. He took the letter with him. It is strictly prohibited to pass out letters through visitors. Jim knew the rules, but he was ready to take a chance. What he didn't know was that the keeper in the visiting room had been instructed to keep an eye on him. The moment Larkin attempted to hand the letter to his visitor, he was caught. The letter was taken away from him. Jim was subjected to a thorough search, in the course of which cash was also found in his possession, and then locked up for violation of the rules. But Jim Larkin was not punished as other prisoners in similar circumstances would have been. He was not thrown into the cooler, nor did he lose good behavior time. It was, however, very apparent that the prison authorities were aroused over Jim Larkin's letter. It was very clear that their attitude toward us changed. I sensed it and so did Harry Winitsky. Jim Larkin became exceedingly angry. He insisted that the prison authorities had committed a great injustice towards him, freely giving vent to his indignation.

A few weeks later, about three in the morning, I was awakened out of a deep sleep by the knocking of keys on my cell door. I jumped up. "Hurry up and pack," commanded the keeper in a gruff voice. "You are on the draft." I generally knew when drafts were taking place, because I was usually informed in advance who was on the draft. But not this time, for this one was what the prisoners called a "sneaky draft." It was kept secret by the warden from the prisoners and the keepers; you knew about it only when it broke upon you. I got dressed in a rush and packed up as quickly as possible. In about twenty minutes the keeper came around again, opened the door and commanded, "Follow me." I did. I was taken down to the wash-room, a large room with a cement floor, where the prisoners take their showers. The room soon filled up with prisoners, about sixty in all. The principal keeper was on hand looking us over. His assistant was also there. About a dozen keepers stood guard. A few of the convicts from the mess hall were also on hand to help get the draft off. We put our prison numbers on the bags which contained our belongings before they were taken from us. Jim Larkin and Harry and I grouped together. But not for long. The handcuffs and shackles made their appearance. We were manacled, two prisoners together, hand and foot. We had to walk in step, or else we could not walk at all. After being shackled, we were marched into the mess hall, where we got some hash, bread and coffee. In the dark we were marched out of the prison to a little station built next to the prison, especially for such an occasion. The special car was waiting for us. We were marched in, a grim, haggard-looking lot of desperados, desperados who had to be shackled—hand and foot.

Before getting into the car the men were in an ugly mood. They muttered curses. Some were worried over what had happened. Some were silent, but sullen and angry. I took in the whole scene. Again a new experience! I had scarcely become used to Sing Sing, when I was being shipped to Clinton Prison in Dannemora, a place noted for its "repeaters," hardened criminals who had long terms to do. Among us was a Spanish fellow who later was to be my friend and co-worker at Clinton Prison. He was sentenced by a judge in New York City to fifty-two and a half years at hard labor. When he arrived in Sing

Sing his long sentence was the talk of the prisoners. So it became the joke of the place. It was as follows: "Do you know why the judge slapped another one-half year on the sentence of 52 years?" "No, I don't," you answered. "Well," came the retort, "that was for war tax."

On another prisoner, a thin Italian fellow, the guards kept an eagle eye. He had been in the death-house, from which he was released because he squealed on some of his companions. They had paid with their lives, but he escaped the chair. The executed men had friends in Sing Sing. Drafting him became necessary for his personal safety. The other prisoners looked at him with contempt. Some remarked, "I wouldn't like to be in that 'Jawbony's' shoes. He'll get the knife in Clinton as sure as you are born."

Another one in the lot was a young red-haired Irish fellow with bumps on his head, a reddened face, pocked and scarred. His had been a life spent in institutions and prisons. To him prison was just another home. He was as hard as a brick and utterly fearless. His coarse ignorance was offset by a happy and jovial disposition. You could get along very nicely with him, provided you were careful not to offend him. We got along very well. "How are you, Bolsheviki?" he would greet me. "Put it here, old-timer," he would say, shaking my hand.

Once on the train the mood of the prisoners changed. They made themselves comfortable as best they could under the circumstances. I was shackled to Jim Larkin, who took the ordeal as good-naturedly as I. Harry Winitsky happened to be an odd one, so his hands were shackled together. He was lucky, because on the train his handcuffs were removed by the keeper, who made him the official water-boy of the shackled crew. He had to answer every call for water, by filling the one tin cup which was provided for that purpose with water and giving it to the one who asked for it. When the train started to leave the small platform of Sing Sing, the prisoners let out a yell, mingled with curses and catcalls. An incessant chatter arose from the human cargo. The keepers in charge of the car were treated to all kinds of verbal jabs and sarcasm. In a few moments we were at Ossining, where we were attached to a regular train. When the whistle blew and the locomotive bell rang the prisoners shouted and cursed again. The gray mist of early morning lifted, the Hudson ribboned her silvery way, and we were off to Clinton Prison. The windows were kept closed, to prevent an escape, and every possible precaution was taken by the guards to see that no one could get away. Shoes came off, cigarettes were lit. The smoke, mixed with the odor of sweaty feet, made the air stifling.

Prisoners told stories of how cons (convicts) on Clinton drafts made their breaks for freedom, some of the breaks happening during my short stay at Sing Sing, so that I knew their stories were true. Whenever one had to go to the toilet, he had to take his shackled partner with him. It was really comical to see how it was done. Nature had to have its way, regardless of the circumstances. When we left Albany, where I had been a member of the Legislature, the sun was shining brightly. There was a beautiful day outside, which to me seemed separated from the train. The car was the world of the prison; outside, a different world. It looked strange and fantastic. I wondered if it could be the same world I lived in a few months ago.

I enjoyed the unfolding scenery of the ride, but my fellow prisoners enjoyed themselves most by using all the power in their lungs every time a farmer came into view. A number of them would cry in unison: "How goes it, Hoosier? You hold him, Sy, while I wing 'im." I understood their attitude, for in their hate first came the police, then the screws of the prison, and third the farmers and residents of the rural communities. I believe this hatred was due to the fact that the so-called Hoosiers despised them just as much and welcomed every opportunity if they lived near a prison to join in the hunt for an escaped convict. For the fifty dollars reward offered by the state the farmers were relentless in pursuit of an escaped convict.

Long before noon the bags, containing two ham and two cheese sandwiches, which were given each of us in Sing Sing, were opened and the sandwiches devoured. That and water was all we were to get until the journey was finished, a matter of about fifteen hours. As the train rolled on north through the beautiful country, the prisoners caught snatches of sleep. Many started complaining about their feet, because as their ankles began to swell from the shackles the pain became almost unbearable. Others talked about their exploits, how they were arrested, of their sweethearts, mothers and friends.

On rolled the train. We were passing through valleys and hills. The brightness of the day was lost in a sunset of riotous colors. When we reached Plattsburg it was already dark. Our car was switched to another track. A small locomotive, puffing in eagerness to be away, was coupled to the car, the whistle of the engine tooted, the bell rang, and before we realized it, we stopped at the small station that is the heart of Dannemora. We were glad the weary journey was over, glad, too, of the expectation that soon the shackles and the iron cuffs would be off our hands and feet.

At the station the whole town was on hand to greet us. The Clinton Prison keepers were there, too. All I could see in the darkness was a small town, above which mountains loomed. It seemed a cold and uninviting place. The keepers were an ugly looking lot. They stood by, holding their long tapering sticks with a heavy metal stub on the end. The sticks were new to me, for in Sing Sing the keepers did not carry them. Their attitude to us was harsh, their manner curt. I got the impression that now I was in for some real prison life, because the whole atmosphere was one of heartless discipline and cruelty. We were counted and recounted as we disembarked from the train. When we were lined up in a row on the station platform we were counted and recounted again. They were taking no chances with the new lot of city desperados that had arrived; they were going to make positively sure that the number of convicts in the cargo was as specified in the papers. The crowd in the station looked sneeringly at us, and I could detect in their eyes a spiteful gleam which seemed to say, "Now, you wise fellows from the city, we will show you what a real prison is like." I hated them for it.

When the principal keeper was sure the count was right, he gave the order to march. We did march between two rows of keepers, silently and sullenly, up the one dusty street that was the town, dragging our swollen feet and shackles along, many a curse being grit between the teeth in silence. The gate of the prison loomed before us in the darkness. An order was given. It swung open. I was a little chilled by the cold mountain air. As we marched through the gate we were counted again. The gate swung back on its hinges. We were now in the prison of the doomed. Still they were taking no chances and counted us once more. Next we were marched into a large room, where we were commanded to line up in a row. The way in which the principal keeper shouted his commands, the manner in which the keepers responded gave you the impression that you were in the drill room of a military academy. Here we were not only counted, but also had to answer a roll call, after which it appeared that they were satisfied that we were all delivered. The order was then given to the keepers to remove handcuffs and shackles, after which we were ordered to undress naked. The room was flooded with light from the large glaring electric bulbs. The screws watched every move we made as we undressed. Soon there stood in their naked innocence over sixty men of different shapes and sizes. I again noticed as I had in Sing Sing that many of the men had their skins pricked by the needles of hypodermic syringes, which they used in injecting themselves with narcotics.

The examination began as soon as we were undressed. First every bit of clothing was carefully searched, every pocket turned inside out, the lining felt, the seams fingered in order to discover if anything was concealed. But the search did not end there, for the keepers looked into our eyes, up our noses, into our ears, under our armpits, combed our hair with their fingers, looked at our hands and at each finger, looked at our feet, between our toes, made us spread our legs apart to discover if anything was concealed between them, and ended the search by making us bend over, after which they spread our buttocks apart and looked to make sure we had not concealed anything there. Yet thorough as this search was, I knew of prisoners who had succeeded in smuggling in dope and other contraband, which goes to show that nothing in this world is foolproof.

When the search was over we were ordered to dress, after

which we were immediately taken to our cells. The cells were a trifle wider and larger than those in Sing Sing, and unlike those in Sing Sing were very dry. The cell block also looked cleaner and better kept. Here, as in Sing Sing, a narrow cot was extended from the wall. I threw myself on the thin mattress stuffed with straw, covered myself with the shoddy blanket and went to sleep. I was too tired to stay awake, for I had been up since three in the morning. I could wait until tomorrow to find out what was in store for me.

At Clinton Prison I went through practically all the formalities that I had been through at Sing Sing. I remember the visit to the Doctor. He was a jovial middle-aged man, whom the prisoners rather liked and called Benny the Dope. The rumor prevalent among the convicts was that he was a drug addict. How true it was I do not know. One day he was found dead in his office. Again the "wise ones" among the inmates were sure it was the result of an overdose of morphine. He greeted me with a smile and asked me to strip to the waist. He gave me a thump on the chest. "Well, you are all right, my boy." That was all there was to his examination.

Clinton was unlike Sing Sing, for in Clinton you knew you were in a tough place. The keepers were strict. You got very little free time. After your day's work you received an hour for recreation in the yard, after which you were marched back to your cells. The guards all carried sticks. Those on the walls walked up and down, their rifles in their hands, ready to shoot at a moment's notice. No prisoners' organization, like the Mutual Welfare League of Sing Sing, was allowed. On Saturday afternoons during the summer months, you spent the afternoon in the yard, where you could watch the prison team play baseball with outside teams. On Sunday you either attended the religious services or stayed in your cell all day long. In the fall and winter months, the prisoners were confined to their cells after working hours. Entertainments were given on rare occasions. Cooking was prohibited in practically all shops. If you wanted to cook up a pot of coffee you did it at the risk of being caught and sent to the cooler (solitary). A prisoner was allowed to spend no more than six dollars every two weeks in the village store, where the prices were extremely high. You were allowed only two packages a year from home. Every one had to go to the mess hall three times a day for breakfast, lunch, and supper. You could only send out a limited number of letters a month. Only one visit a month by relatives or friends approved by the prison authorities was allowed to you. One had to watch one's step, because every infraction of a rule was severely punished. You not only lost time but also spent a number of days in the cooler on bread and water.

I was assigned to the prison tailor shop. Here the prison clothes were made, and suits for the inmates of the prison for the criminal insane, which was adjacent to Clinton Prison. Two keepers were assigned to this shop besides the one who took charge of production. One of the keepers was a French Canadian, called Frenchy by the inmates. The other was a middle-aged rotund Irishman, rather congenial in his ways, an Irish Republican patriot who took pleasure in letting me read speeches made by Robert Emmett and other Irish patriots, which he clipped from the Irish Republican press. At first he tried to make an operator out of me. But I was too tall, my legs too long for the sewing machine. I was therefore transferred and put to work at the basting table. The head of production was an old German. I despised him from the first day I met him. He was round-shouldered, walked with his head outstretched, and, being nearsighted, always kept squinting at you through his thick spectacles.

Working with me at one table was the Spaniard who had received fifty-two and a half years. He made an excellent companion. He was somewhat anarchistically inclined. I learned much about him. He had a mother in Spain. His brother was well off in Cuba in the custom-tailoring business. He was an excellent tailor, having learned the profession from his brother. He always insisted that he was not a criminal, even though he related to me many of his exploits in entering apartments at night for the purpose of stealing. As might be expected, he bitterly hated the judge. It seems that he was robbing a wealthy Texas oil man, who was stopping with his wife at one of the fashionable hotels in New York City. He and his partner had succeeded in getting their pockets full of jewels while the couple were asleep. But his partner was not satisfied. He remembered that the lady wore a brooch studded with large diamonds when they first saw the couple in the dining room. His partner was certain the brooch was worth a fabulous sum.

"We must go back for the brooch," his partner insisted.

"No," replied the Spaniard, "it's hard luck. Come, let's go."

But his partner was obstinate. He would not go. "Come on! Let's go get the brooch."

"So I went, like a big fool, with him. The woman, she woke up. When she saw us, she scream Ow ow ow so loud. I took a pillow and threw it over her haid. But the husban', he woke up. He think I attack his wife. That's the worse thing: when a man is with his women he must act brave. So he gets up and fights me and my partner. And all the time the woman yells like hell. But if I was a criminal, I would take a knife and zip right to the heart. Then there would be no noise. Wad I do? I peek up a shoe and bang over his head and knock him out. The wife she must have fainted. My partner begin to run. But it was too late. The whole hotel was awake. We were trapped like rats. I run to the window; the police were there. Now I am a criminal, they say, and that I wanted to kill, that I was not satisfied to rob the big rich gentleman, that I wanted to rape his wife, too. So the judge send me away for fifty-two and a half years. And my partner, whose fault it all was, he comes to prison and gets religious. You know, I work in the state shop. I work on a keeper's uniform. I decide to make one for myself. My partner find out. And now I am in Clinton Prison."

I used to listen to him moan a Spanish folk song, in a monotone, or marvel as he would go into ecstasy over a photograph that some Cuban ballerina had sent him after he wrote her for it. Then he would tell me about his family, his mother, his sister, his motherless daughter, and how he loved them all. He would end up by sighing, rolling his eyes in a tragic way, as if he knew he would never again see them and would never again be free. I wrote many letters for him, asking the prison superintendent to transfer him back to Sing Sing, though I knew it was useless. He never finished his fifty-two and a half years. He died in Clinton Prison. *"Muy amigo,"* he would call me, as he handed me a cup of coffee. I supplied the coffee and sugar. Fifty-two-and-a-half-years, in spite of his twisted logic, in spite of the fact that he was a thief, had a genuine love and sympathy for humanity.

Life was not without its humor and excitement in the tailor shop. A motley crew worked here, and some of them were very ugly criminals. One of my great dilemmas was the question of getting shaved. In Clinton each shop had a barber or two, according to its size, the tailor shop, a large shop, having two. The barber chairs were crude, wooden, prison-made affairs. Coming up with me on the draft was a young German fellow who said that, though he was a machinist, he would tell the keepers he was an expert barber, in order to get a barber's job, which was considered one of the good jobs in Clinton. Sure enough, he succeeded, for he was assigned as second barber to the tailor shop. But he was not the barber I was assigned to. I was assigned to the old barber, a Puerto-Rican. I went to the Puerto-Rican for my first shave. I gave him one look. When I saw the expression in his eyes I decided it was not safe to shave with him. So I asked the German if he would shave me. He consented. It was an ordeal. He held me tightly by the nose, so that I could not breathe, he pulled my ear, he put his dirty hand in my mouth. He delighted in shaving against the grain. Slips of the razor and cuts there were plenty. But I preferred innocent butchery at the hands of the German barber to the murderous gleam in the eyes of the Puerto-Rican. Nor was I mistaken in my fears. One day a young fellow sat down in his chair for a shave. The Puerto-Rican put the towel around his neck and then proceeded to cut the poor victim with his razor. The fellow got up with a scream. When the other inmates saw what happened they went after the Puerto-Rican. A riot started. The Puerto-Rican grabbed the great big cutting shears and edged himself into a corner. He glared at the attackers like a wild beast. He looked stark mad. The riot call was sounded. In a few minutes the keepers came running in excitedly, with pointed rifles, many of them very much frightened. Our keeper,

Frenchy, in his excitement, swinging his stick in the air, mounted a table and stepped into a pail of water. This broke the tension and caused everyone to laugh. The Puerto-Rican was overcome by the keepers, as were all the other prisoners found with missiles in their hands. The Puerto-Rican was sent to the prison for the criminal insane. The others were sent to the cooler.

Working as a presser at the table next to me was a young Jewish lad of about twenty. He was always in a sullen mood. I thought he was crazy. Very often he would stop his work, turn to a group of prisoners who were talking or laughing and interject, "Stop talking about me. Don't think I don't know. And stop laughing at me, too. Now cut it out, if you want to know what is good for you." One day when no one was suspecting anything he picked up a heavy wooden block which is used in pressing the shoulders of coats, and with terrific force let it down upon the head of an unsuspecting fellow prisoner. His face became distorted, his eyes were red. The prisoner struck fell unconscious to the floor with a large gash in his head from which blood flowed freely. The Jewish lad was subdued, taken away and sent to the prison for the insane.

In my company was a tall up-state Yankee. He was six feet six inches and had the mental capacity of a child. He believed all the wild stories we told him about New York. We finally got him to believe that in New York City the gangsters were so numerous that they pointed their guns at you, from out of the windows of the large buildings, in order to take pot shots at you. Our tall "Hoosier," as we called him, had an enormous appetite. He was always hungry. He ate what every one left over. Fish cakes, meat balls and especially bread pudding found in "Hoosier" a ready customer. He would gather it all together as it was passed to him and at night when alone in his cell would devour it all. No one except "Hoosier" in our company ate bread pudding. It was a concoction made from the week's left over bread boiled in water and soaked in a cheap gooey vanilla sauce, with a few raisins thrown in for seasoning. One day a few of the prisoners went to the doctor, complained about belly aches and received the usual dose of compound cathartic pills.

At supper time, in the mess hall, as they passed their bread pudding to "Hoosier" they dropped in the C. C. pills. The next morning in the shop "Hoosier" in a sweat remarked "Oh gosh, I don't know what happened to me last night. I kept sitting on my bucket all night till the darn thing overflowed." From then on he was known as "Bread Pudding Sy."

In Dannemora I made the acquaintance of one of the two Finnish political prisoners, members of the Finnish I. W. W. who were convicted of criminal anarchy for editing a Finnish Syndicalist paper. He was Gus Alonen, a carpenter by trade, a very shrewd and courageous man. He was not a Communist, but an Anarcho-Syndicalist. At that time he believed in direct action and was ready to practice it. He was sure that a well-trained group of workers who were revolutionists were the equal if not better than an overwhelming number of police or soldiers. He had been active in the I. W. W. and had traveled all over the country working in lumber camps, on construction jobs, everywhere organizing workers into the one big union. Jim Larkin, Gus Alonen, Harry Winitsky, and I formed a quartet. The keepers treated us with respect, but also with caution.

Clinton Prison is situated in one of nature's wonder spots. The Adirondack Mountains rise about it in colorful splendor. From my cell I could see Lake Champlain, majestically at rest in a valley of green and gold. In the fall every leaf was tinted in autumn colors, every bright hue mellowed with a dash of golden brown upon which the sun cast shafts of light, while the tall trees cast their dark shadows to create a phantasmagoria of colors. Yet there was also the village with the ugly cottages of the screws, the prison with its forgotten lost men, the madhouse close by with its maniacs and those who dwelt in the strange lands of their imagination; beyond the wall the hospital for the tubercular criminals who coughed and spat up blood; nearby the cemetery where men rested forever in their plain, wooden, black, painted coffins. Often I watched the scene and pondered how it was possible that amid such beauty so much misery and ugliness could exist.

With winter came the cold and snow. The prisoners prepared for both by making mittens and mufflers, and sewing ear muffs onto caps. The mercury often fell below zero. The wind drove the snow into high drifts of five, six or more feet in height. In the morning during blizzards we walked shivering with our buckets through a path lined by snow banks which rose high above our heads. The Siberia of America the men called the place, and it really looked it. During the winter months we were locked up for the night, after supper, which was served at four. The men amused themselves or passed the time as best they could. Some sang, only to arouse the anger and ribald remarks of others. Others carried on conversations with fellow prisoners on other tiers and in other cells. The studious and serious-minded prisoners read books and magazines. Many artistically and industriously inclined worked at their particular hobbies. Many would pace up and down in their narrow little cells for hours.

The lights went out at nine o'clock. The cell block soon became quiet. One heard the heavy breathing, snores, an occasional moan, the steps of the keeper, marching up and down the cell block. Very often I would lie awake. Events, experiences would go through my mind. The dreams of freedom, the joy of being once more with family and friends were sweet. As the dreams assumed reality in my imagination I fell asleep. In the morning I would jump off my cot just in time to get my tin can filled with hot water. I dressed and washed hurriedly. The doors unlocked. I picked up my bucket at the given command, marched with my company to the bucket shack and emptied it. I was part of a continuous line of men, each carrying a bucket; alongside of me was another line. The two lines spread apart as they entered the shack. A heavy stream of water was continuously pouring down into a large metal bowl. Each line emptied its buckets into the "soup bowl," as the prisoners called it. Then washed them under the pouring stream. One's hands and face always got splashed. We then deposited our buckets on the rack and proceeded by companies straight into the mess hall. What was on the hands or faces of the men did not matter. We marched to the long benches and narrow long tables which stretched across the room. Each company when it reached its table stood at attention until the keeper gave two taps with his stick, the order to sit down and eat the uninviting breakfast. The cereal I never ate, because on a number of occasions I had found long worms in it. The rest of the prisoners ate it, and if they found a worm, just picked it out, threw it away and went on eating. A tap by the keeper with his stick signaled that breakfast was over and that the company had to rise. Another tap, the order to march out into the yard, where the men were lined up for a few minutes before being marched into the shops.

Dannemora was run on the old system. Nevertheless, in spite of the strict discipline, it was possible for one to adjust himself and get along quite well. I found it a little more difficult to get the things I wanted, the things that only currency could buy. But I soon found out how to get cash, what could be used in lieu of money. Cigarettes, Bull Durham and Duke's Mixture were as good as United States currency. In fact, they could be readily exchanged for money. For cash one could obtain special steaks and potatoes cooked by the inmates who worked in the power house. For cigarettes or tobacco one could get better food, from the inmates who worked in the mess hall, delivered just before we were locked up in our cell. Prisoners who had accumulated cash through gambling, or selling goods, would gladly give you cash if you could arrange to deposit an equal amount to their account at the office. This could only be done if you knew how to send instructions out by mail through non-prison sources. Here as in Sing Sing a quarter would do it. A chain worked in Clinton as in Sing Sing. Who made up the chain I never was able to discover. All I did was to give my tier man a quarter and the letter; the rest was taken care of. But in Clinton it could be done only on special occasions and you were notified when you could take advantage of it.

Clinton was considered a punishment prison, a place where the most desperate criminals with the worst reputations, those who were repeaters and had to serve long terms, were sent. Ten years was considered an ordinary sentence. When I told them that I had a sentence of five to ten they laughed and said "Pal, that's nothing at all." I met many lifers and men with twenty, twenty-five, thirty, forty, sixty, and one with ninety-year sentences. Prisoners who could not be controlled in the other prisons were sent here. The worst drug addicts among the state prison inmates were found in Clinton. A large number of the "fairies" (homosexuals) and their partners sooner or later were transferred here. Clinton was a veritable hell of contradictions, where human character in its worst and in its best was brought out in sharp relief. Here too was comedy, but above all grim tragedy.

In Sing Sing it did not take me long to discover that sexual satisfaction was obtained by a very large percentage of the prison population through contact with one of their own sex. The aggressive men were known as "wolves," the others as "kids," "pansies," "fairies" and "sweethearts." It was not unusual for me to hear some one remark, "there goes the big wolf with his two kids." The wolves took care of the objects of their love. They showered them with favors, gave them shirts, blankets, food, money, and above all protected them in every possible way. One youngster in Auburn prison put up a terrific battle to ward off the "wolves." He had to fight with great risk to his physical well-being in order finally to succeed. He was about nineteen, slim and good looking. As soon as he arrived the wolves started to introduce themselves. They showered him with gifts. At first he thought he was fortunate, but when they started to caress him like a woman and to demand what they considered their due, he refused; whereupon, they attempted to terrorize him and beat him into submission as procurers do. But he was strong and courageous. He fought back desperately. It became the talk of the whole prison.

Many youngsters succumb, because state prison is not their first experience with institutional life. They have grown up in either religious or state reformatories from which they graduated into the penitentiaries, finally completing their development in a state prison. Besides, the prison authorities seem undisturbed over these practices among the inmates. Interesting too was the attitude of many of the inmates. They look upon abnormal sex relationships as perfectly normal and proper. I spoke about it to prisoners who were above the average in intelligence and who had a good sense of what was right and wrong. Often I found to my amazement that not only did they consider it perfectly proper but that they also indulged whenever they had the opportunity to do so. I once was struck by the attitude of the inmates over a situation that developed in Yard Two involving two blond fellows just admitted. As soon as they appeared in Yard Two the wolves and other inmates became agitated about them. From what I could see they looked absolutely normal. The other prisoners knew differently. I watched to see what would happen. When they walked in the yard, they were followed. A flirtation with them was started that was as genuine in appearance as between a couple of girls and some shy nervous boys. But the newcomers would have nothing to do with the white inmates. They attached themselves to a group of Negroes for whom they did washing, cooking, errands and the most menial work thrown upon them. The Negroes knew their power over them, for they ordered them around like servants, scolded them and abused them at every opportunity. The inmates called them "nigger lovers." The white inmates were not angry with them because they were perverts—not at all—but only because they did not yield their pervert favors to the white men. It is sometimes very difficult to understand the moral code of some prisoners. Once I overheard the following remark by such a prisoner, when he saw a woman smoking a cigarette in a group visiting the prison: "If my girl smoked a cigarette in public, I'd bat her in the eye."

Clinton Prison was full of degenerates. They flaunted their homosexualist practices. The names they affected included "Princess," "Cleopatra," "Nellie," "Lizzie," as well as those of famous movie actresses. Their mannerisms were feminine, so was the inflection of their voices. They had high heels attached to their shoes, powdered their faces and rouged their lips and cheeks. They remade their shirts to give them a blouse effect and embroidered hearts around the kerchief pockets. During the summer months, the fairies took blankets with them to the yard and spread them on the grass. Here, reclining with their "husbands," as they called their companions, they engaged in amenities of repartee and exchanged darts of vulgar wit. They were extremely jealous of one another, when angry called each other, "hussy," "cat," "lady bum" and similar names.

Perhaps the most popular "fairy" was "The Princess," a man of about forty-five, married and the father of several children. There was not a single mannish trait about him. His walk, his speech, the way he tossed his head, the motions of his hands, his behavior in the company of men were always feminine—never masculine. Next in popularity was a short ugly colored man of about thirty, who was very slim. He was almost jet black, his hair kinky and curly, bright laughing eyes topped a broad nose that almost covered his thin black face. His lips were of medium thickness and edged an enormous mouth which displayed two rows of large snow white teeth. Why this colored man was called a man, I don't know. Not only was he feminine in all his actions and characteristics but in him they were exaggerated. I never saw a person in prison more jolly than he. Always laughing, ever disporting a coquettish smile. The way he rolled his eyes, broke into a laugh, or affected an air of modesty was similar to that of a girl flushed with excitement, during a flirtation. When angry, he was a feminine shrew on fire. In spite of his ugliness, in spite of the revulsion he aroused in me, he was nevertheless a favorite among the inmates, especially the white ones.

How was it possible for convicts in a prison like Dannemora, where the régime was so strict, where freedom of motion was limited, to engage in practices of sex perversion? It is impossible to keep a perfect watch on prisoners unless a guard is attached to each prisoner. The number of guards actually employed, can only do a superficial job, in watching what takes place. Furthermore, the degenerates in Clinton were assigned to jobs where it was possible for many of them to ply their trade quite freely, and I suspect not without the knowledge of the prison authorities, who surely are not so blind that they do not know about this common practice.

At Clinton Prison, as also in Sing Sing and Auburn prisons, much of the trouble that develops between inmates has its roots in the jealousies arising out of these abnormal sex relationships. I have seen convicts cut each other up seriously because of this jealousy. I remember such an incident in Clinton Prison, when a tall French Canadian took a fairy away from one of the convicts I described previously as the red-headed Irish youth with bumps on his head. Just as the men in the yard were given the order to line up with their companies, the red-headed Irish lad threw the Frenchman flat on his back, squatted across the Frenchman's chest, grabbed hold of his head by the hair and brandishing a long knife prepared to cut his head off. The Frenchman gave out a yell like a wild hyena. Frenchy, our keeper, was close at hand. With calm deliberate courage he raised his stick quickly and with all his might brought it down on the attacker's head. The blow was terrific, the Irishman collapsed over his victim. But I could not understand the reaction of the prisoners. A little spark of encouragement and a riot of major proportions would have started. The prisoners became madly indignant at the keeper. "What right did he have to use his stick." They cursed him. An ugly murmur rose from their ranks. They saw nothing wrong in the act if one of their number attempted to murder a fellow prisoner. But that a keeper should use his stick in order to save the life of a fellow prisoner, they considered an outrageous act of brutality. The class lines in prison between the screws and the prisoners were very sharp. Evidently the animosities created by the long confinement of the men and the harsh treatment they received were responsible for their code which held that every act of a keeper against the person of a convict, regardless of its motives, was an attack upon the whole convict fraternity. In no other way can I explain it.

"Hoosier," a lad of about nineteen, was committed to Clinton Prison for perpetrating the terrible crime of stealing a cow, killing it, skinning it and selling the hide for a few dollars. He seemed to enjoy coming to Clinton Prison, where the worst "bad men" from the big city were confined. The minute he arrived he was spotted by the wolves: here was a young country lad from the farm. He was assigned to the mess hall. He seemed to be having one fine time. The wolves showered him with presents. I remember hearing him say one day, "Well, you city fellers can't fool me. I read all about ye. My father on the farm used to get the Sunday paper from New York every week. I'm wised up." Soon he sported a wrist watch, new shirts, a nice new sweater. He was making friends among the old timers, who were initiating him into the ways of prison. And they certainly did! He became very popular with the wolves. When in the yard he was trailed by a score of them. He walked around with a happy air of satisfaction and self-assurance. He was now in big company. Perhaps he thought the Sunday paper from New York that came once a week to his father's farm no longer could teach him anything, for he knew it all. He was thrilled with his prison experiences. He was not only at home in the society of the prison big shots, but he was actually one of them.

In Auburn there was an undersized Jewish lad of about eighteen. He reminded one of a slinking pup that has had its spirit broken by too many beatings. He doubted every kind word, and feared to look one straight in the eye. I never saw him smile. This Jewish lad was the kid of Big Bill Jew, an arrogant Negro who had spent most of his life in penal institutions. He was well built, about five foot ten in height, with a cruel and angular chiseled face. His smile was sarcastic, his demeanor haughty, giving one the impression that he was extremely selfish. He was forty-five or over, strong and well preserved, despite his years of incarceration. He was known as a "cokie" (a dope fiend). When he was released after serving almost ten years in prison, he got off at Albany, spent his money on dope, drugged himself to capacity, and attempted to commit a robbery. He was caught that same night, convicted and sent back to prison. In the bath house he used to admire his physical prowess as he looked over his naked beauty, and would delight in telling all the inmates how he was going to enjoy his first night of freedom with his dark "gal." The Jewish lad was his kid. But he was more than that. He was his slave. He jumped at Bill Jew's beck and call. One day the lad was caught by Bill Jew with a white inmate. I saw the Jewish lad after he had been scolded, cursed and beaten for his unfaithfulness. His eyes were bloodshot, the tears had not yet dried. The story was told to me by one of the old timers, a Jewish safe cracker, who was looked up to by the Jewish inmates. He narrated how Bill Jew cursed and scolded, yelling at the lad, "Yoh is my kid. I take care of you, and as long as I am in this prison yoh better stick to me." Then he slapped him all over the face, while the lad cried for mercy and promised never to be unfaithful again. My narrator spoke in contempt of the lad, not because of what he was, but because a Jewish lad had to associate with a Negro, a *"Schwartzer."* After that the lad continued faithful to Bill Jew, and like a frightened puppy continued to take the abuse and the scorn that was heaped upon him by the Jewish inmates.

In Clinton you felt that you were in a primitive wilderness. The prisoners liked to talk about the jungles surrounding the prison, the impossibility of breaking through them and making good an escape. They looked upon Clinton as America's forsaken spot—the hell hole of America. Nevertheless, there were many who attempted the dash for liberty. My German friend was one of them. Radically inclined, he said that if he ever got a chance he would take it, make for the city and beat it back to Germany. The revolution in Germany was in the making and he was sure he could play his part in it. He got his chance. They gave him a job on the farm outside of the prison taking care of the hogs. He came to me smiling, told me of his good fortune. His smooth oval German face lit up. He would wait for his opportunity. One day in the yard he came to me, nervous but very happy in his agitation: "Tomorrow I go. Good-by." I wished him luck even though I thought his attempt was foolish. The next day he was missing. Two days later they brought him back. I happened to catch a glimpse of him. He was in rags. He had not been able to traverse the jungles. He looked like a man who had returned from a different world. Later, after he had served his punishment in the cooler, I saw him in the yard. His failure was a bad blow. He was a different man. His spirit was broken.

The most daring exploit, based on sheer courage and split-seconds, was the break of an Irish-American lad and a Pole. The Irish-American lad I knew well. He came from the lower Westside of New York City. He was one of the Tenth Avenue mob. In spite of the fact that he was in his early twenties, he was already old in prison years, having spent most of his youth in penal institutions. He was fair of complexion, of medium height, with light brown hair and a broad forehead. They called him Angel Face. He was the kind of boy any mother, from appearances only, would have been proud of. He was a product of New York's streets, poor family environment and sheer poverty. It seemed to me that he was simply puzzled by all the complexities of life. "You are an Anarchist," he would say to me, "I don't know what it means, but if it's what I think it is, then I'm all for it. You are against the present laws. You believe things are not what they should be. I've felt that all along. Maybe you know how to fight it. I've been fighting it all along, and here I am in this dump for life. But if ever I get a chance, I'll learn." And his eyes laughed, as his baby face lit up into a smile that petered out in a puzzled expression of perplexity and he waved his hand in parting. "So long, Bolsheviki," he said, using the common term for us politicals.

I liked him, though he was known as a killer, the kind who, when cornered, fights like a lion and kills without hesitation. Adversity and the struggles of childhood had hardened him, but beneath this veneer was a youth with a heart that could feel deeply and genuinely, with sympathy for the underdog, a sense of justice, and a willingness to fight for what he thought was right. Contemplating him, I came to the conclusion that fundamentally he was a sound young man in rebellion against the social abnormalities of his environment that had crippled his youth by denying him the freedom and opportunities for normal self-expression that were his natural right. He was determined to break his way to that freedom through any obstacle, be it a social barrier or a prison wall. But he knew of only one way to break through—by main force. Patience, subtleties, organization were beyond his intelligence and foreign to his temper. That limitation was at once both his misfortune and the source of his truly admirable courage. What appealed to me most in him was his innate defiance of life as it is. In that, surely he was a revolutionist in temper and truly my comrade.

Angel Face and the Pole did odd jobs around the prison under the supervision of a keeper. Every morning, after mess, the two of them, accompanied by their keeper, would go to a room on a level with the yard and facing it. Here they would wait for their keeper to put on his overalls, and then they would follow him to their assigned chores. At the precise time that the keeper was wont to put on his overalls, a small band of prisoners who worked outside would march across the yard to a small door that was opened for them. On the wall above were six prison guards, pacing up and down, trigger finger on the trigger of their rifles, ready to shoot at a moment's notice. My Irish friend and the Pole had planned to time their escape for the brief lapse required by their keeper to put on his overalls and while the band of prisoners marched through the open door, hoping in that interval to dash for the open door and lose themselves in the woods. The opportune morning came. The keeper was putting on his overalls, the company was marching through the open door. They made a dash for freedom across the yard, using the few breathless seconds between life and death. It was so audacious, so unexpected that the keepers on the wall were dumbfounded for a few moments. These few moments were all the two lads needed. The firing of the rifles came too late. The two prisoners had made their getaway.

Then came the blowing of the siren. The man hunt began. All of us prisoners were locked in our cells. The keepers of both shifts were mobilized. Farmers came rushing into the prison and were enrolled as deputies. From my cell window I saw the automobiles leave with their details of armed men. I watched one automobile and could scarcely believe my eyes. Riding in the front seat with a rifle across his knees was a convict. He worked in the front office. The son of an up-state judge, he had been convicted of murder. The prisoners despised him. He was feared by the keepers. He walked around the prison as if he ran the place. From the expression on his face I could see that he despised the inmates and did not consider himself one of them. Here was this convicted murderer with rifle in hand engaged in the mad excitement of a man hunt, eyes strained, muscles taut, ready for the catch. The prisoners shouted invectives at him, but he was too far away to hear. I listened, and the sentiments of the inmates, regardless of the language in which they were couched, were my sentiments.

Day after day went by. The manhunt continued. If they could only make the jungles! The good wishes of every prisoner went out to the fugitives as the hunt went on. On the fifth day a farmer and his two burly sons brought back the ghost that was once Angel Face. But there were also the glad tidings of the Pole's successful escape. Town after town sent reports that he had passed through. From one farmer he stole clothes, from another a horse, which was later abandoned, and so on, until the authorities lost trace of him altogether.

Later, when the Irish lad was released from the punishment cells, we learned what had happened. The Pole and he had agreed that as soon as they gained freedom they should separate. The Pole evidently knew forests and the open country, had a sense of direction and could make his way. One does not pick up that sort of knowledge on the sidewalks of New York, surely not on Tenth Avenue. One learns how to dodge trucks and automobiles, how sometimes to escape from the clutches of a policeman, but of the ways of nature Angel Face was totally ignorant. Our Irish lad was completely lost. In the daytime he hid in the jungles, at night he ventured out, but all the time he kept running in circles; instead of making headway, he was always returning to the prison. On the fifth day, tired and exhausted, he decided to hit the open road. He proceeded but a short distance, when the farmer and his sons came upon him and covered him with their rifles. The game was up.

I had my troubles in Clinton Prison and so did the other politicals, Harry Winitsky, Jim Larkin and Gus Alonen. First we had trouble with our visitors. Instead of allowing us to talk with them like human beings, we were segregated in wire cages, with a keeper inside each cage censoring all a prisoner wished to say. We rebelled against this and forced the prison authorities to give our visitors the same courteous treatment accorded to all others. One day Agnes Smedley came to Clinton on the pretext that she was interested in prison problems. She was shown the prison, and on her tour of inspection came across Jim Larkin who knew all about her visit. He greeted her with a smile which did not go unnoticed by the prison authorities, who became suspicious, investigated her, took her aside later and ordered her to leave. Then followed a series of articles in the Socialist daily, *The New York Call,* about the dungeon at Dannemora and the terrible treatment being accorded to the politicals, especially Jim Larkin. It was a grim story, part true and part good imagination. It infuriated the prison authorities and particularly State Superintendent of Prisons Rattigan. He looked upon all Reds as dangerous criminals. He really hated us and held us personally responsible for what had appeared in the *Call.*

Rattigan appointed a commission, which included himself, the warden, the chief doctor of the prison for the criminally insane, and an outside psychiatrist, and which was to pass on our sanity. Jim Larkin was the first one subjected to an examination. They were rather rough with him, but he was rougher in his retorts, which he delivered in trenchant Irish brogue. He was followed by Harry Winitsky, who was cross-examined at length, then came Gus Alonen, and I was last. I answered the questions they asked me calmly and deliberately. They seemed chiefly concerned with the treatment accorded to our visitors. I told them that it was discriminatory, that we resented this discrimination and would seek through all means at our command to fight it until it was ended. I told them that while we did not expect any favored treatment or special considerations, under no circumstances would we tolerate obvious injustice. They dismissed me immediately. But I had seen enough to be alarmed. We politicals had a conference in the yard that afternoon. It was obvious from the very nature of this commission and the manner in which Jim Larkin and Harry Winitsky had been interrogated that Rattigan was determined to make short shrift of us by declaring us insane, in order to commit us to the prison for the criminally insane as punishment for our public protest. Word had to be sent outside immediately through some trustworthy underground channel. There was but one that could be trusted implicitly—the Rabbi!

He was a genuine orthodox Jewish rabbi, who lived in Plattsburg. Since he has joined his Maker and is beyond the reach of mundane laws, this sinful world may know that the name of this modern Good Samaritan was Rabbi Judelson. For his sake, I hope there is a heaven, for he surely deserves to be in it. Short of stature, with a pointed reddish brown beard and a merry twinkle in his eye, Rabbi Judelson was as wholesome and hearty a man as any one would care to meet. He was the best friend all the prisoners had, Jewish or Gentile. He understood the men, sympathized with their lot and was always ready to do them a favor, even if it involved infringement of prison rules. He looked upon the prisoners as his children, and they in turn loved him as a father. He was proud of his orthodox Judaism and fought tooth and nail for the religious rights of the Jewish inmates. But he was not narrow and not vindictive. He respected the opinions of others. No prisoner will forget his long black coat, which was far more than a mere garment. It was a sanctuary. Whatever went into its pockets was holy, inviolate—and into its pockets the prisoners would put letters and little slips of paper that bore requests for favors. You had to put them stealthily into his pockets, as if he were not noticing it, and he appeared always unmindful of the fact. When he left the prison and reached his home, he would dig his hands into his pockets, to discover to his assumed surprise the notes and the letters. He would mail the letters and read the notes. Whatever was requested of him, providing it was in his power, he would do. If asked to do so, he would even go to the trouble of calling on friends and relatives of the prisoners for one purpose or another, and on his next visit to prison he would nod to the inmates, to let them know he had received their notes or letters and that he had attended to all their requests. So, Harry Winitsky wrote a letter and dropped it into the Rabbi's long black coat. The letter was mailed. Our friends in New York got busy. Lawyers and visitors came. Instead of going to the "bug house," as the prisoners called the place, a few months later, due to the pressure exerted by our many friends, Jim Larkin, Harry Winitsky and I were on our way back to Sing Sing, and Gus Alonen was transferred to Comstock.

Back in Sing Sing life was more pleasant. There we found Dr. Julius Hammer, serving a sentence for an illegal abortion, having been betrayed to the authorities by political enemies, presumably. Dr. Hammer had financed Martens' Soviet Bureau, had joined the Communist Labor Party and had generously helped to finance its activities. In addition to Hammer there were also Isaac E. Ferguson and Charles E. Ruthenberg, who had both been sent to Sing Sing for five to ten years. These three had arrived in Sing Sing while we were in Dannemora. But soon after our return a fourth Communist newcomer came, a Russian comrade named Paul Manko, the last Communist prisoner to arrive in Sing Sing during our stay there. Manko, an ordinary rank and file member of one of the Russian branches, was arrested for distributing leaflets, indicted and convicted as a dangerous Red leader and sent to Sing Sing. He was obviously a psychopath and probably a paranoic. He had delusions that there was a cosmic plot afoot to poison him, and hence refused all food and drink. The keepers treated him gently and with consideration. We politicals delegated Dr. Hammer, who as a physician understood his mental condition better than any of us and who moreover spoke Russian, to persuade Manko that no one was plotting against him. But that proved the most unfortunate choice we could have made, for Manko detested Hammer as the alleged seducer of his wife. That was apparently another of his phobias. Instead of listening to Hammer, he threatened to settle scores with him in Russia, as one Bolshevik to another. Moreover, the very next time his wife came to visit him, he created a scene, scolded her in voluble Russian at the top of his voice, and the poor woman left dumbfounded and in tears. We were quite sure that she was perfectly innocent of her husband's charges and that Manko, having improvised the seduction charge against Hammer to protect himself from the doctor's intervention, played the irate cuckold to the bitter end with the consistency of a maniac.

Harry Winitsky and I were quixotic enough to try our persuasive powers on him next. Naturally, we couldn't get to first base with him. He spurned our invitation that he eat with us and our offer to taste every morsel of food before he should swallow it. Instead, he would fill his pockets with hard boiled eggs, onions, bread crumbs and other bits of food, at which I presume he would nibble when unseen, for somehow he did manage to keep alive and able to work, notwithstanding his refusal to eat with the rest of us. He behaved in the strangest way, going through breath-taking contortions when let out of his cell in the morning and assigned to his daily job. At times, jovial and in good humor, he would approach one of us and with a knowing look and a mischievous smile would say, "You can't fool me, I know what's happening. There's a revolution and the Red Army is coming. Soon they will be here and we will all be free." Once while Jim Larkin was looking through a book about Mexico, Paul Manko, proudly pointing to a picture of a Mexican wearing a wide sombrero hat, a belt of bullets around his waist, his rifle leaning against the wall, nonchalantly smoking a cigarette, exclaimed, "That, Comrade Larkin, is me. See, that's me smoking a cigarette. I am a general in the Red Army." Knowing, as we did, that he was mentally sick, we could not object when he was assigned to the lunatic asylum for observation. We took steps to see that he was accorded the best of treatment. During his stay at the hospital, Manko, as he passed the linen room, heard someone call for linen. He rushed to the window. "Did you hear that? They called for Lenin and Trotsky." He was very much excited when he spoke: "Do you know that means Lenin and Trotsky are coming for me? You can't fool me, I know all about it." And he went away excited and overjoyed.

Of the many insanity cases I observed in prison, I shall mention only one more. It had to do with that twin of the political passion—religion. Red was an actor who could sing well, dance well and compose popular music. He started getting religion in prison. Every Sunday he attended the services. He went to Bible class as well. His daily job was to sew undergarments in the knit goods shop. There a pipe supplied live steam. The prisoners would put buckets underneath the steam pipe, to obtain hot water for washing their clothes, or boiling water for their coffee pots. One day Red held forth that he was not afraid of anything, nothing could harm him, because he had the "spirit" in him, and to prove it, he said, "Can you put your hand in a pail of live steam? No! But I can, and nothing will happen to me, because I have the 'spirit' in me." However, he was stopped from demonstrating. Several days later he took out his penis in the shop and declared, "It is evil. It does no one any good. I will get rid of the evil." He grabbed a large shears for the purpose of cutting it off. He was stopped, and this time taken to the hospital. When a prisoner is found to be insane, he is put on a special draft, but before he leaves the prison he is dressed as a civilian, in a black suit, white shirt, a tie and a derby hat. One day we discovered Red dressed like that. As he was leaving Sing Sing, he waved good-by to all of us and threw cigarettes at those of the inmates who saw him off. He seemed quite happy.

But Sing Sing had its boisterous madmen as well. I recall the case of a man who went raving mad awaiting his execution. The real inhumanity of the act is psychological rather than physical—the endless waiting which fear and imagination fill with unendurable horrors. The tenseness of that waiting is contagious. It affects the entire prison. It is the doomed man's last strong link with his fellow-men. It stirs all, from Principal Keeper to the least of the prisoners, to a hysterical pitch of excitement, no matter how subdued it may outwardly appear. The P. K. is invariably in an ugly mood on such a day, for he has reason to expect a revolting scene, and he steels himself against it with hate and snarling. All the keepers in the P. K.'s office are ill-tempered, annoyed by the last minute visitors and the reporters, who are invariably on hand and invariably in the way. The entire prison is tense, the impending execution on the lips of every inmate. I remember the executioner, a puny fellow with sandy gray hair, mincing his way across the yard in short quick steps, bound for the power house to see if everything was in order, and I remember that the prisoners never failed to curse him, filling the yard with their indignant imprecations. Before the new death house was opened, we inmates, locked in our cells, would know the exact moment of electrocution, for when the current was on in the electric chair the lights throughout the prison dimmed. An intense hush would fall over the prison. But in a few moments it would be broken by mutterings of indignation and these would rapidly accumulate into a subdued roar, as if of distant waves breaking against the cliffs. Such is the atmosphere through which the condemned man is dragged to his doom—to be "burned" or "fried," as the prisoners call it, terms that describe the effect of electrocution without the slightest exaggeration, for at the end the corpse is actually charred. A keeper in Yard Two who had attended any number of executions told me that in all his experience only one man faced his doom bravely—a dentist convicted of poisoning his mother-in-law—and all others had to be dragged to the chair in a state of utter collapse, petrified with terror or raving mad. I can still hear the shrieks of one such madman. Since he had been sane when first locked in the death house, the keepers were sure that he was feigning insanity on his day of doom. But they were mistaken. He could not be subdued, not even with a hose turned on him full force. He continued to shriek like a wild beast through all the insane commotion. Whatever nightmare he was suffering through in his last moments was communicated to us in our locked cells. That day the entire prison was stark with horror.

But there was also romance in Sing Sing. On the grim stage of the visitors' room Charlie Ruthenberg played the Romeo and Ray Ragozin was his Juliet. Ray was an active comrade from New York City, but far from good-looking, nor was she in the prime of maidenhood. But love being proverbially blind, such things did not matter. Oblivious to all around him, Ruthenberg would woo her in the visitors' room with all the ardor of an impetuous lover. It was a touching sight, even if most of the prisoners disapproved of such demonstrativeness in public. And after the visit ended, our Romeo would stand for hours on end, waving to Juliet, whose balcony now was the hill above the prison walls, from which she waved back. Judged by the ardor of these furtive prison meetings, their love should have endured for an eternity and surely for the duration of their natural life. But there was some inexplicable joker in this affair, for upon release from prison our Romeo turned Lothario and Ray Ragozin was quickly forgotten in the charms of another Juliet.

Ruthenberg's romanticism was merely amusing as long as it

was confined to love. But unfortunately it invaded the domain of politics as well, and then it became rather annoying. Yet it was not untypical of the early period of Communism in the United States, for the tenor of the time was to behave à la Ruthenberg. I remember the day a much excited Ferguson came to me with a tale of Ruthenberg's fantastic plan to escape from Sing Sing. Although I was on the verge of exploding as he unfolded its details, I listened carefully, without interrupting him even once. The plan was as simple as it was foolhardy. A group of Lettish comrades was to explore the terrain around the prison, after which several of the Letts, heavily armed, were to call on Ruthenberg in the visitors' room. At the end of the visit Ruthenberg was to leave the prison, surrounded by his visitors, who were to fight their way out, firing their revolvers as they fled, to the high-powered automobile waiting for them outside the prison gate. From there they were to drive to the hideaway, prepared for the emergency. He was later to steal away to Russia. Ruthenberg firmly believed that in a few years the revolutionary situation in the United States would develop to such an extent that he could return to America, where he was sure he would be acclaimed and become the leader of the American revolution. It was fantastic. But Ruthenberg was all excited about it. He had already succeeded in getting the Letts to survey the grounds around the prison. He even pointed them out to me one day.

Ferguson was more than alarmed, and correctly so. He felt that the plan was a wild romantic dream which would cause great harm to the movement. The others and I agreed with him. We all intervened to stop the scheme. The objections we raised against the plans finally resulted in their being abandoned. Ruthenberg was denied the opportunity of playing the hero and incidentally of making a fool of himself. Had Ruthenberg succeeded he would have played right into the hands of the reactionary forces, who would have seized upon the affair in order to crush all militant and progressive tendencies in the labor movement, because obviously the plan could not succeed without violence and bloodshed. The liberal forces, who were supporting us wholeheartedly in our fight for freedom, would have been alienated. The damage to the Communist movement would have been very costly. Why then did a man of Ruthenberg's caliber entertain such a proposition? Because, I believe, Ruthenberg was motivated mainly by a strong personal ambition to be the head of the American revolution. His actions were based not on what the American conditions demanded, nor on whether they were in harmony with the psychology of the American people, but solely on the romantic aspects of the revolutionary movement in Russia. He was behaving as if America were Tsarist Russia—an adolescent attitude unpardonable in a responsible political leader.

In a few months I was "drafted" again. This time to Auburn, the oldest prison in New York State. My companion in misery was Ferguson. It was his first experience with the "draft." He certainly did not relish it, although he stayed but a few weeks in Auburn, returning to Sing Sing and soon thereafter to liberty on bail. Yet the régime at Auburn was liberal compared to Dannemora. There were, however, no redeeming features about the place. Sing Sing was on the Hudson and had a large yard. Dannemora was surrounded by the natural beauty of the Adirondacks. Its yard was smaller than the one in Sing Sing, but it was nevertheless ample for ball games and other sports. It was bordered on one side by the prison proper and on the other three sides by tall stone walls, yet when you looked beyond the walls the mountains were in view in all their glory. But the yard in Auburn was the smallest of the three. It was oblong in shape, very narrow and completely enclosed by prison buildings. Whichever way you turned or looked, you saw stone walls and brick upon brick. Adjacent to the prison ran a dirty little canal. When the prisoners crowded into the yard there was hardly space for elbow room. In the summer a ball field was improvised that reminded one of a small sand lot in a crowded tenement section of the lower east side of New York City. In the winter time you froze; in the summer it was abominably hot. Unlike the régime freedom of Sing Sing, we were not allowed to use the shop or administration buildings during the free periods. Whether we liked it or not, we had to be in the yard.

Because of its canal, Auburn Prison was infested with rats. I never saw so many rodents in all my life. They were so bold that they came out of their holes in broad daylight. If you left some food in a locker or securely hid it in a machine, the next day it was gone; the rats had gotten to it. The inmates set traps for them, but they soon got wise to the traps and avoided them. I worked in the tailor shop. The rats there were more than a nuisance. One of the inmates, a Swedish-American mechanic, decided to catch the rats en masse. He built a very large rat trap out of steel wire mesh that could accommodate at least a hundred of them. But he decided to educate the rats first. Every night he filled the trap with bread and delicious food morsels, making sure that the trap was left open. In the morning all the food was gone. The rats marched in, ate what was left for them, and departed. This was done for a week. Then the trap was set. The next day it was full of rats, large ones and small ones, about twenty-five in number. After mess, the custom in Auburn was to have the different companies line up in front of their shops for a smoke. With the permission of the keeper, the trap was brought out into the yard. "Beauty," a little black female fox terrier, known for her rat-catching exploits, was on the scene, barking in great excitement. The trap was opened in the middle of the yard. The rats went scampering for freedom in all directions. But their freedom was short lived. With lightning speed, Beauty seized each scampering rat, one at a time, by the back of the neck, threw it into the air, and went after the next one. When each rat fell, it was dead. Not one rat escaped Beauty. It was a marvelous demonstration. The inmates applauded, and aided the dog by preventing any of the rats from escaping back into the buildings.

The Warden of Auburn had a military title and record. The Principal Keeper had also been a junior officer during the World War. The military spirit therefore prevailed in this prison. The most important thing in Auburn was marching. The keepers took time to drill their companies. You had to march in step and in line—old and young, tall and short, crooked and straight, it made no difference. It seemed as if the prison authorities were of the opinion that if the inmates would only straighten out and march correctly, in good military style, they could be cured of their criminal ways. It was "march" three times a day to and from the mess hall and to the cell block. If you were out of step, if you did not keep in line with your partner, if you were too far back of the man in front, you were scolded and often punished. Also, everyone was marked—for perfect behavior, a white disc about the size of a silver dollar sewed onto the right sleeve of the coat; if punished once, a blue disc; if punished more than once, a red disc. Through perfect behavior over a given period of time you could graduate from the red to the blue and eventually to the white disc.

Auburn Prison had its own "police station" and "jail." Prisoners who misbehaved, or were caught breaking prison rules, were "arrested" and locked up in the station house, where they were interrogated by the P. K., who either freed them with a reprimand, or punished them by taking away a few days' time allowed them for good behavior; very often, in addition, they were thrown into "jail," that is, into the cooler. The coolers were dark, without bedding, and those confined to them were fed on bread and water. I have known recalcitrant prisoners who were kept in the cooler for weeks, and who were released only after the doctor reported the danger of a fatal collapse. Pavio, one of the I. W. W. Finnish leaders convicted for criminal anarchy, was kept in one of these dungeons for sixteen days. This frail blond fellow persisted in refusing to admit a wrong which he did not commit. When he came out he was a skeleton, but happy because of the fight he had put up.

A powerful despot in Auburn was the prison doctor. One look at the medico was enough to frighten you. He was a tall austere man, between fifty and fifty-five, who was obsessed with the idea that crime was a mental disease and that all criminals were in some manner, shape, or form insane, purely in a pathological sense. Other factors, such as environment, economic conditions, youthful associations, and the like, never entered into his reasoning. If a man was in prison, he was evidently crazy. The doctor's job was to find out the degree of insanity and whether it was of the dangerous kind or not. He took his job seriously. Every prisoner who came to Auburn was subjected to a thorough physical examination. After that came the mental tests, varied and numerous in form, to determine the mental status of the inmates and to discover mental deficiencies. The mental examination was concluded with one by the medico himself, who sought to find out the most intimate details of a prisoner's personal life. I decided that after I had gone through the physical examination I would not submit further to the doctor's pet whims. I refused to answer the questions of the examiners. I finally reached the doctor himself. He was very polite when I entered his office. But his demeanor changed when I just as politely informed him that I would not answer his questions. I informed him that as far as I knew there was no law on the statute books that gave him the authority to ask the kind of questions he wanted me to answer. He became indignant. His tone of voice changed. He threatened to "arrest" me, to throw me into the cooler until I would answer. I replied very calmly that I knew that he had the power to do what he threatened. However, I made it quite plain to him that I would not answer his questions. If anyone looked crazy in that office, it was the medico. He stood up, his face red with anger, his nervous fingers fumbling the papers on his desk. He hesitated in his attempt to say something, stopped, kept quiet for a few moments, and then dismissed me forthwith with the remark that I would find out soon whether or not I could continue to disobey his orders. I was not a little worried when I left. I soon forgot the incident because I heard no more either from the medico or from the prison authorities.

A few weeks later we learned that a "bug house draft" was in preparation. It spread fear throughout the prison. Many of the inmates who were deficient mentally, or who had been at odds with their keepers for some infraction of prison discipline, began to worry about the draft. No one likes to be considered a lunatic. One day at the movies one of the inmates who worked in the doctor's office came to me and offered the information that the doctor had included my name on the Naponach bug house draft. I decided to lose no time in taking up a fight against the doctor. Right after the movies I asked an old-timer, a safecracker, whether or not it was possible to get a letter out of

Auburn through some underground channel. I told him what I wanted the favor for. He told me to write the letter and to give it to him in the morning. I gave him the letter in the morning. I also decided to let those inmates whom I trusted know of my fight with the doctor, in order, if I was drafted, that the prison should know why. My letter reached New York the following day. The Workers' Defense Committee got busy immediately. One of the lawyers, Isaac Shorr, came to Auburn. He interviewed the warden. He interviewed the doctor. The warden said I was a model prisoner. The doctor, of course, claimed the whole idea was preposterous, because I was rated far above the average in intelligence. Shorr called me out, told me of his interviews, and informed me that he would also take the matter up by long distance phone with the State Prison Department. The draft to Naponach came soon after, early in the morning, while the prison slept. I heard the unlocking of doors, the commands of the keepers, the curses of the inmates. I was wide awake. Only in the morning did we find out who the unfortunates were.

An April 22, 1922, I finally received the telegram which informed me that a certificate of reasonable doubt had been granted in my case. It meant that I would be allowed out on bail pending my appeal to the New York Court of Appeals. I immediately made preparations for the happy event. I was overjoyed when my keeper instructed me to prepare to leave, for I was going home. I had been almost three years in prison. I took the first suit they gave me, a black ill-fitting one, prison-made, of poor material and workmanship. A cap, taken in preference to a derby hat, a white shirt, a celluloid collar, and a black bow tie completed the outfit. I must have looked very ludicrous, because when I met my lawyer, Joseph Brodsky, in the warden's office, he burst out laughing. I did not mind it a bit. I was going out; that was all that mattered. With Brodsky was a detective of the Bomb Squad, one I knew well from the 1919 raids. Brodsky explained that I was going to be taken to New York, where I would be freed on bail, pending my appeal before the New York Court of Appeals, and that Ruthenberg and Ferguson were already out on bail. He further informed me that Justice Cardozo had signed the writ which made my release on bail possible. Brodsky insisted that I get a new collar and tie as soon as we reached outside. Out of prison I felt as though I was walking on thin air. I took deep breaths. I looked at the people as strange beings and was surprised that they looked so well. We went into a haberdashery shop, where I selected a tie and bought a collar. When asked what size collar, I said "17," the size I wore when I first entered Sing Sing. But when I put it on, Brodsky had another laugh on me, because it was ludicrously too big. I had not realized how much I had shrunk, and I was not troubled by it.

Since the train for New York was not due to leave for several hours, the Bomb Squad detective hinted that if I would like it, inasmuch as I had been in prison and away from girls so long, he knew just the place to go. But I declined his kind offer, and so he left me in the custody of my lawyer on the pretext that he had to visit a relative. I had lunch with Brodsky, but was too excited over my liberation to remember what we talked about. Later, at the station, the detective met us. Brodsky had tickets for the three of us in one compartment. As we made ourselves comfortable, the detective showed me his handcuffs, remarking, "Say, Benny, I was ordered to put the cuffs on you. I won't, though, but you better don't try to escape, because I am a good shot. I never miss." He then proceeded to take off his belt and holster with the revolver and bullets. These he placed on the seat next to me. If I had wanted to escape, I could have taken the gun, put the cuffs on his hands, and escaped very easily, his braggadocio notwithstanding. The detective then proposed a game of poker. I refused, but Brodsky played with him, making sure that the detective should win, in order to keep him in good mood. I slept in the upper berth, Brodsky on the side, and the detective in the lower berth. I was eager to get home and to see comrades and friends. Innumerable incidents and ideas concerning the movement and my future activities flashed through my mind. Stretched out on the upper berth, I listened to the pleasant music of the swift-moving train over the rails. I was moving away from the monotonous life of prison, onward to the city where a warm welcome would await me, happy faces greet me, and a life of activity begin. In the morning I was in New York.

When we arrived, it was too early to go straight to court, so I went to police headquarters first, where I was fingerprinted and photographed again. This took a little time. But around ten o'clock I appeared in court, secured my release and for the time being was a free man again. I went straight home. My folks lived on Greenwich Avenue in two rooms that were formerly the mailing headquarters of the underground Communist movement. On the way I passed the places that were familiar to me: Patchen Place, where John Reed had lived, the alley where Jim Larkin had had his quarters, and the office of Dr. Maximilian Cohen, one of the first secretaries of the New York district of the Communist Party. Many comrades came to visit me at Greenwich Avenue.

I saw the Party leaders at the National Office of the Workers Party, located at 799 Broadway, corner of Eleventh Street. Ruthenberg and Lovestone were not pleased to see me then. Lovestone, with Ruthenberg's complicity, had already taken advantage of the fact that Ruthenberg and Ferguson had been liberated a few days earlier than I, to arrange a banquet for them the night before I arrived in New York. Already they were scheming and playing for position in the movement. I also discovered that steps had already been taken to make Ruthenberg the General Secretary of the Party. I visited a number of Party institutions and auxiliary organizations. The Friends of Soviet Russia occupied an entire building on the corner of Thirteenth Street and Seventh Avenue. The movement had grown considerably, its ramifications were many. But everywhere I went I heard about the struggle going on in the Party. I was told of caucuses, that the movement was split, one group having refused to join the united Communist forces. I heard about William Z. Foster and the Trade Union Educational League which he headed. It was all new to me. I had not been informed on all these developments. One thing I did realize, and that was that the virus of factionalism that had been responsible for the violent internecine struggles when the Communist movement was started in 1919 had not been eradicated. Personal animosities were prevalent in all quarters, the comrades hating each other bitterly. I decided to listen, investigate, and learn what it was all about before I made up my mind on the Party situation.

Soon after, a mass meeting was held in Central Opera House, welcoming all the politicals released from prison. The hall was jammed with joyous men and women who went wild with enthusiasm in welcoming us. When I got up to speak I received a tremendous ovation. I thanked the workers of New York for their splendid support. I took the opportunity to reaffirm my Communist ideals, defying the ruling class of the United States to crush the revolutionary working class movement by imprisonment of its followers. I concluded by predicting the victory of the American proletarian revolution which would turn the "sham democracy" of the United States into a Soviet Government of proletarian dictatorship. The years I had spent in prison did not change my political convictions. I returned to freedom a firm believer in Communism.

CHAPTER IV

AMERICAN COMMUNISM COMES UP FOR AIR

THE Communist Party was teeming with life. The most important activity in 1922 was raising money through the Friends of Soviet Russia for the victims of the Russian famine. All the important Party members seemed to be working for that organization, which collected thousands of dollars every day. But this work did not appeal to me. I preferred political activity. I had hoped to tour the country when I came out of prison and spread the gospel of Communism. But I soon discovered that the Party was much more interested in petty politics than in the larger issue of bringing its message to the American people. It was stewing in its own juices of bitter factional controversy. Following the raids, the Communist factions had made several attempts to unite into one organization, but failed each time. Moscow, too, had intervened and had ordered the Communists in America to unite, but no sooner was unity achieved than the movement again split over the question of publicly and legally carrying on Communist activities. The underground Communist Party had organized a number of legal political organizations with which to camouflage its activities. The most important of these, the Workers Party of America, succeeded in drawing into its ranks a number of revolutionary Socialist organizations that had refused to go along with the Left Wing when the Socialist Party was split in 1919 and had steadfastly refused to join the underground Communist movement, although these organizations subscribed in full to the Communist program of the Third International.

The underground Communist Party was affiliated with the Third or Communist International, but the Workers Party was not. Among the members in the movement, the underground

Communist Party was known as the "Number One" organization, while the Workers Party was the "Number Two" organization. A large section of the underground Communist Party split away from the underground movement, feeling that the Workers Party was given too much autonomy and that its program was no more than a remote approach to the Communist program. Regarding the Workers Party as a dilution of Communist principles and a step leading toward the liquidation of the Communist movement, this group, which called itself the United Toilers and was nicknamed by Lovestone the "United Toilets," published in its official paper, *The Workers' Challenge*, edited by Harry M. Wicks, the most violent and vituperative polemics in America. I should say that ninety-nine percent of the United Toilers membership came from the foreign-language federations; they were chiefly Russians, Letts, Ukrainians and Lithuanians, with a handful of Jewish and a sprinkling of English-speaking members.

It soon became very clear to me that the deciding factor in the situation was Number One, the underground Communist Party, where the internal struggle was over the question of its relations with the Workers Party, or in the broader sense, its attitude toward legal public activity. On this issue Number One was divided into three main caucuses. The largest of these was the so-called Goose Caucus. Its leaders were L. E. Katterfeld, Secretary of the Communist Party; Abraham Jakira, outstanding leader of the influential Russian Federation; Alfred Wagenknecht, Israel Amter, and Edward Lindgren. The name "Goose Caucus" originated in the course of a stormy debate, when William Dunne, exasperated by Jakira's unceasing and persistent stuttering, interjected, "Jakira, you make me sick; you cackle like a goose," and Amter, springing to the defense of his fellow-factionalist, retorted, "But the geese saved Rome and we shall yet save the Party," while Lovestone, counter-attacking with ridicule, shouted back, "All right, then; from now on you're the Goose Caucus!" The name stuck. The Goose Caucus looked with suspicion and contempt on those members of Number Two who were not at the same time members of Number One, fought against the immediate liquidation of the underground movement, hoping in time, as soon as the changed situation in the country warranted it, to transform Number One into a legal party openly espousing the Communist cause.

The chief opponents of the Geese were the Liquidators (a name borrowed from the situation in the Russian Social-Democracy after the Revolution of 1905), who allied themselves with the non-members of Number One in Number Two, using them as political leverage for wresting control of Number One from the Geese. The Liquidators were led by Jay Lovestone, Charles E. Ruthenberg, James P. Cannon, William Z. Foster and Earl Browder. Between these two chief contending forces were the Conciliators, who hoped to gain control by pleading unity and by holding the balance of power between the two extreme factions. While the Liquidators sought to have the Workers Party supersede the Communist Party in effect, the Conciliators recognized it as merely the legal front of Number One. But it is really a waste of time to discuss principles in reference to this controversy, for principles played a subsidiary role; they were merely verbose rationalizations to cover up the main consideration—to gain control of the Party apparatus.

I joined neither of the two extreme caucuses nor the Conciliators nor any of the minor ones nor the United Toilers. All of them tried to capitalize on my prestige as a political martyr and courted my support, but it was clear to me from the first meeting of the Central Executive Committee I attended—I was co-opted into it immediately after my release from prison—that personal and factional considerations were of greater moment to all of them than the welfare of the Party as a whole. Perhaps I am stating the matter too harshly; it might be kinder to say that each faction identified the best interests of the Party with its own faction. But it would not be altogether truthful. The fact remains, however unkind it may seem, that factional fanaticism, personal vanity and ambition to rule the roost ranked far above loyalty to the Communist cause. It was this fact that appalled me when I came out of prison; it was a fungus that had grown from the early factionalism in which the Party was conceived into a parasite that was beginning to choke the Communism out of the Communist Party.

The trouble with me was that at the time I understood it only emotionally, not cerebrally, as I see it now I had a feeling about it and merely recoiled from it. Had I understood it better, I might have devised a plan for fighting it—although I can see now that any plan for fighting it was foredoomed to failure. Politically my sympathies were with the Goose Caucus: with reaction still rampant, it would have been suicidal to abandon the underground party, which in turn needed the Workers Party as a front through which to conduct its various open and legal activities. On that issue I happened to be in agreement with the famous Twenty-one-point program of the Communist International for all its affiliates. Knowing that my views coincided with theirs to that extent, at least, although they differed in other respects, the Geese adopted me as one of their own, included my name on their New York delegation to the national convention and supported my candidacy vigorously. So, although I told them frankly that I disapproved of their factionalism as much as of the factionalism of the others, I was adopted by them and became to all intents and purposes a member of the Goose Caucus.

All of this took place while Katterfeld of the Geese, Lovestone of the Liquidators and John Ballam of the United Toilers were in Moscow, arguing the merits of their respective factions before the supreme pontiffs of the Communist International. From the first, Moscow was the final arbiter on the issues and policies in the American Communist Party, as it was on all its affiliates throughout the world. Whatever its decision in this case, it was couched in such equivocal terms that, far from terminating the factional controversy, it merely added fuel to the fire. At any rate, what Lovestone lost in Moscow he regained soon after his return to the United States. All three came back on the eve of the national convention. The air was thick with recriminations and feuds, with charges and counter-charges—nor could the three Communist International nuncios, sent to enforce the decision of the Holy See, do anything about it. The leader of the three Comintern Representatives was a professor of mathematics by the name of Walecki (pronounced *Vahletsky*), a rather aristocratic Polish intellectual, who, notwithstanding his origin, looked like the American cartoonist's idea of a Russian Bolshevik—hooked nose, disheveled mop of hair on his head, an unkempt and unruly beard, looking rather ludicrous in the ill-fitting white linen suit that accentuated the angularity of his frame. But you could not help liking and respecting him, once you saw his eyes, sparkling with intelligence, wisdom, wit, and sheer human charm.

The second of the three Comintern nuncios looked like a Hungarian version of the proverbial traveling salesman. Short and stocky, with a large head and a disproportionately larger nose that proudly bore a pair of gold-rimmed spectacles perched importantly on its bridge, he dressed like a dude, combed his hair sleek and neat, was always clean-shaven, smoked gold-tipped cigarettes, listened attentively to everything that was being said in his presence, and said absolutely nothing. But this man was a genuine Bolshevik, albeit a Hungarian one. A commander of the Hungarian Red Army in 1919, he had fled to Russia after the overthrow of the Hungarian Soviet Republic and along with Bela Kun became an important functionary of the Comintern. In Hungary his name had been Josef Pogány; he came to America as John Pepper. The third "Rep," as we irreverently referred to all three of Moscow's representatives, was none other than Boris Reinstein, a druggist from Buffalo, who until 1917 had been a leading member of the already then steadily-dying Socialist Labor Party, which since the death of Daniel de Leon in 1910 has been no more than a ghost of its erstwhile still-born self. Reinstein was returning like a conquering hero to his home town. He had been practically nothing, even in Leftist political circles in the United States; now he was returning five years later as spokesman of the victorious Bolsheviks. He was about sixty at the time, excitable, enthusiastic, and behaved toward us like an indulgent father toward his recalcitrant children. We saw at once that he was not important, that only Walecki's views were decisive, but all of us underestimated the importance of John Pepper.

L. E. Katterfeld was put in charge of arranging the national convention, which was to settle all controversial issues under the supervision of the Comintern "Reps." Rose Baron, secretary of the Workers' Defense Committee, came to me, very much alarmed, just before the convention was due to open. She told me that one of the detectives of the New York police had confided to one of our comrades in the Tombs that our convention would be raided. He intimated that the authorities were very well informed concerning the secret place where the convention was to be held. William F. Dunne, of Butte, Montana, also spoke to me about the coming convention, asking me, as one who had some influence with Katterfeld, to try to induce him to hold the convention elsewhere. When I saw Katterfeld and spoke to him, I discovered how useless it was to attempt changing his mind. Obstinate, he was very sure that the arrangements he had made were fool-proof and that the authorities would never find out about them. He was obsessed with the idea that the opposition led by Lovestone and Ruthenberg had resorted to circulating these alarming rumors because it wanted to break up or postpone the convention, in order to gain time to manipulate its minority into a majority. I assured him that he was entirely mistaken about that. I argued that it would be folly to hold a secret convention in a place where underground conventions had been held before. When I learned, moreover, that the convention was to be held in a state that had "criminal syndicalist" laws, I launched an attack against him, declaring that, if that were so, he had no right to jeopardize the Party and gamble with the freedom of his comrades. But all my efforts were in vain. Katterfeld was determined to go ahead with his plans.

The convention was held in the latter part of August, 1922. There were regular delegates, fraternal delegates, Central Executive Committee delegates, the representatives of the Communist International, and several lesser categories of others. We were divided into groups of two, three, and five. Each group had a captain who was given the route he was to travel to the convention and instructed when he was to leave. Every route was broken up and circuitous. The trips were so arranged and timed that no two groups were to cross each other en route to the convention or find themselves riding on the same train. Strict orders were given that under no circumstances were any groups to leave for the convention through any of Chicago's railroad terminals, because information had been received that the Chicago railroad stations would be honeycombed with detectives on the watch for Communist delegates, whom they were to follow wherever they went. I left for the convention with Harry Winitsky. We traveled in a round-about way, making about half a dozen changes on the way. To our surprise, at one of the junctions where our train crossed a line directly out of Chicago, Harry Winitsky spotted Ruthenberg and John Pepper. When he informed me about it, I said he was crazy, that it could not be possible. But Winitsky was right. Ruthenberg and Pepper deposited themselves in the parlor car, where Ruthenberg opened up his portable typewriter, sprawled Communist documents and papers all around him and started to type, in flagrant violation of traveling instructions. I considered his actions irresponsible, if not criminal, but I dared not reprove him there and then for fear of violating my own traveling instructions by communicating with him there.

We were to leave the train at Bridgeman, Michigan. The convention place was about a mile away from the station. A small town, Bridgeman consisted of a few ramshackle houses irregularly grouped around the railroad station. Everyone who got off there was immediately spotted. The villagers must have realized at once that there were strange doings going on, by the bands of strangers continuously filtering through the town toward the lake lodge and camp that was to house the convention. The minute I landed I knew it was impossible to prevent detection. The place was picturesquely situated in the wooded section of Lake Michigan. A large rambling building with a very wide and long veranda constituted the main house. A few delegates slept in the main house, but the great majority of them lodged in the cabins in the woods. The proprietor of the place, a German woman of about fifty-five, prepared our meals, which she and several girl waitresses served to us on the porch. The convention itself was held in the very thick of the woods, with night sessions by torchlight. That enhanced the romanticism of the event for the delegates, but it did not in the least deter their penchant for vociferousness. The guards, who were stationed all around the charmed circle in the woods, more to deepen the conspirative atmosphere than to secure real conspiracy (as events subsequently proved), complained that the voices of the delegates carried too far and everything they said could be heard distinctly several hundred yards away. But these complaints went unheeded. In addition, we had scouts stationed in the village, supposedly to detect signs of danger, but really (as events subsequently proved) to betray the presence of rank and suspicious strangers in the Michigan woods. Nor did the convention get down to business at once. A lot of time, fully three days, were spent on preliminaries, held in a large shack in the woods. There, alternating, met the outgoing Central Executive Committee, the caucuses of the various factions, and conferences as to how the praesidium of the convention was to be constituted. After the convention started, that shack was used for the Central Executive Committee meetings, the sessions of the convention praesidium, and the various convention committees.

In the meantime, the delegates were having a wonderful time. They turned our convention spot in the thick of the Michigan woods into a kind of improvised country club. There were avid poker games, swimming parties in the lake, and endless "bull sessions," thoroughly Rabelaisian in spirit, the most ribald stories drawing the lustiest guffaws. A sprinkling of femininity among the delegates added to the enjoyment of life. Not even the most exalted one among us, the eminent chief plenipotentiary of the Comintern, Professor Walecki, to whom we irreverently referred to as "the Rep," disdained to join in the general merriment. Indeed, he proved to be the champion raconteur of risqué stories. That was all right with us, and we liked him for a good sport. But in a couple of days he gave up entertaining us collectively and began to concentrate on Rose Pastor Stokes, who feigned to be shocked as she thrilled at the attentions paid to her by the chief Comintern plenipotentiary. Even that was all right with us—we could even forgive this desertion of the collective for individualized self-seeking as a perfectly human aberration—but we began to lose patience with him when he took to billing and cooing with Rose so close to our bungalow and kept such late hours that we could not fall asleep. Among those who shared this bungalow with me was the impetuous Harry Winitsky, a man of action and no respecter of exalted rank. When our hints and protests failed to restrain the professor's romantic eloquence, we of the bungalow took to yelling imprecations, vowing to murder the lovers if they did not desist from disturbing our sleep. Finally, when every non-violent effort failed, Harry Winitsky picked up a shoe in the dark and hurled it through the fragrant night. In less than a minute we had positive proof that Harry had hit the bull's eye, for the irate Rep was in our bungalow, shoe in hand, matching it, determined to find out whose foot it fitted. Of all things, it turned out to be my shoe!

There were two definite caucuses at the convention. The largest one was the caucus of the Geese, which I attended; the other, the caucus of the Liquidators, led by Lovestone and Ruthenberg. The Geese had a clear majority. Lovestone then organized a so-called "neutral" group, which claimed that it did not belong to either caucus. In charge of this caucus Lovestone placed his crony, Bertram D. Wolfe, who came as a delegate from California. Wolfe had been Lovestone's associate when the National Left Wing was first organized. He had followed Lovestone into the Communist Party, organized jointly with the Russian Federation in 1919. As soon as the raids took place he shirked all Party activities, disappeared from his post and failed to show up at committee meetings, though his wife continued to insist that his Party salary should be paid. After many months news began to trickle in that Wolfe had left the country and had made his residence in Mexico. The rank and file comrades did not relish what seemed to them cowardice in a leader, and openly expressed their disapproval of what looked like flight to Mexico. Through Wolfe Lovestone schemed to cause disaffection in the Geese caucus by using him as a "neutral" spearhead against the Geese majority. It was evident from the beginning that the Communist International delegation favored the Liquidators. But Walecki respected a majority. However, Ruthenberg and Lovestone were indefatigable. They were prepared to drag the convention out for weeks on end—

until they succeeded in dividing and breaking up the majority.

What actually divided the convention was not a fundamental political difference. The Geese were not opposed to a legal organization. All they maintained was that the time was not yet ripe for the Party to come out in the open. The Liquidators were of the opinion that the time was ripe, that the legal expression of the Communist Party, i.e., the Workers Party, had superseded the underground organization and should therefore replace it. This attitude was now adopted by the leaders of the Liquidators' caucus, because they had meantime made secret deals with some of the leaders of the Workers Party and knew that if the Workers Party should supersede the underground Communist Party, they would be in control of the entire Communist movement. Only a very small section of the Geese caucus, represented by Edward Lindgren and L. E. Katterfeld, was definitely committed in principle to an underground Communist Party, but not the majority of the Geese, whose views on this question were in line with the decision of the Communist International, which called for the unification of all groups and acceptance of the Workers Party as the legal expression of the Communist movement.

Before the convention really got under way it was faced with a split brought on by the attitude of the handful of die-hards in the Geese caucus, who rejected all collaboration with the Liquidators. I bitterly fought this tendency in the Geese caucus and finally defeated it. I maintained that the unity of our forces, in spite of the differences on the tactical questions under dispute was of the greatest necessity if our movement was to succeed. Before I made my fight in the Geese caucus the Communist International delegates became panicky and refused to go on with the convention. After the Geese caucus vote was taken and my position upheld, the convention proceeded. By manipulation of the neutral elements on the issue of being against all caucuses, Wolfe succeeded on the minor question of a point of order in dividing the convention by a vote of 23 to 22. However, the important questions before the convention never came to a vote. Had it reached that point, the Lovestone-Ruthenberg leadership would have been decisively repudiated, even though it enlisted the support of two promising newcomers in the Party, William Z. Foster and Earl Browder.

The highlight of the convention took place on the second night, when Foster arrived from Chicago to address us on the Trade Union Educational League and Communist trade union work. The stage was set to make Foster's speech as impressive as possible, in order to win over some delegates from the Geese caucus. In the darkness of the woods, lit by the glare of torches, he started a report, full of personal anecdotes of his experiences in the trade unions. The gist of it was that if the Communists knew how to behave in the unions, they could quickly gain control of them, put through the proposition of amalgamating the craft unions into industrial unions, and thus alter the very course of the American labor movement. It was clear to me that Foster saw himself as the head of this new American trade union movement.

Many delegates resented Foster's presence at the convention. Some felt that he came for the express purpose of diverting attention from the main issue before the convention; others, that Foster's presence was jeopardizing the new trade union activities of the Party, which he was conducting as our undercover man, not openly as a Communist. Nearly all delegates, moreover, expressed the fear that Foster's coming to the convention exposed all of us to imminent danger, because he was being constantly shadowed by agents of the Department of Justice and other operatives, who suspected his hand in the recent railroad strike and the general activities of our Party and the Trade Union Educational League. This apprehension was not altogether baseless. The very next day things began to happen. In the morning a stranger who seemed very suspicious stopped in front of the main house to look the place over.

Another grave situation was caused by Bimba's indiscretions. Anthony Bimba was a fraternal delegate of the Lithuanian Federation, which prior to the convention had maintained relations with the United Toilers. Bimba was discovered mailing convention reports to the press of the United Toilers. Among the convention rules was a strict prohibition on the mailing of any letters, much less convention reports, and certainly not to the United Toilers. Bimba was apprehended by the comrades detailed to look after the safety of the convention, his person and quarters were searched, and copies of his reports were obtained, as well as letters ready for mailing. A special meeting of the convention was held on the Bimba matter, which ended in taking away his convention rights and placing him on probation as far as his future membership in the Party was concerned. A strict watch of Bimba was also arranged. Lovestone and Ruthenberg tried to make capital of the Bimba incident by charging that the Goose caucus was to blame and that it maintained relations with the United Toilers through Bimba. The charge, however, had no truth in it and was knowingly made for factional reasons.

Foster's indiscreet presence, followed by the appearance of the mysterious stranger and the Bimba event, created an alarming situation. We called in the guards from the village. They reported seeing strangers in town who looked suspicious. William F. Dunne, former editor of the *Butte Daily Bulletin*, whose appearance was the opposite of what a Communist was expected to look like, was dispatched to the village to investigate. When he returned the praesidium was called into session to hear his report. He said that detectives were in town looking the situation over, that one of the detectives was the famous Spolansky of Chicago, who had been active in the raids against the Reds in 1919. The Communist International representatives became duly impressed and asked for an expression of opinion. Katterfeld became indignant. He charged that the whole thing was a plot by the Liquidators to break up the convention because they did not have a majority. I disagreed with him. I said steps should be taken in an orderly way to end the convention and disband. The Communist International representatives agreed with me. They decided that in view of the fact that the Geese were in the majority, they should elect a majority on the new Central Executive Committee and that then the convention should adjourn, all records should be destroyed and the delegates ordered to disband in an orderly fashion in small groups of five, leaving at regular intervals.

The order for the disbanding of the groups was as follows:

the first to leave were to be the Communist International representatives; next were to follow those who recently came out of prison and whose cases were not yet completed; next were to follow the non-citizens; the last to follow were a group of Americans, who were to leave the next morning after all traces of the convention had been destroyed. Strangely enough, among the records at this underground convention was a registration of all present, made on mimeographed forms upon the insistence of the Communist International representative. On these forms we had put our party name, our party and labor movement history, including the number of times we had been arrested and confined to prison. Here was a complete record of who's who in the Communist Party—of great value to the authorities.

After all the details were worked out, the convention was again called to order. I made a report on the situation as chairman of the convention. The decisions made by the praesidium were approved. This was all done in the woods under the cover of darkness. Now the comrades spoke in muffled tones. The gathering in the darkness of the great trees, the atmosphere permeated with the danger of an impending attack, the chirping of the crickets, and the buzzing of the insects gave the scene a mysterious, fantastic and conspiratorial air. The election of the new Central Executive Committee proceeded without a hitch, the slates of the two caucuses were elected, the Geese getting the majority, the Liquidators the minority on the committee. By the time the convention adjourned all the comrades had already been assigned to their groups and to the special tasks they had to do. Each captain of a group was given sufficient cash to take the group to its final destination. Special messengers were sent out to nearby St. Joseph, to hire the automobiles which were to take the delegates out of Bridgeman to Chicago and other cities. These automobiles arrived like clockwork at the specified time.

The first group to leave, the representatives of the Communist International, crowded into the first automobile and pulled the collars of their jackets over their faces, so that the chauffeur should not get a good look at them. The second group, which was to follow next, consisted of Winitsky, Ruthenberg, Ballam and me. Before departing I could see in the darkness that all the comrades were in a state of intense excitement and nervousness. Those who had already packed their belongings were standing in huddles awaiting their time to depart. But when our automobile arrived, Ruthenberg refused to come along. He violated the very orders he himself had helped to formulate. When Harry and I insisted that he carry out the instructions of the convention and leave with us, he passed a slurring remark to the effect that he was not a coward and would remain to face the danger. I clearly saw that his determination to stay was grandstand play; he wanted martyrdom, in order to win the applause of the Communist rank and file. Later, when he faced prison as a result of his foolhardiness, he was not so willing a victim, and indeed was greatly disturbed over the prospect of imprisonment. Under Ruthenberg's inspiration, those who still remained procrastinated in violation of convention decisions, which were that they leave the first thing in the morning. They breakfasted, then took a dip in the lake, and wasted hours in just hanging around. Apparently Ruthenberg did not want to lose the opportunity of being arrested; he waited until the Federal and State authorities arrived. Although the convention had voted to have the records destroyed, due to Ruthenberg's interference they were buried in the woods, not only in full sight of all who remained, among whom was one Francis A. Morrow, a member of the Communist Party of Camden, New Jersey, who acted as undercover agent of the Department of Justice, but also in full view of children related to the proprietor of the place.

The authorities came, as was expected. They not only arrested Ruthenberg and all the other comrades who were leisurely awaiting their arrival, but also went directly to the place where the barrel of records had been buried and dug out the treasure they were after. They had no difficulty in finding the burial place, for it was apparent that they had been tipped off in advance about its whereabouts. In addition to the registration of the convention delegates, possession of which gave the Department of Justice a complete history of the important Communists in the United States, that barrel contained some of the most confidential and important Party documents. Those arrested were herded into an army truck and taken to St. Joseph, Michigan, where they were thrown into jail and later charged with violation of the Michigan State Criminal Syndicalist Law, a law similar to the Criminal Anarchy Statute of the State of New York, for the alleged violation of which I had been convicted and sent to prison.

In place of Ruthenberg, the committee put in our car Shachno Epstein, one of the editors of the *Freiheit*, who was so frightened that for a long time he could not talk. When he finally did talk, he spoke in such a low whisper that it was difficult to make out what he was saying. We left Bridgeman about ten o'clock at night and arrived in Chicago the next morning. All the Party headquarters had been closed by the authorities. The railroad stations were full of detectives, who were watching out for Reds. I had to see Bob Minor, according to instructions, to get the money for the trip to New York. I was able to contact him the next day. He rushed in and out of the hallways of Chicago and in and out of the lobbies of the hotels in the Loop, as if an army of detectives were trailing his footsteps. When he finally gave me the money to cover both Winitsky's and my fare to New York, he whispered instructions into my ear that I should watch out for detectives and should under no circumstances take a train out of one of the Chicago railroad stations. Comrade Minor was in a panic.

Upon my return to New York City, I faced prison again, for the New York State Court of Appeals had returned an unfavorable verdict. But the Central Executive Committee, under the inspiration of John Pepper, the Communist International representative who remained in the United States after the Bridgeman convention, had other plans for me. These had been jointly and carefully well-thought-out by Pepper, Ruthenberg and Lovestone, who, for factional reasons, wanted to get me out of the way. They knew I was popular with the rank-and-file and was the only member on the new Central Executive Committee who gave standing to its Goose caucus majority. John Pepper, representing himself brazenly as one of my best friends, advised me in all seriousness to jump my bail and flee to Soviet Russia.

He put it, rather ingeniously, in somewhat this fashion: "Comrade Gitlow, I am sure you realize that the Bridgeman Convention proves beyond the shadow of a doubt that the reaction in the United States will continue for a very long time. I have made inquiries and have learned that after you have served your term in New York State, you will have to face trial in Michigan as a second offender, and, if convicted, you will face a prison term of ten years." He argued that it was foolish to place any trust at all in the law and the courts, something European revolutionists never do. But I was not impressed. He continued: "But, Comrade Gitlow, fifteen years in prison is a lifetime! It means actually spending the best part of one's life in prison. It is not necessary to make such a sacrifice, for today it is possible for a revolutionist to spend his life in worth-while constructive Socialist work in Soviet Russia. There you can gain tremendous experience, so that later, when the revolutionary situation in the United States develops, you can return, just as Lenin did when he returned to Russia from Switzerland, to take command of the revolutionary situation."

I listened to him very attentively, but gave him no definite answer. I told him I needed time to think his proposals over. Others also saw me on the same matter, comrades who could not be suspected of any ulterior purposes—notably, Abraham Jakira, one of the leaders of the Goose Caucus, and Johnny Ballam, who left the United Toilers to work among its membership for putting across the Comintern decision on the American Party question. Ballam was considered a good friend of mine. John Pepper, however, was the most insistent. Whenever he saw me he spoke about it, carefully unraveling to me how it was possible to get the necessary passports, how easily the authorities could be eluded and circumvented. I gave the matter serious consideration. I was young, unmarried, and the adventure of the proposition appealed to me. What then decided me against the proposal? First, I had given my word to the Civil Liberties Union to go through with the appeal. I could not go back on my word. Second, I did not trust in the good faith of those who made the proposal. Third, I did not have such a pessimistic view regarding the extent of the reaction in the United States, even though I, unlike Pepper, Ruthenberg, and Lovestone before the Bridgeman Convention, was of the opinion that the Communist Party could not come out in the open immediately. Fourth, I realized that taking such a step would make me a fugitive from justice and a permanent exile from my own country. Fifth, in Russia, even if it was a Socialist country, I would be a foreigner, with the result that I would be of very little use there, in addition to being cut off from all effectiveness in the United States.

Making the decision did not come easily. Facing, as I did, the possibility of many years of prison in New York and in Michigan was not a pleasant future to look forward to. I was an American. I had already some experiences with the police and prison methods of my country. I knew that what was possible in backward Russia of the Tsarist days, with its crude methods, lack of transportation, and communication facilities, and the attitude of its population, was not possible in the United States. It meant that if I ran away to the Soviet Union, an early return for me, because of my prominence in the movement, was entirely out of question. When I informed the Central Executive Committee about my decision to fight it out in the United States, even if it meant serving many years in prison, they looked dismayed, but finally agreed with Pepper, when he soothingly said, "After all, this is a personal matter which we must leave to the individual comrade himself to decide."

After the Bridgeman Convention the new Central Executive Committee of the Party met in New York City. A flat was hired in upper Manhattan to serve as its headquarters. But we did not meet there often, moving our meetings mostly from one private dwelling to another. Factionalism did not end. Those who were defeated at the Bridgeman Convention were determined to break up the new majority on the Central Executive Committee and to take over the leadership of the Party themselves. In this effort they united with the group Foster and Browder had formed in Chicago and with those forces in the Workers Party who were against the underground Party, even though they now knew that in consequence of the raids on the Bridgeman Convention they could not advocate before the Communist

Party rank and file the discontinuance of the underground. The Foster Group, though many contended that it made the alliance with Lovestone and Ruthenberg, in order itself to gain control of the Party, attempted through the Bridgeman case to discredit the current leadership of the Communist Party.

At the time of the Bridgeman Convention, Foster was advertised to the labor movement as a progressive trade unionist who was opposed to dual unions and who sought so to reform the A. F. of L. within its framework that it would become a militant trade union organization. Prior to the Bridgeman Convention and for some time after Foster emphatically denied that he was a member of the Communist Party, although throughout that period, while he was working most closely with Fitzpatrick of the Chicago Federation of Labor and with many Progressives in the trade union movement, he was attending the sessions of the Central Executive Committee as a highly-placed Communist. His activities through the Trade Union Educational League were supervised by our Central Executive Committee, which made all the decisions, sometimes upon Foster's recommendations, at other times against them, and whatever decisions we made Foster had to carry out. The money for the Trade Union Educational League organization came largely from two sources: the Profintern (the Red International of Trade Unions) in Moscow and from the Communist Party in the United States. The Trade Union Educational League could not have existed one month on the money it raised from its supporters in the United States. The decision for Profintern support was made by the E. C. C. I. (the Executive Committee of the Communist International). In no other way could Foster have obtained that support. Foster was not arrested at Bridgeman; he left right after he made his report, and still continued to insist that he was not a member of the Communist Party, which position he maintained at the time he was tried in the courts.

Placed in charge of organizing the Bridgeman Defense, Foster sought to create the impression that the majority of the underground Communist Party represented at Bridgeman was dominated by spies, that spies determined the policies of the Party.

His factionalism had carried him so far into this crass plot that the matter was brought indignantly into the Central Executive Committee by John Pepper, who demanded an immediate change of the whole defense policy mapped out by Foster, including decisions that would make Foster unable to carry out such a line when he himself came up for trial. Foster pleaded before the Central Executive Committee that it would be a good defense tactic to pursue such a line, because it would lead to the acquittal of the defendants. Foster's stand in 1922 was symptomatic of the downward trend of Communist ethics. In the first Communist trials, in 1919, we Communists took a principled stand. Placed on trial, I realized the responsibility I shouldered. I was the first Communist in the United States to be prosecuted for the advocacy of Communism. I realized that the standing of the movement before the radical workers depended upon making a straightforward principled fight, regardless of the consequences. In the early trials of 1919 all the leaders brought to trial made fearless principled defenses of their Communist beliefs. The one exception was Jay Lovestone, who, faced with prison, came to an understanding regarding his freedom from prosecution in New York and Chicago by appearing as a witness for the State against Harry Winitsky. But even Lovestone did not elevate his defection into a general policy. The Bridgeman cases marked a change in this respect, as far as the Foster policy was concerned. In organizing the Party's defense of the case, Foster, Ruthenberg, Browder and Dunne mapped out a plan based upon an avoidance of the issues of principle involved and pleading that the Communist Party was the plaything of Department of Justice spies. It was only through a bitter struggle in the Central Executive Committee of the Communist Party that this entire plan was scotched.

Soon after the Bridgeman Convention I was returned to Sing Sing Prison. I tried this time to follow the Party situation closely, but was kept inadequately informed by the Central Executive Committee. By the middle of October, 1922, I had concluded that the reactionary trend in the United States was giving way to a more liberal spirit. President Harding had, as early as Christmas, 1921, pardoned Eugene V. Debs. The action of Attorney-General Daugherty, in issuing a sweeping injunction against the strike of the Railroad Shopmen, aroused the resentment of organized labor and a large section of the public. So violent was the reaction against Daugherty that, after the settlement of the railroad strike, impeachment proceedings were started against him. The month of September witnessed the ending of the major strikes in the country and the conclusion of very favorable union agreements in certain industries. Around this time the wage-cutting campaign had come to a close and a definite beginning of wage increases set in. The attitude towards Soviet Russia was also undergoing a slight change. Better contact with Russia was being established, and the Federal Government had sounded out the Russian Government, through its Ambassador in Berlin, on the sending of an American technical commission to their country. The raid upon the Bridgeman Convention, instead of whipping up Red hysteria, had the opposite effect. On the one hand, it put us in a ridiculous position; while, on the other hand, public opinion turned definitely against the raiders. The trade unions rallied to our defense, as did the liberal forces of the country.

At the end of September, Alfred E. Smith received the nomination for Governor on the Democratic ticket, on a platform pledging social legislation, progressive labor laws, the abolition of the Lusk Committee and the repeal of the reactionary "anti-sedition" Lusk laws. Even the Republican Governor Miller, who had a reputation for conservatism, showed how the wind was blowing when he refused to extradite Edward Lindgren to stand trial in Michigan for participating at the underground convention. Around the middle of October, Harding began to commute the sentences of many I. W. W. prisoners in the federal prisons as well as of other political prisoners. These and many other factors convinced me that the time had come for the Communists to emerge from the cellar, to give up their underground party, and to come out publicly as a political party. I informed my parents when they visited me in Sing Sing that the Communist Party must come out as an open, legal, political party, and gave them my reasons. Being party members, they were shocked by what I had to say. They warned me that the membership would never agree to such a change. I told them that the change must be made and that the Party must not lose its opportunity to do so. I instructed them that upon their return to New York, they should immediately inform the Central Executive Committee and the members of the Party of my views. In parting, I said:

> Tell the comrades that, with an open party, we can carry on our Communist propaganda more effectively because we will be able to do so publicly. We will also be able to penetrate the trade unions, engage in political campaigns, increase our membership and gain hundreds of thousands of supporters. For the first time we will become an American political factor of importance. Should we be driven underground again, we will then have an army of Communists spread all over the country, a force that will have to be reckoned with and respected.

This time I stayed only three months in Sing Sing, for my lawyers succeeded in obtaining my release on bail pending my appeal to the United States Supreme Court. I left Sing Sing in high spirits. I was going to help legalize the Communist Party.

Free again, I learned that during the interim of three months many important developments had taken place. Katterfeld, the National Secretary of the Communist Party, had left for Russia after the Bridgeman Convention and had not yet retured with Moscow's decisions. Israel Amter, who was one of the big three of the Goose Caucus in favor of maintaining the underground party, had been won over by Pepper to the idea of an open party. Pepper also succeeded in sending him to Moscow as the official representative of the Party to the Communist International, in order that he might counteract Katterfeld. Pepper was now the political leader of the Party. He sought to re-establish Lovestone's leadership, which was thoroughly discredited, by having the Central Executive Committee assign Lovestone to the task of writing a book on the American Government as a Strike-Breaker.

Our national headquarters was situated in a small three-room flat in the Washington Heights section of New York City. A few chairs, a couple of typewriters, a number of small tables and some filing cabinets constituted its equipment. When not occupied by the Political Committee, it was used by Sadie Van Veen, Amter's wife, as her living quarters. Here the work of the Political Committee was performed. The acting National Secretary during Katterfeld's absence was Abraham Jakira, formerly a member of the Russian Federation. He was very short, not over four feet six inches tall, very nearsighted, and afflicted with stuttering. Jakira was a weakling, with no roots whatsoever in the labor movement. He owed his high position in the Communist movement to the factional situation in the Party and to the fact that he was a Russian. He realized that, in order to maintain his position as a leader, he had to lean upon someone really capable of leadership. Heretofore that someone had been Katterfeld. In addition to Jakira, the meetings of the Central Executive Committee were now attended by Clarissa (or "Chris") Ware, who was in charge of the Research Department of the Workers Party, always with a briefcase full of newspaper clippings which she brought to our uptown hideout from the headquarters of the Workers Party at 799 Broadway, Ruthenberg, Lovestone, Pepper, Minor, and myself. Occasionally Foster and Dunne were also present.

Chris Ware was an ambitious person, who once remarked that if a woman desired to make a career for herself in the Communist movement she had to attach herself to one of the Communist leaders. She was true to her word. It did not take her long to attach herself to Ruthenberg, who was then National Secretary of the Workers Party. Whether by chance or design, even her office was right next to Ruthenberg's private office. Indeed, in order to enter Ruthenberg's office one had to go through the Research Department. It was in the Research Department, however, that Jay Lovestone had his desk placed right up against the partition of Ruthenberg's office; thus, if he desired, he could make sure of keeping well informed regarding everything that went on in the National Secretary's sanctum sanctorum. But after Ruthenberg fell in love with Chris Ware, he not only abandoned Ray Ragozin, but he also moved Jay Lovestone and his desk out of the Research Department. Lovestone was very much peeved over this removal act. The outer office supported his peeve by openly resenting the fact that during office hours, when Ruthenberg wanted to be left in all privacy with Mrs. Ware, he would lock the entrance of the Research Department and keep it locked for hours.

The amorous proclivities of Chris Ware really threatened to create a political crisis of major importance, for her favors became the accolade of leadership. Before long, that indefatigable politician, John Pepper, made an attempt to win her affections when she brought some research material to him while he was alone at the underground headquarters uptown. She described the incident to Ruthenberg, who flared up in anger against Pepper. Chris Ware, quick to recognize that Pepper's ambition for leadership was a challenge to Ruthenberg as the leader of American Communism, took every opportunity to intensify Ruthenberg's anger and to create a wide separation between the two. Lovestone sought to bring peace between Pepper and Ruthenberg at the expense of Chris Ware and not without a thought, I suspect, of having his desk moved back close to the partition. At this point a physiological reaction settled the political crisis. It was a tragic end, for the last of Chris Ware's abortions proved fatal for her. Ruthenberg wept at the funeral, peace with Pepper was established and Lovestone had his desk moved back to the strategic spot in the Research Department.

The first question that the comrades of the Political Committee took up with me was the question of my attitude to the proposed question of the merger of the underground, illegal Communist Party with the Workers Party of America, its legal auxiliary organization. Some of the comrades were fearful that I would be opposed to the merger because, before I returned to prison, I had opposed such a step. They were skeptical of the message I had sent from prison by my parents that conditions now warranted the Party's coming out in the open. When I discussed the matter with Pepper, he at first tried to show me that the Communist International favored the step and would soon order the Communist Party to undertake it. However, when he realized how I stood on the matter, he informed me that he had already assured the others that they would find me not only committed to the step but also ready to carry it out energetically. This occurred at the end of 1922.

Assured of my support, the Political Committee was called together and immediately adopted measures to carry out the merger as speedily as possible. To facilitate matters we received in the nick of time a cable from Moscow, signed by Amter, assuring us that the Comintern favored the step. When Katterfeld, who had gone to Moscow as the leader of the majority, returned, he brought with him the rebukes of the Comintern and its repudiation of his policy. He also returned to a party in which his followers on the Central Executive Committee had deserted him. It marked the end of his leadership. Katterfeld was a sincere, honest American radical, a Kansas farmer, who had given years of his life to the Socialist movement. He was very serious in his demeanor and intensely fanatical. Once he got an idea into his head, he tenaciously held on to it. To him underground Communism was a principle. Its abandonment he looked upon as treachery to the movement. In a brief period of time he was so completely eliminated from the movement that when, in 1928, he started a non-political, scientific magazine called *Evolution,* he was, upon a motion of Lovestone's, instructed that he must be prepared to turn over all the connections and resources of his magazine to the party, which simultaneously was instructed not to endorse the magazine.

Whatever opposition prevailed in the underground Communist Party was soon overcome either by individual conferences or by meetings of the rank and file, held in out of the way places under conditions of great secrecy, at which Pepper usually delivered a long-winded speech, stressed the orders of the Communist International, ridiculed the opposition, and ended in a manner that left his poor rank and file listeners bewildered with the wealth of "arguments" presented. During the discussion he would shout down a rank and filer he did not agree with by crying "schluss" (shut-up) with all the authority of the Communist International, even though the poor fellow had only five minutes in which to answer the tirades of Pepper, which generally lasted two or three hours. In summing up the discussion, Pepper would single out one of the innocent rank and filers who, in his honest simplicity, had left himself open to demagogic attack, and berate him most unmercifully, making him out to be the worst of scoundrels and an ignoramus to boot. He gloried in attacking the weak. His vituperative ability was embellished with abuse and insults. Once, before entering the verbal fray, he remarked gleefully to a friend, "If you want to see how a pig is stuck as you never saw one before, watch me!"

During this period many conferences were held with those leaders of the Workers Party who were not also members of the underground Party or its Central Executive Committee. These conferences dealt mainly with the division of the offices of the merged party. When all the deals were finally consummated and a vote for them assured, a joint meeting of the Central Executive Committee of the underground Party and of the Workers Party took place. Thus, in the early part of 1923, the underground Communist Party—the vaunted Number One—disappeared. During the discussion period we had promised the members of the underground that a skeleton of the underground party made up of the most trusted Communists would be maintained for the conduct of illegal conspirative work and to serve as the framework for an underground party in case reaction in the country once more appeared. The promise was made, but was never intended to be kept. The underground was liquidated thoroughly and completely.

The merging of the Number One, the underground Communist Party, with Number Two, the Workers Party, under the name of the Workers Party, made that party the official Communist Party of the United States, secretly affiliated with the Communist International and recognized by it as one of its official sections. The new party accepted the discipline of the Communist International. Even the Workers Council Group, headed by Trachtenberg, Engdahl, and Olgin, who had originally refused to join the Communist Party because they objected to the discipline it exercised over its membership, accepted as members and leaders of the Workers Party, that kind of discipline and the even more rigid and exacting discipline of the Communist International as devoutly as did the members and leaders of the former underground Communist Party.

It was the first time since 1919 that the Communist Party dared openly to espouse its cause. We had attempted before in a veiled and camouflaged form to propagate our ideas. In 1921 we organized the Workers' League for that purpose. The League ran candidates for office in New York City. I was its candidate for Mayor when I was in Sing Sing and was ruled off the ballot by the Board of Elections. We made a little headway in some of the unions, notably the needle trade unions and the small independent unions. We effectively used our legal defense organization, known as the Workers Defense League, cleverly to carry on Communist propaganda and agitation which could not be done under other circumstances. The most intensive and widespread dissemination of propaganda in favor of Soviet Russia and Communism was carried on through the Friends of Soviet Russia, which we organized for the ostensible purpose of collecting funds for the famine-stricken in Russia. Through this organization we collected hundreds of thousands of dollars, out of which we, to a very large extent, directly and indirectly financed the Party. A large percentage of the funds which we turned over to the central bureau in Paris was credited to our Party instead of being spent for famine relief. The payroll of the Friends of Soviet Russia was swamped with Party bureaucrats who received their salaries out of the monies donated for relief, being thus enabled to carry on Party work. Often when funds were desperately needed, the Secretary of the Friends of Soviet Russia was called in by the Political Committee and directed to turn over money to the Party, the necessary bookkeeping notations being made to cover the matter up. This was easy to do, because practically everyone working on the large staff of the Friends of Soviet Russia was either a Party member or one who carried out Party instructions.

In becoming a legal party we had to turn our attention away from abstract theories of Communism to the problems of the country. This was not an easy task, because our Party, even with the merger, was predominantly made up of foreign-born un-Americanized members. From eighty to ninety percent of the membership belonged to the foreign-speaking language federation of the new Party. The Jewish Federation had about

1200 members and published a daily paper, *Freiheit;* the German Federation had several hundred members, and published the daily *Volkszeitung;* the Russian Federation had about 1200 members and its own daily paper, *Novy Mir;* the Ukrainian Federation had about 1,000 members and also a daily paper; the Finnish Federation had about 3,000 members, published two daily papers and controlled a large and wealthy section of the Finnish Cooperative movement; the Lithuanian Federation had about 1500 members and published a daily paper; the Lettish Federation had a few hundred members; the Esthonian Federation about 100 members, the Italian Federation about 500 members, the South Slavic Federation about 800 members; the Hungarian Federation about 500 and a daily paper, the Polish Federation, several hundred; the Swedish Federation, several hundred; the Greek Federation, several hundred; the Armenian Federation about 150 members; there were a couple of hundred organized Bulgarians; and finally, some Roumanians. In all, nearly 12,000 members belonged to the foreign language branches. Only about 1000 to 1200 members were in the English-speaking branches, and in these branches the overwhelming majority were foreign-born, many of whom were not even citizens and spoke English badly and with difficulty. It was out of this material that the Workers Party had to be built into a Party for the winning of power in the United States. Moreover, a large number of the members were non-workers. Many were professionals, intellectuals, and small business men; if to their number had been added the paid party officials, such as secretaries, organizers, teachers, journalists and professional propagandists, the percentage of non-workers would have been very high. The Party had very little influence in the trade unions; of the majority of its members who were workers, many did not belong to the unions.

Pepper did more than any one else to turn our attention to American problems. He followed closely all the political developments in the country, discussed them at length in the Political Committee, and privately with the party leaders. I had many such conversations with him, conversations in which he prodded me on my views, what my perspectives were concerning the future development of the country concerning the unions and particularly concerning Democratic, Republican and labor politics. But, like all foreign Communists, he did not understand the United States. He expected the Teapot Dome Scandal to result in the overthrow of the Republican Administration before the next Presidential elections, and the emergence of a labor party that would immediately become a serious contender for power. He expected the agricultural crisis which followed the war to bring about a farmers' revolt of great proportions that would result in a farmers' revolution, the farmers taking up arms against the government. He believed that the foreign-born could be welded into a unit of opposition to the capitalist parties because of the anti-foreign-born legislation that was being considered by Congress in 1923 and 1924.

The merger did not give the country a united Communist Party free from factionalism. The Workers Party now contained the leaders of both the Communist and the Workers Party. They were now on an equal footing, because they all were recognized by Moscow. A struggle for power in the Party soon developed. This factionalism was aggravated by the Party's turn to a consideration of American problems. Foster, who had started his career as a Bryan Democrat, and who then became successively a Socialist, an Anarchist, an I. W. W., a Revolutionary Syndicalist and an A. F. of L. organizer supporting Sam Gompers and the World War, ended by becoming a Communist in 1921 and the secret leader of the Party's trade union activity. Foster was imbued with the idea that he could capture the A. F. of L. and take the place of Gompers as its president. He saw little beyond the trade unions. In 1921 he was firmly convinced that the Communist Party could serve his ambition and help him capture the A. F. of L. He did not understand or appreciate politics. He viewed the most insignificant fight in the trade unions of infinitely more importance than the questions of politics over which the country and the press were agitated. It was only natural that the non-political groups in the Party, such as the foreign language federations least active in politics, and those Communists interested in purely inner trade union matters, should gravitate towards his leadership. In addition, he attracted those leaders of the Workers Party who desired to challenge the former leaders of the underground movement grouped around Ruthenberg.

Foster took advantage of all this. He organized his faction secretly, made alliances with the leaders of the former Workers Party, took the various federation leaders into his confidence and enlisted the support of the trade unionists. This marked the beginning of another factional war in the united legal party that raged for six years and kept the cables between New York and Moscow hot with messages transmitted both ways.

The factionalism which developed broke out with particular fury in the Jewish Section and in the staff of its daily newspaper, *Freiheit*. Drastic steps had to be taken in an effort to root out the opposition to the Political Committee. Upon Pepper's suggestion and much against my desires, the Political Committee decided that I should be sent in as its commissar to take over the affairs of the paper. Moissaye J. Olgin, the editor of the paper, became furious. He paraded as the guardian of Bolshevism among the Jewish masses, though he had joined the Communist movement only after he was sure of the success of the Bolshevik Revolution. A native of Russia and active in the Russian Socialist movement, he nevertheless in 1917 wrote a history of the Russian revolutionary movement, called *The Soul of the Russian Revolution,* which mentioned neither Lenin nor Trotsky. Then he made a round-about face and paid particularly obsequious journalistic observances to Trotsky as the guiding genius of Bolshevism since 1905. Alexander Bittleman who was the secretary of the Jewish Federation, opposed both Olgin and the Political Committee. Of medium height, Bittleman was very thin, had drooping shoulders, and squinting eyes. His political manipulations make weird party history. He fought together with Olgin against the underground party and at the same time fought Olgin for control of the *Freiheit*. At the time of the merger of the Number One and the Number Two he became Foster's close political adviser and a leader in Foster's secret caucus. Foster then, with Bittleman's consent and upon Bittleman's advice, made an alliance with Olgin for the purpose of capturing the Party. Bittleman, however, continued, though pledged to support him, to undermine Olgin secretly and to make his position as editor of *Freiheit* unbearable. Obviously, my job to clean up the mess was not an easy one, with the staff against me, the Jewish membership hostile, and the financial affairs of the paper in disastrous condition. I had to watch every line the writers wrote, give attention to the raising of money to keep the paper alive, and convince the membership that the paper was not being destroyed through the changes made by the Central Executive Committee of the Party.

When Foster captured the Party at the end of 1923, he sent Jim Cannon to see me. Cannon hailed originally from Kansas City. He was a member of the I. W. W. and of the Socialist Party before 1919. In the I. W. W. he had gained a reputation for his languid laziness and his aptness in singing and reciting hobo and I. W. W. ditties. I first met him in 1919, when he came from Kansas City as a delegate to the National Left Wing Conference. At that time he edited a small weekly Socialist paper of I. W. W. and Left Wing leanings. He made only a superficial impression upon me, if any: I remembered him merely as a colorless individual of medium height and complexion, who spoke with a nasal twang and in sentimental monotone. He was not then very talkative, perhaps because he was not yet sure where the Left Wing Movement would lead. He failed to show up at the Chicago conventions, but made sure to have one of his emissaries present, to report back to him in Kansas City, so that he could make up his mind. It was clear to me that he did not want to commit himself on the spot, and stayed away so that he could have an opportunity to weigh the events carefully. He joined the Communist Labor Party, soon rose to prominent leadership, and in 1923 united with Foster to oust Ruthenberg from leadership. His mission in New York could not have been a pleasant one, because he came to bribe me, not to convince me. When he spoke, I thought I was listening to a miniature Boss Murphy of Tammany Hall. He hemmed and hawed for a few moments before coming to the point, made some personal remarks, and finally said:

"You know, Comrade Gitlow, you are fitted for big things in

the Party. I, more than anyone else, am interested in seeing that you get ahead and get the position which is your due. Now if you will be reasonable and will comply with my request that you resign, rest assured that I will not let you down."

I replied, "But Comrade Cannon, since when must a Communist be concerned about jobs? It has always been my impression that a Communist must above all be motivated by principles. You are not discussing principles with me but jobs. I am sorry, but under the circumstances I cannot comply with your request."

That ended the parley. Cannon turning red took his leave. But soon after that conversation with Cannon I was removed by the Foster-Bittleman majority. This was my first experience with the practice of trying to obtain political support by bribing with an offer of jobs. In years to come this practice became common in the Party from top to bottom.

I was not sorry to leave and not sorry that I had been assigned to that post, for in the *Freiheit* office I met the girl who, though not a Communist or member of the Party, was destined to become my wife. For a Communist leader to marry a non-Communist was considered by most of my associates an unpardonable breach of Bolshevik conduct. I must confess that in this instance my love for the girl outweighed all the stock Communist objections. I had not become the sort of Communist who regards such intimate personal matters as trivial and as a submission to bourgeois sentimentality. Had I been unable to stand up against Communist prejudices, in this respect, I would have had to give up a union, which through all the years of party strife has been a source of great happiness and has enabled me to overcome the pressure and strain of nerve-wracking events. To have power and to be alone, is the one tragedy which the power-intent politician understands, and the Communist politician who hides his feelings behind the ramparts of so-called "objectivity"—that the needs of the movement cannot tolerate one's personal feelings—knows this better than all the rest.

CHAPTER V

HOW A BRYAN DEMOCRAT CAPTURED THE COMMUNIST PARTY

THE nature of American Communism is incomprehensible without some insight into the nature of its Russian prototype. However vague and inconclusive the relationship between the two in the beginning, by 1923 the leaders of Russian Communism became increasingly involved in the affairs of the American Communist Party. By that time Moscow became quite definitely the Mecca of all American Communists and the source of all Communist wisdom. It is not difficult to understand the reason for this adulation. Nothing succeeds like success. The Bolsheviks alone of all the Socialist sects, groups and parties anywhere in the world, ever since the days of the Great French Revolution, not only seized the state for a short while but held it for years, not only vanquished the enemies that encircled them on nineteen different fronts but won the respectful fear of the great capitalist powers opposing them, signing a commercial treaty with Great Britain in 1921 and entering the concert of great powers in 1922 through the diplomatic coup of an alliance with Germany at Rapallo while the authors of Versailles were plotting to emasculate Bolshevik Russia at Genoa. The Bolsheviks had come to stay. If even the great powers were forced to reckon with them, surely they were good enough for labor leaders in need of allies.

The earliest American votaries of Bolshevism followed in the footsteps of Lenin, because they believed that the Second International and its affiliated Socialist parties of Europe had betrayed the working class of the world by supporting their respective capitalist governments in the World War; whereas, the handful of Socialists grouped around the Bolshevik nucleus constituted the only force in the world that remained loyal to

Marxist internationalism. They believed, moreover, that the Bolshevik Revolution marked the immediate opening of a new era of proletarian revolutions that would culminate in the overthrow of capitalism throughout the world and that the leaders of the Second International and of the organized labor movement throughout the world, being counter-revolutionists because of their careerist self-interest and their political timidity, were hampering the development of this world-wide liberation movement and were determined to defeat the revolutionary endeavors of the most class-conscious workers. Leaders of the Second International and of the organized labor movement were therefore looked upon as an insidious and pernicious agency of the capitalist exploiters inside the working class—an agency that must be rooted out before the workers of the world could be organized for their foreordained victory over the capitalist social order that enslaves them. Therefore, in 1919 the Third International was founded under Communist auspices in Moscow—to destroy the Second International and the existing trade union movement, organize the workers of the world instead into Communist parties politically and through the subsidiary agency of the Red International of Trade Unions (the Profintern) into revolutionary trade unions, and then proceed to the conquest of the Earth for Socialism through the intervening dictatorship of the proletariat, country by country.

Such in bold outline was the Socialist dream as revived and revivified by the victory of the Bolsheviks in Russia—the dream that drew us dissidents of the Socialist Left toward the Communist International. It was no accident that the founding congress of that new international was dominated by the Russian leaders. Lenin opened it and was its presiding officer. All the important reports were made by the Russians—Trotsky, Commissar of War and Commander-in-Chief of the Red Army; Zinoviev, President of the Petrograd Commune, who was elected the first president of the Comintern after its founding; Bukharin, regarded as the chief theoretician of Communism after Lenin; Chicherin, Commissar of Foreign Affairs; and others. From the very beginning in March, 1919, the delegates of the non-Russian parties found themselves in the embarrassing situation of poor relations, dependent on the Russians both for money and wisdom. We who followed them believed with them that the world revolution was just around the corner and that within a few years, under their superior guidance, we would make the whole world Red, provided we did what we were told by them in our own country. We actually believed that they understood the play of social forces in our country better than we, although most of them had never set foot in it. Indeed, through wishful thinking and because of our deference to their wisdom—and subconsciously, perhaps, because we curried the favor and support of these supermen of revolution—we entered into a kind of conspiracy of deception and self-deception, by reporting to them on the political situation in our country in terms most pleasing to the Russian leaders and most in consonance with their theories and expectations of imminent world revolution. Psychologically, thus, the Third International was doomed to defeat from the start, because it began its career as an organization of revolutionists subservient to their political patrons, and hence rapidly developed into an international of toadies and careerists.

This tendency, inherent in the Comintern because of the monstrous political predominance of the Russians in the international organization, had moreover very deep roots in the very character of the Russian Bolshevik Party, which was fashioned by Lenin, himself temperamentally an absolutist, in the course of its hard and dangerous struggle against Tsarist absolutism. From its inception in 1903 until it seized power in 1917, the Bolshevik organization was, with the exception of a negligible interval of several weeks during the early part of the Kerensky honeymoon in the Spring of 1917, a closely-knit conspirative organization ruled from above. Its vaunted principle of democratic centralism became upon application under conditions of conspiracy no more than slightly democratic and no less than overwhelmingly sheer centralism. The Bolshevik Old Guard, schooled to obey the orders of the Bolshevik Central Committee in all its struggles, whether against the Tsarist government, the Russian capitalists or their comrades of the Menshevik faction, were psychologically incapable of undoing this conditioning over a period of years, had they sincerely desired to do so after coming into supreme power. But being after all human, could they be expected to reverse the proportions of democracy and centralism in their vaunted doctrine at the very moment when they came to constitute the personification of that centralism? The fleshpots of power are far too succulent for such self-abnegation, especially when the easiest thing to do is to justify the retention of that centralism in the hands of the revolutionary veterans by the hue and cry of imminent danger to the triumphant revolution on all sides and even inside the fledgling proletarian state. Beginning in coalition with the Left Social-Revolutionaries in 1917, the Bolsheviks became the one and only party in power, the state party, in July, 1918, increasingly identical with the state, the discipline of its ranks increasingly centralized under the sway of its central committee, the latter increasingly restricted by the political bureau, where increasingly the voice of its leading member, Lenin, became the voice of God.

The Russians, who grew up in the struggle against Tsarist absolutism, should have known even better than many of us who hailed from the Western hemisphere, that subservience is an inseparable complement of absolutism and that you can sooner make a revolutionist out of a Tory than out of a toady. Yet, with all the blindness typical of all men in power, the omniscient Lenin and the brilliant Trotsky, not to mention such lesser luminaries as Zinoviev, Bukharin, Radek, Kamenev, Stalin and the rest of them, proceeded to perpetrate the classic error of all rulers by canonizing this fundamental error into a principle. The Comintern became organizationally a carbon copy of the Russian Bolshevik party, and every national Communist party became a carbon copy of the carbon copy. The very cornerstone of the Comintern program, composed by Lenin and concurred in by all his satellites from Trotsky down, proclaimed that every Communist party must perforce be organized on a military basis and subject to military discipline; that, having thus—the *only* way possible, mind you!—overthrown the capitalist government, the Communist party must set up a dictatorship of the proletariat—in which the only party permitted to function would be the Communist party, to whose will the entire country was to be subjected. True, there were important asides on how to mobilize the support of non-proletarian groups, such as, the peasants or farmers, for example, but they were merely of a maneuvering nature, not part of the Communist essence ideologically. The Russian leaders were so certain that they were absolutely right in propagating this sort of pseudo-revolutionary absolutism that they would brook no deviation from this organizational principle among the affiliates of the Comintern, insisting on the "Bolshevization" of all the non-Russian Communist parties. The bed of Procrustes on which all the Communist parties were laid were the famous Twenty-one Points of the Comintern program. It was a case of take it or leave it.

We American Communists took it—hook, line and sinker. We have, therefore, no one to blame but ourselves, nothing but our own moon-calf foolishness in the field of politics, if we got it in the neck as a group and were doomed to political ineffectualness in our own country. What is unpardonable, however, is to canonize your foolishness into a policy and to pursue it wherever it may lead, as long as you stay pretty close to the top, even if the course of events enjoins practices in direct contradiction to the ideals and principles with which you had originally set out. Yet, given the anti-democratic organizational principles of Bolshevism, this course of development was inevitable from the start, although I did not see it then and see it all too clearly only now. I confess that, although I was one of the few who along with John Reed fought against the domination of the peanut politicians from the Russian Federation, when I returned from prison in 1922 and was faced with the accomplished fact of the far more dangerous domination by the Russian Communist Party of Moscow, far from complaining about it, I concurred with the rest of my American comrades. Only the Russian Party was given the unprecedented right—a right no other member party of the Comintern enjoyed—to review Comintern decisions and alter them at will. This organizational poison was implanted in the Comintern by its originators and founding fathers, Lenin and Trotsky. Moreover, while the Russian Party, not only instructed its delegates but even such of its members as were officers of the Comintern, no other Communist Party was accorded the privilege of instructing its emissaries to Moscow, who found out only from the Russian bosses what was what. The internationalism of the Comintern was thus never more than a reflection of Russian desires and Russian policy. As for the national policy of each Communist party, that was merely a reflection in the distorting mirror of the Comintern of whatever happened to be at the moment the policy of the Russian Communist Party.

This dependence on the Russian Communist Party—and more specifically, on the ruling clique and the dominating person within it from time to time—became the condition *sine qua non* for every non-Russian member of the Comintern. Matters concerning the German, French, English, American or any other Communist party were first thrashed out inside the Russian Communist Party by its Political Bureau, and the decisions reached by a half a dozen Russian leaders were handed down to the Communist party in question through the channels of the Comintern. Hence, the policy of every Communist Party became dependent in large measure on the exigencies of the foreign policy of the Russian Soviet Republic, which was the prime concern of the Russian Political Bureau surely since Brest-Litovsk and more definitely and increasingly so since Rapallo, until today it is exclusively so. Official Communism has thus rapidly crystallized into no more than merely the international instrumentality of the Russian Soviet government. That was not apparent when Communism was still in the state of turbulent solution that was being shaken constantly by political winds; now, however, with its stabilization and crystallization under Stalin's personal dictatorship, it is clear that this characteristic of Communism was inherent from the start. This essential characteristic of Communism—I mean, of course, Leninist Communism in practice, not in theory—must be clearly borne in mind, if you are to understand what took place in the American Communist Party from the moment of its emergence as an open political party out of the fusion of Number One and Number Two early in 1923.

We all accepted, without any reservations, the right of the Russian Bolshevik leaders to boss our party. At the same time, we the leaders of the American Communist Party fought each other. Since basic policies were decided upon not by us but by our bosses in Moscow, ours was a struggle for power rather than for principles. In that respect, we were of course no different from Tammany Hall shysters or from any other politicians, for we all became the victims of that strongest of all the social passions, the political passion. Yet the fashion among us Communist politicians—and we believed it to be far more than merely a fashion of thought, we believed it to be an incontrovertible truth—was to proceed on the premise, more readily assumed than practiced, that in the Communist movement the individual factor was of negligible, if any, importance. The individual, we contended when arguing the matter with our aloof sympathizers of the Liberal Left, merely reflected social conditions. In the face of daily experiences with individual Communist leaders of opposing factions who ruthlessly connived to wrest power from us or to keep us from wresting power from them, we insisted to our Liberal friends that pure objectivity was the determining factor in all Communist politics. Therein, indeed, was the crux of the difference between lowly bourgeois politics and the politics of the proletariat's revolutionary priesthood—meaning ourselves, of course. We did not lie with malice aforethought; we lied subconsciously, to ourselves as well as to others; nevertheless, we lied. The truth is, that in the struggle for power inside the Communist Party, the personal ambitions of individuals, their selfish interests, their animal instincts of self-preservation, always come to the forefront and all but completely overshadow the political issues and the principles, which indeed serve mostly as the rationalization for the struggle. In that the Communist Party must be very much like any other political party, bourgeois or proletarian. What makes it worse than any bourgeois party, however, in that respect, is the injection of pseudo-revolutionary amorality; the effect of that is to cast into limbo the last vestiges of human decency as mere "bourgeois prejudices." It is this which flavors Communist politics with horrible bitterness, for the strife among the "comrades" proceeds with all rules suspended and any weapon at all in use, all the way from deceit, chicanery, doubledealing, patronage and bribery, to character assassination and outright assassination, if possible. Anything goes. It is this which makes every Party debate between the leaders a small-scale but highly intense civil war. Indeed, the ethics of civil war against the bourgeoisie and its White Guard defenders are merely applied to the strife among the leaders inside the Party.

When the Communist Party became legal, it was a foregone conclusion that its leader would be Ruthenberg. And he did become its leader. But now the party was different from what it had been in 1919. The most important change was in its trade-union policy. In 1919 we were opposed to the American Federation of Labor and were strongly in sympathy with the Industrial Workers of the World, attacking, however, the anti-political stand of the I. W. W. We were for revolutionary unionism that openly espoused the overthrow of capitalism. The ordinary strikes for more wages and better conditions interested us only in so far as we coud develop them into mass movements for the overthrow of the hated bourgeoisie. Whenever a strike broke out, Communists came upon the scene with leaflets urging the workers to overthrow the government and set up Soviets. But when the revolution in America did not come as quickly as we had expected, and our appeal to the trade unionists to form soviets fell upon deaf ears, we changed our attitude and began to use other tactics and appeals. With these altered means, we soon gained some trade union following; notably, among the foreign-born workers, in such unions as the needle trades, the food workers, some independent unions of metal workers, laborers, and others. The first industrial organizer of the Communist Party who made some headway among these union forces was Joseph Zack. He sought to give the Party a trade union following, by building up a new and independent trade union movement. He achieved some success in this direction by bringing the independent unions of New York and vicinity together into a central organization which was called the United Labor Council. Then, for reasons that had nothing to do with our Communist problems in America, Lenin put an end to this dual union policy when he issued his famous pamphlet, "Left Wing Communism," in which he called upon all Communists to go into the existing unions and there to bore from within for the purpose of capturing them. The publication of Lenin's pamphlet turned the trade union policy of our Party upside down.

In scouting around for some one to organize the boring-from-within activities of the Communists in the trade unions, Foster was discovered. That was in 1921. William Z. Foster was unattached at the time. He had been unsuccessful in leading the steel strike and had lost considerable standing in the A. F. of L. unions. Besides suffering defeat in the steel strike, Foster and his associates also lost their influence among the packing-house workers, who had been organized by Foster during the war through the intervention of the A. F. of L. and the Federal Mediation Commission, because the government then favored trade union organization as a war policy. Foster's Syndicalist League of North America, which was replaced by the International Trade Union Educational League in 1915. The principles upon which they were founded were repudiated by Foster on the witness stand during the steel strike in 1919, even though he had been instrumental in organizing both organizations and was their outstanding leader. After the debacle of the steel strike in November, 1920, Foster organized anew the Trade Union Educational League, with headquarters in Chicago. But this organization had no following in the trade unions, no funds with which to operate, and was destined to die soon, a failure.

Subsequently, the National Committee to the First National Conference of the Trade Union Educational League in Chicago, August 26 and 27, 1922, reported, "For over a year this body lingered along more dead than alive." It was a peculiar organization; it did not charge dues or per capita tax. The first real money it saw came when the representative of the Profintern, or Red Trade Union International, acting in collaboration with the underground Communist Party, contacted Foster, persuaded him to attend the First Congress of the Profintern and gave him the money needed to finance the trip of the Trade Union Educational League delegation to that Congress, to be held in Moscow. This emissary for the Party and the Profintern, was Carl E. Johnson, a Lettish comrade from Roxbury, Massachusetts, and at one time a member of the Lettish Communist Club of Boston, who became a member of the Executive Bureau of the Profintern, under the name of Scott. The very same Scott, entrusted with the work of gathering an American trade union delegation to attend the First Congress of the Profintern, upon the specific instructions of the Communist Party, induced William D. Haywood to head an I. W. W. delegation to Moscow and at the same time skip bail, a decision which had tragic and disastrous consequences for Haywood.

The delegation of the Trade Union Educational League that went to Moscow with Foster in 1921 included Earl Browder and Ella Reeves Bloor. No one in that delegation had official connections or standing with American trade unions. They represented what for all practical purposes was just a paper organization centered around Foster. The Communists paid all their expenses for the trip. In Moscow, Foster joined the Communist Party and together with the Russian leaders worked out the plans for the capture of the American Federation of Labor. President Sidney Hillman of the Amalgamated Clothing Workers was in Moscow at this time. Conferences were arranged between Foster, Hillman and the Russian leaders, at which it was urged that Hillman back Foster's activities in building up a progressive trade union movement in the United States, for the purpose of dislodging Gompers and taking control of the A. F. of L. unions. Foster's Trade Union Educational League was accepted by the Russians as the organization through which the Communists should bore within the American unions. Foster returned to the United States, supplied with funds by Moscow and with the instructions to work under the direction of the American Communist Party's Central Committee. Part of the plan included a strict order that under no circumstances should Foster's official membership in the Communist movement be disclosed and that great care should be taken in so conducting the campaign that Foster should be considered merely as a progressive trade unionist who was not connected with the Party and was entirely free from its domination.

Here let me point out a Moscow paradox. The Bolshevik leaders at the first Congress of the Red International of Labor Unions repudiated the policy of dual unionism to the consternation of the Syndicalists and the I. W. W. delegation from America. They called upon the Communists and all other revolutionary elements to organize cells within the existing trade unions, to bore from within. They completely rejected the idea of building new independent revolutionary unions. But in the international field the Bolshevik leaders adopted a policy that was directly the opposite. They built on the basis of the Russian trade unions an international trade union organization known as the Profintern, a Russian abbreviation for the Red Trade Union International. This international organization was a dual organization to the International Federation of Trade Unions at Amsterdam. The Communists outside of Russia were given the impossible task of, on the one hand, recognizing the unions that adhered to the Amsterdam International, and, on the other hand, fighting to destroy the international organization of these same unions.

Foster returned to the United States in the Autumn of 1921. Backed up by Russian funds and with the full support of the Communist Party, he became active in the campaign to organize the Trade Union Educational League. He became Secretary-Treasurer of the League and the Editor of its journal, *The Labor Herald*. Earl Browder was Foster's man Friday with the title, Managing Editor of *The Labor Herald*. Though Foster denied he was a Communist, he and Browder met continually with the Executive Council of the then underground Communist Party of the United States, the good old Number One. Not a move was made by Foster without the approval of the Communist Party. The only thing the Communist Party did not check Foster on were his expenditures of the special fund given him by Moscow to build the Trade Union Educational League.

Foster steadfastly maintained that he was not a member of the Communist Party, hoping to camouflage the Trade Union Educational League as a non-Communist organization. As late as June, 1923, the Party kept up the fiction that Foster, who was then already a member of the Central Executive Committee of the Party as well as of its most powerful ruling committee, the Political Committee, was not a Communist, not a member of the Communist Party. In the June, 1923, issue of *The Labor Herald,* Ruthenberg wrote:

> These methods and the fact that Foster was not a member of the Communist Party, while I admittedly was a member of the Central Executive Committee of the Party, explains the difference in the results of the second trial as compared to the first.

About a decade and a half later, while writing his autobiography, Foster apparently forgot the period when he masqueraded as a non-Communist, for in his book, "From Bryan to Stalin," on page 163, he states:

> So, when I returned to the United States, in the middle of 1921, I joined the Communist Party and took my proper place in the ranks of the revolutionary Communist International.

Even this statement does not give the actual fact that Foster joined the Communist movement and threw himself under its discipline during his first sojourn in Moscow, in 1921.

The first National Conference of the Trade Union Educational League, held in August, 1922, in Chicago, proved how thoroughly Communist it was. The Editorial Committee consisted of Knudsen, Carney, Wortis, Buck and Foster—all Communists. The report on the Building Trades was by Jack Johnstone, a Communist. The report on the Metal Trades by Knudsen, a Communist. The report on the Printing Trades by H. M. Wicks, a Communist. The report on the Needle Trades by Rose Wortis, a Communist. The report on the Boot and Shoe Industry, by Harry Canter, a Communist. William F. Dunne, Communist, was chosen to lead the Metal Mining campaign. O. H. Wangerin, Secretary of the Railroad Amalgamation Campaign, was a Communist. Representing the Profintern—that is, the Profintern's Commissar at the conference—was Carl E. Johnson, alias Scott.

The program of the Trade Union Educational League combined nearly everything that the radicals and the progressives had been advocating for years. Its main features included the transformation of the craft unions into industrial unions by amalgamating all the craft unions of a single industry into one industrial union; a militant strike policy in place of the policy of class collaboration (the traditional policy of the American Federation of Labor of peaceful negotiations between unions and employers to some working compromise in their mutual interest); and independent working class political action through the unions, although at its inception the Trade Union Educational League did not come out openly for a labor party, at the same time opposing Sam Gompers' policy of supporting the "friends of labor" on the Republican and Democratic tickets. In addition, however, there were other points in the program which had nothing to do with the immediate task of reforming the American trade unions, as, for example, recognition of Soviet Russia, affiliation with the Profintern, wholehearted support of the Russian Bolshevik revolution, and abolition of the capitalist system.

How Russian interests determined all questions that came up before the Trade Union Educational League was demonstrated to me at the convention of the Amalgamated Clothing Workers held in Chicago in May, 1922. I have already mentioned the conferences of Hillman in Moscow, as a result of which it was understood that Hillman would support Foster's activities in the American trade unions. At the same time the Russians agreed to Hillman's proposal to organize the Russian-American Industrial Corporation for the building up of the clothing industry in Russia. The Communist Party of the United States could not be outdone in its praises of Sidney Hillman, the President of the Amalgamated. Olgin, the editor of our paper, *Freiheit,* delivered one of the most flowery eulogies of Hillman possible, at the convention which he had been invited to address. At this convention there was a very strong bloc of Progressive and Left Wing delegates. The underground Communist Party sent two representatives to the convention whose duty it was to advise the Communist Left Wing bloc as to policy. William Z. Foster and Robert Minor were these representatives. Their work consisted chiefly in preventing any opposition from openly breaking out against the Hillman machine. The first important issue came over the status of a Left Wing leader, Albert Goldman, who was also a member of the Party, whose effectiveness the Chicago administration of the Amalgamated undermined by accusing him of being a spy and expelling him from the organization. Hillman supported the Chicago machine against the Chicago Left Wing, which insisted upon justice for Goldman by a repudiation of the frame-up against him. Foster and Minor prevented the Left Wing from making a fight on this issue.

The other issue was even more important. It had to do with a trade union policy. Hillman's main proposal for the Chicago convention was that it approve his policy of "standards of production." Hillman proposed that the union, in close coöperation with the bosses, work out standards of production which should guide the workers in the shops. These standards, wherever they were adopted and applied, its opponents charged, instituted vicious speed-up schedules for the workers. They created impossible conditions in the trade and paved the way for the corruption of the trade-union officials by the bosses, whenever they met to work out standards. Large numbers of workers opposed these standards of production most bitterly. The Progressives and Left Wingers voiced this opposition of the rank and file. At the caucuses of the Left Wing the delegates were determined not to yield on this question. Minor and Foster argued with them. Bob Minor in particular tried to rationalize, to prove that their fears were unfounded, that it was really a progressive measure. When the workers ridiculed his arguments and informed him that his ignorance of the trade was monumental, he switched to other persuasive methods, highly political in their content, arguing that Hillman was rendering a great service to Soviet Russia and the workers' cause by championing the Soviet Union, and besides, that one who had pledged himself in Moscow to further the cause of the Left Wing could be trusted. The Communist Party members were finally whipped into line to support Hillman's proposal under compulsion of Party discipline. Foster in his one speech to the caucus supported Minor, but after that he stayed in the background and let Bob Minor do all the cajoling. I was present at the convention, though not in an official capacity. I had just come out of prison pending an appeal of my case and was sent by the Party to get a donation from the convention for the National Defense Committee. I became alarmed at the anger of the Left Wingers. I called Foster aside, warned him that a grave mistake was being made, that Minor should be called into conference and the whole position on this question changed. He refused to accede to this request. I spoke to Minor in the same vein, but he would not entertain the idea for one moment. With the aid of the Party members in the Left Wing caucus, Hillman's proposal for standards of production was endorsed. Minor jumped up in jubilation over the victory. The workers sat silent when the vote was in. They left in the early hours of the morning, convinced that they had acted wrongly, their dejected faces clearly showing how badly they felt.

Right after the caucus meeting Bob Minor took me aside and tried to convince me what a wonderful man and leader Hillman was. Then he spoke to me about Moscow, about Hillman's agreement to support the building up of a Left Wing movement. "We must be objective," he said, "The interests of Russia must always be our first consideration." I did not realize then, when Bob Minor stated it, that that phrase, "The interests of Russia must always be our first consideration," was to determine all Communistic activities.

The organization of the new Trade Union Educational League proceeded apace. First, all the plans and strategy were worked out by the Central Committee of the Communist Party. Then all the district organizations of the Party throughout the country were informed of these decisions and plans. The district committees proceeded to inform the membership of the decisions. After that, in the industries and union affected by the decisions, fraction meetings were called. The fractions consisted of the Party members employed in the industries or belonging to the unions involved. The fractions were informed about the decisions and minutely instructed how to carry them out. If the decisions were considered of great importance, involving a union in which the Party was strong, then Foster or some other leading representative of the Central Committee reported on the decision to the fraction meeting. Only after the Party membership was thoroughly whipped into line and drilled on how to put the decisions across, was the matter brought up in the section of the Trade Union Educational League covered by the decisions. There the Party membership voted as a bloc and a Party decision was always railroaded through. In fact, it did not take the non-party members of the Trade Union Educational League long to discover that it was useless to take a position on any question that had already been acted upon by the Party. They generally waited to see how the Party caucus voted and either refrained from voting or voted accordingly.

The first National Committee of the League was an appointed body, approved by the Central Committee of the Communist Party. A majority of its members were Communists. Its secretary-treasurer, Foster, was a Party member and a member of the Communist Party Central Executive Committee; the editor of its paper was Earl Browder, a Communist Party member; its two national organizers were Joseph Manley, Foster's son-in-law, and Jack Johnstone, both Party members. When sections of the Trade Union Educational League were formed, such as the Needle Trades Section, the Miners Section, the Metal Trades Sections, the main officer of the section, the secretary, was always a Party member, as was the majority of the Executive Committee. The Communist Party was taking no chances. But notwithstanding all its Machiavellian plotting to pass for non-Communist, the Trade Union Educational League succeeded in organizing only the Communist Party members and their closest sympathizers. It, therefore, became necessary during early stages of the T. U. E. L.'s activities to organize progressive trade union committees to carry on fights within the unions, as for example: in the miners union—The Progressive Miners Committee; in the railroad industry—The Railroad Workers Amalgamation Committee.

These progressive committees were organized in the following way: First the plan for their organization was submitted to the Central Committee of the Communist Party for approval. Second, conferences were arranged between Communist leaders and the dissatisfied elements in the unions for the formation of a leading committee to function as an executive of the Progressive movement. For window dressing, a leading non-Communist Progressive was generally decided upon for president and a Communist put in as secretary, because the secretary carried on the correspondence, had charge of the records and finances, thereby controlling the organization. In the Executive Committee, the Communists were usually a majority by virtue of the fact that they either took a majority outright by agreement, or, if that was impossible, they achieved their purpose by including a number of so called non-Party members who were really Communists disguising themselves as non-Party workers. But the most important source of Communist control and influence was the money the Party supplied for carrying on the work. As for the rank and file control of the progressive movement, it was manipulated, as follows: first the Communist fraction acted as a caucus in the T. U. E. L., where it lined up the closest sympathizers; then, the T. U. E. L. group acted as a bloc in the Progressive movement. The Communist Party left nothing to chance. It worked like a well-oiled machine from the Central Executive Committee down to the most remote Party member.

When the Trade Union Educational League was first organized, Foster had a rather naïve conception of the American Federation of Labor. I spoke to him on many occasions concerning the unions and listened to him at many party meetings during the early days of the Trade Union Educational League in 1922-23. Foster actually believed that if the Communist Party members in the trade unions became active they could in a short time have themselves elected as presidents, secretaries, and executive board members of the thousands of local trade unions throughout the country. Then through the control of the local unions they could easily gather sufficient strength to capture the international unions and finally the A. F. of L. itself. He greatly underestimated the strength of the trade union hierarchy, the strength of its machine control, and its influence over the mass of the workers. Another factor that Foster almost completely left out of his ambitious scheme to become the President of the

A. F. of L., was the government's friendly relations with the American Federation of Labor, and the strength of the Republican and Democratic Parties in the trade unions. Later on in the intense internal struggle in the A. F. of L. which followed the organization of the Trade Union Educational League, Foster had an opportunity to learn that his road to supremacy over the A. F. of L. was not as easy as he visualized, that in the A. F. of L. the Communists faced a powerful adversary.

At this time the Communist International reversed itself on another of its policies and raised the slogan of the "United Front." Moscow called upon the Communists to unite with the Socialists and trade unionists of their respective countries against the encroachments of capitalism, for better conditions, and in support of Soviet Russia. The Bolsheviks hoped that by the United Front maneuver they could gain the leadership over the millions of Socialists and organized workers who had steadfastly refused to follow Communist leadership. In the United States we tried to put the United Front slogan concretely into action by preparing a Labor Party thesis, which we sent to Moscow for approval. When we were assured that the Communist International would have no objections, we launched a campaign to organize a labor party that would include the Communists. Foster's Trade Union Educational League, which at first was very cautious on the question of the labor party, now vigorously espoused its cause. Foster, very enthusiastic over the prospects of a labor party, he expressed high hopes at every meeting of the Political Committee that the organization of a labor party would help him capture the A. F. of L., because Gompers, being opposed to a labor party, would eventually be ousted by the labor party forces. Browder, who was Foster's orderly, made hurried trips from Chicago to New York to report to the Political Committee how Foster was working hand and glove with Fitzpatrick, President of the Chicago Federation of Labor, and Nockles, its Secretary, for the establishment of a labor party. He also reported that hundreds of trade unions were openly declaring themselves in favor of a labor party. Foster would report at length on his conferences with Fitzpatrick and Nockles, giving the impression that both A. F. of L. officials were mere putty in his hands.

The Party threw all its resources into the campaign to organize a labor party. This endeavor culminated in the July Third Convention held in the City of Chicago in the year 1923. Money received from the Comintern helped organize this convention. Important delegates were financed directly by our Party. Trade unionists, Farmer-Labor Party leaders of the Northwest, important liberals, coöperative leaders were interviewed by our agents and every effort made to interest them in the convention and to have them attend. No money was spared. The Party was geared for full speed in this convention. Instructions were sent out to mobilize and send several thousand delegates to Chicago. Every organization in which the Party had some influence, regardless of how small it was or unimportant, was utilized in the sending of delegates, many unborn represented organizations that existed only on paper. Many came representing organizations that never even considered the question of a labor party, let alone electing delegates to this convention. Communists, men and women, formed groups, and hiked to Chicago from all parts of the country, and when they arrived, presented "credentials" and became duly accredited delegates. All the expenses for the convention, every penny of it, were paid for by the Party. The Communists who appeared representing "innocent" organizations denied that they were Communists, but they were all duly registered for a Communist Caucus of the Convention, which caucus included fully ninety per cent of the delegates present.

The steering committee for the Communist Caucus consisted of Ruthenberg, Pepper and Foster. Difficulty soon arose at the convention over the question of the immediate organization of a labor party. President Fitzpatrick and Secretary Nockles of the Chicago Federation of Labor were for waiting. They wanted to see what the Farmer-Labor Party of Minnesota would do, what the Railroad Brotherhoods and the unions represented by the Conference for Progressive Labor Action would do in the immediate future, before taking the step. In this they were supported by some of the genuine state labor-party forces present. However, the Steering Committee wanted to organize a labor party right away. It had the delegates present and they would do whatever the Steering Committee ordered them to do. They came for no other purpose. The Steering Committee also knew that if a labor party emerged from Chicago the Communists would control it. When the Communist steamroller flattened out Fitzpatrick and Nockles, they and their few supporters bolted the convention. Amid fanfare and wild enthusiasm the motion to organize a labor party was carried and the Federated Farmer-Labor Party came into existence. It was just another new premature Communist baby. The Executive Committee elected was dominated by the Communists, its Secretary being Joseph Manley, Foster's son-in-law, who had the unpleasant job of being the new party's wet nurse.

But the break with Fitzpatrick was very costly to Foster. Foster had clung to Fitzpatrick like a leech. He was with Fitzpatrick in the campaign to organize the steel workers, and also in the packing house campaign. Fitzpatrick gave Foster the platform of the Chicago Federation of Labor and on more than one occasion came to the support of Foster and the Trade Union Educational League. Fitzpatrick was Foster's most important ally in the A. F. of L. He played an important part in Foster's plans for the capture of the A. F. of L. Foster had on more than one occasion remarked that Fitzpatrick would make an ideal president for the American Federation of Labor. Moreover, the astute Sam Gompers followed up the break of Foster and Fitzpatrick by unloading the full power of the American Federation of Labor against Foster, the Trade Union Educational League, and the Communists. The few positions which Foster had gained in the trade unions were soon lost. The prospects of capturing the A. F. of L. no longer looked bright and easy. Besides, Fitzpatrick himself followed up this break with an attack upon Foster and the Communists. When he spoke before the Party's Political Committee on the break with Fitzpatrick, Foster almost wept. The break made Foster realize that his efforts to capture the A. F. of L. were at an end. The most important wedge he had in the A. F of L., the Chicago Federation of Labor, with its tremendous membership and powerful unions, was now lost. He looked upon the situation as a tragedy, and, though he shared the responsibility for it, he secretly held Ruthenberg and Pepper solely responsible for this blow.

He had to make up with his followers in the T. U. E. L. for his loss of face in the trade unions. The only way to do it was to blame Ruthenberg and Pepper for the July Third debacle, and to organize to depose them from leadership. For his lost ambition to capture the A. F. of L., he developed a new ambition to capture the Communist Party and become America's number one Communist leader. How crassly opportunistic Foster's new position was is borne out by his actions on the Steering Committee in support of the tactics that forced the Fitzpatrick break; in his support of the actions at the meetings of the Political Committee of the Workers Party, and his writings on the matter. Writing of the July Third Convention in the August, 1923, issue of the *Labor Herald,* Foster declared

> The advent of the Federated Farmer-Labor Party marks an epoch in American Labor history.

and further on,

> The Federated Farmer-Labor Party is a militant organization. . . . The Federated Farmer-Labor Party will break the chains with which the Gompers bureaucracy keeps the workers of this country bound to the political chariots of their industrial masters.

In this article there is no criticism of Fitzpatrick. Foster still had hopes then that he could maintain the Fitzpatrick alliance. At every meeting he raised the Fitzpatrick question, and it was not until the end of December, almost six months after the break, that Foster finally agreed to answer Fitzpatrick's attack. He submitted his reply to Fitzpatrick to the Central Executive Committee of the Workers Party, which went carefully over every sentence and, even after the decision was made, Foster was not so sure about its advisability. The result of the decision was Foster's Open Letter to John Fitzpatrick, which was printed in the January, 1924, *Labor Herald,* and in which, admitting the Foster-Fitzpatrick combination against Gompers, he asserts that the loss of the steel strike of 1919 killed the plan to revolutionize the A. F. of L. Included is an analysis of the personal weakness of Fitzpatrick's leadership, his swing to the Right, his capitulation to Gompers, and the conclusion that in betraying the labor party movement he had thrown the labor movement back twenty years. How completely the line connecting Foster to Fitzpatrick was severed is made clear in the concluding tirade of the letter which states,

> Your retreat from your former progressive position has not only injured the labor movement as a whole, but it has completely wrecked your individual prestige and made you impossible as a progressive leader. Your weakness at the July 3-5 convention, coupled with your re-adoption of the Gompers' nonpartisan method, had killed you as the national champion of the labor party idea. . . You are due before long for a rude awakening on this matter. I wonder how long the reactionaries will let you retain even your formal leadership of the Federation now that you have lost the real leadership of it?

F.

Foster organized carefully and secretly to capture the Party. He raised no political or principled differences with the Central Committee of the Party. What he did was to turn the Trade Union Educational League into a conspirative, factional organization for the capture of the Party leadership. Instead of doing trade union work, the organizers of the T. U. E. L. toured the country as the secret emissaries of Foster and everywhere gathered together Party members for their plan. But Foster could not capture the Party with only the T. U. E. L. He, therefore, secretly made a number of important deals, one with Ludwig Lore and Juliet Poyntz, who jointly had a considerable following in New York City. Ludwig Lore was the editor of the oldest Socialist daily paper in the United States, the *New Yorker Volkszeitung,* through which paper he wielded great influence and dominated the German-speaking members of the Party. Juliet Stuart Poyntz was an American college-bred woman, a forceful speaker, very ambitious, and one who aspired to national leadership. She was popular among the rank-and-file members and could be counted upon to muster a considerable number of votes in New York. The alliance with Bittleman and Olgin of the Jewish Federation gave Foster additional strength in New York and the majority of the Jewish Federation membership throughout the country. Most important, however, was his alliance with the powerful and clannish Finnish Federation, which had a large membership, was rich in coöperatives, printing plants, three daily newspapers, club houses, and other enterprises. The Finnish Federation could be depended upon for considerable financial support in the campaign to capture the Party, and what was more important, the solid vote of its membership, because the Finnish members were never active in the general work of the Party and voted the way the leaders of the Federation told them to. In addition, Foster rallied to his banner some important Party leaders. Foremost was Jim Cannon, who joined forces with Foster. With Ruthenberg removed from the leadership of the Party, Cannon was probably of the belief that he could assume the Party's political leadership, because of Foster's lack of experience in Party politics. Another figure was William F. Dunne, the "wild bull from Montana," as he was known, who was promised the editorship of the *Daily Worker,* Dunne having been editor of the famous labor paper, the *Butte Daily Bulletin.*

Foster conducted the campaign to capture the Party so secretively that Ruthenberg refused to believe the reports he received that Foster was conspiring to oust him. It was only on the very eve of the Party's national convention, with the election of delegates already proceeding in the districts, that he allowed Lovestone, Ballam, and Pepper to organize against Foster's moves. But he was not convinced, for he came to the New York district convention, from which the largest number of delegates to the national convention was to be elected, and delivered a report about the unanimity of the Central Executive Committee on all the important issues before the Party, and squelched all rumors that there was a schism between him and Foster. But no sooner was his speech delivered than it was clear that the Foster caucus and alliances were working smoothly. I was present as a delegate to the New York district convention and led the fight against the Foster forces. I had very little time to organize, because only a few days before the convention Lifshitz, "the little corporal," as he was called, organizer of the New York district, reported to me that there was trouble ahead. Poyntz, Lore, and Jack Jampolsky, the organizer of the New York district T. U. E. L., conducted the fight for Foster. A bitter fight over the election of delegates ensued. When it was over, I was elected as a delegate with a very large vote, but I did not take a majority of the delegates with me to the national convention. Foster had a little more than half of them. But we did manage to retain our majority on the New York district committee.

Ruthenberg went back to Chicago, not at all worried over the result; but once in Chicago, he became alarmed when he received the reports on elections all over the country. He gave Lovestone and Pepper a free hand to see what they could do to remedy the situation. It was clear that Foster had a majority of the delegates, and since the National Convention was the supreme authority of the Party, he could do with the Party whatever he desired. The only way to destroy Foster's majority was to cause a split in Foster's delegation. This Pepper and Lovestone attempted to do by trying to break Lore away from Foster. I arrived in Chicago with Lore. At the station were Lovestone and Pepper. They immediately accosted Lore and invited him into a conference. But Lore hated Pepper. Besides, he was not a man who could be made to change his position easily. The conference with Lore proved futile. At the convention the routine matters prepared by the Central Executive Committee were adopted. The Foster group maintained its majority throughout the sessions, and when the elections of a new Central Executive Committee took place the Foster forces captured it.

At the first meeting of the newly elected Central Executive Committee Foster was a little afraid fully to exert the power of his majority. He hesitated about removing Ruthenberg as the General Secretary of the Party, which he desired, since he feared that such a move would not be welcomed by the membership, and what is more important, by the real boss of the Party, the Communist International. So, Foster had himself designated as the Chairman of the Party and Ruthenberg was retained as General Secretary, but with his wings clipped, because he was subject to the decisions of sub-committees on which the Foster group made sure to have a safe majority. But the Foster majority did request the Communist International to remove Pepper from work in the United States.

This convention brought into life the smouldering fires of factional controversy which were to keep the Communist movement in a state of civil war up to the year 1929. I remember after the convention was over, and the sessions of the newly-elected Central Executive Committee had been concluded, that a small group of the minority met in a restaurant, where over our cups of coffee we discussed the recent events and the future. Present were Lovestone, Ruthenberg, Ballam, and Pepper. Pepper declared,

> Comrades, we must have patience in politics. To gain a majority is one thing, to maintain it is another. We must take a lesson from Foster and organize our own forces, but secretly and carefully.

That night was born our caucus through which we waged the factional fight, not only in America, but in Moscow as well. From that night on, Moscow became involved in practically every important step of the American Communist movement. In fact, so scandalous did the situation become that the following joke became popular among Party members:

> Why is the Communist Party of the United States like the Brooklyn Bridge?
>
> Because it is suspended on cables.

Every week cables to Moscow were hot with messages sent to the Bolshevik Holy Land, or "Mecca," as we called it, protesting or setting forth the position of our group. The Foster group did likewise, and in addition supplemented them by official cables from the Party. Some were sent in code and many were not, even though they carried some of the Party's most confidential matters. These cables were supplemented by letters and long reports. We in return would receive cables officially from Moscow addressed to the Party and unofficially from our caucus representatives in Moscow. Many of these cables were often five, six, and more pages in length. Thousands of dollars were spent in this manner.

No special representative of the Communist International was present at the 1923 convention, because from all indications the Party was united, no serious differences of opinion prevailed among its leaders. Pepper had become a regular member of the American Party. All the Communist International did was to send a letter to the Party, which declared:

> The excellent work that has been done by the Communists in the Left Wing of the labor movement in the United States demonstrates that if all the comrades were members of the trade unions the work would increase manifold. . . The propaganda that the Workers Party has conducted during the past year has been most effective. . . The vast sentiment for Communism that the Workers Party has aroused must be organized. The Central Executive Committee acted right in inaugurating a campaign for membership. . . . The Workers Party has applied Communist tactics correctly. . . . The organization of the Federated Farmer-Labor Party was an achievement of primary importance.

Foster, who had given up as hopeless his ambition to become the head of the American Federation of Labor, had succeeded in his endeavor to become the Communist leader of America. He had traveled a long road from the time he was a Bryan Democrat.

CHAPTER VI

A CASE OF POLITICAL INFANTICIDE

Two cardinal rules of Communist politics are: one, in every important fight for power in the Party, raise only one important political issue or one set of issues as an excuse for the struggle; two, draw up a documentary record of your opponent's "crimes" and "deviations" from the "general line" of accepted Communist policy (if true evidence is lacking, stretch the truth). Foster knew these rules. He was fully aware of the fact that it was not enough to capture the Party. He had to hold on to it. He had to establish a political platform for his leadership and a record of the "crimes" of his opponents—the Ruthenberg group which he had deposed from power. A post mortem on the campaign to organize the Federal Farmer-Labor Party supplied the political issue. But Ruthenberg also knew the rules of the game. That issue therefore became the factional football that was booted around in the Communist Party of the United States and at the Holy See in Moscow. We all played the game, and the way we booted the ball depended on which man we backed for leadership—Foster or Ruthenberg.

Having captured the Party, Foster tried to consolidate his position by using the power which his majority on the Central Executive Committee gave him—and that meant dictatorial powers. The C. E. C. appoints all heads of the district organizations; it has a minority on a district committee, it can either send its representative there with power to nullify all decisions and enforce whatever orders the C. E. C. issues on executive or policy matters, or the C. E. C. can add members to the district committee until it has a majority favorable to itself, even though, according to the Party constitution, the district committee is elected by a district convention. The district committee and all its officers are required to carry out all the decisions of the Central Executive Committee, whether they like them or not. Although elected by the membership of their district, they are in the position of army officers of inferior rank. However, Foster hesitated to use his newly-won dictatorial power—but not because he was a Bryan Democrat. Moscow had even greater power over him, and he was so afraid of Moscow that he moved very cautiously. Many of those who had been with him in the steel strike and the packing house union strangely enough were also members of the Communist Party: he placed them all—his son-in-law, Joseph Manley, Earl Browder, Charles Krumbein, Hamersmark, Otto Wangerin, Jack Johnstone—in strategic positions. It seemed that the cadre he had built up in the days when he confined himself strictly to the trade union field, and upon which he evidently depended in his alliance with the Fitzpatrick forces, was now to make up his lieutenants in the Party.

In a district as large as New York, where we Ruthenbergians had the majority of the District Committee, Foster was particularly afraid to use his power. He moved gingerly. New York was the largest district in the Party, its membership more alive than any other to inner Party developments. On the District Committee were Ludwig Lore, Juliet Stuart Poyntz, George Ashkenusi, myself, and other prominent members of the Party. Foster had removed the District Organizer, "Little Corporal" Benjamin Lifshitz, a short impulsive little fellow, and had put in his place Charles Krumbein, from Chicago, a blustering trade unionist who had got his training in the Chicago Federation of Labor as one of Foster's henchmen. Foster refrained from changing the composition of the district committee. Through this appointment Krumbein automatically became a member of the District Committee with a vote. All Foster needed now was a switch of one more vote from the opposition to his side, to give him a majority on the New York District Committee. Politics works in strange ways. This time it moved along on the Albany night boat, carrying delegates from New York City to Albany, to attend a so-called State Federated Farmer-Labor Party convention, organized and financed by the Communist Party. The Albany boat carried a load of delegates from New York, among whom were all the members of the district committee. The night was beautiful, the moon's silvery sheen enraptured the romantic hearts of the comrades. A Lithuanian woman member of the District Committee who was a supporter of the Ruthenberg group fell under the sway of that romantic night and became enamoured of Charlie Krumbein. After a fateful night with him on the entrancing Albany night boat, she was connected to Fosterism. Krumbein won a sweetheart and a majority on the New York District Committee, but in doing so he broke the heart of a veteran Foster follower on the District Committee; she, however, although slighted by Krumbein, nevertheless remained loyal to her politics and continued to support Krumbein and the Foster group.

Foster was shrewd enough to realize that he had been merely lucky in winning a bare and uncertain majority on the New York District Committee. He had to ground his leadership more substantially. He had to develop political policies which would be in harmony with Bolshevik policy and which would meet with Moscow's approval. One had but to watch Foster at Central Executive Committee meetings to see how cautiously and hesitatingly he developed his political ideas. He was not sure of himself as a political leader, did not feel on firm ground in the domain of internal Party politics. His inferiority complex in this respect was so apparent that we of the opposition took full advantage of it, making his life on the Central Executive Committee just as miserable as we could. We were the bright boys who knew how to sling the Communist lingo; he was the shamefaced dullard. To overcome this deficiency, he brought to his aid—Alexander Bittleman! That was a masterstroke. True, Bittleman was a Talmudist in every respect, completely divorced from all contact with the labor movement and with American life. But he read Russian, followed the Russian Communist press minutely and tried to copy in detail everything the Bolsheviks advocated, in order to apply it to the United States. His sensitive nose was always pointed in Moscow's direction, the better to catch the odor of the political breezes that blew from there. Bittleman became Foster's political brain trust. He bent over the papers, snooped through the books, collected statistics, worked out the policies, which were then presented by Foster. It was teamwork, with Foster in the limelight and Bittleman in the background. (When Foster lost the majority in 1925 and Bittleman was excluded from the Central Executive Committee, Foster acted like a lost man. Finally, in sheer desperation, he came into a meeting of the Political Committee with a special motion on personal privilege, requesting that Bittleman be allowed to attend the committee meetings. The obvious purpose of this motion was to make it possible for Foster to go into a huddle with Bittleman on all important matters that came up before the committee.)

The most important political policy which Foster inherited when he took over the Party was the labor party policy. Let us recover the facts. The policy had been devised by Moscow for the Communists of Great Britain, who were urged to campaign for admission into the British Labor Party. It was John Pepper who had first adapted this policy to the United States. Before it was actively put forward, however, it was submitted to Moscow for approval. When the labor party policy was put into practice the Communist Party was insignificant politically. Our total active membership was 6,862, of whom over two-thirds were not in the trade unions and the rest an insignificant minority there. We could make a lot of noise through our press and at meetings, but we were to all intents and purposes completely isolated from the main stream of organized labor. Through the Labor Party we hoped to attract the workers and penetrate the trade unions. Moscow also was interested in an American Labor Party for purely Russian reasons, for Moscow desired a political party with millions of voters supporting it that would be friendly to the Soviet Union and would fight for its recognition by the United States government. Hence, with the money supplied by Moscow, emissaries of the Central Executive Committee of the Communist Party were sent all over the country to interview trade union leaders, Farmer-Labor Party politicians, Progressives of the La Follette movement, farmer organization leaders and influential people of the coöperatives. These emissaries carried in their pockets complete and detailed instructions from the Party. When they returned, they reported to the Political Committee on their missions, describing in detail the persons visited, their weak points, how they could be influenced with offers of jobs and otherwise.

In order to overcome the opposition of the A. F. of L. to the Labor Party, we attempted to bore within the Conference for Progressive Political Action, dominated by the powerful unions of the Railroad Brotherhoods, the Machinists Union of the American Federation of Labor, and Sidney Hillman's independent union, the Amalgamated Clothing Workers of America. We made no headway with the Conference for Progressive Political Action, for our Party was excluded from its Cleveland Conference. We thereupon took steps to call a conference of our own for the purpose of organizing a Farmer-Labor Party, which would include the Communists and which the Communists would control. The Farmer-Labor Party which in 1920 had run a presidential candidate was induced to support the campaign for such a convention and to issue a call for it, inviting all the political and economic groups favoring the organization of a Farmer-Labor Party. The date of the convention was set for July, 1923. The report of the Central Executive Committee of the Communist Party to the 1923 Convention indicates how completely we dominated the campaign for the July Third convention. It states:

> From the beginning of the campaign for the July Third convention there was close cooperation between the Farmer-Labor Party and the Central Executive Committee. The Executive Secretary (Ruthenberg) of the Party held a number of conferences with the Secretary of the Farmer-Labor Party at which the plans for the campaign were formulated. Our Party did not only give its support as an organization but it assisted in financing the work of printing and sending out the call for the convention.

We were all very enthusiastic over the campaign. Foster was more than enthusiastic, he was jubilant. He very often expressed himself in the Political Committee that the American Labor Party, once it was organized, would bring about the disintegration of the Gompers Machine and would pave the way for the supporters of the Labor Party taking over the A. F. of L. But the July Third convention did not run smoothly. The Communists packed it with their delegates, burdened it with their oratory and stampeded it with their applause. However, the delegates who really represented farmer-labor party organizations and trade unions with standing objected to the platform which was drafted by the Communist Party and presented by Joseph Manley. Then Ruthenberg took the floor and declared:

> The platform we recommend, even though charged with being Red, 'Bolshevik,' ultra-radical, is hard for us, the Communists, to swallow.

And he made this statement even though he himself actually wrote the program. As for Foster, in speaking for the platform, he chided the opposition with being too conservative and out of tune with the radical sentiment in the United States, which in his opinion in the year 1923 was more radical than the sentiment among the Russian masses on the eve of the Bolshevik Revolution.

The real fight of the convention came on the report of the Organization Committee, which included a majority of Communists or Communist sympathizers and which contained the following well known leaders of our Party: Ruthenberg, Foster, Hathaway, Lore, Jay Lovestone, Manley—in all about 23 Communist party leaders were on this committee out of a total of 61 members. In addition, we had a sufficient number of rank-and-file Party members and Communist sympathizers, who could be depended upon to follow the Party line, among the 61, to give us a distinct majority. This committee forced through its resolution to organize immediately a national labor party, to be known as the Federated Farmer-Labor Party, and rejected the proposal of Fitzpatrick, made prior to the Convention, that the Convention of July Third should declare itself merely a conference and create a committee to be known as the Organization Committee, in which the Communist or Workers Party and all other national organizations should be represented, while the local unions and central labor bodies should be affiliated with the existing Farmer-Labor Party. The proposal to organize the Federated Farmer-Labor Party was carried by a vote of 500 to 40. But in carrying the proposal, the Communists, as has been said before, split the convention and forced out the non-Communist forces representing the genuine Farmer-Labor Party movement of the country, as well as the trade unions. We were jubilant about capturing a convention of over 500 delegates, with most of whom we ourselves had packed this convention, with the result that we captured ourselves!

Having organized a farmer-labor party in name, we did not know what to do with it. For weeks after July Third, its office was virtually in the office of the Communist Party. Joseph Manley was appointed its Secretary. His wages and the expenses of his office were all paid for by the Communist Party. Wherever we attempted to organize local or state branches of the new party it became only another cloak or mask for the local or state Communist organization. The Federated Farmer-Labor Party became a joke among the Communist membership. We soon realized that the split was very costly, that we had an illegitimate baby on our hands. Something had to be done to gain a foothold in the Farmer-Labor Party movement of the country. This became an urgent need in February, 1924, when the Conference for Progressive Political Action issued a call for a conference to be held on the Fourth of July, 1924, for the purpose of taking action on the nominating of a Presidential candidate. Besides, there was a lot of talk that Senator Robert M. La Follette would run against the two old parties. The sentiment in Farmer-Labor Party circles was very strong for La Follette. Encouraging the American movement for an independent party of workers and farmers was the recent victory of the British Labor Party, which at about this time took over the reins of government in Great Britain, with J. Ramsay MacDonald as Prime Minister. We were in a panic over these developments, especially as the movement to induce La Follette to run against the Democratic and Republican parties was gaining momentum. We feared that all our efforts in building up a labor party which would include the Communists and be dominated by them would come to naught. The situation created a serious crisis inside the Communist Party. In spite of all the money and energy we had spent, we were facing complete isolation from the movement, because the Conference for Progressive Political Action, dominated by the powerful Railroad Brotherhoods, was the real driving force behind the La Follette-for-President movement. It was very evident to us that we would be excluded from the Convention called by that organization for the purpose of nominating La Follette. Something drastic had to be done to save our political necks in the Farmer-Labor party movement.

A full meeting of the Central Executive Committee of the Party was held in the middle of February, 1924, at which this situation was discussed. At this meeting it was decided that steps should be taken by our Federated Farmer-Labor Party, in conjunction with some of the Farmer-Labor Party leaders of Minnesota, to call a national convention for the formation of a new national labor party, the convention to be held on May Thirtieth, in order that, whatever organization was set up by then should be able to make demands and dicker with the July Fourth meeting of the Conference for Progressive Political Action. The Central Executive Committee of the Communist Party desired to use the Farmer-Laborites of Minnesota as a smoke screen for the new organization, which we would set up on May Thirtieth. We laid down the following policies for the May Thirtieth Convention:

1. We must end our isolation from the farmer-labor party elements under our influence by consolidating our influence over these groups in a definite organizational form.

2. We must hold the May Thirtieth Convention irrespective of the action of the Farmer Labor Party of Minnesota provided we can hold the support of the other state organizations.

3. We must launch an immediate campaign against the July Fourth Convention in order to create doubt and suspicion in the minds of the workers as to its forthcoming action.

4. On May Thirtieth we must form a new organization, adopt a platform and elect a national committee and empower the national committee to take action on the question of candidates for President and Vice President.

5. The National Committee (of the Labor Party) shall go to the Cleveland July Fourth Conference to negotiate. If the National Committee is seated at the July Fourth Conference we shall endorse whatever candidates the July Fourth Conference shall nominate. [This policy meant an indorsement of La Follette.]

6. If the National Committee is refused admittance by the Cleveland Convention and Cleveland nominates candidates for President and Vice President, the National Committee shall immediately hold a public meeting and endorse the candidates of the Cleveland Convention. [Continued endorsement of La Follette even if excluded from the Cleveland Convention.]

7. If the Cleveland Convention does not form a third party, the National Committee shall immediately place in nomination candidates of the May Thirtieth Convention as the Farmer-Labor candidates.

Foster was completely in favor of the May Thirtieth Convention and at the C. E. C. meeting he declared:

> May Thirtieth now becomes the real mass labor party and we close our eyes to the July Fourth Conference.

Ludwig Lore, who opposed the endorsement of La Follette, nevertheless favored the May Thirtieth strategy and stated:

> We must have organizations behind the May Thirtieth Convention. Minnesota must be flooded with our people and activity. The farmers in Minnesota must be organized.

Steps were taken immediately to negotiate with the Farmer-Labor Party leaders of the State of Minnesota, especially with William Mahoney, who edited the *Minnesota Union Advocate,* the political expression of the Farmer-Labor Party Federation, which wielded a tremendous influence in the Minnesota Farmer-Labor Party. We also took steps to flood the state with our organizers and to colonize the important centers with our members. We had considerable strength in the Minnesota movement through the Finnish Coöperative, which had its headquarters at Superior, Wisconsin. They were included in our plans for capturing the Minnesota Farmer-Labor Party movement. Our endorsement of La Follette helped us tremendously in this respect, because the Farmer-Laborites of Minnesota were all for La Follette, but did not like the dominance of the brotherhoods over the Conference for Progressive Political Action. They felt that they were the genuine protagonists of the Farmer-Labor Party idea and that the brotherhoods were not. Since we were in common agreement with them on La

Follette, it was very easy to ensnare Mahoney and the other leaders. They did not realize all the time, from the very first negotiations, that they were just tools in our hands. Most of the negotiations were carried on through Clarence Hathaway. At the time he was a member of the Machinists Union of St. Paul and represented his local at the Farmer-Labor Federation. The Farmer-Labor people did not know that Hathaway was a member of the Communist Party and acting under its discipline. As a disciplined Communist, Hathaway did everything to maintain the fiction that he was not a Communist.

We came to an agreement with the Farmer-Labor Party representatives in Minnesota to call the convention for the formation of a national labor party on June the Seventeenth instead of May Thirtieth. Following this agreement, the Party launched a campaign to discredit the July Fourth Cleveland Convention, and to win over the Party members to the policy of supporting La Follette. The Party members did not like the policy. They were inclined to favor the principled position of Lore that under no circumstances should he be supported. I had great difficulty in convincing the comrades, many of them agreeing not out of conviction, but out of a sense of discipline and loyalty to the Party. Lore and Olgin wrote a thesis, which was published on April Twelfth, attacking our policy. Foster's two main aides on the Political Committee, Bittleman and Cannon, wrote a reply to the thesis, defending our policy, notwithstanding the fact that Lore and Olgin were important pillars of the Foster majority in the Party. The situation for Foster was very complicated. He had to discredit the Ruthenberg group and particularly Pepper on the Labor Party policy, while at the same time accepting their most important premises on this question. In addition, he had to carry on the fight in such a way as not to antagonize Lore and his followers, for the loss of Lore's followers would mean to lose the majority.

Suddenly, while the negotiations with the Farmer-Laborites of Minnesota were going on, a call was issued for a plenary session of the Executive Committee of the Communist International. John Pepper, the initiator and one of the most active spirits in our labor party strategy, was recalled to Moscow, so that the labor party issue was immediately transferred to the Holy See, and we had to await the verdict of Moscow before knowing how best to proceed in the matter. It was Foster who, using his influence with Lozovsky, the head of the Profintern, had succeeded in having Pepper recalled, as we Ruthenbergians learned later. As soon as Foster had assurances that Moscow would recall Pepper, he called a meeting of his caucus in New York City. It was attended by the entire Lore-Poyntz-Olgin caucus. It decided to demand of Moscow that Pepper be permanently withdrawn from the American Party. According to the reports of Ruthenberg's spy at this meeting, Foster ranted against Pepper and welcomed the support of the Lore-Poyntz-Olgin group, even though the latter violently disagreed with the policy of supporting La Follette, should the Senator be nominated by the July Fourth Convention. On this major question of policy, Foster and his group, including Bittleman, Cannon, and Browder, were in complete agreement with Pepper. When the Ruthenberg spy returned with a complete report of that fateful caucus, Pepper became exceedingly nervous. He did not desire to go back to Moscow. During his brief stay he had developed a great liking for the United States. He realized moreover that his political head was at stake. He immediately started to work on his defense. He knew that his greatest fight would be against Foster. He did not want to make this fight alone, because he was wise enough to know that if he appeared alone against Foster, it would be tantamount to committing political suicide. In addition, he realized that he would have to bear the brunt of the responsibility in defending the policies and mistakes of the Party on the labor party question. He therefore appealed to all the leaders of the Ruthenberg group to join him in his fight against Foster and in defense of the labor party policies and tactics. We did not hesitate to do so, not only because of loyalty to a member of our group, but also because we realized that if Pepper was completely discredited by the Communist International, it would be a big blow to our group in regaining the leadership of the Party. We decided not only to back Pepper to the fullest extent, but at the same time to have Pepper develop the fight in Moscow against the Foster leadership. Therefore, in the letters which we sent to Zinoviev, Chairman of the Communist International, we stressed the importance of our own rôle as leaders of the Party; an estimation of Foster and why he could not be trusted with the Party leadership; a defense of the labor-party policy, at the same time showing how Foster was non-politically-minded and hampered the labor party campaign; an attack upon Foster's unprincipledness and factionalism; and finally a laudation of Pepper's services to the American Party and a request that his services on behalf of the American Party be continued.

Before Pepper left for Moscow I had a talk with him. He was rather pessimistic as to the prospects of his returning immediately. Nevertheless, he said:

> Your letter to Zinoviev is an excellent one and every word of it's true. Foster will have to reckon with me when I am in Moscow. I will be the unofficial representative of the Ruthenberg group and will guard its interests every moment of the day. In a political fight one must have patience, for victories are not won in a day.

After Pepper left for Moscow, Foster followed him. He was very bitter against Pepper. At a Central Executive Committee meeting he was heard to boast, "If there is one thing I *will* accomplish in Moscow, it will be to keep him there!" By that time Foster had already developed a critical attitude towards some aspects of the labor party policy. He was not sure of his attitude, his position being the result of developments in the Party. His supporters who followed the Lore-Poyntz-Olgin group were very critical of the Federated Farmer-Labor Party and the endorsement of La Follette. In addition, the powerful group in the New York needle trades, headed by Charles Zimmerman, head of Local 22 of the Dressmakers; Ben Gold of the Furriers; and Rose Wortis, head of the needle trades in the Trade Union Educational League, favored the Lore position. Foster had to yield to the pressure of these forces on the labor party question in order to maintain his majority. He therefore denied responsibility for the formation of the Federated Farmer-Labor Party, in the formation of which he had played as much of a leading part as John Pepper. Besides, placing the whole responsibility for the Federated Farmer-Labor Party debacle upon the shoulders of the Ruthenberg group was excellent factional strategy. Foster went to Moscow in April as the leader of the majority of the Communist Party. He had been its leader since January First, 1924. As the leader of the majority, he did everything possible to hamper the work of the Federated Farmer-Labor Party and to prevent its growth, only in order to discredit the Ruthenberg leadership of the Party. But had Foster then understood the situation clearly, he would have known that nothing which the Communist Party would do could instil life and growth into the Federated Farmer-Labor Party.

In Moscow the Communist International accepted the political line of Lore in reference to the non-indorsement of La Follette and categorically rejected the policy of supporting him. But accepting Lore's policy on La Follette meant a serious repudiation of both the Foster and Ruthenberg groups, which together constituted the overwhelming majority of the Party. Pepper, who was a very shrewd and unscrupulous political adversary, saw this situation immediately and made the most use of it, by launching a most violent attack upon Lore for his heresies and unorthodox Communist viewpoints. Whether one agreed with Lore or not, it must be stated that he dared to maintain an independent and critical viewpoint even when it was at variance with the Moscow position. These heresies, these critical viewpoints, Pepper magnified out of all proportion to their importance. At the same time, Pepper's attack fitted in with the desires of certain Bolshevik leaders, whose fight for the elimination of Leon Trotsky, following the death of Lenin on January 21, 1924, was beginning to take form. Lore had always been an admirer of Trotsky, and in the editorial columns of the *Volkszeitung,* whenever the occasion presented itself, he came out in praise of Trotsky. In addition, it was no secret in the American Party that Lore had no use for Zinoviev, whose leadership of the Comintern on more than one occasion he had criticized in a veiled form. Therefore, Lore became the scapegoat. The Russian leaders attacked him unmercifully. Radek called him an anti-Communist, a Social-Democrat, a German patriot, who entered the Communist movement because he opposed the United States entering the war on the side of the enemies of Germany. Any one knowing Lore and his long record in the Socialist Party, knew that all these charges and especially this last charge of Radek's was absolutely false and was made out of whole cloth, only to destroy the political effectiveness of Lore in the labor movement. Zinoviev, Chairman of the Comintern and member of the powerful Political Committee of the Russian Communist Party, drew up the verdict:

> From what I have read, Lore proves he is in no case a Communist. I really do not know whether he belongs in the Central Executive Committee. In the resolution we have said that very politely. Perhaps we will be compelled to tell it to him less politely. The fact that Lore, too, was against the support of La Follette is of no moment. We know the manners of Social-Democrats who hide behind some barricades, who say they are against the work among the farmers because they are orthodox Marxists.

The Zinoviev-Kamenev-Stalin machine in the Comintern was not sure where Foster would stand on the Trotsky issue, because of his alliance with Lore. In the decision of the Executive Committee of the Comintern, published in the *Daily Worker* of May 18th, 1924, it was stated that there could be no doubt of the loyalty of the Ruthenberg group to the Comintern. In reporting for the American Commission in the Praesidium of the Comintern, Radek put it this way:

> The groups of Comrades Ruthenberg and Pepper appear to be the more radical. . . As far as Comrade Foster is concerned, I believe that we may have very serious difficulties with this comrade.

That was a blow to Foster, who cut a very pitiable figure in Moscow in 1924. He did not defend his position on the Labor-Party question. He merely blamed Pepper for the split with Fitzpatrick and for the formation of the Federated Farmer-Labor Party. But he did not defend Lore, though Lore was one of his most important supporters. Nor did he carry out his promise to Lore and Olgin that he would present their views on the Labor Party for the consideration of Moscow. When he felt how the political winds blew, he kept the famous Lore-Olgin thesis on the Labor Party in his pocket. He talked in the most general terms about the aristocracy of labor and other trade-union matters. On the La Follette matter he begged:

> If we have made a mistake in our policy, then it must be clearly understood why we have made this mistake. And I will be perfectly satisfied with the explanation that will be given.

This subservient attitude toward the Moscow leaders, this cringing before them, this readiness to accept their viewpoint, whatever it might be, even before it was presented, made the erstwhile Bryan Democrat a "perfect Communist."

In the final decision adopted by the Executive Committee of the Communist International, it was decided to work for the establishment of a political united front with the workers and exploited farmers by raising the slogan of the Farmer-Labor Party. Trotsky's proposal that the farmers be dropped was rejected. The trade-union policy of the American Party was now to be in line with the Profintern. An ideological campaign was to be started against the Two-and-a-Half-International* tendency of Lore and his followers. The Party was to be Bolshevized and organized on a shop nucleus basis; that is, the units of the Party were to be organized in shops where Communist members worked. The Foster and Ruthenberg groups were ordered to unite on the basis of equality. On the question of the June seventeenth St. Paul Convention for a Labor Party, a supplementary secret decision was rendered—for Party consumption only, not for publication. In it the Moscow leaders put thumbs down on the endorsement of La Follette under any circumstances. A supplementary decision also contained the point on the removal of Pepper from the American Party, the one Foster demand which Moscow granted. We of the Ruthenberg group had been kept informed almost daily by cable and knew of the Moscow decisions even before they reached the Party.

* So-called because of an attempt by some Left Wing Socialists in Europe to build an international midway between the Second (Socialist) and the Third (Communist) internationals programmatically—B.G.

Upon his return to New York Foster immediately called caucuses of his group, this time without Lore and the Loreites. He was extremely worried about the decisions and tried to interpret them as a victory for his group and leadership. But the Lore group was not satisfied. He could not square himself with them. He met with Lore and Poyntz in an effort to try to convince them that what had taken place in Moscow was only temporary and that it would be straightened out in the future, provided Lore and his followers would meet the decision half way. But the Lore group was not convinced. Feeling that they had been shamefully double crossed by one whom they had helped to put into the position of leadership of the Party, they decided to maintain an independent position as a group, free from entanglements with either Ruthenberg or Foster. Juliet Stuart Poyntz became exceedingly bitter towards the Foster group. She freely expressed her contempt for Foster, Bittleman, and Cannon, the Foster Big Three. The rift of the Lore group expressed itself immediately in the largest district of the Party, New York. The Ruthenberg group gained the majority of the District Committee, because Lore and Poyntz, who were both members of the District Committee, voted independently. There was real consternation among the Foster followers.

The Ruthenberg group decided to take full advantage of the C. I. decision by putting teeth into that clause of the decision that ordered the Party to start a campaign against Lore and his followers. Foster, for his own protection, wanted to pussyfoot this part of the decision, but the Ruthenberg group made life very miserable for him on this issue. In Max Bedacht we had in our group not only a member of the Central Executive Committee but a German expert, so to speak. To him we assigned the task of hounding Lore. He put the writings of Lore under his Communist microscope. Every little deviation of the *Volkszeitung* from accepted Communist orthodoxy was built up into a major departure from Communist principles. Demands were made upon Lore to correct his viewpoint and to turn the *Volkszeitung*, which he edited for a publishing society the majority of whose members were not Communists, over to the Party. While concentrating the attack upon Lore personally, our group tried at the same time, and later with some success, to win Poyntz and the leaders of the needle trades over to the position of the Communist International and against Lore. We practiced the good old maxim: divide and rule.

As to the end of factionalism and the unification of the two groups, as proposed by the Communist International, that did not take place because the Communist International made no specific provisions for such unity. The result of the decision was to create an atmosphere of such intense feelings of animosity between the groups that factionalism flared up within the Party on a scale never before experienced. The caucuses became disciplined military organizations. Party interests, always subordinate to caucus interests, were so far forgotten that caucus members looked upon the leaders and members of rival caucuses as enemies. Each caucus maintained a spy system to ferret out the machinations of the rival caucus, because the caucuses were in theory outlawed by the Party and their activities necessarily had to be conducted with the utmost secrecy.

Most costly to the Party was the Comintern decision on La Follette, for it affected adversely our political prestige as leaders and as a party. We learned of this Comintern decision in the latter part of May. Only a few weeks were left before the June Seventeenth Convention. All the important non-Communists had already been induced to participate, with the understanding that the convention would endorse the nomination of Senator Robert M. La Follette for President of the United States. Now these very same people had to be either convinced, or forced, to reject the La Follette endorsement. Moreover, this could not be done *before* the June Seventeenth Convention, for that would mean its collapse before it even convened and exposure of our Red hand in it throughout. Thus, it was impossible to negotiate the La Follette issue before the Convention took place. The break with La Follette had to be made on June Seventeenth and only then. This was not an easy thing to do. Naturally, we kept the Moscow decision on La Follette a dead secret and prepared to dominate the St. Paul Convention of June seventeenth, 1924 in precisely the same fashion in which we had dominated the July Third Convention the previous year.

By every known conveyance, including a special train from Chicago to St. Paul, the Communist Party delegates converged on St. Paul. Besides, as many Communists as possible who were not delegates were also directed to be on hand. Every Communist leader, every district head of the Party was on hand at St. Paul. Our Party caucus, attended by over six hundred Party members, was like an important national conference of Communists. Here for the first time the Communist International decision on La Follette was taken up with this select group of members and plans worked out for killing any proposal in favor of La Follette that might be raised at the Convention. In addition, the caucus was organized as a functioning body during the life of the convention. The members were informed of the decisions of the Central Executive Committee and ordered under the strictest discipline to carry out explicitly the decisions of the Steering Committee on all questions coming up at the Convention proper. The Steering Committee consisted of Foster, Bittleman and Ruthenberg. The Communist members who were delegates to the Convention were divided into small groups, each one headed by a captain, who was to be in direct touch with the Steering Committee. These groups were even assigned the places they were to take in the Convention Hall.

The Communists who were not delegates were assigned through Clarence Hathaway to positions on the staffs taking charge of Convention arrangements and technical matters. Others were organized into a group of runners, whose duty it was to carry messages between the Steering Committee and the captains of the delegate groups. Certain groups of delegates were assigned to sit in with the wavering elements, in order to influence them to vote as the Party desired. Others were assigned to oversee such elements as the Party knew were not to be dominated by it, in order to spy upon them and report their conversations and attitudes to the Steering Committee. The members of the Political Committee of the Party were directed to sit close to the Steering Committee, in order that if a decision had to be made by that body it could be made forthwith, and to be at the disposal of the Steering Committee when they wanted to fire their big guns at the opposition. Hathaway, who was Secretary of the Committee on Arrangements and in full charge of organizing the Convention, played a most clever Jekyll and Hyde role. Before the non-Communist forces he paraded as a trade unionist and Farmer-Laborite from Minnesota, giving no indication of his Communist entanglements. Before the Party caucus Steering Committee and Political Committee he was a Communist Party member whose double role helped the Party in its machinations against the non-Communist elements. Hathaway reported every matter given to him in confidence by the non-Communist elements and, like a good soldier, carried out the orders given him by his Communist chieftains.

William Mahoney, editor of the *Minnesota Union Advocate*, a genuine Farmer-Labor Party leader from Minnesota, was caught in our Machiavellian plans and plots. He fell into the snares of the Communists and could not extricate himself. He evidently suspected dirty work, for on May twenty-fourth he wrote an editorial on "The Communists and the Farmer-Labor Party," which expressed some of his apprehensions. Mahoney declared:

> The Communists, so-called, closely organized and highly disciplined as a political party, have become a serious problem within the Farmer-Labor movement. The relationship between the two will have to be definitely settled at an early day, as the organized activity of the Communists has become a source of fear and irritation to a great many earnest supporters of this new movement. . . . The presence of an organized revolutionary group within the party and constantly striving to control and direct it, is causing many to question the wisdom of tolerating such activity. . . But the thing that causes most irritation and distrust is the existence of a small group carrying on their intrigues and plots to control. It savors too much of the dictatorship of an insidious minority.

But Mahoney had to go along. He did not know that at almost the very moment he was making an agreement with the Communists for the calling of the June Seventeenth Convention to nominate La Follette for President, steps were being taken in Moscow to repudiate that agreement and to make a complete somersault on the Communist policy toward La Follette. On the eve of the St. Paul Convention, Senator La Follette wrote an open letter in which he unequivocally repudiated the June Seventeenth Convention and in the sharpest terms made it known that, inasmuch as it did not speak for the progressive farmers and workers, he would not accept its nomination or support. He further left no doubts that he would fully coöperate and accept the endorsement of the July Fourth Convention called by the Conference for Progressive Political Action. Old "Fighting Bob" La Follette was no fool; at least, he was a lucky guesser.

Mahoney probably knew that without his support the St. Paul convention would have never been called. He played a very active part in putting the idea across in Minnesota. He resented the La Follette attack, especially since he was one of La Follette's most ardent supporters. The Communists had led him to believe that they could bring to St. Paul a mighty delegation representing millions of farmers and workers. Mahoney believed he could turn St. Paul into an impressive demonstration for La Follette. Imagine his consternation when he found out that the Communists were going to knife La Follette! He soon discovered also what a stranglehold the Communists had on the Convention. About ninety percent of the 600 delegates at St. Paul were either Communists or under Communist tutelage. Outside of a few local unions and the Farmer-Labor Federation of Minnesota, the convention was practically nothing else than a conclave of the Communist forces in the labor movement. The millions of farmers and trade union workers, whose pressure was so glibly promised by us, were conspicuous by their absence. When the La Follette question was raised the Communist steam roller went into action. I opened the fight on La Follette by launching a tirade against him. The Communist faction under orders applauded vociferously every attack and at the end of my speech staged an anti-La Follette demonstration that left the insignificant La Follette minority at the convention almost speechless. But this minority, double-crossed and trapped into the convention as they were, continued to insist upon an endorsement of La Follette, even though their idol had already repudiated them. The Steering Committee called a hurried meeting of the Political Committee members present and decided upon a compromise proposal, which was then presented to the convention by Foster, who declared:

> The only basis upon which the Workers Party will accept La Follette as a candidate is, if he agrees to run as the Farmer-Labor candidate, to accept the Party's program [a program which was drawn up by the Workers Party and contained almost all the Communist demands] and its control over his electoral campaign and campaign funds.

Since the National Farmer-Labor Party organized at St. Paul was a vest pocket creation of the Communists and completely controlled by them, Foster's proposal was tantamount to asking La Follette to place himself under the dictation of the Communist Party, not only as far as the platform was concerned but also in the conduct of the campaign and the control of campaign funds!

I have never been able to understand why Mahoney believed he could go with such a proposal to Cleveland on July Fourth and obtain the approval of La Follette. The fact remains that Mahoney did not split with the Communists at St. Paul. He went along to the very end participating in the nomination of candidates for President and Vice-President, who were handpicked by the Communist Party before the convention convened. Duncan McDonald of Illinois, an ex-official of the Illinois District United Mine Workers of America, was unanimously nominated for President, and William Bouck, a farmer of Sedro-Wooley, Washington, was nominated for Vice-President. We staged a demonstration when the candidates were nominated in true Republican and Democratic Party fashion in a vain attempt to prove that the loud noises represented something more substantial than wind. St. Paul in most respects was a replica of the Chicago July Third Convention of the previous year, with two minor exceptions: One, Foster this time controlled the Steering Committee and engineered the convention instead of Ruthenberg; two, Mahoney, unlike Fitzpatrick, did not split. Later when Mahoney, after he was denied admission to the July Fourth Convention, came out in support of La Follette, we lost no time in attacking him as a traitor to the Farmer-Labor Party movement. There was no bottom to our cynicism.

The Cleveland July Fourth Convention turned out to be a triumph for La Follette. He was nominated to run for President on his own personal program and given the right to choose his running mate. All the organizations participating at the convention representing the unions, farmers' organizations, coöperatives, progressives, Farmer-Labor forces and the Socialist Party united behind La Follette. It was also becoming clear that the American Federation of Labor would soon officially back the La Follette movement. Our campaign to wreck the Cleveland Convention failed completely. All of which placed us in a great dilemma. We leaders of the Party knew that we were completely isolated from the popular opposition movement of farmers and workers, which the La Follette-for-President movement represented. We had hoped to capture the mighty Farmer-Labor movement and had ended again by capturing ourselves.

The plans for the campaign of McDonald and Bouck had already been made. Bouck had already started his speech-making tour of the country, when the members of the Central Executive Committee were called to Chicago for an emergency meeting to be followed by a conference of important Party functionaries the next day. I hurried from New York to Chicago, wondering what the emergency could be. When I arrived in Chicago I immediately went into conference with Ruthenberg. He spoke about the political situation, explained that the Party was completely isolated from the forces that should get behind the new National Farmer-Labor Party, that we would look ridiculous if we ran McDonald and Bouck, because they would receive an insignificant vote, which would discredit the Farmer-Labor Party movement for a long time to come. In order to save the face of the Communist movement and the issue of the class Farmer-Labor Party, it had become necessary to abandon the campaign of the Farmer-Labor Party and run an independent Communist campaign under the banner of the Workers Party.

"But how can we do such a thing?" I inquired. "We cannot take responsibility for wrecking the Farmer-Labor Party right after we organized it with so much fanfare."

"Oh, that has been taken care of already," Ruthenberg informed me. "We have canvassed the National Committee of the Farmer-Labor Party, and the majority of them [the majority were Communists] voted in favor of discontinuing the campaign and endorsing the campaign of the Workers Party. We in Chicago have also decided that our ticket should consist of Foster for President and you for Vice-President."

"But I don't see how we can abandon the Labor Party policy, especially knowing that the Communist International favors this policy."

"That has been taken care of, too. We have cabled the Communist International of our desires and they have replied approving them."

At the meeting of the Central Executive Committee Foster, Bittleman, Cannon and Browder took the lead in proclaiming the new policy. Foster was very excited. He had a wire in his hand from McDonald, the Presidential candidate of the National Farmer-Labor Party, withdrawing from the campaign, but he had no word from Bouck, who was already touring the country. Foster spoke of the million votes Debs received in the last election. He was sure that the Communist Party would rally the Socialist vote, because the Socialist Party was backing La Follette. In addition, he felt we would poll many votes from the progressive forces in the trade unions and farmers' organizations. It was clear from the way he spoke that he expected that the Communist Party would poll anywhere from 500,000 to a million votes. I found out later that he had actually informed Moscow that he expected the Party, running in its own name and on a Communist platform, to make such a showing. After demurring, I finally spoke in favor of the proposal, because the steps already taken by the comrades in Chicago had left no other alternative. I stressed the necessity of making the Farmer-Labor Party question one of the major issues in the campaign, but expressed doubts of the ability of the Party to get anywhere near the number of votes Foster expected. The Party Conference that followed the meeting of the Central Executive Committee was turned into a nominating convention. Foster was nominated for President and I for Vice-President, with organized demonstrations staged and whipped into enthusiastic frenzy. While this was going on, Bouck was notified by wire to discontinue his campaign, because the National Committee of the Farmer-Labor Party had voted not to run in the elections and had endorsed the nominees of the Workers Party, Foster and Gitlow.

Moscow supplied the Party with fifty thousand dollars to get the Party ticket on the ballot in as many states as possible and for the carrying out of the campaign proper. Joseph Manley, former Secretary of the Federated Farmer-Labor Party, was chosen as campaign manager, the position he held for the National Farmer-Labor Party. We succeeded in getting on the ballot in fourteen states. The Party members accepted the change in policy. They welcomed the idea of campaigning for a straight Communist ticket. But the Party organization and membership did not know how to campaign. The Communist movement lacked such political experience, because our members had been primed in the belief that only by a violent revolution could the Communist program be put into effect. Voting in general was looked upon as a necessary evil. The campaign was primarily directed against La Follette. Jay Lovestone wrote a special campaign booklet called *The La Follette Illusion.* The research worker employed to gather the material could find nothing of real importance against La Follette's record. But a case against La Follette had to be manufactured, which was accordingly done by innuendos and drawing conclusions from facts that were in no way germain to the charges made. When the campaign was over and the votes counted, the Communist Party polled exactly 33,361 votes out of a total of almost thirty million. La Follette received five million votes. I had expected at least 100,000 votes, a figure indeed of no real significance. Foster, however, hailed the result as a victory, coupled it with a charge that the two old parties had engaged in wholesale frauds in the robbing of Communist votes, and cabled Moscow that the Party had actually received a half million votes. It was a fitting concluding chapter to the Communist campaign for a labor party and revealed the political weakness of the Communist movement. In the *Liberator* of July, 1924, Ruthenberg had written:

The St. Paul Convention has laid the groundwork for the permanent organization of a Farmer-Labor Party on a mass scale. In the candidates nominated and the platform adopted there is the basis for a nationwide struggle against the capitalist order in this country.

In the *Liberator* of August, 1924, Foster wrote:

For the Workers Party to have continued behind the skeleton National Farmer-Labor Party would have been to accept all the disadvantages of the united front with none of its advantages. . . A militant campaign by the Workers Party for revolutionary ends is the only effective reply to the C. P. P. A.—Socialist Party surrender to the La Follette petty bourgeois movement.

The finale by Browder, in the August, 1924, issue of the *Labor Herald,* declared:

The issues are clear. William Z. Foster, the candidate of the Workers Party, running on the platform of the dictatorship of the working class against the dictatorship of the capitalist class, is the only representative of the struggle against capitalism. The betrayal of the official misleaders of Labor has been complete. Only the struggle for Communism remains in this election for the workers and farmers.

The lightning rapidity with which the Workers Party went through the labor party campaign is indicated by a recapitulation of the dates: July 3, 1923, the Federated Farmer-Labor Party is organized in Chicago. July 17, 1924, the Federated Farmer-Labor Party goes out of business and the National Farmer-Labor Party is organized at St. Paul. July 10, 1924, at a conference in Chicago, Foster is nominated for President and Gitlow for Vice-President, just twenty-two days after the National Farmer-Labor Party is organized and candidates McDonald and Bouck nominated. On the same day Foster, chairman of the Communist Party, had telegrams in his possession signed by Alex Howat, C. A. Hathaway, Alfred Knutson and Joseph Manley, the Communist contingent of the National Committee of the National Farmer-Labor Party, withdrawing the candidacies of McDonald and Bouck and calling for support of the

Workers Party ticket. Alice Daly, of South Dakota, the one non-Communist on the committee, refused to sign and William Mahoney had resigned in order to support La Follette. The hold which the Communists exerted on the Farmer-Labor Party movement they organized ended in the strangulation of their own child just 22 days after its birth.

CHAPTER VII

COMRADES ALL

THE word "comrade" really stood for a fine human relationship between forward-looking persons of exceptional civic courage bound by the common bond of defying all constituted authority in their common endeavor to build a better world for all mankind. But that word sounds hollow today, and in its hollowness mockery resounds. There was a time, even within the span of my own life, when this comradeship of the political Left imposed certain definite restraints on the ardor of partisanship; no radical, no matter how fanatically he championed his particular political sect, would have dared at one time to deny a fellow-radical of opposing views the right to state them publicly without molestation. The radical zealot might go to his opponent's meeting and boo, he might castigate him mercilessly in a meeting of rebuttal or in his own newspaper, but at one time he would never have dared to organize a police raid on his opponent's meeting, no matter how great the provocation. Yet that is precisely what we Communists came down to early in 1925, acting as a kind of colonial police force for the government of the Soviet Union on the territory of the United States. And the victim of our raid in defense of the Soviet Union was a Socialist leader who prior to 1917 had been not only a comrade but a fellow-member of the Bolshevik leaders in the same political party, the Russian Social-Democratic Labor Party. I cite this instance, because it illustrates one stage in the process of moral degeneration that has broken the spirit of the radical labor movement and renders it so utterly helpless today in the face of Fascist reaction.

In its connotation, as used among Leftists, "comrade" has always been a democratic word, an anti-authoritarian word. But with the advent of the Bolsheviks to power in Russia, and particularly as Bolshevik totalitarianism was first consummated in

Russia and then spread through the Communist movement of the entire world, Leftists everywhere began to receive more severe blows from "comrades" of the Bolshevik persuasion than they had ever received from the capitalist police. When Raphael Abramovich came to the United States on a lecture tour early in 1925, the capitalistic government of the United States was not in the least concerned by what that Russian Socialist might have to say; if he were to return this year, it would still be unconcerned. But Nazi Germany and Fascist Italy and Communist Russia would be greatly concerned about the presence of a Raphael Abramovich in their country, bound on a lecture tour, if indeed they would give him an entrance visa. We American Communists lacked the power over visas to visiting foreigners in 1925—an influence the Communist Party of the United States is said to have acquired by 1939 through the intercession of its sympathizers in contact with employees of the federal government—and therefore had recourse to plain ordinary police methods as our most direct way for keeping him from making his criticism of the Soviet Union public in the United States. Abramovich was a member of the Second International, with which in 1922 the Third International had negotiated a common united front against world reaction; Abramovich remained a member of the same Second International, with the French and Spanish members of which the Communists entered into united fronts in 1936. Throughout the intervening years Abramovich has not changed his allegiance to Socialism nor his critical attitude toward the Bolshevik regime in Russia. Yet in 1925 we refused to let Abramovich speak in public in the United States, where we ourselves had been subjected to Red raids only a few years before and were ourselves on sufferance in most parts of the country, although at best Abramovich could address only a handful of foreign-born who attended Yiddish and Russian meetings.

Eighty-seven percent of our Communists were members of foreign-language federations, and of the 1750 in the English-speaking branches, the majority were foreign-born who spoke their English with a decided foreign accent. They had but one homeland in common, these strangers in America, the Soviet

Union, and they were fanatically devoted to the defense of the Soviet Union. They would brook no criticism of their proletarian homeland. Here in America the vast majority of our Party, fully ninety percent, regarded themselves as colonists of Communism among the unconverted heathen, who before long would be either converted or conquered. Anyone familiar with the history of any imperial power knows that a colonist is an infinitely more zealous patriot than his fellow-citizen in the home country; it is the A. B. C. of human psychology that nostalgia for the homeland enhances its attractiveness and love of it, all this being intensified by the necessity to live and work in a hostile environment. Even apart from its subservience to the foreign policy of the Soviet government, the Communist movement was psychologically a movement of political colonists determined to place the world, or as much of it as possible, country by country, under the sway of their government in Moscow. Psychologically we were as imperialistic as the Britishers in the Indian Civil Service, for example. The Englishman in Lahore is a far sterner patriot than the Englishman in London or Liverpool, and a far more zealous imperialist, too. Let us not deceive ourselves. Fanatical zeal alone cannot account for the police methods we employed. Heretofore, fanatical zeal among radicals had not led to police methods. If we Communists resorted to them, it was not only because we were zealots, but rather because, in addition to being zealots, we subconsciously identified ourselves with the ruling caste in our homeland, in the Soviet Union. We were psychologically a new species of radicals—not democratic anti-authoritarians along with the other comrades of the political Left, but, on the contrary, anti-democratic authoritarians, as much so as our superiors of the Communist hierarchy in Moscow, who ruled over one-sixth of the earth. Moreover, we were no longer radicals in the true sense of the word, because we were no longer seekers after the root of social injustice, no longer seekers of the truth that would make men free. We were volunteer members of a militarized colonial civil service, pledged to carry out the decisions of our supreme rulers resident at Moscow anywhere in the world but particularly in the land we were colonizing for Communism, the United States.

How then could we be comrades to anyone outside of our Communist ranks? Why allow any of them to air their views, when these views were bound to be wrong and inimical to our doctrines as revealed by the infallible Russian leaders of the Comintern? We alone knew how to win the world from the capitalists; we alone proved that we knew how to do it through the Bolshevik Revolution. The Socialists, the deviators from the Marxist doctrine in its only true and effective interpretation, or anyone else who was not a Leninist as certified by the Comintern, were only insidious traitors in the ranks of the labor movement, conscious or unconscious agents of the capitalist class in its ranks. To the rank and file of the Communist movement, Communism was not just a political philosophy, it was a faith that was destined to convert the world into a Socialist paradise and solve all of man's pressing problems.

Bolshevik Russia was our country from which we drew inspiration every moment of our conscious lives. Only good could come from Russia. Criticism of Russia aroused our anger, for we regarded all criticism as lies, fabricated by counter-revolutionists and capitalist imperialists. Soviet Russia was our fatherland, its Red Army our army, its red flag our flag. Patriots of Soviet Russia, we would not hesitate to commit any act of violence or treason against the country in which we lived, if ordered to do so by the Party, or if we believed that act would help Soviet Russia. To us the heads of the Soviet government, the leaders of the Communist Party of the Soviet Union, the Russian leaders of the Communist International were supergeniuses, imbued with such political sagacity and knowledge of world affairs that they could make no mistakes and whose decisions were always right and motivated by the highest Communist ideals. We believed that the Communist International knew what was best for us and that to disobey its decisions was tantamount to treason. We who were the leaders did everything to build up this attitude. We did not have to do it hypocritically, because in the main we believed as did the rank and file. We prided ourselves on the fact that we were not only leaders of an international Communist movement but that we also had ties with the Soviet government. Above all, we enjoyed the idea that we were part of a state machine that ruled a mighty empire of millions of people. In fact, we became the most ardent agents of the Soviet government and were prepared to render any service it might require of us. Moreover, whenever the Russian leaders made moves that seemed contrary to Communist principles, as, for example, coöperating with Fascist Italy, we explained it as an example of clever Communist maneuvering by which the Russians would outsmart their enemies, discredit them and gain the upper hand.

This was the highly-disciplined group Raphael Abramovich had to contend with when he came to the United States for his lecture tour. I was in New York City at the time. Upon orders of the Central Executive Committee in Chicago, the New York district was instructed to call a very important and secret meeting of Party functionaries to hear a report by Alexander Bittleman. Though I was a member of both the Central Executive Committee and of the New York District Committee, I was not informed of the nature of Comrade Bittleman's mission. The meeting was held at the headquarters of the New York District Committee. About four hundred party leaders and functionaries were crowded into the room. Bittleman reported that an emissary of the Second International, Raphael Abramovich, a counter-revolutionary scoundrel, was coming to the United States to poison the minds of the workers with anti-Soviet lies, in order to mobilize sentiment against the Soviet Union. He said it was part of a plot hatched by the "yellow" Socialists in league with the White Guardists and counter-revolutionists, to create an anti-Soviet Russian front in the United States. In his report he tried to give the impression that the matters he was going to take up at the meeting were in the nature of confidential instructions from Moscow on how to defeat Abramovich's anti-Soviet campaign. He exclaimed:

> We must give Abramovich the answer of the American working class! We will show him that, in no place in the United States, will the workers permit him to speak.

Bittleman then outlined the policy that every meeting arranged for Abramovich must be broken up.

I objected to this policy and spoke against it then and there. I proposed that the Party and the Friends of Soviet Russia hold counter meetings, at which Abramovich was to be exposed and his charges against Soviet Russia answered. I said:

> The policy proposed is very dangerous, because our Party is a minority party, bitterly opposed by the ruling class. If we deny freedom of speech to others by breaking up meetings because we don't like what will be said there, then we give the opposition to the Communist Party the same right to break up our meetings.

Although my objection was only on the grounds of expediency and self-interest, even my appeal to such motives received no response. The Party functionaries present were either cowed by Bittleman and afraid of the charge of being called cowards, or else welcomed the idea of some real fighting against a "yellow" Socialist. At any rate, the overwhelming majority were in favor of Bittleman's militant policy. That opened the way for Bittleman, who again took the floor and denounced me. He called me to account for not supporting the proposals of the Central Executive Committee, of which I was a member, and considered my position not only an act of hostility against the Central Executive Committee but a crucially serious breach of Communist discipline. He attacked me for giving aid and comfort to the counter-revolutionists and to the enemies of the Soviet Union. Obviously enjoying his own Jesuitic casuistry, he shouted:

> *We* will not be breaking up meetings. The *working class* will break up the meetings. We will do here what the working class in the Soviet Union would do, only not as much, because we haven't the power in the United States as yet.

Does this statement sound familiar? A decade and a half later Dr. Joseph Goebbels was to use similar demagogy in asserting that the German masses had perpetrated the pogroms of German Jews in November, 1938, expressing their pent-up indignation. In those days I did not even dream that such a parallel could ever be drawn.

After the meeting, the District Committee worked out detailed plans for carrying out Bittleman's proposals. They included the appointment of a committee to be in charge of each meeting to be broken up. After that a number of recognized Communist leaders were assigned to the task of rushing the platform as soon as the meeting was opened, in order to bombard Abramovich with insulting questions and charges, all insinuating that he was a counter-revolutionary scoundrel. The committee in charge was instructed to mobilize a sufficient number of Communists, who were to be stationed in all parts of the hall, to start disturbances by incessantly coughing, shouting, catcalls and the hurling of invectives. Another group was assigned to start fights with people in the audience in all parts of the hall. Women were assigned to shriek and throw hysterics. And to climax it all, a group of strong-arm Communists were held in readiness, to go into the fray and start pummeling and blackjacking when signaled to do so by the committee. A conference was held immediately with all the Communist leaders in the trade unions and their strong-arm squads mobilized for the holy war against the politically weak and physically puny Abramovich, who dared to disagree with the policies of the Bolsheviks. The Communist forces went into action immediately and broke up one meeting after another. There was jubilation in the Communist press, but the real jubilation was at the Communist headquarters when the brave Red fighters returned, their scars of battle visible. Flushed with victory, the comrades shouted and laughed, evidently overjoyed, as strong-arm men described how they flattened out the Socialists by terrific punches to their jaws or eyes or by blows on the ear, with a pipe or by breaking a chair over their heads.

But the victories did not last long. The pamphlet which the Party issued, *Abramovich: The Guardian of Democracy*, did not convince those who came to listen to Abramovich. The Socialists and trade unionists who supported him immediately organized to resist the Communists. After the first flurry of success, it was difficult for Communists to gain admission at Abramovich meetings. When a fight started they soon found out that, when prepared to fight, the other side could give more than just blow for blow. Bloody Communist heads coming into Party headquarters soon told the story. Besides, the reaction among the people who came to hear what Abramovich had to say was very bad. A storm of protest arose and a revulsion set in among the Party members. Soon many comrades openly opposed the tactics, so that, when Abramovich spoke in Boston, the Boston District Committee failed to carry out the Central Executive Committee program but instead arranged a counter meeting. For this the Central Executive Committee severely censured them. Thus, we were forced to abandon our anti-Abramovich campaign very quickly. However, this was never done officially. The Central Executive Committee held that this activity was an achievement, for when it reported to the Fourth National Convention of the Party, it stated:

> Abramovich's mission to the United States was completely defeated, and his meetings, instead of mobilizing workers against Soviet Russia, were turned into monster demonstrations in favor of Soviet Russia. The success of this campaign would have been even more complete but for resistance within the Party, such as in Boston, where there was a refusal to demonstrate at Abramovich's meeting and the substitution instead of a rival meeting.

The question of the role that the Party should play at meetings in which the Soviet Union was attacked came up again in March, 1925, at the meeting of the District Committee of New York, when Charles Krumbein, the District Organizer, reported that a meeting was to be held in Town Hall by the International Committee for the Defense of Political Prisoners, an organization started by Roger Baldwin, of which Elizabeth Gurley Flynn was secretary. This committee appealed on behalf of political prisoners in all countries, including Soviet Russia. We, of course, denied that Russia had "political" prisoners. Krumbein proposed that if the committee in charge of the meeting refused to withdraw reference to Soviet Russia, that we attack the meeting. I denounced Krumbein for his position, but he would not listen to me. I felt so keenly on the matter that I drew up a lengthy statement, incorporating the reasons for my position. I knew very well that if I did not do this, the Foster group would send out factional documents from its caucus headquarters, putting statements in my mouth that I did not make and upon those statements interpreting my position as cowardly submission to the liberals and enemies of Soviet Russia. My statement in part said:

> The policy of disrupting meetings of the International Committee for Political Prisoners is not calculated to produce the results we wish to attain. It is more particularly entirely unsuited for the present political situation in the United States, especially in view of the campaign of repression likely to be instituted by the Capitalist and Fascist organizations in the near future. Such a policy only helps to form a united front against the Party, ranging from the liberals to Coolidge, without sufficient compensating results for the Party.

Nevertheless, the meeting, held in Town Hall, March tenth, 1925, was broken up by our Party, when B. Charney Vladeck attempted to speak on political prisoners in Soviet Russia.

We would not let liberals and radicals plead in defense of "political" prisoners in Soviet Russia; instead, we set out to mobilize their money, influence and sympathy for our own purposes at home. In June, 1925, the International Labor Defense was organized. Before that time the Communist Party carried on its defense work through special committees and local defense organizations. The Labor Defense Council, with headquarters in Chicago, was organized to defend Foster, Ruthenberg and the others arrested at the underground convention held at Bridgeman, Michigan, in 1922. The organization of the International Labor Defense, popularly known as the I. L. D., came as the result of a Moscow decision that an American Section of the M. O. P. R.—Russian initials for The International Class War Prisoners Aid Society—be organized at once. The Mopr was run by the Comintern. It was the international defense organization of the Communist movement, with headquarters, of course, at Moscow. To see that the decision should be properly carried out, a representative of the Mopr was sent to the United States and the necessary cash supplied to call a convention and launch the organization. The launching of such an organization was a political plum for any ambitious leader. James P. Cannon, Foster's chief lieutenant, saw in this new organization an opportunity to utilize it for his personal prestige and for furthering the interests of his factional group. It seemed to me that if ever a man was unsuited to head an organization like the International Labor Defense, it was Cannon. He spoke most enthusiastically of the prospects of the new enterprise. In Chicago he explained to me how the I. L. D. could be built into a powerful mass organization. "Here is what the Party has been looking for, an organization with an appeal that can enlist hundreds of thousands." I agreed with him, of course, but I had my own idea as to what was probably in back of his mind. Cannon was smarting under the popularity accorded to Foster. Though in Foster's caucus, he envied him. To him Foster was a simple trade unionist, lacking in political ability. He felt that he was the man of the greatest political ability in the Party, superior not only to Foster but to all of us. If political maneuvering for place is a sign of political ability, then, I admit, Cannon ranked high.

Cannon had organized a caucus of his own within the Foster caucus. He disclosed his true ambitions only to his most trusted caucus comrades and lieutenants. The I. L. D. would give him contact with the masses and with Party members all over the country. He could utilize the organization to build up his reputation as a leader of the masses. He would use the I. L. D. organization to build up his personal machine and to strengthen that machine by the new members that would be brought into the Party by virtue of the I. L. D.'s activities. Furthermore, through the I. L. D. many of Cannon's followers in the Foster caucus could be given berths with pay in the new organization in the same manner in which Foster took care of his followers through the Trade Union Educational League. Of great importance was the added fact that the I. L. D. would publish a magazine. This magazine could become the expression of Cannon and his followers through the able editorship of Max Schachtman, who, together with William F. Dunne, formed the big inner three of the Cannon caucus within the Foster caucus. It was a case of wheels within wheels, and Cannon had hopes through the I. L. D. to become himself the main driving wheel.

All the details for the convention to organize the I. L. D. were worked out by the Central Executive Committee of the

Party. All the officers were selected in advance, and the composition of the National Committee and the Executive Committee of the new organization to be formed was decided by the Party. Even the agenda, resolutions, reports and who were to make the speeches and the kind of speeches were worked out in advance. Yet this was advertised as a non-Party undertaking. The National Conference in Chicago was a poorly attended affair. The trade unions were conspicuous by their absence. Those who had been political prisoners were seated as delegates. Out of the conference emerged a strictly Communist organization. Of course, the fact that it was affiliated with the Soviet Mopr was not then made public. An Executive Committee of eleven members was elected, seven of whom were members of the Workers Party, among whom were James P. Cannon, Ruthenberg and I, all of us leading members of the Central Executive Committee of the Workers Party. The Chairman and Vice-Chairman were genuine liberals roped in as a front, but the Secretary was James P. Cannon. It is important to note that in every so-called non-Party organization or committee organized by the Communists the Secretary is always a Communist. Whosoever controls the secretary, controls the organization, for when Communists organize, the secretary does not merely take care of correspondence, he is the actual full-time paid executive of the organization in charge of all its activities. He is there to guard the interests of the Party in every manner, shape and form, morally, politically, and financially.

The I. L. D. did prove a juicy political plum, if not factionally for Cannon, at least for the Communist Party as a whole. It attained such respectability that its present Chairman is the Republican Congressman Vito Marcantonio, although it continues to be strictly a Communist organization ruled more than ever with an iron hand from Moscow. Cannon lost it, as he lost all his astutely-won prerogatives in the Party, when he attached himself to the wrong Russian leader and ever after has been forced to say B (and pretty much of the rest of the alphabet) to his original A, by continuing to champion the cause of that leader to the bitter end and to this very day. For a politician of Cannon's admitted, not to mention his self-admitted, astuteness, his original bet on the Russian leader in question was an act of monstrous stupidity. On the surface it may appear as if Cannon had acted out of noble, if quixotic, motives. But that is far too unlike the Cannon I knew in the Party, for me to believe.

The measure of the man—and Foster, too, for that matter—and all the Fosterite Caucus leaders, as well—may be judged from his typical reaction to the decision of the United States Supreme Court, which on June eighth, 1925—just when he was founding the International Labor Defense organization—upheld my conviction on criminal syndicalism charges by a vote of seven to two, Justices Holmes and Brandeis dissenting. Had Cannon been the political leader he claims to be, he would never have allowed factionalism to overshadow its significance for the Party, the American labor movement and the cause of civil liberties in this country. Everyone alive to political developments, not only legal experts, recognized at once the importance of this decision as a dangerous precedent for limiting the scope of freedom of speech and civil liberties generally throughout the United States. While my comrade who was head of the I. L. D., together with his caucus chieftain, the erstwhile standard-bearer of the Party, could not think beyond the possibility of having a factional opponent removed, even if that removal was to a capitalist prison in punishment for service to the Party, and both rejoiced at the thought, the American Civil Liberties Union, at that time completely free of any vestige of Communist control and attacked by our Party because its head, Roger Baldwin, had the temerity to champion the cause of political prisoners in Russia, immediately appealed to Governor Alfred E. Smith of New York to pardon me. Since Governor Smith replied that he could not keep his promise to do so at that particular time, because legally the case was not subject to his review until the verdict of the United States Supreme Court had been executed by having me returned to prison, I prepared for immediate imprisonment. It so happened, due to the proverbial delays of justice, so-called, that I did not have to return to Sing Sing until November eleventh, thus continuing to plague Foster, Cannon, Bittleman, Browder, Krumbein et al. for another five months, much to their "comradely" discomfiture.

I do not mention this matter because it involved me personally. As a matter of fact, at the time I, too, was so involved in factional squabbles, a fight I was leading in one of the needle trade unions, and a complexity of trade union and Party problems, that I was too swamped to give the matter of my personal fate or the significance of this decision any thought at all. I left that up to the appropriate department of the Party, administered, as it happened to be, by my comrade then in charge of founding the I. L. D. But I must not be too hard on a man like Cannon. I am not surprised that his political vision did not extend beyond his caucus. What amazes me now, as I look over the correspondence and Party documents of that time, is the indifference to the case on the part of all the Party leaders, irrespective of faction. At the session of the Central Executive Committee of June eleventh, only three days after this important decision that set a precedent for outlawing at will even a reformist, let alone a revolutionary, party, was rendered, the matter was not even discussed. The first person in the Communist Party to be officially concerned about it, according to the record now before me, was a minor official of the New York District organization by the name of Julius Codkin, who on June twenty-second introduced a resolution pledging the New York District to work for my liberation from prison and calling upon the District Committee to forward this resolution to the Central Executive Committee. Chronologically, again according to the record I have, Charles E. Ruthenberg was the second person in the Party to show some initiative in the case. While it is not surprising that Codkin did not appreciate the implications of the decision, I am surprised that Ruthenberg did not, for Ruthenberg wrote me in a letter dated July twenty-eighth:

> I suggested the other day that the New York Party organization arrange a big mass meeting on Thursday, protesting against the sentence, but did not get action. I will make a definite motion to that effect tomorrow, so that we can stir up something.

But Ruthenberg's efforts were in vain. The Fosterites on the Central Executive Committee spiked his attempts, as did Krumbein in New York. As for Ruthenberg, his interest on my behalf was as factional as was the Fosterite effort against me, for in that same letter he expressed the hope for my freedom, "so that you will not have to be out of the present fight for a single day," meaning the Party factional fight. No more! And we fancied ourselves political leaders and liberators of the working class!

This spirit of factionalism was so incorrigible that often it overflowed into the sacred soil of Moscow decisions. The consequences had a touch of the ironic at times, as I look back on it now, although then I took the antics of the opposition in too dead earnest to see the humor of the situation. A case in point concerns the Comintern decision to Bolshevize the American Party. The exalted and then apparently omnipotent Zinoviev himself was in favor of it; so, indeed, were all the Muscovite super-geniuses. Yet nothing more ridiculous could have been thought up, for Bolshevization meant the reorganization on a shop nucleus basis of our little party, numbering all told thirteen and a half thousand members, of whom less than half, and these scattered throughout the length and breadth of the United States, could by any stretch of the imagination be regarded as shop or factory workers. To be precise, out of the 13,556 registered Party members, 2,000 were Party functionaries who registered as workers of a trade of one sort or another, at which they were not working, of course; 4,500 were employed at miscellaneous non-factory jobs, including the liberal professions, business, housewives and students; 1,500 registered as building trades workers, which meant that they constantly shifted from job to job, if and when they worked; thus, leaving about 5,500 Party members for Bolshevization. In February, 1925, I was assigned the Sisyphean task of Bolshevizing the New York District over the sabotage and opposition of its District Organizer, Charles Krumbein. The only reason why I fought for this stupid and thankless job was because the Fosterites wanted to drive me out of New York, in order to separate me from the New York membership, among whom I wielded considerable influence. But the incontrovertible fact that I had not been assigned to definite Party work forced the hands of the Fosterites to agree to my assignment to the important post of shop nuclei organizer for the New York District, the largest and the most important in the United States.

Bolshevization meant a death-blow to branches and federations; it meant that the basic organizations of the Party would now be in the shops, all members working in the same shop constituting the new unit of the Party. By securing the Bolshevization task, our faction had the opportunity to build its support among the membership anew and from the ground up. It was a good move of gerrymandering ourselves into an ironclad majority. Members found to be working in the same shop were organized into a shop nucleus designated by a number, i.e., Shop Nucleus No. 1, or No. 2, or No. 3. I organized a nucleus in every shop of the district that had three or more members. By May I had organized only 25 shop nuclei totaling 126 party members, in establishments employing a total of only 16,022 workers. I had organized ten nuclei in the men's and women's garment industry, six in shoe factories, four in metal and machine shops, one in a restaurant and three others I forget where. My most important shop nuclei were in the Singer Sewing Machine Co. plant at Elizabeth, N. J., employing 7,500 workers; the *Evening Journal* plant printing the Hearst papers, employing 2,000 workers; the Miller Shoe Company's plant, employing 2,000 workers; and in the Board of Transportation of the City of New York, employing 1,500 workers. Since the combined membership of all the nuclei was only 126, they had an average membership of five. The largest nucleus, that in the Singer Plant, had a membership of 24. In the industrial metropolis of the world, this was a ludicrously pitiable record, but I am satisfied it was the best that could then be done. However, Moscow was not satisfied with the slow progress the Party was making in its Bolshevization, and on June twentieth, 1925, sent a letter to the Central Executive Committee of the Party, with detailed instructions on how the Party was to proceed with its Bolshevization. The only intelligible portion in that letter of the Communist International stated:

> During the visit of the representatives of your party to Moscow we held with them a consultation on the immediate tasks of the Workers Party in the sphere of organization and the methods of

carrying out the decision of the Plenum as expressed in the Theses of Comrade Zinoviev on Bolshevisation dealing with the duties of the Workers Party.

The rest was gibberish.

Nevertheless, Bolshevization became a factional football. The Foster group was afraid of it, because the powerful Finnish Federation opposed it. If Foster pressed reorganization, he faced the animosity of the Finnish Federation leaders. Besides, organized in the Finnish Federation branches, the Finnish leaders could deliver the Finnish vote as a bloc to Foster. Without the Finnish vote, Foster could not maintain his majority. In addition, the Lore group, which still was an important factor, opposed Bolshevization as nonsensical. Lore knew even then that Zinoviev was a nincompoop. Foster therefore rendered lip service in support of the Bolshevization campaign and in practice put all kinds of obstacles in its path. Of course, the Ruthenberg Caucus also sought to make political capital out of the reorganization campaign. It became the champion of Bolshevization. In those districts where our group was entrusted with the work of reorganizing, we organized the shop nuclei in such a way that we could control them. Whatever shop nuclei I did organize in District No. 2 were solid for the Ruthenberg group in the next elections for delegates to the District Convention, at which delegates to the National Convention of the Party were elected. But it was all much ado about nothing, and before long the Bolshevization issue died a natural death. Yet how much precious energy was wasted on it by our small group of zealots, how much misplaced idealism and enmity it generated—all because some fools in Moscow quite ignorant of American conditions wanted it. We might have concentrated all this earnest endeavor on something really of moment to America—the United States Supreme Court decision in the Gitlow case, for one.

But of course the crux of all factionalism at the time was the labor party issue. By the end of 1924 the Fosterites became the Anti-Labor-Party Caucus and we Ruthenbergians became the Pro-Labor-Party Caucus. That naturally made the Fosterites appear as simon pure, orthodox, Left of the Left Communists—

and how they wallowed in that glory! As the first act of their recently acquired revolutionism, they merged the *Liberator* (the Party-controlled organ for Left intellectuals and predecessor of the current *New Masses*), the *Labor Herald* (organ of the Trade Union Educational League) and *Soviet Russia Pictorial* (organ of the Friends of Soviet Russia), all of which had previously paraded as independent of the Communist Party, into one official monthly magazine of the Party, *The Workers Monthly*. Immediately we of the Ruthenberg group charged the Fosterites with sectarianism, arguing that they were thereby isolating the Party from the masses. Our emissary in Moscow, the redoubtable John Pepper (nee Josef Pogány), raised a tremendous hullaballoo at the Comintern about Fosterian Sectarianism and got all the Russian leaders in a dither. Thousands of dollars were wasted on cables between Moscow and Chicago, and New York and Moscow. Our caucus was hot and bothered about Fosterian Sectarianism, and the Foster caucus fumed and raged about Ruthenbergian Reformism. That fight went on for months, when subsequently Lovestone wrote me from Moscow:

> It might interest you to know that in the special Bolshevization Committee session this night Zinoviev made the following significant remark: 'Yesterday I had an American day and night. In the afternoon I saw one side. At night another side. The debate in the American Party is now over the question: "Shall the Party be only the Party of the dictatorship of the proletariat or shall it also be the Party of partial demand?" The answer of course is, that it shall be the Party of both.' John laid great stress on this. . . . John feels delighted at this being Zinn's view of the controversy after both sides saw him.

Needless to say, "partial demand" is "reform," "John" is Pepper and "Zinn" is affectionate New York City College style for Zinoviev. And of course the letter speaks for itself.

But how did Lovestone get to Moscow? . . . Thereby hangs a tale intertwined inextricably in the fight between the rival factions. Properly it antedates the Foster seizure of the Party, when Israel Amter was in Moscow as the accredited representative of the Party at the Comintern. Such a "Rep" is the highest in rank above all other representatives of the Party, accredited to the various auxiliary organizations of the Comintern, and he has absolute authority over all of them, including American Communists in the various schools, colleges, and institutes, in training at Moscow as organizers and propagandists. Moreover, the Party "Rep" is the liaison officer in all other respects, often consulted by the G. P. U. and other important branches of the Soviet government on all matters pertaining to the government of the United States, conditions in the country, and American visitors to Russia. His expenses are paid by the Comintern, as are the expenses of all other Party representatives in Moscow, whose number varies from time to time, but has been known to be around a hundred and even more, in the form of living quarters, special food privileges, and a comfortable monthly salary. Incidentally, the Comintern spent millions of dollars a year supporting such official "embassies" of the various Communist parties in Moscow, the largest official families being the Chinese, followed by the Germans, Hungarian and Italian and later the Austrian. In any event, when Foster came to power, he did not remove Amter. Since his policy was to proceed cautiously at first, he merely sent Earl Browder as the new emissary to the Profintern, to scout around and make contacts with the right Russian leaders.

Amter and Browder fell into the thick of this factional war that had been gaining in intensity ever since the 1924 Presidential elections. The Ruthenberg group felt that the time was ripe to deal Foster a body blow from which he could never recover, because of the debacle of the Party in the Presidential campaign. Ruthenberg was stationed at the National Headquarters of the Party in Chicago, and, with Jay Lovestone, handled matters from there for our faction. I took care of matters from New York; John Pepper, from Moscow. Lovestone was our traveling salesman. He toured the country for our faction and was ingenious in putting through proposals that made it necessary for the Central Executive Committee to finance his factional trips around the country. When the Central Executive Committee did not authorize a trip, the money was supplied to him out of the special caucus treasury which our group maintained. The caucus members helped defray the expenses of the factional fight by contributing generously whenever asked to do so. The Communist International decision on the La Follette policy had given us a fighting advantage because, although it really accepted Lore's policy, it savagely castigated Lore. Foster, Bittleman and Cannon, following that decision against Lore, had to engage in two-faced politics. With Lore they had to be confidential, promising him that in the near future he would be freed from the blight of the Communist International attack. They met with Lore, Poyntz and with the leaders of the needle trades who backed Lore, in a desperate effort to keep these lines together. At the same time, they had to give evidence to the leaders of the Communist International that they were fighting the Lore Group and its alleged "anti-Communist" heresy. We of the Ruthenberg group hammered away at this duplicity at every opportunity, recognizing that in so doing we might cause a breach in the Foster group which would give us the majority of the Party.

Every group maintained an organized caucus with well-oiled caucus machinery. The Party members attended secret caucus meetings into the wee hours of the morning, listening to confidential reports on what went on in the Communist International or in the Central Executive Committee and to all the factional gossip that flooded the Party. Besides, each caucus maintained a mimeograph machine and a staff, to edit and issue confidential caucus bulletins, which were "prohibited" by the Party. These bulletins hold a very special place in Communist literature. They are almost literally sizzling with vitriolic attacks against factional opponents. The Party was divided into two warring camps. The comrades, the leaders as well as the rank and file, were virtually at each other's throat. Under such circumstances it was only natural to expect that the issues would reach Moscow and there be adjudicated. After all, we were all acting under orders from our Moscow connections, and the storm we raised in America was to a very large extent raised for Moscow's consumption.

The Executive Committee of the Comintern decided to hold a plenary meeting in the early part of 1925. A meeting of the Central Executive Committee was called to consider the sending of delegates. The Ruthenberg Group decided to send Lovestone and Ruthenberg. The Foster Group picked Foster and Cannon. As soon as the decision was made, Jay Lovestone was off like lightning to Moscow. Every day in Moscow before Foster and Cannon arrived would be advantageous to his group. Foster and Cannon, though they tried, could not outrace Lovestone.

Meantime, Foster had made up his mind about the labor party issue and took a stand on it. That occurred when he publicly hailed our disgracefully small Presidential vote of 1924 as a victory for the Party. Frankly, I was disappointed with the vote and disgusted with Foster's hypocrisy. It was clear to me even then that the pitiable vote of slightly over thirty thousand for us out of thirty million, and the five million for Senator Robert M. La Follette, showed that, while politically we Communists did not have much of a chance with American workers and farmers, the latter were strongly inclined to support a genuine third party, a Farmer-Labor Party free of Communist influence. That, to me, was the lesson of the 1924 Presidential election. It was sad but true, and our only chance was to tie ourselves to the Farmer-Labor Party movement, but do so more subtly than ever, without betraying our hand in it, until we had managed to wear down public prejudice against us, meantime however taking a public stand in favor of the idea and on the basis of that agitation recruit what adherents and sympathizers we could. This was substantially Charles E. Ruthenberg's position. He wrote:

> Our party has made its greatest gains through its united front farmer-labor policy. . . The slogan, 'For A Class Labor Party' is still the best road open for the building of the Workers Party and making it a mass Communist Party.

Not so Foster. Tongue in cheek, brazenly defying facts, he proclaimed:

> Although five million ballots cast amount to a large vote, the outcome in reality constitutes a serious defeat for the La Follette movement in view of the previous overestimates of its strength. . . The Workers Party is now entering upon the third stage of its policy regarding the Farmer-Labor Party movement. This consists

> in going one step further than dropping the Farmer-Labor Party as an organization and also dropping it as a slogan.

Foster did not believe one word of that himself. He took that stand, only because, to maintain his power and his majority, he had to have the support of the Lore Caucus, and Ludwig Lore opposed our labor policy on principle. I thought Lore was doctrinaire about it, yet he was honest and courageous; on this occasion, in my opinion, Foster was neither.

He and Cannon had to spend a few days in New York, to fix up their fences with the Lore group, in order that their house should not collapse while they were away. Lovestone arrived in Moscow in January, 1925, as did Foster and Cannon. Ruthenberg did not arrive until February. An American Commission was constituted, to handle the American Party question, consisting of Nicholas Bukharin, Klara Zetkin and the Finnish exile, Kuusinen, then Secretary of the Communist International. The final decision, however, rested solely in the hands of the Russian leaders then in power, as Lovestone writing to me from Moscow then indicated:

> Tomorrow Zinoviev gets in from the other big city and I will then know definitely when I can see him . . . and at eleven the day after Piatnitsa [Josef Piatnitsky, head of the Organization Department of the Communist International]. These birds are hard to catch.

And in another letter:

> Have not yet been able to get Bukharin. Wednesday he will have me see Stalin.

In 1925 it was already important to get Stalin on your side. In still another letter, which Lovestone, with a humorless eye on his own historic importance, entitled pompously "The Dawes Plan and the American Workers," he wrote of a two-hour talk he had with Zinoviev, in which Zinoviev was ready to make a somersault on the La Follette issue and to instruct the American Party to work inside the La Follette movement, even though less than a year ago the Party was prevented by Zinoviev and the Communist International from so doing. On Lore he reported that Foster and Cannon had opposed the suggestion that Lore come to Moscow to defend himself, and were instead stating that it is their proposal to have Lore and his followers expelled from the Party. Lovestone waxed indignant about that, not, of course, because he loved Lore or justice, but because he wanted to embarrass Foster and Cannon:

> I am going to the Secretariat and will again raise hell about Ludwig, will demand the reopening of his question, that he be instructed to pack up and go at once. I will make the bastards [Foster and Cannon] show their true colors.

But Ludwig Lore did not pack up and did not go to Moscow. The fight in Moscow over the American Party question went on for over three months. For a quarter of a year the outstanding leaders of the Communist movement of the United States were in Moscow.

One may wonder what happened in the United States during those long three months. The Communist Party members all had their eyes focused on Moscow. From Moscow the contending caucus headquarters received cables, letters, documents, instructions, advice on policy. As soon as cables or letters were received by the contending caucuses, the caucus machinery went into immediate operation. Secret caucus meetings were called. The mimeograph machines were flooded with ink, and caucus bulletins went out to every nook and corner of the Party. Besides, the caucus spies were kept very busy during those exciting days. They shadowed their factional opponents, penetrated their caucus meetings, rifled letter boxes to get their hands on caucus documents and at the same time, while covering their own tracks as best they could, collected evidence for a case on the "illegal" factional activities of their opponents. The Foster group did it in all seriousness against the Ruthenberg caucus, and the Ruthenberg caucus did it in the same serious vein against the Foster caucus. Yet notwithstanding this intense factional atmosphere and the turmoil it created, the Party, with most of its leading figures in Moscow, continued to carry on its political and trade union activities, each side utilizing them to gain a factional advantage over its opponent, or to involve or catch the opponent in a serious deviation from what was considered the Moscow-ordained true path of Communism.

As the news began to come in of Lore's disfavor in Moscow, both the Foster and Ruthenberg caucuses began their witch-hunting against Lore and his followers, for whom life inside of the Party became a living hell. Far from ending the factional warfare, the Comintern decision provided for the holding of a national convention in the immediate future to thrash out the issue, and thus served merely to intensify further the struggle for the capture of the majority of the Party. It was full of what in the Comintern was called *Flicken Politik* [indecisive politics]. It was a labyrinthian maze. The more you tried to decipher it, the more difficult it became. Moscow was famous for such decisions, and any one who had anything to do with the Comintern soon became well acquainted with them. There was, first of all, *Flicken Politik* in the decision on the estimate of the vote received by the La Follette movement. Foster had called the election results a victory for the Workers Party and a defeat for the La Follette movement. Moscow declared:

> It must be recognized that in the elections La Follette gained an important victory. . . .

yet:

> Our Party met with a defeat which was not to be avoided under the given circumstances.

But to add to the confusion, it went on to state:

> That does not mean that the tactics of the Workers Party were not correct.

That gave Foster the opportunity to go to the membership and declare that the Communist International approved his tactics in the 1924 elections, though the Communist International did not positively state that those tactics were correct. Some months later, although nothing had changed since 1924, the Muscovite master minds of Bolshevism in 1925 declared in reference to the La Follette movement:

> The path of the proletariat can even lead through such false roads [the La Follette movement] in its first steps towards its constitution as a class.

Every important Moscow decision has its scapegoat. In this decision it was Ludwig Lore, one of the most decent of the Communist leaders in America. We implemented that aspect of the decision by calling it, The Struggle Against Lore's Opportunism. But Lore's opportunism was not separable from Foster's opportunism, because they mutually supported each other's policies. To Lore belongs the distinction of having early in 1924 formulated the very policy on La Follette which the Communist International itself subsequently adopted. But Moscow was not prepared to throw overboard so docile and submissive a tool as Foster, certainly not for a mere Communist of principles like Lore. Therefore, when Foster came to Moscow, none other than Lore was picked for scapegoat, to ward off the fire from Foster. Lore, Moscow declared, represented a non-Communist tendency in the Party and misrepresented the policy of the Communist International on almost every question, spurring on the heresy hunt against him by the following declaration:

> The Executive proposes to the Workers Party to come to a definite decision on the Lore question at its next Congress. In any case the Executive is of the opinion that the Central Committee of the Party is not the place for such an opportunist.

The Communist International executives of course had the power forthwith to expel Lore. But that would not have served their purpose. They wanted his expulsion to come at the end of a campaign in which the Party would be bombarded on the heresies of Lore, while at the same time the pressure of the Party would be used among Lore's followers, who held important posts in the trade unions, to have them break away from Lore and throw themselves at the mercy of the Party. Of additional importance was the fact that Lore, through his editorship, controlled an important and very influential daily paper, the oldest radical newspaper in the United States, *The New Yorker Volkszeitung*. Time was needed to organize the Communist forces in the Volkszeitung Publishing Company for the drive to take over the paper and its valuable property for the Party. And lastly, Moscow had hopes that Lore would listen to the pleas Foster would take back to him, and go to Moscow to take up his case. If Lore would accept, that would lead, for some time, to a voluntary separation of Lore from the American Party. In Moscow they had a much better chance than we had in New York to get Lore to "confess" that his views were deviations from Communism and to agree to spend some time in Communist work under Comintern direction either in Moscow or some other place. Such was the disciplinary technique initiated by Zinoviev, presumably with the approval of Lenin and Trotsky, which, perfected by Stalin, ultimately led to the most obscene of political spectacles, the Moscow Demonstration Trials with their masochistic "confessions." Yet, although Lore was picked as scapegoat, to protect Foster, provision was also made to keep Foster vulnerable. Thus, before the American Party leaders left Moscow, with the well wishes of the Communist International leaders to make a good fight, and thrash things out in their national convention, the Moscow leaders in secret meetings with Lovestone, Pepper and Ruthenberg mapped out for them just how the fight against Foster should be conducted. Whether they did as much for the Foster side against us, I do not know.

Meantime, Earl Browder had been chosen by the Foster majority to act as the Secretary of the Party during Ruthenberg's sojourn in Moscow. He was fanatical in his zeal to promote Foster as the outstanding Communist leader in the United States. At times when he defended Foster, in his deadly monotone, drawing his breath through his mustache, in the manner of the proverbial insidious Japanese spy of popular fiction, heaving sighs of compassion, as he rolled his eyes toward heaven and clasped his hands in the proverbial manner of sanctimonious missionaries, I feared that even his corn-fed Kansas frame would collapse under the emotional burden of his utterances and we might lose a dearly-beloved comrade. He never proclaimed an original idea and was satisfied to walk in the footsteps of his master. In sheer self-defense I would shut my eyes, sorry that I could not also shut my ears when he spoke, and seek some measure of solace in the vision of the dog on the old phonograph advertisement entitled, "His Master's Voice"—a far handsomer vision than Browder's face contorted with his obnoxious style of oratory. Next to Foster, in those days, Browder worshiped Losovsky and the Profintern. He accepted the Communist International authority as a matter of course, but held the Profintern in higher esteem. He diligently read all the Communist tracts and all the bulletins of the Profintern, and accepted them without question as the gospel truth. These he absorbed in his uncritical mind as the acme of intellectual achievement, with the consequence that he soon began to believe himself next to Foster, the greatest intellectual Communist in America. Stalin had his Lenin; Browder had only his Foster.

A greater zealot in a factional cause than Browder was hard to find. I remember one dramatic incident during the feverish days when the leaders of the factions were still in Moscow. Browder happened to be in New York at the district headquarters. Amter, who had his office on the third floor, had just completed typing a factional bulletin against the Finnish members of the Party. In that document he had referred to the Finns as, "the White Guard Finns"—no less. While he was holding the document in his hands and reading it to a number of his caucus comrades, Browder, who was on the floor below, was tipped off by one of the Foster Caucus spies of what was going on in Amter's office. Breathless, the Acting Secretary of the Communist Party of the United States rushed up the stairs, burst into Amter's room and seized one corner of the typewritten sheet which Amter was holding in his hand. I was in the room at the time and saw the whole drama. Panting and breathless, Browder gasped, "As General Secretary of the Party and in the name of the Central Executive Committee, I order you to turn over the document you have in your hand to me." Amter flushed and answered calmly, "This paper which you are holding is my own personal matter and does not concern you or the Party. I will not let you have it." And he tore it away, leaving Browder holding a tiny corner of paper tightly between his fingers. "Under pain of discipline," Browder sharply retorted, his red face turning white with rage, "You will have to answer to the Party for your flagrant defiance of Party discipline." But Amter said nothing, as he slowly and deliberately folded the sheet and clenched his fist around it. Many comrades had gathered by this time. There were angry remarks from members of both factions. Browder shook with anger, his eyes became bloodshot. Turning to me, he said: "As a member of the Central Executive Committee, I, the secretary of the Party, order you to direct Comrade Amter to turn the paper he has in his hand over to me. It is a caucus document and hence a Party document of the greatest importance to the Party." Perfectly unperturbed, I smiled and said, "If what Amter has in his hand is a caucus document and you want it, please turn over all of your caucus documents first." He thereupon left the room, growling, "You will all answer for your factionalism and indiscipline to the Central Executive Committee." But that ended the incident, for his own factional record was far from clear.

That was dramatically illustrated shortly after the Comintern had rendered its decision on the American Question and some time prior to the return of our chief Party leaders from Moscow. The decision had been cabled to each caucus secretly early in April, weeks before it was officially communicated to the Party, each caucus receiving from its own leaders in Moscow lengthy exegeses by cable as to its real meaning. As I have already stated, the decision castigated Lore while adopting his policy. Now, the leaders of the Communist needle trades faction were strictly loyal to Lore on the La Follette issue, and it was quite a job for the Fosterites to make them understand the Comintern decision, not as any normal human being would understand it but as the Fosterites wanted them to understand it. We Ruthenbergians proposed to capitalize on that difficulty by simply proving to the Comintern that the needle trade leaders were Loreites; this was a pleasant and easy job for Lovestone, Ruthenberg and Pepper, because it was obvious and true. Foster, moreover, made that task even easier for our side, for instead of defending the needle trades leaders, who had always supported his caucus loyally, he turned tail, repudiated them completely before the Comintern leaders as incorrigible Loreites and disclaimed all political responsibility for them. At the same time, he sent instructions to his one-man brain trust in Chicago, Alexander Bittleman, on how to save the continued support of the needle trades leaders for the Foster Caucus. I did not read those instructions, but they told their own story in the nature of Bittleman's sudden activity.

First, my spies reported to me that Bittleman had come to New York; next, on April eighth, without previously consulting with me, a member of the Central Executive Committee, Bittleman introduced a resolution before the New York District Committee, which contained in part the following official statement made by the Central Executive Committee at its preceding meeting in Chicago:

> We do not wish to imply, nor do we wish to create the impression, that our comrades in the needle trades are opportunistic.

after sharply criticizing them for their "Loreist tendencies." Finally, again without consulting me, although I was a member of the Party Needle Trades Committee, Bittleman presented the same Central Executive Committee resolution, backed up by a concurring resolution of the New York District Committee, before a meeting he convoked of the needle trades membership of the Party. This was how Foster proposed to whitewash himself before his needle trades supporters after stabbing them in the back. He could execute this maneuver because he had a majority on both the C. E. C. and the New York District Committee, but not without violating the most elementary rules of informing the Ruthenbergian members of both these Party bodies. I caught up with Bittleman at the meeting of the needle trades membership. And there opened up on him. I charged him with all the crimes from malfeasance in office to outright treason. Bittleman counter-charged that I had violated discipline by refusing to support a C. E. C. decision and even criticizing it in public, an unpardonable crime in a member of the C. E. C.; now being magnanimous, he wanted to see whether I was really a good Bolshevik: I could convince him of it, if I forthwith voted for that resolution, notwithstanding that I had just castigated it mercilessly—that would prove to Bittleman that I understood "the highest discipline" and was indeed a good Bolshevik. Whereupon, I told Bittleman to go chase himself and, after consulting then and there with Lifshitz and Weinstone, introduced a statement of censure against the C. E. C. Then, having meantime learned through my spies that the Fosterites were caucusing that day, I sent the following telegram to Earl Browder and Max Bedacht in Chicago, the Party headquarters:

> I prefer charges against Bittleman, Manley, Johnstone, Carlson for holding caucus with Party members New York on Comintern decision laying plans for convention, thus opening convention period letter follows.

and followed it with a letter to Browder, in which I enclosed the following Foster Caucus document stolen by one of my spies:

> Dear Comrade: A very important meeting will be held this coming Saturday evening at six p. m. sharp at Great Central Palace, 90 Clinton Street, Room 11. You must attend without fail. Comrade Bittleman will be present.
>
> M. Unjust.

Then, accompanied by several members of the Ruthenberg group, I went to the meeting. We were refused admission. But our spies were among the seventy-five Party members at that Foster Caucus. To justify his holding that meeting secretly, Bittleman telegraphed Chicago that it was an official meeting of responsible Party workers on confidential matters. As a member of the C. E. C., I was certainly as much entitled to be present at such a meeting as Bittleman, yet I had been refused admission. Therefore, just to rub it in, I wrote a letter to Browder, in which I not only denounced Bittleman for infractions of Party rules but also gave him proof that I had the more efficient spy service and therefore knew what went on in their caucus, by stating in part:

> Comrade Bittleman opened the caucus meeting by giving a lengthy report on the decision of the Communist International on the American Party question. This he did in violation of party discipline. As political secretary of the Party he knew that the Communist International decision must first be submitted to the Central Executive Committee for it to decide how the membership shall be officially informed of it. The significance of the breach

> of party discipline is still more apparent when one realized that this gathering was held a day after the Executive Committee had decided upon Comrade Browder's motion to elect a committee to liquidate the factional grouping in the party.

This time we Ruthenbergians had caught the Fosterites red-handed. But both factions were really equally guilty of scheming, conniving factionalism of the lowest order.

However, the feathers really began to fly when Cannon, Foster, Lovestone and Ruthenberg returned from Moscow early in May. Lovestone and Ruthenberg were elated that they had come back from Moscow with a decision that gave our group a more than fighting chance to win back the Party. They immediately went into conference with the leading comrades in New York, and before they left for Chicago spoke before a large membership caucus of our group. Foster and Cannon did not look so happy. They had to mend their fences with Lore's immediate group as well as with the needle trades leaders, or lose the majority and control of the Party. Foster kept fuming about Pepper and "that bastard Lovestone." It was clear from his attitude that he had no intention of attempting to make peace, as demanded by the Communist International. It was also apparent from the reports we had about the caucus meetings of the Foster group in New York that a rift was taking place between Foster and Cannon, that Cannon, though he did not express it, was disappointed with the political leadership of Foster and held him accountable for the bad showing they had made in Moscow. As for Lore and his followers, they were up in arms. The breach between them and Foster broke out rather violently, not to say openly, at the meeting of the Central Executive Committee, called to consider the Communist International decision, which took place in Chicago on May 12 and 13. This proved to be one of the most dramatic meetings of the Central Executive Committee I had ever attended. It was a setting fit for Homeric heroes, not only for the national convention which was to follow in a few months. Personal feelings ran high and were especially bitter in the speeches of Foster, Lore and Juliet Stuart Poyntz. Cannon and Foster had their administration to save, Lore and Poyntz their political lives in the Party. At this meeting Cannon tried to keep his sails turned to meet the wind and, instead of backing up Foster, straddled, in order to be free to act in the future.

Foster, speaking under a very great strain, recalled that although the year before he had opposed Zinoviev's proposal that the Communist International send a representative to the American Party to assist in liquidating factionalism, he had been the first to propose it to the Comintern this year. He was quite certain, he said, that neither the Ruthenberg Group nor Moscow really took a serious view of his alliance with the Lore Group. He then attacked what he called our fake labor party policy, claiming that on this, the main political question before Moscow, he and his group had been vindicated and upheld. As for his relations with Lore, Foster declared:

> When I was in New York I met Comrade Lore. We talked of the trip to Moscow, whether it would be the best thing for him to go. I put it in this light: If you don't go to Moscow, it will be interpreted as a complete admission of all the charges against you and your group. If you go to Moscow and maintain your position you will be condemned one hundred percent. If you see leaders and say you want to go along, they will whitewash you and you will escape completely.

This statement by Foster gives a good insight into the workings of the Comintern. It was governed by its own rules, which were made by the Bolshevik leaders. These rules involved no ethical concepts. The question of honesty, intellectual or otherwise, did not count and personal integrity was dismissed as only a bourgeois virtue. What did matter, was that Communists of all countries must without reservations accept the control which Moscow imposed upon them. Foster knew the rules, and was perfectly satisfied to play the game of his Moscow bosses. In this respect he acted like most of us who were leading Communists in the United States. To Foster it was perfectly proper for Lore to go to Moscow, in order to give his pledge to the Russian leaders that he would go along with them in everything they did or said. He advised Lore to do so and resented the fact that Lore considered his intellectual honesty and personal integrity above blind obedience to the Communist International.

That Central Executive Committee meeting turned into a lynching bee, with Lore as victim. The Comintern had given the signal to destroy Lore by driving him out of the Communist movement and ruining his reputation in the labor movement. Every member of the Central Executive Committee flew into a rage against Lore. Every Central Executive Committee member present at the meeting and all the officials of the Party who were invited to attend clamored for the floor, in order to put themselves on record against Lore. Lovestone, who in 1923 together with Pepper tried to get Lore's support, took credit as the gallant knight who discovered the treacherous role that Lore was playing against Communism and the working class. Ruthenberg attacked him as an opportunist and a Social-Democrat whose views and activity had nothing in common with Communism. I attacked him as one who as far back as 1919, when the Communist Labor Party was formed, was an incorrigible opportunist and Social-Democrat, and I took prideful credit for the fact that I had been instrumental in keeping him out of the leading committee of the newly-formed Communist Labor Party.

Lore presented a pitiable figure when he took the floor. He appeared like a man thrown into a den of lions who were that moment going to pounce upon him and devour him. His voice sounded as if it came from one who had been painfully hurt. I expected him at any moment to break into tears. Under the circumstances, his speech was one of great restraint. He said in part:

> We have a party of caucauses. . . I left the Minority [Ruthenberg Group] on account of the La Follette struggle. After the last national convention we joined the Foster Group. After a while things changed. The alliance grew weaker. . . We felt that the Majority was beginning to leave the sound sane way and was coming dangerously near to adopting the Pepper policy of adventurism. . . As editor of the *Volkszeitung* I cannot consult the Communist International or the Central Executive Committee on every important event that takes place. I am editor of a daily

paper and must comment on such events immediately. I must therefore write on events as I understand and see them. . . All these articles were written by Lore and he alone stands responsible. . . All the enemies are now branded as Trotskyites. I never made bones of the fact that I am sympathetic to Trotsky. Why I should be, Ruthenberg does not understand, because he does not understand Trotskyism.

Lore then went on to explain how he was condemned for publishing chapters from Trotsky's book on Lenin. But, he charged correctly that William Weinstone, then Secretary of the Workers International Relief, a branch of the Moscow Relief organization, the Mopr, sold the same book to a publisher and turned the money he received over to the Party. Lore further stated on this matter that he knew a Communist publisher, the International Publishers, who refused to do so and warned others not to do so. Lore continued:

The big mistake that I made was not to go to Moscow. The comrades of the Majority know it was not done in defiance to Moscow. The first time when Comrade Gitlow insisted that I should go, I would have liked to. . . The second time I would have liked to go, but we did not have an associate editor. . . I stated that to Comrades Browder, Bittleman and Foster. . . Foster advised me strongly to go. He also told me that it would be bad for me if I would not endorse Zinoviev's program fully. He also told me it might be advisable to go alone because then only John Pepper would be there. I felt that after I had once been betrayed, when Olgin went to represent me, after he stated he stood for everything I had written and could prove it by the Communist International itself, I said that one betrayal was enough and that I would like to go alone.

Lore concluded his speech with these words:

I am not the Social-Democrat you made me out to be. Thirty-nine years ago I joined an illegal young Socialist organization in Germany. Here I joined the Communist movement from its inception, when many who were criticizing me were with Abe Cahan and the *Forward* [Olgin]. I was doing my bit for the Communist movement. I am not going to quit the Party. I don't think you will expel me. You can take all kinds of organizational measures.

Whatever you decide I will try to enforce and carry out. I will try to help the movement as much as I understand. It was I who brought the *Volkszeitung* into the movement. I have brought the revolutionary Germans into the movement. I have never been an enemy but always stood for the Communist International and for Soviet Russia. Nothing you will do will make a reformer of me, less of a revolutionist than I am today.

We were pretty mean and heartless about Lore. But at the time we did not even question the ethics of hounding an innocent scapegoat at the behest of the Comintern leaders. Indeed, we felt no more compunction in hounding out of the Party and out of the revolutionary labor movement, if we could, a man who honestly and courageously, and far more ably than many of us, had served the cause for two score years than in swatting an annoying fly. It occurred to none of us, I am sure, that through no fault of his, but simply because it was his turn in the political game to be scapegoat, we were breaking his heart. All of us took our activity in the Communist movement with deadly seriousness, Lore included. It was a matter of life-or-death to remain in the Party. Yet not a voice was lifted in the Central Executive Committee in defense of this comrade, no one even bothered to recall his previous services in extenuation of his artificially-concocted "crime" and all of us voted for the resolution that branded him as a pariah. Since, moreover the Comintern had decreed that there was a political contagion known as Loreism, we duly passed a resolution, pledging to wage a merciless campaign against it. Had the Comintern decreed that it was our duty to fight the Albegensian heresy in our midst, I wonder how many of us would have paused to inquire first into the nature of Albegensianism before passing by unanimous vote a resolution pledging to campaign against it. Solemnly we laid the ground for Lore's expulsion from the Communist Party. He was as good as out already, since he had the temerity to speak favorably of Trotsky, which sealed his doom in Moscow, if not yet with us. We did not really understand the struggle for leadership that was then raging in Moscow, and, busy with our own squabbles, were primarily concerned with staying on the good side of that omnipotent source of our political prerogatives in the United States, the Comintern. When Juliet Stuart Poyntz took the floor the atmosphere became electric. She was of American stock, fair, about thirty years old, rather tall, rather fleshy, rather good looking. Though her bearing was aristocratic, she was not snobbish, mixed well with the rank and file Communists and was very popular among them. She was headstrong and ambitious. She was the outstanding woman in the Party, an excellent speaker and highly dramatic in her delivery. She craved the public platform, enjoyed the applause of the listening crowds. She delighted in taking part in inner Party politics, aspired to prominent Party leadership, and in the Foster-Lore caucus was a powerful figure who had to be reckoned with. Though a good agitator, she was a poor organizer. Her knowledge of the movement and its underlying philosophy was very superficial. As a fighter for her faction and for her political beliefs she was hard to equal. Her venom and tenacity knew no limits. She was a spitfire when she took the floor at the Central Executive Committee meeting to defend herself against charges of Loreism. Foster and his supporters squirmed and fumed at her sallies. William F. Dunne, the Wild Bull from Montana, shouted and yelled derisively at her. Cannon puffed and chewed away at his cigar, muttering curses under his breath. Foster paced up and down the room, his face flushed with anger, and when her sting hurt most, he would interject, "It's a damn lie." As she hurled one bombshell after another against the Foster group and its leaders, we of the Ruthenberg group listened with glee and often roared with laughter at the discomfort she caused Foster, Cannon, Bittleman, Browder and the others. Her speech laid bare the intrigues, plots and counter-plots of Communist inner Party politics and undressed the leaders of the Foster group, exposing them for what they were. Her very first remark was a bombshell to the Foster group which all the time was trying to create the impression that there was no link between it and Lore. She said:

> After arriving here, I was quite astonished to hear my name brought up by Comrade Cannon as the leader of a supposed group. I was invited once to become a member of a hundred per cent caucus. Perhaps that is why I am qualified to become a hundred

per cent member of the Cannon caucus. Bittleman calls us Right Wingers. In the interest of clarity, what is and what isn't a Lore group? That the majority should determine. There is no Lore group. I am a member and follower of the Foster-Lore-Cannon group. . .

Poyntz continued:

> At the national convention of 1923-4 we joined the Foster caucus at once.

Foster turned crimson at her next remarks and cursed as only Foster knows how, when she said with a good deal of passion:

> During the convention Foster hesitated to take over the power in the Party. He insisted that the only inducement that would lead him to take over the power in the Party would be a pledge by all in his caucus that they would loyally support him until the next convention of the Party. We gave him that pledge. I at last got my main aim in life at the last national convention. I as a member of the Foster Group was to defend and if necessary to die for Comrade Foster.

She then related how she went back to New York as Foster's missionary. The moment she mentioned New York, Charles Krumbein, interrupted her, by hurling insulting phrases, shouting and scowling at her fiercely. But she only smiled ironically, glared at him with contempt and continued:

> There was no group in New York ready to live and die for Comrade Foster. The problem for us was to create a political group for the Majority. . . If any one organized the Lore Group in New York, it was Comrade Foster. . . In New York we gathered into our group Comrade Grecht. . .

Rebecca Grecht was Foster's confidante in New York. He was always with her when he came in from Chicago. She was a short red-haired girl of about nineteen, vivacious, highly emotional and greatly attached to Foster:

> We were the ones who demanded that the Minority district organizer be dismissed. When Krumbein came we took him to our hearts and tried to make him feel at home. Comrade Krumbein did come to caucus meetings, but not to all of them. The

> reason he gave was that while he was in thorough agreement with us it would be advisable for him as the District Organizer not to come regularly, in order to give the impression that he was, in New York, not allied with a group and acting impartially. . . Whenever Foster, Cannon and Bittleman came to New York they caucused with us, and when we met, we met in no other place but the offices of the *Volkszeitung*, 15 Spruce Street, New York.

She charged that Browder came to them and asked them to abandon their opposition to the endorsement of La Follette in the interest of group loyalty. When she spoke on the Bolshevization of the party she exclaimed sarcastically:

> We have heard about fake farmer-labor parties, about fake united fronts, and so forth, but we haven't heard about fake Bolshevization. The Majority is carrying on a policy of fake Bolshevization. . . Their professional Bolsheviser is Comrade Bittleman. He came to New York to Bolshevize New York. . . The group that he has worked with, that has supported him continuously, he is now trying to assassinate.

Nor did she relent when she turned her offensive against Foster and Cannon:

> If anything, we are Left Wing in the Foster group. We are the most Communist wing of that group. We disagreed with their last thesis in abandoning the slogan for independent political action. . . . We did not agree with its omnibus united front policy. We were dissatisfied with the administration of the Party and particularly the New York District. Meanwhile, Foster decided to build up his own caucus and send us to the bow wows. . . Everybody understands that Lore has been a factional football in this factional fight.
>
> At the present time the Lore Group is an ardent supporter of the majority Foster Group. The charge that I have an alliance with the minority is sheer nonsense. I am not even on speaking terms with most members of the minority. I am a disillusioned Fosterite. Browder wants us to remain illegitimate children of the Majority Group, that we should continue to support Foster. Any group that does not publicly announce that I am a member of it will not have me as a part of it—furthermore, I will not under any circumstances be part of it.

She brought her attack to a dramatic closing by loudly declaring:

> I stand by the Comintern. I support it organizationally and ideologically. I support the Old Guard of the Russian Communist Party against Trotsky.

She was greeted by derisive shouts and cat calls from the Foster ranks as she ended, and by silence from the Ruthenberg forces. This silence had been prearranged by the Ruthenberg caucus, which knew in advance that Poyntz would make revelations and attack the Foster group. In her break with Foster, Poyntz however did not break with the Comintern, for she gave her pledge to the Moscow leaders and took a stand against Trotsky, which marked her separation from Lore. She thus saved herself from expulsion. As for her pride, she covered her capitulation to the Comintern and her cowardly desertion of Lore by her fighting attitude against Foster. Yet she it was who had been nicknamed "the Joan of Arc of the Communist movement."

She continued her fight against Foster and for her political life in the Party. In this she was clandestinely supported by us of the Ruthenberg group. The man who carried on the secret negotiations with her was Jack Stachel, known in the Party as "the medicine faker," because before he became a Party official he had sold patent medicines. He was at the time the New York District Secretary of the Young Workers League (The Communist Party youth organization). We of the Ruthenberg group realized that the Poyntz exposures on the Lore question were just the ammunition we needed with which to blast Foster out of control of the Party. Through our caucus apparatus the Party was flooded with mimeographed copies of the Poyntz speech, with copies of her resolutions and whatever dirt she was ready to unload against Foster. However, that did not stop the Ruthenberg group in the Central Executive Committee from agreeing upon a joint resolution against Poyntz, which was published in the *Daily Worker* of July 5th, 1925, calling for the liquidation of Poyntzism as well as Loreism. This resolution declared that Comrade Poyntz was the most energetic leader of the Lore group. But she was safe, because she had eaten the Comintern's humble pie and had made a deal with us. Thus was the game played by all factions concerned, hypocritically and dishonestly. Poyntz subsequently confessed her sins again in a manner satisfactory to the powers that be and the Communist International. In later years she even became an agent of the G. P. U., the powerful secret police of the Soviet Union. This Joan of Arc, who for years was a stormy petrel in the communist movement, whose speeches brought forth thunderous applause from her Communist listeners, finally fell into disgrace, was denounced by Krumbein in the New York press, as an agent of the United States Department of Justice, and disappeared from her living quarters in New York City, becoming the center of a mystery that has not yet been solved.

CHAPTER VIII

THE MOSCOW CAT AND ITS AMERICAN MOUSE

HAVE you ever watched a cat toy with a mouse? You may have in your boyhood or girlhood, when you were still somewhat of a savage, and rather relished the spectacle. Since I am confessing all, I admit that I found the cat-and-mouse game far more fascinating as an observer on the sidelines than as participant, especially on the mouse end of it. This holds both literally and metaphorically. Watching a sleek cat seize a mouse, toy with it, hold it lightly with one paw or with two, release it, flick it suddenly with a rear paw and bowl it over, allow it to escape for a moment only to pounce upon it once more, rebuke it in a fatherly manner, with the feline whiskers like a forest of pikes around its frightened eyes as the mouse quivers between the cat's velvet jaws—it is a cruel game. We all played at this sort of game in the Communist Party, relishing the role of the cat when chastising a deviator for political heresy, real or invented for convenience. But we were tyros as cats by comparison with the Russian leaders, to whom the entire American Communist Party seemed to be no more than a nest of mice to toy with. And the favorite mouse in that nest was William Z. Foster. I suppose he was the favorite as a mouse because he was more playful than the other American leaders: he trembled, he maneuvered, he yielded, he tried again and again, never talked back to the cat, and was always properly mousy with the feline masters of the Comintern. I don't know to what extent the Comintern leaders relished this cat-and-mouse game with the leaders of the American Party, but it seems to me that the game began to gain in intensity around 1924-25, when Stalin, still apparently a member of the Zinoviev-Kamenev-Stalin triumvirate in the Russian Political Bureau, was beginning to emerge as top boss of the Russian Party, of which the Comintern was of course no more than an appendage.

We puny rodents of the American Party leadership took ourselves very seriously. We gnawed through a straw here and sliver there, flattering ourselves that we were seriously undermining the capitalist system of the United States, but most of the time we gnawed each other, chewing catch-as-catch-can at tail or ear or making the fur fly. That was what happened at the Central Executive Committee meeting at which Lore and Poyntz were chewed to pieces and which from our close-to-the-floor vantagepoint was the opening gun in huge strategic operations of the factional war. Foster, intent on maintaining his majority at the forthcoming national convention, reorganized entire districts, brought our followers up on charges, castigated, suspended, expelled, even resorted to outright gangsterism. We in turn protested, sending cables to the Comintern and arousing members of our own faction to savage frenzy at meetings, private, semi-private and public. We also plotted and schemed, finally seizing upon the Comintern decision for a parity commission to supervise the convention arrangements and to settle controversial matters between the factions as a possibility for our side. The Comintern appointed one and the same person as chairman of the parity commission and as its official observer and representative to the convention, investing him with the full authority and all the prerogatives of a top-ranking Communist International Representative. We felt that we could turn the Parity Commission into a mighty weapon for our group, and either check Foster's efforts to hold power under any and all circumstances or at least make life miserable for him by overruling many of his actions in the Parity Commission. We were therefore eager to have it constituted. Foster had the advantage over us in his control of the Party machine; we planned to make the higher-ranking Comintern parity commission our means for wresting that power from him. But it was easier planned than done. Confronted with the accomplished fact that Foster had the power, surely the Communist International was sufficiently power-conscious to respect and recognize his power regardless of the foul means employed in obtaining it. That was at least how Foster reckoned. But he was altogether wrong, because the Communist International could not respect a "power" that was merely the plaything of its own indulgence. In dealing with us, the Comintern respected only its own power.

Within the Central Executive Committee the uppermost question for weeks was, "When would the Comintern Rep. arrive?" The question became an important one in the Central Executive Committee, because the national convention date could not be definitely set without him. Foster tried to utilize the delay by getting the date for the convention set anyway. On June eleventh, 1925, the Foster group of the Central Executive Committee voted that the following cable be sent to Moscow:

> Parity Commission not constituted because absence of essential element. No definite information regarding arrival. In view of this Central Executive Committee requests permission to proceed with organization of convention to be subject to approval of Parity Commission when fully constituted.

The Ruthenberg group on the Central Executive Committee voted against the Foster cable and sent its own cable:

> Party situation such that convention agreements by Parity Commission essential for future of Party. Protest against action before full constitution of Parity Commission which will be possible in one week according to information received.

But in this battle of the cables, about the Parity Commission Chairman, we had the drop on Foster, because one of our men, Jay Lovestone, was aiding the G. P. U. in making arrangements for the arrival in the United States of this very important Comintern Rep., advising the G. P. U. agents concerning the best methods to be used in circumventing American immigration authorities in getting the Communist International Representative into the country. Hence, the Ruthenberg caucus leaders knew more about that than Foster, who on June twenty-sixth, 1925, learned that the Communist International Representative was coming to America via Mexico. A meeting of the Secretariat was hurriedly called together and the matter taken up. The Secretariat of the Central Executive Committee was then composed of Foster, Bittleman and Ruthenberg. Foster made the following motion on the matter:

> That we send a representative to Mexico, to be Gomez, to find out as to the whereabouts of the representative of the Communist International.

But it was useless for Foster to send "Gomez." While "Gomez" was searching Mexico for one lost Comintern Rep., Lovestone had already met him upon his arrival in Chicago. We of the Ruthenberg group were the first to greet him. That gave us a head start on the Fosterites and enabled us to develop our parity commission strategy.

We went to work on the Parity Commission Chairman with a will. We, not the Fosterite leaders, arranged his living quarters, which had to be kept secret. We supplied the liaison officer between him, illegally in the country, and the Party. We looked after all his personal comforts, arranged his entertainment, his social life and provided him with the companionship of women. The home of one of our faction comrades was used as the place for spending sociable evenings and for his relaxation. All persons surrounding the Communist International Representative, all present at these sociable evenings were exclusively members of the Ruthenberg group. The Communist International Representative soon became an intimate of our circle of friends, who very cleverly impressed him with the qualities and excellence of our group. Every want, every slight caprice of the Representative we attended to. We studied his habits, his weaknesses, his tastes and his pleasures, carefully noting all, so that we might serve him most satisfactorily. Taking care of this Communist International Representative did not end even there. His life was delved into, his opinions were carefully analyzed, in order to determine his psychological reactions and mental attitudes. We attached great importance to knowing his role and standing in the Russian Communist Party, and in what phase of Russian political life he was most interested. Sure he was a Stalin man, we knew that we had to be very careful, when discussing the Communist movement, to stress Stalin's importance. Since he was also a military man, we acquainted ourselves with the military problems in which he was interested and with his military record. The "nursing" of the Comintern Rep., as we called it, involved the use of the most delicate and intricate amenities of diplomatic conduct, with an air of such genuine friendship that its ulterior purpose would not be suspected. We did our job so well that we caused consternation in the Foster camp. They lacked the finesse and technique for this kind of activity, with the result that they resented the friendship which came to exist between the Communist International Rep. and the leaders of our group.

His Bolshevik name was Gussev, though he was born a Drabkin. He was a short, rotund, clean-shaven man, who looked more like a prosperous middle-class merchant than like a Bolshevik. Yet he was really both: born into a well-to-do family of Jewish merchants, he abandoned the privileges of a comfortable life for the tribulations of a professional revolutionist, and was one of the twenty-two original Bolsheviks who had rallied around Lenin in 1904 to found the Bolshevik movement. In 1925 he was in his middle forties. Sedate in manner, he spoke his German in a quiet tone and very slowly. He looked at you over his spectacles through eyes that scrutinized keenly. Studied though he was in his demeanor, he was quick in forming his judgment of persons he met and in grasping what they had to say. He had a way of smoking a cigarette, while engrossed in his thoughts, that invested him with an air of mystery. He was a good listener and used words sparingly. Though not a person of passion and dynamic power, the deliberate manner in which he presented his views or imparted his decisions left no doubt as to his strength of character and his ability to force matters through by sheer force of will. A typical Old Guard Bolshevik, he had been a high-ranking officer of the Red Army during the Civil War and was at the time of his sojourn among us a member of the powerful Control Committee of the Central Committee of the Communist Party of the Soviet Union. The Control Committee was made up of the most influential men in the Russian Party who were not members of the Central Committee or of its Political Bureau. To the Control Committee was entrusted the hearing of all cases of misconduct on the part of the highest officials of the Party. It was the supreme tribunal of the Russian Communist Party. A writer on military affairs and a prominent member of the Soviet Military Academy, Gussev despised Trotsky and worshiped Stalin, because, as he told us, during one of the Civil War campaigns Trotsky had threatened him and a number of other officers of the Red Army with death for insubordination and due to Stalin's intervention not only were their lives spared but they were rehabilitated as military commanders and as Bolsheviks. Since he was in this country illegally, having been smuggled in through Mexico, a suitable alias had to be found for him. We christened him, "P. Green."

We soon found out that P. Green was not only concerned with the American Party. He did not neglect to find out all he could from us about the United States in general. He used to exhaust us with his questions. After he had squeezed us dry, he would become confidential. Then he would talk about Russian party affairs and about the Russian leaders. He never lost an opportunity to berate Trotsky. He would tell of his personal experiences with Trotsky in Paris. "Ach," he would say, "Trotsky is not a Bolshevik. We Bolsheviks always despised him for his individualistic vanity and egotism." Then he would tell us, choosing his words carefully, that he would watch Trotsky for hours stand before a mirror and deliver a speech to himself so that he could watch his own expressions and motions and improve upon them. He told how Trotsky would practice and re-practice certain parts of them, in order to get the impression he wanted, finally leaving the mirror, extremely satisfied. He would go at length into the history of all of Trotsky's differences with the Bolsheviks and would maintain that, as an individual, Trotsky was not made of the calibre from which Bolsheviks come and that intellectually he was never able to grasp the real basic foundations of Bolshevism.

But when he spoke of Stalin it was different. He pictured Stalin in the most glowing terms. He confided to us that, as far as Stalin was concerned, not only was he the logical successor to Lenin as the leader of the great Russian Party but that Stalin was prepared to carry out his methods of leadership in the Communist International. From now on we could expect to see

Stalin actively assume the leadership of the Comintern. That would mean, he told us, in the strictest confidence, that Stalin once and for all would end the "Ficken" politics of the Comintern characteristic of the Zinoviev régime. It was the first inkling we got that Stalin did not think highly of Zinoviev. Stalin, he said, was "for a collective leadership." He gave us to understand that Stalin wanted a dependable leadership in the Communist International coming from the affiliated parties whose strength and Bolshevik stamina would center around Stalin. We were sufficiently political to realize that a strong fight was on in the Russian Party and that Stalin, who had not played a major role in Comintern affairs, was determined to play the main role in the future. If Green would support us against the Foster group, we realized it was necessary for us to support Stalin one hundred percent.

The Foster group, however, did not like Green and soon began openly to proclaim their hostility to him. A popular expression among them was, "We got rid of Pepper, only to get a dose of Paris Green." Green was a very shrewd political trickster. He once told me that Lenin told him that "politics is a very dirty business and if one is in politics, he must be prepared to wash dirty linen." Whenever he had private talks with the leaders of the Foster group he would always report them to us. When he met Cannon for the first time he was duly impressed by him and reported to us that Cannon was more political than Foster. "One can play with the young man, and if one is clever, it will not be difficult, by playing on his vanity and arousing his ambitions, to break him away from Foster. If you will permit me, I will try to do it, and I believe I will succeed." Bittleman he considered a Talmudic student, one completely divorced from life. He complained that he had difficulty listening to him because he was bored by his confounded abstractions. He could not understand how Browder became a Communist; he looked and spoke more like a missionary or a minister.

On the American Party controversy he adopted a line which in my opinion was basically correct. He maintained that there were no major political differences which divided the two groups and that, therefore, there was every reason to expect the unification of the two groups and the end of factionalism. He said that, since the Comintern decision on the American Party was accepted by both groups, and since all major political issues before the party were settled in that decision, there was no reason for a continuation of the factional warfare. He would say, "Whenever we Russians are confronted by a factional controversy, we are not interested in individuals. We ask ourselves, what are the political platforms of the opposing factions and wherein do they differ?" He went further and said that the liquidation of Loreism had given the Party the task of the liquidation of that 2½ Trotskyist tendency in the Party, a task which could be successfully carried out only if the two factions would unite. Whenever we insisted upon clarifying the difference between us and the Foster group, he would raise the question of the Party split, by saying: "If you comrades insist on your attitude towards Foster and his followers, then there is no room in the Party for both, and a split is inevitable." When I first met him I was closeted with him for about an hour and a half, talking about the Party situation. I went into details on the crimes and fallacies of the Foster Group. But he concluded, "If the comrades of the Ruthenberg group will continue to insist on their contentions about Foster and his group, then I will have to tell the Communist International frankly that my mission as chairman of the Parity Commission is an impossible task, because the work of such a commission can not be carried on in the factional atmosphere that now prevails. Either the Communist International will have to give me the power to act in a split situation or else I will have to return home." The more Green stressed the danger of a split, the more certain did we become that he sought to utilize as a smokescreen the threat of a split situation for putting through proposals he had brought with him from Moscow. We never lost sight of this important fact and were prepared if necessary to resist to the bitter end any attempt on Foster's part to deprive us of our legitimate gains in the Party.

Soon after the arrival of Green the Parity Commission was constituted, with him as its chairman. The Foster group was represented by Foster, Cannon and Bittleman; the Ruthenberg group by Ruthenberg, Lovestone and Bedacht, all of the National Office in Chicago. The formation of the Parity Commission superseded all the other Party committees. It became the actual boss of the Party, and into its committee hopper were thrown all Party problems, controversies, preparation of convention agenda and resolutions, disciplinary matters—in fact, every matter pertaining to the Party. The Communist International representative, as chairman of the Parity Commission, plus his authority as a Comintern Rep, which gave him the power to overrule every Party decision, became the American Party's virtual dictator. The question of issuing a call for the Party national convention was really left in his hands.

The national convention issue had a complicated history. In the Autumn of 1924, following the miserable showing made in the Presidential election, the Foster group felt that it was beginning to lose its hold on the Party, in consequence of the continuous criticism leveled against its administration by the Ruthenberg group. On November nineteenth a membership meeting was to be held in Chicago on the eve of a full Central Executive Committee meeting. We worked like beavers, preparing to capture it. Since all our top leaders were in Chicago for the full Central Executive Committee conclave, we held numerous conferences with the heads of the language federations, especially the Greek, South Slavic and Lithuanian, we mapped out plans on how to mobilize their members for the momentous meeting, threw sumptuous parties for influential Chicago Party members and there discussed with them the Party situation and plans for the general membership meeting. We were getting ready to railroad through a resolution that would put the Chicago membership on record as opposed to the policies of the Foster-dominated Central Executive Committee. Since Chicago was his stronghold, it would have been a calamity for him to have been thus repudiated and a significant victory for our group. We therefore decided to take no chances at the meeting, and came fully prepared, not only to defend our group politically but physically as well, if necessary.

And it was a good thing we did, for the meeting ended up in

a free-for-all fight and a riot, when the Ruthenberg supporters in the audience demanded that a vote be taken on the resolution we had introduced. Bill Dunne was not allowed to speak. Foster was booed and howled down, when he attempted to take the floor against the wishes of the "rank and file" in order to prevent a vote from being taken. The chairman arbitrarily declared the meeting ended, because he realized that the vote would go against Foster. When the membership protested, the usual trade union tactics of turning the light off were resorted to. The air was thick with personal attacks and recriminations.

The Fosterites were so stunned over the outcome of the Chicago membership meeting that they hurried the arrangements for calling the national convention. Without definitely setting the date for it, they passed a resolution through the Central Executive Committee for starting a pre-convention discussion as a prelude to the holding of the convention, which, according to the Party statutes had to be preceded by a two-months discussion period, which was duly opened on November twenty-sixth, 1924, and was to be closed on January ninth, 1925. But on December nineteenth, 1924, the Central Executive Committee explained to the membership that it could not hold the party convention in January, as it had intended, for the following stated reasons:

1. Under the statutes of the Communist International permission must be secured from the executive committee of the Communist International before a convention of any of its sections can be held.

2. The Central Executive Committee, in October transmitted a request for permission for a convention to be held during the month of January.

3. The Secretariat of the Communist International answered the request suggesting that the advice of the Communist International on policy be sought in advance of the convention of the party and that for this reason the convention be postponed until after delegates of the party, representatives of both viewpoints could present the matter.

After cancelling the January date, however, the convention was again postponed because the representative of the Communist

International was late in arriving. Finally, after the Parity Committee had worked out all the convention matters and after P. Green had succeeded in forcing the Foster and Ruthenberg representative on the Parity Commission unanimously to endorse all political resolutions and decisions to be presented to the convention, the Central Executive Committee issued a new call for the Convention, to take place in Chicago on August twenty-first, 1925. Delegates were to be elected on the basis of proportional representation worked out by the Parity Commission in order to prevent the majority from excluding representatives of the minority. In all fifty-four delegates were to be elected.

But the factional warfare did not stop with the publication of the call for the convention. The unanimous declaration of the Parity Commission calling for cessation of factionalism was completely ignored, for in the campaign to elect delegates the most bitter internal Party warfare developed. The Parity Commission had to sit continuously as a court of final appeal, hearing the complaints and charges of illegality, fraud and high-handed methods, which were used by both sides in an effort to muster a majority of the delegates. Green soon discovered that while he could easily get unanimous agreement on questions of principle and on political thesis and resolutions, he could not get such agreement on matters concerning the question of delegates and power. At one of the meetings of the Parity Commission, when Foster stubbornly refused to set aside an allegedly illegal act on the part of his group and had launched into an attack on Green, the latter for the first time lost his calm and poise and shouted back angrily at Foster, charging him with driving the Party to a split. After that meeting I saw Green. He had regained his calm, and he said: "In politics one must never lose one's temper, one must never show his feelings. One must always be calm, objective."

The Fosterites used their control of the Party machinery to make sure of a majority, manipulating the hierarchy of delegates all the way up to the national convention. The elections to that began really with the basic units of the Party organization, the branches or nuclei electing delegates to the city convention, which elected delegates to the district convention, which elected the delegates to the national convention. The call for this national convention provided that the city conventions be held between August tenth and fifteenth and that all district conventions should be held on August sixteenth. Since the apportionment of delegates was made on the basis of the number of dues stamps sold by the districts, wherever possible the records of dues stamp payments were padded to favor the Foster group, which also did its utmost to suspend opposition members and deprive them of their right to vote in the election of delegates. On top of all this finagling the Fosterites used every conceivable method to gerrymander, pad rolls and obtain more votes than they were entitled to, in order to win. The result was that the Parity Commission was flooded with appeals against the Foster machine. In sections of the Party where we of the Ruthenberg group were able to muster a majority, the Foster group charged gross misconduct against us, and appealed as vociferously as we to the Parity Commission.

Green became alarmed. He called in Ruthenberg, Lovestone and Bedacht and went over with them in detail the critical situation created by the appeals that had swamped the Parity Commission. It was obvious, Green maintained, that, in the limited time left before the convention took place, it was impossible for the Parity Commission to review all the cases. He said two things were clear to him: one, that something had to be done before the convention to prevent a split; and two, that positive guarantees had to be received that under no circumstances would the Ruthenberg group be exterminated from the leadership and the important posts in the party. He pleaded with us as good Communists to be prepared to take whatever steps were necessary, even if it involved great sacrifices on our part, to save the Party. After much arguing, it was finally agreed that Green should propose in the Parity Commission that a fifty-fifty Central Executive Committee be elected at the national convention, but, if the Foster group would not agree, then to compromise on a forty-sixty Central Executive Committee, forty percent to the Ruthenberg Group and sixty percent to the Foster Group, with the guarantees that had been agreed to. After many heated hours of bickering in the Parity Commission, Green finally succeeded in putting across his proposal of a forty-sixty division plus guarantees. As soon as this decision was reached, all the Foster Caucus centers throughout the Party received telegrams that the Communist International had decided to give Foster sixty percent of the Party. I was in New York at the time. I heard of this decision at first indirectly. My wife was working on *Freiheit*. Olgin, who was a Foster supporter, stopped in front of her desk very jubilantly and informed her of the decision in the following words:

> Miss Zeitlin, the Communist International has spoken. It has decided that Foster should lead the Party and should have sixty percent of the new Central Executive Committee to be elected by the national convention. Now that the Communist International has spoken, every comrade must accept its decision.

When my wife told me about that, I called the leading comrades of New York together and gave them the startling information. They were dumbfounded and for a time speechless. It seemed that the fight was all over. I spoke up and told them that, on the eve of the convention, we could under no circumstances accept such a decision. We were fighting and ready to take the consequence. I asked them if they would stand solid in repudiating the agreement and would fight against it. They gave me that pledge. I telephoned Lovestone in Chicago and gave him to understand that the Ruthenberg comrades in New York had most emphatically repudiated the agreement and that we resented the capitulation of our members on the Parity Commission. Lovestone was overjoyed to hear of our reaction. He said that it was precisely what he wanted done. He further informed me that the only chance we had of winning the Party was to contest the Foster group all along the line, even if it meant coming to Chicago with a contesting set of delegates from every district of the Party. He told me that he was sure that Green would not permit Foster to get away with it. Needless to say, I was overjoyed with the conversation. I reported it back to our leading caucus of the New York District and we made plans for a fight to the finish.

And that is exactly the sort of fight it turned out to be, not only in New York but in every district of the Party. Every inch of ground was contested. In New York City we had obtained a majority of the delegates to the district convention from those branches which were active in Party work. What we did not know was how the Finnish branches would vote. The procedure in New York City was to have the branches elect delegates directly to the district convention. This was permissible because this had always been the procedure in New York. Even if all the Finnish delegates were Fosterites, we still would have had a majority. But Foster contested enough delegates to change the picture. He came personally to New York as the representative of the Central Executive Committee to the District Convention. He was not going to take any chances in losing the largest district in the Party, the one that elected the most delegates to the national convention, eleven out of a total of fifty-four for the entire country. Our group now controlled the New York District Committee, because Lore, Poyntz and the other Loreites on it had decided to pursue an independent policy and did not support the Foster faction. The District Committee had charge of district convention arrangements. It decided that I should open the convention as the temporary chairman. The convention took place in Manhattan Lyceum. I made sure that the Ruthenberg delegates should be present at the hall long before the hour set for the convention to open. Our group also came heavily armed and well guarded and protected, should any roughhouse be started. The Foster delegates were also on hand at an early hour, all of them with the exception of the Finnish delegates. As soon as the hall was opened I took the platform and seated myself at the chairman's table. I saw at once that the situation in the hall was very tense. I sat on the platform, watching every one, prepared for any outbreak. Five minutes before the convention was to be opened, the door in the rear of the hall opened and Foster marched in, leading the Finnish delegates, who marched in twos behind him. It was a real military display. It was clear to me that they had come prepared to fight as well as to vote. Who they were I did not know, because most of them had never been seen around Party headquarters nor had ever before been active in the Party's campaigns. I found out later that Foster had these Finnish delegates rounded up by their leaders the night before and that he had slept with them all night, to make sure that he could lead them into the convention the next morning.

The hour for opening the district convention struck. I rose as temporary chairman to open it. No sooner did I do so, when Aaronberg, member of the Chicago Amalgamated Clothing Workers, who had settled in New York to serve Foster's factional purposes, jumped on the platform to open the convention himself and usurp the legal power of the District Committee. The Ruthenberg strong-arm guard formed an iron wall around the platform. To have stormed it would have resulted in terrible bloodshed. Bedlam broke loose. I could not make myself heard. Unless some agreement could be reached on how to run the convention, a free for all fight was bound to take place. And the weapons would not be only bare fists. Lives might be lost. The police would certainly interfere. The Party could stand plenty, but it could not stand the onus of such a riot. All this flashed through my mind as I decided quickly that my voice, powerful though it is, was useless here. Without relinquishing the chair or the chairman's mallet, I held a conference with the members of our steering committee. We agreed to go into conference with Foster and his steering committee before attempting to open the convention. We decided that, if no other way out was found at the conference, both sides should constitute themselves into the district convention, elect the delegates to the national convention, and have the contest decided by either the Parity Commission or the national convention. I held the platform while the other members went to confer. In the face of all this bedlam we kept the utmost vigilance, to ward off any attempted charge by the Fosterites upon the platform.

In about an hour's time the conferees reached an agreement. Then took place the most unusual convention that I had ever attended or had presided over. Practically two conventions went on simultaneously. The Ruthenberg group organized the convention on the basis of its majority and its decisions on policies and proceeded forthwith to elect its slate of delegates to the national convention. The Foster group did the same identical things. There were two chairmen: One for the Foster Group and one for the Ruthenberg Group, both occupying the platform at the same time. There were two secretaries, two credential committees and two sets of motions. This duality was continued until the very closing of the convention, when one motion for adjournment was made by the Ruthenberg convention and carried, and another motion for adjournment made by the Foster convention and also carried.

On the basis of the elections in the Party units, including the votes of the Finnish branches, the Ruthenberg group in New York had won the district decisively. On the basis of the proportional representation rules governing the election of delegates to the national convention, we elected seven delegates of the Ruthenberg group and four delegates of the Foster group. I was elected as a delegate and chosen to head the delegation at the convention. When the reports came in from the other district conventions, it was almost the same story: contests in practically all the districts. The Ruthenberg group, however, did legitimately carry the majority of the largest and most important districts of the party; namely, New York, Boston, Philadelphia, Cleveland and Pittsburgh. In the other important districts, Detroit and Chicago particularly, the vote was very close and the Foster group was able to register a majority only by means of the most flagrant and high-handed manipulations. It was clear to every one in the Party that the national convention would be the most violent one ever held.

And yet, the two contending factions in the Parity Commission had worked out a set of long and detailed resolutions on every important question before the Party. These resolutions were unanimously adopted in the Parity Commission and were laid before the national convention with the unanimous approval of the representatives of both factions. There they were unanimously adopted. The resolution on Lore, with a supplementary motion appended to it, was introduced by Max Bedacht of the Ruthenberg group and Bittleman of the Foster group, calling upon the convention forthwith to expel Lore from the

Party as an enemy of the working class for two main reasons: because he had dared to write editorials in the *Volkszeitung* in defense of his conduct and because although still a member of the Central Executive Committee, he refused to attend the convention to defend himself. Had Lore attended the convention he would have been given no quarter, he would have had to listen to every delegate denounce him as a criminal and renegade, he would have been called upon to submit to the Communist International and confess his crimes and, failing to do so, would have been given no more than a few minutes in which to ward off the swarm of gnats, wasps, flies and stampeding buffaloes. Lore knew in advance the tactics that would be used and acted wisely in absenting himself.

I went to Chicago with the New York delegation, intent on fighting against Foster to the last ditch. I felt that Foster was far from a Communist, that he was primarily interested in his own personal aggrandisement and that if he continued in the leadership of the Party, all those who had fought him would be exterminated and the Party run by the strong-arm methods prevalent in certain trade unions. I arrived in Chicago two days before the opening of the convention. The National Office at 1113 West Washington Boulevard was already jammed with comrades from all over the country. The New York delegation received a hearty welcome. We New Yorkers had come to fight. We found that the comrades in Chicago were in very good shape but lacked our fighting spirit. As chairman of the New York delegation, I intended to utilize it for whipping all the Ruthenberg delegates into a frenzy of opposition. Yet I was not deceiving myself about the outlook of the convention, for that morning I wrote:

> Looking over the field I see a very difficult and bitter fight ahead of us. How it will end I cannot now tell. We will probably see the Parity man this afternoon. Tomorrow he will attend our caucus meeting.

We New Yorkers took a suite of three rooms in the Bradley Hotel, which, besides being the sleeping quarters for our delegation, was also to serve as the caucus headquarters of the

Ruthenberg group. Here we met continually, as the Ruthenberg board of strategy. It was not unusual for us to meet all night. I was added to the Parity Commission as soon as I arrived in Chicago, and was later also included on the Ruthenberg steering committee for the convention. On August twentieth I wrote:

> The situation is not yet clarified. Perhaps at today's sitting of the Parity Commission I will know what the results will be. Contesting delegations are here from practically every district. The Parity man is of the opinion that we were defeated, that a split threatens to divide the Party and that the situation calls for the surrender of the minority. He is very frank in his estimation of the majority. He fears their action. What he will actually do when he will be forced to make a decision I cannot foretell now.

Green maintained a poker face. He spoke slowly, deliberately, without any expression of feeling, presented us with what he thought was the actual situation and let us decide what to do about it. We could not understand what he had in mind. On the twenty-first, the day of the opening of the convention, I wrote:

> Developments have not as yet come to a head. The Parity man is cool and composed and not in a hurry. He sits unconcerned, either puffs away at a cigarette or chews gum, a habit which he has acquired and pursues like a real American.
>
> The situation in the Party is serious. Last night the Parity man spoke before the caucus of the majority. Then he came to us, told us what took place there and what he said. According to his report, Foster said there was the danger of a split. Cannon stated that in the split all the Right Wing, opportunistic elements would go with them and the real Communists would remain with the minority. In respect to Cannon he stated that Cannon was a good school boy who learned the speeches he (Green) made in the Parity Commission and then repeated them as his own in the caucus. The Parity man told the Foster caucus there were two kinds of victory, a bad victory and a good one and that they had won a very bad victory. Green also reported to us that the Foster Group refuses to concede to the Ruthenberg group the five major districts which they won and that he proposed to them as a compromise new elections in those districts under the supervision of

> the Parity Commission after the convention, which compromise Foster rejected. . . . P. Green, the Communist International Rep, addressed our caucus afterwards. The hall was jammed with every important comrade of our group then in Chicago. Several hundred were present. He opened up by declaring that he favors us as the real Communist wing of the Party and declared: "I will do everything in my power to help you. But my hands are tied by the decision of the Communist International which directed that the Foster Group be given at least sixty percent of the Central Executive Committee, which is tantamount to saying that they be given the leadership of the Party. I believe that the decision of the Comintern was a big mistake and must be changed in the future. Nevertheless we must recognize the basis of this decision by the fact that formally the majority won a majority of the party."

He closed by suggesting to us the same compromise that he had made to the Foster group; that we recognize the Foster majority, accept forty percent of the new Central Executive Committee to be elected at the convention and new elections in the contested districts after the convention, with this one concession: that the elections, instead of taking place two months after the convention, shall take place three months after. I took the floor and spoke emphatically against the proposal. I declared that we would never submit to a majority that was secured by violence and fraud and that included the inactive, opportunistic and Loreite elements of the Party. The lead which I gave was followed by the caucus. Green's compromise was emphatically rejected.

It was true that formally and legally Foster had a very slight majority of the Party. This majority was based mainly on the membership of the Finnish Federation, which played virtually no role in the affairs of the Party and whose leaders, with few exceptions, were supporters of the Lore group. Other inactive sections of the Foster majority were made up of the comparatively numerous Scandinavian and Czecho-Slovak Federations. But the Finnish Federation alone had a membership of seven thousand, or virtually half of the total Party membership. These seven thousand were members of the Finnish clubs who were enrolled in the Party as units. They were not Party members in the strict Communist sense, because they did not engage in Party activities. We brought figures with us to the convention which proved conclusively that in the election of delegates to the national convention not even ten percent of the Finnish members actually participated. At some of the meetings that elected delegates to the district conventions more delegates were elected by the Finnish branches than members actually present to vote for these delegates. Had the Finnish representation been reduced to the actual Finnish Communists, and not to those merely carried on the rolls as Communists, the Foster group would have been decisively defeated by the Ruthenberg group. That does not change the fact that the Ruthenberg group also received the votes of many members who should have been included in the same inactive category as the Finnish Federation members, but our proportion of that was far from being as large as in the Foster camp.

The national convention was opened and organized by the Fosterites on the basis of alloting us twenty-three delegates and taking forty for themselves. It should be noted that the Foster group seated eleven more delegates than were provided in the convention call. In fact, Foster seated all the contested delegates he had brought to Chicago from all parts of the country. In the report of the minority of the credentials committee the Ruthenberg group claimed a majority of the delegates for its group. For two days, while the convention was in session, between the many conferences and caucuses that went on, the fight continued on the report of the credentials committee. The Ruthenberg group decided as part of its strategy not to refer to itself as the minority but as the Left Wing of the Party and to brand the Foster group as the Right Wing. The Ruthenberg group represented then a solid block of determined fighting delegates. Every opportunity was taken for staging demonstrations and flaying the Foster "Right Wing." When Martin Abern as Chairman of the majority of the Credentials Committee reported in his dull sonorous voice, the words coming slowly through his nose, he cast a slur on the Communist integrity of the Ruthenberg group. We immediately staged a demonstration, demanding a retraction. One Ruthenberg delegate after another rose and indignantly stated that the convention would not go on unless the statement was withdrawn. Abern was flabbergasted. He was purple with rage as he bit his lips. The chairman kept banging the table with his gavel. Had a fight broken out, it would have been a very bloody affair, because both sides came very well armed. The Ruthenberg group was taking no chances. The Foster group had barricaded the National Office on Washington Boulevard, which housed the *Daily Worker* plant. Behind the barricades were Fosterites armed with automatic revolvers, to prevent any attempt on the part of the Ruthenberg group to seize the National Office. We knew also that the Foster group had a heavily armed guard at the convention, with revolvers ready to go into action if given the order. The backbone of the Ruthenberg defense were members of the South Slavic Federation, each one a husky of six feet or over, who had been actively engaged in fighting in the old country and who had been hardened in the steel mills and coal mines of the United States. As for us, we brought to Chicago everyone who knew how to fight and wield weapons. The Fosterites knew that. There was therefore a lame semi-retraction by Abern and a bloody fight was averted.

But the next day the Fosterites were as arrogant as ever. On the twenty-fifth Foster served notice that we would have to submit to the arbitrary rulings of his majority; that our leading comrades would have to go back to their districts on probation, since the Fosterites would henceforth be in control of all districts, including the ones in which we had a majority. This was his answer to all the painful negotiations and all the conferences we had held with him under the aegis of the Communist International Rep! We attempted to come to some understanding which would make some semblance of unity possible, but Foster made it plain that he was determined to annihilate any and all opponents that did not submit to his authority. Yet in his private talks with us P. Green kept pressing that we yield. He always confronted us with the threat of a split, and his famous phrase in German was, "Kapitulation oder Spaltung!" [capitulation or split]. At that time it looked as if the convention would soon break up and mark the beginning of a new internecine war in the Party. But in view of Foster's ultimatum, we did the only thing we honorably could do—we broke off all negotiations with the Fosterites. If they wanted blood, we would give it to them—but only fighting, not by surrendering. I was not the only one of our group who felt that way, yet I was singled out for a bitter personal attack by James P. Cannon, Foster's chief lieutenant, who, holding me responsible for the adamant attitude of the Ruthenberg group, declared accusingly:

> Gitlow is . . . the most intransigent of the minority, he is the leader of the extreme Left Wing of the minority caucus.

He argued, moreover, that if the extremists represented by Gitlow could be overcome there would be some basis for coöperation between the two groups. He then made a weak plea for some sort of coöperation between the two forces. When we heard that, we knew that the Foster caucus was cracking.

It became increasingly clear to us that Cannon was beginning to withdraw from Foster's leadership. Two factors were responsible for this situation: Cannon's feeling that he was the actual leader and organizer of the Foster caucus but had failed to gain the recognition he deserved; and the clever intriguing of the Communist International Chairman of the Parity Commission, who was always availing himself of the opportunity to flatter Cannon, whispering innuendos into his ear and firing his ambition. The steering committee of our group was fully informed on the progress of Green's intrigues by Green himself. He filled Cannon with the idea that Foster had no political judgment, that he was nothing but a trade unionist, and that it was about time that such an able political thinker and tactician as Cannon should assert himself. He urged Cannon to prove himself a Communist leader in his own right and follow his own political line, in keeping with his own judgment rather than continue to bear the brunt of responsibility for Foster's mistakes and deviations. He even promised Cannon recognition by the Communist International and an outstanding position of leadership if he would only assert his independence as a leader. All this was grist to our mill.

On August twenty-sixth I debated Foster on the trade union question. Foster looked upon my efforts as sheer effrontery, for he considered himself the only man in the Party qualified to speak on that subject. Yet I not only spoke on the policies of trade union work, but went further and ridiculed Foster's activities and policies. Foster spoke for over two hours, while I was given only forty-five minutes to make the minority report in answer to him. But these discussions on the convention floor served only to maintain the illusion that the convention was really proceeding, meantime affording us the opportunity to keep up an incessant barrage against the Foster group. The decisive developments were going on behind the scenes. On the morning of the twenty-seventh, a few hours after the debate on the trade union question, I learned that, in consequence of Cannon's impending break with Foster and our refusal to capitulate (which was what P. Green wanted all the time, although he did not say so), Green had cabled a draft of his decision on the American Party situation to Moscow, with the request that the Communist International cable it back to the convention with all its authority behind it. I was therefore able to record in a letter I wrote to New York:

> Yesterday as a climax to our bombardment of the majority we received news from across that definitely gave us the Party. Great jubilation arose in our ranks. Everyone was smiling, laughing and joyful in the camp of the minority. The cable we received from the Communist International states the following: "Under no circumstances must majority suppress Ruthenberg group, because it has finally become clear that the Ruthenberg group is more loyal to the Communist International and stands closer to its views, because it has received a majority in most important districts or an important minority, because Foster group employs excessively mechanical and ultra factional methods. As minimum, Ruthenberg Group must get not less than forty percent of the Central Executive Committee. Ultimatum to majority that Ruthenberg must remain as secretary and Lovestone a member of the Central Executive Committee. Ultimatum to majority, to refrain making removals, replacements and dispersions against minority. Ruthenberg Group must retain co-editorship *Daily Worker*. In contested districts Ruthenberg group gets 50-50 district commit-

tees and 50-50 on sub-committees of the Central Executive Committee. If majority does not accept these demands, then in view of circumstances that elections were unclear who has real majority and methods of majority raise danger of split, Communist International proposes then only a temporary Central Executive Committee with equal representation for both groups and a neutral chairman be elected to call new convention after passions have died down. Those who refuse to submit to this decision will be expelled.

Green called a conference of the Parity Commission for five o'clock of August twenty-eighth. I shall never forget the scene. I can still see Cannon, Bittleman and Foster seated beside each other on a couch; Green, cool and unconcerned, sitting at a table, busily engaged in writing; and seated on chairs around the room Ruthenberg, Lovestone, Bedacht, Ballam and myself. Foster had just come from a session of the convention, where he had been unmercifully pounded by the Ruthenbergians in the debates on his report. Perfect quiet reigns. Then Green nonchalantly gives the Moscow cable to Ruthenberg. As Secretary of the Party he reads it, calmly and very slowly. A more dramatic setting could not have been staged. Foster's eyes become liquid, his jaws set. Cannon squints out of his eyes, and his jaws lock with a nervous twitch. Bittleman collapses into dejection and hopelessness. Minutes go by. For some time they cannot talk. Then the Parity man, cool and deliberate, no sentiment, no emotion, explains the cable and lays stress on the point that the Communist International has now corrected the very bad mistake it had made in its last decision on the American question. Foster asks for time to confer. The trio go into another room. When they return, Foster speaks. He is excited and bitter. He offers us the majority of the Central Executive Committee. He states with great emotion that he wants to be relieved from membership in the Central Executive Committee. He says that under such a decision it is impossible for him to shoulder responsibility and work. He is a bundle of quivering nerves as he speaks. It seems that any moment he will collapse. The Parity man quiets him down, tells him he cannot accept such an attitude. Foster then agrees formally to accept the decision. He further agrees to hold an executive session of the convention at which the cable will be read. Flushed with anger, Foster curses and says he knows who is responsible. He departs, followed by Cannon. Bittleman, shoulders drooped, dejected, blue in the face, completely flabbergasted, remains seated on the couch. He looks around, is surprised when he realizes his associates have departed; so, hurriedly picks up his hat and jacket and leaves. It is the tragedy of politics. The victors remain. The Parity man smiles. Wolfe's wife comes dancing into the room, and the Parity man wittily remarks: "Why are you dancing? Do you think this is a love affair? This is a Lovestone affair," and so victory is snatched from the victors.

With this decision the convention was practically over. The Foster group was wrecked and divided. They had to caucus for thirty-four hours before they could reach an agreement on the decision. What Foster did not know in his caucus was that Cannon, who was leading the fight against him, was following the strategy suggested to him by Green, was Green's tool against him. Cannon fought to accept the Communist International decision, while Foster fought to withdraw and give the Party to us outright. For hours Foster maintained a majority in his caucus. The change came when Cannon won over Bill Dunne to his side. Together they hammered Foster's position and finally won the majority of the caucus for accepting the decision. At half past ten in the evening of August twenty-ninth the Parity Commission held another session, to get the answer from the Foster caucus. Of that meeting I wrote:

> I witnessed something I will long remember. If ever a group looked broken and beaten, it was they. Bittleman especially was a picture of misery, as he sat hidden away in a corner, trying to obscure himself. His face was virtually black. His thin frame seemed to shrivel up. Cannon was a nervous mass of human flesh. Weary and exhausted, he stared out of his bleary, bloodshot eyes like a trapped fox. He pressed his thin hands against his forehead in a supreme effort to suppress his emotion. Foster was disheveled and unkempt, like one shipwrecked, hopeless and helpless. Politics is a cruel game.

The last two days were jammed with drama and tragedy. The day before, Dunne's seven year old boy was buried. He was killed by an auto on Chicago's busy streets. The comrades gathered around the grave. A little in the distance stood the bulky wide-chested Bill Dunne, the Wild Bull from Montana, tenderly holding his frail wife in his arms. As Norman Tallentire spoke, I saw Dunne, a picture of sorrow silhouetted against the background of trees, and heard the sobbing of his poor wife. The *Internationale* was sung. The earth thudded down on the coffin. We were for a moment caught by the mystery of life in the grim reality of death. But it was only a momentary respite. As our footsteps turned back to the city, we who had mourned together at the great sorrow that had befallen our comrades, split into our factions, to resume the fight where we had left it off.

The Foster group had decided to accept the decision of the Communist International on the basis suggested by Green. Cannon had fought for Green's proposal, which was that the new Central Executive Committee should be on a fifty-fifty basis, with the Chairman of the Parity Commission as the neutral member. The Foster group finally decided upon this course, because it refused to take responsibility for the leadership of the Party after the Communist International had implied that it was not as loyal to the Communist International as was the Ruthenberg group. As for Cannon, in fighting for Green's proposals, he had reckoned without Green. At the first meeting of the newly-elected Central Executive Committee following the conclusion of the convention, the Parity man made a significant statement which completely baffled Cannon. It arose on the question of the organization of the Central Executive Committee in the elections of its subcommittees. Green stated:

> Of course, we now have a Parity Central Executive Committee, but it is not exactly a Parity Central Executive Committee. With the decision of the Communist International on the question of the groups in the American party there go parallel instructions to the Communist International Representative to support the group which was the former minority. If the Communist Inter-

> national continues to support this policy, that will always be the case; that is, the Communist International Representative will be supporting that group, and therefore, although we have nearly a Parity Central Executive Committee, we have a majority and minority in the Central Executive Committee.

The result of this declaration was that Green, representative of the Communist International, member of the Bolshevik Party and of its Control Committee, voted as a member of the Central Executive Committee with the Ruthenberg group, thus giving the Ruthenberg group a majority of the Central Executive Committee. Thus did Moscow deliver the Communist Party of the United States to Ruthenberg. But this was not yet the end. The game of the cat and the mouse was to continue.

PART II

AMERICAN COMMUNISM IN ACTION

CHAPTER IX

COMMUNIST PARTY LIFE

IN November, 1925, I was ordered back to Sing Sing Prison, to finish my sentence. When I arrived there, I was greeted humorously by my fellow-prisoners as the man who goes in and out of prison at will. The authorities, treating me as an old-timer, transferred me immediately from the receiving flats of the old prison cell block to the new prison on the hill. The old cell block had everything to condemn it; the new prison everything to commend it. I was assigned to the company that had to keep the place clean. I scrubbed two tiers of stairs with soap and water every day. They had to be scrubbed spotlessly clean in order to satisfy the inspection of the keeper in charge. It took me about three quarters of an hour maximum to do this job. Then I had to clean the bars of the cells on my tier with a rag dipped in oil and do a few odd cleaning jobs which the keeper assigned to me. If I worked more than an hour a day, I considered it a long day's work.

The new prison was kept immaculate. A cleaner place was not to be found. Here the cells were larger than those in the old cell block. The walls were of steel and smoothly painted. Every prisoner had his own private cell, which included a wash basin with running hot and cold water, a window opening to the outside that let in plenty of fresh air and a hospital cot with a spring and comfortable mattress. The greatest convenience was the inclusion of a private toilet bowl with a modern flushometer. Had a bath been included, it would have been equivalent to a good small room in a modern hotel.

Each prisoner had to keep his cell spotlessly clean. The basin and toilet bowl had to be polished and white, the bed made up neatly, the window cleaned. The slightest infraction on the part of the prisoner against the rules for cleanliness was called to the prisoner's attention and, if repeated, he was punished.

Besides, each cell was heated and ventilated by a most modern hot air system, which was fed by ventilated air, to keep the dust out, and which could be regulated to suit the desires of the inmates of each cell. Many of the men in the new prison had never before lived so comfortably and so cleanly. The régime in the new prison was very liberal. Radios were permitted. The cell doors were left open until the men returned from the movies. One could stroll all over the cell block, visit fellow prisoners and engage in conversation or games. The place was prison nevertheless, and I was anxious to be free.

I expected to be pardoned soon, because the Civil Liberties Union had assured me that they had a promise from Governor Smith. But he did not pardon me at once. The last word I received from my lawyers was to the effect that I could obtain my parole from Governor Smith after the meeting of the parole board. I sent back word that I was not interested in parole and would not accept it. I had already made plans for finishing out my term. On December tenth I wrote my wife about it:

> Our hopes did not materialize. In a few days I will be able to form a definite opinion on what will take place. This letter will probably reach you Friday morning. I very strongly desired to be out by that time in order to be with you. You know why and what a memorable day it is for us. Perhaps, Badana, you will be able to come here Friday.

Friday, December eleventh, was the first anniversary of our wedding. On that memorable Friday my wife paid me a visit. She showed me a letter from Forrest Bailey of the American Civil Liberties Union stating that if I would consent to go out on parole it might be arranged, but that a pardon was now out of the question. The letter was very discouraging. I did not want to go out on parole. I wanted to be free to carry on my Communist activities without any restraint. When I explained the matter to my wife, she agreed with me that it would be better to finish the term, so that I could leave Sing Sing feeling that I was a free man, free from the supervision and restrictions of the parole board.

While we were talking about the not-too-happy turn of events, the keeper in charge of the visiting room approached my wife: "Mam, you are wanted on the telephone." As my wife went to answer, she half-jokingly remarked: "Wouldn't it be funny if the call is on the matter of your pardon?" I replied: "It would be like believing in miracles." My wife returned from the warden's office greatly excited. She stopped at the keeper's desk and happily said: "Well, don't be surprised if you will lose one of your steady guests soon. I just got word that the Governor has pardoned my husband." When I got the news I was more than surprised. It was a very pleasant and unexpected shock. I could not get myself to believe it. My wife told me that she had received the call from the editorial offices of *Freiheit,* which had been informed that the convention of the International Ladies' Garment Workers Union in Philadelphia had received a wire from Governor Smith to that effect. She had asked them to recheck, in order to make sure. A little later my wife was again called to the 'phone. The news of my pardon was confirmed. I then asked my wife to wait, in the event the Warden received the pardon from Albany, because as soon as a pardon is received the prisoner is released. But the pardon did not come that day. My wife had to leave for New York. It was like a moving picture climax to a prison scene, liberation coming at the darkest moment and on the very day of the first wedding anniversary. The following morning Warden Lawes received official notification of my pardon. I was immediately notified by him and went once more to the State shop, where I again got into an ill-fitting prison suit, put on a heavy ugly prison overcoat and left the prison a free man.

On the train I was informed of the circumstances that led to my pardon. The National Convention of the International Ladies' Garment Workers Union was in session in Philadelphia. The sessions were torn by a bitter factional dispute between the Left Wing forces led by the Communists and the so-called Right Wing forces led by the President of the International, Morris Sigman. A split in the organization was threatened. Sigman was trying to prevent the split. The Party's three representatives in Philadelphia, Bedacht, Weinstone and Dunne, likewise opposed a split. Those in the Left Wing who advocated a split, did so as a tactical maneuver, believing that, if a split should take place, Sigman would enter into negotiations with the Left Wing, which controlled the majority of the membership, and would come to such terms with them as would result in the Left Wing virtually taking over the organization. Dr. Henry Moscowitz was present as the representative of Governor Smith. He, in consultation with Sigman, engineered the plan to prevent a split in the organization by having Sigman present the convention with a resolution calling upon Governor Smith to release me from prison. It was arranged that, when Governor Smith received the telegram, he would wire back the convention that upon their request he had pardoned Gitlow. In fact, the convention was informed by Governor Smith that he had released me hours before the official papers had been signed and the authorities at Sing Sing notified. The introduction of the resolution asking for my release resulted in a spontaneous demonstration in which both the Left and the Right Wing participated. When the news of my release was received, a wild demonstration took place at the convention, which wired me at once to come to Philadelphia to address the delegates.

When I arrived at Grand Central Station in New York City the place was jammed with Communists who cheered wildly, giving me a rousing welcome. I had just time to greet my parents, for as soon as I was out of the station, my wife and I were pushed into a taxi and rushed to the Pennsylvania station, to make a train for Philadelphia. The Left Wing and the Communist Party of Philadelphia had planned to stage a demonstration on my arrival there and gathered at the station long before my train was due. But the police precipitated a riot, and the demonstrators were dispersed. Upon my arrival in Philadelphia the large headlines in the local papers informed me that I had caused a riot in Philadelphia, the news being so written as to give the impression that I had purposely come to Philadelphia to stage the riot, which took place in my absence.

Dr. Henry Moscowitz came to see me at my hotel. He was very nervous and very much disturbed. He wanted to make sure that the kind of speech I would deliver would not lead to disorder and a split. I assured him that I appreciated his efforts on my behalf and that I had come to Philadelphia in order to thank the union and its membership for what they had done. The convention hall was packed when I arrived. I received a very impressive welcome. I spoke very carefully and guardedly. I thanked the union and its membership for their efforts in my behalf, stressed the need for unity, and without engaging in personal attacks, I criticized what I believed to be disruptive trade union tactics. My speech, punctuated by repeated applause, took about an hour and a half to deliver. I was of the opinion that it was the best speech I had delivered during my many years in the labor movement.

But evidently what I said did not please the administration, because more than half of it was expunged from the printed record of the convention. It also did not please the Left Wing, which felt that it was my duty as a Communist, to ignore the reason for my invitation to attend the convention, by availing myself of the opportunity to attack Sigman and his administration, implementing my popularity into a call for the ousting of Sigman and his reactionary lieutenants. I disagreed with their position, since such action would have been tantamount to creating a situation from which a split might result, with the blame resting squarely upon my shoulders and the Communists whom I represented. Foster and his group, who opposed a split, nevertheless did not hesitate to attack me for my speech, spreading versions of it that were distorted and altogether false. More than once I challenged Foster himself to come out in the open and prefer charges against me, for the kind of a speech he alleged I had made left the Party no other alternative but to censure me or expel me from the Party.

The years 1925 and 1926 witnessed a development of the Communist movement in all directions. The membership, in spite of the factional warfare, was devoted to the Party and fanatical in its belief in Communism. The greatest ambition of a Party member was to serve the cause and become a professional revolutionist—a paid Party official or organizer. The members were highly disciplined. They functioned like privates in a military organization. Orders given were carried out. Personal or family considerations were never taken into account; to take them into account was to be considered a petty-bourgeois, the greatest insult to a Communist. The Party was dynamic, intensely active in whatever it did. This was possible because our members gave every moment of their spare time to the Party.

This is difficult for one who has not been active in the Communist Party to understand. It can best be described by a typical Party member's daily routine, a rank and file comrade, a union member, who works during the day. In the morning he buys his Communist newspaper and reads it going to work. He may arrive a little earlier than his shopmates in order to spread Communist leaflets around without being noticed. At noon he will be engaged in some noon day activity of the Party or of his Communist trade union faction. After work, instead of going home, he will rush to Party headquarters, to attend committee meetings of the Party or of the Trade Union Educational League, of his trade union faction, and the like. Later, after eight o'clock, he may have to attend a union meeting or a meeting of his Party branch. After the meeting he probably will go back to Party headquarters to get instructions for the next day's activities.

A Party member is always meeting, for he belongs as a rule to the following organizations: The Communist Party, the Trade Union Educational League, the union of his trade, the Communist fraction * in that union. The International Labor Defense, the International Workers Aid, and a fraternal organization. In all the organizations to which he belongs there are Left Wing organizations organized by the Communists into fractions of Communist Party members. All of them hold meetings. The Communist Party member must attend them all. Besides, he must attend the Party school, help circulate the Party papers, attend the caucus meetings of his faction, and be present at all the general important meetings called by the Party. In addition, all the organizations, and the organizations within the organizations to which he belongs, have special

* *Fraction* is a term used by the Communists to denote an organized group of Communist Party members functioning as a unit in any organization other than the Party itself for the express purpose of furthering Party policies and carrying out Party orders; *fractions* are not to be confused with *factional* groups *within* the Party.

committees, with the result that the Communist Party member is always hurrying from one committee meeting to another. Sometimes an active rank and filer attends half a dozen meetings in the evening, until late into the night. Saturday afternoons are particularly crowded with numerous meetings, with perhaps an occasional demonstration thrown in. At night either his attendance is required at a Communist lecture or forum, or else he must be present at a Communist ball or entertainment. On Sunday, too, meetings and conferences take place, followed by Communist lectures and other affairs in the evening. In the summer time, if the Communist Party member finds it possible to take a few week-ends off or to take a vacation for a few weeks, he will invariably go to a Communist summer camp, where as part of his vacation enjoyment he will engage in innumerable Communist camp activities for the Party, the *Daily Worker* and the multitudinous campaigns in which the Communists are active raising money.

A Communist's life is in and of the Movement. He is like a squirrel in a cage, always running around in circles. He is so busy, so feverishly active, that it is impossible for him to see what is going on around him. His world is the Party and its incessant round of meetings. His personal associations are almost completely confined to Communists. He reads the Communist press and the numerous party tracts and magazines. A Party member even speaks a language peculiar to the Communists and foreign to others. The Communist Party members talk and think almost alike, because they keep absorbing the phrases, arguments and expressions which the Party lavishly feeds them through its press, propaganda and cultural departments.

The fanatical zeal of the Communist Party member is founded on his belief in the power of the Soviet Union and in its ultimate victory over the capitalist world. To the Communist Party member the Soviet Union is a workers' paradise, the most desirable place in the world to live in. Not only does the Communist Party member give every moment of his time to the cause but every dollar he can spare as well, often giving much more than he can afford. In fact, the contributions

Communist Party members are called upon to make are out of all proportion to their earning power. There are the dues to the Party, to the union, to the Trade Union Educational League, to the International Labor Defense, to the Workers International Relief, to the Left Wing in their union, to the Communist fraternal organization, to the workers' club, besides contributions to the Party branch, the *Daily Worker,* the special appeals of the National Office for funds, and the numerous financial drives constantly carried on by the Party. In some of these drives, like support of the *Daily Worker,* members are assessed from time to time as much as a day's pay. In addition, there are always tickets to buy and sell, dozens of them every week, for every kind of affair. The Party member gives freely, happy to be able to do so. The individual Communist is a generous contributor; the Party bureaucrat, an extravagant spender. We would not hesitate to spend twenty-five thousand dollars for a single demonstration, if we deemed it politically necessary. I doubt if Chinese "bandit generals" ever taxed the Chinese peasantry more heavily than Communist officials tax the Party membership.

Courageous and disciplined, the rank-and-filers of my days were ready to give up their lives for the Party. They carried out unflinchingly the Party's order to go out on dangerous demonstrations, to do picket duty in strikes, to defy injunctions, to resist the police. The Party member would not hesitate at any time to give up his job, to leave his home and family, to engage in Party activities in some remote part of the country or anywhere in the world. Yet in most cases all this was done not only as a free sacrifice, but also in large measure as an investment in a future career. All rank and file Party members considered themselves potential political leaders of the working class. We developed this leadership psychology by impressing the members with the idea that they represented the vanguard of the working class. Hence, imitating us, their leaders, they became adept in political intrigue and trickery. The result was that Party members did not trust one another. Whenever Party members met they generally talked deprecatingly about other members. The Party was a regular gossip factory, in which the most intimate personal relations of the members and leaders were discussed and all kinds of rumors about them circulated. And of course, being embryo politicians, Party members magnified their own importance and exaggerated the extent of their activities and achievements. If they were unable to make headway, they would exaggerate the difficulties confronting them out of all proportions to the actual facts, because a Party member who did not succeed in carrying out an activity assigned to him was subjected to the harshest kind of criticism. They were afraid of this criticism and did everything to avoid it.

Many Party members were given over to fads. In Russia the men and women wore leather coats and caps. The Communists in America followed suit by wearing caps and leather coats. A Communist girl could be recognized in a crowd by her swaggering walk, her bobbed hair, her low-heeled shoes, her leather coat and boyish cap. Communists were a boisterous and jolly lot. After midnight, the meetings over, they would swarm into their favorite cafeterias, to discuss and wrangle in a more care-free vein over the problems they had been discussing, or to digest over the coffee cups the latest factional developments in the Party. This was especially true of the New York Communists, who had a night life all of their own, never getting to bed before two or three o'clock in the morning. One who joined the Party was soon caught in the Communist whirlpool. Family ties had to be broken almost immediately, the non-Communist friends dropped and one's social life completely changed. If a man was married to a non-Communist, in many instances, he would be separated from his wife and family before very long and would be found living with a girl Party member.

From 1919 to 1925 the membership of our Party was almost static, around thirteen thousand, in spite of the fact that thousands of new members were recruited. Too many newcomers stayed in the Party for a short period of time and then dropped out. Only a handful remained. The turnover in membership was about eighty-five percent. The real growth began during the first two years of the Ruthenberg administration, 1925-

1927, when we made the first serious effort to gain a foothold in the United States. It was during this period that American Communist methods and tactics were developed.

The Purcell Tour

In 1925 the Communist International decided to make an energetic campaign on behalf of international trade union unity. Through it Moscow sought to gain a foothold in the trade unions of the important capitalist countries for the purpose of furthering the interests of the Soviet Union, by having the trade unions exert pressure on public opinion for more favorable trade relations with the Soviet Union and for *de jure* recognition of the Soviet government. Albert A. Purcell, a member of the General Council of the British Trade Union Congress, was enlisted by the Communist International in this campaign and sent on a tour of the United States, to see what he could do to enlist trade union support for American recognition of the Soviet Union.* Purcell's expenses in the United

* The question of the Purcell tour came up for consideration in the meeting of our Secretariat on July second, 1925. The following motions were passed:

1. That we accept the proposition as received from Comrade George Hardy relative to the tour of Purcell in the United States.

2. That we make applications for meetings by Purcell in all the principal cities of the country, at least sixteen in number.

3. That we propose the tour be handled by a routing manager who is a close sympathizer of the Party and who shall be appointed formally by Purcell to handle his tour.

4. Trade Union Committees shall be established in all the cities to organize Purcell meetings. These committees shall be organized by the routing manager, who shall first send out circular letters to all the trade unions in the given city, inviting them to send delegates to organize for the meeting. Arrangements shall be made so that our comrades fully control such committees.

5. These committees shall be utilized eventually to build a Left Wing movement in the trade unions. Just before the meeting is held in each city the organizing committee shall be made permanent and given a Left Wing program, important points of which shall be, to fight for international unity, recognition of Soviet Russia, amalgamation, a labor party and other Left Wing demands.

6. Arrangements shall be made to have Party and Trade Union Educational League speakers at the Purcell meetings and to circulate our literature. In addition to the regular pamphlets there shall be printed a condensed version of the British Trade Unions' Report on Russia.

7. We should propose that Purcell make at least four meetings per week and offer him terms of $50.00 per meeting and railroad expenses.

States were paid by Moscow. The money which the Party paid out to organize the Purcell tour, as well as the minimum of two hundred dollars per week plus railroad fares paid out to Purcell, came out of a special fund which was supplied by the Profintern and which was in William Z. Foster's custody. In New York the so-called Trade Union Committee to Organize the Purcell Meeting was headed by M. Rosen, a member of the Communist Party and the Carpenters Union, as President, and Elias Marks, a member of the Communist Party and of the International Ladies Garment Workers Union, as Secretary-Treasurer. Out of the thirteen who made up the Provisional Advisory Committee, ten were Party members. We tried to give the impression that the Communist Party had nothing to do with Purcell meetings. Whenever we were charged with running the meetings, we denied it most emphatically, by declaring that Purcell was not a member of the Communist Party of Great Britain, that his routing manager in the United States was personally appointed by Purcell and that we supported his meetings because he supported world trade union unity and the Soviet Union. But the Purcell tour turned out to be a failure. We found it practically impossible to inveigle the trade unionists who were not under our influence to support the campaign.

The Purcell tour shows some of the means resorted to by our Party to camouflage its activities. It employed these methods in defense activities, strike activities, relief activities, and wherever it was necessary to give the impression that the Communist Party was not directly involved. But in all these camouflaged activities we always took the greatest care in so organizing the machinery to conduct them that our control was secure, in order that the policies dictated by the Party would not be countermanded. Many of those who were put in charge were either secret Party members, who paid their dues directly to the National Office of the Party, or sympathizers, who were, if not organizationally affiliated, actually Party agents, because every move they made was in consultation with Party agents, whose orders they followed as explicitly as did disciplined Party members. Only we who were in the inner circle knew who these individuals were. Their actual connections with the Party were kept secret even from the regular Party members.

The American Trade Union Delegation to Soviet Russia

The Soviet government, through its Commissariat of Foreign Affairs and the Communist International, had worked out elaborate plans for publicizing the Soviet Union abroad. Among them was the ingenious scheme of trade union delegations from important capitalist countries journeying to the Soviet Union to investigate for themselves presumably at first hand the actual conditions, as they found them, in Russia. The Soviet government hoped through the reports which these delegations published after their trip, not only to refute the anti-Soviet publicity appearing in the press of the capitalist countries but also to win over the support of a large section of the trade union movement. The Communist parties of the countries sending trade union delegations were instructed by the Comintern to use the reports of the delegations as the findings of fair-minded, impartial investigators, who, though they were not Communists, had to admit that conditions in Russia were excellent and that the workers received many advantages they did not enjoy in the capitalist countries. The greatest emphasis in the reports issued was put on the lucrative trade which could be established with the Soviets, a trade which would be profitable for the capitalist countries and would offer increased employment to their workers.

After the success of the British Trade Union Delegation in 1924, our Party was given instructions to survey the field and to lay plans for the sending of a trade union delegation from the United States. The idea of sending a delegation of prominent trade unionists from the United States to Soviet Russia, to investigate for themselves the conditions prevailing in Russia, was first raised in the Central Executive Committee of the Party while the Purcell tour was under consideration. The C. E. C. decided first to arouse the interest of American trade unionists in the idea through the Purcell tour itself. When that came to an end, we began to translate the idea into action. The

Communist International informed us that all the expenses involved, including the trip to and from Soviet Russia, as well as the cost for preparing and printing the report of the delegation, would be paid by Moscow.

But organizing the delegation was not an easy task. Of the six members who constituted it only four were active trade unionists and trade union officials. Of these four, one, L. E. Sheppard, the Honorary Chairman of the delegation, did not even go to the Soviet Union. The three other unionists were: James H. Maurer, President of the Pennsylvania State Federation of Labor; John Brophy, President of District Two of the United Mine Workers of America; and James William Fitzpatrick, President of the Actors and Artists of America. The two non-union members were Frank L. Palmer and Albert F. Coyle, both Party sympathizers. This small delegation was accompanied by technical, advisory, research and secretarial staffs numbering nineteen persons, including—besides such prominent persons as Professor George S. Counts, Professor Arthur Fisher, Professor R. G. Tugwell and others—disguised Party members. Although Coyle was officially Secretary of the delegation, his duties were really performed by Robert W. Dunn, a secret member of the Party. We thus had a disciplined Party member in actual control, with the concurrence of a close sympathizer, and were in position to have our orders carried out explicitly.

First to go to the Soviet Union were members of the technical staff of the delegation—the Party contingent—which left in June, 1926, to prepare the ground for the genuine trade union members, who left for Moscow on July twenty-seventh, 1926. In the Soviet Union the trade union delegation of *three* actual trade unionists divided itself into *five* separate parties, which toured the vast areas of that country, covering in one month's time thousands of miles and visiting over thirty-five cities, doing a lot more listening to speeches, speech-making, attending of receptions and sheer traveling than even beginning to investigate conditions. So cleverly was the whole trip of the delegation planned that its non-initiated members never suspected that they were just pawns in the hands of the Communists who were directing their tour. They were kept busy seeing what the Soviets wanted them to see, getting the reactions that the Communists wanted them to get, and were so lavishly entertained, so subtly flattered and so deftly impregnated with the Soviet and Communist viewpoint that they had very little or no time for independent investigation and the gathering of free and uninspired opinions. They were on a tour, the details of which were known in advance, and wherever they went the scenes were dressed up for them in glamorous colors.

In 1927 I had a talk with the head of the Comintern department for this work. He jokingly remarked on how cleverly the work was done and how easy it was to put the naïve visitors in the right frame of mind. He told me an interesting story about the visit of some British trade unionists. On the way from the border to Moscow, the train was suddenly stopped because of some "engine trouble." When the passengers got out of the train and walked up and down the small station they were suddenly surprised to hear the strains of a band of music. As they looked around, they saw a group of workers carrying banners marching merrily behind a Red Army band. When the procession reached the station they stopped, one of the workers stepped forward and made a little speech, in which he said the workers in the factory had heard of the coming of the delegation to visit their country, and, when they heard that the train had stopped at the station, they had rushed to give their comrades and brothers a welcome as is befitting such visitors to the land of Socialism. He called the head of the delegation by name, flattered him with praise for his good work and working-class solidarity, and thanked him for the greetings he brought with him from the British workers. The Russian workers cheered wildly, surrounded the delegation and made them feel that they were the recipients of a most hearty spontaneous welcome in some small insignificant little village in the vast Soviet territory. The effect upon the British trade unionists was startling. That little unexpected welcome melted away whatever misgivings they may have had. But my informant said laughingly in German, "*Nicht wahr?* They did not know that that welcome was well planned weeks in advance and was most carefully executed. Even the unexpected stopping of the train at that spot on account of assumed engine trouble was also planned."

But the tutelage of such delegations went further. They were so loaded with affairs, functions, wined, dined and what not, that they had no time or desire to take upon themselves the responsibility for writing up an objective report on the investigations of the delegation. The Trade Union Delegation gladly entrusted that work to Robert W. Dunn, who, in collaboration with Communist International and American Communist Party representatives, drafted the report and put it into final form. Every word of it was then edited by the Party. Incidentally, out of the money allotted by Moscow for organizing the delegation and printing its report, the Party saved several thousand dollars, which it put in the Party treasury for general Party expenditures. The report was signed by only two of the three actual trade unionists who went to Russia, James H. Maurer and John Brophy. The latter could not be considered unbiased, because he had for years worked together with our Party in the campaign to oust Lewis from the leadership of the United Mine Workers of America. The report, which was nothing but a rehash of what we of the Communist Party had been saying in defense of the Soviet Union, tried to hide the fact that most of the money involved in financing the trip and the work of the delegation was paid by the Soviet government, by inferring that the money came from contributions of workers and liberal friends, who supplemented a nucleus from the Purcell fund. But we had no Purcell fund. Purcell's tour did not pay for itself. His meetings were far from profitable and the campaign we organized around his meetings to raise funds cost much more in administration than what was raised. The contributions from workers and liberals were less than negligible. The cost of the whole publicity stunt, which was what the delegation tour really was, a rather expensive proposition, was met by the Soviet government. The publicity was bought and paid for.

Friendship and Politics

The Communist Party is an impersonal organization in which nothing is left to chance. All human relations are mangled, in keeping with the Procrustean standards of political schemes and plans. Long before it could hope to attain the expropriation of capitalist property, the Party had expropriated our very souls, controlling not only our behavior in public but our private actions and our thoughts. If we had friends prominent in public life, the party was bound to know about it and to determine our relations with them. That placed me very often in a very embarrassing position among friends who were not Communists. As a blanket apology to all friends I lost through the Party's control over my personal affairs, I cite one illustration—the case of Elizabeth Gurley Flynn, who is herself now under Party control.

On February fourteenth, 1926, The League for Mutual Aid, of which I was a member, tendered a banquet to Elizabeth Gurley Flynn in honor of her twenty years of activity in the labor movement. I was a member of the dinner committee, which included the names of such opposites of political opinion as Harry Kelly (Anarchist), Victor Berger (the first Socialist Congressman), Abraham Cahan (Editor of the *Jewish Daily Forward*), Mrs. J. Sargent Cram, Eugene V. Debs, Waldo Frank, Emma Goldman, Sidney Hillman, Isaac Don Levine, Morris Sigman (President of the International Ladies Garment Workers Union), Norman Thomas, B. Charney Vladeck and Art Young. The Committee in charge of arrangements was eager that I attend the banquet, because Elizabeth Gurley Flynn had inquired whether I would be present. It also informed me that if I would attend, I would be called upon to speak.

I took the matter up with the Party, as was the custom. I explained that, even though I did not agree with Gurley Flynn politically, I nevertheless had the greatest regard for her as a friend. I explained that the Party must not forget that Gurley Flynn was among the first to rally to my defense and that of the Party and its leaders when we were under fire in 1919.

I further stated that her efforts on behalf of the I. W. W. prisoners, her work in the National Defense Committee on behalf of myself and the other comrades who were sent to prison, put her in a special position and imposed upon us the obligation to treat her as a friend, not as an enemy. I made it clear that such an attitude did not imply that we were to be uncritical of her actions. My comrades, however, stressed that we could not honor Elizabeth Gurley Flynn for her past activities without holding her responsible for her support of the movement on behalf of political prisoners in Soviet Russia, her Anarchist and Syndicalist leanings, all of which put her in the camp of the enemies of the Communist movement and made her a part of the counter-revolutionary forces fighting Soviet Russia. I then pointed out to them that Flynn was now traveling in our direction and that we would make a serious mistake in snubbing her by having me fail to attend the banquet. I added that I could make my speech political, approving her activities as a militant I. W. W. strike leader and criticizing her for her present inactivity, at the same time utilizing the occasion to castigate the critics of the Communist movement and of the Soviet government in such a way as to cause a rift between Flynn and her anti-Communist friends. That argument appealed to my comrades and I was allowed to attend the banquet, the Party decision being that I should speak politically and critically. Whereupon a committee of the Party worked out my speech in all details along the lines of my proposal.

This was the speech I delivered at the Gurley Flynn dinner. Those who heard me were greatly shocked, because I criticized the one honored by the banquet and injected into an otherwise nonpolitical occasion a controversial political tone. The fact remains that these Communist methods do bring home the bacon when properly applied; that is, my speech was not in vain. When Gurley Flynn rose she took special note of my speech, and from her answer I knew that it had had the proper effect. Some years later when I spoke about the banquet to her she told me that my speech had greatly impressed her, that at the time she had no doubt that I had made the speech in a spirit of genuine friendship and in all sincerity, but that, after having worked with the Party, she now had doubts. She said: "Tell me, Ben, was not that speech planned by the Party? If the Party did, it was very cleverly done." But I only shrugged my shoulders and remained noncommittal: even as comrade to comrade, as a very close friend, I could not be frank with her.

Representing the Soviet Government

In addition to being a branch or "section" of the Communist International, the Communist Party also acted as an agent of the Soviet government. Indeed, it is the link between the American Communist Party and the Soviet government that accounts for the tight grip of the Party upon its membership. The typical American Communist regards himself by virtue of his membership in the Party as an important cog in the world-wide Communist machine that serves the Soviet government. He is compensated for his opposition to the United States government by being impressed with his importance to the government of the Soviet Union. It is this tie-up with a mighty government that holds the Party and the leadership together more than any other single factor. Of course, the Soviet government has repeatedly argued that it and the Communist International are two separate entities. But their separation is as real as, say, the separation of the President of the United States from the U. S. State Department. Soviet spokesmen have always insisted that the Soviet government and the Russian Communist Party are two entirely different organizations, like, let us say, the United States government and the Republican Party during a Republican administration. Yet in Russia the Communist Party is the state even more so than the Nazi Party in Germany and the Fascist Party in Italy. Stalin, the head of the Russian Communist Party, is the recognized ruler of the Soviet government, and has been for years, even though the nominal head of the government is that political nonentity, Mikhail Kalinin. The Communist Party of the Soviet Union directly considers all the policies of the Soviet Union and its decisions then become the laws of the state. In its turn the American Communist Party has always argued that it had no connections whatsoever with the Soviet government, but the fact of the matter is that the American Communist Party is in the same relation to the Soviet government as the paid agents of Nazi Germany in the United States are to the government of the Third Reich.

Before the Soviet government was recognized by the United States, visas were issued in this country for the Soviet government by the Society for Technical Aid to Soviet Russia. This was a Russian organization which was run by the members of the Russian Federation of the Communist Party. Its affairs were subject to the control and decisions of the Party. Individuals who desired to visit the Soviet Union would get approval for their visas either from this organization or from the Party. If the Party O. K.'d them, the procurement of visas was facilitated. Very often the Party would directly notify the Soviet government that it was opposed to certain persons obtaining visas. In one case, that of Abraham Cahan, Editor of the *Jewish Daily Forward,* the Party held up the granting of a visa to him for a long time, and when a visa was granted to him, the Soviet government made sure that his trip in Russia should be supervised and carefully watched by the G. P. U. At the same time, the Party has always served as an agency of information on American visitors to the Soviet Union. The Soviet government was supplied with a detailed report on particular visitors. When Party members traveled to the Soviet Union they received special credentials from the Party which were recognized by the customs officials and the G. P. U. agents on the border. Presentation of such a Party credential, which was typed on a small strip of white silk, stamped with the Party seal and sewed into the lining of one's coat, immediately gave the bearer special consideration. Furthermore, Party members who went to the Soviet Union to settle permanently or for a period of years obtained transfers to the Communist Party of the Soviet Union only after the American Party received the membership request of the Russian Party and approved of the transfer.

The opening of the Amtorg Trading Corporation, the Soviet's trading corporation in the United States, gave the Party many advantages. In staffing the Amtorg with technical help, bookkeepers, stenographers, translators, salesmen, advertising personnel and publicity agents, the Party was consulted, the important, confidential and well-paying positions being filled by Party members. Several hundred Party members were employed by the Amtorg. These workers became in fact part of the Party bureaucracy, their jobs depending definitely upon the good will of the Party. The Party members working in the Amtorg were organized into an Amtorg Nucleus, but this nucleus was kept a strict secret. The head of the nucleus was the confidential liaison officer between it and the Party. Party members in the Amtorg had to pay whatever assessments or taxes were levied upon them by the Party. Failure to do so would have meant loss of their job. But the influence of the Party in the Amtorg did not apply only to Party members. Others who sought jobs in the Amtorg did not hesitate to court the favor of Party leaders, and many who were job-conscious rather than class-conscious joined the Communist Party in order to obtain jobs. When Soviet trade or technical missions came to the United States, it was a rule that the Amtorg sought to obtain from the Party not only advice and other help for these missions but that Party members were also given posts on the missions as translators, interpreters, guides and the like. Party members who obtained these jobs consulted with the Party on what they could do to be of service to it and from time to time gave special reports to the Party on matters of importance. Moreover, the heads of the Amtorg very often conferred with the members of the Party Secretariat on political matters pertinent to their activities. Jay Lovestone and I had a number of conferences with Saul Bron, head of the Amtorg, on how a movement could be started in the United States Congress for the recognition of the Soviet Union. At another time, when the Amtorg arranged an exhibition in New York City, employing Party members almost exclusively in taking care of the various phases of the exhibition, we were requested by the head of the Amtorg to discourage Party members from attending the exhibition, because they wanted to create the impression that it was a bourgeois affair.

But the Party was tied to the Soviet government by stronger strings as well. Most important of these was the G. P. U. Directly upon the request of the G. P. U., the Party supplied it with Party members who could be added to its espionage staff. These Party members became full-fledged G. P. U. agents, employed and paid by the Soviet government. These agents were the link between the Party and the G. P. U. Contacts were made for them by the Party Secretariat, who from time to time advised them how to proceed. A Party member who became a G. P. U. agent dropped out of Party activity the moment he was selected. He became subject to the severe discipline which the G. P. U. imposes upon its agents. Only very few of the Party leaders knew when a Party member became a G. P. U. agent, and they kept this information strictly confidential. Every time the Party was called upon by the G. P. U. to help, it was paid for any expenses involved far above what was actually spent, the surplus going into the Party treasury. But we, the Party leaders, who greatly cherished every opportunity to be of service to the G. P. U., aid in its work and be in its confidence, knew that the G. P. U. kept a close watch on us, too. It was an open secret among us, the Party leaders, that the G. P. U. was supplying Moscow with a complete record of all the leaders of the American Communist Party along with reports on the activities of the Party as a whole. But it was impossible really to find out whether the G. P. U. agents who came to the United States, many of whom were unknown to the Party leadership, favored or disapproved of the Party leaders and their activities. However, we all knew that the Soviet government did not consider our Party merely a section of the Communist International, which the leaders of the Soviet government dominated, but that they looked upon the American Communist Party as one of its agencies.

Nor were the Party's services to the Soviet government confined to the borders of the United States. The Soviet government utilized members of the American Communist Party over a far-flung area that included China, Japan, Germany, Mexico and the countries of Central and South America. Charles Krumbein, a leader of the American Party, was sent to England, presumably to work for the Profintern. Jack Johnstone went to India, from where he was deported by the British government.

H. M. Wicks went on special missions to Germany and Central America. Earl Browder headed a bureau, known as the Pan-Pacific Trade Union Secretariat, with headquarters in Hankow, China. Party members traveled as representatives of the Communist International and the Profintern to the four corners of the earth, not only to carry out the particular policies of the Comintern and Profintern, which were adopted as part of the intricate policies of the Soviet government in the spheres controlled by these two organizations, but the representatives of these two organizations also served directly as G. P. U. and all sorts of other agents of the Soviet government as well. This was strikingly brought out by the activities of the Soviet government in China during the rise to power of the Kuomintang in 1924-1927. Not only were Russian Communists poured into China, but also Communists from other countries. They made up the trusted corps of confidential representatives who watched out for Soviet interests and helped guide Soviet policy through the difficult maze of Chinese politics.

At times, taking advantage of its connection with the Soviet government, the Party would even play the picaroon. Thus, on February eighth, 1927, I wrote Ruthenberg:

> Enclosed is a copy of a letter I mailed to Comrade Amter. I saw Mrs. Falk when I was in Ohio. Her property if sold now could realize five to ten thousand dollars. However, the property, if held, provided it cannot be sold immediately, will increase in value tremendously in a year's time. . . . I believe you should grant Comrade Mrs. Falk's request that she be transferred permanently to the R. C. P. [Russian Communist Party] provided she transfers the property. Amter was foolish enough to create the impression that the Party needed workers like her and would oppose her permanent transfer. You should advise Amter accordingly and instruct him to proceed immediately to have Mrs. Falk turn her property over to us.

The letter to Amter was as follows:

> Enclosed is a Russian letter and a *poltinnik* [a half-ruble silver coin] for Mrs. Falk from her son. This was sent to me by Bob Minor [then the Party representative in Moscow] through Comrade Wishnyak, who just arrived. It is necessary that you forward

> the letter and the coin to her at once. When you see her, and you should see her personally, you ought to make definite arrangements about the turning over of her property to the Daily concern [Daily Worker]. I think we ought to get the Central Executive Committee to promise her that she can obtain, if she transfers the property, a permanent transfer to the Russian Communist Party.

The sending of the Russian letter and the coin was arranged through Bob Minor in Moscow, as was the matter of Mrs. Falk's transfer to the Russian Communist Party. Mrs. Falk got her transfer and we received from her valuable Canton, Ohio, real estate. Anything for the cause!

The Propaganda Machine

During this period the International Publishers was organized for the purpose of publishing Communist books and pamphlets for sale in the United States. The idea originated in Moscow. Such publishing houses were started in all important countries. Through these publishing houses an attempt was made to popularize the works of Lenin and the other Bolshevik leaders among the general book-reading public as well as among the membership of the Communist Party. To all intents and purposes it made its appearance as a purely private enterprise. The heads of this book company were two Party members, Alexander Trachtenberg and A. A. Heller. The latter supplied the original capital needed for its organization. The manuscripts for most of its books were supplied by the Comintern Publishing Society. Many of the books were printed either in England or Russia and shipped to the United States in sheets, to be bound here, in order to avoid the high printing costs and duty. The books were sold at regular publishers' prices. The gifts from Russia as noted above were actually a form of subsidy to the International publishers. The financial books of the company were fixed so that Moscow was charged for translators or books to an equal value of the sheets received from them. The Party advised and approved original books published on American subjects, but otherwise International Publishers was subject to direct orders and control from Moscow. When the company was first organized, Heller controlled a majority of the stock of the corporation, but when I was in Moscow in 1928 the head of the Communist International publishing department asked me about the stock question and I explained to him that in the United States the one that controls fifty-one percent of the stock of a corporation practically controls its outright. He said that while the Comintern was safe in its control because of the nature of the business, he was nevertheless of the opinion that, inasmuch as the Comintern paid the greatest cost involved, steps would have to be taken to give the Comintern an actual majority of the stock.

The International Publishers activity, coupled with the publishing activities of the Party and the schools and forums run by the Party, was woven into a plan for the spreading of Communist propaganda and the development of Communist ideology. This important phase of Communist activity was centralized in the Central Executive Committee through a special department known as the Agitprop (a contraction of Agitation and Propaganda) department. The work of the Agitprop department also included the drawing up of answers to all important questions on Party policy confronting the Party membership. For example, when the Russian Party expelled Trotsky, it became necessary that the Party members should know the official reasons for the expulsion. The Agitprop department answered the questions on Trotsky's expulsion, with the result that all Party members had the same hackneyed answers to the question of why Trotsky was expelled. Because of the energy of the Agitprop department, the Communist Party from the top down spoke like one man with one mind. The Agitprop department was headed by a member of the Central Executive Committee, whose main duty was to be guided in all the many intricate questions arising in the various fields by the declarations of the Communist International and the Soviet press. Involved in this work was the task of creating a so-called Left front of writers and intellectuals, who could be depended upon to defend everything that the Party did, and especially everything that came out of Communist Russia. That activity also went under the name of building up proletarian culture and proletarian literature and art in the United States.

From Chicago to Union Square

In January, 1927, after obtaining permission to do so from the Central Executive Committee, the New York District, managed since the advent of the Ruthenberg administration by William Weinstone, who styled himself General Secretary instead of merely Secretary, purchased a building at 30 Union Square with a down payment of seventy thousand dollars. Since the Comintern was dissatisfied with the record the *Daily Worker* was making, Moscow decided to transfer it from Chicago, where it was making no headway, to New York, and house it and the Party printing plant in the Union Square building recently purchased by the New York District. The *Daily Worker*, far from paying its way, was constantly losing money; the Comintern had poured many times over the initial sum of thirty-five thousand dollars it had invested to start the paper, to the growth of which it attached tremendous importance as organizer of the American masses around the banner of Communism. Our hope was that with the transfer of its headquarters to New York, the *Daily Worker* would begin to yield better returns on its investment in the form of increased circulation. The total cost of the building, general repairs, the new printing plant and incidentals ran well over three hundred thousand dollars. With the Party's official organ in New York, Moscow gave the Ruthenberg group permission to move the National Office from Chicago to New York, and in October, 1927, shortly after the national convention of that year, the National Office established its headquarters at 35 East 125th Street, away from the madding crowd that almost immediately began to mill around 30 Union Square and made Union Square synonymous with American Communism.

The crowds around our Union Square center seemed to be always on hand, pushing through the stairways and corridors and the Party stores. They milled around on the sidewalks in front of the building all day and all night, discussing mostly "inside" Party matters among themselves and Communist ideology with sympathetic outsiders. Opponents of Communism who dared to air their heterodoxy in that part of the city were handled roughly and often beaten up severely. We took advantage of the advertising value of our location to cover our building with Communist slogans and with large signs advertising our important meetings and affairs. Soon not only we but all the United States began to look upon Union Square as our Red Square. On the slightest provocation we staged Union Square demonstrations, which ended in wild and boisterous cheering before our headquarters. "Thirty Union Square" had given Union Square a reputation and had put our Party on the map. Neither a hostile police nor the professional Red baiter could dislodge us from that fortress of ours. Yet in less than two years "30 Union Square" housed dress bargains. How that came about is part of a bigger story told elsewhere in this book. But at the time none of us could have foreseen that Stalin would have had a lot to do with taking away the color and life for which Union Square had become nationally famous.

Curiously enough, one of the leaders who to this day remains a pillar of Stalinism in the Party was the first to introduce among us ways hitherto unknown among American Communist leaders—and he did it, strange to say, under our very eyes, at 30 Union Square. That was William Weinstone. We had punished him for his opposition to us at the 1927 convention by depriving him of his self-designated title, General Secretary (in obvious imitation of Stalin's office in the Russian Party), and ordering him henceforth to be what all his predecessors had been, merely Secretary of the New York District. Weinstone had to swallow this "demotion" in silence—and in silence he more than made up for this affront to his dignity by providing himself with an enormous office. I don't know how many walls between adjoining rooms were demolished to attain the impressive spaciousness of Weinstone's office, but the effect was like Mussolini's at the Palazzo Chighi, for Weinstone placed his desk at the furthest corner away from the door, and anyone calling on him had to submit to the embarrassment of walking an insufferably long distance before coming within talking range of this petty bureaucrat's presence. Moreover, the average comrade could not gain access to this sanctum sanctorum. But all this mechanism of grandeur did not overcome, any more than his pompous manner and his deep stentorian voice, his chronic fear of making decisions. Notwithstanding all the outward trappings of a powerful and important satrap, Weinstone remains a victim of chronic hesitation, a little man in a state of perpetual panic.

Communist Coöperatives

On the ground floor of 30 Union Square a coöperative cafeteria was established, with murals on its walls by the talented Hugo Gellert, a comrade. This was not only the center for Communist "bull sessions" lasting far, far into the night, but also a gold mine for the management of the *Daily Worker*, the New York District organization and the National Office. All these functionaries were important Party leaders and ranked far above the obscure comrade (Pollack was his name, I think) who managed the cafeteria very ably, garnering thousands of dollars daily in profits, mulcting the money, as it were, out of the Communist enthusiasm of the comrades. Daily peremptory notes would be sent to Comrade Pollack, *ordering* him to send a stated amount of money with the bearer. This was done so often that even the humble Comrade Pollack forgot his reverence for exalted leadership and protested. But it did him no good. All the leaders indulged in this malpractice. The result of this mulcting was that the only paying Party enterprise went bankrupt and the owners of coöperative shares in it were done out of thousands of dollars. Pollack was rewarded for his "coöperation" with the Party leaders in mulcting the coöperatives by being placed in charge of the finances and accounting books of the National Office.

But this was a mere bagatelle compared to another coöperative enterprise venture, this time in housing. When this idea was first propounded, I thought it was fantastic that poor, exploited comrades should be able to swing a three-million-dollar coöperative apartment building proposition. I wondered where the money would come from; as things turned out, I should have been wondering rather about where the money would go, for the money came, all right—but it vanished into thin air, millions of it. When I was licked on my financial argument in the Central Executive Committee, I protested that it was bad policy to concentrate the most active comrades in one little sector of the Bronx, taking them away from important trade union and other highly-valuable activities to make coöperators of them instead of good Communists. I warned, moreover, that should the venture fail, as it was bound to, it would give the Party a black eye. But all my arguments and warnings were overridden, and the coöperative apartment houses were actually built in a beautiful section of the Bronx. Near these apartment houses, moreover, a restaurant and food stores were built to supply the tenants with meats, groceries and baked goods.

The financing part proved simple enough: the comrades and sympathizers were simply informed that if they wanted to live in genuine Communist coöperative apartment houses, they would have to put up several hundred dollars each before the houses were even begun to be built, in order to secure the right to an apartment. And since living in such a house was almost in the nature of a step toward the supreme happiness of living in the Soviet Union itself, the comrades and sympathizers, thousands of them, somehow raised the several hundred dollars apiece and subsequently more besides. And then the fun began. In the first place, these proletarian domiciles were equipped with the lavishness of Park Avenue apartments. This led to the second step, excessively high building cost, which led to the third step, the unforeseen deficit, which led to stoppage of construction activities. Whereupon, Joseph Brodsky, a member of the Party and of the Party's legal staff, who was attorney for the United Coöperative, suggested a simon-pure capitalist bond issue. Being revolutionary statesmen, *Realpolitiker* and Machiavellians, we of the C. E. C. not only consented to the bond issue but designated it even as consisting of "gold bonds" only, to give the impression that they were worth more than the paper on which they were printed, and decreed a sales campaign of these so-called Gold Bonds. We out-krugered Ivor Kruger himself in conducting the sales throughout the Left Wing labor movement, for our sales talk included pretty ingenious arguments, including the one to the effect that instead of crooked capitalists, the men behind these bonds were proletarian leaders of sterling integrity with a reputation to maintain in the labor movement. No one in that crepuscular world of utopian shadows thought of inquiring what that had to do with financial solvency, and these purely hypothetical Gold Bonds sold to the tune of a quarter of a million dollars.

And then the whole financial structure collapsed. First went the bondholders and after them the coöperators. I shall never forget the tragic scenes at 30 Union Square, in the offices of *Freiheit, The Daily Worker* and the United Coöperative itself. I proposed in the Central Executive Committee that every bondholder should be repaid ten percent yearly until his entire investment was repaid to him. Notwithstanding Foster's opposition to this motion, it passed. But it was never acted upon. The bondholders had nothing but a printed piece of paper to show for the hard-earned money they had saved and borrowed and scraped together through heaven only knows what heroic efforts. As for the coöperators, they not only lost their investments, which in some cases ran over a thousand dollars per person, but also their titles to their respective apartments. When during the reorganization that was instituted subsequent to the debacle sixty-five thousand dollars became available, all of it went to cover a debt to Grace Burnham, a wealthy Party member who could afford to lose that amount with greater ease than the average Party investor his pittance. Moreover, to add insult to injury, we organized without much effort a system of mass browbeating against any incipient critic of this venture. The Party had such a grip on its membership and such prestige in the Left Wing labor movement, that it was never held responsible for this fiasco. Instead, a few individuals were blamed for mismanagement and, without even so much as a breath of scandal around its name, the Party continued to prosper, growing in membership and increasing its influence in the labor movement. No capitalist corporation could ever have survived so disastrous a financial debacle.

Communist Morality

When Stalin expelled two of the foremost Communists from the Russian Communist Party—Trotsky, the junior partner in the Lenin-Trotsky team that had guided the revolution from its inception, and Zinoviev, Lenin's chief lieutenant and first president of the Communist International—all of us, including the future leaders of American Trotskyism, rushed to pass a resolution endorsing this outrageous expulsion, declaring with unmitigated sycophancy:

> . . . the Russian Party has been amazingly patient, but the time for patience is past.

Most of us behaved just as shabbily when Stalin maneuvered Bukharin, Rykov and Tomsky out of the first place in the Russian hierarchy. It was therefore no surprise to me when not only the American Communist Party leadership and membership but even the entire periphery of sympathizers, stooges and others of the pseudo-intellectual Communistic riffraff rallied in one voice of enthusiastic approbation when the entire Old Guard of Bolshevism, its founders and leaders, demoralized by the political ethics of their Bolshevism and broken on the wheel of the Bolshevik-perfected political police, made of themselves the most obscene spectacle in the political history of this sinful earth at the notorious Moscow Trials in 1936-1938. Here indeed was a new low in arrant knavery. Yet it was indulged in by people whom even many of their opponents regard as idealists, as persons in all essentials on a higher moral level than the average. I daresay that even intelligent Fascists harbor the delusion that Communists, having renounced all selfish interests and all desire for worldly goods, are saints seeking martyrdom in the hope of redeeming the world, or, at least, the working class. Certain liberals and others who had always believed in the honesty of Communist intentions, disagreeing only with certain of their methods and objectives, were the most flabbergasted people in the world when the Moscow Trials and the Communist-organized reaction to them took place. Consequently, all sorts of theories were spun to account for the show-trial "confessions" of the old Bolsheviks "on trial" and for the role of Stalin and the Communists in that show. Everything from esoteric drugs to the shade of Dostoyevsky was invoked in the spinning of these theories. But the explanations satisfied no one. After spending the better part of my life in the Communist movement, it seems to me that one would get further with an attempt to understand Communist ethics, Communist behavior, and Communism in practice, if he proceeded on the assumption that Communists, too, are merely human, subject to all the corrupting influences of this world, even as you and I. Shocking as the Moscow Trials were, they really did not surprise me, because I knew in my very bones the whole sordid story of corruption and degeneration that comprises the latter-day history of Bolshevism. I cannot tell it here, for the very nature of an autobiography limits me to eye-witness accounts only and to America mostly, but I shall cite a few instances in substantiation of my main premise—that Communists are only human after all and no different from the rest of the people.

For example, the matter of drunkenness among the staff of the *Daily Worker* and among Communist leaders generally, who made asses of themselves in public, was the subject of several plenums in the Central Executive Committee. Several protests on the subject by high and low Communists had been received concerning this matter. Something had to be done. But what to do concretely to remedy this situation was never proposed, because some of us felt that it would raise in the Party the issue of personal morals, something the Party could not afford to have aired.

The Party was going through a moral crisis which was in a measure a reflex of conditions in the country but which was also intimately connected with the general development the Party was undergoing. Upon the insistence of the Comintern we were intensifying our trade union activities and making a serious effort to Americanize our movement. It was only natural that the trade unionists of American stock should come to the fore. The group around Foster took advantage of this development by claiming that they were both the trade unionists and the genuine American elements. Since they had no actual roots in the trade union movement and an insignificant influence among the trade union masses, they attempted to overcome their shortcomings in this respect by assuming what they considered to be the true mark of American trade unionists. They cursed like troopers and prided themselves upon their drinking abilities to such an extent that it soon became the accepted theory in the Party that one's Americanism was determined by his ability to swear and his capacity for drink. This form of Americanization took on a particularly ugly form in Chicago. At important Party affairs Party leaders, Party members and members of the Young Communist League became so drunk, so abusive and so vulgar in speech that drunken brawls took place. When the matter was raised at the meeting of the Central Executive Committee, Bill Dunne took the floor and shouted that if the Party was interested in probing the personal morals of individual Party members and intent on conducting a witch hunt into their personal conduct, he would demand an investigation of the activities of the Communist youth, among whom Saninism * was rampant.

The entire matter was dropped, including the investigation of the youth, precisely because what Dunne had charged against our youth was true. Every leader of the Party and of the youth was aware of it. Many of the young people who joined the Communist youth organization joined out of strong emotional sentiments and not because of an understanding of the principles and philosophy of the movement. Their ages ranged from fifteen to twenty-five, the majority being between sixteen and twenty. They were young and impressionable. In the Party they were accepted as the favored ones. They heard that the Communist movement depended upon its youth, that youth makes the revolution. The older Party leaders courted the support of the youth by going out of their way to play up to them. Their importance was exaggerated. They were extolled as the ones who knew best how to keep the Party on the straight revolutionary path. The youth leaders were taken into the Party councils and the inner circles of the Party leaders. They were initiated into

* From Artzibashev's "Sanin," a novel written after the defeat of the 1905 Russian Revolution, which inspired loose morals in place of revolutionary activity. It is interesting to note that at the same time a similar "moral crisis" was considered by the Russian Communist Party and was referred to as Yesseninism, from the name of the poet who was Isadora Duncan's husband. Note also that in the choice of our terminology we American Communists were about twenty years behind our Russian comrades, constantly aping them (to this day) approximately a generation late.

all the Party controversies and intrigues. They in turn accepted all this attention as their due and soon began to look down upon the older Party members and leaders with disdain. They paraded in the Party like cocks of the walk, looking forward to the time when they would replace the older leaders. They became most malleable morally as well as politically in the caucus of the most unscrupulous among the leaders.

The young people often joined the Party in opposition to their parents. Many came from homes where the parental influence was not very strong. A few were the sons and daughters of Party members. They were drawn into a hectic whirl of activity, which interlocked with that of the Party, mingling and rubbing shoulders with the older Party members. A member of the Young Workers (later Communist) League soon became so engrossed in the life of the League and the Party that he cut loose from all family ties. He was greatly impressed by what went on all around him and imitated what he believed to be the accepted Communist thing to do. Our young member soon changed not only his mode of dress but his demeanor as well, and as his head became stuffed with Communist phrases and ideology, he lost all his youthful attributes, turning into a hard, sophisticated cynic who knew the alpha and omega of all questions confronting the troubled world. A youthful Communist ended by becoming the most conceited and intolerant person one could meet. The young Communists, drawn into a life of their own, sure of their own importance and maturity as Communist leaders of the working class, fell easy prey to all the vices in the Party, which to them were not vices but expressions of rebellion against bourgeois society and the hypocrisy of bourgeois and morals.

They broke with their families because the family was a bourgeois institution which stood in the way of their Communist activities. Many completely divorced themselves from their parents. It was not unusual for parents of young Communists to come to our offices, to plead with us that we induce their children to show them some kind of consideration. One case in particular involved the father of one of the leaders of the young Communist movement. His son despised him and would have nothing to do with a father he considered ignorant and a sentimental petty-bourgeois. The father spoke to me for hours, tried to explain that he loved his son more than anything in the world, that he was a hard-working man and had made tremendous sacrifices to give him an education. Perhaps I could persuade the young man at least to greet him and show him some of the courtesy due a father. He said:

> I am now getting on in years. You know what a worker can expect. I am very poor. But believe me, I don't want a penny from my son. What I want is to know that I have a son.

Very often mothers would come to the office, complaining that their young daughters failed to come home at night and that they had lost all influence over them. One mother explained:

> My daughter is only fifteen. Before she joined the young Communists she was a very quiet and good girl. But now she is different. She smokes. When I tell her something, she laughs and tells me I am ignorant and think like a bourgeois. She has neglected her school and studies. She is seldom home. When she does come, it is around two or three o'clock in the morning.

We knew the situation very well, but the complaints and pleadings fell on deaf ears. Another tragic case occurred at the National Offices in Chicago. An irate father came into the office and deposited an infant on a desk. He shouted: "Here, take your bastard!" The child was the infant of a sixteen-year-old girl who had been seduced by one of the Party leaders.

Loose morals were general. Party leaders changed their wives sometimes as often as one does an overcoat. The young Communists had but to see what their elders in the movement were doing. It was no wonder that they defied all moral codes. If a young girl who joined the Communist youth organization insisted upon maintaining her chastity, she was frowned upon as bourgeois by the self-styled revolutionists who had just emerged from their knee-breeches. Many of the young Communists considered the giving up of one's chastity as a mark of distinction. Young Communists did not long remain single, but the common-law marriages between them, as a rule, were short lived.

Under such conditions it was not surprising to hear the question of Saninism raised in our leading Party committee, for the situation in New York and Chicago had become really scandalous. The orgies and debaucheries among the youth were spoken about in whispers in the Party, never seriously discussed and considered. We felt that the profligate sex relations among the youth was something we could not control and that as long as the youth could be depended upon to serve the interests of the movement it was best to leave the matter alone. What we failed to realize was that the Communist youth, which came to us imbued with a spirit of rebellion against injustice and motivated by the highest ideals (in breaking with bourgeois society and its code of morals so categorically), had lost the most precious heritage of youth. Many of them turned out to be really tragic figures—intellectually infantile; otherwise, cynically worldly and senile.

Had we probed the situation more closely, we would have realized that what was going on in the youth movement was but a reflection of the movement as a whole. It was we who had set them the example of placing no moral limits about anything we found expedient to do. A minor incident will illustrate this point. It had to do with our support of the Nicaraguan rebel leader, General Sandino. The Party was sponsoring a lecture tour through Europe by his brother; and the New York District, sponsoring protest meetings against American intervention in Nicaragua, advertised that at a certain meeting in Madison Square Garden it would display an American flag which had been captured by Sandino's forces from the United States Marines. When the meeting date approached, Weinstone came to the National Office very much worried and asked for a private talk with Lovestone and me. It developed that Weinstone was worried because the district did not have a flag that was captured by Sandino, and Weinstone wanted to know what to do about it. He suggested that a good way out would be to buy an American flag, take it down to the basement of 30 Union Square and shoot it full of holes, to make it look genuine. But Lovestone and I opposed the scheme as pure adventurism that would arouse the ire of the United States government as well as the people and would end in causing the Party much more harm than good. Note that even our opposition to this bit of knavery was purely on the grounds of expediency. It occurred to none of us to consider the matter in the light of ordinary human decency.

Though dedicated to the task of bettering the world through Communism, the Communist Party is as amoral and immoral in its practicality as any organization of racketeers. Moreover, today it is less interested in serving the ideals of Communism than in promoting its own career within the ambit of Stalin's world-wide political machine. But even during the heyday of radical idealism no Communist ever forgot that in order to achieve his objective, power must be achieved, supreme power. The question of control and power was therefore always uppermost in our minds. That question was at the base of all the questions we considered. In order to gain influence and control over the masses, it was necessary to influence and control the organizations to which they belonged. If a handful of Communists controlled an organization to which thousands of workers belonged, it would be possible for us to speak in the name of these workers and, whenever necessary, mobilize them for action along Communist lines. Once we gained control of an organization, we considered it of the greatest importance to maintain our control by flooding the organization's employed staff with Communists. First sent in were Communist stenographers and clerical help, then Communist publicity and educational directors. Whatever paid positions were open, we saw to it that Communists were employed. This helped the Party in many ways. First, it put into the organizations a large number of Communists whose jobs depended upon the Party. Second, the Party now had groups in the organizations who were obligated to carry out its orders. Third, these job holders became part of a tightly-webbed Party bureaucracy which dominated the rank and file of the Party and were useful for factional purposes. Fourth, in unions that exercised job control in their particular industries, the Communists saw to it that Party members and their supporters got the best jobs, that their opponents were victimized, and often while Party members new in the industry got jobs, old-timers in the trade who were not Communists remained unemployed. In this scramble for Party power, through catering to self-interest, whatever there was of social idealism petered out into pious phrases.

From Lovestone's Stachel to Stachel's Browder

But Communist ethics and Communist psychology as practiced in America may perhaps be best understood through the nature of some of the Party's most successful leaders. Of the Communist *crème de la crème* no two persons typify the personal characteristics that go into the making of Communist leaders better than Lovestone and Stachel. Lovestone discovered Stachel and Stachel recognized in Lovestone a kindred spirit. They became two of the most intimate cronies in the Party. Lovestone depended upon Stachel's uncanny understanding of the political and personal motivations that determined the activities of Party members and leaders. Lovestone himself was of course a master in the art of political maneuvering and trickery. However, he was responsible for the general political direction of the Party—which entailed the formulation of programs and the drafting of theses that analyzed from the Communist standpoint the economic, social and political conditions of the country—and needed someone who could relieve him of the details of inner Party politics, one who would quickly grasp his methods and in whom he could have confidence because they would understand each other. At the same time, Lovestone made sure that the one he selected was of such caliber—had such shortcomings intellectually and in his appeal to the masses—that he would never be able to aspire to that leadership which he had attained, but rather would recognize that his standing as one of the inner circle which ruled the Party depended upon his collaboration with his leader. Stachel fitted into the picture perfectly. Stachel became Lovestone's privy councilor, and in his crafty hands he held the strings to all the intrigues and political manipulations which constituted the daily life of our Party. Lovestone and Stachel, whenever that was possible, ate together, schemed together, went to the movies together and always put their heads together. To know them is to understand the important events which followed.

I first met Lovestone at a meeting of the New York County Committee of the Socialist Party in 1918, when the fight between the Left and the Right was in full progress. He was a young man in his early twenties, who had been brought into the party by Trachtenberg. A long large nose protruded from the center of his face and hung over his upper lip. His eyes shifted constantly and seemed to avoid you when he engaged in conversation. He was dignified, well-built, about five feet ten inches tall. When he spoke, in a sharp sarcastic tone as was his custom, his face would become livid and break into a contemptuous sneer, his words coming at a rapid clip. His remarks sounded downright insulting, and what he said always aroused the most bitter ire among those whom he attacked. His command of English was good, his speech substantial and well thought out. His was a new voice among the socialists. It spoke in a tone and used expressions which were new to Socialist gatherings. This lad sounded sincere enough, though he did not look it. Facing the shouts and angry insults thrown at him by the enraged Socialists, he stood up defiantly, erect, answering mere insults with caustic, sarcastic rejoinders that were deadly. His was the voice of Bolshevism, which was calling for the tearing down of the whole structure of Socialism built up by the Socialist Party.

In the early stages of the Left Wing of the Socialist Party and in the days when the Communist Party was in the process of being organized Lovestone already demonstrated that he was a master of political intrigue, one who resorted to the most unscrupulous and dishonest acts in gaining his objectives. In those early days of 1918 and 1919 he displayed an almost superhuman energy in the pursuit of his ambition to establish himself as the leader of the movement. He not only attended to all the routine duties which activity in the organization demanded, but he also utilized every moment of his spare time and the early morning hours after Party meetings were over to devour Marxian and Communist literature, at the same time following world events and the developments in the United States.

The Left Wing rank and file, and later the membership of the Communist Party, that followed Lovestone did not trust him and did not like him. Nevertheless, he was able to attach himself to a group or a leader in such a way as to make his services indispensable, his reward being inclusion in the top leadership of the movement. In his first test with the government, which he was organizing a party to overthrow, Lovestone, of all the outstanding Communist leaders, collapsed and proved to the membership that he lacked that staunch revolutionary courage which they believed the movement had a right to expect from its leaders. At the very first meeting of the New York organization of the Communist Party, Lovestone was chosen Executive Secretary, but categorically refused to accept the job because it was too dangerous, it being his belief that the first one among the comrades to be arrested in the event of a raid would be the executive secretary of the organization. Nevertheless, in 1919 Lovestone was indicted, as were other members of the Communist party, including Harry Winitsky, the Secretary of the New York organization. Lovestone was also indicted in Chicago, and a Chicago warrant for his arrest had been issued. He was apprehended in New York and was released on bail. The night before Winitsky went on trial Lovestone told Winitsky that he was sorry he ever got into the movement, and if freed, would have nothing further to do with it. Furthermore he advised Winitsky, if he wanted to win his case, to get out of the Party and take care of himself. In a statement which Harry Winitsky sent from his cell in Sing Sing Prison to the Central Executive Committee of the Communist Party he wrote:

> A few days later, during the progress of my trial, I saw Lovestone talking to a certain Mr. E., a wealthy and influential business man, whom we both knew. They were talking together in the lobby of the Criminal Courts Building. Lovestone later told me that he had asked this Mr. E. to go and see Mr. Rorke, the prosecuting attorney, and promise him that if he would drop the case against him, he would promise to leave the movement and stay away for good. Mr. Rorke turned down this offer, but promised Lovestone his freedom, if he would publicly make the statement in open court. This Lovestone refused to do, stating he felt he could never look a comrade in the face again.

Lovestone appeared as a witness for the state in the trial against Harry Winitsky after he had been promised his freedom in New York and immunity from arrest on the Chicago warrant. Lovestone gave the prosecution the testimony it needed to obtain for Winitsky the maximum sentence of five to ten years at hard labor. Notwithstanding this unpardonable act of cowardice and betrayal, Lovestone succeeded in whitewashing himself. So low was the moral and intellectual caliber of certain leading comrades that his political chicanery was successful. He called together C. E. Ruthenberg, I. E. Ferguson and Rose Pastor Stokes, and induced them to issue an official Party statement exonerating his actions. True, Rose Pastor Stokes did not concur in the statement, but Ruthenberg and Ferguson were personally involved, because they were facing trial in New York, and Ruthenberg and Ferguson, being paid officials of the Party, were members ex officio of the Central Executive Committee of the Party, the only committee that had the power to exonerate Lovestone. The trio—Lovestone, Ruthenberg and Ferguson—were the inner circle which worked as a unit inside of the Communist Party at that time. But Lovestone's effrontery did not stop there; he set out to win also the good will of the very victim of his treachery. After Winitsky was convicted, Lovestone visited him in prison. Winitsky wrote about the visit:

> A few weeks after I went to prison, Lovestone visited me and tried to explain that his testimony was for the best, that I would have gone to jail anyway, and that it merely saved him from jail. He tried to induce me to write an article for the *Communist* stating that I was not opposed to his testifying and that he consulted me before he did so. This I refused to do. He then told me that he would see to it that my case was appealed immediately, and he was sure that I would be set free. At this time he again reiterated his former statement to the effect that I was foolish to remain in the Party, and that I ought to accept the offer made to me by my relatives, and go into business as soon as I was free.

Yet Lovestone was no ordinary witness for the prosecution. He was the prosecution's *chief* witness. An examination of the record proves how important the prosecution considered Lovestone's testimony, for *the prosecutor asked him more questions than any other witness. Lovestone was asked 245 questions.* In their brief before the Appellate Division of the New York Supreme Court, Winitsky's lawyers said of Lovestone:

> In a direct examination covering almost 22 pages of record (fols. 1224-1288), *he answered all questions* frankly and fully; *in fact, where his information was not specific, he was so ready to give full answers that on more than one occasion* (fols. 1274; 1283) *parts of his answer had to be stricken out.*

Lovestone's actions aroused a storm of protest in Communist circles, many suspecting him of being a Federal agent. But in those early days of the Communist movement spy mania was very strong. There was a basis for it, of course, because of the energetic activities of the Department of Justice against the movement. The case of Louis C. Fraina, a brilliant young Italian-American, now known as Lewis Corey, caused quite a furor in the Party when Santeri Nourteva, Secretary of the Russian Soviet Bureau in the United States, accused Fraina, who was the first representative of the newly-formed Communist Party to the Communist International, of being an agent provocateur in the employ of the Department of Justice. Nourteva went so far as to charge that agents of the Department of Justice wrote some of the planks into the platform of the Communist Party which enabled the government to deport Communists out of the country. A trial of Fraina was held by the Central Executive Committee of the Communist Party before he left for Russia. Present at the trial were Lovestone, Bittleman, Nourteva, Fraina, Martens and several others, among them a certain Dr. Nosovitsky, a friend of Fraina who had traveled with him to Europe and who later publicly admitted that he had been an agent of the Department of Justice employed especially to investigate radical activities. When objections were raised to his presence on the ground that he was a police spy, both Bittleman and Lovestone insisted that he remain. The trial, of which a stenographic report was published by the Party, is a very enlightening document. It proves that the spy Dr. Nosovitsky had the confidence of the highest officials of the Communist Party, was a very good personal friend of Fraina and was considered a trustworthy member of the movement. Dr. Nosovitsky was not only permitted to be present at the trial, but he was in fact the one who asked most of the questions, using the occasion to cast doubt on the trustworthiness of Nourteva's witness, cross-examining him as if he were on trial, not Fraina. Right after the testimony was completed Fraina asked everyone present to state whether he thought that the matter had been sufficiently cleared up, so that he could leave for Moscow. Those present, including Dr. Nosovitsky, answered yes, with the exception of the Chairman, Houdin, and Nourteva, who answered No, and Weinstein, who reserved his opinion. A few months later Fraina, who was accused by the Comintern of embezzling funds entrusted to him, dropped out of the Communist movement for several years.

I was bitterly opposed to Lovestone in those days. He had originally helped split the Left Wing of the Socialist Party. He and his associates had been instrumental in organizing the Communist Party, from which I was excluded, while Reed and I organized the Communist Labor Party. When I read about his actions at the Winitsky trial I became furious. I sent word from prison that he must be removed at once from the ranks of the revolutionary movement, since he had violated the most sacred trust placed in him by testifying for the government against his comrade in the movement. I continued my opposition to him when I left prison. I opposed him bitterly at the Bridgeman underground convention of the "Number One" Communist Party. But such is the nature of the Communist movement that in its development a period was reached at which my political views on what was best for the movement coincided with the views of Jay Lovestone, and from that day in 1924 on, when the Party emerged from the celler into the open, I collaborated with him in the Ruthenberg caucus and shared the leadership of the Party with him. Though I never liked Lovestone's methods, I nevertheless developed the highest regard for his abilities, and as time passed the incidents of 1919 and 1920 faded into the background. Lovestone grew in my esteem. Like many others, I considered his services of great value to the revolutionary labor movement.

Lovestone was the one leader of our group who never lost

sight of the importance of holding on to the majority in the Party, come what may. He was a veritable Tammany chieftain among us Communists. He shuffled the Party jobs this way and that, all in order to build up a dependable Party machine. One of his most successful methods was to call a comrade into his office, tell him extremely confidential information, obtaining in return a solemn promise that the matter would not be disclosed to a soul. In that way he won the support of numerous Party members, who believed they were particularly favored by him. Naturally, at first none of them suspected that this information was common knowledge to scores of Party members who had received it in identically the same way they had. Lovestone was a high-pressure super-salesman of Communism. He sold it with particular success to ambitious intellectuals; especially, the naïve and the uninitiated, with the persistence of a Fuller brush salesman. Always holding forth a prize package free in the form of some Party honor, recognition, publicity, or important Party mission for accepting the bid to join the Communist Party, to act for the Party, or to donate large sums of money, Lovestone seldom failed. Inside the Party he high-hatted no one. He could stoop to the plane of the most backward Party member. Nevertheless, he was the man about whose private life little or nothing was known.

He was unmarried, as far as anyone knew, but beyond that not a man in the Party knew anything more about him. But Lovestone knew everything about everybody in the Party. He was a walking Walter Winchell of the lives and scandals of the important Party members. To him many Party comrades would confide their innermost secrets, yet he confided nothing. The leaders of the Party feared and hated him more than any other man because he knew too much. His personal file was the talk of the Party. Whenever he could get a leader of the Party down in black on white, it went into his file, and when one least expected it, the letter, foolishly written, the remark, damaging to one's character, was publicly used if the occasion demanded it.

Lovestone's weakness was his distrust of those who served him most loyally to the bitter end and his dependence on scoundrels. It seemed that he was afraid of honest, straightforward people. Instead, he put his greatest trust in Jack Stachel, who in turn did not trust Lovestone. In Stachel's estimation of human beings, there is no such thing as an honest and sincere man. He saw in everyone he met someone to guard against and someone to use in his schemes. He was Lovestone's junior by about five years. His main interest in Party affairs had to do with factional politics, the division of jobs and the control of Party committees. He won his place in the Party early as the organizer of the Young Workers League in New York. He aligned himself with the Ruthenberg group when it lost the control of the Party, becoming immediately influential in it through his control of the New York youth organization. In the Foster Group he could not have gained the same recognition because the outstanding national leaders of the youth were all in the Foster caucus. But he never allowed his attachment to the Ruthenberg group to sever his relations with Foster and Cannon. He was always ready to confer and to bargain. He was almost invariably up to date on the positions of the powers-that-be in Russia, but once he did make a mistake on the so-called Russian question. At a meeting of the Central Executive Committee in November, 1926, he sharply criticized a speech of Molotov's, but he soon more than corrected this slip by becoming the most loud-mouthed opponent of Trotskyism in the Party and by being the first one to rush in with an endorsement of every expression of the Russian leadership.

He did the dirty work in the Lovestone partnership, and did it gladly. He arranged the slates, made up the compositions of committees and decided who should get the jobs. Appeals from his decisions were made to Lovestone, those appealing little suspecting that the original lists had been worked out in collaboration with Lovestone. Stachel knew the Party rank and file better than any other man in the Party. He knew what they were thinking, how they were lined up and how they would vote. He could be as slimy and as slippery as an eel. But when that was not necessary, he acted brusquely, with authority, the perfect autocrat. On such occasions he would shout at Party members as if they were his chattels. But public work did not interest him. The recognition that comes with leading public struggles or public demonstrations had no attractions for him. He did not aspire to acclaim. He was rather determined to wield power inside the organization, not in the sense of building it up from scratch, but rather in the sense of fashioning a machine inside it which he could use for tightening his grip upon the Party. The public attracted by the Communist Party did not know Stachel, for he was what he desired to be—the man behind the man before the public. With Party leaders as his Charlie McCarthies, he was the Boss Tweed of American Communism, a Stalin within the limits of the Stalin-controlled Comintern.

Only in the Communist Party, ruled by the inner circle from the top down, could a man like Stachel rise to such a high position of power and leadership, for Stachel was despised by such of the Party membership as knew him and most despised by the very members of the faction to which he belonged. The membership of the faction more than once served ultimatums on Lovestone for Stachel's removal from his position of power and leadership in the Party. When Stachel was finally removed, it was only nominally, for he virtually ruled the Party organization together with Lovestone. Stachel the medicine man is today the National Secretary of the Communist Party, the most powerful figure behind the scenes, about whom little is heard. Today Lovestone, expelled from the Party, leads an insignificant sect which is in the ridiculous position of both trying to reform the Communist International and declaring that Stalin's Soviet policies are one hundred percent correct.

When Stalin removed me as the General Secretary of the Party in 1929, Max Bedacht, a member of our group who remained loyal to Stalin, was given the post. Stalin, however, made it clear that Bedacht's appointment was a temporary one. A struggle took place among the leaders of the Party for Bedacht's post when the time approached for replacing him by a permanent General Secretary. The members of the Political Committee split into factions, one headed by Browder and the other by Weinstone. The factions knew that Moscow was considering the American question once more and had not yet decided who was to be given the coveted post. At this time Browder had made a couple of serious blunders. Moscow had ordered the

Party, in view of the repeated Japanese provocations on the Siberian border, to stage anti-Japanese demonstrations. Browder, always eager to do the bidding of his masters, overreached himself by sending out instructions to the membership publicly through the Communist press, stating that the members must do everything in their power to make the demonstrations against Japan a huge success because they were ordered by Moscow. For exposing the hand of Moscow in the anti-Japanese demonstrations in this clumsy and stupid manner, Browder was severely censured by the Communist International, but the censure was never made public even before the membership of the American Party. Another issue within the ruling cliques of the Party involved the participation of the Party in the famous Bonus March during the Hoover Administration. The idea of a "Bonus March" was first formulated by the Workers Ex-Servicemen's League, an organization established by the Party. But Browder rejected the idea. It was, however, taken up by the veterans' organizations and groups with which the Communists had little to do and developed into a mighty movement. When the March was actually under way, Browder instructed the Communist veterans to proceed to Washington as an independent force. In Washington the Communist veterans, upon the direct instructions of Browder, sharply denounced the non-Communist leaders and organizations who had made the Bonus March a success. The Weinstone group sharply criticized Browder's group for its hesitation and lack of bold leadership in the Bonus March and held him responsible for the Party's failure to gain leadership and control of the movement. Weinstone then received word from Kuusinen, the Secretary of the Communist International, that Browder was slated to go, and advising him to make the bid for the secretaryship, Kuusinen assuring Weinstone of his support and that of the Executive of the Comintern.

Browder, a very gloomy figure in those days, confided to his friends that he had made many serious blunders, for which he was prepared to go into exile in Moscow for a number of years and do penance there. But Browder did not know Stalin. When Weinstone's name was suggested, Stalin put his thumbs down on the proposition. He did not want a Jew to be General Secretary of the American Communist Party. Moreover, precisely because of Browder's numerous blunders and his repentant humility, Stalin looked with favor upon him. Stalin said that Browder could be trusted to carry out orders implicitly precisely because he lacked independence of both thought and spirit; and besides, he was by birth a Christian and a native American. So Stalin chose Browder for the post—but not before Stachel had again made one of his remarkable acrobatic flip-flops, this time from the Weinstone group to that of Browder, personally exposing to Stalin all of Weinstone's factionalism in his effort to become General Secretary. Earl Browder, Stalin's choice, became the General Secretary of the American Party, and Weinstone was exiled to Moscow for a number of years.

Browder is a typical Midwesterner from Kansas, who instantly impressed me as a man of limited intellectual dimensions. Before he became General Secretary, it had never occurred to me that a man of his caliber could become head of the Party. When members of the Foster caucus used to complain to Foster about Browder's stupidities, he would remark, "But what can you expect from an errand boy?" When he was in his middle twenties he became enamored of a Party member who was about sixty years old, a much-married lady with numerous children and grandchildren. I saw him at the Bridgeman convention in 1922, his arm around her waist, strolling through the woods in the most romantic fashion. But soon after the Bridgeman convention Browder met a member of the Foster caucus by the name of Kitty Harris, a youngish and fanatical Communist engrossed in factional politics, whom he married. She became his loyal collaborator, serving him in every capacity, from that of secretary to confidential messenger on important trips to all parts of the world. However, when he came to aspire to the highest leadership after Stalin had swept Lovestone and me out of office, Browder began to woo Ruthenberg's last sweetheart, Anna David, who longed once more to move around in the high Communist court circles, an opportunity Browder gave her. That alliance lasted until Browder's trip to Moscow as General Secretary, for Browder was not allowed to leave Moscow without making his Russian sweetheart his legal and official wife. That

Russian woman is still his wife. A former judge of the revolutionary tribunal important enough to mete out death sentences, the present Mrs. Browder has been simultaneously in an important secretarial post of the Profintern and on the staff of the G. P. U. The latter is a connection that is never severed, except through death or flight from Soviet service. Kitty Harris, who was of far less political use to Browder than his Russian wife and whose presence in America might have proved embarrassing to him, was disposed of with the assistance of the Comintern and the Soviet government, which, playing upon Kitty Harris' loyalty to Communism above every other consideration, induced her to leave America for work in the G. P. U. abroad.

Browder, who was paraded as the leader of the American Party, was in fact nothing but a figurehead and a mouthpiece who spoke as ordered. Stalin, now that he had the American Party in his clutches, was not taking any chances of a slip. The result was that, in addition to one representative of the Comintern with plenipotentiary powers, representatives were sent from Moscow to head every important department of the Party. These representatives, whose identity is kept secret from the Party members, and who are known only to the leaders of the Party, constitute the real bosses of the Party. They determine the important Party policies and appointments to important posts. Similar organizational changes took place in the other Communist parties after Stalin assumed complete control of the Comintern.

Browder fits in perfectly with this setup. He is satisfied to do whatever he is told, since he knows that only by such subserviency can he hope to continue his glamorous public rôle as the leader of American Communism. The position which Browder holds has many advantages, one being that he does not directly assume responsibility for initiating and developing Party policy. Browder has been surrounded by an able staff that does his thinking for him, his speeches being written for him and his activities directed for him. He is, however, given freedom to deal with the lesser Party functionaries, and he has taken due advantage of this privilege, acting towards them like a little Stalin, subjecting those who displease him to severest condemnation and disciplinary action. Enjoying only the outward signs of leadership and power, he can taste its real attributes only in this fashion. Lately even the outward significance of his leadership has been circumscribed by the Party, for at the last convention the wings of the office of General Secretary were clipped by creating a new post in the Party, that of National Secretary. Browder is still the General Secretary, but he has actually little to do with the Party organization. That is left in the hands of the National Secretary, Jack Stachel, who has demonstrated to Stalin that he is able to see eye to eye with the supreme boss.

Stachel is the "big boss" of the American Communist Party. The American public knows nothing about him. Yet he has whatever substance of real leadership is permitted an American Communist leader. Stachel's position is a very important one, because, through his hands, the Communist organizational network is controlled and directed. It is not confined to the Communist Party alone, because, due to the Party's support of the New Deal and the C. I. O., it reaches into practically every walk of American life. The C. I. O. has augmented the Communist machine politically and financially beyond the fondest hopes of the Communists. Thousands of Communist Party members, who are under the direct orders of the Party, either acting openly or as concealed Communists, are holding down paid positions in the C. I. O. and its affiliated organizations. Stachel's department takes good care of that. Besides, the Party's support of the New Deal has made it possible for many Party members to parade around as non-Communists, and others without joining to work under the direction of the Party, with the result that the Party's interests are being served in many important quarters and even in government circles. A weird system of hypocrisy and deceit has been built up to maintain this structure, so that it can effectively accomplish things, which the Party openly as the Communist Party could never do. This weird system, this chameleon superstructure, is operated by crafty Stachel so stealthily that it hoodwinks many well-wishing innocent people, motivated by idealism and lofty sentiments.

Browder, who enjoys being allowed to bask in the Communist

limelight, has never lost sight of his self-interest. And Moscow has taken that fact into consideration, for Browder is given every opportunity to earn a sufficient income to live comfortably. During our régime in the Party we seldom received our wages in full. For weeks at a time I often went without receiving a penny in wages. Lectures, articles, extra work was never paid for. But today it is different. Wages are paid regularly. Royalty is paid on books that are printed and sold to the Party members, who must buy them as a Communist duty. Besides, the Russian press now pays Browder for articles he submits to the Russian magazines and newspapers, in American valuta. We got paid for articles before, but in Russian rubles, which we had to spend in Moscow, and the sums were never large enough to make a substantial amount. Today Communism is a paying proposition for the Party's spokesman, who, for value received, speaks exactly as he is told, with small regard for consistency, let alone honesty or decency.

For years Browder had been insisting that the Party should have nothing to do with any labor party because it was a Fascist development. He was called in to Moscow, and returned so thoroughly converted that he not only favored the organization of a labor party but called upon the comrades to do everything possible to help bring about its organization. For years he had been calling the American Federation of Labor a Fascist reactionary organization, and insisted that the party must build its own revolutionary unions. Again, upon a return from one of his trips to Moscow, he suddenly developed a change of opinion and succeeded in having the Party liquidate the unions it had organized in order that its members might go back into the A. F. of L. In 1932, after Roosevelt was elected and came out with his New Deal program, Browder attacked Roosevelt as a potential Fascist and the New Deal as Fascist. Then he went to Moscow, saw the light, and returned a stanch champion of President Roosevelt and the New Deal. Then the Republican Party was attacked by Browder as the seat of reaction and Fascism. He went so far as to charge that it was under Nazi influence. But, again a fateful trip Kremlin-ward, a fateful return from Moscow, and lo! a declaration that the Communist

Party must work with the progressive forces in the Republican Party. He is a man of such diversity and of such elasticity that it is possible for him with the most serious and pious demeanor to profess his belief in the very same thing he denounced in the sharpest terms only one day before. To him—and he is merely the best-known example of the typical Communist career man—"honor is only a bourgeois prejudice"—the phrase that epitomizes Communist ethics. Given the opportunity, Browder may yet endorse the Nazi régime in Germany, should his Moscow masters require it of him.

CHAPTER X

STORMING THE TRADE UNION FORTRESS

I HAVE already told how in 1921, following upon a swing to the Right in Russian internal and foreign policy—(the New Economic Policy restoring a certain amount of private trade, following upon food strikes in Soviet factories, peasant rebellions like the one in Tambov, and the never-to-be-forgotten Kronstadt Rebellion of Soviet sailors, once hailed as the pride and glory of the Bolshevik Revolution; as well as the signing of trade agreements with capitalist countries, of which the most important was the one with Great Britain, the opening up of Russian natural resources to foreign concessionaires, and the like)—the Comintern policy changed accordingly, a change signalized by the publication of Lenin's pamphlet, "Left Wing Communism: An Infantile Disorder." At the same time the Communist policy of revolutionary trade unionism, which looked upon the struggle for improved labor conditions and higher pay as merely levers for developing a revolutionary mass movement, building revolutionary unions along parallel lines to the established conservative trade union movement, was dealt a death blow by this very pamphlet of Lenin's, and the diametrically opposite policy of boring from within the existing trade union organizations was suddenly instituted. As I had already pointed out, this sudden about face was not caused by any change of conditions in our own country, but was instituted for the sake of consistency with Russian internal policy and in the service of the foreign policy of the Soviet government, which through control and domination of organized labor hoped to exert pressure on the public opinion in the democratic capitalist countries in favor of *de jure* recognition of, and trade with, the Soviet government.

As far as the United States is concerned, while prior to 1934 the Soviet government exploited American labor and liberal opinion principally in the interests of recognition by the Washington government, it concentrated with increasing intensity to exploit those layers of American public opinion to arouse a mass hysteria against the alleged Japanese menace along lines analogous to the "Yellow Peril" propaganda in the yellow journals of our country, to interfere with American policy toward Spain, toward Germany, toward Italy and even such recent matters as the Ludlow Amendment and so-called "neutrality" legislation before the Congress of the United States. The Soviet government, vitally interested in jockeying the American government into a position analogous to its own on these and other issues of international significance, has exerted its influence on American public opinion through numerous organized channels, some open, others *sub rosa.* One of these has been the organized labor movement. Since 1921 our task has been to storm the fortress of American trade unionism with Bolshevik resoluteness and capture it—we thought, for the Bolshevik Revolution in America and throughout the world; but our Russian masters, more practical and realistic than we, wanted it only as diplomatic leverage for their People's (sic) Commissariat of Foreign Affairs. Our revolutionary enthusiasm was thus exploited to help maintain in power the political gang that had seized the reins of the Russian State. Bear that in mind as you read the story of what we Communists did to American labor organized in trade unions, at the behest of a foreign power.

I do not mean to imply that the Russian leaders rejected out of hand the prospect of a proletarian revolution in the United States after 1921. As I see it, they began in 1917 with the most fantastic illusions, the most puerile ideas, about the possibilities for revolution in the countries of Europe and even the United States—childish visions to which Leon Trotsky and a small band of political ghosts still cling with the firmness of rigor mortis—and as they were knocked on the head in Hungary, in Bavaria, in Bulgaria, again and again in Germany, in China, and elsewhere, the Russian attitude toward revolution gradually developed into the classic example of Soviet policy in Spain, the policy of exploiting a revolutionary situation to seize control of a revolutionary government for the sake of making the country ruled by that Soviet-dominated government a pawn in the diplomatic game. If that much cannot be achieved, the Soviet government is satisfied to play the game inside of a foreign country through its policy of *Front Populaire,* as demonstrated in France since 1936, or by an adaptation of popular-frontism to American conditions, by tacking Communist sails to the national administration under Roosevelt, a municipal administration under La Guardia, or a trade union movement like the C. I. O. under the redoubtable John L. Lewis. Object? Less and less proletarian revolution, hope in which has been practically abandoned, and more and more the interests of the Soviet state. The advocates of world revolution are about as inimical to the democratic order in the United States—or anywhere else, for that matter—as the Seventh Day Adventists. The real danger comes from the totalitarians of the Soviet-Communist persuasion, who have worked out a gospel attuned to the wishful thinking of maladjusted intellectuals and the restless youth of the country, tempting them with all sorts of ideological and organizational shortcuts to a more abundant life. All that Stalin's intricate power machine demands in return is the defense of its interests. That this Soviet system of social corruption and intellectual pollution is today dangerously contaminating American life is attested to by such manifestations as the control exercised by the Communist Party in the publishing field, among book reviewers, among actors on Broadway and in Hollywood, among scenario writers and playwrights as well as the general run of writers, among college teachers and college students, among clergymen and in church organizations, in political clubs of both major parties as well as the third-party movements, and last, but far from least, among organized labor.

My purpose here is to tell as briefly as possible how we first began to make inroads into the field of organized labor, how we established Communist control of certain trade unions, what effect this Communist intervention has on the welfare of the workers, and to trace the origin of the Communist system of penetration into American trade unions. One cannot understand the workings of the Stalin power machine in American life today without knowing the story of its inception—first of all, among the needle trades unions of New York City. That was the testing ground for the methods that are now yielding a rich harvest of influence and control to the Communists in more phases of American life than the average American realizes. I shall therefore have to go back a decade and a half, to the year 1924, when the Central Executive Committee of the American Workers (Communist) Party placed me in charge of our campaign in the needle trades unions. These were selected as the point of least resistance to Communist penetration at the time, because we already had some two thousand of our members scattered in those unions, some of them held important minor posts, and the majority of members in those unions were the sort of foreign-born who had been for years under Socialist influence and hence attuned to our ideological approach.

We began by ranking the needle trades unions on the basis of our chances to make progress inside of them, as follows: first came the Furriers International Union, second the Ladies Garment Workers Union, then the Amalgamated Clothing Workers of America, followed by the Hat, Cap and Millinery Workers Union. Our so-called "industrial policy" was founded of course on the strategic principle of boring from within. Keymen from the locals of the various unions we were intent on capturing would meet with me from day to day, bringing me first-hand information on conditions in their particular locals and in their entire union, as far as they knew, and I in turn would collect all this information, collate it, and on the basis of it translate our strategy into concrete tactical steps for each local and each union. Naturally, our tactics and policies would vary in accordance with the equipment of our agency in the unions, local conditions and various other circumstances. To what extent and just how they varied will become apparent as I describe certain concrete experiences.

At the end of the World War the conditions in the needle trades industries were far worse than they had been before the war, with chronic unemployment, strikes and lockouts rampant. Negroes, Latin Americans and Italians on a much greater scale than heretofore considerably diluted the hitherto preponderant

Jewish immigrants. These were drawn in as the industries spread out on an unprecedented scale to parts of the country free from unionization. The manufacturers resorted to professional gangsters in an effort to keep their employees ununionized, trade union officials fought back with the same weapon, and before long the unions in many instances fell a prey to racketeering gangsters. In protest against this corruption, against the increasingly undemocratic methods of trade union officials, and in a desperate effort to improve their lot, trade unionists here and there organized themselves into opposition groups within the needle trades unions. Our first move therefore was to insinuate ourselves into the leadership of these opposition groups wherever possible and to capitalize the discontent of the organized workers for our own Communist purposes. We hoped to oust the old trade union officials, displace the influence of our chief political rival in these unions, the Socialist Party, and capture the leadership of almost three hundred thousand organized workers. Using the needle trades as a base, we proposed to reach out for certain locals of the building trades, the shoe workers unions, the silk branch of the textile industry, the jewelry workers, leathergoods, upholstery, raincoat workers and the unions of the United Hebrew Trades. With these phalanxes as an opening wedge, we planned to launch a war for the capture of the American Federation of Labor through a network of our agents, who were to be placed in key positions in these unions as paid functionaries and who were to secure access to union treasuries, our idea being that the American Federation of Labor should also finance its own transformation into a Communist-led organization. The capture of such an important sector of American public opinion and sheer voting strength was of tremendous importance to the Soviet government, which at the time was primarily interested in securing recognition by Washington and in promoting trade relations. Moscow therefore concentrated its financial aid to us on this major effort to colonize American organized labor with Communist leaders.

Needless to say, our campaign developed behind a camouflage of high-minded principles. We drew up elaborate programs for the needle trades as a whole, for each of the four great unions, for every union election down to the smallest local. Under that smokescreen we laid our barrage on the union leadership. If we cast all decency to the winds in this struggle for power, the entrenched labor leaders were no more squeamish than we in defending themselves against our onslaught. Lies, treachery, character assassination and sanguine battles between the opposing forces became the order of the day. While castigating the trade union officials as gangsters and racketeers, we did not hesitate to negotiate with them and make deals that suited our purposes. While denouncing every agreement with the manufacturers concluded without our participation as a sell-out, the same sort of agreement concluded under our sponsorship was hailed as a brilliant victory for militant trade unionism. We savagely attacked the entrenched trade union officials for resorting to the services of professional gangsters and drew the bitter moral that this was the morass into which reactionary leadership was leading the honest trade unionists, but when we hired gangsters and resorted to gangster methods, we pointed with pride to the heroic achievements of the rank and file, glorying in the revolutionary upsurge of the class-conscious masses. What venom we spilled on the heads of certain Socialist officials in the unions for alleged squandering of union funds on bribes to police officials, while at the same time some of our Communist officials far outstripped the Socialists in this branch of trade union technique!

As the fight developed we began to attract to our banner a number of trade union office seekers, who joined the Communist Party only because they became impressed with our omnipotence in securing trade union elections of candidates sponsored by us. But we did not rely on these climbers; we had sincere Party members in strategic positions, among them Ben Gold and Aaron Gross of the Furriers and Sasha Zimmermann, the brilliant manager of the Dressmakers Local 22 of the I. L. G. W. U. These Communists in key positions in the needle trades discussed every phase of trade union activity, including the most confidential, with the proper Party officials. This was first, the Political Committee of the Party's Central Executive

Committee, highest in rank in our hierarchy, which carried out policies approved by the Comintern and the Profintern. Next came the Needle Trades Committee of the Central Executive Committee (of which I was the Chairman), which functioned on the spot in New York City, the center of the fight. Then followed the National Committee of the Trade Union Educational League in Chicago, headed by Foster, of which Committee I was also a member. Then came the District Committee of the New York District of the Party, which carried out the orders of the Central Executive Committee's Needle Trades Committee. The Leading Fraction of the Needle Trades, composed of the outstanding Communist leaders of the needle trades unions, ranked next in importance. Right below them was the National Needle Trades Committee of the Trade Union Educational League. Then followed the leading fractions of each one of the unions, which included not only the leaders of the unions but also the Communist members on the Joint Boards and all Communist officials plus the Communist leaders of the opposition movement, if they had no official place in the unions. Besides, each local union had its Party fraction divided into a small leading fraction and the all-embracing fraction of all the Party members in that local union. In addition, there were Trade Union Educational League members and writers, who participated in the unions as so-called "progressive movements" and "blocs," both representing a united front with the Communists. In all these organizational ramifications the Communists were organized into fractions in which Communist policy was first decided upon and then rammed down the innocents' throats. As Chairman of the Needle Trades Committee of the Central Executive Committee of the Communist Party I had to supervise all of this intricate network.

The Party's Central Executive Committee followed closely every development in the needle trades fight. It made decisions on all phases of the struggle. Between October fifth and twenty-ninth, 1925, it sent me nineteen separate communications containing suggestions on policies, and over a hundred decisions. These communications and decisions from the Central Executive Committee and the National Office of the Trade Union

Educational League, including the suggestions in the letters from Ruthenberg, Foster and Lovestone, were in turn taken up by the Central Executive Committee's Needle Trades Committee and its detailed decisions passed on in turn to the New York District Committee of the Communist Party and the needle trades leaders and fractions. These letters and decisions did not deal with Party policy alone, but also with the most intimate union matters which should have been the concern of the unions alone.

In the course of the needle trades fight we developed a special set of epithets against our opponents. The uses of language in Communist trade union fights has a history all its own, which begins with the inception of the Trade Union Educational League. At first we were careful what names we called trade union officials. In those days Moscow nursed the hope of establishing a progressive labor bloc friendly to the Soviet government, with the aid of Sidney Hillman and some of the progressive trade union leaders in the railroad brotherhoods and in the A. F. of L. unions. That was in 1921. Foster was then on very friendly terms with a number of these officials and had entrée to still others because of his close and friendly association with Fitzpatrick of the Chicago Federation of Labor. After Foster's memorable break with Fitzpatrick in July, 1923, Gompers took the offensive against the Trade Union Educational League and the Communists. Foster lost his privilege to use the platform of the Chicago Federation of Labor as a sounding board for his policies and campaigns against Gompers. His former trade union friends shied away from him. He became a very troubled man. One day at a meeting of the Central Executive Committee he began, as was his habit, to fish in the troubled waters of the trade union fight. At this meeting he finally came to the conclusion that, in order to instill the proper spirit into the forces leading the fight, their hatred must be aroused against Gompers and his lieutenants. Foster insisted that we had been too gentle in the fight. To call our opponents "conservatives" and "reactionaries" was not enough. It didn't describe them properly and by branding them as such you could not expect to arouse the proper fighting spirit among the workers. Even the characterization of them as "misleaders of labor" was much too mild. From then on we had to brand them for what they were. "Call a spade a spade," Foster reiterated. "'Labor fakers,' that's what we'll call them. We must use every epithet that will arouse the hatred of the workers against them." We followed this advice and soon improved on Foster. In the needle trades fight we used every vulgar characterization that we could invent, to precipitate a revulsion against the officialdom. The *Freiheit* became particularly adept at this game and certain members of its staff proved themselves to be veritable geniuses in billingsgate.

Outstanding among them was that newspaper's labor editor. A carpenter by trade, Yuditz was not much of a newspaperman, but he was peerless as a reviler. His Yiddish bristled with the slang and vulgarisms of the shops, and he transferred them all to the columns of *Freiheit*. Since no word was too vile for him to write, his contribution to recorded calumny is unique in labor journalism. Some of the gentler names he called the labor leaders we opposed were: *Vorwaerts Menschen* [creatures of the *Forward*, Jewish Socialist newspaper], crooks, gangsters, crooked politicians, *Starker* [strong-arm men], gunmen, agents of the bosses, yellows, mobsters, fakers, traitors, police agents. These are mere samples. The objective of such linguistic exercises was to assassinate the character of our opponents and arouse the mob spirit against them. This soon became common practice for all of us, and was resorted to in all Party campaigns. We managed to develop it into such a portentous weapon that many in the labor and liberal movement were cowed and terrorized into silence or submission rather than brave a barrage of our invectives.

Exploiting to the utmost the harrowing economic situation in the needle trades market, which declined steadily since the end of the War, we used our weapons of villification for all they were worth in whipping up the discontent of the workers into a frenzy of opposition. We Communist leaders did it deliberately and "with malice aforethought," but the rank and file who followed us earnestly believed that they were engaged in a great mission of reform. They believed that a Communist victory would end the abuses from which they suffered, would install an honest and idealistic trade union leadership in place of the old bureaucrats they despised and blamed for all their ills. The radicals among them believed moreover that, in addition to an improvement in conditions, the victory of the Communists in the union would bring the workers nearer to the goal of working-class liberation through the overthrow of the capitalist system. Whatever may have been the political ambitions of the Communist leaders at the time, whatever may have been the reasons for the actions of the Communist trade union officials, the rank and file trusted us implicitly and followed us blindly. With the idealistic spirit of self-sacrifice for which the radical needle trade workers are known, they went into the fight and fought courageously. And they paid very dearly for it. Many were crippled for life, as bones were broken and heads were smashed. Very often they went down before the blackjacks of gangsters and the blows of policemen's clubs. Thousands were thrown out of their jobs and their families made destitute. But they never failed to rally to the call of the Communists. When employed, they responded unstintingly to all Left Wing appeals for money and literally emptied their pockets to contribute hundreds of thousands of dollars to the Communist Party.

The Furriers Strike

The New York Fur Workers Union was the first bona fide affiliate of the American Federation of Labor to come under Communist Party control. It had a membership of about thirteen thousand, or three-fourths of all members in its parent organization, the International Fur Workers Union of North America and Canada, of which it was the financial and organizational mainstay. The industrial plants in which these thirteen thousand unionists were employed produced moreover four-fifths of all fur garments manufactured in the United States. In 1925 we Communists took over the New York Furriers Union, through an alliance with leading racketeers and gangsters that had broken away from the notorious Kaufman machine, centering around Morris Kaufman, then the President of the International Fur Workers Union of North America and Canada. The very gangsters who formerly had used knives and blackjacks against the Communists now protected them instead of protecting Kaufman. The Kaufman machine correctly described the new alliance in its letter to the New York membership of July ninth, 1925, when it declared:

> The first unholy act of this united fraud was the deal of its chief leaders . . . for years the bitterest foes, with ex-manager Brownstein. These have entered into an alliance with the so-called Furriers Civic Club whose members have been recruited from the picket committee in the strike of 1920.

Kaufman knew the members of the Furriers' Civic Club very well. They were the very same strong-arm boys who had been paid by his machine to terrorize and beat up the opposition when he controlled the organization. Now that the situation was reversed, he complained of the unholy alliance. And we Communists, who had made the fight against gangsterism the main issue among the Furriers, had no qualms in making a deal with the gangsters, accepting their protection and services, including the most nefarious gangster activities, just as long as they controlled the union and dominated its affairs.

We had two able leaders in the Furriers Union, Ben Gold and Aaron Gross. They complemented each other. Gold was the dynamic personality. He was of short stature and fair complexion, vain, quick-tempered and a fiery orator who always succeeded in arousing his audience to a high pitch of enthusiasm. He rode to glory on the crest of their acclaim. He knew his furriers, knew that he could play on their emotions as no one else could. Old and young, men and women regarded him as a demi-god. They believed he could relieve them of all their troubles and difficulties. He was a young man, physically strong, courageous, audacious. A furrier himself and a member of the union since his boyhood days, he had a combination of qualities which, reinforced by the backing of the Communist Party, raised him to outstanding leadership in the union. Gold took particular delight in his ability as a leader of the union to mete out physical punishment to the union's internal as well as external enemies—and of course any member of the union who fell afoul of Ben Gold's whims was an internal enemy. He was the bosom companion of the strong-arm boys of the union and was continuously seen in their company. They in turn reciprocated his admiration for them by looking upon him as their master whose merest glance was law.

Gross was the direct opposite. He was not an orator. He spoke quietly and with great reserve. He never lost his temper. He was shrewd and calculating in all his actions. Gross was the brains behind Gold. Never spectacular and seldom acclaimed by the masses, Gross was the man who thought out the moves in overcoming the difficulties that beset the Communists in the union. He was the man of committees and conferences whose judgment Gold always respected. Many of the moves which Gold dramatically executed in public and for which he was thunderously applauded by the masses were actually the product of Gross's well thought-out decisions. Gross was also a furrier, a few years older than Gold. He was gentle in his habits, physically not strong, boasting was not in his sphere, and he did not seek the public acclaim which Gold relished. Both were Communists. But both were narrow in their conception of Communism. They were so intimately bound up with the affairs of their union that they failed to see the union's limitations and the greater political arena of which the affairs of the union were but a small part. Gross, being the more intelligent, and intellectually the more honest of the two, was nevertheless sufficiently cognizant of his own shortcomings as a Communist leader and aware of the broader aspects of the movement to break in 1929 with the Party and with Stalin's dominance over it.

Our leadership of the Furriers Union met its first test of battle in the furriers' strike that broke out on February sixteenth, 1926, after the manufacturers had flatly rejected the union's three main demands—(1) the forty-hour, five-day week, (2) equal division of work throughout the year, and (3) the establishment of an unemployment insurance fund, to be raised by contributions from the manufacturers at the rate of three percent of the wages paid, distribution of the fund to be completely in the hands of the union. The immediate antecedents of that conflict are recorded in my correspondence with the National Office of the Communist Party, for it was my duty to keep it fully informed of the situation. Thus, on February first, 1926, I wrote to Ruthenberg:

> A general strike of the Furriers is absolutely certain. Our comrades during the negotiations offered a compromise on the question of equal division of work. The compromise was not even considered. The manufacturers demanded the withdrawal of all three points. . . . It would have been better for us if the strike could have been avoided. Now we will have to strain every effort to push the strike, when it will be officially called, to a successful conclusion.

At the Central Executive Committee's Needle Trades Committee meeting of February fourth, at which both Gold and Gross were present, the question of the strike referendum was considered, and a decision was made for actually delaying the calling of the strike. At that meeting it was also decided that "we cannot give Shachtman, President of the International Fur Workers Union, as was the custom, the chairmanship of the general strike committee . . . Gold must be the chairman, and Shachtman must be given an office compatible with his position." As to the Communist Party's role in that strike, the minutes of this meeting state the following: "Comrade Gross pointed out, the Party would have to determine policy throughout the struggle."

And the Party did. At the very beginning of the strike, a steering committee, composed entirely of Communist Party members, was chosen by the National Office of the Communist Party to direct the strike and determine its policy. It was this steering committee, with which I met continuously as the representative of the Central Executive Committee, not the official strike committees selected by the union that actually directed the strike. It was this committee which met at the Union Square Hotel, where secret headquarters were established by Gold, and at such places where the most important problems of the strike were discussed and strategy decided upon. Yet the real leadership of that was even more select than the clandestine Communist steering committee, for within it was an inner circle, which very often met separately and determined in advance questions which were considered too important and confidential to take up without adequate preparation with the entire steering committee. This inner circle consisted of Gold, Gross and Potash of the Furriers Union, myself for the Party and, at times, William Weinstone of the New York district, or one or two other Communist leaders.

I recall a typical meeting of this esoteric little group which was held on February twenty-third at the headquarters of the Party, 108 East Fourteenth Street. At this meeting Zack, Weinstone, Gold, Gross, Potash and I were present. According to the minutes of that meeting, Gold gave a confidential report on certain phases of the strike's activity. He stated that during the first week of the strike the finance committee had spent about eight thousand dollars; that for the first four to five weeks, the committee would have to spend at the rate of about ten thousand dollars per week; and that the law committee had made "arrangements" with a Tammany Hall lawyer for the sum of about four thousand dollars per week. This lawyer was supposed to cover all the territories affected by the strike, "fix" police captains, and get rid of "gorillas." It was proposed by the law committee, according to Gold's report, that two automobiles be bought for two detectives, who would use them in chasing away the gorillas. Further, in reporting on the police situation, Gold stated that

> the 5th Street police worked well. Police angry. Mercer Street was all right. 27th Street O. K. 30th Street O. K. . . . The [lawyer] pledged to create a favorable situation. Chief of the detective bureau was not in game. Now everything O. K.

Reporting on the picketing committee, Gold boasted of its achievements. In breaking up fifty-two corporation shops—shops run by small operators on a contract basis—everything in them was destroyed and two of the bosses were so badly beaten up that they thought they would die. Indeed, the chairman of the picket committee had to go into hiding, because the District Attorney's Office was making an investigation. Reporting this, Gold concluded with obvious satisfaction,

One of the chief of detectives said, "You can't tell me you have no gorillas."

The expenses of this strike were staggering, far beyond our expectations. Eight days before the outbreak of the strike I had written to Ruthenberg:

> Another conference with the manufacturers takes place this week. I doubt if the strike will be avoided. . . . A settlement would be of the greatest help to us . . . would make it possible for the furriers to back us up with sufficient finances for our textile struggle in Passaic, which must be broadened to include Lawrence, if we want to have it culminate successfully. . . . It would stiffen up our fight in the whole of the needle trades considerably. But, as Gold states, dreams of a settlement are nonsense. The manufacturers will give the union the stiffest and worst struggle it has ever experienced. . . . The Furriers Union has not sufficient finances for such a struggle. . . . They will need close to a million dollars. . . .

I wrote that on February eighth, 1926. But a few weeks later it began to look as if even the optimum estimate of "close to a million dollars" was rank understatement. The law committee alone spent at the rate of ten thousand dollars weekly minimum and more often a good deal more—how much altogether being still a dark mystery, since the nature of its expenditures was always so strictly confidential and its disbursements were so thoroughly camouflaged in the course of bookkeeping that subsequently no one was able to solve that puzzle. Bribing the police cost us at least fifty percent more per average police station than we had been led to believe by the Tammany Hall lawyer who was our fixer. Over six hundred thousand dollars was spent only in strike relief. Besides, there were: the maintenance of a very populous picket committee, the rental of halls, printing, automobiles, the upkeep of an out-of-town department, sundry lawyers, and the like.

Although Jack Schneider, a Party member, was Chairman of the Picket Committee, its guiding spirit was really Ben Gold. The backbone of that committee were members of the Greek Federation, fearless and able fighters, who were exemplary in wielding the knife, the blackjack and other weapons. All Party members assigned to the Picket Committee were paid for their services, as were the professional gangsters hired by the Picket Committee. Its members were accorded special considerations, because they were the shock troops of the strike, the ones who did the actual fighting and faced the greatest danger. The Party members on the Picket Committee, especially the Greeks, were all loyal and devoted Communists. They did the work assigned to them not because they were paid but because they believed that they were serving the working class and especially the Communist movement. We indoctrinated our membership with the idea that violence in strikes was necessary and that the revolution for which the Communists were striving could be accomplished only through violence. Anyone who resorted to violence against "scabs" and "bosses" was glorified. The members of the Picket Committee were heralded as heroes. The very type of knife they used—a knife in which the blade was let loose immediately by the pressing of a button—became an object of admiration, and many such knives were acquired by Party members who had no occasion to use them yet prized them highly and attached fetichistic significance to them. As for the actual members of the Picket Committee, they were a wild audacious lot, who went into action like ferocious beasts, unafraid of the enemy, be he gangster or policeman. They spread terror among the scabs. The gangsters in the hire of the bosses were no match for them. In their eagerness to make good, it was not unusual for them to attack the police as well. I believe now that a great deal of the braggadocio displayed by them was due to their awareness that their violent actions were being effectively protected by the activities of the Law Committee. Whenever they were arrested they were freed as soon as their lawyer appeared in court.

In this strike an unusual institution was established, known as the Butcher Shop. It consisted of a room in Astoria Hall. Here one of the powerful members of the Picket Committee officiated. Known scabs and workers who were suspected of treachery to the strike were brought to the hall, where a hearing was given to them, and then they were turned over to the one in charge of the torture chamber, where they were given "a lesson in unionism that they would never forget." Gold once reported to one of our meetings with a sort of sadistic delight what happened to one scab there. As revolting as the gory tale was, there was not one among the Communist leaders including myself who did not consider the treatment accorded the scab as justified by the theory that, since a strike was virtual warfare, violence was essential.

One result of the furriers' strike was that violence ceased to be considered by Party members as a means towards an end. It began to be regarded in practice as an end in itself. Violence *per se* began to be worshiped. Party members would gather around members of the Picket Committee, their faces aglow with excitement and enjoyment, as they listened to the tales of violent deeds well done. Little did the Party members realize that later members of the very same Picket Committee, especially the "Greeks," would be used as effectively and with as much violence against those Party comrades who disagreed with the Party line. Nor could they foretell that many of the members of the Picket Committee, especially the "Greeks," who had joined the Picket Committee out of idealistic considerations as Communists, would degenerate into professional gangsters in the pay of the Communist Party.

Our leadership of the Fur Workers Union ran contrary to all Communist theory. We had always maintained that we represented primarily the unskilled and the most oppressed workers. We considered the American Federation of Labor an organization largely based upon the skilled, the "aristocracy of labor." Our theory held that the skilled workers, because they were better paid, represented a privileged class, whose better wages actually represented "bribes" in the form of special privileges accorded them by the capitalist class. We, therefore, concluded that the skilled, the backbone of the A. F. of L., were a force of reaction and stood for the maintenance of capitalism. But the furriers were not unskilled workers. They were highly skilled, and, whenever employed, received good wages. It was not unusual for a furrier during the busy season to go home at the end of a week's work with over a hundred dollars in his pay envelope. The trade could not be learned easily; it took years of apprenticeship to become a good fur worker. Theirs was not a basic but a luxury industry, mainly catering to the wealthier section of the middle classes and the very rich. Yet we gained our greatest influence among these highly skilled and privileged workers.

To meet the attack of the Socialists, of *The Jewish Daily Forward* and of the opposition in the furriers' union itself, we adopted the strategy of conducting the strike as a recognized union of the A. F. of L. No expression of dual unionism was tolerated. At the outset of the strike the endorsement of the Central Trades and Labor Council was secured. In fighting against the Right Wing, we attacked not only those dislodged by the furriers from power in their own union, but also the Right Wing in the International Ladies Garment Workers Union and the Hillman machine in the Amalgamated Clothing Workers. We thus succeeded in splitting the Socialists, by winning the support of Norman Thomas, who publicly repudiated the activities of *The Jewish Daily Forward* and of all the Right Wing Socialists.

Following the failure of the Right Wing to break the Communist grip on the strike, Hugh Frayne, organizer of the American Federation of Labor in New York, and William Green, president of the American Federation of Labor, were brought into the strike situation in an effort to outmaneuver the Communists and to settle the strike without them. The policy for counteracting the interference of Frayne and Green was worked out in detail by me, with the aid of the Steering Committee, and was immediately reported to the National Office, so that in turn it could be embodied as a decision of the Communist Party's Political Committee. Frayne's first salvo against us was in the form of a referendum instituted among the strikers on the following question: "Shall the International Union forthwith go into a conference with the Associated Fur Manufacturers for a settlement of the strike?" This question was formulated in Yiddish as well as in English. But the vote on this referendum was an emphatic, No, in both languages, Frayne's attack turning thus into a boomerang, for it brought out beyond cavil or doubt that the union members preferred the leadership of the New York Joint Board and its inimitable chieftain, Ben Gold.

A meeting was then called by Hugh Frayne, to be held in Carnegie Hall, at which William Green was to speak and at which the terms of the strike settlement were to be announced. We decided to send our numerous adherents among strikers en masse and early to Carnegie Hall. After carefully planning our strategy, we instructed our strikers to call for Ben Gold as soon as the meeting was opened. This was only an initial move of a carefully-organized procedure of disruption. Not a thing was left to chance. The moment the doors of Carnegie Hall swung open, our stalwarts rushed in, led by veteran members of the Picket Committee. The latter, reinforced by other battle-tested Communists, were assigned to key posts in various parts of the hall. Our people had that hall filled to capacity in one steady press of pushing humanity. We had an army of over four thousand inside the hall and another fifteen thousand fur workers with Communists scattered judiciously among them milling around outside. To make the success of our strategy doubly sure, we took precautions to arrange that the police should not interfere. As soon as the doors were closed, the signal was given, and four thousand throats merged in the "We Want Gold!" "We Want Gold!"—spurred on by the Communists. When Frayne took the platform as chairman of the meeting, he was immediately greeted by thousands of voices shouting lustily, "We Want Gold!" Frayne was as powerless against the cries for Gold as was King Canute against the rising tide of the ocean. He looked silly and pathetic, gesturing in vain, his lips moving without producing a single audible sound. In sheer desperation and helplessness, he finally gave up. The meeting had to be abandoned. Green did not even appear on the platform.

Having won a complete victory by routing the enemy on his own stamping ground in the Battle of Carnegie Hall, we were ready to make peace with the vanquished foe. A diplomatic mission, headed by Ben Gold, was delegated to negotiate with William Green. This was all the more possible, because the terms of settlement Frayne had secured from the manufacturers, and publicly announced immediately after the meeting that did not take place, were not too far afield from our own conception of such terms. Indeed, with the exception of one point, they proved to be identical with the terms on which we ultimately settled the strike. That point dealt with hours: Frayne obtained a forty-two hour week; we secured a forty hour week—surely, an unsubstantial difference. Nevertheless, our diplomatic mission induced Green to reject Frayne's eight-point settlement. Moreover, it was agreed that another mass meeting would be called, at which William Green was to reverse himself by publicly endorsing the strike and its continuation. At this meeting both President Shachtman and Ben Gold were to join Green in indorsing the strike. And so it happened that Green, grateful to us for this face-saving device, was cheered lustily by our organized cheerers, led by our cheer-leaders, at the mass meeting in the Sixty-ninth Regiment Armory on Thirty-fourth Street after he spoke his little piece in accordance with our instructions. But even then our lads did not overlook the finer points in the game of prestige: the organized cheers for the President of the American Federation of Labor were mere bleatings by comparison with the organized ovation accorded Ben Gold.

Several weeks later, in an effort to settle the strike, we called upon William Green to help us. He responded. But the negotiations between the strike leaders and the manufacturers at which Green was present turned out to be unsuccessful. After the break-up of these negotiations, Green supported us further by issuing a statement in favor of the forty-hour week. But it did not do us much good.

The inner circle of the Steering Committee met right after that to find a way out of a desperate situation. Gold, Gross and the other strike leaders were very much worried over the turn of events. They were afraid that Green was now in position to force a settlement. Gold expressed the opinion by endorsing the strike and by speaking under the auspices of the New York Furriers, Green had outmaneuvered us, had created a favorable impression among the workers, and through his endorsement of the forty-hour week could force a settlement over the heads of the strike leaders. Gold was also of the opinion that Green could use the strike politically to discredit its Communist-controlled leaders by claiming that they alone stood in the way of a peaceful settlement of the dispute. *What to do?* was the perplexing question. The only suggestions that came from Gold, Gross and the others was the old stock-in-trade one of launching an attack upon Green, by "warning" the workers that, like Frayne, he was preparing a settlement of the strike that was a sell-out. But I argued that such a course would be ruinous, because it would throw Green and the A. F. of L. against the strike, particularly at a time when the workers were becoming tired of the long struggle and finances were low. I insisted that we had everything to lose and nothing to gain by such a policy. I then proposed a policy which Gold and Gross immediately accepted. In view of Green's endorsement of the forty-hour week demand of the strikers, I advised that we build a united front movement in support of the strike, as the beginning of a movement for the establishment of the forty-hour week in all industries.

Plans were immediately made for the calling of a forty-hour-week mass meeting in Madison Square Garden. Telegrams and letters were ordered sent to all labor organizations in the United States, asking them to endorse the forty-hour week. Endorsements came from all over the country. The Central Trades and Labor Council of New York endorsed the campaign and participated in the Madison Square Garden meeting. The meeting raised the spirits of the workers to a high pitch of enthusiasm. Green was put in the position of being a champion of the forty-hour week, for which the Furriers were fighting not only for themselves but also for the entire labor movement.

But Foster was not satisfied. He attacked me for making the proposal. He branded it as a rank opportunistic proposition that the labor movement could not accept. He insisted that the only proper demand would have been for the eight-hour day five-day week. Foster's criticism however was not taken seriously, because its basis was factional, a stab at a member of the Ruthenberg group who was directing the strike for the Party.

Soon afterwards the strike was settled, when the manufacturers granted the forty-hour week and a ten percent increase in wages. The workers accepted the settlement as a tremendous victory for the union. The settlement of the strike was also followed by a very busy season in the industry, which meant fat pay envelopes. The settlement of the strike plus the combination of favorable circumstances which followed the settlement gave the Communists the undisputed leadership of the New York Furriers and considerably increased our prestige in the trade union movement.

Two phases of the settlement contract indicated how we ourselves ignored some of the very principles we were advocating in the unions. We were outspoken against the signing of contracts which ran over a period of years. The contract signed by the Furriers Union ran for three years. We opposed in principle any and all forms of class collaboration—the system of impartial intervention and arbitration of labor disputes—one of the main issues in the unions. We advocated instead direct negotiations of the union and the manufacturers in the settlement and adjustment of complaints. In the Furriers settlement there was not even the hint of opposition, let alone a fight, against the impartial machinery in the industry. In fact, the settlement provided for a most elaborate system of class collaboration in the settlement of disputes. Communist theory was one thing; Communist practice in the face of realities, another.

After the settlement of the furriers' strike, the A. F. of L. sought its revenge against us by appointing a committee to investigate the conduct of the strike under the chairmanship of its leading Communist-baiter, Vice-President Matthew Woll. He conducted the investigation in a biased and extremely highhanded manner, determined to make a case against the Communist leaders of the furriers' strike and then, on the basis of his findings, launch a concerted drive against all Communists in all the needle trades unions. He was facilitated in that enterprise by the stupidity of Ben Gold, who, without authorization from me or any member of the Party Political Committee, agreed to allow the A. F. of L. to conduct the investigation, granting that point in the course of his negotiations with William Green. We of the Political Committee were not even informed of that agreement, and the investigation began without our knowledge. It was well on the way before we became aware of it, when the cat was out of the bag, as it were, and we could not very well object to it, let alone stop it. Nor could we discipline Gold, for any action against the hero who had just led a successful strike would discredit us rather than Gold and besides would lend added weight to Woll's charges of misconduct by our leadership in that strike. After hours of fruitless discussion and resentment against Gold and Woll, we finally decided to do but one thing—denounce Woll's report of his investigation as a pernicious frame-up, although when it was made public we knew that for the most part it was true and on the whole not as damaging to us as the full measure of actual facts. Woll's report charged gross mishandling of funds and police bribery. The A. F. of L. implemented it at once by appointing Edward F. McGrady as its emissary to the Furriers, suspended the Communist-dominated Joint Board of the Furriers, set up in its place a Joint Council and invited all honest union members to register with the new body. We in the Political Committee had decided to make a public exposure of Woll as a labor leader who had sold out to the manufacturers, and to hire Frank P. Walsh to defend the Fur Workers Union. But the money for putting these two decisions into effect could not be procured.

The shops in the industry became divided into Joint Council and Joint Board affiliates. The gains of the strike were soon dissipated and the conditions of the workers became materially worse. Finally, just when the A. F. of L. was getting sick of the situation and there was every possibility of bringing about peace in the strife-ridden industry, the line of the Communist International on dual unionism changed. The Communists were instructed to organize their own unions. Though Gold and Gross were opposed to the policy of dual unionism, no opposition was manifested to the new line in the furriers' unions. Following the lead of the Communists, the furriers left the A. F. of L. and, together with the Communist followers in the International Ladies Garment Workers Union, organized in 1928 the Needle Trade Workers Industrial Union and the Fur Workers Industrial Union.

The Cloakmakers Strike

Shortly after securing domination of the Furriers Union in 1925, we had succeeded in making considerable inroads elsewhere in the needle trades, and by 1926 we had gained control of the New York Joint Board of the International Ladies Garment Workers Union, which had a membership of about sixty thousand workers. But here the control was not as secure as it was among the Furriers. A number of the large locals—notably the Italian locals 89 and 48, which had a large membership, and the Cutters' local 10, of which David Dubinsky was the manager—as well as several of the smaller ones, were in the hands of the Right Wing. Moreover, the membership ouside of New York City, which constituted about two-thirds of the entire union, was largely controlled by forces in opposition to the Communists. Besides, we shared our leadership of the New York Joint Board with several Anarchists and independents. Nevertheless, notwithstanding the precariousness of our control, we did not hesitate to impose our will upon the organization and to use the Joint Board, as much as possible, as a rubber stamp for our decisions.

This was resented by the non-Communist Left Wing leaders of the Joint Board. Louis Hyman, then an independent although a Communist sympathizer, protested and threatened to resign his post as General Manager of the Joint Board. At the time his was the highest position on the Board. The matter came before the Central Executive Committee's Needle Trades Committee on March tenth, 1926, the minutes recording the following:

> Comrade Zimmerman also reported that they have a very critical situation with Hyman, the general manager of the Joint Board. Hyman resents the fact that policies are made without consulting him, and that he is in a position where he must carry out orders. Hyman disagrees with many of the policies of the Party. Hyman's resignation at this time would be a serious blow to our Party. It was decided that our comrades should take all possible steps to prevent the resignation of Hyman and that, on the question of relations, steps be taken to bring Hyman in touch with members of the Central Executive Needle Trades Committee in order to straighten out the difficulties.

But there were other difficulties as well. The Communist leaders in the union were members of the Lore Group. Very often the Lore Group was designated as the Lore-Poyntz-Zimmerman group. Zimmerman was the outstanding Communist leader in the International Ladies Garment Workers Union. In the campaign against Lore we had sharply attacked our Communist leaders in the I. L. G. W. U. as deviators from Communist orthodoxy and as unprincipled opportunists. We branded them the Right Wingers of the Party. Being under attack, they were always on the defensive. They seldom took responsibility for boldly executing policies, preferring to throw the responsibility into our laps. They were always afraid that their proposals would be either misunderstood or deliberately used to attack them as Right Wingers.

The strength of the Communists was concentrated in locals Two, Nine, and Twenty-two, the same locals which made up the Joint Action Committee that had fought against expulsion from the Joint Board. Their fight for readmission was a very costly one, depleting the local treasuries as well as the Joint Board treasury, so that there was little money left in the treasury with which to conduct a strike. The audit of the accounts of the Joint Action Committee from June twenty-fourth to November thirtieth, 1925, gives the total expenditures of the fight for readmission as $122,261.51. This audit was made by a Party member, a chartered accountant who carried out all the instructions and desires of the Party in making the audit. Lack of money was a serious matter and greatly increased the difficulties facing our leaders on the eve of the Cloakmakers Strike. I wrote about that to Ruthenberg on May twenty-second, 1926, in part as follows:

> We are on the eve of a general strike . . . Our position in the union is not a pleasant one. From reading the minutes of the last few meetings [of the Central Executive Committee's Needle Trades Committee] you can get an idea of how insecure we are. Our position in the International cannot be likened to our position in the Furriers. The Right Wing is still in a very strategic and powerful position. The Right Wing machine has a capable leader in Sigman. . . The New York Joint Board of the International is bankrupt, heavily in debt. . . There are serious divi-

sions in our own forces. Hyman is wavering. He is afraid of the struggle. He is prepared to give the struggle over to Sigman. . . With Hyman as Chairman of the General Strike Committee, the strike will be in danger of being compromised at any time. Hyman is also in favor of arbitration. . . If Hyman had his way, he would have adopted a policy of dealing most intimately with the Governor's Commission. . . We also lack a dynamic personality like Comrade Gold in the International. In fact, we are hard pressed for persons with ability. The strike will involve about forty thousand workers. I am fearful of the situation. It is not a good one.

On the eve of the Clockmakers Strike our Party was actively engaged in two other important labor wars, the Passaic Textile Strike and the Furriers Strike. For a small Party like ours, with a membership of approximately fifteen thousand, a third strike involving an additional forty thousand workers would have been a great strain upon our organization even under the most favorable circumstances, while in this case all circumstances were unfavorable. To go into the strike was sheer folly. I personally believed this, and so did a number of other Party leaders. I definitely knew, as did they, that all the important leaders of the Left Wing, the Communist and non-Communist alike, did not favor the calling of a strike. The only one who favored strike action was Foster, who in spite of his boasted knowledge of trade union affairs, never really understood the needle trades or their strike problems. Though he gained his reputation as a leader of a Steel Strike, he never assumed responsible leadership in any strike situation for the Party. In my opinion, he was for a strike of the Cloakmakers for purely factional reasons. The Ruthenberg group was in control of the Party. To dislodge them, it was necessary to discredit them in some sphere of important Party activity, and nothing was more important than trade union work. In favoring a strike he could speak in a militant manner for uncompromising action against the bosses and could brand those who opposed strike action as cowardly opportunists who were afraid to fight.

The winds blowing from Moscow were Left winds. The Party was prodded to take leadership in strikes. The attitude of Moscow, the internal factional situation in the Party, and the fact that the Communist leaders in the I. L. G. W. U. were made the scapegoats for the Lore Group created a combination of circumstances in which no one among the Party leaders wanted to take the responsibility for adopting the only logical position in the Cloakmakers situation—namely, to avoid a strike, even though such a move would have meant a partial retreat on the part of the union. In addition, our Communist leaders in the Union, who knew the situation, never once proposed the strategy of trying to avoid the strike, because they knew that to have done so would have played into the hands of the Party leaders of both the Ruthenberg and Foster groups, who would have pounced upon them as horrible examples of opportunist leaders ready to sacrifice the interests of the workers in order to avoid a struggle with the bosses. They did not relish being held up as an example of "where Loreism leads to."

The Cloakmakers Strike was therefore called on July first, 1926, after the terms of the Governor's Committee were rejected. A month and a half before the strike was called the Central Executive Committee's Needle Trades Committee met and considered the question of the personnel of the various strike committees. At this meeting, on May eighteenth, 1926 it was decided that Hyman should be Chairman of the General Strike Committee and Charles (Sasha) Zimmerman, Secretary; and that David Dubinsky should be Chairman of the Settlement Committee, despite the fact that he was a leading figure in the opposition to the Communists. Like Dubinsky a number of other Right Wingers were given responsible posts in the strike machinery in order to make them share responsibility.

The main demands of the union were for the forty-hour week, increase in wages, limitation of jobbers and rejection of the demand of the manufacturers for the right to reorganize their shops by being permitted to discharge ten percent of their workers at the end of each season. The main objection to the terms of the Governor's Commission was that it granted the manufacturers the right of ten percent reorganization. In September the leaders of the strike had a conference with the manufacturers for the purpose of reaching a settlement. A tentative basis upon which the manufacturers were ready to settle the strike was handed to the union. It included acceptance of the forty-hour week, an increase in wages and a modified form of reorganization. Following the conferences with the manufacturers, a meeting was held at the District headquarters of the Party, 108 East Fourteenth Street, to consider the terms of settlement. Present at the meeting were our Communist leaders of the strike, Burochovich, Zimmerman, Rose Wortis and others. The party leaders present were Weinstone, Ben Lifshitz, Jack Stachel, a number of members of the New York District Committee, and I.

Burochovitch reported. I realized from the way he reported that a basis had been reached by which the strike could be settled. Zimmerman also spoke on the conferences with the manufacturers. He indicated that the terms embodied a compromise settlement which could get the approval of the workers, the obnoxious feature being that, if it were made, the Left Wing would have to take responsibility for inaugurating the principle of reorganization in the industry. It was also clear as the discussion on the proposals proceeded that, if the terms were rejected, the Cloakmakers would have to face a very long and exhausting struggle, the final settlement of which could not be foretold. The discussion went on for hours, but during the entire discussion not one of the strike leaders dared to propose that the strike be settled. They wanted the Party leaders to take the responsibility for the settlement. As the meeting was coming to a close, I turned to Weinstone and whispered, "We have an opportunity of settling the strike. If they would only come out and state that they favor a settlement on the basis of the reported terms, I would support them and move for the settlement of the strike." Weinstone, however, was in a fit of perplexity and afraid to take decisive action. He knew that we were in no position to lead a prolonged struggle. But he did not want to take responsibility for a settlement which would become a football of factional Party controversy, a settlement which Foster would brand as a flagrant sellout. He replied: "Unless Zimmerman and Burochovitch definitely come out with a proposal that we accept the terms of settlement, there is nothing we can do." I began to prod the strike leaders with questions, in an effort to make them take a definite stand. They circumvented all my questions. They were determined not to take responsibility. I asked them if they could continue the strike to a successful conclusion. They answered that under certain conditions, which in their opinion could be obtained in coöperation with the Party, they could. Finally, it was decided to reject the terms and to intensify the strike activities in order to get better terms. The strikers never knew the inside story. Had they known, our Communist leaders would have been stoned. The strike, which should have been settled, was not, and the workers were made to pay for it in months of suffering. When the strike was finally settled in December, the terms offered by the manufacturers in September formed the basis of the settlement and the obnoxious reorganization clause in a modified form was agreed to.

After this memorable meeting Foster came to New York and received a report on the situation. When he returned to Chicago he reported to the Political Committee at its meeting on September ninth. But he made no proposal in the Political Committee that any definite action be taken to settle the strike on the terms offered. Later, however, as the strike dragged on and it became clear to the Political Committee of the Party that the Sigman forces would interfere and take over the strike and the New York Joint Board, it made desperate efforts to bring about a settlement of the strike, but without any success. When finances became low, a drive for funds was made, to help our Communist leadership continue the strike. But not enough money was collected. Finally, Sigman stepped into the situation and reached a settlement with the manufacturers. Hyman as Chairman of the General Strike Committee signed it. Following the settlement of the strike, Sigman brought charges against the leadership of the strike, ousted the Left Wing leadership and proceeded to reorganize the New York organization. The Communists fought against his reorganization of the New York organization, but, due to the protracted unsuccessful strike, they could not rally the workers to their support. The positions they lost they were never able to regain. The strike was a very costly affair. For the entire strike period of twenty-four weeks about three and a half million dollars of union funds were spent.

But what it cost in human suffering and misery, all of which could have been avoided, has never been estimated.

The Passaic Strike

But the most significant strike of all was the one at Passaic, New Jersey, which began on January twenty-fifth, 1926, among the textile workers of that city, because it was entirely initiated and led by Communists. The man who started the ball rolling was Bert Miller, industrial organizer of District Two of the Party, which then included most of industrial New Jersey and Connecticut as well as New York City. Comrade Miller called to my attention the fact that the Botany Mills of Passaic had announced a wage cut of ten percent, beginning with October, 1925. I immediately instructed Miller to get in touch with our New Jersey comrades and explore the matter further, agreeing with him that on its face the situation seemed favorable enough for initiating agitation for a strike in retaliation for the wage cut. Miller was a veteran of the Party since its underground days and carried out his assignment expeditiously. His report convinced me that there was ample ground for developing a successful strike.

About the same time, a young Harvard law student, who had recently abandoned a high position in the Young People's Socialist League to become a rank-and-file member of our Party local in Boston, was transferred to Paterson, New Jersey, where we hoped to utilize his oratorical gifts in our campaign to "unify" the textile unions there. But Albert Weisbord became a thorn in the flesh of our Paterson local. Thoroughly saturated with Marxist-Leninist lore, including all the exegeses and homilies thereof, Weisbord took it upon himself to berate all comrades who disagreed with him as ignoramuses, eclectics, or opportunists. The Paterson comrades found him insufferable, complained of his overbearing manner to the district office and finally demanded his removal. Since that happened to coincide with our need for a man of his talents in Passaic, we ordered his transfer there. Weisbord's first public appearance at Passaic was in the capacity of Chairman at a meeting at which I, advertised as a candidate for the office of Mayor of New York City, was the main speaker. This meeting was the prelude to the strike.

It is germane to note that an overtone of petty fraud was played into this prelude. Although the advertisements of the meeting described me as a mayoralty candidate in the biggest American city, there was no mention of the party that sponsored my candidacy. Needless to say, I entertained no hope to be elected Mayor. One of the main political purposes of the mayoralty campaign was to throw mud on the Socialist Party and its standard-bearer, Norman Thomas. The problems confronting the city of New York had nothing whatever to do with the issues as we saw them. These were formulated in the open letter I addressed to Norman Thomas, as my principal opponent, by beginning with the rhetorical challenge, "Why not unity in America, Mr. Thomas?"—note the deadly slur of calling a Socialist and fellow-Marxist "Mister" instead of "Comrade"—and winding up with the following exercise in political malapropism:

> We further invite you and your party to join with us and other labor forces in issuing a joint call to the unions and workers organizations of this country to promote recognition of Soviet Russia, world trade, union unity, independent working class political action through a labor party. . .

Judging by this document, the Communist Party's candidate for Mayor of New York City in 1925 was first of all an agent of the Soviet government (recognition and world trade), only secondarily a protagonist of the trade union and political movement of American workers, and, as far as his specific candidacy was concerned, a candidate without a platform. Moreover, before Norman Thomas could respond to my open letter, I sent another open letter to the members of his party, denouncing him and all other leaders of the Socialist Party as betrayers of the movement for a labor party, branded Thomas as a "sky pilot"—(he had abandoned the church of which he was a minister in 1917 because of his opposition to war and had joined the Socialist Party)—unfit to lead labor, and invited all Socialist Party members to desert Thomas's party and join mine. This sort of tactic is generally known as "the united front from below." It is certainly "below"—or rather, *beneath* contempt—but what it has to do with a sincere "united front" policy remains a mystery to me. However, at the time it seemed the height of Bolshevik wisdom in political strategy. The campaign itself was conducted lackadaisically, because our propaganda against the ballot box as futile in accomplishing our revolutionary tasks, conducted since 1919, was then still too fresh in the minds of our members to reverse their attitude toward campaigning for office. On top of all, New York City authorities informed me on October thirteenth, 1925, that my name would not appear on the city ballot, because as a convicted felon I was ineligible for nomination to public office. Nevertheless, I was advertised for that Passaic meeting as a mayoralty candidate, and indeed many who came to that meeting believed that I was not merely a candidate but actually the Mayor of New York City. About fifteen hundred textile workers, men and women, crowded into the hall to hear me. The meeting was a success. Its keynote was enthusiasm, the workers present enrolling immediately into the mill councils we were organizing. Thus began the organization campaign for the Passaic strike.

As representative of the Central Executive Committee in charge of the Passaic situation, among other trade union activity elsewhere, I placed Albert Weisbord directly in charge of the preparatory organizing campaign in Passaic, and he went to work under my close supervision. When in the midst of this campaign I was obliged to return to Sing Sing, the Central Executive Committee continued to keep a sharp eye on Weisbord, who, for all his erudition in Communist theory, was rather young and inexperienced in such practical matters as organizing and leading a strike. Upon my release from prison in December, I resumed supervision of the Passaic field, which the Party regarded as part of a greater whole, and therefore on January eighth, 1926, I was appointed Chairman of the Central Executive Committee's Textile Committee, which was the Party's general staff in charge of the entire textile field. Within seventeen days after that appointment we opened the textile war at Passaic—a war that was subsequently to spread throughout New

England and Southern textile regions—a strike at the Botany Mill, on January twenty-fifth. The strike spread from mill to mill in Passaic and its environs, until we had seventeen thousand textile workers mobilized in the walkout. But we did not have everybody out in those mills. Many of the skilled workers stayed on the job, our following consisting mostly of the unskilled, predominantly foreign-born—chiefly Poles, Hungarians and Italians—so that, counting even the children of these foreign-born employed in the mills, the percentage of American-born among the strikers was under thirty. In charge of the strike was the United Front Textile Committee, which established its headquarters in the same building as the Passaic local of the Party, which was more convenient than discreet, for that committee, nominally in charge of the strike under the leadership of Weisbord, was no more than a Party instrument from beginning to end.

After the first week of the strike, it was clear to me and to the entire Textile Committee of the Party that we had not made the happiest choice in Weisbord. He was a hard worker—in fact, indefatigable—but he lacked common ordinary horse sense. Instead of attracting non-Party elements into strike activity, he antagonized them with his narrowness and sectarianism. He lacked the human touch so necessary to a leader in such a situation—something I shall always hold against Harvard, for I was certain that men trained in law in any good college were bound to have that attribute, at least. On top of all, this Harvard-trained lawyer proved such a poor judge of men and was so gullible that he was completely taken in by a rather simple-minded police stool pigeon and provocateur, whom he put in charge of pickets, thus exposing the picket line to police provocation. A sample of Weisbord's stupidity with reference to the participation of non-Communists is recorded in his own report to us of the Textile Committee at the meeting of February second, over which I presided and at which Weisbord said in part:

> Messina of the *Il Nuova Mondo* wanted to speak. Sormenti [Secretary of the Italian Federation of the Communist Party and certainly more competent than Weisbord to pass on the reliability

of an Italian radical journalist in America] thinks he is all right, but I have my doubts. Said he would also get Giovanitti [ex-priest and revolutionary poet, whose name was magic among Italian workers] to speak. I stated we would drive him and Giovanitti out of the hall. [!?] I also learned that Hoffman [of the Hosiery Workers Union] was trying to secure Gurley Flynn to address the strikers. I had adopted the policy not to allow such speakers to speak, only accredited Communists and unionists should get the platform.

He had adopted a policy! . . We instructed him to turn his policy inside out and from then on concentrate on building up as wide a support for the strike as possible. He simply did not know how to be all-embracing in scope while maintaining firm control of his strike organization. As for his gullibility, here is a sample of the sort of report from the chief of pickets, the stool-pigeon Bryan, which Weisbord swallowed hook, line, and sinker, personally vouching to us for Bryan, whom we expelled from the Party and drove out of Passaic before the strike was a month old:

On Wednesday, Dec. 27/26 Hoffman arrived here with Art Shields of the Federated Press the purpose seemingly was that of a desire to get first hand information as to the strike situation. Hoffman took a place in the demonstration also Shields.

Hoffman left that day but returned the next day and showed me what was alleged to be a sort of credential from the Central Bureau stating he was to stay here and act in the capacity of a Proletarian News Reporter. He seemed very anxious to be friendly with me and I admit I became suspicious at once as before this strike I had met him and at that time he was not very friendly and true to the type of renegade that he has shown himself to be he at once began to tell me the usual story of dual unionism saying that the UTW (United Traitors of the World) was the only legitimate union and we should amalgamate. He stated that a Delegate of the UTW had been in town and after looking around had told him (Hoffman) that they were going to take a hands off attitude during the strike.

He at once began to tell me what a wonderful man I was and that I had a glorious future ahead of me in fact he painted a picture that was as splendid as Paradise Lost told me That I should go to see a (Lady Called Sarah) in the New York Office of the UTW. He told me that Sarah would do business with me (Monkey Business) but not with Wisebord because he was a WP (Wild Person). He began to harp on the question of the methods conducting a strike offering petty criticisms.

He then told me he could get nine miners from some College in New York and all so a girl called Anny Something who was connected with the road to the bug house (Road to Freedom) an Anarchist Group of Steelton New Jersey and I let out a squawk as this same snake Anny had been the cause of what might be truth fully said the wrecking of The Marine Transport Workers of the I.W.W. I told him I had many a battle with her and would take direct action on her if she came here.

He then in a diplomatic way suggested that I could be worth from 30 to 40 dollars a week to the UTW. Well I told him I did not belong to the Parasite Class that Marx Calls the Dangerous Class. He all so said he would like to have act as an out side man for him if any strike his sock makers society might pull in the futer. Since then he has had became very repulsive as he makes remarks that will lead to open conflict between me and him

For the Class Struggle All Ways
Jack Bryan

This Jack Bryan was presumably a former I. W. W., the type of element we generally welcomed into the Party; whether this ex-Wobbly had been a police spy in that organization, too, I don't know. But during the initial period of the strike he exerted a malefic influence on the well-intentioned, hard-working Weisbord.

I do not mean to imply that Weisbord was an utter fool. On the contrary: he was an intelligent, broadly-cultured chap. But there was a queer quirk in his mind: he lacked judgment. Part of that deficiency was due to inexperience in trade union work. That could be overcome in time. But deeper than that was the lack of mental balance peculiar to a fantasist. For example: after deep cogitation, no doubt, he voiced the opinion that in dealing with the Passaic textile workers as a body, we must first come to understand the underworld, because the textile workers were intimately bound up with the activities of the underworld. Where he got that notion is beyond me; it may have been a modification of one of Bakunin's wild theories of mass action, but I wouldn't swear to it. Although easily amenable to the dictates of the Central Executive Committee's Textile Committee, he became so puffed up with his importance as a strike leader—which was no more than a byproduct of our publicity for the strike, since he was the leader in name only—so vain about his talents as a Communist philosopher and tactician that he became overbearing toward his subordinates in office. Those who did not worship him found it extremely hard to get along with him. In fact, our greatest single difficulty during the strike was to get people to work with Weisbord. Yet he was utterly unsparing of himself in his devotion to the strike and to the Communist cause. It was not unusual for him to address ten meetings a day and be twenty hours a day on the job. He was a dynamo of energy. Fanatical in his zeal, he literally ate, slept and talked nothing but the strike and Communism. He was an effective speaker, a good agitator.

His tragedy was that he overrated himself. His ambition stumbled over his inordinate vanity. Nationwide publicity, often on the front page under blaring headlines, was his undoing, for he was not smart enough to know its true value. Although a good deal of it came from his own facile pen, he took it for gospel truth. He was like a spinner of yarns who comes to believe in his own fairy tales. Measuring his worth by the synthetic and utterly irresponsible hyperboles of publicity, he came to regard himself as the Party's outstanding, if not the only, authority on trade union matters. Yet he was docile and meek, whenever the Textile Committee rejected his fantastic proposals one after the other, and accepted without a murmur of protest the committee's proposals in their stead. For fantasist though he was, he was practical enough to play politics. He aspired to outstanding leadership in the Party. So, this dreamer, too, became a slave of that ineffable blight, the political passion. The strike became his stepladder toward Party leadership. He became a member of the Ruthenberg faction, then the dominant faction in the Party, and he made no bones about the fact that he expected to be rewarded for his loyalty to our faction by a prominent position in the Party after the next national convention. It was finally this same ambition that led him eventually to break with the Lovestone-Gitlow caucus, when his hopes did not materialize, and when in turn the Stalin machine failed to satisfy his political ambitions, he began to behave so obstreperously that he was expelled from the Party. He then joined the Trotskyists. But his career with the latter was also brief and explosive. He then proclaimed himself the only true Trotskyist, without benefit of Trotsky, and only stopped short of proclaiming himself the only true Trotsky. From then on he sank into oblivion as the leader of a group which literally numbers less than a baker's dozen, counting himself and the ever-faithful Vera Busch.

But let us return from this fortuitous nominal leader of the Passaic Strike to the real leadership of that strike and to the meeting of February second, 1926, which, in addition to rebuking Weisbord, turned to the more important business of formulating the strike demands and the method of their presentation. After these demands were formulated, they and the instructions on their presentation were passed on to the general strike committee, the United Front Textile Committee, by Weisbord. We also decided to start a relief campaign for the strikers, our object being to use the funds so raised among the general public for financing our strike activities. The men who made these decisions, present at the meeting of February second, were, in addition to Weisbord and me, William W. Weinstone, General Secretary of District Two; Joseph Zack, one of the Party's real trade union experts and a member of our New York Industrial Committee; Kovetz, representing the Hungarian Federation, for there were many Hungarians among the strikers; Clarence Miller, then representing the Young Workers (Communist) League, who subsequently became involved in the Gastonia, North Carolina, textile strike, was framed on a charge of complicity in the murder of the Chief of Police there, and fled to the Soviet Union to escape a sentence of seventeen to twenty years in prison; and three members of the Passaic City Central Committee of the Party—Blumkin, Baylin and Dyaik.

The general strike committee had as little to do with formulating strike demands as with the conduct of the relief campaign for the strikers. The most intimate questions of strike policy were settled without even consulting it, let alone the strikers. For example, we decided that an application be made to the United Textile Workers for affiliation, as a clever maneuver to prevent the A. F. of L. from attacking the strike and the officials of the U. T. W. from interfering with the strike, our avowed purpose being to "prevent the disintegration of the movement by the treacherous activities of the officialdom." We sent in our missionaries. We swamped Passaic with Party organizers and organizers of the Young Workers League. But perhaps the best help of all came from the minions of law and order. By clubbing the strikers, smashing picket lines and arresting prominent liberals, whom we succeeded in getting to go to Passaic to speak and lead picket demonstrations, the Passaic police gave us nationwide publicity. No amount of money and no agitation effort could have secured us this publicity otherwise. We exploited the stupidity of the police by provoking dramatic situations, which made stirring news stories and interesting action pictures for the newspapers.

The fact that Passaic was near to New York, from where we could draw upon large liberal and Socialist elements for assistance, helped us materially in this respect. We staged parades. We dressed the pickets in uniforms and steel helmets and paraded them as ex-service men. We utilized the young girl strikers to give the strike feminine attraction and color. Our publicity staff consisted of Mary Heaton Vorse, who was a Party member and acted directly for the Central Executive Committee's Textile Committee, but who operated in the situation as a liberal; Robert W. Dunn, who also operated as a non-Communist and a liberal; Art Shields of the Federated Press; and Margaret Larkin, who was brought into the situation upon the recommendation of Mary Heaton Vorse. Miss Larkin and Art Shields later became Party members. Vorse and Dunn upon our instructions held conferences with William Green, Sidney Hillman, with manufacturers, with United States Senators, with Congressmen, judges, ministers and priests, in fact with all who might be interested in investigation of conditions, strike settlement moves and legal defense. As Communists, we could not make these contacts, but through fake "liberals" like Vorse and Dunn we could, and in that way get assistance as well as be more or less adequately informed of what was afoot. Passaic became the most important Communist activity. Every branch of the Party was drawn into the strike. Party members flocked into Passaic in such large numbers that Weisbord had to complain that they interfered with the conduct of the strike. But we organized the children of the strikers from six to fourteen in the Young Pioneers, the young workers in the Young Workers League, and the older strikers in the Party, which grew like a mushroom. The strikers did not differentiate between the Union conducting the strike and the Communist Party, because the activities of both were interlocked and the leaders the same. That gave our Party great prestige among the strikers, who regarded us as the foremost champions of their union.

The Party organizers were paid out of the relief funds, which source also supported all the strike activities. At first the relief was organized as a strike activity through a committee set up by the General Strike Committee and known as the General Relief Committee for the Passaic Textile Strikers. On February thirteenth the Central Executive Committee's Textile Committee decided to put Alfred Wagenkneckt, who had the reputation of being the financial wizard of our Party, in full charge of the relief. We decided to introduce him to the General Strike Committee as the representative of the Mopr, or International Workers Aid, in line with the specific instructions of the Central Executive Committee of the Communist Party, to place the relief in the hands of that Moscow organization. It was not as easy to carry out that decision as the Central Executive Committee thought. I had to formulate a set of motions on March the eleventh which virtually put the decision of the Central Executive Committee into effect in such a way as to hide the fact that the I. W. W. dominated the relief situation. My motions provided that the General Relief Committee for the Passaic Textile Strikers in the future continue its functions as in the past; that the I. W. A. form a joint committee with the General Relief Committee for the purpose of starting a national campaign; that new relief stations be opened in Passaic under the auspices of a joint committee; that the Joint Committee shall consist of three members of the General Relief Committee and two of the I. W. A.; that the expenses for conducting the relief stations conducted under the auspices of the Joint Committee shall be paid by the General Relief Committee of the Passaic Textile Strikers; that all other organizations that desire to carry on relief activity shall function through the General Relief Committee; that the Central Executive Committee of the Party utilize the national campaign for relief for the Passaic strikers to organize sections of the I. W. A. all over the country. On March the twelfth I was able to declare in a letter to Jay Lovestone, then Acting Secretary of the Party:

> We have sufficient influence in the General Relief Committee to prevent any activities in the relief field against our interests.

These decisions were very important, because they enabled the Party to build up in all the districts so-called I. W. A. machinery for the collection of relief funds for the Passaic Strikers and to use part of the sums so raised to pay for Party organizers, who were engaged in doing Party work, by having them placed on the books of the I. W. A. as working for the local sections of the I. W. A. In fact, the Central Executive Committee's Textile Committee on March the eleventh made a decision as to how that was to be done:

> All the New York Sections of the I. W. A. and all other sections that may collect money independently of the National Office of the I. W. A. shall expend the sum and shall transmit to the national office of the I. W. A. duplicate copies of all other financial transactions.

Thus, the national office of the I. W. A., not the Joint Committee, was the clearing house for the expenses of the local sections. In the national campaign for funds, money could be diverted to the national office, from which expenses could be paid out without the knowledge of the Joint Committee. In that way thousands of dollars of Passaic strikers' relief money could be paid out for Party work and for the support of the *Daily Worker*. Furthermore, such disbursements would never show in the bookkeeping record of the General Relief Committee or the Joint Committee. Their books would show a minimum of expenditure for administration expenses. Even in the expenditures of the General Relief Committee and the Joint Committee, there were moneys paid out that had absolutely nothing to do with the strike or with relief. This mishandling and juggling of relief funds accounts for the fact that there was no real audit of the relief at the termination of the strike. The money collected totaled several hundred thousand dollars.

In the Communist movement, *control* is a factor of the greatest importance. Every Communist, no matter in what organization he belongs, has it continually hammered into his head that the objective of a Communist must be to gain control. As soon as Communists gain control of a union, a strike, or any kind of activity, the Party steps in and runs the union, leads the strike and directs the activity. That was true of Passaic. The strikers and their leaders did not lead the strike. The strike was led by the Party, which appointed the union organizers, determined strike policy, led the strike. The union and the General Strike Committee were just the Party's rubber stamp. Weisbord was put in the leadership not by the workers but by the Party. But even he did not lead the strike, because every important move in the strike was decided upon by the Party's Central Executive Committee and the Textile Committee of the Party, of which I was chairman. Weisbord had to carry out our decisions and orders. The General Strike Committee was just a perfunctory committee through which Weisbord and the Party Fraction on the General Strike Committee carried out the orders of our Party. The textile workers who showed signs of leadership during the strike were either drawn into the Party, or so impressed with the Party's authority that the Party was recognized as the final arbiter in all differences that arose among them. Just a casual examination of the minutes of the C. E. C.'s Textile Committee will show how completely the situation was in the hands of the Party:

February 2, 1926: The question of demands was considered and it was agreed that a uniform set of demands must be issued. . .

February 9: Motions passed instructing Weisbord and the General Strike Committee how to conduct picket lines, how to resist the efforts of the police to stop picketing and to make an issue of the same, drawing in influential persons and organizations in support of the strike and for relief activities. Concentrating the strike on the Forstman Hoffman Mill. Directing the organization of the Rubber Workers of Passaic in order to bring them also out on strike. [On the question of the rubber workers the possibility of developing the strike into a general strike was discussed and the consensus of opinion among the members of the committee was that if we should be successful with the Rubber workers we would have a general strike and we could make Passaic another Seattle or Winnipeg.]

February 13: The question of the role of the party was discussed. It was decided that as the strike support was being broadened the role of the party should be brought more and more prominently into the strike situation. At this meeting the question of the Mayor's proposal to settle the strike was considered and motions passed how to resist the mayor's proposals and utilize the settlement proposal to get the workers who had not yet joined the strike to do so.

February 19: The following motions were passed: That the name of the strike bulletin be called the Textile Strikers Bulletin. . . That the editorial Board of the Bulletin shall consist of Comrades Weisbord and Gitlow.

March 3: Consideration of Rabbi Wise's proposal for attempting to bring about a settlement of the strike and a series of motions adopted that so tied the hands of Rabbi Wise that he could not effect a settlement.

March 10: A motion was passed that as far as the publicity given out by Margaret Larkin, who is publicity agent for the strikers, is concerned, that Weisbord look over all publicity in order to be sure that such publicity is in line with Party policy, and to give proper credit to the work of the Party and its organizations.

March 25: At this meeting the Washington situation was discussed. The Committee had sent Mary Heaton Vorse to Washington to line up Congressional support for a Congressional Investigation of Passaic and also to get in touch with President Green of the A. F. of L. for the purpose of getting his support for the strike. Her mission was unsuccessful and she blamed the spurt of party activities in Passaic for her failure.

Mrs. Vorse also sharply attacked H. M. Wicks for the kind of a speech he made before the strikers, Wicks had the reputation of being the most vitriolic speaker in the party. In the speech she referred to he said: "Let the American Legion come on. . . Bring with you your Red Cross ambulances and nurses."

March 29: Question of the A. F. of L. was discussed, policy outlined and motion made that a letter be sent to President Green which letter should be sent in the name of the strikers. I was instructed to draw up the letter to Green.

April 8: The Mayor refused a permit for a children's parade. We must hold the parade in spite of the refusal, and if clubbing takes place, we must then call the children out on strike to protest against the kind of Americanism that is in force and to demonstrate their solidarity with their parents out on strike.

On April eighth I received a letter from the Trade Union Committee of the Party which stated:

> Inclosed find a copy of Trade Union Committee of April 7th. In regard to the motions in the minutes regarding the Passaic strike, these motions are only for information of the Central Executive Committee sub-committee and must not be taken outside the committee. Any action along the lines of the motions on the minutes must be taken by the Strike Committee, itself, at least seemingly so.

This letter showed how Communists run the affairs of the union without even consulting the union, confident that they can use the union, once they control it, to put through automatically everything the Party decides. This point was also brought out by the cryptic telegram which I received from Ruthenberg on May eleventh. It read as follows:

> Has Textile Committee included in call for conference invitation to all mill committees to send delegates. Political Committee decided this should be done.

The Passaic strike lasted almost a year. Most of the workers either returned to the mills or left Passaic. Those who remained were the recipients of relief, of which there was plenty, because our Party through its publicity machinery kept the strike alive before the public, with the result that contributions for relief continually flowed into the relief treasury. We knew after the strike had dragged on for many months that we could not get a settlement. We decided, when it was no longer possible to continue the strike, to get the strikers into the A. F. of L., in order that the United Textile Workers should be burdened with the responsibility of settling the strike. After a series of negotiations through intermediaries who spoke in the name of the Passaic strikers and after much correspondence between the strikers' organization and the United Textile Workers, the way was cleared for the strikers entering the A. F. of L. But the A. F. of L. laid down conditions. The conditions were that Weisbord must be removed as the leader of the strike. The Political Committee of the Party at first did not want to accept this condition. Every effort was made to circumvent it, but without any success. Weisbord was removed. The strikers entered the United Textile Workers Union, and eventually the United Textile Workers settled the strike. We had lost the strike. The Passaic textile workers got nothing out of it but bitter experience. In a short time there was no semblance of an organization left. Weisbord toured the country for the Party, and was later made a Party District Organizer. Because of our masterly publicity, the Passaic strike became a historic event in American labor history, and our Party ably used this to enhance its standing as a force in leading strikes among trade unionists and the workers generally.

Undermining the Coal Miners' Union

The influence we wielded in the needle trades unions made no impression on the Communist International. Our venture into textiles, as in Passaic and later in New England and the South, which came later, was also regarded as not of prime importance by the Russian leaders. They insisted that the capture of the American masses by the Communist Party must be grounded in the capture of the basic industries—and of these, coal and steel above all. Foster's prestige in the Communist International rested on his record as leader of the Steel Strike of 1919. Unfortunately, he never even came near to duplicating his record since then; indeed, in view of his performance during the subsequent twenty years, with almost unlimited resources from Moscow for "industrialization"—that is, for the capture of American unions for Soviet purposes—one wonders whether his vaunted record of 1919 was not in large measure plain exaggeration. However that may be, Moscow has always been consistent in insisting on Communist penetration of the basic industries. That was true under Lenin; it is still true under Stalin. For a while—a short period in the late 'twenties—the method of attaining this task changed; that is, dual unionism was tried instead of boring from within—a harking back to early Communist sectarianism—but that was soon abandoned, and today the classic method of boring from within persists with more subtlety and insidiousness and with less regard for the classic Marxist tenets than ever before.

Our first notable attempt in that direction was the organization of the Progressive International Committee of the United Mine Workers of America in 1923. With that we hoped to capture the miners' union. At the time the Political Committee of the Party proposed to exploit the failure of the miners' general strike of five months' duration in 1922 and the widespread unemployment in that industry to develop a revolt against the leadership, John L. Lewis, President of the United Mine Workers. Among the Russians, Finns, Poles, Lithuanians and South Slavs who worked in the mines there was a contingent of Communists and sympathizers. Our members in the coal industry were concentrated at strategic points in the important coal mining districts around Springfield, Illinois; Pittsburgh, Pa.; and the anthracite coal fields of Pennsylvania. They could therefore constitute our first important centers of organization. We had already conducted a preliminary investigation, from which we learned that there were many important forces in opposition to John L. Lewis ready to make a united front with us. An important factor in causing us to select the mining industry for the scene of our first major battle in a basic industry had to do with the attitude of our Party's membership. We knew that they could be depended upon to push the campaign enthusiastically and to support it generously, because among radical workers miners have always symbolized heroic working class traditions.

When Moscow gave the campaign its approval and the money

necessary to start it, the fight against Lewis was on. The Political Committee and the Central Executive Committee worked out all the details and gave Foster and the Trade Union Educational League all the necessary instructions how to proceed and what policies to pursue. A program was drafted for the campaign by the Political Committee and published by the Progressive International Committee of the United Mine Workers of America. We selected the personnel of that Committee, including its Secretary, Tom Myerscough, who was a Communist, as well as the date for a miners' conference to be held on June second and third, 1923. We then called conferences of Party organizers, Party officials and Party members in all the mining districts, at which the plans of the campaign were explained and our Party forces organized. Special organizers were put in the field. Conferences were arranged with progressive and opposition elements. Instructions also went on to all the language federations, Party papers and the factions in organizations that were connected with the mining industry or could be utilized in the campaign, stressing the importance of the campaign and explaining in detail how the Party desired the instructions to be carried out.

As our drive developed the miners' union was thrown into a controversy, the bitterness of which was seldom equalled in the labor movement. When the Trade Union Educational League was first organized it did not attack or criticize John L. Lewis. It took the defeat of the miners' general strike in 1922 mildly, because Foster was of the opinion that Lewis could be used at the conventions of the A. F. of L. as a wedge in opposition to Samuel Gompers, the President of the American Federation of Labor. At the first conference of the Trade Union Educational League, in the resolution that was adopted and in the report to the conference, not even a reference was made to Lewis. What is even more indicative was the fact that no demand was raised for the reinstatement of Alexander Howat, who was expelled from the miners' union by Lewis because he had fought Governor Allen's Compulsory Arbitration Court in the Kansas coal fields. But this was in August, 1922. In April, 1923, when the program of the Progressive Miners was first published, it was very different, for the line against John L. Lewis was sharply drawn in several declarations, such as:

> Of all the crimes of the Lewis administration, none has been more flagrant and cowardly than the brutal expulsion of Alexander Howat and the fighting Kansas miners. . .

or these statements:

> Lewis Violates Miners' Policies. . . Lewis has violated his duty, times without number. . . Lewis failed to vote in favor of independent working class political action. . . The district and international elections at the present time in the U. M. W. of A. are a shame and disgrace to the cause of unionism. "Payroll" agents of the various administrations employ bribery with money and liquor and the most brutal forms of intimidation to accomplish their corruption of the ballot.

We Communists painted John L. Lewis as Workers' Enemy Number One. As the campaign developed Moscow became more and more interested. The Comintern and the Profintern not only approved the plans but also sent us special instructions, and the Profintern additional money which was turned over to Foster, who, as always, personally controlled its expenditure. Later the Political Committee decided to check on the expenditure of the Moscow money, because a number feared that Foster was using part of the money for factional purposes within the Party, that instead of being used to oust Lewis from the miners' union, it was actually being used to build up the Foster faction.

This April, 1923, program further called for the nationalization of the coal mines, for the building of a Labor Party, for the organization of the unorganized coal fields, for an alliance between the coal miners and the railroad workers, for the reinstatement of Alexander Howat and the expelled Kansas miners, for one national agreement for both bituminous and anthracite fields in place of their separate agreements, direct election of organizers, endorsement of the movement for the amalgamation of the craft unions into industrial unions, the six hour day in the mining industry and the five day week, against dual unionism, for international affiliation with miners' organizations of other countries, against the Lewis leadership, for its replacement by a militant leadership and the calling of a progressive miners' convention. At the conference about two hundred delegates were present, most of whom were either Communists or Communist sympathizers, although no known Communist addressed the convention, which adopted the program we submitted. A new committee was elected and then the conference adjourned. Foster, writing of it, said:

> The progressive rank and file of the miners are sick to death of the corruption and treachery of their reactionary leaders. They are going to clean the organization from top to bottom.

The Pittsburgh Miners Food Relief Conference, which was organized to gather relief for the striking miners in the coke regions, was also converted into a vehicle for the Progressive campaign. Under its auspices organizers were routed and paid who ostensibly were sent on missions for the collection of relief. Naturally, Earl Browder was also in the fight against Lewis, prophesying in 1923:

> It is safe to say that the Progressive International Committee will bring about a revolution in the leadership, tactics and policies of the miners' union within the next couple of years.

But two years later the war still raged on in all its fury. Lewis fought the Progressive with all the weapons foul and fair at his command. Miners were expelled, locals were suspended, districts were reorganized, strong arm tactics were used. Foster, writing on the Miners' Convention of 1924, stated:

> Another manifestation of the reaction was the stand taken by the administration regarding the Ku Klux Klan. Although the reactionary Portland convention of the A. F. of L. had flatly condemned the hooded order, Lewis and his official cronies lent it aid and comfort. . .

The Progressive concentrated on the union elections held in December, 1924, by nominating a slate in opposition to Lewis. But Lewis took no chances. He ruled Howat off the ballot in Kansas and fought the Progressive, giving its followers no quarters in the union. After the elections we charged that fraud on a great scale was practised. The Progressive claimed to have been robbed of its victory, Foster summing up the case, as follows:

> The fakers would steal 100,000 votes if necessary to keep themselves in power.

The rulers of the Soviet Union and of the Comintern were now greatly incensed at the campaign which John L. Lewis was conducting against the Soviet Union through his union and its official organ, *The United Mine Workers' Journal.* The Comintern and the Profintern decided that a campaign should be started against Lewis personally. The Profintern was to supply the money necessary to carry it on. Again the funds were to be turned over to Foster. The first installment received by Foster was fifty thousand dollars. Strict instructions were given to the Party that the campaign against Lewis must be conducted as a broad rank-and-file opposition movement against him personally and against his leadership of the miners' organization. We were to do everything in our power to mask the Communist face and to camouflage our control of the campaign. On September second, 1926, our Political Committee adopted a detailed program for the campaign against John L. Lewis. Its objective was formulated without equivocation, as follows:

> To discredit and drive Lewis out of the labor movement for the principal reason that he initiated the fight against our Party and began the expulsion policy in the A. F. of L. and typifies the anti-Communist forces in the A. F. of L.

The methods by which this was to be attained were stated with equal clarity:

> The organization of an oppositional bloc in the union around a group of candidates, which include all honest oppositional elements, from Brennan on the right, Brophy in the center, Hapgood, Stevenson and others close to our Party and certain of our Party members.

The leaders of this opposition movement against Lewis were not in the least ignorant of the Party's rôle. They knew perfectly well that every cent was supplied by the Workers (Communist) Party. That was especially true of John Brophy, who conferred with Foster or Lovestone on the affairs of the campaign almost weekly. The liaison officer between Brophy and the Party on such occasions when Brophy did not confer directly with its representatives was Powers Hapgood. His part was to play an independent miner who was in close touch with the Party but was not a Party member. As a matter of fact, Powers Hapgood was one of the secret and most trusted members of the Workers (Communist) Party, bound by its decisions and discipline.

Meantime a strike broke out in the anthracite fields in September, 1925. In accordance with instructions received from Kuusinen on behalf of the Executive Committee of the Comintern and Lozovsky of the Profintern, dated April thirtieth, 1925, reminding us again that

> The Party must actively engage in every strike and wage movement. It must also arouse the masses to take up such movements. It must skilfully utilize these movements for political ends. It must have a program of demands for each mass movement of this kind, and the Communists must fight for leadership in the struggle. . .

we of the Central Executive Committee of the Party injected our Communist cohorts into the anthracite strike. We drafted a strike policy and rushed organizers into the strike territories with instructions to operate under the name, Progressive Miners Committee. I was put in charge of these operations by the Central Executive Committee.

Outside of a handful of mining union organizers and a score of foreign-born members of the Lithuanian, Russian and Italian federations of the Party, who were rank-and-file miners, we had no forces to start with in the anthracite fields. These miners as a whole had about as much use for Communists as for the bubonic plague. However, Bolsheviks never hesitate to storm any fortress, no matter how formidable. We distributed over two hundred thousand leaflets which embodied our ideas of the demands the miners should fight for. We held scores of meetings at which John L. Lewis and all his lieutenants were castigated as traitors and turncoats, as betrayers of the miners to the mine owners. But the hardy anthracite miners were not impressed by our agitation. The few that did drop in occasionally at our meetings maintained a sphinx-like silence. Then the police got busy. It arrested our organizers at a meeting in Scranton. That was a boon and a blessing. I immediately launched a united front free speech fight, hoping to rally the miners under that banner as an opening wedge. But whatever steps I took in this direction were nullified by the Central Executive Committee, which opposed a free speech fight on the grounds that it did not desire to dissipate the struggle for the miners' demands in that way. I tried to convince the Central Executive Committee that we could not fight for our miners' demands at all if the authorities prevented us from appearing and speaking before the miners. But they would not listen to me. Three of our organizers arrested at the Scranton meeting were sent to jail for a few days. Their plaints about it made one think that they were sent to prison for life. The Secretary of the Progressive Miners, Alex Reid, a Party member, became so frightened that after he was released he disappeared from the district without letting anyone know of his whereabouts.

Our main organizers were two youngsters, Pat Toohey and August Valentine. Pat Toohey was an impulsive Irish-American about twenty years old. When he spoke his face took on a fighting expression that was very effective. But he was unstable: he would be very enthusiastic one moment and thoroughly dejected the next. He was a recent convert to the Communist movement, having joined the Young Communists about a year before. He had already married a young Communist girl, with whom he was greatly in love. Often, whenever he became despondent, he took to drink, becoming profane and obstreperous. On such occasions he was a hindrance and not a help to the work. He lacked experience and judgment and was unfit for handling a strike situation which involved 150,000 organized miners, most of whom were married and had families to take care of. Valentine was a more serious and steady type. He had become acquainted with the miners' union at an early age, but was inexperienced and unfit to deal with the problems confronting the Party in the strike. Besides, he lacked Toohey's pugnacity and courage.

The Anthracite Strike was the first test of the Ruthenberg group in a strike situation. The Fosterites sabotaged this activity for factional reasons. They came into the Central Executive Committee with a long list of motions on what should be done, motions which under the circumstances could not be carried out, because they were not based upon the actual conditions and left out of consideration the forces the Party had to work with. Having thus read their interest into the record of the Central Executive Committee minutes, they then proceeded to do everything in their power to hamper the actual work in the field. When the Central Executive Committee decided to send the Fosterites, William F. Dunne and Joseph Manley, to the Anthracite Fields, both got lost and could not be found when wanted most. Foster, who had in his possession special funds from the Profintern for work of this kind, especially among the miners, did not release a penny for it. The work was also sabotaged by Lozovsky, who strongly supported the Foster faction, with the result that the Party got no support from the Profintern. Had Foster been leading this activity, the Profintern would have supported it handsomely. The Trade Union Educational League, of which Foster was the head, maintained a passive neutrality and failed to assist in the campaign. At the same time, the Fosterites criticized every step made by us.

While the strike was still in progress, I was returned to prison. Upon my release, I again took charge. When the strike was settled, the Party made a hopeless attempt to prevent John L. Lewis from putting the settlement into effect. On February thirteenth, 1926, the Political Committee made the following confidential decisions in regard to the anthracite settlement:

1. Fight for the seating of all delegates who attended the last sessions of the Tri-District Convention. [We were unable to get a single delegate to raise his voice for our demands.]

2. For the re-affirmation of the Tri-District Convention strike settlement terms.

3. Failing to win on reaffirming old demands, we shall fight for agreement terminating simultaneously with Jacksonville agreement.

4. Repudiate setting up fake arbitration board, as an agency to kill effectiveness of strike as weapon and expose ninety-day deadlock clause as class collaboration scheme and betrayal of miners.

5. Progressive Miners Committee to issue an open letter to Ratification Conference on basis of this program.

6. Send Reid and Gitlow immediately to coal field, Comrade Gitlow to be Central Executive Committee representative.

7. Call out maintenance men for hundred percent strike, if they don't accept settlement terms and strike continues.

8. Tallentire to continue for minimum of two weeks to strengthen Party organizations and connections.

9. Toohey to stay for minimum of one month full time as Progressive Miners organizer, if this cannot be done—

10. If possible Toohey should get job as miner and work for Progressive Miners in spare time—all expenses to be paid by Party.

11. In case of the strike being settled, local miners relief committees to make public announcement that they are ready to return funds to donors upon request. That they are ready to suggest that relief money collected should be used for the relief of Passaic Strikers. Or to turn over the use of the funds for the defense of the convicted Zeigler miners, or any other working class activity or agency specified by the donor.

These instructions are strictly confidential and should be treated as such.

P.S. Instruction No. 11 is not to go into effect until the earliest March first. There is considerable suffering among the miners that must be alleviated, therefore, all miners' relief campaign must be prosecuted with added vigor until March 1st.

These instructions were signed by Ruthenberg as General Secretary of the Party. They show how completely we controlled the Progressive Miners' Committee and the relief agencies, which had really been set up by us. The relief campaign for the Anthracite Fields was conducted by the International Workers Relief, a branch of Mopr, with main headquarters in Moscow. The money collected by this organization up to March first did not go for the purposes for which it was collected. It helped to finance our Party organizers in the Anthracite Fields. Yet all our activity petered out into a demonstration of Communist futility in this important strike involving 150,000 workers in a basic industry.

After the convention of the Party in 1927 and when the Party was established in its New York headquarters, the question of the expenditures of money in the miners' campaign was taken up and a motion was made that, hereafter, no more money should be spent by Foster in the campaign without the knowledge of the Secretariat. In June, 1928, most of the Party leaders went to Moscow as delegates to the Sixth World Congress of the Communist International. Lovestone and Foster, both members of the Secretariat, went to Moscow to attend the Congress. As the third member of the Secretariat, I became the acting Secretary of the Party during Lovestone's absence. The decision was therefore made that all the money in Foster's possession for the miners' campaign, as well as all other confidential funds, should be entrusted to me and that I should be empowered to make the necessary expenditures therefrom.

By 1928 the trade union policy of the Party had been stood on its head by the decisions of the Fourth World Congress of the Profintern. Our Party with no opportunity for discussion was suddenly ordered to give up its policy of working within the frame-work of the existing unions and to begin the organization of unions of its own independently. In spite of the heavy subsidies received from Moscow for the fight against Lewis, Lewis had always emerged victorious. The Party now, in line with its new policy, decided to conduct a campaign among the miners affiliated with the United Mine Workers for the purpose of splitting the miners' organization and forming a new union. A committee was formed, this time almost entirely of Communists, with headquarters at Pittsburgh, known as the National Miners Convention Arrangements Committee.

The special funds turned over to me in the miners' campaign amounted to a total of $29,329.46, to be exact, the bulk of the money having been transmitted to me by the comrade who had charge of the Party's archives. Arrangements were made in

Moscow for additional money to be transmitted through him. Every time money was forwarded we were notified by cable to that effect. In the short period of two months over five thousand dollars was spent for the miners' campaign. I also turned over to the National Office of the Party, to be dispensed as I ordered, $21,650.40. In addition, I paid out $1,000 to Marcus, a representative of the Organization Department of the Communist International. The money the National Office received from me was entered on its book as loans and donations from fictitious persons without addresses.

The money which the Communists received from Moscow for the support of Communist activities in the United States has a history. During the early days sailors who acted as couriers brought into the United States diamonds and jewelry which we sold far below their actual value in order to obtain the cash we needed. Communists who went to Russia were given large sums of cash, diamonds or jewelry, which they smuggled into the country. One of the leaders of the Lettish Federation, who was in the inner circles of the Slavic Federation's council, was given fifty thousand dollars in cash when he was in Russia in 1920 for transmission to the Party. He kept the money for himself and with it went into business in Chicago. This comrade's great revolutionary ability consisted in stamping his feet when he did not like what someone was saying. Fraina was given a sum reported to have been twenty thousand dollars, to start a Communist party in Mexico. After a short time in Mexico he lost interest and what actually became of the money remains a mystery.

In the early days thousands of dollars were lost by these crude methods. In 1922 the Party received a large shipment of money from Moscow, which it used to speculate in German Marks, upon the advice of Lovestone and one of his business friends, only to lose several thousand dollars in the transaction. As the Comintern organization was improved, better ways were developed for shipping money. When the Arcos was first established in London, the money destined for the United States and Canada was shipped through the Arcos. The raid on the Arcos stopped this, because all the names of all the persons to whom the Arcos cabled money for the party were obtained by the British authorities in the raid. New names and methods were then devised. In later years most of the money was cabled to us through an office maintained for that purpose in Berlin. The money was cabled to relatives of party leaders, business men who were party members or sympathetic to the party, through firms of these in Canada and in New York. Our Party members, usually when they returned from trips to Moscow, brought back with them money for the Party's activities.

The Party today has branched out into so many new fields, its importance to the Soviet Union's foreign policy on account of the Japanese situation makes it necessary for the party to carry on an unprecedented propaganda campaign through every avenue of publicity, even including the expensive use of the radio. Recently the Party has started the publication of two new daily papers, one in Chicago and one in San Francisco, even though the yearly deficit of the *Daily Worker* has always been over fifty thousand dollars. Obviously the Soviet Union must now subsidize the American Party more heavily than it ever did before. I do not know all the methods it resorts to nowadays to overcome financial difficulties, but, as Stalin has been reported to have remarked, there is no fortress a Bolshevik cannot capture, and, when with the advent of the Five-Year Plan, which placed a strain on Soviet foreign valuta resources, the G. P. U. found itself short of foreign valuta needed for its world-wide machinations, it secured an expert engraver from the German Party and established a counterfeiting plant in Berlin. Much of this counterfeit money found its way into the treasuries of the various Communist parties of Europe. American money was the last to be counterfeited, the G. P. U., which handled the matter in the United States, concentrating on the counterfeiting of one hundred dollar bills.

Communist Unionism

The policy of splitting the unions did not work out successfully. The National Miners Union, notwithstanding the money that was spent on its organization, failed to attract the miners.

They preferred to remain in the United Mine Workers of America, in spite of all our charges that Lewis and his machine were selling them out to the mine owners. The National Textile Workers Union which we organized gave us a union which could shout against the A. F. of L. but could not organize workers and win strikes. We attempted to start organization campaigns in the steel and automobile industries. But these efforts proved ludicrously futile. The workers were simply not responding to our call for new unionism under Communist domination.

The real problem in carrying out the new policy came in the needle trades. All the outstanding leaders with years of experience as union officials were sincerely opposed to leaving their unions and organizing new ones. On this they had the secret approval of most of the Communist Party leaders, who looked upon the organization of the needle trades workers in new unions as the height of folly. But orders were orders. Moscow had ordered a split to take place. The new unions, therefore, had to be organized. Never mind that it ran counter to our convictions and to common sense. Moscow's decision must have been formed on considerations of that "higher strategy" for which the Bolshevik leaders were held to be famous. We believed that the Russian leaders, who apparently had better sources of information than we, must know that the great sacrifices entailed in organizing the new unions were necessary, if not for American reasons, then for international or, most important, Russian reasons.

Though we believed, as did the leaders of the needle trades, that the step was suicidal, we prodded these leaders on and hurried them into taking the step. Our motives in this respect were not based upon principles, nor were they concerned with the interests of the labor movement as a whole. We did not want to be found in opposition to the Russian leaders, even if we believed they were wrong, because the Russians never tolerated opposition. They always made it a point to take "organizational steps" against opposition elements by removing these elements from all important posts of leadership. We had to curry favor with the Russians in order to maintain our leadership of the American Party. The Russian whip could drive us out just as quickly as the Russian pat on the back had put us in. Hence, we did not hesitate to split the unions and to wreck what it had taken years of tremendous effort and great sacrifice to build up.

The Bolsheviks from the time of Lenin to the present have never given up the hope of capturing the trade union movement of the United States. Our Party received more assistance, more advice, more decisions on the trade union question than on almost any other question. Lenin was particularly anxious to win over the American trade unions. It was Lenin who conceived the idea that it would be possible for the Communists in the United States, by hiding their identity, to form an opposition bloc in the trade unions, which would enable them to dislodge the reactionary forces in control of the American Federation of Labor. The one policy of the Party that has not undergone any changes has been this policy, with but one exception, when, for a short time, the Party attempted to organize its own unions. Immediately after the failure of that policy the Party again, with some degree of success, put through the policy of an opposition bloc.

Lenin first worked out the policy when William Z. Foster and Sidney Hillman were in Moscow in 1922. At that time Lenin hoped that Foster, who was not to disclose his identity as a Communist, would succeed in building up a powerful progressive opposition in the A. F. of L. It was hoped that Hillman would be able to enlist in the opposition movement the powerful unions of the Railroad Brotherhoods, which, like his own union, the Amalgamated Clothing Workers of America, were not affiliated with the A. F. of L. At the opportune moment, the two forces were to combine in a concerted drive against the Gompers machine. It was hoped, through such a movement, one part of it resting on the base of the powerful independent unions outside of the A. F. of L. and the other on a large progressive force working inside the A. F. of L., to bring about that situation in the trade unions which would lead to the ousting of Gompers and his lieutenants from control.

Lenin demanded but one condition for his support of such a movement: namely, a change in the policies of the unions toward Soviet Russia. The Bolsheviks hoped that the success of Lenin's plan would create a very great sentiment in the trade unions for American recognition of Soviet Russia and trade with it. Lenin was also of the opinion that if such an opposition movement could be launched, its success would help transform the Communist Party from the small underground sect it then was into a powerful mass party.

However, Lenin did not know Hillman. He did not know that Hillman pursued a two-faced policy in his own union. On the one hand, he gave expression to progressive and radical phrases, which he took care were widely publicized, and on the other hand, he pursued as conservative a course in trade union matters as did Gompers in the A. F. of L. Hillman, who was not a Communist and never was even a Socialist, was at best a lukewarm liberal. His actions as President of the Amalgamated were always characterized by extreme opportunism. The trade-union machine with which he controlled the Amalgamated consisted of a mixture of radicals and Socialists, who had lost all their Socialist and radical idealism, and a crowd of corrupt, reactionary trade union officials, racketeers and gangsters. Hillman had his general executive board exert pressure upon Local Big Four of the Amalgamated to expel me as a member of the organization because I had exposed the corrupt and racketeering machine of Beckerman in that local when Beckerman had the full support of Hillman. Later Hillman himself had to expel Beckerman, because the charges which I had made were not only proven true but because they became widely known. When Hillman returned from Moscow, he made all the capital he could out of his visit, as far as the members of his organization were concerned, because a large number of them were radically inclined and supported Soviet Russia. But he did nothing for the idea of helping to form an opposition bloc in the trade unions.

Though Lenin's plans failed to materialize, the idea was not given up. Attempts along that line were being made repeatedly, but without success. In 1926 the Communist International sent special instructions to our Party, directing us to take steps to organize an opposition bloc in the trade unions. In line with these instructions we drew up a detailed program on how it should be done. The campaign in the miners' union against John L. Lewis was part of a move to form such an opposition bloc. It was hoped that, by defeating Lewis and electing Brophy as President of the United Mine Workers of America, a base of operations would be established which would enable us to create a broad oppositional movement under Communist control. These attempts finally culminated in a measure of success ten years later, with the organization of the Committee for Industrial Organization. The Communist Party not only supported Hillman and Brophy, with whom it had had relations before, but it went further. It threw its wholehearted support to John L. Lewis, the same John L. Lewis who ten years before was to be driven out from the labor movement. John L. Lewis now became not the blackguard but the hero of organized labor.

From the Communist standpoint the rapid strides made by the C. I. O. in gaining a strong foothold in the trade unions and in organizing workers in industries never organized before was a vindication of its opposition bloc policy. The sudden friendship of the Russian Ambassador for John L. Lewis had more to do with the C. I. O. position on international affairs than it did on trade union matters. John L. Lewis had been for years one of the most outspoken critics and enemies of the Soviet Union. Suddenly he was invited to the most important receptions arranged by Ambassador Troyanovsky. Had not the C. I. O. taken a position on international affairs in line with Soviety policy, I am certain that John L. Lewis would not have been a welcome guest at the Soviet Union Embassy in Washington. The political consequences of the C. I. O. are more important to the Communists than its trade union policies, because the Communists hope through the vehicle of the C. I. O. to establish a political front in the United States that will be the counterpart of what the People's Front of France was. The Communist Party has closely followed the political ambitions of the C. I. O. and has supported each one of its political moves.

The Communist Party hopes through the political activities and pressure of the C. I. O. to force the Democratic Party to adopt a policy which will lead the United States either into a war against Japan or into a combination including the Soviet Union. It is a conscious policy for the embroilment of the United States in war. The Communist Party is prepared to support John L. Lewis in every adventure, provided he will continue to favor those policies which in their opinion are in the interest of the Soviet Union.

As I have pointed out, our Party sought to gain a foothold in every trade union, especially in the basic industries. This was in line with the instructions of the Communist International. To demonstrate the ramifications of the Communist Party in the trade unions, let me give a typical meeting of the Trade Union Committee of the Central Executive Committee, held on June second, 1926, in Chicago. The agenda consisted of sixteen points, as follows:

> Mining, Railroads, Metal, Textile, Needle, Shoes, Rubber, Food, Printing, State Federation of Labor Programs, New York Port Bureau, British Strike Relief, Montevideo Conference, Youth, Trade Union Educational League Literature, Pullman Porters.

This meeting considered the organization of subcommittees for every trade. Dunne and Johnstone were instructed to submit plans on how these were to be organized. Programs for Communist and Left Wing activity were worked out for the metal industry, the textile industry, the needle trades, and matters concerning the other industries were considered.

Let us take rubber as an example of how each situation was considered. The report to the committee was that the situation in the rubber factories of Akron was a very difficult one, because there were two organizations in the field—an A. F. of L. union with three hundred members and a club with five hundred members opposed to the A. F. of L. The Party had two nuclei in the shops, but no capable leaders among the local comrades. Since real dynamic leadership was necessary, it was decided to get some one to take charge of things and give direction to the struggle for organizing the rubber workers. Meanwhile we were to penetrate whatever existing organizations there were in the field as well as the unions. Dunne, Johnstone and Bittleman were designated to draw up a program for the industry. Foster made a series of motions, which were generally made in such situations. They were:

1. That the district organizer in Cleveland district be instructed to concentrate upon the establishment of shop nuclei in every rubber plant.

2. That we instruct our best comrades to join the club and also the A. F. of L. organization, and undertake to get control of both.

3. In the club we should follow the policy of quietly building up committees based upon the respective plants and departments in these plants, in preparation for the shop committee system.

4. That active preparation be begun in Akron for developing a campaign to approach the workers directly on the basis of economic demands. This campaign to be organized so that the club itself does not appear to take the initiative.

5. We propose that Jack Bradon be sent to go to work in the mills and undertake to take charge of the organization.

It was at this meeting that steps were first taken to organize a Port Bureau in New York City. Port Bureaus were being organized all over the world upon the direct instructions of the Communist International and the Red Trade Union International, which supplied ample funds for their organization. The purpose of a Port Bureau was to establish a center in each port that would be active in contacting sailors and workers on ships. Through the activities of the Port Bureaus it was hoped an effective Communist network of seafaring workers could be organized in the ports and on the ocean liners, who could be of invaluable service to the Soviet Government for espionage purposes and in the event of a war.

Through our membership of fifteen thousand, insignificant in number, we kept a careful watch on every trade union situation. The National Office of the Party was like a railroad center from which tracks led to every important trade union and industrial district of the country. We were building up an intricate network of these important centers, for the express purpose of eventually dominating the trade union and industrial centers of the country. Our contacts kept the National Office fully informed on all important developments. Our National Office acted as a clearing house, and the Political Committee as a board of directors for this intricate Communist industrial network. The information received was digested by the Political Committee, which made the decisions. Linked up with this network were the Party terminals in the various centers, the district offices of the Party, each with its district committee and industrial subcommittees, and the various branch and industrial organizations of the Trade Union Educational League. We were perfecting the network for reaching the masses, the winning of the masses depending upon our ability to organize the workers and capture the trade unions. Taking care of this network was no easy matter, for it taxed to the utmost the national leaders of the Party and the district leaders. We had to work a minimum of from eighteen to twenty hours a day to take care of the problems and situations that accumulated incessantly. We the leaders became so wrapped up in the industrial affairs of the Party, in the exciting internal fights and politics of the unions, that we had little or no time left to consider what we were doing and where all our confusing intrigues and complicated maneuvers would end.

PART III

FROM LEADER TO OUTCAST

CHAPTER XI

THE PASSING OF AMERICA'S LENIN

As I look back on those years of feverish activity, I begin to understand that many of our errors were the inevitable consequence of overwork and nervous tension. We were so engrossed in immediate tasks of great urgency that we lost sight of political developments in the United States which were a challenge to us as revolutionary Marxists. It would take me too far afield to discuss or even to itemize these errors of omission. Moreover, any consideration of what might have been done and was left undone is bound to be controversial, and I prefer to confine myself chiefly to what was done. Yet I do nurse to this day a profound regret with regard to one of my own errors of omission in the realm of the factional struggle that rent the Party asunder. I do not shun my share of responsibility for the loathsome factionalism that wore down the Party's moral standard until nothing was left of it. The malpractices indulged in during the struggle for power were perpetrated by both factions. It is nevertheless a fact that in our faction the initiator of these malpractices was chiefly Jay Lovestone, with the assistance of Jack Stachel. That was due to the fact that Lovestone was the factional leader, while Ruthenberg headed the Party as a whole and I was in charge of trade union activities. Had either Ruthenberg or I been the factional leader, we might have been no better than Lovestone, it may be argued. Moreover, did we not approve of Lovestone's machinations? Did we not act in concert with him? Of course, we did. Yet I cannot help regretting that out of a sense of loyalty to the faction, out of a sense of political expediency, as well as out of sincere conviction that we of the Ruthenberg faction knew better how to lead the Party than the Fosterites, I suppressed many a misgiving and fell in line with the malodorous plots hatched by Lovestone and his Stachel. No, I did not concoct those plots, but I approved them either overtly or tacitly, and hence my responsibility is no whit less than Lovestone's or Stachel's. I mention this fact, because the Moscow Trials of 1936-1938 showed dramatically the ultimate end of such a course. We in America sank so low in our ethical standards that we resorted to gangster tactics against fellow-Communists because they disagreed with us. That confronts me with the horrible speculation: had we Communists attained power in America, myself included, would we hesitate to go through with blood purges? I confess that I am constrained to answer in the negative. With that in mind, are not Stalin's purges far less startling?

For months after the National Convention of 1925 had given us the leadership, we were engaged in reconstructive work, to repair the damage of the factional strife. We intensified trade union activity, on which Foster claimed a monopoly, increased agitation, propaganda and educational activities under the direction of Bertram D. Wolfe, spurred the new organizers we placed in important districts to establish new records of achievement, and it was during those months of reconstruction that we succeeded in capturing leadership and control of the New York Joint Council of the Furriers International Union. We had also successfully combated the attempt to exclude our members from the International Ladies Garment Workers Union by capturing the largest locals of the union—1, 9, and 22. Preparations were laid for an extensive drive among the miners for the ousting of John L. Lewis and the capturing of the United Mine Workers of America. New fields were penetrated, new elements were brought into the Party orbit, and plans were laid for the wave of strikes in the needle and textile trades which were to make labor history in 1926.

But the factional war did not stop. Foster did not give up his caucus. Its activities were conducted much more secretly than heretofore, through underground channels. Cannon was peeved because in the deal he made with the Communist International Representative the Party was not handed over to him. From the remnants he pulled out of the Foster Caucus he organized a caucus of his own. The organizer of Cannon's Caucus was Martin Abern, whose pretensions to leadership lay in the fact that he had been formerly a trusted lieutenant of the Foster group and had held some important posts in the Party, which he managed from a factional standpoint to the satisfaction of the Foster caucus. Included in the leadership of the Cannon caucus was Max Shachtman, who had just graduated from the Young Workers League into the Party. He was a capable youngster, well read in Communist literature, thoroughly convinced of his own importance, one who carefully studied his Communist phrases and was able to broadcast them in an authoritative tone but, to many of us, with a ring of insincerity. Besides, Shachtman was endowed with a sense of humor and a contemptuous sarcasm towards others, especially his opponents. He was a gifted and very prolific writer.

Although we of the Ruthenberg group were the administration that talked in the name of the Party, we did not give up our caucus, which became the privileged inner circle within the Party. At our caucuses the most confidential matters were considered and the most delicate political situations disposed of without sanction of the Party as a whole. Our caucus was the military wing of the Ruthenberg administration and a sort of secret police within the Party. It was the dictatorship over the Party. The caucus was dedicated to the task of defending the Ruthenberg majority against all enemies and for the purpose of preventing any serious defections from its ranks into the camp of its factional enemies. It maintained a loyalty and discipline above that of the Party. Ruthenberg was the leader of the Party. Jay Lovestone was the leader of the Ruthenberg caucus.

Foster now changed his strategy. He supported the position of the Ruthenberg majority, with few exceptions, on all political questions. But on organizational questions, especially questions concerning the appointment or removal of Party organizers and officials, he fought like a tiger for his people and against our appointees. Towards the Communist International he adopted a very clever and well thought out policy. He decided to colonize Moscow with American Communists who were his supporters. He succeeded in having the Ruthenberg Central Executive Committee send some of Foster's most important followers to the Lenin Institute, to learn in three years how to become full fledged professional Communist leaders. Lozovsky, head of the Profintern, upon Foster's request, assigned many Fosterites to jobs in the headquarters of the Red Trade Union International in Moscow. He took advantage of every opportunity to send his people for special work in Moscow. At the same time he pressed in the Political Committee that his appeal against the decisions of the last national convention be taken up immediately with the Communist International.

When a tentative date for the holding of a plenum of the Executive of the Communist International was announced for the end of October, 1925, Foster immediately served notice on the Party that he and Bittleman were leaving to present their appeal. The executive of the Communist International did not meet as scheduled, but met instead from February seventeenth to March fifteenth, 1926. This gave Foster and Bittleman about four months in Moscow, four months which they used to great advantage against our group. They visited all departments of the Comintern and Profintern and made reports which were grossly colored to suit their factional purposes. They visited all Soviet institutions closely allied with the Comintern and spread propaganda against the Ruthenberg group. They zealously sought interviews with the leaders of the Russian Communist Party in order to impress them with their own importance and the mistake they made in supporting Ruthenberg. The Fosterites colonized in Moscow worked along similar lines, with the result that Foster was being publicized and advertised with all the characteristic American ballyhoo.

Our group felt so confident of Moscow's support that it made a big mistake in not cultivating the Moscow Front. When in January, 1926, it became necessary to send delegates to the Comintern Plenum, Ruthenberg moved that Max Bedacht and Cannon present the case of the Party against Foster. Ruthenberg made this decision even though he knew that Cannon had failed to support the Party majority and was maintaining a caucus of his own, his independence being maintained in such a way that on important questions he was free to throw his support to Foster. Our caucus opposed Ruthenberg's proposal. We realized that Foster was using his Moscow center very effectively to spread all kinds of information by calls, letters and confidential reports; that Moscow was dissatisfied with the Ruthenberg leadership, and was prepared to give the Party back to Foster. The battle on the question of who should go to Moscow was fought out in our caucus. The culmination of this fight was that Ruthenberg, as much as he disliked to do so, had to pack his grip and embark for Moscow once more.

Foster in Moscow demanded that he be recognized as the leader of the American Party and be given thirteen members of the Central Executive Committee to eight for the Ruthenberg group. Moscow rejected Foster's demand for a majority, but to appease him, gave him a majority on the Trade Union Committee and one more member on the Political Committee, Alexander Bittleman. Upon Ruthenberg's arrival in Moscow, we received a cable informing us of Foster's charges and the effect they were having upon the Moscow leaders. A meeting of the top leadership of the Ruthenberg caucus was held immediately in Chicago, at which we decided that every important Fosterite should be offered an official position in the Party. The resistance to this move among the rank and file of the Ruthenberg caucus was very strong, and we had to use considerable pressure to force them to agree to what we had decided to do. When the American Commission of the Comintern met to consider Foster's charges of political knifing, cables were produced by Ruthenberg to prove that every Fosterite whom Foster charged with being removed and prevented from serving the Party was on the Party payroll.

In its new decision on the American Communist Party, the Comintern stated:

> The hegemony of the imperialists of the United States of North America over the capitalist world renders the work of the American Communists an important and specially responsible one. The Communist Party of America is called upon to play a tremendous role and in many respects even a *decisive* role. Even for that reason alone all the sections of the Comintern and the Comintern as a whole will attentively follow the activity of the American section and support it in every possible way.

This declaration meant to us that Moscow was not only interested in American developments, but that the activities of our Party would be carefully scrutinized by the watch dogs appointed for that purpose in the apparatus of the Comintern. They would be delving not only through our Party press, but through Party documents and minutes, to check up on us. We knew that from now on we would have to watch out carefully that our record of activities and especially our political line should not displease Moscow.

Upon his return Cannon conceived a clever political idea. It consisted in breaking away a section of the Ruthenberg group, making together with it a new combination with Foster for the purpose of capturing the Party. He had private talks with three important leaders of the Ruthenberg group—Weinstone, Stachel and Wolfe. Weinstone, self-styled General Secretary of the New York District, pompous, ambitious, craved leadership and sought to build up in New York City a center which would rival the political importance of the Party's National Office in Chicago. He strutted around like a Fuehrer and never lost an opportunity to impress the rank and file and even outsiders with his importance. But he lacked one necessary qualification for leadership—courage. He was afraid of making a mistake, he was afraid of making deviations of Communist policy. The result was that he hesitated in making an important decision. Very often when he had to write and sign a letter involving a disputed question of policy, he would stamp it with a rubber stamp, "Dictated but not read." This stamp gave him an opportunity to squirm out of situations, if they became untenable, by claiming that his stenographer had not correctly transcribed what he had dictated to her. Among the followers of the Ruthenberg group, he was known as William "Wobbly" Weinstone. He, Lovestone and Wolfe had been active in the Left Wing of the Socialist Party before they had assumed positions of leadership in the Communist movement. The Foster faction had dubbed them the "City College Boys." Of the three, Lovestone had achieved national and international prominence as a Communist leader. The other two were in the second category. Weinstone was very jealous of Lovestone. He craved

Lovestone's position of leadership and importance. Jack Stachel was a youngster who had just joined the Party, and in the factional situation had proven his qualifications as an expert political maneuverer. Both Lovestone and Wolfe had been responsible for Stachel's speedy and phenomenal rise to leadership, solely because of the youngster's aptitude for dirty factional politics. His leadership had nothing to do with carrying on of Communist activities among the people or with activities in the labor movement, to which he remains a stranger. Wolfe and Weinstone were members of the Central Executive Committee. Stachel was not.

Cannon's conversations took place in preparation for the full meeting of the Central Executive Committee which had been called to consider the recent Comintern decision. This meeting was almost as powerful as a Party convention, for it elected all sub-committees of the Party, and, if it desired, could elect a new set of Party leaders and officials. The Central Executive Committee at the time was composed of twenty members, ten for the combined Cannon and Foster group and ten for the Ruthenberg group. If Cannon could succeed in switching Weinstone and Wolfe to vote with the ten Cannon and Foster members, the majority of the Central Executive Committee would automatically be changed, a new political committee could be elected and the Ruthenberg group ousted from the leadership.

In carrying through his plot, Cannon met with some difficulties. He easily convinced Weinstone and Wolfe, but he was unable to make Foster see the advantage in the new setup. Foster evidently wanted to be *the* leader and not one of the leaders. He had every reason to distrust Cannon because of his previous break with the Foster group. Cannon proposed that he take the Chairmanship of the Party, Weinstone become the General Secretary and Foster the head of the Trade Union Department, which the Communist International declared was to be his special field in the American Party. But Foster no longer desired to be the trade union "spetz" as, from the Russian, we called a specialist in the Party. He knew that in the Communist movement political leadership was what counted, and that unless you were recognized as the political leader of the Party you were no leader at all. Foster was not quite as naïve as Cannon took him to be. He knew enough about the workings of the Comintern to realize that such a putsch could not be made without first getting its approval.

The first inkling that I got of Cannon's plot was in a conversation I had with Weinstone. First, he complained that Ruthenberg was too rigid, that he was a poor mixer, who did not know how to utilize all the forces of the Party. He blamed Ruthenberg for the failure of the Party to give Foster the place in the leadership which he deserved. He explained with an air of authority what he believed a good secretary of the Party should be like, and intimated that if he were in Ruthenberg's place he would be the ideal man. He ended by declaring, "What we need is a collective leadership. Ben, we must recognize that we have two main streams in the Party—the trade union stream, made up of the members who came from the trade unions, represented by Foster; and the political stream, made up of the elements who came from the Socialist Party and its Left Wing, represented by Ruthenberg. What is necessary is to join the two streams together. The one force that can do that is the Cannon group, which has some of the best elements that came from both streams. Once we can get such a collective leadership, the factional warfare will be over."

I did not like the way Weinstone was parroting Cannon's phrases about a collective leadership, so I replied: "Comrade Weinstone, what you want is not a collective leadership but a collecting leadership. If you will play Cannon's game, you will not end factionalism for you will throw the Party into a more bitter factional controversy than ever."

I lost no time in informing our caucus headquarters in Chicago of the new factional lineup. Lovestone came pell mell to New York. He talked to Wolfe for two hours and finally persuaded Wolfe to remain loyal to the Ruthenberg group. Then Wolfe and Lovestone closeted themselves with Stachel. After many hours of talk Stachel followed Wolfe in declaring his loyalty to the Ruthenberg group. Then a caucus of the top leaders of our group was held at the Hotel Albert in New York City, without Weinstone. At this meeting Wolfe gave as an excuse for his conduct that the only way in which he could get the real inside information about Weinstone's and Cannon's plans was to join up with them. Everyone was skeptical. However, we were not going to drive Wolfe out of the group and jeopardize our hold on the Party by calling him a liar. Such political stupidity would have driven him permanently into the hands of Cannon. At this meeting we discussed all afternoon and all night our relations to Cannon and how we should act towards Weinstone. It was decided that under no circumstances should we break with Weinstone, for that would mean losing the New York District and the majority of the Central Executive Committee. We finally decided to discuss the question with him, dragging the discussion out for an extended period of time, in order to prevent him from precipitating action on his proposals.

Another caucus meeting was called for the next evening, and to that meeting Weinstone was invited. The status of our group was discussed. As had previously been decided, the question of Cannon was not raised. We wanted Weinstone to raise the question himself. But Weinstone was very cagey. He talked about everything except what we wanted him to admit. The meeting dragged on for hours. It was early morning when the management of the hotel, after guests had complained of the noise, moved us to a remote and secluded section of the hotel. We talked the following morning and afternoon. Sandwiches and coffee were served in the rooms. But Weinstone did not weaken. He talked at random on all kinds of petty questions, but failed to raise the question for which the meeting was called. Finally, having lost patience, Lovestone and I called Stachel aside and induced him to raise the question. A discussion followed which dragged on for hours. Weinstone spoke, but did not unfold the full scope of his deals with Cannon. When he raised the question of a collective leadership by uniting with the trade union stream of the Party, we listened and pressed for more information. Then we told him his ideas were well worth considering, but that before he put them into practice he owed it to the group to which he belonged to present his point of view fully, and that we, as a group, were not opposed to a collective leadership, if it could be honestly attained. We asked him to give the important national leaders of our group who were not present an opportunity to consider the question. We suggested that it might be possible for us to formulate a basis of agreement which we could present to our national caucus when the Central Executive Committee met in Chicago. Weinstone hesitated. He did not know whether to take us seriously or not, for he did not know that the approach to him had been worked out beforehand. The vague friendly speeches of Wolfe and Stachel puzzled him greatly. Pretending to see much in his position, they nevertheless cautioned against precipitous action and pleaded with Weinstone that he try first to come to some understanding with our group, which they said they were convinced would be possible. After thirty-six hours of wrangling, Weinstone, hesitant and afraid to make a break, agreed to the appointment of a sub-committee of three, consisting of Lovestone, Wolfe and himself, to work out a draft resolution for final consideration by the national caucus in Chicago.

Weinstone was given every opportunity to talk his head off in our caucus. He was permitted up to a certain point to amend resolutions before they were introduced for adoption by the Central Executive Committee but, under no circumstances, was he given an opportunity to vote against the Ruthenberg group. Thus, Cannon's schemes to break the Ruthenberg majority on the Central Executive Committee were forestalled. At the plenum of the Central Executive Committee, no shift in power took place.

Although Weinstone was determined to carry through his policy, he did not want to break with the Ruthenberg group simply as an individual; he wanted to break with a following. We gave him a following by instructing many members of our group to tie up with Weinstone. We instructed them to act just as cautiously, just as hesitatingly as he did. We had to spend days and nights in caucuses with Weinstone. Ruthenberg, Bedacht, Lovestone and others traveled repeatedly between Chicago and New York. Caucuses were held generally at the Hotel Albert, where Ruthenberg and Lovestone stopped when in New York. Most of them lasted continuously for twenty-four hours or more. This precarious situation for the Ruthenberg group, due to Weinstone's vacillations and leadership ambitions endured up till Ruthenberg's death in March, 1927.

Charles E. Ruthenberg was the most ambitious of us all. He was insufferably egotistical, resented passionately any challenge to his preëminence in Bolshevik leadership, conceiving himself as the American Lenin. Yet unlike his Russian prototype, it never occurred to him to assume leadership of the revolutionary forces in his own country independently of Moscow—something, I am sure, Lenin would not have hesitated to do had he found himself enmeshed in the trap of foreign domination. Ruthenberg made deals with both Pepper and Foster in the hope of climbing to such a pinnacle of leadership as would place him above all factional controversy and beyond the reach of attack. He abided by only one principle, and its name was, Ruthenberg. Anything that would advance that principle was right; anything inimical to it was counter-revolutionary. I have already told how he united with Foster to ditch the labor party idea and how a few months later he championed the same idea, each time for the sake of advancing his fortunes as a leader. I have also told how Ruthenberg, along with Lovestone and the rest of us (for that matter), went out of his way to court the Lore group, holding conferences with Ludwig Lore, promising him the fullest support and a high place in the Party leadership, and how, when Lore, for considerations that had to do with political ideas and principles, turned down these overtures, Ruthenberg led the campaign against the same Lore, denouncing him as a dangerous Social-Democrat, a Menshevik, an opportunist, a traitor to the labor movement, and drove him out of the Party.

Ruthenberg was a complex of mutually-exclusive contradictions. Vain, he was conservative in his dress and bearing, yet most radical and reckless in his political views. His pleasures were simple: a walk in the woods or a quiet afternoon in the country gave him adequate enjoyment and contentment. But his romantic spirit could never be appeased, and he constantly sought satisfaction for the restlessness it engendered in him by worshiping as a slave at the feet of one woman after another.

He was calm and deliberate. He definitely did not give one the impression of a rabid Communist leader. Rather, one would expect from looking at him to find a man who would like ease and retirement, to ponder the philosophic aspects of life. Yet, in pursuit of his ambitions to become the undisputed leader of American Communism, he threw himself into a life of ceaseless excitement, nervous tension and activity. He had a Messianic complex, carrying himself among us as if he were the incarnation of Communism, the one destined by intellectual and other measurements to be the leader of our movement, the ordained one to bring about the Revolution, and the one to rule Soviet America. I marveled at this sincere conceit, because he was obviously both dogmatic and shallow in his views. He could think only along the lines set down in the accepted Communist and Marxian formulas. Even those he could interpret only in an inflexible and narrow way, revealing a mediocre mind. Yet, he did become the one in whom the power of our Party seemed vested for all eternity. Ruthenberg epitomized the Communist Party. He was the hub around which the wheel turned. We of the Ruthenberg group built up our régime, the stability and endurance of our rule over American Communism, around him. The fact that Ruthenberg's bearing was so unlike that of all other Communist leaders as to become an enigma before the membership, helped us to establish our régime, because it was a factor in causing the members to accept his leadership. Like good slaves, they recognized their lord and master when they saw him. Not only members of our faction but the Party membership as a whole trusted and worshiped him.

On March first, 1927, we received news in New York that Ruthenberg had been operated upon for peritonitis and that his condition was very serious. I discussed it at the time with Ben Lifshitz. He was worried because he was afraid if Ruthenberg died that the Ruthenberg group would disintegrate and a new combination of forces would take over the leadership of the Party. But before we had time to consider the Party situation, a telegram received on March the second announced that Ruthenberg had died.

The news of Ruthenberg's death caused a distinct shock, because he died suddenly, in the prime of his life. Only two weeks before, he had been in New York in an effort to straighten out William Weinstone, who was again trying to build a bloc which would hold the balance of power between the Foster and Ruthenberg groups. At that time Ruthenberg did not look like a man who was to die two weeks later. In fact, he sat through a caucus meeting with Weinstone which lasted over thirty-six hours. He went back to Chicago after the meeting, feeling confident that he had at last straightened out Weinstone and that the latter would remain loyal to our group. I did not share his optimism. After Ruthenberg returned to Chicago I had on more than one occasion to telephone both him and Lovestone of Weinstone's factional activities against our group and his secret negotiations with Jim Cannon. Unlike Ruthenberg, Lovestone was alarmed. Ruthenberg was sure that the promises Weinstone had made to him in New York were bona fide and would not be broken. He never lived to find out how mistaken he was. The news of Ruthenberg's death, while it depressed all the leaders of the Ruthenberg group in New York, had quite the opposite effect on the leaders of the other factions and on Weinstone. They were jubilant. They saw in Ruthenberg's death the end of our reign and their own rise to power.

I left for Chicago on March fourth. When I arrived there, I found out immediately that behind the curtain of death an intense struggle for power was going on. Ruthenberg's body was lying in state in Carmen's Hall. Beside the coffin which contained the blond Ruthenberg, his face thin and pale, stood a Red Guard of Honor. The personnel of the guard changed, for the vigil of the Red Guard was kept up every hour of the morning and night while the body lay in state. The leaders of the Party as they arrived in Chicago rushed to Carmen's Hall, to stand guard at the bier of their departed leader. Carmen's Hall was visited by a steady stream of Party members and sympathizers who displayed genuine emotion over the loss of their leader. But at the Party headquarters on West Washington Boulevard the atmosphere was entirely different. It was the atmosphere of a royal court torn by intrigues. The Fosterites scurried around like ants over a dead beetle, nor were the Cannonites far behind. Lovestone called me aside and expressed the opinion that the Foster group had been only waiting for Ruthenberg to die in order to seize the Party. The round-faced German barber, Max Bedacht, fuming at the Fosterites, said to me, "These vultures would snatch up Ruthenberg's corpse and feed upon it for their own enjoyment!" I turned away, for that humorless comrade would not have understood my smile.

Even in the arrangements for the funeral and for the funeral mass meeting we were motivated by factional considerations. The Foster group tried to take over the funeral arrangements, in order to capitalize on the sentiment which Ruthenberg's death would arouse by appearing in the rôle of his chief mourners and as his rightful heirs to the Party leadership. Foster was like a hawk that scented his prey. He could not wait. Now was the opportunity to capture the Party leadership.

At the first meeting of the Political Committee which I attended, on March fifth, Foster moved that a plenum of the Central Executive Committee be held right after the Ruthenberg memorial meeting in New York. At that meeting Foster figured that, in a deal with Cannon and Weinstone, he could obtain a majority for reorganizing the Party machinery in such a way that he would have the power in the Party. But we of the Ruthenberg group were not to be found napping. Comrade Kalfides, a leader of the Greek federation of the Party, had learned about the intentions of the Foster group the day Ruthenberg died. He called Lovestone and Bedacht into conference. A plan of battle was drawn up. All the Ruthenberg leaders in Chicago, including the leaders in the language federations, were called into a caucus at the editorial offices of the Lithuanian Communist daily *Vilnis* on North Halsted Street. At that meeting it was decided to mobilize all the forces of the Party to resist Foster's efforts. Moreover, knowing that the issue would not be decided in the United States, we immediately sent cables to Moscow, informing our representatives, Bob Minor and John Pepper, of the situation and advising that cables be obtained from the Executive of the Comintern restraining Foster from using the present Party situation to stage a coup.

Lovestone had his own plan for capitalizing on Ruthenberg's death. In conference with Anna David, Ruthenberg's intimate companion in the Party at the time of his death, Lovestone arranged for a report on the dying words of Ruthenberg to the Party and to the group. To the Party it was, as given by Anna David, "Tell the comrades to close the ranks and build the Party. The American workers under the leadership of our Party and the Comintern will win. Let's fight on." To the group at the caucus meetings held later on it was reported by the copiously weeping Anna David that it was Comrade Ruthenberg's wish that Comrade Lovestone should take his place as the Secretary of the Party.

The memorial meeting in Ashland Auditorium and the funeral which followed took place on the sixth of March. Ashland Auditorium was jammed with the thousands who came to pay homage to Ruthenberg. The hall was draped in black and red bunting and with the red and gold banners of Communist and sympathizing organizations. The small East Room where Ruthenberg's body lay was a mass of flowers, red banners and red ribbons. The large platform of Ashland Auditorium was adorned with flowers. Seated on the platform were the comrades selected by the Political Committee to act as the Guard of Honor during the memorial services. They included all the important leaders of the Party in the districts and unions from all parts of the country.

The pallbearers selected by the Political Committee consisted of Lovestone, Bittleman, Cannon, Foster, Bedacht, and myself, actually the Political Committee of the Party as constituted, with the exception of Ruthenberg. Sam Darcy and Kaplan were chosen as pallbearers for the Young Workers League. The pallbearers gathered in the East Room. When it was time to begin the services, we carried the coffin into the hall. The emotion aroused in the audience was very intense. Women shrieked and fainted. Sobbing was audible in all parts of the auditorium. There was no doubt in my mind then how the audience felt—that the Party's great leader, America's Lenin, was dead. Ruthenberg's wife and son did not attend the meeting or go to the funeral. He had been estranged from his wife and son from the early days of the Communist movement in 1919. She had come, as did his son, to take one last look. The wife sobbed, standing hopelessly by and looked at the man she had loved. "Oh, how he needed my care! If I had been with him, it would never have happened." But the son, a young man going to college, seemed unmoved and displayed an obviously unsympathetic attitude towards the ambitions and work of his father.

The funeral was held right after the meeting. The day was cold and windy. A light drizzle fell steadily. I rode in the automobile with Anna David and Jay Lovestone. Anna David mourned the passing of Ruthenberg with genuine emotion. She cried all the way to the cemetery, interminably repeating in a lugubrious chant that the day was a fitting one and in harmony with the sad occasion. At the cemetery there were no speeches, no services. The body was cremated. After the cremation was over Shachno Epstein came over to me as I was standing talking to Lovestone and Bedacht. He carefully unrolled his handkerchief, as if it contained something precious, and disclosed a few white bones. "These are the remains of some of Comrade Ruthenberg's bones." Lovestone winced and turned away. Revolted by his joy in the macabre relics he held, I could only look at the man.

The funeral over, a few of us gathered to discuss the future. Ruthenberg was gone. His ashes were already enclosed in a small urn, which would be taken to Moscow, to be buried in the Kremlin Wall in accordance with his alleged "request," of which I heard for the first time only after the funeral. Lovestone was present, as was Bedacht. We knew that we faced a severe test in holding on to the Party. We knew that without support from Moscow it would be a hopeless task to attempt to hold power in the Party. We knew very well that Weinstone and Cannon had been negotiating with Foster from the moment Ruthenberg's death was announced. We also knew that Weinstone would be followed by other members of the Ruthenberg group into the new setup. We decided that our chances depended on action from Moscow and the fact that at critical moments Weinstone always vacillated and hesitated to act. We mapped out our strategy accordingly: to keep bombarding Moscow with cables; to complicate Weinstone's negotiations with Foster and Cannon by negotiating with him ourselves; and by priming the Ruthenberg caucus for the intense factional war which would immediately break out in the Party.

I went back to my hotel that night, tired and dejected. Ruthenberg was now just a vision. I recalled all the years we had spent in the movement and in prison together. I could not help feeling that life had toyed with Ruthenberg, and had cut him off at the height of his power and prestige in the Party.

I had every personal reason for detesting Ruthenberg because of his shabby action against me in the past. When we were in Sing Sing, he and Ferguson won their case on appeal by charging me with sole responsibility for the publication of *The Revolutionary Age* and the articles it contained, alleging that I, as its business manager, had taken the copy to the printer. The fact was that I did not even once take the copy to the printer and that Ruthenberg, who was a member of the National Council, and Ferguson, who was its Secretary, shared equal responsibility with me. At the time I wrote from prison that "I am glad that my shoulders are broad enough to sustain both Ferguson and Ruthenberg." But in the stress of Party work and in what I considered to be in the best interests of the movement, I put aside my personal feelings. Since the emergence of the Communist Party from underground, I had been a close collaborator and friend of Ruthenberg's. Now death had removed him from the American Communist scene, in which he had considered himself indispensable. I admit that I was sad about his passing.

On Monday we left for New York with the urn that contained Ruthenberg's ashes. The New York district had been unable to get Madison Square Garden. Memorial meetings were scheduled to be held on Wednesday night in Carnegie Hall and at the Central Opera House. We arrived in New York Tuesday evening and were met at Grand Central station by a guard of honor consisting of the district Party leaders. Lovestone and

I carried the urn as the procession marched to the district headquarters. Later the urn was placed on a pedestal at the Manhattan Lyceum on East Fourth Street, where it was attended by a guard of honor until the memorial meetings took place. Both halls were crowded to overflowing. After the meeting the Political Committee decided that J. Louis Engdahl should be the special representative of the Party to take the ashes to Moscow. He left shortly afterwards without any ceremony whatsoever. The Ruthenberg era in the Party was closed forever.

A new factional war now flared up. On the twenty-first of March, 1927, Weinstone came to Chicago. Jay Lovestone, Bedacht and I had a conference with him. We offered him the Executive Secretaryship, the highest position in the Party, provided he would agree to the immediate holding of a national convention, and that, if we should have a majority of the delegates at the convention, we should take a decisive majority on the new Central Executive Committee and the Political Committee. But he was afraid once we had the majority that we would go back on our promises to him. He said we could throw the secretaryship out of the window as far as he was concerned. After that conference we agreed to give Weinstone a jolt at the Political Committee meeting the next day by deciding to hold an immediate convention without his consent. At that meeting Weinstone opposed our motion for a plenary session of the Central Executive Committee on May fourth, to be followed by a national convention. He was supported by Foster and Cannon. We then knew that Weinstone had made a deal with them. I wrote then, bearing in mind that we could not hold the convention without permission from the Communist International,

> If we do not get permission for a convention, in all probability the new alliance will, through the course of fate, double-dealing, and treachery, become the leadership.

At the April eighth meeting of the Political Committee Jack Johnstone protested that his files had been rifled. Our group had of course arranged for the rifling of his files, because they contained some factional correspondence on the Foster caucus connections which we desired to obtain. We nevertheless solemnly ordered an investigation and promised to punish the guilty party if he was found. On the same day we also received a long distance call from New York. We had already informed New York that we had received information that the Comintern would support our group and our proposals for the holding of an immediate convention. The call from New York came from Jack Stachel, who informed us that "Wobbly Weinstone" had finally made up his mind that he would support the Ruthenberg group, that he wanted our group to have a definite majority on the Political Committee and on the Central Executive Committee, that he favored Lovestone for Secretary and that he would not send his appeal against our actions to the Communist International.

Important developments then came quickly, proving that our strategy with the Communist International was correct. At the meeting of the Political Committee on April twenty-fifth the following cable received from the Communist International was reported:

> We hold the coming of Jack [Jay Lovestone] comma Ben [Gitlow] and Bill [Foster] to be necessary stop the coming of Jim [Cannon] and Weinstone would also be desirable but in case the polbureau [our Political Committee] holds this to be inexpedient comma then we ask that written reports on part of these comrades be sent stop regarding Ben we would excuse him from session of executive [Executive Committee of the Comintern] only in case all members of polbureau including Ben himself are against his coming stop we say latter because we do not sufficiently know present needletrades situation stop no other comrades shall come stop this telegram is to be shown to all five comrades mentioned stop signed ECCI (Executive Committee Communist International) Kuusinen.

At this meeting Weinstone had again wobbled into an opposition position and had made a united front with Cannon. Foster fought against my going. He said all our work in the needle trades unions in New York would collapse if I went. But I had also received a confidential cable from Nicholas Bukharin, the Chairman of the Communist International, ordering me to come to Moscow, stating that under no circumstances should I fail to do so.

On the twenty-seventh of April we had another cable from Moscow. It indicated that the Communist International was paying very close attention to our Party. This cable read:

> We are of the opinion that the Plenum of the Central Committee must be held immediately and before departure of delegation Stop however the decisions of the central plenum are not to be considered as final without ratification by the ECCI [Executive Committee of Communist International] and shall not be published before such ratification. . . ECCI Kuusinen.

This cable was a distinct victory for our group. We knew that at the plenum to be held on May fourth we would be in a minority. Now the Communist International had decided that the plenum could not make any definite decisions, that all its decisions had to be ratified by the Executive Committee of the Communist International, before they could be enforced. This cable was notice to Foster that he could not seize the Party and reorganize it, even if he had a majority at the plenum. We knew that he would have a majority, because he had come to an understanding with two members of the Ruthenberg group on the Central Executive Committee, William W. Weinstone and John Ballam. Since previously we had a fifty-fifty Central Executive Committee, this meant that by political trading Foster had obtained a majority of the committee. Foster raved like a madman when this cable was read. His group sent a cable to Moscow immediately, appealing against the Central Executive Committee, in which they demanded the holding of a plenum with full authority, that Weinstone and Cannon be added to the delegation going to Moscow and that I be prevented from going. Their appeal was ignored by the Communist International. Instead, when the plenum took place, we received an additional cable from the Communist International stating that the plenum could make no organizational changes.

Before the plenum took place I had rushed to Canada and made arrangements to obtain a Canadian passport under a fictitious name with which to travel to Russia. I arrived in Chicago on May third, just in time to attend a meeting of the Political Committee. There was no mistaking the fact that the inner Party war was on in real earnest. After the Political Committee meeting our group on the Central Executive Committee went into a caucus that lasted all night long. Weinstone and Ballam were not present. We discussed the situation in detail and came to the conclusion that our group would gain nothing from the plenum, and the quicker it was over the better for us. Furthermore, it was decided that Lovestone and I should leave for Moscow without delay and should try to get there in the quickest possible time. When the plenum opened we had a real demonstration that our majority on the Central Executive Committee was a thing of the past. For the first time, instead of electing a chairman for each session of the plenum, as was the custom, a praesidium of three members, consisting of Lovestone, Foster and Weinstone, was elected. Weinstone acted as the Chairman. After the adjournment of the plenum for the day, Lovestone, Bedacht, Wolfe, Stachel and I had a caucus on the situation. After talking almost all night long, we decided that it would be best, in view of the fact that the plenum had no power to make decisions, to ignore its sessions and leave immediately for Moscow.

On the fifth of May, Jay Lovestone and I checked our bags at the Union Station. That same morning we conferred with a number of the other comrades, informed them of our decision not to participate at the plenum and leave immediately for Moscow. The plenum opened without us. It was reported to me later that on the afternoon of the day we left the plenum discussed the Chinese situation and that Bill Dunne took the floor in his stocking feet and with his shirt tails out of his pants—drunk, of course—presumably out of deference to Chinese customs. We had not missed much by missing that plenary session.

I arrived in New York three hours before the boat was scheduled to sail. Saying good-bye to my father, just as my wife and I were stepping into the taxi that was to take us to the Cunard docks, I saw that he was deeply worried and depressed. It was not opportune to ask him why. Perhaps my going recalled memories of his homeland. As an obscure young Russian revolutionist, he had fled from Tsarist Russia to the haven of democratic America, and had fought on for Socialism here; as an American revolutionary leader, I was going to Socialist Russia, the fountainhead now of world revolution. Yet I wondered then, and I still wonder, what was really in his mind, for it struck me that at the time he was going through a deep emotional experience. I am still sorry that we parted without a long and unconstrained talk. A few comrades met us on the dock. A little before midnight we boarded the Olympic. About an hour past midnight the boat departed. It was my first trip to Soviet Russia.

The next morning I wrote:

> We have received no word yet of our situation. We are a little bit worried because what we did was a very bold act. I doubt however that we made a mistake.

Later I found out that when the plenum discovered that Lovestone and I had run off without so much as a By-your-leave from that exalted conclave, Weinstone, Foster, Cannon and other members of the opposition became indignant, protested and threatened to prefer charges against us before the Communist International. But they did not continue the farce of the plenum much longer. That very night they adjourned. The leaders of the various factions packed their bags and prepared to leave forthwith for Moscow. After all, it was Moscow that had the final say. But, before leaving for Moscow, Cannon and Weinstone in alliance with Foster banded themselves together into the United Opposition Bloc. In doing so, they made a serious strategic mistake—one I am sure they did not intend to make—because at the time the most damaging single accusation against the Trotsky group in Russia was the charge by the Stalin group that the Trotskyites were plotting to split the Communist movement by trying to form a United International Opposition Bloc to the Russian Party leadership.

Lovestone and I arrived in Paris, intending to leave the same night for Moscow. But we had to stay over till the next day in order to obtain our Polish visas. When we arrived at the Polish Consulate the place was jammed with people, many of whom had been waiting for days in an effort to obtain visas.

We introduced ourselves as British subjects who wanted visas. We were immediately given application blanks. "How shall we fill them out?" I inquired of Lovestone. "Oh, just put down that you are a business man going on business to Russia and give as your status during the war some important military post." I put down that I had been an officer in the Commissary Department during the war, and Lovestone put down that he had been in another branch of His Majesty's Service. Having thus filled out our applications, we handed them to the clerk. He took them inside immediately. Then I observed what went on in the adjoining room, the door to which remained open. I saw the clerk open a file. He was evidently looking for our names on the official blacklist. He did not find them there. We were both using fictitious names. A few moments later we received our visas. The crowd in the Polish consulate regarded us with awe and respect. The next day we took a train straight through Berlin and Warsaw to the Soviet Border, to the land set free by the Bolsheviks under Lenin and Trotsky, with Lenin now in a mausoleum and Trotsky on his way out.

CHAPTER XII

STALIN CONFIRMS OUR LEADERSHIP

How strange that my first trip to the first workers' republic turned out to be on a mission of entrenching myself in political power! It was a far cry from the dreams of Socialism in my callow and idealistic youth. Curiously, although I was playing power politics, I had not lost my idealistic faith in Socialism; indeed, I was playing politics for the sake of that faith. I was merely being practical about my idealism, the ethics of my conduct resting on the doctrine that the end justifies the means, any means. I would have dismissed at the time as stupid prejudice any notion that the means might corrupt the end, no matter how noble the latter. As a matter of fact, that attitude was so deeply lodged in me, so instinctive, that it did not even occur to me then to question its merits. I was a Bolshevik, a revolutionist, guided by the supreme law of revolution—what is beneficial to the revolution, is right; whatever mitigates against it, is counter-revolutionary and must be exterminated. The logic of that position leads to appalling consequences—for one thing, because human intelligence is so very, very fallible in estimating just what is beneficial to the revolution. I was to discover that for myself, but not at once. I thought as I was approaching the borders of Soviet Russia that I was to discover there above all a new source of inspiration for my life's work. Now I see that, in spite of myself, it was the beginning of a new turn in my life. My first trip to Russia became the prelude to those misgivings and doubts, at first subconscious, which eventually were to culminate in my break with Communism.

Needless to say, I was unaware of all that at the time. I was concerned rather with my immediate mission, which I discussed with Lovestone, and with the cursory impressions of the trip itself. This was the first time I had crossed the ocean, my first trip anywhere abroad. I confess that I was discovering the new strange world outside the United States not without a measure of eagerness and even avidity. I noted details that the seasoned traveler might deem too trivial for his attention. I recall, for example, that when our train stopped in Poland for about an hour, the German porter in charge of our *wagon-lit*, fuming against the Poles, advised us that in his opinion it was a waste of time to visit Warsaw, saying: "Warsaw is a big ugly city full of dirty Poles. You will be wasting your time to see the Polish pigs." But we had no time to visit Warsaw. Besides, we were afraid to leave our bags alone or in the care of the porter. They were full of documents we had taken along for the hearing on our Party question. So we remained in our compartment, to make sure that our bags were safe.

As the train sped on, it seemed to me from what little I saw that Poland rested on police and military force. The police looked even better equipped and more terrifying than the military. It seemed to me that there was either a soldier or a policeman to every dozen civilians. The marks of the war had not yet been completely erased. Winding lines of trenches followed the railroad tracks, at regular intervals appeared large wooden crosses marking the common burial grounds of the thousands of soldiers who had fallen in battle. Many buildings which had been bombarded were grim reminders of the time when the armed battalions hurled themselves at one another. As we approached Stolpce, the last railroad station on the Polish-Russian border, night was approaching. I was nervous and excited, moved by deep emotions. Soon I would be in the land where the red flag waved as an inspiration to the oppressed of the entire world.

When the train stopped in Stolpce I was a little worried, because I did not want to lose the documents we carried when the Polish customs examined our baggage. As soon as the train stopped Englishmen entered the train and carefully scrutinized everyone. I wondered what they were doing in this capacity in Poland. Next, Polish officials inspected our passports. Then we were allowed to get off the train with our baggage for customs inspection. The station in that God-forsaken border town of Stolpce must have just been built. It was an all-white stone structure very elaborate for so insignificant a town. I suspected it was done in order to mock Russia for its station on the other side of the border, which was a rather crude wooden affair, reminiscent of Western frontier days in our own country. The baggage inspection was actually carried on with an eye to finding things! As the clerk looked through my bags I saw that he carefully examined a number of books I had purposely placed on top. But he was looking at them upside down, indicating either that he did not know how to read or did not care to read. I gave him a knowing look, put my hand into my pocket, with the result that he did not look through the remaining bags and put the customs labels on all of them. For his kindness I gave him a tip of half a dollar, for which he fell all over himself in thanking me.

When the train started for the Russian border, all the blinds were pulled down. But I looked through and could see that the Poles had stretched barbed wire across the border, an expression of the hostility which existed between the two countries. The German porter was very glad to get out of Poland. He became happy and jubilant and had only praise for the Russians. All on the train seemed to me to be relieved, smiling and happy to be in Russia. I peeked through the curtain to catch the first glimpse of Russian soil. Before we reached Negoreloye, the Russian authorities entered. The first to appear was a Red Army soldier, a young sad-looking Slav, dressed in a long army cloak that brushed the floor as he walked. He was followed by the chief of police, a young man dressed in civilian clothes, soft collar and tie. He displayed no signs of officiousness. When he politely thanked the German porter for the papers he turned over, it seemed to me that I recognized the new spirit of Soviet Russia. When he passed through the car we showed him our credentials, and from that moment on we had no difficulty. Our baggage was immediately O.K.'d without inspection. We were surrounded by the ticket agent and other officials. The ticket agent was a young man who had been in the United States before the Revolution and spoke English fluently. In the United States he had been a member of the I. W. W. I was very happy and felt perfectly at home, as if I had come to my homeland from which I had been absent a very long time.

The Russian station was full of people, as Russian stations always seem to be. There was plenty of commotion and lots of shouting, expressive of the genuine heartiness and expansiveness of the great Russian people. But at the time I was sure it was more than that: it was the very warmth of the Russian revolution, the enthusiasm of those living in a country where the most far-reaching changes in society were taking place. When I approached the Russian border I eagerly watched for the first glimpse of the Red flag. Failing to catch sight of it, I was disappointed. But my disappointment was only for the moment. I was greatly moved by my first contact with the country. I swelled with emotion. Before me flashed the whole panorama of its history, its glorious struggle for liberty, as told to me during my childhood days. Here was a country for which I was patriotic. Here was the country where the dreams of the future were being enacted in the realities of today.

We arrived in Moscow on May twenty-first, 1927. Three American comrades met us at the station: Robert Minor, the representative of the American Party to the Comintern; Bill Kruse, a student at the Lenin Institute and unofficial representative of the Ruthenberg group in Moscow; and George Askenuzi, a former member of the Russian Federation of our Party who had transferred to the Russian Communist Party and was at the time working in the Coöperative Department of the Comintern. We boarded the Comintern automobile and went straight to the Lux, the hotel of the Comintern people resident in Moscow, situated on the Tverskaya. We were bombarded with questions about the American Party situation and were informed that the Tenth Plenum of the E. C. C. I. (Executive Committee of the Communist International) would open in the evening. We considered ourselves lucky that we came in time to be present. We deposited our baggage at the Bristol Hotel opposite the Lux, in which rooms had been assigned to us. We went straight to Pepper's room at the Lux, where dinner was already prepared for us by Pepper's wife. Pepper had two rooms in the Lux which he shared with his wife and two daughters, about eight and ten years of age respectively. His wife worked in the Censorship Department of the Soviet Foreign Office. She was a short woman, a typical Hungarian, who worshiped her husband and was ready for any kind of sacrifice on his behalf. She considered Pepper one of the most brilliant men in the movement. His daughters were young, vivacious, and full of the devil. They spoke Russian fluently. But they steered clear of Pepper, who dominated his household. Pepper's room was piled with books on China. He seemed to have every available book on the Chinese situation. He was of the opinion that the Chinese developments would be of the greatest importance to Russia and to the future of the Comintern. When we asked him about the plenum sessions, he informed us that the most important issue would be the fight against Trotsky and his complete elimination from the affairs of the Comintern, that the second question would be on the war danger facing the Soviet Union, and the third question would deal with the Chinese situation. But we had little time to discuss details. After our dinner, which was excellently cooked, Pepper phoned the Comintern for an automobile, and in a few minutes the five of us, including Minor and Kruse, packed into an ancient Italian Fiat that went recklessly tearing through the crowded streets on its way to the Comintern.

The Comintern headquarters—which were opposite the Manège, an old riding academy infamous in Tsarist days for housing Cossacks to use against the student demonstrations at the university nearby and now used as a government garage, with the Kremlin in the background to the left—was a typical old unassuming ramshackle Russian building. Here was planned the strategy for the Communist parties of the world. The plenary sessions of the Executive Committee of the Communist International took place in what was called the Red Hall on the first floor. The room was long, narrow, oblong, capable of accommodating a maximum of about 300 to 400 persons. A very expensive oriental rug covered the floor. In the front of the hall, where the windows faced the riding academy, was a raised platform for the Praesidium and the Secretary. To the left of the platform was the raised speaker's lectern. In the center of the platform was the Chairman's table; on the side, the Secretary's desk; and between the two windows, a large portrait of Lenin. The delegates were disposed in the hall proper at long narrow tables with chairs facing the platform.

The first session was a formal affair with opening speeches and routine announcements concerning the composition of the various committees and rules of procedure. Trotsky was not present at the opening. Neither was Stalin. The next day I saw Trotsky for the first time. He arrived with Andres Nin, a member of the Executive Committee of the Profintern and an outstanding leader of the Spanish trade union and Communist movement. Trotsky took a seat directly behind me. Delegate after delegate rose, and in every question discussed made sure to lodge an attack upon Trotsky. The latter muttered to himself, hurled some invectives or sharp questions at the speakers, and then left the hall. That day after the sessions were over Lovestone, Pepper, Minor and I discussed the plenum. Our opposition, Foster, Cannon and Weinstone, had not yet arrived. If we could only propose something on the Trotsky question, we would put ourselves in a good position with the Russians, who, Pepper informed us, were very much worried over the Trotsky issue. They wanted his complete elimination from the Comintern, of whose executive he was still a member, but were not yet certain how to bring it about.

That day a so-called *Senioren Konvent* was formed. This was a gathering of the oldest and most trusted members of the Comintern. It was somewhat of a steering committee of the plenum. But it was much more than that. It was actually the real plenum which drafted and approved the decisions finally adopted. Besides, to it were entrusted the confidential matters which it was advisable not to raise at the sessions of the plenum. We decided to raise at the *Senioren Konvent* the question of Trotsky's removal from the Comintern and to present a resolution in the name of the American, German and other important parties, calling for Trotsky's removal from the Comintern. When the matter was brought up at the meeting of the body the next day, the Russians expressed approval of the idea, and a sub-committee was appointed to work out the resolution. Trotsky knew nothing about this maneuver, although I am sure he must have suspected that he was slated for some such action. This move against Trotsky on our part was done purely for selfish reasons. We believed that in so doing we would indicate to the Russians that we were with them against Trotsky and in return could get a more favorable settlement of our own issues, which were in their hands. That was all that mattered to us.

The Trotsky issue laid bare the whole system of the Comintern. Delegate after delegate took the platform, representing parties from the four corners of the earth, accepted the official anti-Trotsky position as a matter of course and then proceeded to attack Trotsky as being responsible for every failure of the Communist International. They went even further. They attacked him as a disrupter who would betray the very purposes of international Communism. From the attitude of the speakers one could see that they really did not mean what they were saying. But the more they did not mean it, the more denunciatory they became. When Thaelmann, the leader of the German Communist Party, took the floor, he barked like a dog, and it seemed as if the whole edifice would collapse under his verbal and explosive bombardment. When I finally got the floor to speak for five minutes during the general discussion, Trotsky was present. I felt a little uncomfortable, because it was the first time I had spoken to a gathering with representatives from all over the world. In drafting my short speech, I had to include mention of Trotsky and a denunciation of his position, even though it had no place in the speech. I did not like to do it, but in discussing what kind of a speech to deliver we had agreed that in every one of our speeches we must devote a little of the time allotted to us to attack Trotsky very sharply. Trotsky taunted me for what I had to say, but I cannot recall what he said, although his remarks were in English.

When Trotsky spoke in his defense, the hall was jammed. The representatives of the various parties, in spite of their expressed hostility, showed an evident delight in hearing the brilliant Trotsky fling his wit and sarcasm at his opponents. He answered interruptions with lightning rapidity and with shafts of wit and humor that demolished his interrupters. The Russians squirmed as he spoke. Bukharin's face turned red. However, when Bukharin took the rostrum to answer Trotsky, Trotsky left the hall, evidently unwilling to face the attack that was to follow his speech.

Stalin also from time to time attended the sessions of the plenum. He generally arrived in an unassuming manner, dressed in a simple Russian military uniform and black boots. As soon as he made his appearance he was surrounded by a coterie of delegates who seemed to relish close proximity to the ruler of a great country and to have the opportunity of a snatch of conversation with him. He carried his arm in a sling, because, according to the information given me, he was suffering at the time from a severe attack of hardening of the arteries. He put on no airs, smiled occasionally, and gave one the impression at first of a very ordinary congenial individual. But when you looked at him closely you caught a faint glimpse of his cynical expression and his cold piercing gray eyes. When he spoke, he spoke slowly and little above a whisper. His listeners had to draw close to him and cup their ears in order to hear him. When he finished one thought, he allowed it time to sink in before beginning his next. I looked at him intently as he toyed with the fate of Trotsky, for before me was standing the most powerful Communist leader since the death of Lenin.

I soon had an opportunity to view him more closely, for he had granted us an interview. Our delegation included, besides myself, Lovestone, Pepper, Kruse, Minor, Askenuzi and Engdahl. Our interview took place at his office in the large building of the Central Executive Committee of the All Russian Communist Party, one of the buildings then recently erected in Moscow of which the Bolsheviks were very proud. The room we met in was a spacious one with huge windows. On the side stood a long oak table surrounded by massive, hand-carved oak chairs. The table was covered with a green felt cloth. The wall displayed large paintings of the old revolutionary leaders of Russia. Prominently resting on a chair was a large oil painting of Lenin in one of his speaking positions. On a pedestal in a corner, enclosed in a glass case, was an excellent sculpture of the head of Lenin. Stalin greeted us very cordially, shook our hands, and asked us to be seated on one side of the table. He took a seat on the other side. He did not know a word of English, or of any other Western language, and we knew no Russian, so that the entire conversation between us had to be carried on through interpreters.

In the course of this long interview Stalin indicated that he was very much interested in American affairs. He especially showered questions upon me. He wanted to know how many wage-earners there were in the country, how many workers in industry. He inquired about the incomes of the workers, what social benefits they enjoyed. He asked many questions concerning social legislation in the United States and expressed surprise at the backwardness of the country in this respect. When Pepper tried to supplement one of the questions which he put to me, Stalin curtly and with a great show of anger interrupted him and told him to remain silent. Pepper winced and turned as red as a beet. After I had answered all the questions that he had put to me, he turned to his secretary and asked for something. The secretary rushed out of the room and immediately returned with a folder, which he handed to Stalin. When Stalin glanced at the folder he actually jumped from his seat in anger and cursed at the top of his voice at his secretary, calling him *durak* —literally, "fool"—in Russian one of the worst of insults. The secretary was shaking with fright as he took the folder and returned running with the one Stalin really wanted. The scene did not speak well for a leader of Stalin's rank, especially before Communists of other countries.

Stalin opened the folder, resumed his talk. He informed us of the advantages the workers in the textile industry of the Soviet Union enjoyed in social benefits as contrasted with conditions which we described as prevailing in the United States. Then he gave us some advice. Stalin insisted that the most important problem for the Communist Party in the United States was the fight for social insurance and for the betterment of the workers' conditions. He told us that the proletarian revolution in the United States could wait, that it was a long way off, that we ought to build up a good and powerful press, enter the trade unions and gain influence in them, develop our party methodically, especially attempting to draw into it leaders in organizations which exerted influence over the masses.

Our interview with Stalin lasted over three hours. He bade us good-by in the most cordial manner and seemed to imply that he was pleased with the interview. We felt that in granting us this interview Stalin had given an indication that he favored our leadership of the American Party. In this respect we believed that we had made a scoop on our opposition, who were not invited and did not participate in the interview.

The days I spent in Moscow were very stormy ones. A few months before, the British government had raided the Arcos, the Russian Trade Delegation's offices in London, and had obtained some very valuable papers concerning the relations of the Soviet government to the British Communist Party. In fact, it was no secret in Moscow that, among the papers seized, was a complete list of Comintern connections, codes, and confidential material, not only pertaining to England, but to other countries as well, and particularly to the United States. The raid on Arcos was followed by a rupture of trade and diplomatic relations between Great Britain and the Soviet Union. The Chinese revolution was getting tremendous support from Russia in men, advice, money, and munitions, and the campaign in China was being directed against all foreign imperialist powers, but especially Great Britain. Furthermore, the relations with Poland were near the breaking point. The Soviet rulers looked upon the entente between France and Great Britain as a move directed against Russia, and believed that through this alliance England had gained a strategic advantage over the Soviet government, because it was now possible for Great Britain to unite the small countries surrounding Russia for an attack upon her.

During my first days in Moscow news was received that Voikov, the Russian Ambassador to Poland, had been assassinated when he went to meet Rosenholtz, the returning Soviet Ambassador to Great Britain, at a Warsaw railroad station. Voikov was shot four times in the abdomen, and collapsed as he pulled out his own revolver to answer the shots of his assailant. When the news reached Moscow, a mighty demonstration of the people poured out of the factories and offices into the streets. Red flags draped in black made their appearance everywhere. *Izvestiya* carried a cartoon which showed an assassin's hand shooting a revolver; and beside it the arm that pointed where to shoot emerged from a cuff on the cuff-link of which the Union Jack was engraved. The demonstration was directed against England. Men, women and children, carrying all kinds of banners, shouting, singing, dancing, kept marching through Red Square from half past three in the afternoon until ten o'clock in the evening. I was impressed with the might and spirit of the Russian people, the strength of their numbers. It seemed as if no power on earth could conquer them and there was no obstacle which they could not overcome. The Russian people were the backbone of the Communist movement, the Russian Revolution the inspiration of mankind. Both were the strength that assured Communism of its ultimate triumph over the world. I joined in the demonstration and was proud of being a Communist and sharing with the Russian people their indignation over the treachery of Great Britain.

On the tenth of June Voikov's funeral took place. It was a very impressive affair. The funeral cortège from the station to the Red Square was led by six Red Cavalrymen who rode on jet black horses. Then followed a long column of Red Army soldiers who carried the wreaths and flowers sent from organizations all over Russia. Behind the soldiers marched a large Red Army band playing the funeral march. Then came the casket, carried on a gun carriage and drawn by black horses. Behind the casket followed a square mass of men and women, the leaders of the Russian Revolution and of the Soviet government. They were all there—Stalin, Bukharin, Rykov, Lenin's widow, Krupskaya, members of the powerful Political Bureau of the Russian Communist Party, Red Army commanders, ambassadors, every person of importance in Russia was in that column. No wonder the G. P. U. took great precautionary measures. For a block away on each side of the line of the procession the streets were closed and no one was allowed to pass. Along the line of the procession all stores were closed, the windows in all the houses along the way had their blinds drawn and their shutters closed. G. P. U. men with drawn revolvers scampered over the roofs of the houses and cleared them of all persons. Wherever a window was left open or a person was seen standing at the window to watch the procession, G. P. U. men rushed up to the house and ordered the window shut and the person to depart. Not a soul without a pass from the government, the Russian Party, or the Communist International was permitted on the street where the procession passed.

The Red Square was lined with soldiers standing at attention. The grandstands were filled with people, only the people who had the proper passes. After the funeral cortège entered, workers' delegations carrying banners began to pour into the tremendous square and through it. Banners in all kinds of languages appeared. This was no mere funeral. It was a political demonstration. It was the first workers' republic, backed by the Workers of the World, organized for revolution everywhere, defying the hegemony of the chief imperialist powers of the world, the British Empire and France, with all their satellites. Amid the bizarre splendor of the Kremlin, on a platform in front of the Lenin Mausoleum, the coffin was rested. When the band played the funeral march, all heads were uncovered. Then all was quiet, except for the swallows flying overhead in the gray sky.

The speakers mounted the Lenin Mausoleum. They spoke, the amplifiers broadcasting their voices across the square, so that everyone in that huge crowd heard them distinctly. The buildings reëchoed their words with metallic resonance, words spoken in defiance of Great Britain and the capitalist world. Premier Rykov spoke for the Soviet Union; Bukharin, for the Russian Communist Party; Engdahl, for the Communist International; Melnichansky, head of the Russian Textile Unions, for the Russian Trade Unions; and Litvinov, for the Soviet Foreign Office.

At the conclusion of the speeches the funeral march was played again and the coffin taken to its final burial. Behind the coffin walked Voikov's frail little mother, who seemed about four feet eight inches tall, dressed in black. Her face was buried in the palms of her hands as she walked behind the coffin and cried. Slowly the procession moved. All the tragedy of life was in the little mother who walked hesitatingly with stooped shoulders behind the coffin which contained her son. Further back walked his wife, head erect, restraining her tears, biting her lips. The band kept playing the funeral march all the time. The grave, which was beside the Kremlin wall, reached, the coffin was lowered. The cannons in the Kremlin roared their salute. The whole square reverberated with their echoes. The square quickly emptied. The funeral was over. As I left, I thought: the living keep ever moving on, fighting and struggling towards new accomplishments and greater victories; the Russian Revolution is only the beginning.

Under these conditions the discussion on the war danger took on real significance. We were not only left to digest these incidents, but we were informed that the G. P. U. had unearthed spies in places very close to the government, in important government offices and in some of the institutions of the Russian Party and of the Communist International. At the plenum every effort was made to impress the representatives from other countries that the outbreak of war against the Soviet government was to be expected immediately. Lovestone and I visited Gussev, who under the name of P. Green had been the representative of the Comintern to the American Party in 1925-1926. Since he was a military expert, we spoke during our conversation about the coming war against the Soviet Union. He declared that the Soviet military authorities had reached the conclusion that, in spite of all the advances in military machines, the infantry still was the decisive factor. "We not only have the preponderance of infantrymen, but in addition to infantry such a vast territory that the invaders will need millions of soldiers to hold the territory they once conquer," he said. "We have worked out our strategy. We are even prepared to give up Moscow if necessary and retreat far into the interior, even into Siberia. The further inland we go the more difficult it will be for the invaders, for we will never submit and will continue to fight and harass them as long as they occupy our territory. The costs for them will be tremendous. Besides, the rigors of our climate will take a heavy toll."

The discussion with him brought the notion of war much closer home. In addition to the war, we discussed Trotsky. Gussev informed us that at the last meeting of the Central Committee of the Russian Party, Trotsky had accused Stalin of Thermidor. "That," said Gussev, "is an either-or proposition. If one is guilty of Thermidor, he is a counter-revolutionist, and any action, even an armed uprising against the one guilty of Thermidor, is justifiable. This charge is flung at Stalin to give Trotsky an excuse for his counter-revolutionary activities against the Bolshevik party, Stalin, and the Soviet Union. We will have to arrest Trotsky and send him out of Moscow."

This was the first time I heard it even hinted that the arrest of Trotsky and his expulsion from Moscow was contemplated. Gussev also informed us that the Trotsky faction was being broken up, that Zinoviev and Kamenev had broken with Trotsky and were ready to confess to the errors of their ways and to the counter-revolutionary tendencies of Trotskyism.

At the plenum the discussion of the war danger did not only hinge on how we were to organize the force in opposition to the war and in defense of the Soviet Union. First, the Communists of the world were ordered to adopt the slogan that the workers of the world have only one fatherland, which is the Soviet Union. Second, that in view of the fact that in a war against the Soviet Union the workers' fatherland is to be attacked, the Communists must work for the victory of the military forces of the Soviet Union. The Communists in the capitalist countries that attack the Soviet Union must work for the victory of the Soviet Union and the defeat of their own country. But they must not do this as pacifists. They must enlist and, if drafted, not resist service, because in the army the Communists can best work to undermine the military power of the enemies of the Soviet and can use their contact with the soldiers, if the possibility presents itself, to foment civil war. Third, in those countries which would enter into a military alliance with the Soviet Union the Communists must support the alliance until a victory is won by the Soviet Union, and only afterwards are they to organize for the capture of power by civil war and revolution. This fundamental structure of Communist policy towards a war involving the Soviet Union has been adhered to up to the present time, and will not be relinquished as long as the Soviet Union continues to be the supporter and dominating influence over the affairs of the world's Communist parties.

During the course of the plenum we entertained the German delegation, in order to establish a better understanding with the Germans who represented the party next in importance to the Russian Party. The affair was held in Minor's room in the Lux Hotel. The German delegation to the plenum with its secretaries came down in full force, for we always had plenty of cognac, vodka, wine and champagne on hand. A tray was loaded with sandwiches of all kinds and another tray with cakes and cookies. Music was supplied by a small portable phonograph which Kruse had brought with him from America. Everybody drank and danced and had a good time. In between we discussed politics and acquainted the Germans with our particular affairs.

An interesting figure at this little junket was Heinz Neuman. He had been ordered by Bukharin to stop drinking. He did not touch a drop but was able nevertheless to hypnotize himself into a hilarious drunken condition. He climbed up the corners of the walls, tried to hang from the chandelier and acted like a man completely out of his senses. Heinz Neuman was of slight stature. He was an exile from Germany who came to the Communist movement from the Zionists. He was an intellectual of the romantic type, with fine features and a pleasant smile. One could not help but like him. He spoke Russian and French fluently and was a very excellent talker and debater, full of fiery repartee and wit. Bukharin liked him very much. He did for Bukharin and the other Russian leaders whatever they asked him to. In the fight against Trotsky he was one of their main non-Russian supporters.

The Germans drank liberally, and when they became drunk, they acted vulgarly and boisterously. The Americans, strange to say, drank with moderation. Had the Foster-Cannon crowd been there instead of us, it would have outdone even the Germans. Members of other delegations kept drifting into the room from time to time. It was four o'clock in the morning before we broke up. Such affairs took place very often in the Lux. The Germans reciprocated very soon by playing host to us. Their affair had the atmosphere of a party in a German *Bier Halle* deep in some subcellar in Berlin. The place was dimly lighted, the small room thick with smoke. When I arrived, all the Germans, men and women, were already drunk. I got the impression from that party that there was something fundamentally wrong with the German delegates. They seemed to me to be very morose. I failed to find among them the morale indicative of a political force that could be depended upon to regenerate the social and economic life of Germany. I often asked myself the question: *Is it possible that a political organization as large and as influential as the German Party is, cannot bring forward a better leadership, a leadership that can measure up to the problems which confront the German movement?*

The Chinese question played a very important role at this plenum. It was tied up with the Trotsky question, because Trotsky had made the policy of Stalin in China the object of his criticism. Trotsky maintained that Stalin was betraying the interests of the workers and peasants in China. In April the Communist Party of Russia declared that the Chinese Revolution was a national bourgeois-democratic revolution whose main driving forces were the proletariat and the peasantry, and that the revolution showed during its development the tendency to become a Socialist revolution. The Soviet Union supported Chiang Kai Shek and his party of the democratic bourgeoisie of China, the Kuomintang.

Trotsky maintained that the Communist Party of China should pursue an independent course and should not put itself completely at the mercy of the Kuomintang. Stalin and the leadership of the Russian Party considered this policy of Trotsky tantamount to demanding that the Communist Party of China leave the Kuomintang. Such a policy was declared to be equivalent to the isolation of the Communist Party of China and the proletariat it represented from the national movement for China's emancipation.

But at the Plenum in May the turn of events in China had

become very discomforting to the Stalinists. Chiang Kai Shek, the important Chinese generals and the Kuomintang, had become openly hostile to the Communists of China. The Communists were not only driven out of the army and important posts, but thousands were seized and executed. The anti-Communist turn of Chiang Kai Shek and the Kuomintang was branded as a betrayal of the Chinese revolution necessitating a sharp change in Chinese policy. However, Stalin did not blame his own policies for the tragic events in China. Instead, the Comintern lashed out in a severe condemnation of the leadership of the Chinese Communist Party, which had faithfully carried out the Comintern's instructions. The Chinese Communists were made the scapegoat for the mistakes of Stalin, mistakes which cost them persecution, imprisonment and death. In fighting the leadership of the Chinese Communist Party, a plan carried out against other parties as well, the Young Communists of China were praised as the true revolutionary fighters in China and entrusted with the task of carrying out the new policies proposed by the Communist International. They were called upon to fight against the opportunist deviations of the Chinese Communist Party leaders, "who have pursued a policy of damming back the masses from revolutionary struggles." The Communist International called for the ousting of the leaders and their replacement by young Party members who had matured during the time of the civil war.

The Chinese developments caused a complete shift in Chinese policies. Such shifts are the usual thing in Communist politics. Communist policies swing like a pendulum from one extreme to the other. From the extreme right the policy shifted to the extreme left. Stalin not only followed Trotsky's advice belatedly, but, as usual, went far beyond what Trotsky had proposed. After the plenum a large group of selected Communists were sent into China to revive the revolutionary movement. Now that the situation was hopelessly worse than ever, they tried to precipitate a social revolution and to establish a Soviet government. There were many who voiced opposition to the move, declaring that in a country as backward as China was, with the overwhelming majority of the population engaged in agriculture, with the factory workers constituting an insignificant minority, it was folly to imagine that the establishment of a Soviet government in China was possible. But Stalin and the Comintern gave the order. The Canton uprising took place. The Chinese Communists, workers and peasants were slaughtered by the thousands and a brutal reaction against the Communists and the entire Chinese labor movement set in. This was precipitated by Stalin's panicky shift Left of the Left. The Canton uprising and Soviet, which was set up simultaneously with the uprising, were a monument to the reckless folly of Communist policy and the disregard for human life on the part of the Russian communist leaders whenever it suited their political expediency.

The discussion of the Chinese situation at the plenum showed that the majority of those present knew little of what was going on in China, for most of the delegates left the room and congregated in the hallways or sipped tea in the Comintern lunchroom in the basement. When the Chinese delegates spoke, they were lucky if a baker's dozen listened to them. At one of the sessions on the Chinese question, a delegate from Korea spoke. There was not one translator present who knew his particular dialect. As he kept on speaking in all sincerity to an audience that did not understand a word he was saying, his listeners began one by one to leave the hall. Finally one man remained, and that man was Bob Minor. Bob Minor was not seated. He was standing, his head stretched forward, his right hand cupped over his ear, listening intently to the jumble he did not and could not understand. Bob Minor stood that way for almost half an hour, until the comrade from Korea had finished. This was his brilliant sacrifice to the cause of the Chinese revolution. The three important figures of the Communist International apparatus in 1927 were Bukharin, the Chairman; Kuusinen, the Secretary; and Piatnitsky, the head of the Organization Department. Josef Piatnitsky was a short man of about fifty, with a slight tendency to stoutness. Sandy gray hair surrounded his bald pate like a halo. His prominent nose, gray mustache and piercing eyes were characteristic of the man. He spoke a poor German with great rapidity, and his anger flared up at the least provocation. His shirt or blouse was never pressed and seldom looked clean, while his suit, ill-fitting, baggy and creased, always appeared as if it needed a brushing badly. But he was a power in the Comintern. His department took care of the finances, the passports, secret service work, and kept a check on all the Communist parties of the Communist International—of course, with the exception of the Russian Party, which was a power unto itself and was the real boss of the International. Piatnitsky was a trusted member of the Russian Party. In the Comintern he was feared but liked. Behind his outbursts of anger one could detect a man who had gone through a great deal during his lifetime, not only persecutions during Tsarist days but the rigors of the revolutionary civil war as well. He was very modest in his habits and expected all Communists to live by his standards. He guarded the interests of the Communist International as his own child. However, if he took a dislike to you, especially if that dislike was based upon a belief on his part that you were squandering Comintern funds, he would never forget your alleged misdeeds and would throw them into your face at every opportunity. The desires of the Russian Party were laws to him which had to be explicitly carried out. His office, unlike other Russian offices, was kept immaculately clean, with a semblance of order that was remarkable. In Piatnitsky the Comintern had a good watchdog, one who could bark and also bite.

Kuusinen, the Secretary, was a Finnish Communist, a refugee from Finland upon whose head the government of his country had put a price. He was very slim, shoulders slightly drooped, and short. A typical Finn, he was fair of complexion, had thin lips and a pointed nose, above which two eyes squinted sharply at you. Reddish brown hair topped his skull. He stuttered and blustered when he spoke, his voice never loud. He was the human equivalent of a mouse. He never ceased working. After he left the Comintern building he continued working in his apartment in the Lux. He usually sat humped up at his desk with little stubs of pencils about an inch and a half to two inches long, sharpened to a very fine point. He would scribble minutely over the documents before him. Like his little pencils, he was a master of details and little things. He seemed a tragic figure. Never once did I see him smile. His Russian sounded as monotonous as his German. Never was he the father of an original idea. He always phonographed the official tune of the time. He lived on in the official family of the Comintern in spite of all the drastic changes which took place. The Russians needed a man as methodical and as hard working as Kuusinen, who effaced his own personality and ideas completely, only to serve his masters. They needed him also because they could point to him as a non-Russian who held down the important post of Secretary. Such details for foreign consumption were not overlooked by the Russians.

In Nicholas Bukharin, the Chairman, the Comintern had a man of great attainments and rare personality. Bukharin was very short of stature but very well built. Everybody liked him in the Comintern. He was known as the darling of the Russian Party. One could not help but like him. A kind, open face which broke out readily into a pleasant smile always greeted you. His light brown hair and reddish beard and eyes that sparkled with childish gaiety were those of a man of great intellect and deep philosophic convictions. Here was a Bolshevik who had not lost the human touch. At meetings he would sit lackadaisically, listening to what was being said, penciling with his delicate artistic hands pictures and caricatures, never for one moment losing track of what was going on, for he would often interrupt with a pointed remark or a humorous sally. In addition to being Chairman of the Communist International, he was a powerful figure in the Russian Party, being a member of its small and exclusive Political Bureau.

Bukharin was the real power in the Comintern, because he spoke, as the Chairman of the International, with all the authority of the Russian Party. Yet he was never officious. In spite of the tremendous amount of work which was put upon him, he always had time to see you, always had a pleasant greeting and was always indulgent with what you had to say. But his gentleness of manner was no sign of weakness. Bukharin was a stubborn fighter. When necessary he fought like a tiger. When genuinely angry, all his muscles would become taut and his face aflame with rage. He was very cosmopolitan, for he had been during his exile from Tsarist Russia in many countries, including the United States. He spoke German and French, but did not speak English, which he understood when spoken to only with great difficulty.

After the plenum our group had arranged a Ruthenberg memorial service at the place in the Kremlin Wall where his ashes were buried. A little procession was organized, consisting of a score of Red Army Cavalrymen, a band, and representatives of the Comintern, which was to proceed from the Comintern to the Red Square. Bukharin was one of the speakers. A few days later the ashes of one of the leaders of the Communist Party of Great Britain arrived. I was in Bukharin's office at the time the British delegation insisted that he speak at the services when the ashes were interned in the Kremlin Wall. Bukharin paced up and down the room. He did not want to speak. But he could not refuse the delegation. He stopped abruptly, looked out of the window and remarked (he did not know how prophetically!), "When I die I do not care what becomes of my *dreck*. They can throw it wherever they want to."

During my short stay in Moscow I had seen many things which I did not like. But I drew a balance sheet of the handicaps and difficulties facing the revolution, the great cost of the revolution in lives and the destruction of property, and came to the conclusion that the results were in favor of the revolution. In May of 1927 conditions in Soviet Russia were considered very good. In fact, when I was again in Russia in 1929, the Russians spoke of 1927 as the prosperous year. But one had to be blind not to see that there was a great deal yet to be done, for the mass of the people were still very poor. Housing conditions were abominable. I also noticed that there were class distinctions in Russia. Some people had plenty and others nothing at all. In the restaurant near the Moscow Soviets, when the Soviet bureaucrats and Party workers took breakfast, they had tea, eggs, bread and cheese. The tea was served with sugar. Earlier in the morning ordinary workers took their breakfast in the same restaurant. It consisted of a pot of hot water with a little tea, no sugar and a plain roll without butter, a breakfast that would have been rejected on a Bowery breadline. Beggars, tramps, and the homeless waifs were everywhere. Thievery was practiced on a grand scale. At night in the main street of Moscow, Tverskaya, there were many prostitutes who plied their trade. They were both young and old. I noticed extremely young girls, no more than eleven or twelve, among them. Fights and drunken brawls were not uncommon. When I asked how this came about, I was told that there was nothing to worry about because the prostitutes came from the former bourgeoisie and petty bourgeoisie, who would not and could not work. When I asked about the elderly women who stood for hours in the street selling newspapers, I was given the same answer.

The officials of the Government and the Party rode around in automobiles, always driving at a reckless speed, disregarding all regulations for traffic safety and the people in their way, who had to run and jump for dear life. In the amusement parks I could see that the ordinary run of workers were not present. Here many would strut around in good clothes, swinging canes like dandies and when meeting friends of the opposite sex, kiss their hands. All this was rather foreign to the equality of Communism I had expected.

What struck me most in Russia was the failure of the government to give serious attention to improving the living conditions of the workers. This, coupled with the fact that the class distinctions were being maintained on the railroads, with the first, second, and third class prevailing as in Europe, led me to question the Russians about it. The answer I got was always unsatisfactory—namely, that the Russian masses were culturally at too low a level to appreciate the better things of life. If they obtained them, they would not know how to utilize them. This excuse of the so-called better classes and the aristocracy I had heard before. It did not appeal to me. I often pointed out to them that in the United States people came from all parts of the world, including the most backward countries, and that they soon learned to appreciate and use precisely those modern improvements which lightened their burdens and made their lives more enjoyable. But my protests did not go beyond that—nor could they.

Our opposition was late in coming to Moscow. When they finally arrived, the plenum was coming to a close. Steps were immediately taken to constitute an American Commission, which was to consider our question. Braun, one of the leaders of the German Party, a chap liked immensely by Bukharin, was appointed its Chairman. After the plenum was ended the Commission went to work. First came what we termed the fireworks. The Commission held a public meeting in the Red Hall, at which all the Americans were given an opportunity to blow off steam. All of us made long speeches defending our point of view and attacking the position of our opponents. Then the Commission got down to work methodically in order to draft a resolution on the American question. At these meetings documents, letters, and minutes were produced by all sides. The work of the Commission was very painstaking and took weeks. We had two advantages over the opposition. Bukharin did not like Foster. He told me personally that he did not consider him a Communist and thought him very shallow in his views. Braun, the chairman of the Commission, was one of our best friends in Moscow. In Communist politics friendship counted just as much as it did in Tammany Hall. We would dine together, and, what was much more important, we very often drank together, Braun, like most of the Germans, liking his liquor.

The drawing up of the resolution was a give-and-take proposition. The Commission included sections from each one of the resolutions presented to it, three in all, one by Lovestone and me, one by Foster, and another by Cannon and Weinstone. In the drafting of the final resolution it was clear to me that we were being given an advantage over our opposition, for in the resolution our opposition were given what we termed "flowers," something they could present to the membership back home as favorable to them, while, at the same time, their leaders were very sharply criticized. On organizational questions, which was what really counted most, our group was given most of the favorable decisions.

After the Commission had drafted the resolution it was presented to the Executive Committee of the Communist International for further consideration. This procedure gave the Political Bureau of the Russian Party an opportunity to review the question and give its final O.K. Then the Executive reported the resolution at a meeting in the Red Hall, where the representatives of all the Communist Parties, as well as the delegates who came from the United States, had an opportunity to discuss it. The Executive adopted the resolution as a basis and referred it back for final formulation to a small sub-committee of the Executive. This committee went over the draft and then appointed another sub-committee to put the resolution in proper form. Again to our great satisfaction Braun was appointed to the task. Lovestone and I were jubilant, for that appointment gave us an opportunity of polishing up the resolution to suit ourselves. The final act was a meeting of the Praesidium of the Communist International, which adopted the resolution in its final and authoritative text. At this meeting of the Praesidium the selection of a representative from the Comintern to the United States was also decided upon. Lovestone and I had conferences with Bukharin on this matter and we agreed that a good selection would be Braun, also known as Ewert, who was Chairman of our Commission. He was selected, and the American question for all intents and purposes was settled. But not for Lovestone and me. Braun's appointment as representative of the Communist International gave him the power of the Comintern over the American Party. After he was appointed, Lovestone and I had him draw up an interpretation of the decision. This interpretation became supplementary to the decision and carried with it the full weight of Comintern authority.

The Resolution on the American question was a long document of nineteen pages which went into all phases of the problems confronting the Party in the United States. All this verbiage merely paved the way with flowers for the decision, which came at the close of the resolution, and set the Party national convention for the end of August, 1927. It provided that a commission for the preparation of the Party convention be constituted, consisting of three members of the Majority and three of the Opposition, with Comrades Foster and Lovestone functioning as deputy chairmen; that the election of delegates to the convention should be on the basis of proportional representation; that, at the convention, a broad Central Executive Committee should be elected, into which proletarian elements should be drawn; that ample representation to the Minority on the Central Executive Committee must be assured; that, until the Party convention, Comrades Lovestone and Foster should function as Secretaries of the Party and Comrades Foster and Gitlow as Secretaries of the Trade Union Department; that, at the convention, a motion should be passed that the newly elected Central Executive Committee must elect a Secretariat of three members, one of whom would be a representative of the minority, and that Comrades Foster and Lovestone must be on the Secretariat. The resolution ended with Point Five:

> The Praesidium thinks it advisable that the Party convention discuss and decide the question of the expediency of transferring the seat of the Central Committee.

This clause referred to the proposal to move the National Office of the Party from Chicago to New York. The matter was argued for over a year in the Central Executive Committee of the Party and the decisions of the Executive to move were appealed by the Opposition. Moving of the Party headquarters had been held up by the Comintern, which had, however, granted permission to move the *Daily Worker* to New York. Now the Comintern permitted the Convention of the Party to make a decision on moving. The decision on the American question and Clause Five shows how completely the Comintern bossed and controlled the affairs of the American Party.

The supplementary decision drawn up by Braun was adopted one week after the adoption of the main resolution. The gist of this decision was in its declaration as to where the Comintern stood with reference to the groups in the American Party. That was in the closing lines, which may seem rather turgid to the layman, but were clear enough to the initiates:

> The line of the Comintern has been: on the whole for the political support of the Ruthenberg group, and for bringing Foster

> nearer to the general political line of the Ruthenberg group, at the same time, however, following the course towards the correction of the trade union line of the Ruthenberg group on the line of Foster through closest cooperation in the Party leadership.

In other words, the Comintern was giving control of the American Party to us, at the same time holding the Fosterites in reserve—in case. . .

Before the American delegates left Moscow, they had to sign a pledge that they would abide by the resolution and carry out its instructions. In this agreement the details of the discussions and elections of delegates to the convention were decided upon as well as the election of a Central Executive Committee of thirty-five members, of whom the minority should have thirteen. The agreement, which was signed by Lovestone, Pepper and me for our group; by Cannon, Foster and Weinstone for the Opposition, and by Braun for the Comintern, was to be sent to all Party units, but was not to be published in the Party press.

After the Praesidium adopted the American Resolution, Lovestone and I were accepted as the leaders of the American Party, it being a foregone conclusion that we would carry the convention. I was called in by the comrade in charge of the confidential archives of the Comintern and shown the material which they had on hand concerning the American Party. I was shown copies of all the letters and reports, personal as well as official, which members of the Foster group, including Foster, Browder, Bittleman and the others, had sent in to Moscow and out of Moscow. The Comintern had a file of the most confidential letters of these comrades. I looked them over and obtained a number of copies of some, which I thought it might be helpful for me to have at hand in the United States. It showed that the Comintern maintained an elaborate spy system to watch and report on the leaders of the Communist parties that adhered to it. It was clear to me that they made every effort to follow up their activities and scrutinize their correspondence.

After the decision on our question, I was made to feel part of the official family of the Comintern for the first time. I was well satisfied with my mission to Moscow. I was now convinced that our group would continue to get the full support of the

Russian leaders. That, I thought, would enable us to eliminate factionalism in the American Party and make it possible for us to develop the Party into one of the strongest and most influential of the Comintern. I flew with Lovestone out of Moscow on the morning of July eighth, full of hopes and eager to get into harness in America. I had been in Moscow for two months, a long time to be away from one's party, and was glad to return. The Russian plane flew to Koenigsberg, where we changed to a German plane and arrived in Berlin in the evening.

The next morning Lovestone and I visited the Embassy of the Soviet government. There we had a brief conference with the confidential agent of the Comintern, who was also a member of the G. P. U. He was a very short stocky fellow and very well informed on Comintern matters. He was displeased with the lack of progress the German Communist Party was making and explained that what it needed was better leadership. We discussed with him the question of the possibility of the Comintern opening a European Bureau in Berlin, which was being discussed in Moscow. He declared that that might be a good step for Germany because then much closer direction could be given to the German Party. From Berlin we went to Paris and then back to New York. I had no time to visit the Communist parties of Germany or France. We had to return to the United States as quickly as possible, because the Party convention was scheduled by the Comintern to take place on August thirty-first, which left us very little time for organizing our forces. I arrived in New York on the eighteenth of July and plunged immediately into the Party fight.

Braun, the Communist International representative, arrived about a month before our national convention of 1927. We dined him and wined him in grand style. The days he spent in Chicago consisted of one party after another. At one of the parties, he got so drunk that he began to vomit, and one of the comrades shouted, "Whoop, there goes the decision of the Communist International on the American question!" The Foster group just didn't know the technique of entertaining Communist International representatives. We knew Braun's weaknesses and his likes, and catered to him accordingly. In spite of his drinking propensities, Braun was a very honest and devoted Communist. He had been very active during the fighting stages of the movement in Germany. He and Remmele, a gruff proletarian type who in Moscow enjoyed singing as loudly as he could the German Communist song, "Blut muss giesen" (Blood must flow), were the leaders of a group that was in opposition to Thaelmann. Braun took Communist discipline very seriously. If the Comintern had made a decision that he should jump into a fiery furnace he would have carried it out without wincing. All the members of the German Party with whom I had spoken had the highest regard for Braun and trusted him for his honesty and devotion to the movement.

The opposition made a desperate effort to fight its way into a Majority. But the Fosterites were in a very bad position for contesting the election of delegates, because, at the membership meetings at which the Communist International resolution and decisions were discussed before elections took place, they were decisively voted down by the membership. Neverthless, at the convention they brought in a minority report on credentials, claiming by the most fantastic presentation of imaginary facts that they had elected a majority of the delegates. They took their report seriously and fought for hours for the adoption of their utterly spurious minority report. Their action greatly angered Braun. When the convention adjourned he called the leaders of the Party together. He rapped the oppositionists over the knuckles. He criticized them for wasting the convention's time. In his German accent, he declared: "You are violating the agreement you signed in Moscow. Your proposals are nothing more than an attempt to block and sabotage the convention." He turned to Foster and said, "Your tactics are wrong and I will hold you responsible for your remarks." Foster fumed with rage: "I am sick and tired of the one-sided remarks of the Communist International Representative. Twice the majority was taken away from me. This time with the supplementary decision. It is not good for the American Party. I will not stand for it." Braun bounded to his feet and roared: "Let me tell you, Comrade Foster, the decision that was made in Moscow was made purposely all in your favor, to help you and not the others."

That ended the convention trouble and the filibustering. The Majority report of the credentials committee was adopted and the convention rolled along to its conclusion, which was the election of the new Central Executive Committee. Before the election of the new Central Executive Committee the United Opposition Bloc broke up into two groups, being unable to agree on the choice of Central Executive Committee members to represent them. We proposed to add Pepper as a regularly elected Central Executive Committee member, though he had not been in the country since the beginning of 1925. The Opposition indicated that it would bitterly oppose the election of Pepper. A concession was made to them to induce them not to oppose Pepper and elect the slate for the Central Executive Committee unanimously. We agreed to give them fifteen instead of thirteen members and to take twenty-three instead of twenty-two for ourselves. They agreed. The slate agreed upon became the new Central Executive Committee.

At this convention our group made great strides. The comrades in the needle trades had made peace with our group. Zimmerman appeared before the convention and confessed the errors of his ways. Foster fought against giving him the floor, while I defended his right to speak before the convention. After the convention Weinstone began to wobble once more, abandoned his opposition and made peace with our group. A very large number of Party leaders in the districts and in the unions, as well as leaders in the federations and writers on Party papers who formerly supported the Opposition, gave up their opposition and pledged their loyalty to the new Central Executive Committee.

But in spite of the swing towards Party unity, Foster and Cannon continued their opposition. Foster's strong card was Lozovsky and the Profintern. Lozovsky not only kept Foster informed on the political trends in Moscow, but he also used the apparatus of the Profintern to help Foster and his group in every way possible. The Profintern established the Pan-Pacific Trade Union Secretariat in the middle of 1927. Browder was given one of the leading posts on that Secretariat and was made the editor of its official organ, *The Pan-Pacific Worker*. Members of the Foster group were given important positions in the Profintern. The Lenin Institute students who belonged to the Foster group spent most of their time at the Profintern looking out for the interests of the Foster group instead of studying how to become first line Communist leaders. Foster fought on in the Party. He kept his caucus intact and continued as his main objective the capturing of the Party majority. He did not conduct an open political fight. He used the method of the ward politician—personal contact. In his travels all over the country he made it a point to talk on the Party situation individually to as many Party members as possible. He could carry on the conversation to suit the particular taste of every Party member he so favored. The result was that the Party was flooded with all kinds of information on the activities of the National Office, on the affairs of the Communist International and on the personality of the majority leadership. The wildest rumors were circulated throughout the Party. In his most confidential manner towards the Party membership Foster kept alive the flames of factionalism.

How low Foster sank in his factionalist zeal was revealed by a document which Foster himself reported to the Party Secretariat in an effort to throw the Secretariat off his own trail of chicanery. On the twenty-eighth of September he reported that he had received the following letter from a Comrade Dunbar:

> Here is good news from the jungles. No Jews there tho—no Rebeccas even—no Levins. Wasn't that 'ell?
>
> His report was all wind as usual—He'll elect himself DO [District Organizer] I presume but Jay is likely to confirm him; tho there's no telly what Jay will do next. The Party has gone to the Jews—but it can't be helpt. We shook out the old thin-skinned socialist, only us wobs [members of the I.W.W.] and them Jews remained—and they outnumbered us—We'll get them next time, maybe. Yours as ever, Robt. Dunbar.

Robert Dunbar was an ardent Fosterite. He responded to the kind of propaganda for his group that Foster disseminated in the Party fight. The expression of anti-Semitism in the Communist Party was not new to me. The Dunbar letter indicated that the anti-Jewish question was being made an issue by the Foster group, even though their political head, Bittleman, was a former Talmudic student. If Dunbar had not had confidences of that sort, he would never have written the letter. We had not until then suspected that such a campaign was being conducted in the Party. The Dunbar letter was an eye-opener. The letter was so crass that I imagine Foster was afraid to hold on to it, for fear it would fall into our hands or for fear one of our group had seen it before it reached him. It was not unusual for such letters to find their way into our files. He brought the letter into the Secretariat, believing, I surmise, that, in so doing, he washed himself of the whole affair.

But this letter proved symptomatic of Communist anti-Semitism in a much broader aspect. I am convinced that if events should dictate, it would not be out of the realms of possibility for some of the leaders of the Communist movement openly to espouse an anti-Semitic course. The German Communist Party leaders, under instructions from Moscow, were not hesitant in inviting outstanding Nazis, who had broken with Hitler, but had not given up their anti-Semitism, to join the Party. Belief in Communism did not stop Heinz Neuman, a former Zionist, from following the instructions of the Comintern and proposing a united front with the Nazis, nor did it stop the German Communist Party from making a united front with Hitler for the dissolution of the Prussian Diet when that body was controlled by the Social Democrats. The politics of the Communist movement is above every other consideration power politics, and, with power politics as the main objective, ideals are soon lost sight of and forgotten. The fact that Dunbar's letter was condemned by the Secretariat and the organizer of the California district was instructed to conduct an investigation, does not mean that the Communist Party can be depended upon to remain true to any of the ideals it preaches. In the final reckoning, political expediency is the supreme law in the Communist Party's quest for power.

CHAPTER XIII

AT THE PINNACLE OF POWER

I WAS now deeply engrossed in my work. I was a member not only of the Political Committee but also of the Secretariat of Three, which managed the affairs of the Party day by day and was entrusted with the Party's most confidential matters. In addition, I was a member of the Trade Union Committee, and had charge of all the districts and the foreign language sections of the Party. There were also numerous other activities entrusted to me. But, before I had time to put the affairs I had charge of in order, it was decided that I must make a national tour of the country which would take me about two months' time. When I returned from my tour, I found that the Political Committee had under consideration the election of a delegation to the Profintern Congress, which was scheduled to open around March tenth, 1928, in Moscow.

Since the Profintern was presumably an international organization of trade unions, delegates to its congress should have been elected by trade unions. But the American delegates, including the two non-Communists who were sent to this Profintern congress, were elected at a meeting of the Party's Political Committee. Although the Profintern pretended to be a trade union organization, it did not function as such. It was in effect a branch of the Comintern specializing in the trade union phase of the Communist program. The Russian trade unions, which were nothing more than government labor agencies, were officially affiliated with it, but the Profintern had absolutely no jurisdiction or control over them. Its membership was made up almost entirely of the Communist oppositions in the regular trade unions of countries outside Russia. On the international field it served the Soviet government as a negotiating and bargaining body with the powerful Amsterdam International of trade unions, which really represented the trade unions of Europe and other countries.

Foster did not attend this Profintern Congress, although as a member of the Profintern Executive Committee he should have, and, notwithstanding several cables from Lozovsky urging him to come to Moscow, Foster remained in the United States on the plea that the campaign among the miners could not proceed without him. Of the American delegation, which consisted of about twenty-five, all, with the exception of two, were Party members. The latter functioned as a caucus in the delegation, although there was no need to do so. The result was that the two non-Party delegates greatly resented the fact that matters of policy were being settled behind their backs. Several more delegates were added to the delegation by Lozovsky from among people who happened to arrive in Moscow and claimed that they represented workers' organizations. Noteworthy in this respect was George Mink. This comrade when a member of the Philadelphia district of the Communist Party was a taxi driver. He claimed to be related to Lozovsky. When the Profintern began to organize port bureaus in the important seaports of the world, Mink suddenly blossomed out into a full-fledged seaman, though he did not know the difference between the bow and the stern of a ship. He was amply supplied with funds by the Profintern and unexpectedly showed up at almost all the important Profintern conferences, regardless of where they took place. Upon arrival in Moscow, he insisted on becoming a part of our delegation, though he was not officially selected by the Party and his election to the delegation was voted down by the Party's Political Committee. But Mink was a Foster supporter, so Lozovsky made him a delegate. Lozovsky not only added delegates at random, but even appointed Foster supporters to important posts in the Profintern apparatus against the direct wishes of the Party. Thus, although we expressed doubts about the reliability of Comrade Smith, and some of his dubious activities were being investigated, Lozovsky gave him a job in the Profintern's information department.

One who arrived late at the Congress was James Ford, a Party member who was sent as a Negro delegate representing the Negro workers of the United States. He had recently joined the Party in Chicago and a number of speeches he made had impressed Max Bedacht. Besides, in the Party fight he supported the Ruthenberg group. Bedacht therefore suggested that he be sent to the Congress. I never saw a man who, arriving in Moscow for the first time, was so obviously intent on using his visit to make a career for himself. Ignorant of trade union matters, representing no organized Negro workers, and even more ignorant of the Communist movement, he had an innate shrewdness and a canny ability to take advantage of situations that had to do with his own advancement. When he arrived in Moscow, he made sure to have a personal interview with Lozovsky before he made his appearance among the American delegation. Lozovsky, who would have made an excellent horse-trader in American politics, soon came to an understanding with Ford. The ambitious young Negro sensed at once that he could get more out of currying favor with Lozovsky than out of being loyal to a Party leadership that might soon be replaced. He knew that Moscow was boss, not we.

When he spoke before the American delegation, I looked at him with astonishment, for in one day he seemed to have learned what was the trouble in Russia. He did not speak on American questions. He did not speak on trade union questions. He did not even mention the problems which were being discussed at the Congress. He spoke on the menace of bureaucratism in Russia and the necessity of stamping it out. It so happened that at the beginning of 1928, for purely Russian Communist Party reasons, a campaign was begun by the Russion Party to stamp out bureaucratism, which was held responsible for the ills which were besetting Russia at the time. In a few hours' time Ford knew enough of this subject to speak about it oratorically and seemingly sincerely, and to berate the delegation for not being aware of the need of concentrating all our efforts to stamp out this menace from Soviet life.

Ford was seldom present at delegation meetings, except when his vote was necessary to support some proposition in which Lozovsky was particularly interested. He was very busy being wined and dined by Lozovsky's official family. He was showered with flattery, given many testimonials and loaded with pins, badges and presents of every description. His emergence as the outstanding Negro Communist began. From that time on he has fawned before his Moscow superiors. His rise to Communist fame and high position has been rapid. I doubt that he ever had an independent thought. Yet Ford is paraded not only in the United States, but throughout the world, as the outstanding champion for the *liberation* of the Negro people.

Most of the delegates to the Profintern Congress were housed at the Hotel Europa. The accommodations were modest indeed, though for Moscow it was considered one of the better hostelries. Rooms that should have accommodated two or three persons maximum accommodated six to eight delegates. The Chinese delegates were virtually packed into their rooms. The hotel was so overcrowded and its inadequate sanitary conditions so overtaxed that this greatly inconvenienced the delegates from America and the other countries of higher living standards.

The Congress was so organized that the Russian leaders left nothing to chance or even to Lozovsky, in spite of the fact that Lozovsky, as a member of the Russian Party, was strictly under its control. The Congress elected a praesidium, which was only ostensibly its presiding body. The power that really ruled this Congress functioned behind the scene and had absolutely no public or official standing. It consisted of the members of the Executive Committee of the Profintern, the chairmen of the delegations from the various participating countries, all of whom happened to be the outstanding leaders of the Communist parties of their countries, and a committee appointed by the Executive Committee of the Communist International, whose function it was secretly to guide and control the affairs of the Congress. The Communist International Committee was the real boss. Of the two most important figures of this committee, both members of the Russian Party, one was Joseph Piatnitsky, of the Comintern apparatus and the other was Gay, a leading figure in the Russian trade unions. The men of the Comintern committee represented not merely the Comintern but the Russian trade unions and the Russian Party. The meetings of this body were, to use popular American slang, "the real works." It made all the decisions and was the final arbiter on all disputed questions.

The American delegation was divided into three parts. One consisted of a group of loyal supporters of our leadership in the American Party, and held on to its majority in the delegation by the skin of its teeth; another, of the loyal supporters of Foster; and the third group, of William F. Dunne's drinking companions. This last group was the talk of Moscow. Included in it were two students of the Lenin School, a certain Comrade Bell and Clarence Hathaway, who subsequently became chief editor of *The Daily Worker*. Every night drunken carouses took place. They always broke up into fights after "Auld Lang Syne" and "Sweet Adeline" were butchered. On one occasion glass doors were smashed amid such pandemonium that many thought a serious riot had broken out. On the ground floor of the hotel was an all night café and cabaret. All night long, bottles of every kind of liquor traveled from the café to Dunne's room. How all this liquor, which was very expensive in Russia at the time, was paid for I was never able to find out.

On the whole, the rest of the American delegates and the delegates from the other countries deported themselves in an orderly manner. Most of the time of the Congress was taken up with entertaining the delegates who came from all parts of the world. The very large delegation from China took its participation most seriously. The delegation was interested above everything else in obtaining arms for its members in China and instruction on how to use them. China was going through a period of reaction. To be discovered as a Communist meant to have one's head chopped off.

The Congress itself was turning sharply to the Left. Stress was being laid not so much upon boring within the existing unions, which were branded as reactionary organizations beyond redemption, but rather upon the organization of new unions, which would be revolutionary organizations and which would affiliate with the Profintern. This Congress actually marked the complete reversal of Communist trade union policy, for, instead of working inside of the unions for the purpose of capturing them, the Communists decided upon a dual union policy of splitting the old unions and building new ones of their own. Lozovsky, who from the time he was appointed the first Chairman of the Profintern had harbored dual unionist principles, lashed out against all the Communist leaders who had stubbornly resisted the tactics of dual unionism. He attacked the American Party in the severest terms, and held it up to ridicule by declaring that the American Communist Party instead of fighting the A. F. of L. was dancing quadrilles around it.

At that Congress I had an opportunity to study Lozovsky and his methods closely. Although listed as a capmaker, I doubt that he worked at his trade for any length of time. He was short of stature. Thin locks of brown hair covered his head, while his beard was a dirty red. His eyes, narrow and squinting, lit up like those of a fanatical dervish doing a holy dance, every time he was under sharp attack. He was a bitter, unscrupulous antagonist. Originally one of the Menshevik leaders, he had joined the Bolsheviks when certain that they would maintain their power and at the price of being given the Chairmanship of the Profintern. Shrewd, he was not only unscrupulous and tricky in his actions, but basically unprincipled. To this day he has been able to weather all the storms through which the Communist International has gone without once losing favor with those who continued in power and, most important, with Stalin. Zinoviev disliked him. Zinoviev has been stood up against the wall and shot. Bukharin despised him and considered him an ignoramus and a fool. Bukharin, whose great popularity Lozovsky envied, has been disgraced and killed. But Lozovsky remains.

Michael Tomsky, that short, dynamic chief and driving force of the Russian trade unions, looked upon Lozovsky as a necessary and expensive evil, often threatening to oust him; yet it is Tomsky who was driven to "suicide," while Lozovsky lives to tell the tale. In the executive of the Profintern were many figures, who in the Trotsky, Bukharin, and Tomsky purges paid dearly; but so cleverly did Lozovsky manipulate and so quickly did he change his views, that this ace of turncoats, who more than anyone else I have seen gave me the impression of a court jester, was able to hold on without loss of position, or harm to himself. Today Lozovsky is Assistant Commissar of Foreign Affairs under Premier Molotov.

As head of the American delegation, I had my hands full because of Lozovsky's opposition and because of a development concerning the United States of which I was kept ignorant. When I arrived in Moscow for the Congress I was met by Bill Kruse, who was finishing out his term at the Lenin School, and by J. Louis Engdahl, who had replaced Minor as the representative of the Party. I had expected to meet Pepper, for, before departing, Lovestone and I had mapped out a campaign of strategy against Lozovsky which included the assistance of Pepper. When I asked about Pepper, they looked at me with surprise, and Bill Kruse remarked: "Why, haven't you seen Pepper in the States?" "No, I haven't," I answered. "He certainly is going to cook up a lot of new trouble, now that Party affairs seem to be going along fairly well." Then Kruse and Engdahl informed me that Pepper was not very popular in Moscow and that in their opinion his going to America was not going to do the Party any good. I later found out after the Profintern Congress that Pepper was sent to America with a mandate to bring about the unification of our group with the Foster group. He did not only promise the executive of the Comintern that he would carry out its mandate. He went further and informed it that he was the only man who *could* bring that desired result about.

The first thing that Pepper did when he arrived in the United States was to go into conferences with Jay Lovestone and Foster. He tried to sell them the idea that Lovestone, Pepper and Foster could form a triumvirate that would not only unify the Party membership but lead the Party so effectively that it would make great progress. He argued that the three of them complemented each other and that there was no reason why they should not join their forces and work together. But Foster had to be shown. The only demonstration that would convince him that Pepper and Lovestone meant business was for them to carry through a drastic shakeup in the Party. It was this shakeup that took place while I was in Moscow. Throughout the two months I was in Moscow, Lovestone purposely kept me uninformed of a development that would have been of the greatest importance in guiding my conduct. I did not receive a single letter from him and only a cable to explain why the Political Committee and the Secretariat had voted contrary to my wishes on matters that I cabled him about. Always his explanation was general and not specific. Meantime, doublecrossing me, my partner in the leadership collaborated in the Party which consisted of accusing the most trusted and loyal members of the Lovestone-Gitlow group and of the former Ruthenberg group of following a hard line, of being factional, having them removed from their posts and followers of the Foster faction put in their places.

When I had fought against Mink's inclusion in the delegation, I pulled Lozovsky off the floor virtually by his whiskers. I raised a row about it in every committee and department of the Profintern. Finally it came to the special body that actually ruled the Congress. Lozovsky went to all lengths to prove why such a valuable seaman as the taxi-driver from Philadelphia should be added to the delegation. I ridiculed each and every one of his arguments. Finally, Piatnitsky, who had the final say on such matters, asked if I was willing to let the Political Committee of the American Party decide the question by cable. I agreed. I drew up the cable. The cable was sent to Lovestone. To my amazement, when the answer came back, it was to the effect that the Political Committee had no objections to Mink's being included as a delegate. This sort of doublecrossing, which was part of the Pepper plan, and evidently done to please Foster and hence further his triumvirate plan, was repeated a half a dozen times, so that, after every fight against Lozovsky, I was left holding the bag.

Lozovsky and the Opposition, unlike me, were very well informed, for Lozovsky was always ready to let the Political Committee of the American Party decide. But Lozovsky was not satisfied with the advantage Pepper and Lovestone gave him. He used all his other tricks as well. The translators at the conference deliberately twisted my words and the words of other American delegates Lozovsky did not like, to mean the opposite of what we said. When I discovered this, I had Gross of the Furriers Union, who was a delegate and who knew German well, take a seat among the German delegates, and another comrade who understood Russian take a seat among those who understood Russian, and they immediately notified me when translations were falsified. I then had them interrupt the translators and call attention to the errors. But imagine my surprise when I discovered that the falsifications went into the Russian Press. The most deliberate alterations of meaning occurred in one of my remarks. I procured a stenogram of my speech and took the matter up in the special unofficial committee. Lozovsky promised that he would see to it that a correction was printed in the press. But that was where it ended—with a promise deliberately made, never to be kept.

During the Congress, together with Zimmerman and Gross, who came on behalf of the needle trades, I tried to get the Communist International to vote a considerable sum of money for the needle trades fight. Our unions were under terrific pressure from the Right Wing and were bankrupt. Money was badly needed to continue the fight. We proposed that a minimum of a hundred thousand dollars be given for this purpose. Bukharin was very glad to receive us. But I saw that it was not the same Bukharin, and he indicated that he did not enjoy the power he formerly had. He said the matter would have to be considered by the Political Bureau of the Russian Party. Then a special committee was appointed to study the question. Bukharin told us we would have to take the matter up with Tomsky, because it was a trade union matter, and, if the money were voted, it would have to come out of the treasury of the Russian unions. But Tomsky was the most difficult man to contact. He was always on the go. Finally, when we did get to see him, he listened impatiently, flew into a rage, and told one of the Russian clothing workers' leaders present, "How can you propose to give such a sum of money? What kind of an excuse will you be able to give your unemployed workers when they ask for assistance?"

I knew that conditions in Russia were not good. Workers were unemployed even in the land of Sovietism. Prices of certain commodities had gone up. There was an acute shortage of dairy products, meat was far from plentiful, and in manufactured goods, like shoes, clothing and textiles, there was a shortage and the prices were exorbitant. Workers in 1928 were far worse off than in 1927. During the ten years of their rule the Russians were still at grips with the elementary economic problems of the country.

The Profintern Congress ended with a grand ball, which took place at the Hotel Metropole. In the center of the banquet hall was a fountain, the sprays of which were spectacularly illuminated by colored electric lights at its base. The tables were set in very elaborate style with the most unusual dishes, including salads worked out in designs of exquisite architectural beauty, all of it the ultimate in culinary art, to please the eye as well as the palate. Each table was loaded with bottles of the finest champagne, cognac, vodka, wines and liqueurs of every description. An orchestra played on a platform surrounded by palms. Artists from the opera, concert singers, and entertainers of all kinds supplied amusement all night long. As soon as one bottle was finished, another took its place. The waiters were kept busy running to and fro with the bottles. The more liquor disappeared the more hilarious the party became. There was dancing, of course. Then the Russian custom of throwing one into the air amid applause took place. But as the hours ran on the fountain became the center of attraction. Delegates threw one another into the fountain.

Around the table at which the Americans sat, a fight took place between William F. Dunne and a non-Party delegate from Detroit. The fight started, as most drunken brawls do, over a woman, one of Lozovsky's secretaries. She came to the affair in dazzling evening clothes. She could have transported herself to one of the elaborate balls at the Waldorf-Astoria. The delegate from Detroit, who had been buying whisky for Dunne all the way from America to Moscow, and in Moscow as well, insisted that Dunne, who was dancing all evening with her, introduce him. Dunne refused. They quarreled, and during the argument our American from Detroit opened up and spoke some very harsh truths in his drunken candor. "You can't pull the wool over my eyes," he blurted out. "I know what is going on outside. I know that while you are wining and dining here, thousands of poor Russians haven't got bread to eat. I know you are putting on a show and you want the rest of the world to believe that things are wonderful here. But you won't stop me from telling the truth." Resentful of these blasphemous remarks, Dunne threatened to beat him up. But others intervened, and they were separated. The man from Detroit was rushed out of the banquet hall. Dunne continued to dance with the glamorous secretary. The gay ball continued.

When my wife turned to me and asked me why this lavish display, why this hilarity, I remarked, "These comrades must enjoy themselves now. Many of them when they return to their tasks will face great dangers. Many will never return again because they will be killed in line of duty, others will be in prison. It happens after all only once at a Congress."

I took a walk after the ball for some fresh air. I passed the riding academy and its wide stone wall. On top, huddled in their rags, like mice, one on top of another, lay a group of the homeless waifs of Russia. Soon there would be another dawn, for them when they would rise, shake the sleep from their tiny limbs, scratch the lice on their dirty carcasses and begin the day's search for food.

After the Profintern Congress I received a cable from Lovestone that I must return home immediately, after taking up the matter of "a consignment of goods" to America. The "consignment" concerned the bringing over ten thousand dollars as the initial payment of the thirty-five thousand dollars voted as a contribution to the American Party for the Presidential campaign of 1928. In the cable I was informed that I must return in time to be present at the national nominating convention, which was to take place in New York City from the twenty-first to the twenty-seventh of May. Before departing for the United States I requested that I be permitted to return home by way of Leningrad, because I desired to visit the city and to enable my wife to see some of her relatives there. Unlike other Party leaders who had visited Russia with their wives, I made it a matter of principle personally to pay for all her traveling and other expenses. This request was refused on the ground that the nature of my return to America was so important and its circumstances kept so confidential that I could not take the route via Leningrad. I was instructed to leave Moscow immediately, and left by train via Negoreloye, Warsaw, Berlin, and Hamburg.

I had been given a sealed confidential letter which I was to present to the Organization Department of the Communist

Party of Germany before leaving for America. Besides, I had in my possession all the decisions and documents of the Profintern Congress. On the same train with me, a large number of delegates were going home to their respective countries. They all displayed large Soviet buttons on their lapels. When the train pulled into Stolpce, the Polish authorities gave them a very strict search and confiscated a large part of the books and literature which they brought with them from Moscow. When I traveled I made it my business always to go dressed conservatively and not to look or act like a Bolshevik. I never displayed buttons or other incriminating material on my person. I greeted the Polish customs official with a smile and had a tip ready in the palm of my hand. When I opened the first bag he just looked on top, then motioned to me not to open the other, stamped them all, and when I gave him a tip thanked me profusely.

In Berlin I went to the German Community Party headquarters in the Karl Liebknecht house, a very large building that occupied almost a whole city block. It was a place of great activity. However, the first thing which struck me was the way in which the German Party aped the Russians. Before one could enter the building, one had to appear at a small room where permits to see some one were issued. It reminded me of Russia, of the Comintern and the headquarters of the Russian Communist Party, where the same procedure was carried out.

As soon as I got my pass I was taken to the office of Wilhelm Pieck, one of the Secretaries of the German Party and its contact man with the G. P. U. He had been informed in advance about my mission. He simply greeted me, took the letter I gave him and then called one of the clerks, with whom I was directed to go. The clerk took me to another part of Berlin, where I was introduced to a young man who spoke German but looked to me like a Lett. I soon discovered that he was an agent for the G. P. U. while also working for the Comintern. He proceeded by a circuitous route, by bus and subway, to take me to another part of the city. Here I was taken to a basement in an apartment house. The basement apartment was kept by an old German lady in her middle sixties. I was introduced by my companion, who left immediately.

The old lady was a very striking personality. She was rather tall and stately. Her straight chiseled features seemed to be those of a woman with great courage and of fanatical devotion to the cause in which she believed. She told me that I would have to wait. While I waited she informed me that conditions in Germany were very bad, that the Socialist *Hunde* [dogs] were complicating matters, but that the Communist Party was growing and would soon gain the upper hand. But before the conversation could proceed much further, my Lettish companion returned with a Russian. We left the basement apartment, which was furnished very much like a poor workman's apartment in the United States. On the street I was handed the consignment for the United States, which consisted of $3,500.00 in American bills of small denominations as the first instalment instead of the $10,000.00. As soon as I got to my hotel I counted the money and put it in a money belt I had bought for that purpose.

I returned to America after my first trip to Moscow as a member of the Executive Committee and the Praesidium of the Communist International. I returned after my second trip as a member of the Executive Committee of the Profintern. I held the highest offices that it was possible for a Communist to hold in both the political and trade union organizations of international Communism. The Profintern Congress did not impress me. Most of the delegates saw through its bluff and pretenses. Most of the delegates who came represented the Communists only and had no real standing in the trade unions of their respective countries. This became apparent when the newly elected executive held its first meeting after the Congress adjourned. Lozovsky half-seriously suggested that it would be advisable to put the Profintern on a more substantial basis, that the affiliated organizations pay a per capita tax for each and every one of their members. The members of the executive became disturbed. Fritz Heckert of Germany jumped to his feet. He said that while it was true that his delegation represented millions of adherents to the Profintern, they were not yet in a position to pay the per capita tax, because most of them had to pay into the treasury of their respective unions, which were still controlled by the Social-Democrats. When he made that statement the other members let out a roar of laughter and even Lozovsky looked silly. They all knew that exaggerated claims had been made by all delegations. Lozovsky then let us know that it was only a formal resolution, for the record.

A few days before I left Moscow I went to visit Bill Haywood. I had known of Big Bill over a period of twenty-five years, and intimately since 1919. I went to the hospital with mixed feelings. The Comintern literature department had only a few days previously handed me Haywood's manuscript of his autobiography, which he started in 1927 with the assistance of Lydia Gibson, Bob Minor's wife, and a Party member. She left before the work was completed. Haywood, however, was fortunate enough to get the services of a former I. W. W. member who helped him conclude the book, which was to serve as his last testament to the labor movement and especially to the I. W. W., which he cherished to his last days. It was my job to read the book from the Communist angle and to suggest any changes or eliminations which in my judgment should be made. I was, in fact, acting as a censor for the Comintern. It was not at all unusual for the Comintern to change the text of books and to falsify history if it was considered in the interest of the movement to do so.

I approved the book in my report, but suggested that one item be stricken from it. This concerned the activities of Elizabeth Gurley Flynn during the strike in Northern Minnesota on the Mesaba Iron Range. Haywood was embittered against Flynn, one of the most popular organizers of the I. W. W., because she had, in his opinion, obtained immunity from prosecution for an intimate friend, at the expense of a group of rank-and-file miners who were sent to prison for long terms. I did not go into the merits of the case. However, I knew that Gurley Flynn was traveling in the direction of the Communist movement, that she had been of invaluable service in the defense of Communist political prisoners and in the Sacco-Vanzetti case. I pointed out that, in the Passaic Textile strike, she coöperated to the fullest extent with our people and that the Party had made her one of the prominent leaders of the International Labor Defense. Not only was that reference to Elizabeth Gurley Flynn eliminated, but much more was changed when the book was turned over to International Publishers, with instructions to complete editing and print. Not only were references of Haywood to the I. W. W. eliminated and changed, but paragraphs were added to make it appear that Haywood was a full-fledged Communist, which indeed he never was. Alexander Trachtenberg of International Publishers was intrusted with the job of editing in the United States.

The Kremlin Hospital, which was considered the best hospital in Moscow and to which the important Bolshevik leaders went for treatment, would be considered a very poor and dilapidated hospital in the United States. Russian hospitals require visitors to take off their coats and put on a smock, which is supplied by the hospital. (I often wondered why this custom was insisted upon, because as soon as you were through with your visit the smock you wore would be hung on the rack and given the next person who came in. It was not sterilized.) As I entered the room where Haywood was lying, his Russian wife greeted me with tears in her eyes and said some words to me in Russian, which I did not understand. Bill Haywood had married a Russian woman many years his junior who spoke no English. And Haywood spoke almost no Russian. There was nothing in common between the two intellectually or even socially. But she made life more comfortable for him and acted as a good nurse and housekeeper. Whether she loved him or not I could not say.

"Hullo, Ben," Haywood greeted me, "awfully glad to see you." I grasped him by the hand. His bulky form showed through the white sheets. He seemed to have grown much stouter. I said very little to him, for he did all the talking. "You know, Ben, this time the attack got me in such a way that it felt as if all my insides were jumping up and down. I thought I was a goner for sure. But they got me here and I am feeling much better."

Then he began to talk about America and about the I. W. W. He wanted the latest news about both. I gave them to him. About the Wobblies I told him that I thought the organization had practically gone to pieces, that many of its leaders were out of all sympathy with the revolutionary movement. I could see that he was pained, for sick as he was he propped himself on his elbows, and looked at me with his one eye, full of a pathos and yearning that I will never forget.

"Ben, it can't be true. I am sure that at heart the old spirit of the Wobblies is still there. If I could only get back to the States and see and talk to my boys I am sure the whole situation would change."

The effort exhausted him. He spoke of his lonesomeness in Russia and then again about his sickness. I could see that he felt that his end was near, an end he regretted because it was so hopeless and an environment so foreign to every fiber that made up his being.

I tried to reassure him. Jokingly I remarked that there was plenty of fight left in him still. The attendant came, tapped me on the shoulder, and beckoned me to leave. I clasped Bill's hand. He held my hand firmly in his grip: "Good-by, Ben, and remember me to the boys back home."

Back home was what Bill Haywood dreamt about. It was this back home which the Bolsheviks could never understand.

After Haywood and some others were induced to skip bail, on April twenty-first, 1921, Charles Edward Scott, the former Lettish comrade from Boston, writing as the secretary of the Pan-American Agency of the Communist International who induced Haywood to flee America, promising him at the same time that the Soviet government would pay back every dollar deposited for his bail, wrote:

> Comrade Haywood did not leave the United States of his own accord, but at the direct command of the Communist International of which he is a disciplined member and whose authority he recognizes as the highest in the world.

And further,

> Openly and undisguised, Haywood will return to America; but the time and manner of his coming will be determined by requirements of the revolutionary class struggle and not by the decrees of capitalist courts. . . Fellow-workers, do not be deluded into the childish belief that the ruling class will listen to pleas for clemency. Put no faith in petitions—those scraps of paper

> which our oppressors only laugh at and throw into the waste basket. Revolutionary mass action of the workers is our weapon to force open the prison doors.

The Communist promise to pay back the bail money was never kept. But the I. W. W. paid back every cent of it.

Haywood was never a Communist, as Scott implied. He was not a man who could be ordered and commanded about. Nevertheless, they had snatched him up from America, wilfully made him a fugitive from his homeland, and deposited him in Russia, a land which was strange to him and to which he could never get accustomed. Once in Russia, they forgot him completely.

But Haywood never forgot, nor could he forget, the land of his birth. He was typically American. He embodied the youth, the romanticism, and the individualism of our country. In Haywood, the frontier and the wild recklessness of the western metal mines blended into a rebellious courage which comes only with freedom. He sensed power in the workers. He believed that if they were organized into one big union they could become masters of the world and make it a better place to live in. But Haywood was not a Bolshevik. He was not that person of objectivity that drives sentiment and feelings out of his breast as "bourgeois virtues" that presumably undermine the revolutionary will. Haywood was the typical American sentimentalist. He could feel for the suffering of the hobo panhandling for a dime. He had the most tender compassion for the sufferings of human beings, though he was an advocate of force in the struggle of the workers for economic emancipation. In Haywood, American life sang out in all its simplicity and in all its individual splendor. This intense feeling for one's fellowmen, this morality of being fair and honorable in one's dealings with others, this comradeship with all on a plane of equality and genuine friendship, with its typical admixture of American sentimentality—this was Haywood's. It was America's gift to Haywood. No wonder that Big Bill with his simplicity and boyhood enthusiasm was shipwrecked when thrown into a sea of intrigue, of duplicity, where people who called themselves Communists, revolutionists, instead of being independent, fawned and sniveled before the new aristocracy power. Haywood's life in far away Russia was a tragedy. The news of his death reached me when I was on the high seas. As I read this news on the ship's bulletin board, it occurred to me that Haywood had really died when he first landed in Russia as a fugitive from his native land.

Back in America again, the vortex of unceasing activity on behalf of the Party and the Majority faction drowned out the very time for reflection. It was a case of one damn thing after another occupying my attention practically twenty out of every twenty-four hours, robbing me of sleep, of normal intercourse with family and friends, undermining (although I did not even think of it then) my naturally great reserve of vitality. Every breath I took was laden with politics, politics, politics; every reflex action became political in content, not to mention every convolution of the brain. For the most part it was petty politics, conniving, scheming, purblind to larger issues because of its absorption in the tangible and immediate realities step by step. Along with this politics was the constant attention to raising the money for the sustenance of our varied activities. Moscow was a generous donor, but far from all of our activities were paid for by the Russians. With a membership never exceeding sixteen million in those days, we spent on an average of a million dollars a year, of which the better half was raised right in the United States. Some years we spent much more than that, without taking into consideration strike situations under our control. The Central Executive Committee alone averaged about a quarter of a million dollars annually in expenditures. In addition, the various language federations, district organizations, and subsidiaries like the Trade Union Educational League, the International Labor Defense, the American Negro Labor Congress, and the like, had budgets, fund-raising campaigns and separate bookkeeping records of their own, which received only cursory supervision from the National Office. Yet with all this investment of money and energy, of political conniving and propaganda, we made no appreciable inroads into the body of American public opinion until about the advent of the New Deal administration of Franklin D. Roosevelt. Why that was so, is another question. It may be mere coincidence. But such is the fact.

An example of our financial juggling was our fund-raising campaign on behalf of the British coal miners in their strike of 1926. *The Jewish Daily Forward* caught up with us and charged that the money the Party collected through its Relief Fund never reached the British miners. The charge was true. But of course we denied it with vehement counter-charges and character assassination against those nosey Social-Democrats. Since the *Forward* persisted, however, by pointing out that the British miners had no records of having received any money from the American Communists, and the whole affair created a considerable scandal, the Central Executive Committee, after due deliberation, reached the following official decision at its meeting of November nineteenth, 1926:

> That we issue a reply to the *Forward* attack, to be printed in the *Freiheit* only for the time being, stating the total collection for the British Miners Relief, dividing the expenses on the basis of overhead and publicity, and making the argument that the overhead was used for the purpose of propaganda to get contributions from the unions, which contributions went through the Executive Council of the A. F. of L.

With slight variations, this became the classic formula for justifying the transference of such funds to unauthorized channels. It is based on the assumption that all moneys collected by Communists were *invested*, so to say, in propaganda expenditures for the purpose of stimulating contributions from other sources—unions, fraternal bodies, and other organizations of a public character. This alibi persists to this day in all Communist fund-raising campaigns, the money going of course to the Party in large measure.

Not even the Sacco-Vanzetti campaign was immune from this sort of scheming. Independently of the official Sacco-Vanzetti Defense Committee the Party carried on a campaign of its own, agitating and collecting funds through the International Labor Defense. Hundreds of meetings were held, gigantic demonstrations organized, the Party contributing greatly toward the extension of the movement to Europe. Yet the Sacco-Vanzetti Defense Committee had the temerity to complain that the funds we collected for the Sacca-Vanzetti cause were never turned over to it. The complaint was true, of course, and could be easily substantiated. Some of the money went to *The Daily Worker,* which financially has always been a bottomless pit, and the rest was spent on campaigning to enhance the prestige of the Party. We saw nothing reprehensible in such handling of funds. The Communist Party has always regarded a *cause célèbre,* particularly with a labor or Negro angle to it, as a golden opportunity for advancing the Party's own fortunes politically and financially, the latter being in the final reckoning also political, of course. As for the immediate occasion itself that presents the opportunity for campaigning, the personal fate of the individuals involved is of no moment to the Party, which looks down upon the puny human beings enmeshed in trouble from the Olympian heights of the Historical Perspective through that objective telescope known as the Class Angle. While pettily interested in our own individual political fortunes, we Communists have always been sublimely cool, aloof, objective about the individuals we exploited for our purposes. Come to think of it, there is nothing strange in that. It is a classical attitude. You will find it in the heroes of Homeric legend, in the myths of the Greek gods on Olympus, in the accounts of Roman tyrants, Oriental despots, and the kings and princes of Medieval Europe. But what has it in common with Socialism and a free society? Nothing.

It was in that spirit that we carried on our campaigns for the recognition of Soviet Russia, on behalf of China, India, Nicaragua and Mexico; it was thus that we worked among farmers through the United Farmers Educational League, among Negroes through the American Negro Labor Congress, among the trade unions, social and cultural organizations, conducting shop activities, publishing pamphlets and periodical literature. Always, no matter how far afield from the objective may seem the policy or conduct of the moment, the Communist keeps before him his objective, the seizure of power, of ultimate power, through capturing the machinery of the state, through becoming the government of his country. Meantime, he trains for this objective by behaving like the overlord of every organization he touches. The gospel of control, of securing the actual power

—that is the heart and soul of Bolshevik philosophy, that is the fascination that draws such a varied assortment of the disgruntled and the dissatisfied to the banner of Communism, backed as it is by a government that holds despotic sway over one-sixth of the earth, populated by more than one and a half times the population of the United States, and having its colonies of political control over the entire face of the earth. It is a fascination virtually irresistible to the power-hungry.

We Communists have always considered the anti-militarist work of the Party from two distinct angles. On the one hand, we considered that it was necessary systematically to work to undermine the military structure of the capitalist class. We believed that if the military power of the capitalist governments was not undermined, it would not be possible to dislodge the capitalists from power. But we were not pacifists. We did not decry the use of force and violence. Quite the contrary. We firmly believed that without the use of force and violence it would not be possible to carry through the overthrow of capitalism and the seizure of power. Our anti-militarist work therefore was divided into two parts: one was positive, the other negative. Our negative policy consisted in criticizing all the military activities of the government, opposing expenditures for armaments, characterizing the army and navy as weapons of imperialism and in attempting to create hostility between the population and the military power of the government.

Our positive policy however was very subtle. As Communists, it was our duty to penetrate the armed forces and win the support of the enlisted men. Very small beginnings were made in this direction. First we attempted to organize a left organization of veterans. Our first organizer in this field was Jack Braddon from Minneapolis, a very excitable and erratic man. The first organizations established were of a local character, attracted very few ex-service men and wielded very little influence, even though every step necessary was taken to hide the Communist initiative in this work. We also attempted to raise certain questions in the organization of the Veterans of Foreign Wars and to a lesser extent in the American Legion. But there we met with complete failure.

A real spurt was given to our efforts to penetrate the armed forces during the fight to free Trumbull and Crouch, two soldiers who had been arrested in Hawaii for propaganda among the soldiers at Schofield Barracks in Honolulu. Both were members of the Communist Party. Upon their release from military prison they not only toured the country under the auspices of the Young Workers League but also helped to develop the Party's work among the soldiers and sailors.

Finally we decided upon "colonizing" the armed forces, in order to establish contact with the men in the service, propagandize them, learn about their conditions and grievances, and finally, learn military tactics for future use in the event of a revolution. An insignificant number of young men were ordered to enlist in the United States Army. The largest number, however, were ordered to join the Citizens Military Training Camps run by the National Guard. We did not hesitate to send scores of selected young men into these camps even though we had been most outspoken in branding the National Guard as the most vicious strike breaking agency. As for the Reserve Officers Training Corps, in many colleges a compulsory course, we continually fought against it as a military organization. However, we also sent all young Communists in college into the R. O. T. C., to learn military tactics. After we learned a little of the soldier's and sailor's conditions, we formulated a program of reforms for the Army and Navy and a set of proposals for giving the enlisted men more democratic rights.

However, we realized that in carrying on this work, the greatest precautions had to be taken not to involve the Party, because we were sufficiently aware that in working within the armed forces we were engaging in very dangerous activity, which, if discovered, would have probably resulted in serious prosecution of the Party and its leaders. In carrying out our anti-militarist activities, however, we were not working upon our own initiative, but upon the direct instructions of the Communist International, which insisted that that kind of work be done.

The anti-imperialist work of the Party was considered in some respects its most important activity, because it was closely linked with the machinations of the Communist International and of the Soviet government. It was Lenin's premise that capitalism would break at its weakest links; that is, in the colonial and undeveloped countries. To undermine the great capitalist powers, he maintained, it was necessary to undermine their imperialist grip in Asia, Africa and South America. The Communists were directed by their leaders in Moscow to support practically every nationalist struggle against the imperialist aggressor. The anti-imperialist activities of the Communists were closely tied up with the Foreign Office needs of the Soviet Union and with Soviet interests in the particular countries involved.

The American Party had for its special sphere of anti-imperialist work the countries of Central and South America and the Philippines. We supported every movement in the Latin American countries against the United States. Our Party supported the movements of opposition in the countries to the south of us, not only by aiding them financially but also by having representatives in the important centers. From time to time the Communist International and the Profintern arranged important international conferences in the Latin American countries to further the anti-imperialist work of the Comintern, in an effort to win influence over the unions, peasant organizations and the leaders in the movements of opposition to "Yankee Imperialism."

But the activities of our party were not only confined to Latin America. They were also closely tied up with the activities of the Soviet Union in China. It was no secret to us in America that the Bolshevik leaders hoped to utilize the class of American and Japanese interests in China to their own advantage. This fact had a great deal to do with the important role given the American Party in the affairs of China.

Communist activity found its most dramatic expression during a hectic period that began in 1929, with the proclamation by a Comintern Plenum of the so-called "Third Period" in the historic development of the revolutionary trend throughout the world. The year 1929 marks the beginning of this period of Communist insanity and Gargantuan boasting. The world was divided schematically into two separate and distinct parts. One was the Soviet Union, where the Five-Year Plan was marching toward complete Socialism in seven-league boots—indeed, at such a rapid pace that the industrialization and production standards of American capitalism would soon not only be reached but surpassed. Presumably, such standards would be surpassed in the land of the Five-Year Plan, not only in terms of increase money wages for the workers but in real wages—in the tangible form of better living standards and a wider distribution of commodities among the masses. Furthermore, the revolution in agriculture, the so-called collectivization of agriculture, which involved the elimination of private peasant holdings, would bring the fruits of Socialism enjoyed by the urban population to the rural population as well. Stalin and Molotov boasted that the tremendous advances that would be made by Russia in successfully completing the Five-Year Plan and going far beyond its fondest hopes, would so inspire the peoples of the other countries that the Bolshevik example would soon be followed in other countries. Traditionally backward and chaotic Russia was transformed by these braggarts into the haven of planned economy.

On the other hand, the rest of the world, the remaining five-sixths of the globe, populated by the remaining nine-tenths of the human race, was pictured as a capitalist nightmare. Capitalism, it was proclaimed, was now in the so-called "third period," the period that would mark the beginning of the end of capitalism. During this period the misery of the masses would increase, their living standards be reduced far below the level of subsistence, gigantic class struggles, revolts and wars would take place. In the third period the Communist parties of the capitalist countries were ordered to be prepared to lead revolutionary struggles, to get ready for the assumption of power. In Russia, the Soviet workers were filled with paens of praise on what they were receiving, in contrast to what the workers were receiving in the capitalist countries. They were fed on stories that in the rest of the world the workers were not only starving but that they were allowed to die of hunger and privation on the streets of New York, London and Paris, not to mention Warsaw and Tokio. The workers of Russia were promised that soon their brothers in other countries would revolt and set up Soviets and Soviet governments of their own.

To lend greater credence to this propaganda campaign, which was created for home consumption and in the interests of the bureaucrats administering the Five-Year Plan, and also in order to enlist wide circles of liberals and workers in support of the Soviet Union, steps were taken by the Comintern to put a semblance of plausibility on the fantastic publicity campaign which had been instituted throughout the world on a gigantic scale. Before the close of the sessions of the American Commission in 1929, the Comintern was aroused to a feverish pitch in regard to the coming events in Germany. Its activities were cloaked in a great deal of secrecy, but it was purposely and confidentially allowed to leak out that the Comintern was expecting and preparing for a Bolshevik revolution in Germany. Representatives from all the parties of the Comintern were being hurried to Germany, to be on hand when the great event would take place. H. M. Wicks was sent from the American Party. He made a hurried stop-over in the United States, to give his comrades of the American Party advance information on what was going to take place. The members of the American Party were keyed up to a high pitch of enthusiasm.

The Communist International in this period executed a right about face on its policy of the united front. During a revolutionary period, like the third period, the Communists were warned to trust no one but themselves. The greatest enemies were those in the working class who refused to accept the leadership of the Communists. These paved the way for the counter-revolution and Fascism. These, the Comintern insisted, together with the Right Wing in the Communist movement, constituted the main and most immediate danger. The Socialists, the liberals, the trade unionists were branded "Social-Fascists," more potentially dangerous than the Fascists themselves. Against them a war of complete elimination from the labor movement—indeed, of extermination—must be started at once.

The convention of the Trade Union Educational League, held in Cleveland on August thirty-first, 1929, three months after its regular date of opening, the postponement being ordered by Lozovsky, was attended by close to seven hundred delegates, most of whom were Party members who were selected by the Communist Party to attend it. Among them were over a hundred and fifty youth delegates, who represented no trade union organizations; seventy-two women delegates, in the same category; and no less than one hundred and eighty-one delegates from its largest constituent body, the newly-formed National Miners Union, which did not have over three thousand members. Nevertheless, this convention went on record to change its name to that of the Trade Union Unity League and to organize as a national trade union federation rivalling the American Federation of Labor. The new organization was given a Communist political program, which proclaimed that the new unions "aim to sharpen, deepen and unite the scattered economic struggles of the workers into a general political struggle aiming at the abolition of capitalism and the establishment of a workers and farmers government." It characterized the A. F. of L. as a Fascist organization which must be destroyed. Revolution was just around the corner in the summer of 1929—very much like Hoover's prosperity.

The Communist International called upon the Communist parties of all countries to arrange demonstrations in protest against unemployment on March sixth, 1930. The American Party answered the orders by calling for a general strike on that day. The largest demonstration was held in New York in Union Square. The demonstrators, reinforced by those who came to watch the demonstration because Grover Whalen had issued an order against its proceeding to City Hall, numbered altogether around sixty thousand. The Communists flaunted banners demanding the overthrow of the United States government and the establishment of a revolutionary workers' government. Orders were given to the Communists to resist the police if any attempt would be made to stop the demonstrators from marching to the City Hall. In charge of the demonstration were Foster, Amter and Minor. As the march to City Hall was about to begin, Foster, Minor and Amter took a taxi and drove off there. That was good practice after the style of Mussolini's "March on Rome"—in a railroad car. When the demonstrators attempted to form columns for the march down to City Hall, the police interfered and a fight took place. Amter, Foster and Minor were picked up like fugitive pickpockets, arrested and sent to jail for a short term.

But the Union Square demonstration was used by the Communist International in Russia and throughout Europe as evidence that bloody revolutionary battles had taken place in the United States. *Die Rote Fahne*—the mouthpiece of the Comintern in Berlin—reported that the demonstrators were confronted by an army of twenty-five thousand policemen. But the demonstrators, according to this inspired story, refused to budge. When the police opened fire from the roof tops with machine guns, a bloody street battle developed which lasted into the late hours of the evening. Europe was informed that barricades were raised in Detroit and that, in the alleged demonstration of eighty thousand before the White House in Washington, D. C., thirty were wounded and over forty arrested. Thus Europe learned that the third period spelled the doom of capitalism, for even in the most powerful capitalist country in the world, and surely the richest, the masses were in revolt and revolutionary struggles were taking place, including street fighting and the rearing of barricades.

The same story was repeated with the instruction by the Communist International to organize and lead the Negro masses of the United States, for which the Comintern provided a lot of money. The attitude of the Communists was based upon the belief that the Negroes constituting, as they do, the most impoverished and most exploited section of our population, a section which has special problems and grievances because of racial discrimination and persecution, would constitute, if once properly organized and led, the front rank fighters in a revolution to replace our present republic with a Soviet form of government. Hence, the Party created a special Negro department, built special Negro organizations, issued Negro papers and periodicals, made every inducement for Negroes to join the Party, took advantage of every opportunity to penetrate existing Negro organizations and to participate in Negro movements, for the purpose of bringing its program before the Negro masses. The Party membership was impressed with the importance of Negro work. Every new Negro member brought into the Party was looked upon as a Communist achievement, and the Negro Communists were actually accorded special privileges.

Our Negro program was originally built around the demand that the Negro people in the United States be accorded full racial, social and political equality. Yet in spite of our efforts and the large sums of money spent on that sort of propaganda, we made very little headway among the Negro masses. The Negroes in the United States refused to flock into the Communist Party and gave little credence to our promises. At the Sixth World Congress of the Communist International in 1928 a special commission was therefore constituted to study the Negro question. This commission, on which the American Party was well represented, reached some startling conclusions, which brought about a very radical change in our Negro policy.

I first received word of the change in policy when I was touring the South during the Presidential election campaign of 1928. I received a telegram from the National Office that, in addition to our regular Negro demands, I should add the demand for the right of the Negroes to national self-determination. This demand of the Comintern that the Negro movement in the United States be considered as a movement of national liberation, the ultimate objective of which was the establishment of an independent Negro state and government in the South, though it originated in Moscow, did not appeal to me. I was against the whole proposition and during the closing weeks of the campaign I did not once refer to it or advocate it. In all my speeches I did not venture beyond the advocacy of full racial, social and political equality for the Negro. The demand for a Negro republic I considered dynamite, which would be so explosive in the South that it would do the Negroes more harm than good.

At the close of the campaign when I returned to New York I made it my special point to discuss the whole question with Pepper, who had written a pamphlet for the Party called, "American Negro Problems," in which the new Comintern policy on the American Negro question was outlined. I asked Pepper: "What do you want to do with this policy? Create a situation in the South where you will bring about a civil war between the whites and the blacks? Do you realize where that will lead to? Do you not realize that such a policy will lead to the butchery and massacre of thousands of Negroes?"

I explained to him that, if properly presented, the Negro demand for justice and equality could be offered to the people of the South in such a way that they might lend a receptive ear to what we had to say on the subject. I gave him example after example of cases in which blacks and whites united against landlords and industrial exploiters. I gave him examples of what had taken place among the sharecroppers, to show that there was a possibility, if we fought on economic and political issues, of overcoming the race lines and uniting both white and black in a common struggle. "But," I concluded, "now you propose a policy which would make the white population in the south a minority group, who must subjugate themselves to the political dominance of the Negroes. Remember the tragic experiences following immediately after the close of the American Civil War, which clearly indicate that against any such Negro domination the white people of the South, irrespective of class divisions, would rise like one man. If you advocate that policy, you are certain to close the South to the Party and to inflict great harm upon the Negro masses, for which they would indeed not be responsible." I expected Pepper to flare up. Instead, he answered quite calmly, "Comrade Gitlow, there is much truth in what you say; but we could not help ourselves in Moscow. The Russians on the Commission could only see the American Negro question in the light of the minorities question which existed in Russia before the Revolution. Had we not fallen in line, we would have been severely condemned as deviators and *khvostists* * who neglect work among the Negro masses."

The fight for Negro self-determination was therefore put in the forefront of the Party's Presidential campaign of 1928. Fol-

* *Khvostist*—one who lags behind a [horse's] tail.

lowing Comintern instructions, the Party made every effort to attract the Negro masses. In this respect the Gastonia case and later the Scottsboro case played a large part, though the Gastonia case did not involve Negro workers. The campaign for a Negro republic in the South was tied up with a campaign in the Party ranks against white chauvinism. Party members who failed to carry out the Negro policy or disagreed with it were accused of white chauvinism. However, if they recanted and admitted their guilt and promised to be unprejudiced in the future, their membership was continued. The Negro question was injected into every situation, in every campaign. The Negroes were looked upon as the chosen people who were to be the vanguard of the Communist revolution. Party members were urged to make every effort to establish personal as well as social relations with the Negroes. Negroes were brought into the Party, not on the basis of their Communist convictions, but on the promise that in the Party they could enjoy a sociable evening together with whites on a basis of equality. Negroes who had recently joined the Party were pushed into places of leadership simply because they were Negroes and as a demonstration that the Negroes enjoyed preferred treatment in the Party. This was done not out of sympathy or consideration for the Negro masses, but for purely political reasons.

Behind the Negro agitation and the stress laid on exploiting the Negro issue was the desire to comply with the orders from Moscow. It was hoped through a Negro minorities movement in the United States to give leadership to a colored nationalist movement of world proportions in the countries of South and Central America, Africa, Asia and the Antipodes. The American Nationalist Negro movement, Moscow believed, would provide the leadership for such a world movement. Besides, the Communist Party could dominate the American Negro movement, because it was believed possible for a small handful of American Communists to organize and control the two million Negro workers in American industry, which force could be the most decisive in the broader world-wide Negro movement. The Party was instructed by the Comintern that to fight for the admission of the Negro workers into the unions was not enough; the

Party must immediately begin the organization of the two million Negro workers into purely Negro unions. Said the Comintern resolution:

> To the extent to which the Party succeeds in developing a strong revolutionary Negro movement in the United States, it will also be able to exert a decisive influence upon the revolutionary movement of the Negroes in all parts of the world.

It was hoped by the development of this Negro nationalist movement on a world scale to bring millions of new supporters in defense of the Soviet Union, ardent supporters, who could actually fight against Russia's enemies over a far-flung territory. The Negro nationalist movement was thus part and parcel of Russian political imperialism.

The "third period" was taken very seriously by the Communist Party. Grace Burnham, heiress to a substantial capitalist fortune, wrote a pamphlet on the unemployed situation called, "Fight or Starve!" Every opportunity was taken to stage demonstrations. Party members were organized to turn the demonstrations into militant affairs and particularly into pitched battles against the police. The slogan was issued that "Only the communists fight for the working class." All others in the labor movement were branded as Social-Fascists. A campaign was started against the Social-Fascists, which term generally implied the Socialists. Bands were organized to break up Socialist street meetings under the slogan of, "The right to the streets belongs to the Communists!" The labor party—an idea that was beginning to take root in the United States—was denounced as laying the basis for Fascism. In order to attack it, the comrades brought in from over the ocean that Pied Piper of Stalinism and nephew of a distinguished Englishman, John Strachey. Every act of the American government was denounced as Fascist. So was everything else not sponsored by Communists. When the trade unionists and the Socialists of New York called an anti-Fascist mass meeting in Madison Square Garden, the Communists were sent down by Earl Browder to demand that the platform be denied to the "Fascist La Guardia" and turned over to the Communists, and, when their request was refused, they turned the meeting into an "anti-Fascist" riot and broke it up. Red Front Fighters units were organized. Its members were dressed in uniforms that imitated those of the Red Army. They drilled assiduously and prepared for the day when real fighting was to take place against all who did not approve of the Communists and were therefore ipso facto either Fascists or worse—Social-Fascists.

This was the peak of the period when the members of the Communist Party wore leather jackets and caps and when the girls went also dressed in leather jackets, and walked as a matter of principle on low-heeled shoes. The Communists were living in a play world of their own. In Russia the Five-Year Plan was achieving miracles in Socialism; in the United States capitalism was tottering. The Communists, who gave color and life and romance to Union Square, lived on the vision of a Soviet America in the making. No wonder the Russian magazine *Stroika* wrote on May twenty-fifth, 1930:

> Across the ocean in the land of democracy there is great social unrest. It expresses itself in great strikes and demonstrations and in individual terrorist acts. Those responsible for these acts are never discovered. Last April on Broadway, the main street of New York, fifteen bombs exploded in one day, making lots of noise and damage.

These bombings were never heard of and never took place. This bit of Russian fiction, directly or indirectly supplied by Union Square, reflected the state of the movement in the United States, which in all its phases was completely out of step with the realities and the life of the country.

Shortly after the Seventh Congress of the Comintern in August, 1935, Browder returned from Moscow with a new program, which completely reversed this wild-eyed revolutionism, and instead entailed support of the New Deal. The third period was forgotten. American capitalism was no longer in the process of decay, American democracy was no longer a snare and a delusion, but such a vital prerequisite for the well-being of the country that the people ought to be prepared to defend it with their very lives. The comrades discarded their leather jackets and low-heeled shoes for the haberdashery of Babbitts and for high-heeled shoes. Communism found its way into Park Avenue pent-houses, put on sophisticated airs and sipped cocktails. The thousand and one strictly proletarian art and literature clubs, which had begun at the end of our leadership with John Reed Clubs and Worker's Theater Leagues, shifted to the arts, theater and writers projects under Roosevelt's W. P. A., which were developed into a special sphere of Communist influence to such an extent that they captured this New Deal domain for their own Party uses. They did not stop here, but invaded the haunts of the Roosevelt Bohemians. The latter, being truly innocent, have fallen for their long talk, which all seems innocuous. Yet even back of this policy stands Stalin, who underwrites it for his own selfish reasons. The Stalinist axiom, which underlies all Communist policy, whether it be in China, Madagascar or the United States, is that Communism triumphs or fails with the Soviet Union.

To Stalinists, Communism and the Soviet Union are synonymous. The defense of the Soviet Union takes precedence over all other considerations. All Communists are Soviet Union patriots first. The policy which Stalin has launched in the United States rests upon deceit. As far back as 1927, when I was in Moscow, the attitude toward the United States in the event of war was discussed. Privately it was the opinion of all the Russian leaders to whom I spoke that the rivalry between the United States and Japan must eventually break out into a war between these two. The Russians were hopeful that the war would break out soon, because that would greatly secure the safety of Russia's Siberian borders and would so weaken Japan that Russia would no longer have to fear an attack from her in the East. Stalin hopes through the activities of the American Communist Party to create a public opinion in the United States that would favor a war, presumably in the defense of democracy against the encroachment of Fascism, but actually against Japan. Stalin is perfectly willing to let Americans die in defense of the Soviet Union, even if they are not members of the Communist Party.

In order to help Stalin in this, the American Communist Party had to become ostensibly both respectable and patriotic.

Instead of seeking the overthrow of the government, the Party now pretends to be its most loyal supporter and defender. Instead of decrying American democracy as a cloak for the capitalist "strike-breaking Fascist government of the United States," the Party declares no sacrifice too great can be made in its defense. Russia is proclaimed as one of the great democratic powers and the United States is called upon to line up with the democratic dictatorship of the Soviet Union in defense of democracy. The anti-militarist, the anti-imperialist positions of the Party have been relegated to the background, the charges against American imperialism in Mexico, Nicaragua, the Philippines, Latin America and China have been entirely forgotten.

Should Russian international policy shift tomorrow, it would be followed immediately by a shift in policy by the Communist Party of the United States, which today, even while wearing the heavy cloak of respectability, is but a propaganda agency of the Soviet Union. Its protestations of patriotism towards America are as insincere as those of the Nazi German-American Bund. Both fly the American flag, yet both owe their allegiance to a foreign power. Both support dictatorships, one the red, the other the brown. Both bow before Fuehrers—the one Hitler, the other Stalin.

Before the Party became "respectable," its position as stated in a Party resolution was, "American Imperialism to an interesting extent leads and directs the war preparations against the Soviet Union." Today Browder proclaims that the United States is against aggression and for peace. Before the Party became "respectable," it proclaimed:

> The Pope, the British Archbishops, Protestant Churches, Jewish Rabbis, the Salvation Army, all religious sects, all peddlers of religious opium, were mobilized for the defense of the Russian Kulaks, thus giving a clear example of the international imperialist united front of cross and cannon against the Soviet Union.

This declaration did not stop Browder, after he was ordered to do so by the Comintern, from appealing to the Pope and to all Catholics to make a united front with the Communist Party of the United States in defense of the workers' living standards, in defense of Democracy and for a common front against the Fascist countries. Should Stalin conclude a pact with Hitler or Japan, and Soviet foreign policy change its course, the Communist policy in the United States would shift accordingly, and Browder would go forth to laud it ardently. Such acrobatics are executed with an agility that is marvelous. They constitute what the Communists call flexible tactics and clever maneuvering. Basically only one principle dominates the Communist program—power. The power of the Stalin regime must be maintained and extended throughout the world. Towards this end everything is justifiable.

But I admit that this was not apparent to me—certainly not with such lucidity—while I was myself a leading member of the Communist Party. Nor did I then see with any degree of clarity the parallel developments inside the Comintern and inside the American Party. I do not believe that any of us really understood where our factionalism was leading. Yet it is clear today that by 1928 the Communist movement all over the world was beginning to crack up and that out of it was emerging the totalitarian regime of Stalinism parallel to the Mussolini regime in Italy and presaging the advent of Hitler. The Trosky fight inside the Russian Party, which had started a half a dozen years before, was the first symptom that all was not well with the affairs of the Communist International. By 1929, the Russian Party, the largest party and the one that dominated the International, was split into a number of factions. The Trotsky faction was the largest and most important. Together with the Bukharin faction it included the most popular and powerful figures in the government and the Party. Against them Stalin had to use the most ruthless methods in the Russian Party and the Communist International in order to hold on to his power. By 1929 every Communist Party was drawn into the crisis created by the intense internal war raging in the Russian Communist Party.

Stalin had decided to clean out the Communist International, to drive out all elements that might be suspected of developing, at some future date, independent views. He was determined that the leadership in every Communist Party should be made up of persons of whose lack of independence there would be no doubt and who would be completely subservient to him. Only those leaders were continued in the Communist Party or given leadership over parties who realized that their leadership depended upon Stalin's favors. Thaelmann, the head of the German Party, was continued, precisely because he had been involved in the Wittdorf scandal (an account of which is given in Chapter XV) and owed the saving of his neck to Stalin. Browder, the leader of the American Party, was put into the leadership of the American Party for precisely the same reasons, because Stalin had saved Browder's neck in the Chinese scandal. In every party the most tried and trusted leaders of the movement—tried in battle and trusted by the masses—fell under Stalin's axe precisely because of their integrity, prestige and independence, and their places were taken by sycophants beholden only to Stalin.

The crisis in the Communist movement manifested itself in numerous splits and the formation of opposition groups in all the parties. An examination of the German Party, the one next in size to the Russian, will disclose how deep had been the disintegration in Communist ranks. Practically every important leader of the German Communist movement, from its inception up to the advent of Hitler, has been either expelled from the Comintern or executed as a traitor in Russia. The Party which once boasted a membership of close to four hundred thousand and a vote of almost six million has disintegrated completely. It has no membership that is worth considering, its leadership is unknown and inarticulate. That this should happen to a party which had in back of it the resources of the Soviet Union and was subsidized by Moscow with millions of dollars is evidence that the source of the trouble in the international Communist movement is basic and deeply rooted. The unfortunate personality of Stalin, his twisted psychology, his narrowness of vision and his inability to understand the western world are all contributing factors, not the basic, the fundamental cause. The Communist movement is, in my opinion, quite beyond redemption. It is doomed to progressive degeneration.

Stalin's frantic swings in policy, his desperate efforts to force issues by exercising the sheer power of his will, his blood-letting purges always culminate in new and more serious crises, which drive him on to ever more desperate measures. The opposition elements, the real and fancied enemies from within, continue to germinate and to spread throughout the Communist movement as well as in the most vital branches of the Soviet government. These manifestations are not only an expression of opposition to Stalinism but, what is much more important, they are symptomatic of the fact that Communism in practice does not work. True, in its early stages Communist theory was predicated on the concept of world revolution. Hence, certain Communists (Trotsky is the most prominent among them) apologize for the failure of Communism in practice by pleading that the very attempt to establish Communism in one isolated country, even one as rich as the Soviet Union in potential wealth, land and people, is responsible for the crisis in Communism. But I find this position untenable. It is not only utopian but asinine to assume the simultaneous fruition of developments in a sufficient number of countries and to such an extent as would guarantee the victory of the Communist revolution on a world scale. That has been made so crystal clear by post-War history that only the most self-deluded of wishful thinkers fail to see it now. Moreover, the least that could be expected of a regime that has held continual sway for over twenty years, with complete control over the entire economy of the country, is that it would satisfy in some measure the most elementary needs of the masses. Communism in practice has failed to pass even this test. Indeed, it is this failure which has found its political counterpart in an autocratic and corrupt machine, a super-Tammany Hall. Notwithstanding the widely-publicized fabrications about the prosperity and the happy Stalinist life in the Soviet Union, it is precisely because of its economic failures that Communism was obliged to seek refuge in absolutism. Only a diseased social organism leans heavily on the crutch of police power to maintain its authority and the vestiges of its tatterdemalion prestige. The reaction to this illness was slow in asserting itself.

In the Russian Party the reaction, as a rule, came over immediate economic issues. In the Communist parties of other countries the reaction is predominantly political and strangely enough for that very reason far more important, for it signifies that the Communists of the foreign countries who have broken away from the Russian orbit are beginning to have some very serious doubts about the infallibility of the Communist International. No matter how vehemently or how often these opposition elements may proclaim from the housetops that they are the original and the only true disciples of Bolshevik Communism and of its founder Lenin, back of their words is the germ of those doubts, implanted in the belief, however thoroughly suppressed inside of them, that the whole organic structure of Communism is probably at fault. Among many of these opposition elements is now developing a profound differentiation from official Stalinist Communism. Sooner or later Communism itself is bound to become the object of their most devastating criticism. The apparent numerical insignificance of the oppositions at the present moment is no criterion of their symptomatic importance. The Communist International and the Soviet power which backs it up, notwithstanding the unlimited resources, cannot squelch the oppositions. Their criticisms, their exposures keep mounting as the prestige and sanctity of Communism diminishes.

The struggle against Trotsky and Trotskyism, which began in the Russian Party even before the death of Lenin, and the campaign against the so-called Right Wingers headed by Bukharin, which started in 1928 and culminated in Stalin openly becoming the supreme power in Russia, had its repercussions throughout the Communist movement, including our American Party. In the years 1928 and 1929, the Communist parties of all countries were subjected to purges. As a result of these purges the outstanding leaders of the parties were expelled, and the parties split. The parties officially recognized by the Comintern after these purges became known as the Stalinist parties, their members being called Stalinists. The oppositions were either Communist parties which refused to obey Stalin, as the Swedish Communist Party, or oppositions which assumed different names.

The Communist Party in the United States did not escape

this purge. The first ones to fall were the Cannonites, who had an alliance with the Foster group. Cannon, with his followers, were expelled in 1928 for organizing a Trotsky opposition. Cannon's conversion to Trotskyism was a complete surprise to us, because Cannon and Shachtman, the leaders of the newly-formed Trotsky opposition, had never before indicated any sympathy for the views of Trotsky. If Cannon was a Trotskyist why did he not spring to defense of Lore when Ruthenberg castigated Lore for Trotskyism in 1924? An examination of the Party records will prove that both Shachtman and Cannon had always voted against Trotsky. They had been active as Party leaders in conducting the campaign to counteract Trotskyism as Menshevism, as an anti-Soviet tendency. What caused the sudden conversion? Trotsky has never kept his political views a secret.

The expulsion of Cannon and his disciples was followed up by a campaign of violence against the Trotsky movement in the United States, which at first called itself the Opposition Group, Workers (Communist) Party. Every effort was made by the official Communist Party to tie up the Trotsky movement with the counter-revolutionary forces fighting against the Soviet Union. After Cannon's expulsion from the Party, Lovestone arranged a raid upon Cannon's living quarters, in order to steal his personal records and those of the Trotsky movement, which were stored there. Cannon's apartment was broken into by his erstwhile comrades, Jack Stachel and Ravich, then the business manager of the *Daily Worker*. All of Cannon's records were stolen and brought to Stachel's house, where they were examined by Lovestone, Pepper and Stachel. No counter-revolutionary material was discovered, of course, but that did not prevent Lovestone from preparing a story for the *Daily Worker*, illustrated with photostats of Comrade Cannon's correspondence, to prove that Cannon, the American Trotskyite, aided and abetted by Max Eastman, was leading a world-wide counter-revolutionary campaign against the Soviet Union. The whole business was not only nasty; it was stupid—and so utterly futile!

Whatever was Cannon's game, the Trotsky group succeeded in enlisting only a fraction of the Cannon caucus. Most of the

Cannonites preferred to remain in the Party. However, the handful of about fifty Trotskyites were a determined group, for we soon discovered that all the strong arm tactics which the Party employed against them, far from dispersing them, drew them closer together. We invested them with the strength and the halo of martyrdom by persecuting them. In power, we repeated the stupidest errors of the most provincial police department.

CHAPTER XIV

STALIN SETS HIS TRAPS FOR THE LOVESTONE-GITLOW LEADERSHIP

THROUGHOUT this book I have laid perhaps undue stress on the evils of factionalism. That factionalism is a bitter potion to swallow and one that poisons the organism, is, I believe, beyond dispute. But as long as individual differences persist and opinons vary, the natural and human thing to do inside any political party, as in any other social organism, is to band together into a faction and defend those beliefs jointly. I cannot see anything wrong in that; on the contrary, I believe such a course to be fundamental to the democratic processes. Man is a thinking and emotional animal. He may find his convictions and ideals more precious to him than his daily bread. Some may look upon this as an aberration, overclever psychologists may dismiss such a manifestation as a "defense mechanism" or a form of "compensation" for some defect in the personality, yet this tendency in mankind is a factor that has laid its impress on history. It is only fitting and proper that men of convictions should proclaim them and defend them, individually and in groups. Naturally, when groups holding opposing views clash, passions are aroused, bitterness is engendered, feelings are hurt, recriminations take place, conniving is practiced—all distasteful consequences. All of that is the seamy side of a democratic regime. I have been unsparing in presenting it—not because I repudiate the democratic way of life, but, on the contrary, because I adhere to it more than ever before, with full knowledge of its negative aspects. I have no illusions about democracy. Its defects are legion. But I am convinced that there is but one way to rectify its faults—by more democracy, by extending and deepening the democratic way of life.

The perniciousness in the factionalism that existed in the American Communist Party leadership and affected the entire membership, the amorality it fostered, the corruption it spread was not due to the democratic regime that prevailed in the Party but rather to the constraint placed upon that regime. And the source of that constraint was Moscow. The prestige of the Bolsheviks was so overwhelming that it instilled in us far too much humility toward the Russian leaders. We Communists in America were convinced that they alone knew the magic formula for effecting a proletarian revolution. It is beside the point at this juncture of the discussion that we were wrong in entertaining such a belief, that time has proven conclusively the non-existence of any such magic formula. At the time we believed that the Russian leaders were super-strategists of revolution. We looked upon them as our teachers. We came to them with unbounded faith in their wisdom, brushing aside our own judgments as erroneous or irrelevant, whenever they disagreed with the judgments of the Russians. That was our mistake. The crime of the Russians was that they not only encouraged this attitude of humility, but demanded it as their due. They were puffed up with pride. They played around with the leaders of the non-Russian Communist parties as a boy plays with his tin soldiers. They turned us into flunkies—and we let them, because we loved Communism more than our very lives. That was the beginning of our degeneration as revolutionists, as Communists and as decent human beings. That turned us into servile courtiers intriguing against each other, to win the favor of the Russians. How could we practice party democracy, with that blight upon us? We were competing servitors who could not call our souls our own. Everything we might decide among ourselves was subject to the whims and desires of the men from Moscow. Everything we thought and did was by the grace of Moscow.

The advent of Stalin in the Comintern political machine, as his advent to supreme power in the Russian Party, merely crystallized, organized and solidified a condition that had previously been in a fluent state. Stalinism is the *reductio ad absurdum* of Leninism. It is the proof of the pudding. Lenin was dodging responsibility when he predicted that Stalin is a cook that would prepare some peppery dishes. Stalin's dishes were all prepared by Lenin—with the aid of Trotsky, Zinoviev, Bukharin and the whole Bolshevik Old Guard—and Stalin has been serving them from time to time as they cooked and were ready to serve. True, he might have thrown some pepper into the pot as he watched the dishes cook—pepper is a seasoning to which that cook is rather partial—but Lenin was not averse to pepper, either, and used it liberally in preparing his dishes. Take the treatment of Paul Levi in Germany, of Serratti and the Italian Socialist Party in the days when Zinoviev was head of the Comintern under the personal tutelage of Lenin, and you will find astounding similarity between the ways of Lenin and Stalin in the treatment of non-Russian Communist leaders and the non-Russian Communist parties. It is Lenin who taught cold cynicism to the Bolsheviks. It is Lenin who sowed the seeds of mistrust and toadyism in the Comintern. Stalin garnered the crop. What was in the process of maturing under Lenin has matured under Stalin.

The removal of the Lovestone-Gitlow leadership marks the advent of Stalinism in the American Communist Party. Stalin's Juggernaut rolled over that leadership, and, as it moved, practically all American devotees of Communism flung themselves under its wheels. The American Party, having thus achieved a state of political coma, if not Nirvana, was then added to Stalin's collection of puppets. He put an end to factionalism in the American Party, even as he put an end to it in the Russian Party and throughout the Comintern—even as he put an end to it in Russia itself and for a time in Spain under the Loyalists, although not completely—even as Mussolini put an end to party politics and all expression of independent thinking in Italy and Hitler in Germany. He did it by directly appointing the Leader of the American Party and subjecting him completely to Russian plenipotentiaries with full powers derived directly from Stalin. The decisions of these secret emissaries of Stalin are translated by the Party leader into immutable laws for the entire Party. Whatever latitude today's leader—Earl Browder—happens to enjoy in the exercise of his office, he has by the grace and indulgence of these emissaries from Moscow, who administer the American Communist Party as a branch of Stalin's worldwide political machine. Thus the semblance of hundred percent harmony and unanimity is achieved. Now liquidations of dissidents take place quietly, without any back talk. Peace and harmony have been achieved in the American Party—just as peace and harmony have been achieved, say, in Nazi Germany. It's a case of you gotta eat strawberries and you gotta like 'em. It is the Lovestone-Gitlow leadership that fought the last and losing battle against the institution of this totalitarian régime in the American Communist Party.

Of course, the seeds of that totalitarianism already existed during the Lovestone-Gitlow régime. For example: I returned from Moscow to attend the 1928 Presidential nominating convention of the Party with five thousand dollars of Russian money in my jeans, as the first installment of Moscow's contribution of thirty-five thousand dollars to our Presidential campaign. That in turn was part of the quarter million dollars we used to receive annually under special grants for specific purposes. For our 1924 Presidential campaign Moscow had contributed fifty thousand dollars. Having started *The Daily Worker* on its career with an initial donation of thirty-five thousand dollars, Moscow has continued to feed into that hopper never less than that sum annually. Of course, Moscow's financial contributions to the American Communist Party in my day were only a very small part of what they are today, when Moscow is undisputed boss; but the seed of financial control was already planted then. Similarly with political control. We had our Comintern emissaries. True, we could argue with them and even have them overruled by appealing over their heads directly to Moscow, playing one Russian leader against another on occasions—something utterly unthinkable today, when Browder has only the privilege of accepting orders not only from Stalin's Russian emissaries but even from Jack Stachel—but Moscow was already the court of last resort. Thus were the seeds of Stalin's totalitarian control over the American Party already planted. Nor were we ourselves remiss in behaving like totalitarian bosses. Although a nominating convention was called, staged in imitation of such conventions as held by Republicans and Democrats, with four hundred and fifty regular and fraternal delegates on hand, there was really no need for holding it, for months before it convened the Political Committee had decided that Foster would be the Party's candidate for President and I for Vice-President of the United States.

The convention was called for the purpose of approving the choice of the Political Committee and to get publicity for the Communist candidates. All the resolutions, the Party platform and even the campaign committee and manager had already been decided upon. Naturally, the convention, which listened to speeches for several days, ran as smoothly as a well oiled machine. On the last day, when nominations were to take place, every delegate knew in advance who the nominees were to be. Horns, rattles and all kinds of noise makers were supplied to both visitors and delegates. When Foster was nominated the Communist candidate for President of the United States, cheerleaders whipped the gathering into a frenzy which lasted about half an hour. The same thing happened when I was nominated for Vice-President. Jay Lovestone stood behind the curtains with a watch in his hand, to make sure that the tumultuous and spontaneous demonstrations lasted the required length of time. Comrades shrieked and bellowed, blew their tin horns, jumped on tables and stamped with their feet. Snake dances were organized and bedlam reigned supreme. In this way we served notice upon the United States that we were an American party and were nominating our candidates in the traditional American manner. After it was all over the comrades looked at each other sheepishly and burst into laughter, because they realized it was a huge farce and staged for outside consumption. The whole affair lacked the tone of sincerity.

But after the nominating convention the things that did matter were taken up. The delegates who came from all over the country actually represented the important Party leaders. A Party conference followed at which the real Party problems were taken up. This was followed by individual conferences for the purpose of lining up important people from the districts with our group. Pepper's policy of appeasement toward the Foster group was not proceeding as that wily Hungarian had expected. Foster had agreed to make a number of political statements jointly with Pepper and Lovestone, but he never could be pinned down to agree to definite organizational proposals. On the question of Party jobs he always demanded his pound of flesh, which depended upon the removal of one or more of our people and putting Fosterites in their places. I had many conferences with Pepper and Lovestone on the relative merits of an appeasement policy and the so-called hard line. I told them frankly that I was opposed to appeasement and would support the position of our rank and file. The Pepper policy finally collapsed, when Foster revived the war against the Majority and openly intensified the activities of his caucus. He had evidently received inside advice as to the new currents manifesting themselves in Russian political life.

The first sign we had that our status in Moscow was not in good shape reached us in a cable from the Comintern, which sharply condemned the Party for its lack of principles in the election campaign. The cable was ostensibly based on information the Communist International had culled from one of the documents issued to the Party members in the form of instructions on how to gather signatures for the petitions which were needed to put our candidates on the ballot. In this document the comrades were instructed that the most important thing was to obtain signatures, for only the required number of signatures could put us on the ballot.

In securing signatures the comrades were advised to refrain from mentioning the fact that the candidates were Communists, to avoid rousing the anti-Communist bias. In addition, the Political Committee decided that, in the states where we were unable to obtain the required number of signatures, we should hire professional signature-gatherers. Alexander Trachtenberg was the one who had reported on these matters in the Political Committee, and his report was unanimously approved, because there was no other way possible for getting our candidates on the ballot, and we took the position that since the presentation of Communist principles and issues could most effectively be done during the election campaign, it was folly to think that it should be done while gathering signatures. The Communist International trounced us severely on a matter about which it knew absolutely nothing.

Foster immediately assumed a righteous attitude and made a factional issue of it in the Party, although he had voted for the signature-garnering procedure along with the rest of us. He deserted the ship, as it were, when it was up to all of us to find a way of squaring ourselves with the Communist International criticism. The purpose of Foster's maneuver was, of course, to make the Lovestone-Gitlow leadership take the blame for it all alone. But Lovestone found a better way. He obtained a scapegoat in Julius Codkind, who, as Trachtenberg's assistant, had sent out the letter of instructions. He induced Codkind, who was a loyal Lovestone supporter, to take all the blame entirely upon himself. Codkind was forced to confess that he sent out the unprincipled letter of instructions without the knowledge or approval of the Central Executive Committee. For this he was censored publicly in the press and removed from his post.

The Political Committee drew up a resolution fully agreeing with the Comintern criticisms and drawing the necessary lessons from the same for the benefit of the Party membership. Codkind, who was a very loyal and devoted Communist, among the founders of the Communist movement, did not take his condemnation lightly. He spoke to me and complained that, while he had made the sacrifice in the interest of the Party and its leadership, he was of the opinion that the Party acted wrongly in making him the scapegoat. He resented particularly Trachtenberg's attitude. Trachtenberg was the campaign manager and his direct superior. In the Political Committee Trachtenberg attacked him with bitterness and as if he alone were criminally responsible. Codkind, who was more of a rank-and-filer than a Party official, went around a beaten man.

But Codkind's sacrifice on the altar of Party unity did not change matters. Signatures continued to be obtained as outlined in the famous letter of instructions. Indeed, during the closing weeks allotted for obtaining signatures, in those places where some of the comrades could not get away with copying names out of telephone books, professional signature-gatherers were hired and thousands of dollars were paid out to them. Our Party leadership had learned from the Russians not only how to supply the scapegoat, but also how to get him to confess to crimes he never committed. This should be kept in mind when considering the confessions of Russian Communist leaders.

The Sixth World Congress of the Communist International opened in Moscow on July seventeenth, 1928. The American delegates to the Congress, over twenty in number, representing the Party's outstanding leaders, left the country about the middle of June. In the present delegation practically the entire Political Committee of the Party departed, two-thirds of the Secretariat and the heads of most of the important departments. Foster, the Party's candidates for President of the United States, was among those who had left, although it meant that the Presidential candidate of the Party would be away during practically the entire campaign. Since February the Party had been traveling on ocean liners. From February to the end of September, when the Sixth World Congress adjourned, was a period of seven months. The situation might be used as a comical setting for a light opera laid in Moscow and New York with scenes aboard trans-Atlantic liners thrown in sidelights. But behind it all was the underlying fact that to us the situation in the United States was of minor importance to what was going on in Moscow. It furthermore proves more effectively than documents and records that the real center of the Communist organization for the United States as well as for other countries has always been Moscow. During the Sixth World Congress Moscow was like the capital of a far flung Red Empire whose emissaries came from all corners of the world to demonstrate their loyalty and to pay tribute to their masters.

With the departure of the delegates the factional war broke out in the Party on a scale never before equaled. Upon the arrival of the delegates in Moscow it seemed as if the events at the Congress were adding hot coals to the factional war spreading in our midst. The official reports on the Congress emanating from Moscow indicated that at the Congress there was no friction, that perfect Communist unanimity prevailed. I kept sending cables to Lovestone on the factional situation in

America, and in return got replies that were reassuring and gave no key to developments at the Congress.

The most active agent of the Foster group in New York was a small man whose name was Costrell. He had never been connected with the English-speaking movement of the Party, being a leader of the Jewish Federation. His leadership depended upon his loud mouth, his intense factional background and his ability to make deals with the important people in the Jewish Federation. He never engaged in constructive Party work, was not active in the unions and had no standing whatsoever with the masses.

But precisely because he was a harmful person, he was a "power" in the Party with whom one had to reckon. Not only was his English so atrocious that one could hardly understand him, but he was unable even to speak the Yiddish language correctly. Yet this cog in the Foster caucus was Bittleman's chief adjutant. In the factional fight, on which he thrived, he displayed tireless energy. He worked morning, noon and night for his faction. When he could not win an argument on intellectual grounds he would disregard all rules of procedure, all time limits and attempt to make up for his shortcomings by shouting and refusing to stop. And when Costrell began to shout, victory was his, for his voice was so rasping and his manner so exasperating that it caused me unendurable pain. Imagine the sharp grating of gears, the rubbing of coarse sandpaper and the smashing up of a china closet, and you will get some idea of the tone of his voice. He was about four feet two inches tall and strutted around erectly like a game cock. His intense activity, running in and out of all Party offices and headquarters, caused me great anxiety. I knew something important was up, so, I decided to have him watched.

I called in Comrade Levitch, who was one of the most trusted members of our group and who in the past had engaged in confidential work for us. I told him of my concern over the activities of Costrell, informed him that it would not be amiss to keep a close watch on him and if possible to obtain the black brief case which he hugged closely wherever he went. I had already received reports that Fosterites were going around crowing in the Party and claiming that Stalin was supporting them. We also decided on a plan of action. We knew that every week end the Fosterites went to Camp Unity, one of the Party's camps, in Wingdale, N. Y., and that Costrell was in the habit of going there. Levitch was to pick himself a trusted assistant and that week end both of them were to go to Wingdale.

With his assistant, Levitch went to the camp and found Costrell there in all his glory. He had his black brief case with him. Levitch and his aide, a young comrade by the name of Stanley, dogged each and every one of his steps. On Sunday afternoon before going into the mess hall, Costrell put down his brief case in one of the tents. Levitch immediately snatched it up and deposited it under a mattress in another tent. After the dinner, Costrell, I was told by Levitch, who still continued to dog him, emerged with a large group of the leaders of the Jewish Federation, writers on *Freiheit,* and workers in the Amtorg. He proceeded to the tent, where he had left his brief case. When he could not find it, he became ashen gray and was speechless for a few moments. The tent was turned upside down. Costrell began to shout like a madman. Then a large group of Fosterites who were at the camp were rounded up and divided into groups to search the place for the ones who had stolen the brief case. They armed themselves with sticks, beat bushes, and gave every evidence that they were on a real man hunt. Levitch decided it was time to leave. The rain began coming down in torrents. Levitch grabbed up the brief case from the tent in which he had hidden it and together with Stanley beat a hasty retreat out of the camp through the woods.

On Monday morning Levitch appeared in my office drenched to the skin, a broad grin on his face. "Comrade Gitlow, I got the stuff. Everything." He gave me the brief case. What I read was a revelation to me. I had obtained copies of the latest documents issued by the Foster caucus for underground dissemination in the Party. I read confidential letters sent by Bittleman, Foster, and the other Fosterites from Moscow. The letter I was after, the most important one, was a two-page single-spaced letter from Foster telling about a private confidential interview he had with Stalin. The letter made some startling disclosures.

Foster claimed in his letter that Stalin informed him that Bukharin was a Right-Winger and supported the Right Wing elements generally in the Communist International. He told Foster that that accounted for the support which Bukharin gave to the Lovestone group. He informed Foster that his differences with Bukharin extended over a long period of time, but that the time had come when Bukharin's Right Wing deviations could no longer be tolerated. He further let Foster know that he was ready to support him in the American Party. But when Foster explained to him that the Lovestone group was in the Majority, Stalin replied, "We Bolsheviks know how to reward good fighters. When you go back to America make a good fight. You will get my support."

I had such faith in the probity and decency of all Russian Bolsheviks, "the heroes of October" so-called, that I considered the Foster letter merely a very treacherous piece of factional connivance. I was certain that what Foster reported were his distortions of what Stalin had really said to him. I had known Foster to do that before. I had seen letters of Foster distorting Moscow developments which were against him into victories for himself. Acting on that presumption, and ignorant of the actual state of affairs, I did something I should not have otherwise done. Nor was I alone of the leaders left in America kept in ignorance of the facts we had a right to know. Jack Stachel, who had Lovestone's confidence even more than I, had also received no information as to what was really happening. After consultation with Stachel and other leading comrades in America I sent a long cable to Moscow, giving in detail Foster's letter. I was subsequently told that upon the receipt of my cable a meeting of the Russian delegation at the Congress was called, at which both Bukharin and Stalin were present. It was at this meeting that the reply to my cable was drafted, in which it was stated that there were absolutely no differences among the Russian leaders, that they were in complete accord on all the decisions of the Congress and on all the issues in the Russian Party as well. When I received this authoritative reply from the Russian comrades I was convinced that Bill Foster was a liar and a forger. I publicized the cable throughout the American Party as proof that the rumors the Fosterites were spreading, that Stalin would give Foster the leadership of the Party, were absolutely false. I gradually learned—blow by blow, as it were—that at least one "hero of October" excelled all other mortals in the capacity for lying and intrigue.

As subsequent developments proved I had been completely misled about Foster's letter reporting his interview with Stalin. The information given in that letter as to what Stalin had said was correct in every detail. Furthermore, in sending my naïve cable of inquiry I had committed the unpardonable sin of exposing Stalin for the double-crosser he was, a crime he never forgives. The meeting of the Russian delegation was no more than a subterfuge to gain time. Had I known all this, I would not have been surprised when the Russian bear did pounce upon me.

Immediately after this incident I had to start on my vice-Presidential campaign tour, a tour which took me all the way from New York to the Pacific Coast, down through the South and back to New York for the windup. The platform of the Party was called the "Platform of the Class Struggle." The meetings were a little more successful than the meetings in 1924, but on the whole they showed that the Communist Party was not yet able to impress the people of the country with its message. The trip kept me away from the National Office of the Party for over two months.

The delegates to the Sixth World Congress returned in September after I had already started my tour. I met Foster in Pittsburgh on the ninth of September. He was among the first to return and immediately went to Pittsburgh to check up on how our mining campaign was getting on. He was very bitter and very factional when I spoke to him. He did not give me the impression of one who returns a conquering hero. Evidently he had been disappointed in his fight for the Party leadership too many times, and he was not so sure of the future, especially when it was evident to him that our Party leadership had the overwhelming support of the membership. At the same time, Jay Lovestone wrote me about routine Party matters, intimating that I would have to wait until I returned to New York to learn about the real situation in the Comintern and in the Party.

My campaign tour went along without any incidents, until I reached San Diego, California. At my mass meeting in San Diego in Woodbine Hall I received a telegram from William O'Brien, the Party organizer for Arizona, informing me that he was canceling my speaking dates for Tucson and Phoenix and suggesting that I proceed directly to Houston, Texas. I thereupon prolonged my stay in San Diego for one day, and made a stop over on the way to Houston at El Paso, Texas, because I was personally interested in the city, my brother having crossed the border at El Paso during the war in order to avoid being drafted into the Army. After a day in El Paso I proceeded by train directly to Houston. As soon as I arrived there and registered at the Sam Houston Hotel, I was besieged by local newspapermen and representatives of the press associations. Then I learned from the reporters that I had been kidnaped. At least, such was the report issued by the National Office of the American Communist Party. For several days the Party press and newspapers all over the country had been featuring the news of my having been kidnaped, when I left the train at Phoenix, Arizona, by a band of men and left all alone in the middle of the desert. I got rid of the news-hawks and continued with my duties. I spoke in Houston.

From Houston I proceeded to San Antonio, where the press was carrying on a campaign to prevent me from speaking. Screaming headlines appeared in the San Antonio papers insisting that I be not allowed to speak. Halls originally hired for the meetings were closed. However, we were able to secure a hall in the Mexican quarter of San Antonio. About five hundred persons were present. I launched an attack against the press and their whole campaign of trying to prevent me from speaking. From San Antonio I went back to Phoenix, Arizona, to speak. As no hall could be secured, the meeting was held in the public square.

Just before the meeting in Phoenix, I had occasion to discuss the kidnaping farce with O'Brien. I showed him his telegram. He admitted that he had sent it to me. I asked him why he had sent that telegram. He explained that he had been informed by a prominent member of the American Legion that they were organizing a committee of vigilantes to prevent me from speaking in Arizona. He said they had also informed him that they were prepared to drive me out of the state and to dump me into the Mexican part of the desert. I then told him that if that was the true story I would have gone anyway. "Well," he said, "you don't know these regions. One should never travel alone here and unarmed. Our people out here are very polite. But they can be very nasty, too." Then I asked, "Did you notify the Party that you canceled my meetings and the reasons for doing so?" He swore to me that he did. I had every reason to believe him. However, when I returned to New York and asked Lovestone about the incident, he stated that he had received no word from O'Brien and that he knew nothing of the cancellation of the meetings. He reiterated time and again that he based his action in playing up the kidnaping story on the Associated Press report which came from Phoenix. I asked him why he did not try to get verification of the report from O'Brien before he acted. He claimed that he did and that O'Brien wired him that he did not know of my whereabouts.

Lovestone was always reckless in his search of sensationalism. I would never have believed, however, that on so slight a provocation—the most flimsy unverified reports—he would plunge the Party into a situation which made us ridiculous in the eyes of the entire country and over which I was very much ashamed. The rest of the Presidential campaign was virtually reduced to the making of explanations of the affair and trying to justify in some rational way the Party's inexcusable stupidity in this matter.

On October twenty-fifth I reached Chicago. There I met both Bedacht and Kruse. Bedacht had been left in Chicago when the Party headquarters were moved to New York, as the organizer of the district, the second largest in the Party. Kruse, upon graduation from the Lenin School in Moscow, was slated to replace Bedacht as organizer. From them I got the first inkling that important developments were taking place in the Party and in the Comintern. They informed me that Cannon, upon his return from the Sixth World Congress, had secretly begun the organization of a Trotsky group in the United States. I was also informed by Max Bedacht that Cannon was removed as Secretary of the International Labor Defense and was on trial before the Political Committee. "The whole opposition is in a terrible mess," said Bedacht, "Foster and Bittleman are trying to save their faces by making charges and attacks against Cannon. By insisting that his line was that of the United Opposition, Cannon is making them look most ridiculous."

The original charges against Cannon were brought in by comrades Foster and Bittleman. They had known ever since their arrival from Moscow that Cannon's leanings were in that direction, but they had kept quiet about it. They were trying to make Cannon change his views, in order to maintain the unity of the opposition against our leadership. Bittleman and Foster rushed into the Political Committee with the charges only after they had become aware that we were secretly conducting an investigation on our own account into Cannon's affairs. I had a very long talk with Lovestone when I returned to New York, and he gave me a good insight into the situation that existed at the Sixth World Congress.

Lovestone gave me the first inkling that there were differences between Stalin and Bukharin. "There were two Congresses going on at the Sixth World Congress," he said. "One was the official Congress, over which Bukharin presided, whose plaudits he received and the decisions of which were passed unanimously. Then there was the Corridor Congress called together by Stalin. This was an unofficial Congress. It took place in the corridors. Through it, a devastating campaign was carried on against Bukharin as a Right Winger. I collaborated with Bukharin at this Congress and for that reason aroused the enmity of Stalin. The cable which you sent about the Foster letter on the interview with Stalin was the worst thing you could have done. It played into Bukharin's hands, because it gave him proof of Stalin's factional activities against him in the Comintern. Stalin did not like that nor did any of the other Russians. They resent having an outside party interfere in their family affairs."

From Lovestone I learned also that our Opposition when it

arrived in Moscow was torn with dissension. Foster and Bittleman had developed serious differences. The Cannon delegates had developed sharp differences with Cannon because he wanted them to form a center group with Weinstone and Foster. Pepper had taken care of Weinstone, however, by taking him under his wing. But as the Congress went on, the Opposition succeeded in uniting against us and in making the charge that we represented the Right Wing in the Party. Foster and Bittleman had been drawn into the Corridor Congress and were getting a great deal of encouragement. Lovestone also informed me that, when the decision on the American Party was reported out, the opposition, including Foster and Bittleman and Johnston, accepted the decision "with reservations," a procedure highly unusual in the Comintern.

As to Cannon's Trotskyism, it was not new to Lovestone. Before he left for America he was called in by Bukharin, who showed him a report by the G. P. U. on Cannon's activities in Moscow. The report indicated that Comrade Cannon in talks with Russians had disclosed that he had strong Trotskyist leanings. According to Lovestone, Bukharin was of the opinion that Cannon's conversion to Trotskyism gave our leadership an opportunity to smash the Foster Opposition.

The situation looked very serious to me. I now knew that what Foster wrote in his famous letter was true. The political winds in the Comintern were changing and I knew that the changes were not motivated by any other than the internal considerations of the Russian Communist Party. The fight to eliminate Trotsky from the Comintern and from the leadership of the Russian party was carried on under the battle-cry of the fight against Left Sectarianism. After the Sixth World Congress the clarion call was for the fight against the Right danger. If it was to be a fight against the Right danger, then I knew that there would have to be victims in this fight who would be branded as Right-Wingers.

Lovestone was very silent on the effects of the new situation on our leadership. However, when I spoke to Pepper, who had meantime assumed the name of Swift, I learned a great deal more. From Pepper I knew that the future was not a bright one.

Pepper was very much worried. He confided in me that he expected to be recalled to Moscow, a prospect which he looked forward to with the greatest dread. Lovestone was not in good repute in Moscow, he told me. Stalin was preparing a fight against Bukharin, and all in the Comintern who were under suspicion of being Bukharin supporters would be made to suffer if Stalin got the upper hand. Pepper was of the opinion that Stalin would gain the upper hand, even though the situation in the Russian Politbureau was uncertain, because Voroshilov, who held the balance of power, was wavering.

But we had worries other than the situation in the Russian Party upon which our Party leadership depended. Weinstone, who supported us, was in serious trouble. The New York newspapers, especially the tabloids, were featuring in scandalous headlines the news about the "Eugenic Baby." According to the papers, Grace Burnham, when she gave birth to a baby girl, refused to name its father and stated that hers was a "eugenic baby." She said that she had chosen as her mate the man, a union with whom according to her estimate, would yield the best progeny. The tabloids carried big headlines asking the question, "Who is the Eugenic Father?" The matter came up in the Secretariat of the Party because it involved Grace Burnham, who was a prominent Party member, and William Weinstone, a member of the Political Committee and Secretary of the New York District. Harriet Silverman, Weinstone's wife, who had recently joined the Party, threatened to expose the whole matter to the newspapers. Harriet Silverman was a director in one of the institutions established by the wealthy comrade Burnham. It was through Harriet that Weinstone came to know Miss Burnham, who had inherited a fortune from her former husband.

We of the Secretariat were afraid that if the newspapers got the story they would feature it in such a way as to discredit the Communist Party by holding it up to ridicule. Jack Stachel and I were therefore appointed as a special committee to confer with Grace Burnham, Harriet Silverman, and the clerk in her office, who sided with her. Harriet Silverman cried and became hysterical. Her supporter wanted to know how she could continue to work in Grace Burnham's office under such conditions. She saw no reason why Harriet should not expose the whole mess in the newspapers. Mrs. Burnham was calm under the circumstances. After all, it was only a personal matter. She reiterated that she was ready to abide by whatever decision the Party made, and she hoped that Harriet Silverman, who had just joined, would prove worthy of her membership by not letting her emotions lead her into a step which would help no one and greatly injure the cause.

No sooner had one finished talking than the other began to spitfire back. Our Party, however, had a very marked influence on its members. We pleaded in the interests of the Party, that even though personal feelings had been hurt, all concerned ought to work out a solution together with the Party which would not bring the mess out into the open. By cajoling and using the threat of Party discipline, we finally persuaded Harriet Silverman to agree to a settlement of the matter by the Party. She had to promise us faithfully that she would keep all reference to the matter out of the press.

Betram Wolfe, who had been a delegate to the Sixth World Congress, did not return to the United States. He remained in Moscow as the representative of the Party, replacing Engdahl, who returned for work in the American Party. Wolfe, unlike Engdahl, was wide awake politically. The reports we were getting from him were not very encouraging to us.

The election results added to our worries. All of us expected a very marked increase in the Communist vote. I was much more conservative than the rest and expected a vote of between 75,000 and 100,000. The general expectation among us was for a vote of between 150,000 and 200,000. But when the results came in, our vote amounted to only 48,770. It was far from impressive. It did not even register a gain over the 1924 results, because we had been able to get on the ballot in many more states than we had been on in 1924. We were fearful that the results of the elections would have a bad effect upon the prestige of our leadership in Moscow and would encourage those who were working for our removal from power.

On November twenty-eighth we announced to the Party that

the National Convention would take place on February first, 1929. This notice was a signal for the resumption of open warfare between the factions. At the Political Committee we had our skirmishes with the Foster group. In Stachel's apartment, where Pepper did most of his work, our board of strategy usually met. Here Lovestone, Stachel, Pepper, Bedacht and I would meet almost every day. We knew we were under fire. I told Lovestone repeatedly that "if we have a majority of the Party and the Communist International attempts to take it away, we ought to break with the Communist International and maintain our hold on the Party."

The strategy we worked out for the convention was to carry on the fight against the Foster group for disloyalty to the Communist International because they accepted the decisions of the Communist International with reservations while we accepted the decisions of the Communist International without reservations; carry on a fight against Trotskyism and Cannon, its American expression; link this fight up with the fight against the American Right Wing, by exposing the close relations between the Foster group and Cannon. We thus did our utmost to cater to Stalin. At the same time, the substance of the strategy we decided upon was to carry on such an energetic fight among the membership for their support that we would roll up an impressive majority. Lovestone was of the opinion that, if we could do this, the Comintern would have to respect and recognize that majority. In spite of all his trips to Moscow—and he had been to Moscow more often than any of us, conferring there with all the Russian leaders—Lovestone thus proved that he still had much to learn about the ways of the Russian Bolsheviks.

The Foster group became bolder and more defiant as the convention date approached. They were spreading all kinds of rumors about what Stalin was going to do for them. Bukharin was now openly attacked in the Comintern as a Right Winger. Yet the pre-convention discussion meetings that took place in the principal cities around the middle of December resulted in a crushing defeat of the Foster opposition. Our side was jubilant. We were now certain that if we did not slacken in our drive to win the convention that we could roll up an enormous majority.

But our jubilation did not last long. One day Pepper received a cable ordering him to return to Moscow immediately. This was Moscow's first thrust at our leadership. Pepper almost collapsed under it. He became panicky and depressed. We decided to answer the cable in such a way as to assure the Comintern that Pepper's departure would take place immediately but on account of his illegal status he would have to return to Moscow in a round about manner through Mexico and the Far East, which would take a very long time. By dispatching this reply we hoped to keep Pepper in the country and to benefit by his advice. Pepper indicated to us that he dreaded going back to Russia. His opinion was that we had lost on the Russian Front. Jay Lovestone, however, did not share that opinion. He had hopes of coming to a satisfactory understanding with Stalin. I again raised the question of not capitulating to Stalin, even if it meant a break with the Comintern.

At this time we again decided to intensify our fight against the Foster opposition and to win the convention by such an overwhelming majority that there could be no doubt that the Opposition was decisively crushed. In addition, we took steps immediately to prepare our followers for what was coming from Moscow. We held caucus meetings with our trusted group leaders. At these meetings we talked about the Comintern situation and about its leaders. We exposed the role of the Corridor Congress and supplied the comrades with all the current spicy stories and gossip of official Moscow. Lovestone especially went out of his way to describe Stalin and to poke fun at him. But all of Lovestone's remarks on such occasions ended on the same note. He would wind up his talks with this assurance: "Comrades, we have always been disciplined Communists and loyal members of the Communist International. I want to give you my word of assurance, whatever the Comintern decides in relation to me I will carry out. That you can depend upon."

The letters and cables coming from Wolfe added to the gravity of the situation. The Executive of the Comintern stressed the need of taking very drastic steps to end factionalism in the American Party. He informed us that the Executive was seriously considering the removal of both Bittleman and Lovestone from the American Party for work in the Comintern, because these two comrades were guilty of the worst factional behavior. This information led us to believe that the Comintern was contemplating the removal of Lovestone as Secretary of the Party and replacing him by Foster.

Upon the receipt of this news we intensified our campaign against Stalin. Jay appeared before our caucuses as the victim of a plot against the Party. We decided to raise the cry that under no circumstances would we turn the Party over to Foster. We strengthened our campaign against Foster. We dug out his record in support of the World War and his activities in selling Liberty Bonds, to prove that he could not be trusted with the leadership of the Party during this period, when the fight against the war danger and in opposition to war was one of the most important tasks confronting Communists. We stressed the fact that the decisions of the Congress characterized the present period as "the third period of post war capitalism," a period which would witness the collapse of capitalism and the outbreak of great revolutionary struggles. We maintained that during such a period a man who had drifted from the extreme Left, to become a lieutenant of Gompers and a supporter of the A. F. of L., one who, when the revolutionary leaders of the country were being imprisoned for their opposition to the imperialist war, was supporting that war and selling bonds to the workers to finance it, that such a man could not and must not be entrusted with the Party leadership. We berated Foster for his factionalism, for his lack of principle, and prepared the grounds for his expulsion from the Party. I believed every characterization against Foster, because it was true. Foster's entry and rise in the Communist movement was an accident based upon his failure to become a dominant figure in the A. F. of L.

Lovestone now appeared before our caucuses as an injured party, as the sacrificial lamb. He said that as far as he was concerned he was not interested in retaining the leadership as an individual, but he would never sacrifice the Party leadership, which represented the majority and the best interests of the Party to the minority represented by Foster. "Even if I have to put a turban around my head and go to India, I will go. Wherever the Comintern will send me, there will I go—to China, India, Korea, Madagascar or the Sandwich Islands." But he did not mean a word of it. He was interested in personally retaining the leadership.

The election of delegates to the National Convention exceeded all our estimates. If we so desired we could have prevented the Foster group from having a single delegate. But we decided not to exclude the Fosterites from representation and gave them ten percent of the delegates, so that they should have a voice in the proceedings. This was not on a proportional basis. On such a basis they would have had about twenty percent of the delegates. But in Bolshevik politics ten percent can be more than ninety percent. This we learned soon enough. We received an open letter from the Communist International sharply criticizing our Party. This open letter did not harm us because in Communist parties the leaders always know how to trim their sails to political statements and how to turn sharp criticism to their own advantage. We were no exception. But we did expect the open letter and its political importance to be followed up with organizational proposals. We knew nothing of the nature of the organizational proposals that Moscow would send us. Our Opposition did. Before we received the cable officially from the Executive of the Communist International, the text of the cable was being circulated by the Opposition. We later learned that the organizational proposals were made behind Wolfe's back and that, although he was the sole official representative of the Party in Moscow, he was not given an opportunity to present his opinions on them, a most unusual procedure even for the Executive of the Comintern. At the same time a letter was circulated in the Party which was sent by William F. Dunne concerning an interview he had with Stalin. In this letter Dunne claimed that Stalin accepted him as the kernel of the future leadership and that was why the Communist International was for the Opposition and against the present Party leadership.

The organizational proposals provided that Lovestone and Bittleman should be removed from the American Party for work in the Comintern, that Foster should be made the Secretary of the Party and that the newly elected Central Executive Committee and Secretariat should be so constituted that, including the decisive votes of the Communist International representatives, the Majority should be changed into a Minority and the Minority take its place as the new Majority. In addition, we were sent two Communist International representatives, Harry Pollitt from the British Communist Party and Philip Dengel of the German Party. Dengel and Pollitt were both members of the Executive of the Communist International. The head of the Communist International delegation was Dengel. His word was final in all matters.

By this time Pepper, who had been ordered to Moscow, had gone into hiding. His whereabouts were known to only two comrades of the Central Executive Committee and to two stenographers, who were in the employ of the National Office and who had been assigned to help him in a secretarial capacity. The two members of the Central Executive Committee were Jay Lovestone and Jack Stachel. The only other member of the Central Executive Committee who knew that he had not left for Moscow was I. But at the time even I did not know where he lived. During the National Convention, Jay Lovestone and Jack Stachel invited me to take a taxi ride through Central Park. When I got into the taxi I found one of the stenographers of the National Office already sitting in the car. As soon as we were all seated in the taxi, the conversation began. The girl was very angry. She told us a story of how, while working with Pepper, she had become decidedly intimate with him, and that he had made very definite promises. Now it seemed he had abandoned her for the wife of one of the leaders of the Young Communist League and an arch Fosterite. She threatened that, unless we did something to remove the interloper and keep her as Pepper's sole secretary, she would expose the whole affair to the Party, even letting the convention know where Pepper lived.

Here was a real problem in entangling alliances. If this

matter ever saw the light of day, we would be completely ruined. We had already notified all our forces that Pepper had left the country and boasted of that departure as proof of our absolute loyalty to the Communist International. I knew the girl well. It was clear that this was her first important love affair. But it was also clear that she was enamoured of Pepper's glamour as a great leader and that she rather relished the role of heroine in a melodrama of political intrigue. She knew of course that Pepper was married and the father of two children. But she had been one of the most loyal and devoted members of our group since its very inception, and as a secretary in the National Office had been entrusted with our most confidential matters. We played upon her loyalty to the group, sympathized with her plight, explained to her the difficulties we were now facing and what her exposure would mean to our group and the Party, asked her to have patience, that we would do everything in our power to straighten out the affairs between her and Pepper. She agreed.

The convention was one of the most riotous which I had ever participated in, and I had participated in all kinds of conventions, under all kinds of circumstances. But never had I attended a convention like the one held in Irving Plaza Hall, New York, in February, 1929. It was not a convention of an American political party, because over it hung the shadow of Stalin from the moment the sessions opened. The Communist International plenipotentiaries tried to force us to accept their interpretation of the Communist International organizational proposals, which was tantamount to giving them the decisive vote on the newly-elected Central Executive Committee for carrying through any kind of a reorganization of the Party they desired.

Under the statutes of the Communist International, its representatives had the power to make any ruling they desired, and it was our duty as members of the Communist International to accept them as binding upon us. But we had decided not to accept their rulings, to defy them and to carry the fight to Moscow. Dengel spoke before the caucus of our delegates, who were prepared for the event. Pollitt spoke also, at many meetings. At all the meetings, they faced a stone wall of opposition. We had tried to curry favor with the Communist International delegates. But this time they were instructed how to act. They would not let us find quarters for them; they would not let us wine and dine them. We realized that they had definite instructions from Stalin to do a dirty job and that they were intent on serving his wishes, for if they did not, their own skins would be scorched.

The Foster Opposition had undergone some important changes. The Pan-Pacific Trade Union Secretariat had been abandoned, with the result that Browder, a former member of this Secretariat, arrived in the United States from Shanghai via Moscow. A break took place between Bittleman, Browder and Foster. Browder became the virtual leader of the Foster caucus. Stalin temporarily cemented the Opposition together, which was solid in its univocal endeavor of giving three rousing cheers for Comrade Stalin on the slightest pretext or none whatever. Such sycophancy was a new low. From the day the convention opened, this opposition sought to force through a resolution condemning Bukharin as a Right Winger and hailing Stalin as the outstanding leader of the world Communist movement. We resisted the attempt. Most of the time I was chairman of the sessions, and the hall was always packed with milling delegates and other Party members, who came because they knew the Party was going through a crisis of major importance. Often fights took place. But of course the real convention took place behind closed doors during the caucus meetings of both groups, in conferences with the Communist International representatives, sometimes with our steering committee, and sometimes jointly with the steering committee of the Opposition.

During the course of the convention we raised the cry that we wanted no labels, no buttons, that in our Party there was no room for either Bukharin buttons or Stalin buttons. At our caucus meetings we informed our adherents that the Communist International had to be composed of a leadership based upon mutual understanding, that hereafter our Party would assert its independence, that in the future we would not accept

Communist International decisions blindly just because they came from the Communist International, that we would consider the decisions on their merits and take our stand accordingly, of course always recognizing the right of the Communist International to enforce its decisions on the basis of the discipline upon which the Communist movement rests.

Our steering committee had another difficulty. Weinstone, who had been elected a delegate on our slate as a member of our group, began to wobble again and came to a definite understanding with the Communist International representatives, supporting each and every one of their proposals. He was supported by only one other delegate from our group, Albert Weisbord, who had ambitions to become an outstanding Party leader. His support came after a conference with Dengel and Pollitt, in which they promised to support his ambitions.

The Communist International representatives tried to put terrific pressure upon us. Our steering committee often would meet with them in sessions that lasted for twenty hours at a stretch. On a number of occasions Stachel, Lovestone, and I had conferences with Pepper, who was of the opinion that the whole line we were following was wrong and that we had only two courses open to us: either accept the Communist International decision and take its consequences; or break with the Communist International by expelling Foster and his group from the Party and by taking over the Party organization. In the heat of the convention fight he said such a course could be put through. But we were misled by our big majority. We believed the Communist International could not fly in its face. Never before had the Communist International faced a party with such a majority. We recalled from past Communist International experiences, recalling the time when Lenin was still alive, that a party majority was always respected by the Bolsheviks.

At one of the conferences with the delegates of the Communist International which lasted all night long we finally came to an acknowledgment on the part of Dengel that we were slated for removal from the leadership, because in Moscow we were considered supporters of Bukharin and the Right Wing.

He further stated that if we could give the Russians assurances that we were not Bukharinites, we could regain their confidence and perhaps the leadership of the Party. When we protested that the accusation that we were Bukharinites was unfounded, that the issues between Bukharin and Stalin had nothing to do with the issues before the American Party, he smiled and said, "But the actions of Jay Lovestone at the Sixth World Congress is decided proof to the contrary." "But," I said, "the Sixth World Congress is considered the highest body of the Communist International. All its decisions were passed unanimously. Besides, when I obtained Foster's factional document and cabled its contents abroad, Stalin himself came into the Senioren Konvent of the Congress and personally declared that there was no dissension among the members of the Political Bureau of the Central Committee of the Communist Party of the Soviet Union. How then could we be accused of being Bukharinites at the time of the Sixth World Congress when according to Stalin's own personal declaration there were no differences between him and Bukharin? If those differences developed, they evidently developed after the Congress and we must have an opportunity of considering the differences and formulating our opinions on them before we can be branded as either Bukharinites or Stalinites." But there was as much use arguing with either Dengel or Pollitt as with an Egyptian mummy. Pollitt, like most of the English Communists, was too naïve politically and too sluggish mentally to give answers to the arguments we made. He left most of the answering to Dengel, who was a short thin German, colorless and unimpressive. He rigidly adhered to his instructions and repeated monotonously his worked-out formulas on all questions, to our utter exasperation.

After that famous session we held a meeting of our own steering committee on March eighth, at which Bedacht and Minor presented us with a resolution condemning Bukharin and demanding his removal as Chairman of the Communist International. Minor was the father of the idea and wrote most of the resolution. He believed he had made a master political stroke. It is to the credit of Lovestone that he was the only one against the resolution when it was first introduced. I favored it because it was made necessary under pressure as a result of a situation which was based upon the most crass unprincipledness. I stated that I was interested most in saving the American Party and that to do what the Communist International wanted us to do would mean to wreck the movement. I was determined that the twenty years of effort which I had given in trying to build a movement should not be wrecked. My position, I stated, was not unlike that of a person held up by a bandit who sticks a gun under his nose and demands, "either your money or your life!" "Dengel," I said, "has proven to me that Stalin has the gun before our noses. Either give him what he wants or pay with our lives." Coincident with the adoption of this resolution we decided to send a cable signed by the proletarian delegates to the convention appealing against the decision to prevent the convention from registering the will of the majority.

When Bob Minor introduced our resolution on Bukharin, which Lovestone also finally endorsed, and which Pepper declared was folly and unprincipledness of the lowest order, Bittleman rushed to the platform and introduced the Opposition's resolution, which he had been trying to introduce ever since the convention opened. When he concluded his reading of the lengthy document, which ended in "Hail to Stalin!", the Fosterites staged a wild demonstration, stamping on the floor, throwing hats into the air, yelling and madly singing the International. It was a disgusting, sickening affair. Here we were, representatives of American Communism, yet our sole interest was as far removed from the interests of the workers and farmers of the United States as that of the lowest Tammany jobseeker. Our constituents had been completely forgotten. We who claimed to be the leaders of the oppressed and exploited millions in the United States were falling all over ourselves to prove to a ruler in a country over six thousand miles away from our shores that we were his subservient bootlickers and ready to curry his favor under all circumstances. We had traveled far from the original rebellion against authority that had drawn us into the revolutionary movement, and were now but blind worshipers of a new authority more autocratic than any Tsar.

The cable of the proletarians received a prompt reply from Stalin personally to the effect that there was no intention on the part of the Comintern to prevent the majority at the convention from asserting itself, that the majority had the full power to elect a new Central Executive Committee and a Secretary for the Party, but that Lovestone and Bittleman, because they were factionalists, must go to Moscow for work in the Comintern.

Foster was dumbfounded by this cable. Again his hopes of becoming the Secretary of the Party were blasted. But Browder was not dismayed. He held the Foster group in line and served notice that he was continuing the factional war. As for me, I was completely fooled by that cable. I believed that now Stalin had had a change of heart because of our majority. I agreed with Lovestone's proposal that the convention elect a large proletarian delegation, which, together with Lovestone, Bedacht and myself, should appeal to the Comintern against its decisions on the American Party. The new Central Executive Committee elected me as Secretary of the Party. When we served notice of our appeal, we named Bob Minor as the Acting Secretary during my absence.

We saw Pepper that day after the Central Executive Committee meeting. We met in a restaurant on 125th Street. We told him of our plans. He stated that we were making a major mistake in relying upon Stalin's cable and that, in our decision to appeal, we were playing into Stalin's hand. Our cause, he said, was a lost one. But Jay, who did not want to break with the Comintern, had high hopes that, in taking a large delegation with him to Moscow, he could save his own neck and return to the United States. Jay said he knew Stalin, and that if he had an opportunity to speak to him, everything would be straightened out. I disagreed with Pepper on two grounds: I said that Stalin's cable proved that, with the kind of a majority we had, we had more than an even chance on appeal; secondly, I was of the opinion that, unless we went to Moscow and finished the fight there, we could not hope to maintain our support in the Party. Pepper was right; Lovestone and I, wrong.

However, we took no chances as far as the future was concerned. We took steps that, if a split should take place, we would hold on to all the Party institutions and property, which were very valuable and could give us the wherewithal to continue the fight against such a powerful adversary as Stalin, who had all the resources of the Soviet Union at his command. We called in the comrades important in this respect. We had a conference with Joseph Brodsky, the Party lawyer, who was in thorough agreement with us. He made out the legal papers, which were necessary to transfer the property to us, and they were left in his care, to be executed whenever he received the word from us. But Brodsky, when the time came, refused to execute them and kept the property safe for the Communist International. He likewise kept safe his job as the Party's attorney.

The proletarians chosen by the convention to appeal our case to the Executive Committee of the Communist International consisted of William Miller from Detroit, a machinist who worked in the automobile industry, but was employed most of the time as a Party functionary; Tom Myerscough, a coal miner from the soft coal district of Pennsylvania, who had been an important leader of the Party in the campaign among the miners and was in the employ of the Party; Edward Welsh, a Negro comrade who had recently joined the Party; William J. White, a steel worker who, in recent years, had been editor of the official organ of the steel workers' paper and was at times engaged by the Party as an organizer; Ella Reeves Bloor, who had been a paid organizer for the Socialist Party and later for the Communist Party for over twenty years, and who was one of the oldest living members of the Party; Otto Huiswood, a Negro Communist, who had been a paid Party official almost from the organization of the Party in 1919; and Alex Noral, a six foot recent convert to Communism, who claimed to be half Indian and an expert on agriculture. Each one was supposed to be working in a factory at the time chosen, but they were really chosen for their proletarian looks and political reliability.

Each one of them was a native-born American with the exception of Huiswood, who was a West Indian. However, being a Negro was considered a mark of distinction among us. We brought this delegation along, to prove to Moscow that the charges that we were a group of foreign-born Communists was false, and that our group had the real native Americans in its ranks. We knew that the Comintern had repeatedly insisted that we must draw the native Americans into the Party if we really wanted to bring about its Americanization.

Our delegation embarked from New York on March twenty-third, 1929. Traveling on the same boat was Alexander Bittleman, who was obeying the orders of the Comintern to leave America and take up work with the Comintern. A selected crowd of Party officials was on hand to see us off, including Robert Minor, who was to be the Acting Secretary during my absence. Minor was in the most jubilant spirits. It seemed to him that we were going on a picnic rather than on a mission that might cause the loss of our political power. I spoke with him and he assured me, a little too sincerely, that he would hold the fort while we were gone and that we could depend upon him.

When the time came to say good-by he grabbed my hand and as he bade us farewell the crafty glimmer in his eyes gave me forebodings. I told Lovestone about it as soon as I saw him.

"Jay, I am afraid of Bob Minor. Did you see how happy he was that we were going? That sly grin he gave me when he said good-by worries me. I'm afraid we made a mistake in making him Acting Secretary. I have a premonition that he will double-cross us the minute we are out of his sight."

"Don't worry," Lovestone replied. "After all, we have Stachel to depend upon. Bob Minor will have to wake up very early in the morning to pull any tricks against us."

We were tied up in the bay for almost a day by a heavy fog which spread a gloomy blanket over the waters. The fog horn blew in monotonous intervals, the bell at the stern kept ringing. New York was in the background and Moscow before us. I was in a fog, and so was Lovestone, because, for the first time, we did not know what fate awaited us in Mecca.

CHAPTER XV

INNOCENTS ABROAD SEEK JUSTICE FROM STALIN

THE trip to Moscow was a new experience for us. It was the first trip we had made to defend our political heads from decapitation. Leaders of other parties had gone through that experience before, and we had helped in their decapitation. We could not get ourselves to believe that we would follow in their footsteps so quickly. We knew that we were in for a fight with a powerful adversary, and that the fight would be the most difficult one of our political careers, but we believed that we would succeed in convincing Stalin that we were the rightful leaders of the American movement and deserving of his support.

I often paced the deck, exasperated at the idea that I had to defend myself before a Communist tribunal for crimes I did not commit. I often pondered: "Why must we in America be punished because Stalin doubts our reliability and believes that we are supporters of Bukharin? Doesn't Stalin know that we are primarily interested in America? Doesn't Stalin realize that we are ready to make every sacrifice for Communism?"

I reviewed the past, and concluded that we had always supported the Russians in whatever they did, that Stalin should have no doubts about our supporting him and his policies. We were always loyal to the Communist International and especially to the Russian Communist Party. Why should we change now? If Stalin would only leave us alone to work out our problems in America, as the Bolsheviks were allowed to work out their problems for Russia, he need have no fear of our loyalty to him, for we would follow him, wherever he would go.

But I could never get around to the idea that, in order to

suit Stalin's whims, I must voluntarily give up the leadership of the movement I had labored for ten years to build. He was asking too much.

On the high seas our delegation planned the appeal we would make in Moscow for justice, for the right of the majority to rule the American Party. However, we overlooked one important strategy of warfare. It is that the generals should never go in advance of their armies. In modern warfare the generals are always in the rear. In our delegation the three generals of the party, Lovestone, Bedacht, and I, left our army, the Party membership, in the United States, in order to fight it out with Stalin like knights at a joust, in single combat. Separated from our army by over six thousand miles of land and ocean, it was folly on our part to expect that we could make an effective fight in Russia and at the same time hold our lines in the United States.

When we arrived in Germany we received word that Wolfe had cabled that it was not necessary for the delegation to come, that only Lovestone should come. At the meeting at which we discussed this cable we decided that Wolfe did not understand out situation, that the cable contained nothing to make us change our line. Stalin, however, was not asleep. In Berlin we were already made to feel that difficulties were being put in our path. When we applied for visas at the office which took care of such matters for Comintern delegates, we were politely informed by those in charge that they could do nothing for us until they received word from Moscow. This was an unusual procedure, because we had informed the Comintern that we were on our way and that we would stop over for our visas in Berlin. We were well known at the office. We had to wait in Berlin, nevertheless, spending our money on hotel bills and extra telegrams to Moscow. We were kept waiting in Berlin for five days.

Berlin was alive with Comintern news. We met a girl by the first name of Lu, who had been a member of the German Party and had worked in the Comintern and for the G. P. U. She had accompanied Green to the American Party when he was sent over as the Comintern representative in 1924. She was no longer a member of the German Party, because she was married to the Communist leader of India, M. N. Roy, who had just been expelled by the Comintern. She gave us very disturbing news about what had been going on. She told us of expulsions in the German Party, of expulsions from the Austrian Party, and that the Czecho-Slovak Party was practically non-existent. The news about the German Party was most illuminating. Ernst Thaelmann was in Moscow to settle the crisis in the German Party caused by the Wittdorf incident.

Wittdorf, Thaelmann's brother-in-law, was Political Secretary of the Hamburg organization of the German Communist Party. The Central Committee of the German Party declared him guilty of embezzling Party funds over an extended period of time.

During Wittdorf's trial before the Central Committee, Thaelmann admitted that he knew that his brother-in-law had been embezzling Party funds and that he had deliberately refrained from reporting the matter to the proper Party authorities. He gave as an excuse that he was waiting for a more favorable opportunity to do so. The Central Committee of the German Party censured him for his conduct, but did not remove him from the Central Committee or from the leadership of the Party. For censuring Thaelmann, who had admitted shielding the guilt of his brother-in-law and who himself joined in the unanimous vote to expel the latter from the Party, the German Central Committee was called to Moscow, where those who had been instrumental in exposing the Wittdorf scandal and in justifiably censuring Thaelmann were themselves most severely censured and removed from the Central Committee, from the Political Bureau, from the Secretariat, and from the editorship of the *Rote Fahne,* the official daily newspaper of the Party. They were accused of being conciliators, of having sought to make peace with the Right Wing and of being Right Wingers themselves as well. Thaelmann was exonerated by Stalin, his policies and leadership declared to be in the best interests of the movement, and the members of the German Communist Party were called upon to rally to his support.

The outstanding leaders other than Thaelmann were ordered

to leave Germany and put themselves at the service of the Comintern for work in some other country. The one most severely condemned was Ewart, who, under the name of Braun, had been sent as the representative to the American Party in 1927. He was considered a good friend of Bukharin, so the ax fell upon his neck. He was ordered into exile by the Comintern for work elsewhere, but not in Germany.

Lovestone, Bedacht and I visited Roy during our stay in Berlin. We found Roy a tall, handsome, scholarly man who spoke English in the most polished manner. He told us his story. The account of his experiences should have been a warning to us. Roy had been part of the original committee of four which had been sent by Stalin to China to execute the Leftist swing in Chinese politics which Stalin had decided upon after the Kuomintang and Chang-Kai-Shek had broken off relations with the Communists. This committee consisted of Heinz Neuman, of the German Party, Lominadze of the Russian Party, a staunch supporter of Stalin, Roy, and Jacques Doriot of France. As I have already written, the policy led to the Canton uprising and the unnecessary butchery of thousands of Chinese. Besides, it played into the hands of the reactionary forces, who were enabled by the Canton Putsch to carry on a campaign against the labor and peasant movement more effectively and extensively than ever before. Stalin, in the true Bolshevik style of self-criticism, looked around for a scapegoat and found the scapegoat in the very man he had entrusted to carry out his policy. Roy was the man. Roy, however, was never on good terms with Bukharin. They disagreed on too many important questions. He had been one of Stalin's first supporters in the Comintern. But Roy refused to take the blame for Stalin's mistakes. He was thereupon denounced as a traitor and counter-revolutionist and expelled from the Comintern and the Communist Party of India. Lominadze later also fell into disgrace and was executed, as was Heinz Neuman in the recent Soviet purges. Doriot broke with Stalin after years of corruption in the Stalinist morass and graduated from the Stalin school into one of the Fascist leaders of France.

Roy, however, took the situation quite philosophically. He

was already collaborating with Brandler and Thalheimer, two German Communists who had been kept exiles in the Soviet Union for years. When they demanded once too often to be permitted to go back to Germany, and threatened to take the matter up with the German Consul, they were expelled from the Comintern and their Party as Right Wingers and renegades. In those days such a purge did not yet lead to the firing squad. But Brandler and Thalheimer could not be accused of being Bukharinites. I recall a meeting of the Executive of the Comintern at which Bukharin himself flew into a rage when these two comrades insisted that the question of permitting them to go back to Germany be taken up.

When we told Roy of our plans, he laughed at us. He turned to Lovestone and said: "You have been to the Comintern often enough, and yet you speak as if you have never learned anything about the Comintern. Your majority means nothing. Stalin is a ruthless man. Once you are in Russia, you are like a trapped animal. Don't you see, you have nothing to gain and everything to lose by going to Russia?"

But Lovestone argued to the contrary. The American situation was different. That much we knew because all the Communist circles in Berlin were buzzing with what Stalin had done and was attempting to do to the American Communist Party. There were some who cautionsly expressed the opinion that perhaps the fight that the American Party would put up would end the system of vassalage to the Russian leadership on the part of the other parties.

The delay in getting our visas was not our only trouble. We had to protect our delegates against the Moscow system of corruption. We warned those to whom the experience of going to Moscow was a new one that they should expect all kinds of trouble. We also explained to them the ways of the Comintern. We told them the Comintern had tremendous resources, that its agents would entertain them lavishly, that every kind of temptation would be thrown their way, to make them change their views, that, if temptation did not work, pressure would be used. Our delegates solemnly pledged to remain loyal and to fight for the justice we sought, to the bitter end.

We traveled to Moscow via Riga, in order to gain time. One incident happened which convinced us that conditions in Russia must be bad. Before we crossed the border a Lettish peasant lad entered the train and asked if any of us wanted to change our currency for rubles. He informed us that across the line the Soviet exchange people would pay us only 2.94 rubles for a dollar; he, on the other hand, was ready to pay us 40 rubles per dollar for as many dollars as we would care to exchange.

At the Russian border town of Borgosovia we were detained for a long time and our baggage searched, something which was never done before. We were made to feel we were in for trouble. Trouble came quickly enough when the G. P. U. arrested two members of our delegation: Ella Reeves Bloor and William E. White, who were traveling on one passport, as man and wife under one fictitious surname for both—quite the regular procedure in the Comintern. The confusion was due to the error of the Russian Consulate, which had issued one visa for both instead of two visas. The visa was in the name of the man only, and we understood that it covered the wife as well. We pleaded with the G. P. U. We showed them our credentials. Lovestone proved to them that we were a delegation from the American Party, that he was a member of the Executive of the Communist International, and that I was both a member of the Executive and the Praesidium. But it did not help. It was only after we reached Moscow that we were able to effect their release from prison. Fortunately, instead of being put out by their experience, both of them rather enjoyed the incident.

Upon our arrival in Moscow on April seventh, 1929, we were met by Wolfe and a number of our supporters who were students in the Lenin School. Our question, we were told, was considered a personal matter by Stalin. The commission that was appointed had for its chairman the newly appointed head of the Comintern, Vyacheslav Molotov, who subsequently took Rykov's place as Premier of the Soviet Union and more recently took over from Litvinov the Commissariat of Foreign Affairs as well. Molotov was considered the most powerful figure in the Russian Party next to Stalin even then. We were also informed that Stalin would personally attend the important sessions of our Commission and of the Comintern Executive Committee meetings, at which our problem would be taken up.

When Lovestone, Bedacht and I closeted ourselves with Wolfe, we learned a great deal of what had been going on in Moscow. Bukharin was no longer Chairman of the Comintern. His place had been taken by Molotov, who never before had figured prominently in Comintern affairs and was considered in the Russian Party an authority on Russian agricultural matters. It seems that Bukharin was guilty of a number of crimes, besides being opposed to Stalin's Five-Year-Plan. He was charged with having called Stalin a Ghengis Khan. He had opposed the exiling of Trotsky to Turkey, Stalin having obtained the approval of the Politbureau for Trotsky's exile by the slim majority of one vote. But the real cause for his removal from the Political Bureau of the Russian Party and from the Presidency of the Comintern was the fact that, after the Russian Party had voted to send Kamenev and Zinoviev into exile in Russia, he had the audacity to visit both of them, in order to express his regrets and to bid them good-bye. Kamenev, who was a weakling and a coward, afraid that the G. P. U. would find out about the meeting anyway, reported it to the Russian Party in the hope that he could thereby save himself. Bukharin was hailed before the Control Committee of the Russian Party. In Berlin we had already learned that Bukharin had capitulated to Stalin and had confessed his errors, but we did not know under what circumstances. At the meeting of the Control Commission it was made clear to Bukharin that he would be exposed as a Trotskyist plotter. Stalin was present at the meeting. The cold, calculating Stalin, in whom every human feeling was suppressed for the political advantage he personally sought, conducted the proceedings in such a star-chamber fashion that Bukharin collapsed, broke into tears, and capitulated to his master.

On Trotsky's exile to Turkey, Wolfe gave us some additional information. His information made a lasting impression upon me, because, when Trotsky was exiled to Turkey, I had protested to the leaders of our group on the Political Committee of our Party. I stated that the exiling of a revolutionist from a workers' country to a semi-fascist capitalist country like Turkey was obnoxious to me and a crime against the labor movement. I charged that the move played right into the hands of reaction, because it gave an excuse to all capitalist governments to exile their political opponents and that as Communists we had more to lose than to gain by Stalin's acts. "The partnership of Stalin with Mustapha Kemal stinks to high heavens," I had said. Of course, my remarks went into Stalin's dossier against me. But what Wolfe told us proved to what perfidy the Stalin regime was stooping. A letter was sent out by the Executive of the Comintern to the representatives in Moscow of the Communist parties of all other countries and to all non-Russians working in the apparatus of the organization, inquiring of them what in their judgment they would think would be the reaction if Trotsky was outlawed from Russia. Wolfe replied that in his opinion it would have a bad effect. After he had handed in his reply, he found out from the Russian papers that Trotsky had already been exiled to Turkey three days before the Comintern letter of inquiry had been sent out. The letter of inquiry was sent in order to trap "secret Trotskyites" in the Comintern, for all those who had written that Trotsky's exile would be looked upon unfavorably were indexed as Trotskyites or as having leanings toward Trotskyism. Yet Wolfe had written the main attacks on Trotsky for the American Party.

In 1929 Moscow was going through a crisis. It had changed drastically to the worse since the year before. If conditions were bad in Moscow proper, they must have been frightful in the provinces. Food scarcity prevailed. Milk, meat, fruit, vegetables, all kinds of dairy products were very difficult to obtain. They were rationed off. Even the amount of bread sold to a person was limited. Besides, there was an extreme shortage in manufactured goods for personal consumption; such as, clothing, textiles, shoes, implements, and the like. The prices of clothing and shoes were prohibitive, quite beyond the reach of the ordinary worker. There were long lines everywhere before the stores. People stood in line for hours before the textile stores waiting for them to open, so that they could be the lucky ones to obtain the textiles on hand for sale that day before they were sold out. From my window I watched the lines of women gather in the early morning waiting for the main coöperative stores on the Tverskaya to open. They began forming the line at four o'clock in the morning, each one hugging her position on the line and firmly gripping the pot, pitcher, can, or other receptacle she had brought along. When the store opened at seven o'clock in the morning, a pitiful cry arose from the women in the line. They pushed forward. Before a quarter of the line obtained the coveted portion of milk allowed them, the doors were closed. The milk was sold out. The women cried pitifully and rushed frantically to the next store to join another line in the vain hope of obtaining milk, perhaps for an invalid or an infant who was badly in need of it.

But there were residents in Moscow who received milk which was delivered to them in bottles in the American style every morning. The dairy supplying the milk was known as the G. P. U. Dairy. It supplied milk regularly to the members of the G. P. U., to the important leaders and functionaries of the Communist Party, to the employees and officials of the Comintern and the Profintern and to the foreign representatives of both these organizations. They received the milk whether they needed it or not. It was among them that one had to look for the privileged in the Soviet Union.

The Comintern headquarters, the Lux, which housed the employees and representatives of the Comintern, and the Hotel Bristol, which housed Communist delegations, were very gloomy places in 1929. There Communists spoke in whispers. Every one seemed to fear his comrade. Comrades who had been our best friends in 1927 and 1928 now failed to greet us and hurried on when they saw us. Moscow was a city of rumors about the drastic purges which were going on in the Comintern and in all the Communist Parties. Party leaders from the German Party, from the Czecho-Slovakian Party, from the Polish Party, from the Chinese Party were being kept for months with nothing to do, as virtual prisoners and exiles in Moscow. Men who were ready to give up their lives for Communism were being treated as traitors and criminals.

The most tragic figure of those days was the charming and brilliant Nicholas Bukharin. The first time I saw him that year was in front of the Lux Hotel. I greeted him. All he did was to stare at me. He did not greet me and feigned not to recognize me, though we had always been the best of friends and had talked at length together. We had served on committees together. I was not an ordinary comrade. I was a member of the Executive Committee of the Communist International and of its Praesidium. But the look he gave me was not unfamiliar to me. I had met with it before in prison when convicts were caught after they had made a desperate attempt to escape. It was the look of one hounded, for whom everything had been lost. His face had become very thin. His eyes had sunken in. He looked worried and like a man who had failed to sleep for many nights. The jaunty smiling Bukharin was no more. The complexion of his face, which usually was fair and blended with his reddish brown beard and blond hair, had assumed a pinkish tinge as happens to fair women when they cry incessantly. He looked morose and beaten. Could this be the fair, lovable Bukharin, or was this his ghost? I watched him walk down the Tverskaya. The quick gait was that of the short lively Bukharin, but with one new attribute. He kept continuously looking back and to the side, as if afraid of being followed and watched. Stalin's Juggernaut had left the man a wreck of what he had been just a few months before. Would it crush his spirit? The future would tell. I looked at the man who had been the best-liked man in the Russian Party, until he disappeared in the distance. What a price Bolshevism is exacting from its own people!

Bukharin was a Russian. Ewert was a German. He made two mistakes. One: he was Bukharin's friend. Two: he exposed the Wittdorf scandal involving Thaelmann, the leader of the German Party, who had been in Stalin's caucus at the Sixth World Congress and a leader of Stalin's Corridor Congress. To be the friend of someone Stalin disliked and to expose the corruption of one of Stalin's henchmen was to Stalin a double crime that must be ruthlessly punished. Ewert paid the price. The incident first came up when we had a meeting in Wolfe's room with the Lenin Institute students who supported our group. Around eleven o'clock at night we heard a tap on the door. When we opened it, a thoroughly scared young woman in a bathrobe drawn over her pajamas entered, closed the door hurriedly, walked a few paces, and hesitated before she spoke. Gathering courage, she beckoned to Lovestone and in a frightened whisper told him that Ewert would like to have a talk with him that evening in his room. She explained that everything had been taken care of and it could be so arranged that no one would know anything about it.

Lovestone took the matter up with Bedacht, Wolfe, and me, and we agreed that he should speak to Ewert. Given the answer, the girl, who was Ewert's secretary, opened the door, looked up and down the hallway, to see that no one was looking, and hurriedly departed. But what happened afterwards was significant to me. The Lenin Institute students, our Moscow-trained successors, the future leaders of the American Communist Party, became indignant. We had no business having any kind of intercourse with Ewert. He was a discredited man, a conciliator. How could we have any relations with a man who in the eyes of Stalin had given aid and comfort to the Right Wing in his own party and to the enemies of the Comintern? If we should speak to Ewert, they argued, we would immediately be branded as a part of his group. No, they said, we must sever all relations with him of a personal and political character, and we must go on record in condemning him for his crimes. We fought it out at the meeting, obtained the support of the delegation from America in opposition to the Lenin Institute students and it was decided that Lovestone, Bedacht, and I see Ewert.

Ewert had been to America in 1927 as the Communist International representative. We had built up a genuine and warm friendship. He was remembered as the jovial German Communist who liked the Americans and was always ready for fun and deviltry in a sociable way. Ewert always used to smile. Even in his angry moods he often had to laugh. That he liked to drink more than was good for him was characteristic of most of the German Communist leaders. But Ewert was not the jovial German and Comintern Rep Braun we had known back in America. He grasped our hands with great emotion. Tears he tried to suppress welled in his eyes. Then he spoke to us in whispers, nervously, as he told us his story of the injustice being done to him. He had just returned to the German Party after many years of absence. The workers and Party members greeted him with joy. Then the Wittdorf scandal. Now he was blamed and was being attacked. The Comintern had removed him from the German Party. They were going to send him to some outlandish place for special work. We pleaded with him not to take it lying down, to fight, as we intended to do for our rights, to refuse to be exiled. And the broken man replied: "Never will I be found guilty of formally breaking discipline. A Communist above every other consideration is a disciplined soldier. Whatever decision is made in my case, I will carry it out. You see, comrades, I am a Communist. My life is bound up with the movement and the Comintern. There is no other existence possible for me. Never, regardless of what the circumstances may be, will I put myself in a position where I will be expelled or driven out of the Comintern." With that our visit ended.

Ewert was one of Moscow's many tragic figures. He was a man truly alone in what he called his own, his workers' fatherland. In the Comintern building not even the clerks spoke to him unless they had to in an official routine manner. No one associated with him. He sat in the restaurant alone at a table, his thoughts his only companion, nibbling his food and sipping his beer. At the Lux, where he was quartered, he was shunned and avoided by everybody. It was the kind of ostracism which is well known in Moscow. One becomes its recipient the minute one falls from the good graces of the powers that be.

Another troubled man in Moscow was Charles E. Johnson, alias Comrade Scott, the Lettish comrade from the United States who went back to Russia in 1919. He had been the one who was instrumental in having Haywood flee to Moscow. He was a tall handsome man, courageous and able. He lived with his wife at the Lux. She was a head shorter than he, looked more like an Oriental with her high cheek bones and narrow searching eyes. She was a very clever, shrewd woman and a tried Communist. Scott had served the Communist International and the Profintern in the most dangerous situations. He was a Number One trouble-shooting globe-trotter for them. Up to recently he had an excellent standing and was greatly trusted. Now he was in difficulty. He held Earl Browder responsible for his difficulties. He had been assigned by the Profintern to work under Browder, who was put in charge of the Pan-Pacific Trade Union Secretariat. According to his story, secret offices running as a commercial concern were established in Shanghai involving a great outlay of money. Browder was in charge of the Shanghai center. All people sent into China for special work reported at the Shanghai headquarters. It was the center for all confidential work and revolutionary preparations. One day everybody had to take to their heels and flee, because the police and intelligence services of the Chinese and other governments interested in China had discovered the place and had prepared to raid it and arrest everybody connected with it. The arrival of the personnel in Moscow aroused the ire of the Comintern. Browder was brought up on charges of incompetence and criminal negligence. Piatnitsky raged at what he called the criminal squandering and wasting of money at a time when Russia was so badly in need of valuta.

But in Lozovsky Browder had a friend in court. Lozovsky put all the blame on Scott. But even Lozovsky was not able to save Browder. Stalin had to step in. Stalin was casting around for some one of the American Party upon whom he could depend and who would be indebted to him in more ways than one. Browder fitted into the picture. Stalin is credited with the remark in this connection that a good housemaid can put even a cracked chamber pot to some use. Stalin saved Browder's neck. Scott was condemned for something he knew nothing about and was now among the castoffs in Moscow. He vowed to us that he would clear himself. He wanted to know what we knew about Browder. His wife, however, held him in check. She was very careful and treated us with some disdain, as if she already knew or sensed that we were being slated for the ax.

We knew a thing or two about Browder insofar as his activities were connected with the American Party. Browder had a Fosterite by the name of Aronberg as his Chinese Bureau's confidential contact man in the United States. A very large amount of the money required by the Shanghai headquarters was sent from Moscow through Aronberg in the United States to China. A bill of very large denomination, five thousand dollars or larger, was received by Aronberg for transmission to China. He consulted us about it, but hesitated to have the Party break up the bill into small amounts for safe transmission to China. Kitty Harris, Browder's wife at the time, having been instructed to come to Shanghai to work in a clerical capacity in Browder's office, Aronberg entrusted her with the bill. Since the bill was in United States currency, Browder decided to cash it in Manila. The moment it was presented either by him or by one of his assistants at one of the most aristocratic hotels there, the management declared that it was unable to cash it without first cabling an inquiry to the United States, because the government kept a record of all bills over a certain denomination. Browder decided not to cash it. From that moment on, the Intelligence Service of the Far East was on his heels. The bill was presented for exchange at several cities, including Tokio, but could not be cashed. In consequence of Browder's carelessness, the entire personnel of his Shanghai Bureau barely escaped arrest, having been warned in the nick of time by a Chinese employee who had discovered that the police were investigating the place. By this final act of stupidity he had jeopardized the entire conspirative setup of his Chinese Bureau, which ostensibly functioned as a respectable commercial office.

The final act of this little comedy was written in the United States. While I was a member of the Party Secretariat we assigned a certain Cosgrove to confidential work in China. Weinstone was indignant that the assignment was not made in consultation with him, because Cosgrove was a member of the New York District and a leader among the organized shoe workers. He protested the assignment. After we were expelled from the Party, aspersions were spread on the reliability of Cosgrove. It was intimated that he was a government agent, that he had disclosed the information which led to the breaking up of the Shanghai headquarters, and as one example of his untrustworthiness, he was accused by the Party of violating Party discipline, abandoning an important post in the Shoe Workers Union against the express orders of the Party in order to go to Shanghai, and was forthwith expelled from the Party. Cosgrove closed the Shanghai story. Stalin saved Browder and Browder is today the leader of the American Communist movement. Corrupt political machines in our own country can take many a leaf out of Stalin's notebook.

The naming of Molotov as head of the American Commission was a signal to us that our question was one of the most important before the Communist International. However, the Russians had decided not to rush through with our appeal. They had lots of time and sought to wear us out by procrastination. Before the Commission got under way they informed us that its sessions would have to wait until after the Plenum of the Central Committee of the Russian Party. This gave us time to prepare our appeal and to visit friends.

A party was arranged for our delegation by Deutsch, a prominent member of the Moscow district organization of the Russian Party and of the G. P. U. Before the Revolution, Deutsch had had a checkered career in the United States, having been both a member and organizer for the I. W. W., as well as an employer involved in labor difficulties. Deutsch was known in the United States for his recklessness and courage. He was an adventurous type, one who liked to go out and face danger; the more dangerous the situation was, the better he liked it. His attachment to the radical movement in the United States was based upon this personal trait rather than on conviction or understanding of the philosophy upon which the movement was based. At the outbreak of the Russian Revolution he lived in Detroit. He was among the first Russian immigrants who sold out their belongings and left for Russia. He immediately joined the Red Army and became one of its most trusted spies. He went through the most hair-raising experiences and in later years suffered a nervous collapse. He had the highest Soviet decoration in recognition of his bravery—the Order of Lenin.

America had made a lasting impression upon Deutsch. In spite of his Russian origin, he was more American than Russian.

He dreamed of the United States and cherished everything American. A Wobbly song would raise him to the heights of ecstasy. One could see that he could never forget the reckless abandon and freedom he had enjoyed when he lived in America. Yet he lived well. In overcrowded Moscow he occupied an unusually well-kept apartment of several rooms, which were lavishly and even gaudily furnished. It was in a house reserved exclusively for higher officials of the G. P. U. Besides, he was one of the very few Russians who could boast the ownership of a piano. In spite of the food shortage, his table was generously laden with rare food and choice liquor.

It was at this party that Deutsch spoke to me about the Five-Year-Plan. He showed me the plan as finally worked out by the Party commission, the very plan that was later presented to the Party for adoption at the coming plenum. He was very proud of the fact that he was one of the recipients of the elaborate book which described the Plan in its minutest details. He was sure that Russia was embarking on a plan of industrialization that would startle the whole world. He was very enthusiastic and was sure of the fulfillment of the plan, although at the beginning it would require the exertion of superhuman effort on the part of the Russian people. "We will succeed," he said, "we will not only solve the problems for our own country but we will also set an example for the whole world." He showed me the book and explained to me where the gigantic undertakings would be built and the enormous figures set for production. "Stalin has the will. He is the driving force behind the people. With him and the great Russian people we will triumph."

Bukharin, Rykov and Tomsky were under fire as Right Wingers because of their opposition to Stalin's plan. Bukharin had written an article called "The Notes of an Economist," in which he warned against the extreme tempo set by Stalin. In his article he showed that the maximum figures originally worked out for the plan had been changed by Stalin to the minimum figures and that the question of light industry, consumers' goods, and the question of the market had been neglected. Rykov made dire predictions and sought a more balanced plan in conformity with Russian conditions. Stalin falsely charged them with being against industrialization. He charged that they were opponents to the Five-Year-Plan and against the building up of heavy industry for the manufacture of capital goods.

A couple of years before Stalin had opposed the far more modest industrialization figures proposed by Trotsky and others of the Left Opposition as fantastically impossible. (Similarly, prior to the arrival of Lenin in 1917, Stalin did not dare to dream of a Bolshevik-led "proletarian" revolution.) Stalin constantly underestimated the revolutionary capabilities of the Russian people. Yet suddenly he turned and not only accepted Trotsky's proposals, which he had formerly denounced as thunder on the Left, but went so much further than Trotsky that he found himself far to the Left of Trotsky's Leftism in the matter of industrialization plan figures. This was not a case of conversion in Stalin's economic thinking, but purely a political maneuver for disorganizing Trotsky's adherents and forcing them to choose between Trotsky and his program. They chose the latter, returned to the Party after eating humble pie, and left Stalin free to turn his attention to the so-called Opposition of the Right. Stalin then coined the slogan that at this stage of the development of the Russian revolution, "the main danger is the danger from the Right."

He now had a free hand to deal with the Bukharin-Rykov-Tomsky followers, who were very numerous in the Russian Party, since, unlike Trotsky, these three had been part of Lenin's Bolshevik Corps before the Revolution, and moreover, they had retained their prestige throughout the six year battle to drive Trotsky out of the Bolshevik Party—in the name of orthodox Leninist Bolshevism. The leaders of the so-called Right had secure positions in the Political Bureau of the Russian Party and were powerful in many of the district organizations. They had served Stalin's purposes in the campaign against Trotsky, even as Zinoviev and Kamenev had served that purpose. They then coöperated with Stalin to eliminate Zinoviev and Kamenev, Lenin's closest collaborators and the most serious contenders for leadership after Trotsky. Now the contest had narrowed to a struggle between these three and

Stalin, who had the advantage over them because the Party machine was firmly in his hands. His task was to pillory them and make them squirm in public. The Five-Year Plan became that pillory. Economics were beside the point, merely a pretext, merely the scenery. With the might of the Party machine on his side, anything Stalin would say was right, was the law; and anyone opposing him was sinning against the Party. The three old Bolsheviks were doomed.

I received an invitation to attend the sessions of the Plenum which were scheduled to take place in the Throne Room of the Tsar's palace in the Kremlin. Lovestone did not receive an invitation, though he asked for it and was really entitled to one as a member of the Executive of the Comintern. He was informed that the number of invitations allowed the Comintern were limited, that only members of the Praesidium were given invitations. This was mere pretext. It was a slap against Lovestone for having coöperated with Bukharin at the Sixth World Congress in 1928. The Tsar's Throne Room was a large long hall ornamented with gold frescoes. At the head of the room was a raised platform with a long table at which the presiding committee sat. Below the platform sat a corps of stenographers and clerks. Towards the left, facing the audience, was the speaker's box. Behind the table was ample room for members of the Praesidium to pace up and down or to hold hurried conferences while the sessions were going on. At the right was a large anteroom, which was filled with about fifty typists busy with the hum of banging typewriters and the incessant reading of stenographic notes and the orders of clerks and secretaries. Members of the Central Committee and the delegates invited to attend its sessions sat on long benches. Loudspeakers transmitted the speeches to the very rear of the hall. On the platform were to be seen Stalin; Voroshilov, natilly dressed in his military uniform; Kalinin, the figurehead President of the Soviet Republic; Molotov; Ordzhonikidze, the Chairman of the ruthless Control Committee of the Russian Party, whose large mustache and bearing were strikingly Georgian in character; Rudzutak, a

Lettish member of the powerful Political Bureau; Kuibyshev and Rykov.

The members of the Praesidium, including Stalin, munched Indian nuts and sun-flower seeds. During important speeches Stalin would pace up and down the platform like a panther about to pounce upon his prey, listening intently to every word that was said. If he disliked what a speaker was saying he would jump to the front of the platform, lean over the table and scoff at the speaker, to let the listeners know he was dissatisfied with the speaker's remarks, or he would interject a question or a few words. It was apparent that he was the leader of the pack. In the group that listened to Boris Reinstein, who acted as our English translator, was Sirola, the representative of the Communist International to our Party in 1926 and 1927. He was a Finnish Communist and active in the affairs of Karelia. In the American Party he went under the name of Miller. He said to me, "Stalin takes his time in making decisions. But once he makes up his mind, he goes through with what he has decided to the end. He is firm and inflexible. Nothing can deter him from his course, and all who are in his way are ruthlessly swept aside and crushed. He is the typical expression of Bolshevist will and leadership." That the Five-Year-Plan would be accepted was a foregone conclusion. The main fight was against Bukharin, and his associates Rykov and Tomsky. All interest centered on this fight.

Molotov was the rising sun at that plenum. It was evident that Stalin was bringing him into a position of prominence. Lenin had called Molotov an incurable fool [*durak*]. Molotov had the faculty of changing his opinions to suit the powers that be in the Russian Party as one changes his socks. He was an unimpressive figure. He spoke for several hours, sputtering and stuttering through his long speech, which he interspersed with numerous statistics. Lenin's widow spoke. She presented a pitiable figure. The audience paid her the greatest respect. Stalin leaned over the table and took great pains to note every word she uttered. She pleaded for the unity of the Party. She claimed the differences between Stalin and Bukharin were not so great that they could not be recovered and unity achieved. She said that, even though she agreed with Stalin and considered his views correct. Stalin showed by the expression on his face that he was disappointed, and in his speech he categorically rejected her plea. Another man whose speech was listened to with great interest, and who made an impression that what he had to say counted, was Andreyev from Ukraine. He spoke well and with conviction. He had been one of Bukharin's supporters. Now he took the lead of Lenin's widow, but with this difference: he lashed out against the views of Bukharin and praised Stalin's stand, especially on the grain collections and industrialization. He called for the eradication of the errors and deviations of the Opposition and called upon them to confess to their errors for the sake of Party unity. Stalin was pleased with his speech. Tomsky spoke like a wildcat at bay. He made an impression upon me as a fighter, a man of convictions, who was ready to fight for his convictions against all odds.

A sorry figure that I met at the plenum was Melnichansky. He was formerly the head of the textile unions of the Soviet Union. He had been an I. W. W. organizer in the United States. That was before the revolution. During the October uprising he was one of the leaders of the Bolshevik forces that captured the Kremlin. He displayed in those days unusual courage and leadership. He was a supporter of Tomsky. Since the Profintern Congress in 1928, he had been removed and disgraced. Stalin did that to him—and rather crudely, too, to say the least. Melnichansky had gone on a mission abroad. When Soviet officials went abroad, invariably they not only brought back merchandise for their own immediate use, but they also brought with them many things which their friends asked them to obtain for them, their friends generally being other Soviet officials. As officials, they were not subjected to customs duties, which in the Soviet Union were exceedingly high. Melnichansky on his return from abroad was held up by the Soviet Customs at the border and accused of trying to smuggle goods into the country. Simultaneously the comical sheet of the Soviet Union printed a caricature of Melnichansky as a peddler who was caught with his contraband at the border. Now the brave jovial Melnichansky, still smarting under the sting of that public ridicule, hid behind the columns of the

Tsar's Throne Room so as not to be too conspicuous. His genial smile was gone and in less than a year's time he had aged considerably.

At this plenum the fight against Bukharin was not only political. It was also personal. His revolutionary integrity was challenged. It was insinuated that he had collaborated with agents provocateur. Letters by Lenin were produced attacking Bukharin's reliability. Molehills were made to look like mountains. Every rumor or insinuation ever current in the Party before and during the Revolution was revived to undermine and destroy the man. He took the platform and tried to defend his character and to present his political views. This he did ably and in a defiant voice, much to the chagrin of Stalin. He made a vain plea for a code of Bolshevik law, so that persons in the Soviet Union could know what they could and what they couldn't do. Rykov's speech was that of a wounded bleeding lion. He spoke with intense emotion. One could see that here was a man in stature and intelligence far above Stalin. From the way he spoke you realized that he knew it. Yet Rykov was at Stalin's mercy.

Stalin's concluding speech was that of the ruthless conqueror. He demanded complete capitulation. He was not satisfied with the speeches that had been made. The culprits had the audacity, in supporting the resolution of the Central Committee and in voting for the Five-Year-Plan, to defend their criminal past. They had not yet given evidence that they could be trusted. He proposed their removal from important posts and giving them an opportunity to prove that they were good Bolsheviks by abandoning their Right Wing policies.

The plenum, which lasted for a couple of weeks, was followed by a Party conference, which included all the important Party functionaries from all the districts of the Party. Here the days droned on endlessly with speeches in favor of the Five-Year-Plan and in condemnation of the Right Wingers. The Party conference ended, as was expected, by endorsing everything the Central Committee Plenum had done. After the Party conference, the proper Soviet government authority met and in a perfunctory manner adopted the Five-Year-Plan.

If Stalin had acted so cavalierly with Bukharin, Rykov and Tomsky, what chance had Lovestone and I? If the rightful heirs of Lenin were disposed of like recalcitrant schoolboys, what treatment could be expected by us, the poor relations from across the seas? The fact that Molotov was appointed chairman of the American Commission of the Comintern signified that the American Party matter was considered by Stalin a problem of the greatest importance to him. We soon learned that Stalin had already committed himself on the American question, even before our delegation had arrived. When the leaders of the German Party were in Moscow, before the arrival of our delegation, in order to come to an understanding with Stalin on the Wittdorf scandal and the April Convention of the German Communist Party, Thaelmann and the other German Party leaders had a conference with him and Molotov, at which not only was the American Communist Party situation discussed, but also plans made for the passing of a resolution condemning the American Party. In other words, Stalin was prejudging the case before the American Commission was constituted and the hearings on the appeal heard. The German Party convention in the resolution worked out by Stalin declared:

> While Comrade Bukharin was publicly declaring his agreement with the decisions of the Sixth World Congress, he was trying in reality to form a factional block with Kamenev against the leadership of the Communist Party of the Soviet Union. The Rights and Conciliators in Germany are ideologically connected with all opportunist groupings in the Communist Parties of Italy (Serra), France, England, America (Lovestone, Pepper), Czecho-Slovakia (Hais, Jilek), Switzerland (Humbert Droz), Austria (Schlamm), and others.

If we had not been blinded by our loyalty to the Communist International, still believing that those in charge of the Comintern were our comrades and could be convinced that in our case they were wrong, we should have packed up our bags and left Russia immediately, declaring that not only was the court prejudiced, but the judge who had been appointed had already gone on record, before even hearing one word from our side, in declaring us guilty. We merely protested, because we trusted in the good faith and the Communist integrity of the Comintern—and of Stalin.

How closely the American Party was linked to the Russian Party was brought out at the Plenum of the Central Committee. Bukharin charged that when he was in thorough agreement with the Sixth World Congress decisions and after Stalin personally had declared there were no differences between them and after he had loyally pledged to carry out the line of the Party, a campaign was being conducted against him in the United States. As proof he referred to the famous resolution against Bukharin adopted at our Party convention. Dengel, the representative to our Party, thereupon issued a statement to the effect that he was totally innocent of having anything to do with the resolution, that it was an example of the unprincipledness of the Majority of the American Party. He was referring to the resolution proposed by Minor and the competing one by Bittleman. This matter caused a furor at the Russian Party Plenum. When Bukharin spoke about it, Stalin listened with the greatest attention. It was Stalin who had Dengel advise us to issue the statement. However, I was not going to let the matter rest with Dengel's statement. I reported the matter to our delegation. We decided that it was necessary that I issue a statement in answer to Dengel's charges, in which it should be proved that the resolution was the direct result of Dengel's pressure. The next day I handed in the statement to the Plenum. I requested that it be immediately translated into Russian and read to the Plenum. Stalin became very much perturbed. He asked what it was about. The translator informed him. He became very angry. The Praesidium on the platform went into conference immediately. As soon as the statement was translated, a copy was handed to Stalin. Another conference took place. I knew what they decided by the action which followed. The Plenum session was adjourned. My statement was never read to the Plenum, for it was a startling exposure of Stalin's campaign in the International for the extermination of Bukharin.

Upon our arrival in Moscow, we also learned that the Comintern had invited Foster and Weinstone to come to Moscow to oppose our appeal. We also knew that pressure was being exerted upon all our people in Moscow, especially upon the Lenin Institute students and workers in the Comintern and Profintern apparatus. Those in charge wanted to know where they stood in the controversy, with Lovestone and Gitlow, or with the Communist International. A number of them capitulated, the most important one being H. M. Wicks, whom we had sent as the Party representative to the Profintern. Wicks had been one of our supporters for years. During the underground days of the Party, he was one of the most vociferous supporters of the underground organization. When the Communist Party made its first attempt to begin public work, he split with the Party and became a leader of the United Toilers, from whose platform and press he heaped the most vituperative abuse upon the Party. In strike situations and during demonstrations, he generally made the most provocative speeches, but nothing ever happened to him. John Reed, who met him upon his return from Russia, disliked him and did not trust him.

We also faced another problem. The Comintern had made a decision that Bertram D. Wolfe, our Party's representative to the Comintern, must go, on Comintern business, to Korea. But in the Comintern, Korea was considered the graveyard of Communist representatives. The Japanese intelligence service was so efficient there that the moment a foreigner entered Korean territory he was shadowed and, if a Communist, he was immediately apprehended. When the Comintern wanted to get rid of some one, it sent him on a mission to Korea. Pepper was sent there at the behest of Stalin in 1927. But he was shrewd and never reached the place. He took his money to go to Korea, but instead he got lost and turned up in time to participate with the special Comintern committee for China consisting of Lominadze, Neuman, Doriot, and Roy. Pepper opposed Stalin's policy and the program worked out by the Committee, and gave his reasons for the same. Stalin's policy, as I have already written, caused the criminally disastrous Canton Putsch. When the Comintern Committee returned to Moscow together with Pepper, Piatnitsky hailed Pepper before the International

Control Commission for violating discipline and misusing Comintern funds. But the matter had to be dropped, because Pepper had been correct on the Canton events. This enabled Bukharin to come to his defense and prevented Stalin from getting his pound of flesh. Thus Pepper narrowly escaped being persecuted by either the Japanese intelligence service or by Stalin. The same choice now confronted Wolfe. He refused to go and submitted a long statement, giving his reasons.

The move against Wolfe was of course directly tied up with our fight. We saw in it a move of hostility against our group. But what could we do about it? We could no longer get help from Bukharin. Hostility was now openly shown against the leaders of our delegation, while the so-called proletarian members were treated with the greatest friendliness. Every opportunity was taken to give them the time of their lives. The girls of the Comintern were put at their disposal. Parties, trips, amusements, every kind of enjoyment was lavishly thrown at them. Fortunately, our preliminary talks with them had not been in vain. This "tactic" on the part of the Russians did not work. With but one exception the members of the delegation remained loyal to us in Moscow to the bitter end.

At the opening sessions of the Commission in the middle of April, Stalin was present, to serve notice that he personally was interested in the outcome. I opened the case for our side and spoke for over two hours, presenting the demand that the Majority be given the right that belongs to every majority. The fight was on. We were sufficiently familiar with the Communist International to know that battles are not won at the public sessions of its commissions. We knew that these sessions served the purpose of creating atmosphere and undermining the viewpoints of the opposition. If we were to win, we would have to come to an understanding with the leaders of the Russian Party, now Stalin and Molotov. We first sought an interview for our delegation with Stalin. But every time he granted it, he called it off just before it was to take place. Finally, we obtained assurances for a definite appointment on a Sunday morning at the offices of the Central Committee of the Russian Party. We arrived on time and were asked to wait.

We waited for hours, and then were informed that Stalin had been busy all night and was now indisposed and could not come.

We did secure a meeting with Molotov, at which Kuusinen was present and acted as interpreter. Lovestone, Wolfe, Bedacht, and I represented the delegation. Molotov outlined to us the kind of a decision he had in mind, one that would condemn us sharply. In his talk all of us present could clearly see that he was uncomfortable, because, in his hesitating and stuttering manner, he proved that he knew little about our party and almost nothing about the United States. We fired questions at him which he could not answer. It seemed incredible then that this ignoramus could be Zinoviev's and Bukharin's successor as Chairman of the Communist International. Yet soon he was to succeed Lenin and Rykov as Premier of the Soviet Union; and more recently, Trotsky, Chicherin and Litvinov as Soviet Commissar of Foreign Affairs. He reminded me strongly of silent Cal Coolidge, only less intelligent and far, far less decent. He seemed drab, dull and petty. Before the conference really got under way, he burst into a fit of anger against Kuusinen, who immediately terminated the interview.

Lovestone and I also went to see Kuusinen. He had always been one of our good friends. Perhaps he would give us some clew to the situation. Kuusinen at first refused to see us. He said he was piled up with Comintern work, that he could not spare the time. But we would not take No for an answer, and forced ourselves upon him. This time he proved to be a good listener and a poor talker. We used every kind of an argument to demonstrate to him that our unbearable situation in the Comintern must be changed and that he must support us in our fight. But Kuusinen shrugged his shoulders and made what to me was a remark which explained the helplessness and the dejection of the man. "You," said Kuusinen in German, "you have a country to go back to, but I am an exile from my country and a refugee here. You must understand that there is nothing I can do." He was, of course, a refugee from Finland.

On April thirtieth, John Pepper came to town. Pepper's return was not just an ordinary routine compliance with the request of the Communist International that he return to Moscow. We were sure that Pepper finally showed up because something had happened in the United States that left him no alternative. For weeks before Pepper returned, his wife had been crying before us, asking us what had happened to her husband. She told us that she had not heard from him for months. She suspected that another woman was involved. Would we not please let her know the truth? "When a man is away from his wife for such a long time, it is unreasonable for his wife to expect him not to have affairs with other women. That I can understand. But why does he not write?" she cried out bitterly. But we told her that everything was all right. She did not believe us. We dared not tell her what we knew. Every time she spoke to us about Pepper, she ended by telling us that there was something we knew which we were hiding from her. Often she would exclaim because she was a devout Communist, "Oh, the stupid fool! What has he done to himself? Why did he not obey the Comintern and return to Moscow? Doesn't he know that he has killed himself? Oh, what can he now do to save himself!"

Pepper was very glad to see us, but he was not the Pepper of old, who was so sure of himself. He was like a little school boy who had committed some indiscretion and was ashamed of himself. A number in our delegation were inclined to have nothing to do with Pepper. In fact, when I first heard the news that Pepper had arrived in Moscow, I felt very much hurt that he should come at this time to complicate our political situation after we had taken every precaution to protect his reputation. But I soon got over my original feeling. I felt that Pepper was a victim not only of his own ambitions and egotism, but also of circumstances and of the Communist International system of dealing with individuals as so many pawns to be sacrificed in the interests of the political objectives of the Russian leaders.

Pepper told us the whole ugly story. He had become enamoured of his little secretary. She had given him her word of honor that she would not give him away to the Party. They had planned to leave the country together and to settle in Mexico.

He had been very careful about his movements, for fear some one would discover him. He was generally confined to his room. His condition of voluntary confinement, because of its uncertainty, was even worse than prison. One day when he ventured forth, he was accosted accidentally by Lifshitz, a member of our faction. Lifshitz, instead of approaching him as a comrade, regarded him as a criminal. He immediately saw in Lifshitz's expression that he was hostile and that the first thing Lifshitz would do would be, not to take the matter up with the comrades of the group, but to report the matter to the Party. Under such circumstances there was nothing left for him to do but to report to the Party and make a declaration that because of his illegal status he was unable to effect his return to Moscow. Such a step put him in the position of being obliged to leave the country immediately. He was certain that he could trust her. She would not expose him; he had implicit faith in her. Their's was no casual affair; they were deeply in love. He also informed us that he had written her from Germany and had warned her about the necessity of keeping quiet.

Jay and I were skeptical about her dependability. We knew her too well. She had worked as my secretary in the National Office. She lacked all the qualities that one would expect in a strong woman who would defy all conventions to protect the man she loved. That she did not love Pepper I was certain. She was typical of a large number of girls in the Party who did everything to shine in the orbit of some outstanding leader of the Party. Her husband was originally a Fosterite. We were about to convert him to our group, since his conversion would be important, he being one of the leaders of the Youth movement. But he was extremely jealous of his wife. He suspected that she had become more than a secretary to Pepper. He fought with her over the matter continuously and dogged her footsteps in order to find out where Pepper lived. We were not satisfied with the Pepper story. Minor and Stachel had handled the situation very badly. What was worse, they had not informed us about it, so that we were surprised when it was reported to us that Pepper was in Moscow.

On May sixth came the final meeting of the American Commission. Stalin and Molotov both spoke and indicated that an address would be sent to the American Party and that its Secretariat would be enlarged. The address would criticize both Foster and Lovestone sharply for factionalism and for speculating on the divisions in the Russian Party. For Foster, Stalin's speech was a bombshell. He had come to Moscow to collect on Stalin's promise to give him the Party and make him its Secretary. Now Stalin attacked him, told him he did not deserve the Party, that the Majority could not be disturbed, that only the Secretariat would be enlarged. We immediately knew that when Stalin proposed the enlargement of the Secretariat he was really proposing a Secretariat that would take the place of the Political Committee. Such a Secretariat would rule the Party and through such a Secretariat the ninety percent of the Party, which we represented, would be reduced to nothing.

Foster showed his disappointment. This was the third time, according to his interpretation of Party history, that the leadership of the Party had been snatched from him by the Russians. He had been under constant fire during the sessions of the Commission. We had raked up his record as a lieutenant of Gompers, his role in the Steel Strike, his support of the War. So hot was the barrage against him that he came into the Commission with his hat in his hand, confessing to his errors and mistakes, but declaring that now he could be trusted to lead the Party in a true Bolshevik manner. We tore his confessions to shreds, proved by records that he had not told the whole story, that he twisted records to suit himself and that even by his confessions, through which he desired to show himself off in the best light, he condemned himself and forfeited his right to the dominant leadership of the Party.

Now Stalin attacked him, said he lied in his letter about the interview he had with him, explained that he did not promise him the Secretaryship, and in the cable to the convention in which he had been given the Secretaryship, the Executive Committee of the Comintern had made a mistake. Stalin wanted the world to believe that it was possible for the Executive of the Comintern to make such a decision, involving as it did Stalin, without his consent. It was clear to us that Stalin was playing a game. He was using Foster as a rag to mop up a dirty mess. But after the mopping up process and after the rag had been wrung, would he throw it away? If ever a man looked like a squeezed-out dishcloth, it was poor Foster. Surely, it should have been apparent to him that when Browder and Bittleman broke with him at the Foster caucus meeting in Chicago on the eve of the national convention, they had done so on very definite advice from Moscow.

Stalin spoke as if he were the angel of purity. The comrades gathered around him closely, to imbibe every gem of wisdom that fell from his lips in slow, low, and deliberate tones. "The Comintern is the holy of holies of the working class. The Comintern must not be confused with a stock market." But that was precisely how Stalin was running the Comintern, buying, selling, and ruining its leaders. It is the holy of holies; therefore, those who control it, namely Stalin, do all manner of things by divine right. Their rule is holy. They can make no mistakes. That racket is as old as the hills. Here is a curious sidelight on the psychological make-up of Stalin, who claims to be a Marxist, a materialist, yet his mind runs along the line of religious reference to the holy of holies and his emphasis was on the sanctity and infallibility of the Comintern, as if it were a church rather than a revolutionary organization.

But there was one expression Stalin used on that day which became one of the most widely used expressions in the Communist movement of the world. When it was translated to me at the time, I could not help but grin sarcastically in derision. It was used in the following sentence, when Stalin, putting the tip of his thumb and index finger together, looked at them sharply and closely and remarked: "We are Leninists, and our relations one with another, as well as the relations with the Comintern, and vice versa, must be built on mutual confidence, must be *as pure and as clear as a crystal,*" and he continued, "in which case there should be no room in our ranks for rotten diplomatic intrigue." He said it with a straight face, too. One would imagine when Stalin spoke, if you took him literally, that Bolshevik politics were not confined to this earth but to an ideal state in heaven and that in this Bolshevik heaven the little Stalinites together with the Big Stalin himself flitted about in their white robes and held a crystal in their hands to see that everything they did was pure and clear. In the face of such rank hypocrisy it was refreshing to recall Lenin's frank admission—one, I am sure, Stalin must well remember: "Politics is a dirty business, and to be a good Bolshevik politician, one must be prepared to wash dirty linen." One has but to study the record of Stalin in the Bolshevik Party against Trotsky, against Bukharin, against Zinoviev, against all who dared to oppose him, to get an idea of how free his own politics were from rotten diplomatic intrigue, how crystal clear they were. Was it crystal gazing that led Stalin to torture his comrades and associates in G. P. U. dungeons and order their eventual murder on cynical pretexts?

After this meeting, our delegation was certain that the verdict would be a bad one for us. But we were determined to fight on. We drew up a statement on what we considered would be an acceptable decision on our appeal. At first, the meagre news we received from the United States was to the effect that our lines were holding well. And then confusing cables began to come from our chief supporters. On May third we received a cable from Bob Minor and Jack Stachel which suggested that the home front was beginning to crack. This cable denied that there were any differences between Minor, Lovestone, and Stachel, and called for the quickest return of the delegation, including Lovestone. After the receipt of that cable, we sent a number of cables protesting against certain actions which indicated to us that Stachel and Minor were playing into the hands of the Opposition. We received on May ninth a long, reassuring cable to the effect that they were carrying out our instructions and were fighting against Browder's opposition and sabotage. This cable included the interesting information that Pepper's *inamorata* had appeared before the Party and had confessed her relations with Pepper and his meetings with Lovestone. The cable claimed the testimony was a result of her reunion with her husband. Pepper almost collapsed when we told him about it. He now knew that his case before the International Control Committee would end in his expulsion from the Comintern.

We sent a cable in a code we had worked out before our delegation left for Moscow, instructing them what to do as the fight in Moscow progressed, and preparing them for the adverse decision which was to come.

On the tenth of May we attended a farewell party by an American member of the G. P. U., one whom we had assigned to that post. At the Grand Hotel, Lovestone and I were greeted by our friend, the G. P. U. chief in charge of his department, and two women G. P. U. operatives who were engaged in foreign espionage work. The Russian Chief was a tall, handsome fellow. According to him, the Comintern was in an awful mess. The whole house was threatening to collapse. Some of the best elements were being expelled and incompetents were taking their places. "Yes," he said, "there is a great difference between the régime of Lenin and that of Stalin. Stalin rules by virtue of his power; Lenin ruled by virtue of his authority." At the close of the party, where we drank rare wines, champagne, dated brandies, and ate the sandwiches of caviar, *pâté de foies gras* and other delicacies, our American G. P. U. friend informed us that he was leaving Moscow on the twelfth of May and was taking with him to Berlin a pouch under diplomatic seal, which meant that it would not be opened until it reached its destination. We asked him if he could take in it mail of the most confidential nature which we must be sure would not be tampered with. He promised to do so.

On the twelfth of May the American Commission held a full meeting, at which it reported the Address it had decided to send to the American Party. I described the meeting in my letter of May twelfth to my wife—the letter I sent in the safe keeping of the diplomatic pouch with my G. P. U. friend. It was actually mailed from Berlin as promised, but only after it was kept in Berlin for two days and thoroughly "examined." The letter was so crudely opened by the G. P. U. in Berlin that they had to paste a piece over the back of the envelope to hide the fact that they had examined its contents. I believe they sent the letter as I wrote it to the United States because they wanted to check up on Stachel, for I had written in the letter that its contents should be shown to Stachel immediately. This letter proves that as late as May twelfth we still had confidence in Stachel's loyalty and honesty. Its opening paragraph also indicates that we were afraid to write openly from Moscow because we knew that our mail was being tampered with:

> This letter will be mailed to you from Berlin. That does not mean that I am in Berlin. It means that some one who has left before me has mailed it. I am sending it thru that way because I will be able to write about such matters that it would be inadvisable for me to write otherwise. You will give the contents of this letter concerning Party matters to my mother, so that she can take them up with Jack Stachel.

Further on in it, I wrote about the Comintern Address or Open Letter to the American Party:

> It is a document which proposes thoroughly to discredit the present Party leadership and to turn it over to the Opposition. In the Letter, Lovestone, Pepper, myself, and Bedacht are very sharply attacked. We are called unprincipled opportunists, rotten diplomatists, our political views are attacked unjustifiably. The Opposition is treated with silk gloves; the only one of the Opposition mentioned by name is Bittleman. The basis for the expulsion of thousands of members on formal lines is laid down in the Letter. The Letter is to be sent over the heads of the Central Committee to the Party membership.

At this meeting Molotov and Stalin both spoke again. They set the tone; the others followed suit. All the countries were lined up against us, and their representatives all outdid themselves in the viciousness of their attacks. After this meeting we prepared a statement on the Open Letter, or the "Comintern Address," as it was called in Moscow. Our delegation had held firm. Bedacht insisted on the sharpest kind of a statement. That the delegation had not crumbled before the onslaught of the Comintern was indeed a surprise to me. We also drafted some very important code cables to America, informing Stachel and Minor to carry out all the plans we had made before departing, laying particular stress on the transfer of the Party's property into our hands, for with the resources of the Party we would be in position to fight against the Comintern decision in the United States, which was what mattered most to us.

We did not know at that time that Stachel and Minor were sending us one set of cables and another set to the Comintern. We did not know then that the Comintern sent Stachel every coded cable which we sent him and that he in turn decoded it and cabled it back. Stachel the medicine faker merely saw his opportunity of breaking loose from his master Lovestone, in order to serve a more powerful and resourceful boss—Stalin.

In the meantime Max Bedacht was going through a terrific personal crisis. We shared a room at the Hotel Bristol. Frightfully sick with diarrhea, he moaned and cried all night long. Previously I had suggested to our Steering Committee the necessity for determining Bedacht's intentions. But whenever the question was raised at our delegation meetings, he pledged us his loyalty and said he would fight on with us regardless of the consequences. The night before the Praesidium meeting was to take place Bedacht tossed around in his bed and cried like a baby. He had come to the crossroads and had to choose between breaking with the Comintern or with us. With our future uncertain, for Bedacht to break with the Comintern was to break with every hold he had on life in an economic, political, and social way. I doubted when the supreme moment would come that he would stand firm. I decided to watch his reactions at the meeting.

The Praesidium met on May fourteenth. The meeting, which was very important because it was to give its seal of approval to the Executive's decision, lasted until three in the morning. Stalin personally took charge of this meeting of the Praesidium. The whole world of the Comintern was mobilized against us. We introduced a letter signed by the members of our delegation, stating why we could not vote for the Comintern Address. Stalin attacked our letter by calling us names and by ridiculing our leadership, which he had only a few months ago praised as outstanding. Then he did what is always done by those in power in the Communist movement. He demanded that now that the decision was made, we demonstrate that we are loyal Communists by voting for it and pledging ourselves that we would carry it out loyally.

But in asking us to ratify this decision, Stalin was asking us to admit that we had committed the crimes alleged against us. Had we signed the pledge demanded of us, we would have been condemned by our own confessions of guilt. It was the G. P. U. method of forced confessions, which has since become so prominent in Stalin's Russia and which enabled him to liquidate the Old Bolsheviks, the leaders of the Bolshevik Revolution who had been Lenin's closest collaborators. Had we obeyed Stalin, we would have declared to the Party membership that we were unprincipled, Right Wingers, "rotten" diplomats, that we supported the slanderous attacks of the Right Wing upon the Communist Party of the Soviet Union, that we did not know the nature of American capitalism, that we overestimated its strength, that we overestimated American Imperialism and were weakening the struggle against it, that we distorted the line of the Comintern, that we were gross intriguers. Moreover, the speeches by Stalin, Molotov, Bela Kun and others shed a blinding light on the nature of this Address, this confession Stalin wanted us to sign, for they called us glorifiers of American Imperialism, Hooverites, Fascists. Stalin even called us Babbitts, said that we were drawn into the old outworn path of opportunism, that we were guilty of deceitful maneuvers, that we were, indeed, no more than shyster lawyers. The Praesidium's vote was taken right after this scurrilous attack. It was no surprise to me that I was the only member of the Praesidium who voted against the "Address." With the vote of the Praesidium, the Address became forthwith an official decision. Stalin rose and stated that now the comrades of the American delegation individually had to state whether they would obey the decision or not.

It was a very tense moment. Every one was on his feet. It was the fourth hour past midnight. In addition to every important Communist Leader, the American students of the Lenin School were also on hand. The Germans, the French, the Hungarians, the Italians, the English, the Chinese, and many other representatives of Communist parties throughout the world, were on hand. The important figures of the Comintern apparatus attended. Piatnitsky had just returned from a long absence, ostensibly due to illness but which had really been taken in order to avoid the ax which fell upon Bukharin's head. Boris Reinstein was on hand as interpreter.

One by one the members of our delegation took the floor and stated that they adhered to the declaration which we had submitted. I believe that never before had the Red Hall of the Comintern witnessed such a dramatic closing to a decision by one of the sub-commissions of the Executive Committee of the Communist International. Bedacht was pacing up and down in the rear. He turned to me. His face was pale and covered with a cold sweat. "Comrade Gitlow! It is now a decision! The whole situation is changed! We must accept! I will accept!" I looked at him with disgust. I turned to Lovestone and told him about Bedacht. But Lovestone was much more worried about his own situation and what he was going to say than about Bedacht's collapse. A check-up of the delegation showed that all would stand by our declaration. Ella Reeves Bloor made a preliminary statement in which she said her conscience did not permit her to support the decision because it was contrary to the best interests of the Party. The other members just stated that they stood by the statement submitted. Only when Max Bedacht in a wavering voice made his submission to Stalin's demand known did the crowd applaud. It was the thing that had to be done, but there was no enthusiasm in it. Piatnitsky looked sick. His Comintern was going to pieces.

Then Lovestone rose to speak. He ended with the declaration that he stood by the statement of our delegation. I was to speak last, after Lovestone. I had been reviewing the whole situation in rapid-fire succession in my mind. Could I submit to a decision in which I made myself guilty of crimes I did not commit? Could I capitulate to Stalin who was using the discipline of the Comintern to force his will upon the world Communist movement? What right did the Russians have to boss the movement in the United States and make its course subservient to the interests of the Russian Party? Could I submit to the dictates of men who did not even begin to understand the problems confronting the United States? No, I could not. On the contrary, it was my duty to fight against such a decision and declare my intentions to do so to the entire world.

I was called upon to give my answer. I made a speech criticizing the decision. I stated that I could not accept it without grossly violating my deepest convictions, for the decision was detrimental to the American Party. I stated that I could not accept the demand put upon me to discredit myself before the American working class, for I would not only be discrediting myself and the leadership of the Party, but the Party itself which gave rise to such a leadership. I spoke slowly and calmly. Yet my whole being was aflame with the deepest emotions, for I was taking a stand that would cut, perhaps forever, the knot that tied me to the Communist movement, the movement I helped to build in the United States, the movement for which I had gone to prison. I was about to sever my relations with the first proletarian country, the country I considered my true fatherland, the country I stood ready to serve with my very life if need be. I recalled with what joy I had received the news, when in Sing Sing Prison, that the Soviet government had offered to trade an American spy by the name of Kirkpatrick for my liberation. I knew that I had been honored by the government which had elected me an honorary member of the Moscow Soviet. I had given all of my time and efforts to the movement, never seeking position, honor, or reward, because I believed that Communism paved the way to economic betterment and freedom never before enjoyed by the individual. But what Stalin was proposing went against my grain. In it I recognized the seeds of a despotism that would be more ugly, more brutal than the despotism of the Tsars. I spoke out. "Not only do I vote against the decision, but when I return to the United States, I will fight against it!" As I said this, I looked straight at Stalin. I left the crowd aghast for a moment. Then a long drawn-out whistle arose from the crowd, as if it wanted to say, "Whew, did you hear that?"

Stalin heard it. The action of the American delegation was bad enough. It was an indirect defiance of his course in the Comintern. But I had gone beyond that. In Soviet Russia, where he was supreme, in a room filled with important Communist leaders from all over the world, I had told him frankly what I thought of his actions against the American Party, and followed it up with a declaration both of defiance and fight. I knew what I was up against. I knew that I was facing Stalin in his own realm, where his word was law. I knew that it might mean detention in the Soviet Union indefinitely and perhaps worse. But I had made up my mind that, regardless of what the personal consequences would be, the fight had to be made openly and started right in Moscow, if our fight was to lead to a change in the Comintern and change the system of puppetry which prevailed at the Bolshevik Court.

Stalin rushed to the platform. I had never seen him so angry before. His reserve was gone, and the low, slow delivery supposedly characteristic of the man, a delivery which he affected, was gone. He burst into a tirade against us. The American Party published a version of his speech. The full speech he actually delivered will never be published, because it was replete with personal abuse and name-calling. When he ended his outburst, he declared that we could go back to America, adding, "The only ones who will follow you will be your sweethearts and wives." An answer to the question, what weapon is used to force Communists to yield against their innermost convictions and confess to crimes of which they are not guilty, is contained in the following portion of the published version of Stalin's speech:

> We ought to value the firmness and stubbornness displayed here by eight out of the ten American delegates in their fight against the draft of the Commission. But it is impossible to approve the fact that these eight comrades, after their views have suffered complete defeat, *refuse to subordinate their will to the will of the higher collective,* the will of the Praesidium of the E. C. C. I. True Bolshevik courage does not consist in placing one's individual will above the will of the Comintern. *True courage consists in being strong enough to master and overcome one's self and subordinate one's will to the will of the collective, the will of the higher Party body. Without that there is not, and cannot be, any collective leadership.*

Stalin did not express himself quite so urbanely at the meeting. But I am sure he checked this edited version, which represents the substance of the Bolshevik attitude. Complete subordination of one's will to the higher Party body, without reservations, even if it result in one's annihilation—that is the essence of Bolshevik Party discipline. The higher Party body may be a committee representing a collective of dictatorial power over the Communist Party, or it may, as it has become in Russia under Stalin and for the world Communist movement, be assumed by one man whose will is inexorable law, a law to which all Communists must subordinate themselves. Before his absolutism, his unlimited dictatorial power, so extensive and far reaching in its attributes, all must bow, all must humble themselves. To fail to do so under all circumstances is, as Stalin has put it, to be denounced as a strikebreaker, a traitor to the working class, to be branded for all time by the powerful organization of the Communist International as a renagade, to be vilified in its press of a hundred tongues, and to be hounded even unto death. This is the fate that awaits all Communists who have the temerity to stand by their convictions. Stalin could not get over my defiance of him, for again and again he referred to it, appealing to my fellow-delegates: "Members of the American delegation, do you think that the conscience and conviction of Comrade Gitlow are above the conscience and conviction of the overwhelming majority of the Praesidium of the E. C. C. I.?"

When we left the Red Hall it was past four o'clock in the morning. The gray dawn was just coming to life. A fruit vendor was selling oranges at an exorbitant price. The members of our group bought one apiece and began sucking them. Jay, Bedacht and I went back to the Bristol. Not a word passed between us. We were fagged out. The nervous strain of the long day had taxed our energies to the breaking point. Bedacht and I went to our room. He moaned, groaned, and tossed about in his bed, crying, "Oh, mama, mama, mama! I had to do it, I had to." Three days later in a letter to my wife I wrote:

> Max [Bedacht] is sleeping the sleep of the disturbed. I am think-of you and Sonny. I expect soon to be with both of you. I have not heard from you for a long time because you expected me home much sooner. But now it is only a matter of a few days before I start back. Our fight is the talk of every one. We put up the kind

> of a fight that will be long remembered. I am not sorry for that fight. I am of the opinion that it will do a lot of good. I will have to pay for it, but I am not sorry. . . But our question is not looked upon as satisfactorily settled. The whole affair has left a bad taste. I am convinced that such methods of treating parties will never again be resorted to. Perhaps it will be very costly for us who made the fight. That we shall see. It is not the first time that fighters have paid dearly for the gains to be enjoyed by others.

The afternoon after the Presidium meeting, Lovestone and I went to call on Dr. Julius Hammer. He was very glad to see us, for he had some very startling news to give us concerning the American Party. We wondered how the news reached Hammer so quickly. It was supposed to be kept secret until the Central Executive Committee in the United States had an opportunity to act upon it. He volunteered the information without our asking for it. His son Armand had seen Walter Duranty of *The New York Times* that morning. Duranty informed him that he had been given the news of the decision on the American Party with the request to cable it to the United States immediately. He had shown Armand a copy of the cable, which he had sent that morning upon Stalin's request. This was a new angle for us of the way in which the Comintern under Stalin's direction was fighting us. He was using the capitalist press to prejudice the American public against us before we were expelled from the Party and before the Party membership was officially notified of the action taken by the Comintern.

Only two days before Stalin had denounced our factionalism as leading to the disclosure of Communist Party matters to the bourgeoisie. And the very practice which Stalin accused us of and denounced us for, of which we were, of course, not guilty, he now used himself. It was a fitting tribute to his statement that the relations of the Communists must be pure and clear as a crystal. Duranty's cable to *The New York Times* opened the "Enlightenment Campaign," initiated by the Comintern for enlightening the Party membership and the American public on the reasons for its decisions.

I told Lovestone, after the Hammer meeting, that when we

returned to the United States we would be met by a hostile membership, a membership which would be poisoned by a campaign of lies and vilification. Lovestone believed that the membership would wait to hear his version of the decision, provided he could arrange for his speedy return to the United States. I laughed at him and told him that he had grand illusions and that he would be shocked when he was confronted with the reality. And, strange to say, in spite of all of Stachel's double-dealing, Lovestone still had faith in him.

In Bolshevik circles it was axiomatic that all political decisions must have their organizational consequences. The organizational proposals came soon enough at a meeting of the Executive of the Comintern. Molotov himself announced them. Lovestone, Wolfe, and I were removed from all positions in the Party and in the Communist International. I was removed as Secretary of the Communist Party of the United States and from its Secretariat. Then followed my removal from the Executive Committee of the Communist International, from the Praesidium of the Comintern and from the Executive of the Profintern.

But the proposals did not end with the removals. It was decided that Bedacht and Minor be added to the Secretariat, to maintain the fiction that the majority of the convention was continued as the Majority, but with a difference. A committee of three was to be sent to the United States immediately under the chairmanship of a Russian. Upon their arrival in the United States, the members of this committee were to become members of the Secretariat, with power to vote on all American Party matters coming before the Secretariat. Its authority was broadened to include all political matters, making the new Secretariat of six actually the leading committee of the Communist Party of the United States, three of whose members were put there by Stalin, they having never been members of the American Party.

But even this arrangement was not a sufficient guarantee for Stalin. He proposed that the Russian chairman of the committee of three have plenipotentiary powers over the Secretariat, the Political Committee, the Central Executive Committee and all the districts of the Party, that this single individual have the sole right and power to make decisions which would have the full weight of Comintern authority back of them and would have to be obeyed without appeal. It was also decided to help the Party's fight against us with all the resources at the command of the Comintern. Following that meeting, Bedacht was called in for a private conference, at which the strategy of the fight in America was worked out and the decision made to send the Party an initial sum of fifty thousand dollars with which to finance the fight. These decisions were made on May eighteenth, when the Communist International had received information from Stachel that the Political Committee had accepted the "Address" and endorsed it unanimously! This did not stop these crystal-pure American Bolsheviks from cabling to Moscow at the same time their pledges of loyalty to our delegation and to the fight we were making. This duplicity was part of Stalin's strategy. Stachel kept it up by connivance with Stalin, whom he was thus able to keep informed of our plans. Sure that he had the situation of the American Party in hand, Stalin immediately shipped Bedacht, Weinstone, Foster, and his Russian Communist International Representative to the United States. The so-called proletarian members of our delegation left about a week afterwards. Lovestone, Wolfe, and I were ordered to remain for the hearing of the Control Commission on Pepper's case.

I was kept in Moscow for two weeks. My routine consisted of walking to and from the Comintern building and the Bristol Hotel. At the Comintern building we were generally kept waiting for hours on end in an anteroom, waiting day after day for the Control Commission to call us in. It was quite evident to us that we were being deliberately detained while our personal fate was being further considered. Every day I demanded that I be permitted to go home. But the only answer I got was: "When the Control Commission decides that you are no longer needed on the Pepper case." On May twenty-fourth I wrote to my wife in part:

> I did not write you also because of the uncertainty of my departure. I expected to be on my way long before. But we are being

> kept. How much longer I cannot say. . . Regardless of what happened or may happen, as far as I am concerned, I made a clean, principled fight. I have not lost my self-respect; that is important. I can look everyone square in the face. . . If I had been unprincipled, I could have risen to the zenith of power and place. Now I have lost whatever place I had.

My letter of May twenty-eighth declared:

> How much longer I will remain I cannot now say. I am trying to get out as soon as possible. I hope I succeed. . . You may wonder why I do not write you at length. Feeling the way I do, always uncertain, hoping against hope, it is quite impossible to write. So my letters are brief, say almost nothing. We are completely shut off from news of the States.

The inquisition of Pepper was a subterfuge to keep us in Moscow indefinitely. I know that the question was debated in Stalin's inner circle for hours. Had we been citizens of one of the Balkan countries, we would have been kept prisoners in Moscow indefinitely or until we capitulated to Stalin's superior will. The fact that we were Americans, citizens of a great power with whom Russia was anxious to establish friendly relations, frightened Stalin from doing his worst.

I was finally released by the Control Commission. I got my passport from Abramovitz, in charge of the passport and secret service department of the Comintern, a branch of the G. P. U. When he gave me the passport, he remarked that one is either with the Comintern or against it, that every one who started by being in opposition to the Comintern on some issues soon traveled the road which makes one a renegade. He then gave me a letter, which he said, if I handed to the customs officials, would facilitate my passage out of the country. He warned me not to break its wax seal.

I was overjoyed and decided to leave by plane early the next morning, on June second. I made arrangements to wait for Wolfe and Lovestone either in Berlin or Paris, so that on our way we could discuss the plan of battle for the United States. At the Moscow airport, I fingered the sealed letter and then decided, since I did not know its contents, not to give it to the customs officials. Instead, I showed them my Comintern pass as a member of the Praesidium of the Comintern. It worked like a charm, as it always had in Russia. My baggage was immediately stamped without even the formality of an examination. I was most courteously escorted to my plane. I bid good-by to Lovestone and wished him luck in getting out of Moscow soon. The plane took off and soared high into the heavens. I was leaving Moscow perhaps never again to return. It was my departure from the land of Communism.

Once outside of Russia, I opened the sealed letter. When I met Wolfe in Paris about ten days later, he translated it for me. It contained instructions to the customs and G. P. U. officials on the border to give me the most thorough search and to take away from me all my documents and papers. The clever trap did not work. Wolfe, on the other hand, did not receive a letter. The officials were notified in advance. His search lasted for hours. Everything, including his person and that of his wife, was searched for material that the Comintern did not want to be taken out of Russia. Lovestone was still being kept in Russia. Stalin did not want to let him out.

In order to get permission to leave the country, Lovestone had to withdraw the statement he had made in the Praesidium on May fourteenth regarding our insubordination, in return for which he would be allowed to go to America for two weeks, beginning June twelfth, provided he pledged to return to Moscow and work in the Comintern. But the Comintern did not want to allow Lovestone to go without the approval of the American Party. The new Secretariat of the Party opposed permitting him to leave for America. After the receipt of this information, the Comintern stated it had no objections to Lovestone leaving the country, provided he would carry out his promise, but delayed in setting the date for his departure. Lovestone took advantage of an American friend who happened to be in Moscow at the time and had considerable influence with the Soviet Travel Bureau, to obtain his visas and airplane tickets without the knowledge of the Comintern. The next morning he flew out of Moscow. The American Party immediately expelled him from the Party for leaving the Soviet Union without the Comintern's permission.

I arrived in New York together with Wolfe in June, 1929. The campaign against us was on in full swing. *The Daily Worker* and all other Party papers carried screaming headlines against us as renegades, splitters, petty bourgeois politicians. Every vile word in the political dictionary was used over and over again. The Comintern Address became the most important Communist document in existence. The Party demanded that every member must vote in favor of the Address, declare that he believed in it and would loyally carry it out. The Party members who failed to do so were brought before the Control Committee, under the Chairmanship of Dr. Mindel, a dentist. If they persisted in having any doubts concerning the correctness of the Address, they were generally given twenty-four hours in which to confess that they were wrong and to admit their errors or else be automatically expelled from the Party as renegades.

The Party sent out instructions that Party members must have no social contacts with the renegades. Such contact would lead to expulsion from the Party. Additional instructions went out that in families which belonged to the Party, if some of the members supported the renegades, there must be a break with such members of the family, those loyal to the Party denouncing the renegades. The Party forced husbands to denounce their wives and wives to denounce husbands. There were cases where sons publicly denounced their fathers in the severest terms and pledged themselves to have nothing further to do with their parents.

I was expelled from the Party for refusal to submit to the Comintern Address. I had sent a letter to the Party stating that I was ready to accept any kind of an assignment the Party would give me and carry it out faithfully, but would not vote for or approve the Address. Attempts were made to bribe me. I was offered a lucrative position doing confidential G. P. U. work in the Latin-American countries at a very good salary, including traveling expenses, which would enable me to travel first class and stop at the best hotels. In return I would have to promise that I would keep quiet on the American Party question and disassociate myself from the comrades in opposition to the Comintern. I would have to stay out of the United States for a year or two. In return the campaign against me in the Party and in the press would be stopped. This offer I turned down, even though, upon my arrival in the United States, I did not have a penny to my name and I was badly in debt. I had been away from the United States for over two months. During all that time my wife received two and a half weeks of my wages, amounting to one hundred dollars. She had to get work in order to maintain our one-room apartment in the Bronx, provide food for herself and our son, then two and a half years old. I turned the tempting offer down, because I recognized that it was a bribe and because I knew that if I once put myself in the employ of the G. P. U., I would be at its mercy for ever after.

Before I went to Europe I had left in the National Office a trunk which contained an old suit of mine, an overcoat, some shirts, and some of my son's clothes. The National Office refused to return the trunk to me on the ground that I owed it some money which I collected for dues and subscriptions from Dr. Julius Hammer when I was in Moscow. The money I collected from Dr. Hammer amounted to a few dollars, which was spent for cables. Since I had been the Secretary of the Party and our delegation was an official Party body, I had a perfect right to make those expenditures. I spent every available extra ruble I had in Moscow for that purpose also. Besides, I had given Bedacht, who was appointed to the Secretariat, a complete accounting of these expenditures. I informed the Party accordingly. After many weeks, they decided to return the trunk to me. My wife went to the office to pick it up. She was met by Comrade Pollack, an accountant who had been placed in charge of technical and accounting matters of the National Office. When she saw the trunk in the store room, she noticed that the lock had been broken open and the trunk battered. She decided to look inside. All our personal belongings, the clothes which we needed badly, for we had no money to buy others to replace them, had been taken. The trunk without the clothes was worthless. My wife turned to Pollack and said: "Haven't you taken enough from us that you had to steal our clothes? This is just some more of your Party wrecking. Since you are so badly in need of funds, I donate the trunk to you also." When I met her, she had tears in her eyes.

I soon felt what it meant to be expelled from the movement which had been part of my life since 1919. My comrades who had been my best friends turned their heads away when they met me, muttered curses, and often spat upon the sidewalk to show their contempt. Bob Minor and Jack Stachel, in charge of the national office, did not have to rifle my trunk, for it contained no documents. Yet they allowed it to be sacked of my clothes and the clothes of my little son—all because I had refused to do Stalin's bidding. It was petty and mean and typical of the Stalin régime. I felt Stalin's whip on all sides, for his arm stretched from far off Russia into the United States to direct a campaign of vile personal slander and fanatical intolerance against us. I was to learn in due time upon further reflection that Stalin, the fanatic and despot, the personification of Communist ruthlessness and evil, was but the natural outgrowth of Bolshevism and its system of politics.

CHAPTER XVI

FRAGMENTS THAT FLY APART

UPON our expulsion from the Communist Party, Lovestone and I organized our faithful followers into the Communist Party, U. S. A. (Majority Group). Let us recall in passing that when Lenin's followers organized as a faction or virtually outlawed splinter group in the Russian Social-Democratic Labor Party a generation earlier, they called themselves the *Bolshinstvo* (Russian for "majority group"), on the pretext of a passing and accidental majority at a preceding party congress. The Lenin group began with twenty-two members, counting Lenin and his wife. Lovestone and I began with a hundred and fifty. We had fully fourth-fifths of the Communist Party membership with us when we were its acknowledged leaders, yet hardly one percent followed us out of the Party into our American neo-Bolshevik organization. Our program at the time was certainly more sensible and had more reference to American conditions than the official Party's adventurist and ultra-ultra-Leftist "Third Period" nonsense, which I described in an earlier chapter. But of course there was no fundamental difference between us and the official Party. Neither organization renounced Leninism either in theory or in practice. There were only passing differences as to the interpretation of Lenin's theories—differences that time ironed out and subsequently reversed the relative position of the two groups, so that, whereas in 1930 our group was Right Wing, by 1935 the Party proved itself far more Right Wing than the Lovestone group. But it is a waste of time to recount the programs in detail. Neither program led anywhere.

The American Trotskyites under the leadership of James P. Cannon, Max Shachtman and Martin Abern started with a following of fifty, when we expelled them from the Communist

Party a year before our own expulsion. For six years, until 1934, they regarded themselves stubbornly as merely the Left Wing of the official Party, hoping against hope and against their better judgment, I daresay, to reform the Party and the Comintern and be readmitted eventually. The Lovestonites pursued a similar course as the Party's Right Wing. The Party, however, not only spurned traffic with either self-styled opposition wing, but castigated both as counter-revolutionaries and as enemies of the labor movement. The Lovestonites did not attain a membership in excess of three hundred and fifty throughout my connection with the group. The numerical strength of the Trotskyites remains a mystery, but I do not believe that it exceeded that of the Lovestonites until after 1934, when they began to make raids on other organizations in the traditional Bolshevik manner. Having organized as an independent party, the Trotskyites first merged with the followers of the former preacher A. J. Muste until they demolished Muste's organization and swallowed a goodly portion of his following. Then they merged with Norman Thomas's Socialist Party, which expelled them before they succeeded in utterly annihilating it, as they had annihilated Muste's organization. Even at that they succeeded in raiding the Socialist Party considerably, particularly of its more impressionable Youth section. But with all these raids and notwithstanding all of Cannon's political conniving, I doubt that today the entire membership of the Trotskyites, currently known as the Socialist Workers Party, exceeds a thousand—after more than ten years of propaganda activity in the United States, where they are far stronger than anywhere else in the world, not excluding Russia. What the membership of the Lovestonites is today, I do not know, but I do not believe that numerically they can compete even with the American Trotskyites.

The reason for this chronic weakness is clear. Neither group has anything to offer to the dispossessed of America. Their programs had and have nothing whatever to do with American realities. From the moment of their expulsion neither group had the intellectual strength to break with the fundamental concepts of Communism. They continued to stew in the embalming fluid of the mummified Lenin. Both criticized the Party for real or alleged deviations from the course of true Leninism—the Cannonites in pale imitation of Trotsky's trenchant style, the Lovestonites somewhat more diffidently. Both called for clarity—in turgid verbiage that reduced their political reasoning to so much gibberish. Both called for Communist unity, each on the basis of its own pet notions. Decrying the policies that were splitting and wrecking the Communist movement, the Trotskyites lashed out against the Lovestonites as Right Wingers and rotten opportunists, while the Lovestonites taunted the Trotskyites as exponents of international Menshevism (that is, of reformist Socialism), which, being anti-Communist, was *ipso facto* anti-Soviet and hence counter-revolutionary. They might as well have been discussing the momentous problem of how many angels can stand on the point of a needle, for all the relevancy of their polemics to the political problems confronting the United States and the world. Their bodies were mostly in Lower Manhattan, the Bronx and Brooklyn, but their minds were still in the Kremlin.

For years I have been reading their literary effusions, for ten years of earnest seeking, and I have failed to discern any real difference between these oppositions and the official Communist Party. All three are Leninist in the basic sense of accepting the dictatorship of the proletariat through a so-called Soviet or council form of government under the thumb of one party, their own brand of Communist Party. All three favor the establishment of a Communist totalitarian state.

The Trotskyites and Lovestonites did not break with their Communist past, for they took over with them into their oppositions the morality, or rather the lack of morality, which characterizes the Communist Party. They organized their oppositions on the organizational principles and discipline of the Communist Party. They proceeded to work inside of other organizations—trade unions, cultural societies and political movements—in identically the same way that the Stalinists did, however lacking the power and the resources to make themselves as effective as the official Communist Party. They have developed an intolerance for the views of others and a conceited belief in the correctness of their own views which was not to be distinguished from the intolerance of the Party. They were small replicas of the Communist Party, which worships Stalin: the Trotskyites idealize Leon Trotsky, while the Lovestonites idealize the very much smaller figure of Jay Lovestone.

But these two oppositions could not keep their own forces together. The louder they called for unity, the more they split up. Weisbord, though he followed Trotsky, could not stand being bossed by Cannon, so he formed the Communist League for Struggle, which solemnly declared in its mimeographed official organ, *The Class Struggle*:

> The little old Communist League for Struggle is forging ahead valiantly on its own account. Within the past three months we have doubled our membership. The Fourteenth Street tea-drinkers will inquire cynically of one another—did they have fourteen or fifteen members before they doubled? Never mind! As we said at the beginning, if we are a family group, at least we are a prolific family, and the offspring are strong and vigorous. Our members are for the most part sturdy proletarian fighters, some of them of long experience in the Communist movement. We have won two members from the Communist Party of the United States of America and two from the German Communist movement.

The Weisbord Communist League for Struggle, which never had more than fifteen members by actual count, caused Trotsky many sleepless nights, I dare say, in trying to bring about its unification with the Cannon forces. But without success.

Nor was this the only split in Trotskyist ranks. Every important international event, as well as every programmatic discussion or venture into trade unionism, involves the small Trotsky group in a crisis, which leads to a number of splits. From these have emerged, to mention only a few, the Field group, which seeks to weld its handful of pure Leninists and Trotskyists into a Revolutionary Workers Party that shall bring about proletarian dictatorship in the United States; the Oehler group; the Stamm group; the Marlen group. Nor are these groups immune to splits. Even the Weisbord group had a split when one of its members sold the communal mimeograph machine.

The Lovestone group, too, has had its troubles. The first split came when a group headed by Bert Miller sought to have the Lovestonites unite with the Committee for Progressive Labor Action, a non-Communist group, headed by A. J. Muste. I split with the Lovestone group when it insisted that Stalin's policies were a hundred percent correct. I wrote Lovestone, who was in Europe at the time, that, in my opinion, conditions in Russia proved that there was something fundamentally wrong there:

> Another point upon which we must be very careful in considering is the question of the present economic collapse of the Soviet Union. I have been getting reports . . . of such gravity as to indicate an acute situation. The conditions in Russia today are frightful. I suppose that in Germany you are able to get some first hand information on the same. To hold that the present situation there is due to a fall in export prices, in my opinion, is taking too shallow a viewpoint of the situation. There are other factors involved, including the whole line, methods and regime of the leadership of the Communist Party of the Soviet Union.

To this Lovestone replied from Berlin on July twenty-second, 1932:

> Your remarks on the Russian situation: I still believe that our resolution was correct and is correct. Yes, I have quite a bit more information. Information from critical high officials rather than from disgruntled, declassed Jewish peasants. . . Finally, the crop this year, through no fault of Joe [Stalin] and through no virtue of Trotsky or Bukharin happens to be a bad one. . . Without minimizing the difficulties and certainly without excusing Joe's factionalism, we must admit that if it hadn't been for the substantial achievements of the Five-Year-Plan based on a general correct line the situation in the U. S. S. R. today in the face of the aggravating world market situation would be far worse.

That winter millions of Russians starved to death.

When the group supported Lovestone on the proposition that Stalin was correct, I told them that they ought to go back to Stalin's Communist Party and resigned. But my break with the Lovestone group did not mean a break with Communism. I was still a firm believer in Communism, though I had the boldness to break with many of its cherished traditions and prejudices. I declared that there was something fundamentally wrong with the Communist movement, its tactics and leadership. Communists, I said, must face this fact frankly, courageously, and with a desire to go to the roots of the trouble. I went even further and declared that the Stalin régime must be held responsible for its criminal actions, that the line of the Communist International and its disruptive tactics in the labor movement must be abandoned, that the united front must not be considered a maneuver, but a necessity, if unity in the labor movement was to be achieved. I demanded that serious consideration be given the question of winning the support of the middle class in the struggle against Fascism, and concluded that the Communists must end the domination of the Communist International by the Russian leaders.

All the Communist opposition movements pounced upon me for my stand. They declared that I was going over to reformism and away from Communism. When Hitler came into power, all of them believed that Stalin would become sufficiently alarmed to reunite the movement. Stalin, however, took the position that the victory of Hitler was a victory for the working class and the Communists, because it shattered the democratic illusions in the working class and thereby hastened the day when the Bolshevik Revolution would break out in Germany. Trotsky was of the opinion as late as the end of February, 1933, that

> The Reichsweher, to say nothing of the Steel Helmets, is not in Hitler's hands. His own armed forces represent a problematic quantity which is still to be verified. His millions of reserves are human rubbish. . . In this manner there remains no short distance from the ministry headed by the Fascist Chancellor to the complete victory of Fascism.

And if this seems overly optimistic, to say the least, consider the declaration made by the Trotskyist International Left Opposition to the World Anti-Fascist Congress, published in *The Militant* of May 20, 1933:

> The dénouement [of Hitler] can come very much sooner than the masters of the day think.

As for Lovestone, he went to Europe and after putting his head together with that of Otto Brandler, who had been expelled with his group from the German Communist Party as a Right Winger, the two decided on behalf of their so-called International Opposition that Stalin was basically correct on Russia and that the issue of democracy in Germany was now dead. Before the triumphant beat of Hitler's brown-shirted hordes, the Communist movement—right, center and left, Stalinists, Trotskyites, Brandlerites, and Lovestonites—was left stunned. Their theories failed to work, and all they could offer was the vain hope that Hitler's collapse would usher in Bolshevism.

After leaving the Lovestone group, I attempted to form a bloc of all the Communist oppositions against Stalin. But I found each one of them as monolithic as the Communist Party itself. The Trotskyites were ready for unity, provided everyone accepted Trotsky's program of opposition. The Lovestone group insisted that it wanted unity *with* Stalin, not a bloc against him. Notwithstanding the failure to form a bloc, I made another attempt to unite the Communist oppositions and forces into a new party. Again I was faced with the fact that each Communist opposition wanted to be boss in its own little house, and that the trend was toward splits and splinters rather than unity.

My belief in the Communist movement was beginning to weaken considerably by this time. I could not help but sense that the Communists were so hopelessly divided, so impregnated with their own dogmas, that it was impossible to build through them any serious political movement in America. They had not learned anything from their conflicts with the Communist International. They still accepted Lenin as their infallible prophet, and to them life still ended with Russia. Cannon and Lovestone were both little Stalins in their own groups.

In 1934 the Socialist Party began to show, what I considered then, signs of life. I was still a Communist. The fight in the Socialist Party interested me because the issues between the Left Wing and the Right Wing were being drawn sharply. I had said right after the death of Morris Hillquit that without his leadership the Right Wing of the Socialist Party would go down to defeat and that Norman Thomas would take the leadership of the Socialist Party away from it. His assumption of leadership made the Socialist Party more resilient than it had been during the last ten years of Hillquit's tenure. The Left Wing in the Socialist Party was represented by two organizations. The older one and the one with the largest following was called the Militant Group; the other went under the name of the Revolutionary Policy Committee. I got in touch with the leaders of both of these groups, in order to learn more about the issues in the Socialist Party and to determine my own course.

The leaders of the Revolutionary Policy Committee did not impress me favorably. One of them, Francis Henson, a minister by profession, expressed to me his strong belief in Communist fundamentals, his categorical opposition to the official Stalinist Communist Party of Browder, on the grounds that it was impossible to build a Communist Party in America if it were dominated by the Russians, and declared that he did not agree with Lovestone because Lovestone supported Stalin's Russian policies. This position coincided with my views and made me feel hopeful about reaching an organizational understanding with Henson. But subsequently I discovered that Henson maintained the most friendly relations with the Stalinists and was working completely under Lovestone's direction. Through him and others in the Revolutionary Policy Committee Lovestone hoped to split off a substantial number of Socialists who would immediately join his group. Upon further investigation, I discovered that the Revolutionary Policy Committee swarmed with agents of the Communist Party, the Lovestonites and the Trotskyites. I was nevertheless hopeful enough to believe that I could induce this group to unite with the Militants, who in my opinion represented the more decisive and numerous Left Wing elements in the Socialist Party. I failed.

On the eve of the Socialist Party's Detroit convention in 1934 I had a long conference with J. B. Matthews, who lectured under the auspices of the League for Industrial Democracy in which Norman Thomas was the leading figure. I knew that Matthews had been working closely with the Communist Party, but I believed he had disassociated himself from it when he resigned as President of the League against War and Fascism, a

Communist-inspired organization, the building of which was financed in the main by Moscow and which the Communists dominated. Matthews showed a surprising lack of knowledge of the inner politics of the Socialist Party. He was lackadaisical in discussing matters in which he should have been very vitally interested. Moreover, he seemed to me essentially a weak character, one who could not stand up in a crisis. I spoke to him of the necessity of uniting all the Left elements in the Socialist Party and of keeping free from Communist corrupting influences, if the Left Wing was to succeed in uniting the radical forces into a genuinely American revolutionary movement. He assured me that that was precisely what he was after. At the end of our conversation he pledged himself to work for the unity which I desired. About that time I received reports that the Communist Party expected that most of the members of the Revolutionary Policy Committee would join it when the split of the Socialist Party occurred and that Stachel boasted that J. B. Matthews was fully collaborating with the Communist Party.

Then I came in contact with Irving Brown. The minute I heard him talk I knew that he was a Lovestonite. An investigation brought out the fact that Brown was employed by the Educational Department of Local 22 at Lovestone's request. Brown had worked on the draft of the program of the Revolutionary Policy Committee which was issued as "An appeal to the Membership of the Socialist Party." Lovestone at one of the membership meetings of his group declared: "We have the Revolutionary Policy Committee in our vest pocket; we even wrote their program." I was told that when Lovestone made this statement Brown was present at the meeting as a Lovestone member.

At the Convention of the Socialist Party a split took place in the Revolutionary Policy Committee. The split was the culmination of a fight for the control of the committee between the Lovestone Group and the Communist Party. As a result of that friction, J. B. Matthews was expelled from the Committee, Brown and Henson emerging as the dominant leaders of the organization.

When the Left Wing captured the Detroit Convention, I joined the Socialist Party. But by that time I was beginning to go beyond the Communist opposition standpoint. I was beginning to drift further and further away from Communism. Once in the Socialist Party, however, I became aware that the young elements, who made up the bulk of the Militants, were falling like flies on fly paper for the very Communist program from which I was extricating myself. They were accepting practically all the positions which another Left Wing had adopted in 1919 before it split the Socialist Party in order to organize the Communist Party. What was more, I saw that the methods and caucuses, discipline, clique control and lack of moral scruples, which characterized the Communist movement, were coming to the fore in the Socialist Party, which had degenerated from a political party into a conglomeration of factions and a happy hunting ground for the intrigues of the Communist Party and the Communist oppositions. Their agents, like the agents of a foreign power, did their utmost to undermine its structure, in preparation for blowing it up altogether.

In the Militant Group I discovered much evidence that the influence of the Communist Party was very strong among its members and that prominent Militant leaders favored united front action with the Communists. The Socialist Party was a headless monstrosity with many legs, all pulling away in different directions. The result was so much confusion, such chaos that the Socialist Party was impotent. But what was even more disastrous was that distrust of one another was seeping into the organization. This one was suspected of being a Lovestone agent, that one of being a Trotskyite and the third one of being a Stalinist. The one man who after the Detroit convention might have steered the party in one direction or another was Norman Thomas. But Norman Thomas was like a ship without a rudder. He did not agree with the Militants, yet he allowed them to steer his course. He was a sorry figure of indecision.

Mary Fox, of the League for Industrial Democracy and one of Thomas' trusted collaborators, was too engrossed in the work of the League to pay sufficient attention to the internal politics of the Socialist Party. Her views on the party situation, especially her opposition to pushing on to a split with the Right Wing, were sound and showed an appreciation of reality. I agreed with her, because, if the Socialist Party was to amount to anything, it first had to prove its ability to unify all its available forces. In the past, the Socialist movement had been torn apart by too many splits. To promote more splits would reduce the party to an insignificant sect. But the forces for a split were working overtime. The Militants were not alone responsible for that, since the Old Guard in large measure forced the younger elements into a split by hampering their activities in the party. Norman Thomas, who was opposed to a split, was so engrossed in his own activities, which kept him moving all over the country and busily speaking day and night, that he had no time to watch his own house. The Communists and their sympathizers entered and secured themselves so firmly that Norman Thomas had to bend to their proposals. I was very much alarmed when this took place, and my failure to get the Militants in the Socialist Party to interfere had much to do with my disillusionment with the organization.

Joseph P. Lash, now Secretary of the American Student Union, was at the time head of the Students' League for Industrial Democracy. For years this organization had been able to withstand Communist pressure, maintaining its independent program among the students of the high schools and colleges. Then the Communists won over Joe. He became one of their secret agents. The Communists had organized a students' organization of their own, the National Students' League, in an effort to gain control of the radical student movement and to eliminate the influence of the Socialists in this field. With Lash's support certain, the Communists started a movement for the unification of the student organizations, knowing full well that once they should succeed in uniting the two organizations into one, the Communists would control it. Suspecting Joseph Lash from the very start, I advised against the amalgamation of the student organizations as a move that would play into the hands of the Communists. Norman Thomas, though with many misgivings, supported Lash's move, as a move demanded by the students. When the matter was discussed in the Socialist Party and among the Militants, I strongly disapproved of the merger. But the Communists, it seemed to me, had sufficient backing in the Militant group to carry their point. Amalgamation carried. Norman Thomas's Student organization disappeared off the map, although the general League remained and continued, besides its other activities, to send lecturers to the colleges. Joseph Lash got his reward in a trip to Moscow, the trip serving two purposes, to introduce him to the Russian leaders and to tie him definitely to the Communist machine.

The same thing happened with the Workers Alliance, which organized the unemployed. This body owed its organization to the initiative and support of Norman Thomas and the League for Industrial Democracy. The leader of the Worker's Alliance was David Lasser, an ambitious politician.

The Communists were not slow in playing up to Lasser's ambitions. Here again the issue of unity was used. Norman Thomas again gave this unity his blessing. The Communists gave up their own organization, the Unemployed Councils, and threw them into the Alliance branches. Lasser was continued as the national head of the alliance, but the real boss, acting for the Communist Party, remained Herbert Benjamin. The Communist program for the unemployed, as well as its political program—support of the C. I. O., Collective Security, the Japanese Boycott, and the like—became the baggage of the Alliance. After unity was effected, Lasser, like Lash, made his pilgrimage to the Soviet Union and upon his return wrote fantastic stories about the wonderful conditions there, stories even more amazing than the astronomical fantasies that he wrote for the pulp magazines before he became a leader of the unemployed. In a very short time the Socialists were squeezed out of the Workers Alliance and the organization became definitely a Communist auxiliary.

Just as I had decided to drop out of the Socialist Party because I did not want to be the leader of another split, a split which would have resulted in the Socialist Party breaking into half a dozen splitlets, I was excitedly told by Lazar Becker—a former Communist Party member who had supported me during my fight in the Lovestone Group, and had entered the Socialist

Party when I did—about the marvelous relations that were developing between the Socialist Party and the Communists. He informed me that the Communist Party had not only agreed to work jointly with the Socialist Party in conducting a debate between Earl Browder and Norman Thomas at Madison Square Garden, but that the Communists had gone even further. They paid all the expenses for hiring the Garden, gave in to all the proposals the negotiating committee of the Socialist Party made, and agreed upon a division of the proceeds that was very beneficial to the Socialists. They had also advanced a considerable sum of money to help advertise the affair, which was a great help to the *Socialist Call.* The Communists sold most of the tickets, the Socialists got most of the money. I argued with Becker that the move was motivated by Communist policy, not by a desire for unity. "Since when," I asked Becker, "is Stachel so magnanimous with Communist funds and so solicitous of the welfare of the Socialists?" But the Militant leaders thought otherwise. It was clear to me that some of them were happy because it was a step in the direction of possible future collaboration with the Communists. Years later the Socialists, realizing the direction in which the united front was taking them, reversed their emerging policy, as was indicated by their refusal to take part in the May Day parade in 1938 and 1939 with Communist elements. But by that time they had almost no party left.

The Socialist Party got another headache when the Trotskyites joined it in a body. Needless to say, the American cohorts of the former Red War Lord did not join as Socialists but as an invading army advancing behind camouflage. The Trotskyites had but one purpose in view: to change the Socialist program into a Trotsky program and transform the Socialist Party into a part of Trotsky's Opposition. They functioned inside the Socialist Party as an organized caucus with caucus loyalty and discipline, issued their own literature, published their own paper and denounced everyone in the Socialist Party who did not agree with them as opportunists, reactionaries, Right Wingers, Centrists, calling them all the pet names for which the fountainhead of Trotskyism is famous. The Trotskyites were too much for the Socialist Party to digest without getting the most violent cramps. A factional war started between the Trotskyites and all the others which was reminiscent of the worst days of factionalism in the Communist movement. When the Trotskyites were finally expelled, due largely to pressure from Stalinist agents, they took with them the Socialist Party's Youth organization, including the officers and most of the membership of the Young People's Socialist League, and set up a rival organization, the Socialist Workers Party. In 1938 committees on Socialist unity were appointed by the National Executive Committees of both the Socialist Party and the Social Democratic Federation, the organization of the "Old Guard Socialists," with a view of exploring the possibility of unity among the Socialist, as opposed to the Communist, elements. But this is still in a nascent state.

The Socialist Party continues to lament like Hamlet, "To be or not to be." It has succumbed not to a Fascist onslaught, like the German and Italian Socialist Parties, but rather to the Communist virus that has been eating at its vitals. Yet the Communist virus is only one symptom of the general decay which characterizes the Marxian movement all over the world.

The Communist opposition movements continue to grow, not in power and influence or in the number of their adherents but in the number of their organizations, for every Communist opposition organization continues to split, so that in the place of the original opposition there are many oppositions. All claim to be the only true Marxists in existence. But Marxism cannot hold them together, for they are fragments that automatically fly apart. How can the working class realize the Marxian slogan of "Workers of the World Unite," if the Marxians themselves cannot unite?

The Balance Sheet

I visited the venerable old lady of the Communist International, Clara Zetkin, when I was in Moscow in 1929. She was under doctor's care and confined to bed. With effort she propped herself up, the better to talk to me. Her body was old and feeble but her mind active and alert, for her conversation proved that she was fully informed of everything that was going on in Moscow and had definite opinions on it.

Her features—large head and prominent brow—were those of a determined and courageous character. First she plied me with questions, and then she began to talk. I forgot that she was an old woman, who was sick and weak, who had to be attended to constantly, for her voice was clear and strong. We spoke in German. She said, "Yes, I know what is going on. Don't give in. Stand by your convictions." She castigated Stalin, called his actions "Dumheiten" (stupidities). She was indignant over the treatment Bukharin had received. She was in thorough disagreement with Stalin's actions towards the German Communist Party.

But my visit was cut short by the nurse in charge, who brought Clara Zetkin a glass of milk, ordering her to drink it and stop talking. She insisted that the conversation had gone on too long and must be terminated forthwith. Clara Zetkin protested. As she took my hand to say good-by and to remember her to my mother, I detected a sign of hopelessness in her eyes, occasioned by the fact that, at a time when there was so much to do and fight for, she had to take orders from a nurse and be fed milk like a baby. Her closing words were, "Good luck! Keep up the fight, for you have everything to win by being principled."

After I left Russia, Stalin demanded a statement from Clara Zetkin as to where she stood on the recent developments in the Comintern. She did not hesitate, and made the following defiant statement:

> I have always had the courage to take a stand even if I had to stand alone. My highest judge has always been—this I declare openly—not formal decisions but a regard for the advancement of the revolution, for the winning of the masses to the revolution under the leadership of the Communist Party. And precisely from the point of view of this highest duty, I must declare that I cannot recognize every single decision of the Executive Committee of the Communist International and of the Central Committee of the Communist Party of Germany as the last word of wisdom. On the contrary, I am of the opinion that what has been decided and done by the Executive Committee of the Communist International

> and the German Communist Party will operate against the achievement of our aim—the mobilization of the masses under the leadership of the Communist Party for the struggle against the bourgeoisie and for the development of the world revolution.

The statement took Stalin by surprise. It was not what he had expected. But he could not proceed against an old lady who was expected to die at any moment. He was afraid, if he proceeded against her, of the public resentment that would take place throughout the world and in Germany, where she was held in the highest esteem. Clara Zetkin was not molested. After all, an old lady confined most of the time to her bed could do very little harm.

In its very first sentence the Zetkin statement runs counter to the whole intellectual system upon which the official Communist movement stands. Zetkin had the audacity to declare, at a time when all Communists were outdoing themselves to be in agreement with Stalin on everything, that "I have always had the courage to take a stand even if I had to stand alone." The Communist movement, in contradistinction, always demanded the subordination of one's convictions to the "majority" decisions of the Party. Under Stalin, this position of Lenin found its logical fruition in the submission of all Communists to the will of the one man, the leader and dictator of the movement, who fashioned "majorities" by corruption and violence. Intellectual convictions became, if they were in opposition to the opinions of Stalin, treasonable. Persons suspected of holding such convictions were either thrown into prison or lined up against the wall and shot. The Communist movement of the world, represented by the Communist International, is the only organization on a world scale which can boast of unanimous decisions on all matters. The *Communist International* magazine of September twentieth, 1934, proudly boasted about this "virtue" by declaring:

> It is an International of people who think and act alike, and only as such can it ensure the success of the proletarian revolution, the establishment of the dictatorship of the proletariat, and the victory of Socialism.

This enslavement of the human mind, this proscription of independent thinking more than anything else caused me to break with Communism.

I joined the Communist movement because I believed in it, not because I wanted to be a blind follower of either Lenin or Stalin. I believed that the Russian Revolution gave the Socialists an answer to the question of how Socialism was to be achieved.

My first trip to Moscow in 1927 gave me a picture of the Communist International. It was altogether different from what I had expected it to be. I did not like the court attitude which prevailed. I did not like the hypocrisy and the ready professions of belief in things I knew the delegates to the Communist International did not believe in. I did not appreciate the way in which the rulers of the Communist International juggled with individuals and parties. I expected to find men in the Communist International of high intellectual caliber, but found that most of them were of very mediocre stock, who enjoyed their places in the Communist International because of their readiness to bend the knee before the Russian leaders.

The European Communists disappointed me. The German leaders were unfit to lead a German revolution. They drank too much, made blustering speeches, and were too willing to do the dirty work in the Comintern for their Russian masters. Not once did they give expression to an independent idea of their own. Bela Kun, the head of the short-lived Hungarian Soviet government, was an uncouth individual physically and mentally. He was the center of intrigues against his former comrades. He always fawned before the Russian leaders and showed no capacity for leadership.

The Communists of Great Britain, with the exception of Murphy, who was expelled from the Comintern because of his intellectual integrity, were a group of pettifogging nitwits, as expressionless and dull as a fog over London. Gallagher, Pollitt, and the others I found narrow in their views in inverse proportion to the expanse of the British Empire. The British Communist Party was treated like a sickly child. The Party had to receive assistance from Moscow for every step it took. The British people were cold to the Party and its leaders. The Comintern tried to force the British Party to raise a certain quota of the money necessary to start a British Communist Daily. The leaders made all kinds of excuses as to why they could not raise the money. When the paper was published it was done with Comintern money, the Russians supplying practically all the money needed to launch the paper and keep it in existence. What was true of the leaders of these countries was in lesser or greater measure true of other countries as well. But I would be doing many individuals in the Comintern an injustice by lumping them together with this conglomerate of poor heads, for there were many of rare intellectual accomplishments and real ability who were restricted by the Comintern system and dwarfed by its intellectual straitjacket.

The treatment of Trotsky personally and the methods employed in opposing his views shook my faith in the Russian leadership, even though at the time I did not believe in Trotsky's program.

My break with Stalin in 1929 forced me to reëxamine in a critical way the activities and tenets of the Communist movement. My break with Communism, however, did not come suddenly, as I have indicated. It was not easy for me to sever the associations that I had built up in the movement, associations that had become, so to speak, part of my life. I knew that I was drifting away from the movement, but I was not yet ready to take the step that would cut me definitely loose from it. Some important event had to take place which would shake my faith in Communism. It came when Hitler obtained power in Germany. In smashing democracy, Hitler smashed my Communist belief that democracy was an illusion. I realized that, when the German people lost their democratic rights, they lost their freedom and their most valuable possessions. One had to be blind not to see that the labor movement of Germany was infinitely better off when it had the right to organize, to hold meetings, to strike and to publish newspapers. When these rights were lost its existence came to an end.

Stalin's statement that Hitler's victory in Germany was a victory for the working class, because it shattered the democratic illusions of the German proletariat and prepared them for proletarian dictatorship, sounded to me like a mockery against the working class to which it was addressed. I recalled that in the Socialist Party we always tied up Socialism with democracy. Socialism to us meant the extension of democracy, not its repudiation. When we left the Socialist Party, we railed against democracy, called it a cloak for capitalist dictatorship, and called upon the workers to overthrow democracy in favor of proletarian dictatorship. In our fanatical zeal for Bolshevism we forgot the lessons we learned from the pages of history. We forgot that man throughout the ages fought for the right to be a *free* man, for the right to communicate his ideas to his fellow man, and to express his opinions. We were ready to discard the liberties man had paid a very dear price to obtain for the blessings of dictatorship. Now we are able to see where this faith in dictatorship has brought us. Reaction rides on the totalitarian Juggernaut, which bears down upon the terror-stricken defenseless people, who, deprived of their liberties, must submit to their misfortunes in silence.

I have come to the conclusion that the Communists more than any other force were responsible for the development of Fascism. They turned the tide of the Russian Revolution from the course of democracy into the blind alley of dictatorship. We must look to Lenin, not to Mussolini or Hitler, for the father of the modern totalitarian state. Lenin, in the name of Socialism, not only practiced the absolutism of the Tsarist State, but improved upon it. When he set up his "proletarian" dictatorship in Russia, he played right into the hands of the post-War reaction, for the reactionary forces reasoned that, if in Russia freedom of speech and freedom of the press could be abolished by Socialists, it should also be possible for rulers in other countries to abolish these liberties. If the Bolsheviks saw fit to abolish all other political parties, including all shades of Socialist and later of Communist opinion, in favor of the rule of only one party, their own, the reigning Communist Party, why should it not be just as permissible for non-Communists to do the same things in their own countries? The post-War reaction was quick to grasp the implications of the Bolshevik system of maintaining power. They learned from the Bolsheviks how to deprive the people of their liberties in order to fasten a military, economic dictatorship upon them. Mussolini was the first reactionary politician who found in Lenin a good teacher. He learned from Lenin how to apply Bolshevik methods in destroying the Socialist movement, the trade unions, and the liberal movement of Italy.

But Lenin's service to post-War reaction went further. Possessed of an indomitable will, he was determined to force the world labor movement to accept his views. At a time when the labor movement should have been kept united, he started a civil war which divided its forces and destroyed its morale. As a result, labor lacked unity. Weakened and divided, it fell an easy prey to the Fascists. The destruction of such powerful labor movements as those of Italy, Austria, Germany, and now Spain are evidence of labor's inability to fight effectively and successfully against Fascism.

The Communists did not hide the fact that Communism and Fascism had much in common. As early as January, 1923, an article appeared in the *Labor Herald*, then under Foster's editorship, which stated:

> In two countries where the battle is bitterest, Russia and Italy, the final forms have probably been produced. On the workers' side it is Bolshevism and on the capitalists' side Fascism.

The article further praised the social implications of Fascism; to wit:

> Strangely enough Fascism and Bolshevism in their modus operandi, greatly resemble each other. The essence of both is dictatorship; the one is the dictatorship of the bourgeoisie, the other the dictatorship of the proletariat. Both are compact, enthusiastic, highly disciplined military organizations composed of militants of the two warring groups; both are based upon the principle that in the supreme crisis, all the riff-raff of ignorants and inconcients in the respective classes must be pushed to one side, and that the direction of the struggle shall pass into the hands of the active spirits, who not only understand the true interests of their social group but who also have the energy, courage, and initiative to battle for them relentlessly to the end.

But Fascism does not kill the riff-raff of ignorants in the capitalist class so much that you can notice it, while it does kill thousands of those who dare to oppose it from the working class and all other classes. And in Russia today under Stalin's rule, firing squads are exterminating not the ignorant riff-raff of the Communist movement, but its most intelligent exponents. However, let us return to the comparison:

> The fact is that the organization methods of Italian Fascism are patterned after Russian Bolshevism. Mussolini, the tool of Italian capitalism, is a pale reflection of the great proletarian leader, Lenin. His organization is copied after that of the Russian revolutionary working class.

Then, after proving that Italian Fascism destroyed democracy for precisely the same reason that the Russian Communist Party did, this article contends:

> When the Fascisti overthrew the Italian parliament and set up their dictatorship, it was an act comparable to that of the Bolsheviki dissolving the Russian Constituent Assembly and establishing the control of the Communist Party.

In Russia we now have, as in Italy and in Nazi Germany, a one-man dictatorship in the person of Stalin. Stalin enjoys more supreme power than either Mussolini or Hitler, for in Russia all private ownership has been abolished in the important economic and cultural fields. Stalin rules a vast empire as a dictator over all phases of its life. He dominates the government, for he is the state. He dominates the Communist Party, for he is the party. He rules the factories, the newspapers, the theaters—his power is everywhere. No wonder that one of the Russian poets writing on Stalin's fiftieth birthday greeted him as the *Cosmic Leader*, the leader not only of our earth, but of all the worlds in the cosmos as well.

Many Communists in opposition to Stalin would like the world to believe that what is wrong in Russia is due to Stalin. Remove Stalin, they cry, and everything will become better. The Communist Party will again become the glorious party of Revolutionary Socialism that it was during Lenin's leadership.

They fail to see that Stalin is a product of Leninism. The state that Lenin set up was a totalitarian state. The fact that it claims to work for Socialism does not change the nature of the Soviet State. Hitler also claims to be a Socialist. He calls his ruling state party the National Socialist Labor Party. If what Hitler, Mussolini, and Stalin stand for is Socialism, then it is different from my conception of Socialism, for under Socialism as I have always understood it the workers were not only to benefit economically, but at the same time were to enjoy more freedom than they had under capitalism. However, we know that in the totalitarian states, including Russia, the workers have not improved their lot economically. As far as freedom is concerned, they have lost whatever freedom they once enjoyed. In Russia, the workers in the land of proletarian dictatorship enjoy less representation in the affairs of industry than is allowed the workers in Nazi Germany and Fascist Italy. The factory committees and other agencies of workers' control, and representation, which was set up right after the Bolsheviks came into power, has been abolished in favor of giving the state managers of the industry complete control over the productive and labor conditions of the plants they manage.

Many Socialists in Russia and many of them outside of Russia, who were acquainted with Lenin's philosophy, warned that, if his program would be applied it would lead to despotism that would defeat the very aims of Socialism. Trotsky himself had at one time criticized that tendency in Lenin. Rosa Luxembourg, who has been idealized by the Communists, until Stalin purged her from the Communist Valhalla years after her heroic death, was one of Lenin's bitterest opponents in this respect. We did not heed Lenin's critics. We fell under the spell of his phrases and slogans. Deprive the people of a country of all their liberties, put them at the mercy of one political party that is ruled like a military machine from the top down, and under these conditions a dictatorship follows which must soon express itself in the absolute power of one man. But it may not stop there, for the one-man dictator, as ruthless as he may be, Stalin for example, may in the near future be replaced by a new dictator who will come riding into power on horseback, and will represent the dictatorial state's final form—that of a military dictatorship.

There are many who claim that what we are witnessing in Russia is a great experiment in social planning that will transform our social institutions into an earthly paradise. In Russia, they inform us, is taking place the birth of a new society, which will benefit all mankind. The Bolsheviks, they say, know what they are doing. In spite of formidable domestic difficulties and the antagonism of the world, they will succeed. These sycophants of the Russian régime, who are comfortable in their smug security, justify everything that is going on in Russia as sacrifices for Communism. But what we have in Russia is neither Communism nor Socialism. The Russian people live under a system of Monopolistic State Capitalism. The state owns and runs everything—not the workers in the enterprises, or the working class as a whole. The Soviet Union is like a giant trust, a monopoly that has succeeded in seizing possession of everything in Russia. This monopoly surpasses the wildest dreams of the monopolist titans of Wall Street.

The gigantic Russian corporation, which is a state unto itself, wielding economic, political, judicial, and military power, rests upon a vast bureaucratic structure. These bureaucrats constitute the ruling class of Russia. They are the officers, the board of directors, and the managers of the huge corporation. The maintenance of this bureaucracy is a very costly affair. The Soviet bureaucracy, which is largely in the Communist Party, is like a super-Tammany Hall, which exacts its toll from the Russian workers and peasants. Acting in the name of the proletariat and the toiling masses, this bureaucracy is contemptuous of the masses.

This bureaucracy is the new aristocracy of Russia. They enjoy the special privileges and favors which accrue to every ruling class and aristocracy. These they are determined to maintain. There is today a wide gulf between the bureaucracy and the Russian workers and peasants. The bureaucracy is well fed, gets good wages, rides around in automobiles, lives in the better apartments, travels, and has a thousand advantages which the worker has not. The gap between it and the workers, instead of becoming narrower, as Soviet industry and economy in general is being developed, is actually becoming wider.

Under such conditions we cannot expect the Soviet state to wither away, as Lenin promised it would. We cannot even expect it to grant the elementary liberties which are the attributes of a free people. On the contrary, the monopolistic nature of the Russian state can be maintained only by the most rigid form of dictatorship. Stalin may grant constitutions, he may grant the people the right to vote by secret ballot, only to give evidence next morning by treason trials and purges by firing squads that Russia is not a free man's country. Since the people enjoy no rights in Russia, the ruling bureaucracy has license to mistreat the masses. Consider one characteristic little detail: in Russia, to be late to work is a crime against the state. The Russian worker is not free to move around from one place to another, from one job to another. His boss, his master, is wherever he goes and wherever he works, for it is the state, the government which rules over him.

The Bolshevik rulers of Russia are extreme nationalists. All their actions are predicated on Russian national interests. But what the Bolsheviks have been taught by Lenin they have never forgotten, and that is that propaganda is a very valuable and effective weapon. The Bolsheviks have never been parsimonious with their propaganda machine. They have spent lavishly for propaganda, with the result that they have impressed millions of people with the belief that in Russia a new society is being built which is greatly benefiting the people, and that the Russian form of dictatorship surpasses all democracies in the freedom and liberty its people enjoy. They go further and seek to gain the loyalty and support of the masses throughout the world for the Soviet Union, by instilling in them a patriotism for the Soviet Union as the fatherland of the exploited and oppressed people of the world. The *Pravda* greeting the Eighteenth Party Congress on March tenth, 1939, bore this out, when it declared:

> The exploiters and oppressors in all countries feel and know that the decisions of the Eighteenth Congress of the Bolsheviks will make the Soviet Union—*the fatherland of the working people and the oppressed of the whole world*—even stronger, more powerful, will hasten the triumph of Communism throughout the world.

No other government in the world enjoys or can afford to maintain the kind of a propaganda machine the Soviet government maintains in the name of Communism and for the liberation of mankind from exploitation and oppression. The Communist propaganda machine is built up on the basis of idealism. It does not depend upon the sending of paid agents from the Soviet Union to other countries, as the Nazis do, to carry on its propaganda. In all countries it has Communist parties made up of the countries' nationals, which constitutes the kernel of its propaganda machine in that country. But its propaganda agents are not confined to the Communists, for many liberals and other well-intentioned people are impressed with the Soviet's virtues and become its most ardent supporters and propagandists. Besides, through the activities of the Communist Party machine, the Soviet government is able to maintain contacts for information and all other purposes it deems necessary in the key industries of the country, in the newspapers and agencies of public information, in the schools and colleges, in the government, and even in the armed forces. Moreover, Communists seek support for the foreign policies of the Soviet government from the government of the United States, while simultaneously organizing for the ultimate aim of turning the United States into a Communist totalitarian state.

In every country where the labor movement has fallen under the spell of the Communists, the people as a whole have had to pay very dearly for it. We must not forget that the Russian rulers are primarily concerned about the affairs of their own country. If their nationalist interests require the sacrifice of hundreds of thousands of people in foreign countries, they will not hesitate to offer them as sacrifices. We have had many examples of that. The Soviet government sacrificed the Ethiopian people in the interest of Soviet trade with Fascist Italy. The Soviet government has needlessly sacrificed hundreds of thousands of Chinese for its interests in the Far East. The Soviet government has sacrificed the German people on the altar of Nazism, because Soviet policy against the Versailles Treaty and for a German rapprochement coincided with that of the Nazis and of the German militarists with whom Russia was collaborating. That this orientation was never wholly abandoned, notwithstanding avowals on behalf of so-called collective security and the "defense of the democracies" against "totalitarian aggression" is attested to by the signature of a new commercial treaty for seven years signed in August, 1939, between the Nazi government of Hitler and the Red dictatorship of Stalin. As for the Soviet government's role in Spain, it is no longer a secret that the defeat of the Loyalist forces by Franco was in large measure due to the intrigues and machinations of the Soviet G. P. U.

Russian Communism as an economic system and a political régime is the fulfillment of Communist promises. Shall we in the United States follow the Communist course? Can we thus improve the lot of our people, eliminate poverty, extend our liberties? This question is crucial in the face of the rival claims of Fascists and Communists, both of whom are storming the citadels of democracy, seeking its destruction, for the promise of a better life.

My emphatic answer to the claims of both Fascists and Communists is, No! The record of Fascism in Italy and Germany speaks for itself, and it is not a savory record. As for Communism, we can achieve it in America only through a violent revolution in which millions of our people would perish, in which basic and irreplaceable human values would be destroyed, in which the most intelligent, the most independent-thinking and the most socially-minded among us would be exterminated. In the course of the civil war that would rage over the land our economic structure would be devastated, our industries wrecked, our fields laid waste. The loss in material values alone would be so great that many decades of hard work would be required to repair the damage done.

But what would be our gains? What about the idealistic claims of the Communists? What about their vaunted slogan of bread and freedom? What about their promises to the masses that Communism would abolish poverty, rid them of their exploiters, deepen democracy and provide them with economic security?

Few are they who today harbor any illusions about the sort of "democracy" that prevails in Russia today. It is virtually indistinguishable from the "democracy" practiced in Nazi Germany and Fascist Italy.

As for economic security, the evidence is clear that, like the people of Germany and Italy, the Russian people have much less food than we, and even that little is ephemeral because it is predicated on the feverish preparation for war. In the twenty-two years of its existence Communism in Russia has failed to fill the bread basket.

To yield to Communism is to permit the abrogation of our liberties and the institution of a system of state exploitation of labor that would make of our people chattels of the dictatorial régime. Communism is universal conscription of labor. Communism is forced labor. Free labor cannot exist under Communism any more than it can exist under Fascism. Free trade unionism is impossible under either régime. Neither régime recognizes the rights to life, liberty and the pursuit of happiness.

Democracy is something more than a shibboleth. The history of Man is a sanguine record of stubborn struggles against oppression, of countless sacrifices for the sake of freedom. We cannot lightly surrender this dearly-won heritage. The Russian people, who in the course of their heroic struggle against Tsarist despotism fell under the yoke of Communism, are today confronted with the greater task of overthrowing Stalinist absolutism. Let us learn from their misfortune. If democracy in America, precious for all its imperfections, were to be replaced by a Communist dictatorship, a new American Revolution would have to be fought to reëstablish the rights of Man. Economic security and freedom go hand in hand. Only through the democratic process can both be achieved.

FINIS

INDEX

INDEX